Early Bicycles and
the Quest for Speed

Early Bicycles and the Quest for Speed

A History, 1868–1903

Second Edition

ANDREW RITCHIE

McFarland & Company, Inc., Publishers
Jefferson, North Carolina

An earlier version of this book was published by the author in 2011 as *Quest for Speed: A History of Early Bicycle Racing 1868–1903*

Frontispiece: High-wheel racing in Winona, Minnesota, probably in the late 1880s. The photo (lightly cropped) is by Chas. A. Tenney, of Winona. Winona is located about 100 miles southeast of Minneapolis, on the Mississippi River across from Wisconsin, just north of La Crosse, and must have been an outpost of bicycle racing when the photo was taken. The photograph shows a relatively primitive stage of the sport, with a flat, dirt track, and a grain elevator in the background. Nevertheless, all the elements of the early sport are there, with a small grandstand and officials lined up by the side of the track.

LIBRARY OF CONGRESS CATALOGUING-IN-PUBLICATION DATA

Names: Ritchie, Andrew, 1943– author.
Title: Early bicycles and the quest for speed : a history, 1868–1903 / Andrew Ritchie.
Description: Second edition. | Jefferson, North Carolina : McFarland & Company, Inc., Publishers, 2018 | Includes bibliographical references and index.
Identifiers: LCCN 2017049310 | ISBN 9781476671079 (softcover : acid free paper) ∞
Subjects: LCSH: Bicycle racing—History—19th century. | Bicycle racing—History—20th century. | Bicycles—History.
Classification: LCC GV1049 .R48 2018 | DDC 796.6/2—dc23
LC record available at https://lccn.loc.gov/2017049310

BRITISH LIBRARY CATALOGUING DATA ARE AVAILABLE

ISBN (print) 978-1-4766-7107-9
ISBN (ebook) 978-1-4766-3046-5

© 2018 Andrew Ritchie. All rights reserved

No part of this book may be reproduced or transmitted in any form or by any means, electronic or mechanical, including photocopying or recording, or by any information storage and retrieval system, without permission in writing from the publisher.

Front cover: Track officials can be seen gathered beside competitors in this undated photograph, probably at the start of an N.C.U. championship event from 1885 or 1886. G.L. Hillier in white, probably H.O. Duncan in black with black bowler, to his right (author's collection).

Printed in the United States of America

McFarland & Company, Inc., Publishers
Box 611, Jefferson, North Carolina 28640
www.mcfarlandpub.com

Acknowledgments

I could not have brought the first edition (2011) to press without the help of Rob van der Plas, John Weiss, Christian Wignall, Lorne Shields and Teresa Fagan

For this edition, once again, thanks and appreciation to all the people in the bicycle history world from whom I have benefitted with a constant exchange of photocopies, photographs and email discussion. Especially helpful has been the ongoing exchange of information with members of the International Cycling History Conference and the Veteran Cycling Club, whose combined knowledge and research expertise now constitutes a body of informed opinion which someone who tackles any aspect of the history of the bicycle neglects at their peril.

Table of Contents

Acknowledgments   v
Preface   1
Introduction: Sport, Speed, Technology and Modernity   5

Chapter One. The Origins of Bicycle Racing
  1. The Earliest Bicycle Racing   15
  2. The Beginning of Commercial Bicycle Production, 1865–69   19
  3. Velocipede Developments in France and the United States, 1867–69:
     Their Influence on the British Sport   20
  4. Charles Spencer's London Gymnasium   27
  5. Bicycle Competition as Athletic Novelty and Public Spectacle   30
  6. Links Between Manufacture and Sport   34
  7. Varieties of Competitive Activity   38
  8. An Elite Emerges: Match Racing and Championships   45

Chapter Two. Expansion of Bicycling in Britain
  1. A Cutting-Edge, Modern, Technological Sport   50
  2. Technological Innovation at the Birth of Cycle Sport   54
  3. Amateurism and Professionalism in the 1870s   59
  4. Cycling at Oxford and Cambridge Universities   62
  5. "Muscular Christianity": The Cycling Career of Ion Keith-Falconer   65
  6. "Gentlemen, Not Players': The Establishment of the Bicycle Union, 1877–78   69
  7. John Keen (1849–1902)   77
  8. A New Athletic Liberalism   78
  9. The Bicycle Touring Club, 1878   80
  10. Public Recognition of Bicycling   83

Chapter Three. The Beginnings of Bicycle Racing in the United States
  1. American Cycling in the Late 1870s   88
  2. The Foundations of American Cycling   91
  3. Harry Etherington: Bicycling Entrepreneur and Promoter of Endurance
     Spectacles   101
  4. Etherington's 1879 "Anglo-French" Tour of America and Its Repercussions   105
  5. The Founding of the League of American Wheelmen   113

Chapter Four. Expansion of the High-Wheel Sport
  1. The New Sport Expands and Matures   121
  2. Bicycle Racing Infrastructure: Road Conditions and Track Construction   125

3. Competition in Britain: Amateurism and Professionalism in the Late 1870s and 1880s … 133
4. Two Professionals: George Waller (c.1855–1900) and H.O. Duncan (1862–1945) … 138
5. Competition in France: The Tendency towards an "Open" Sport … 141
6. British "Meets," the Springfield Tournaments and the Growth of International Competition … 143
7. New Departures: Tricycle Racing and Recreational Tricycling … 155

Chapter Five. Sport, Speed and Safety, 1885–93
1. Design and Technological Ferment within the Bicycle Industry and the Sport … 163
2. Alternative Designs: the "Facile" and the "Kangaroo." … 165
3. The Rear-Driven "Rover Safety" and the First "Safety" Races … 169
4. The Rise of Road Racing … 176
5. Competition and the Invention of the Revolutionary Pneumatic Tire … 181
6. The Cycling Revolution, 1888–93 … 188

Chapter Six. The Foundations of Modern Road Racing
1. Road Competition in Britain and France … 193
2. The Foundations of Modern Professional Road Racing in France: Sport as Business and Athletic Celebration … 195
3. Opposition to Organized Road Racing in Britain … 205
4. George Lacy Hillier: Amateurism Versus the "New Professionalism" … 209
5. Road Racing in the United States … 216
6. Racing Bicycles on Public Roads: Danger or Celebration? … 222

Chapter Seven. International Competition
1. Bicycle Racing as a Global Sport … 228
2. National Championships, International Competition and Early "World Championships" … 229
3. The International Cyclists' Association, 1892 … 238
4. World Champion: The International Career of Arthur Zimmerman … 245
5. Amateurism, Professionalism and Licensing Schemes … 254
6. The 1896 Olympic Games … 257
7. Rival Philosophies of Cycling Competition and Sporting Excellence in the 1890s … 260

Chapter Eight. Bicycle Racing and Modernity
1. The Transformation of Bicycle Racing in the 1890s … 263
2. Long-Distance Races on the Road … 267
3. Stage-Riding and Stage-Races on the Road and the Origins of the Tour de France … 269
4. "Stayer" (Paced) Races … 272
5. Six-Day Races … 277
6. Professionalization and Commercialization … 280
7. "Gigantism" and the Pursuit of Records … 284

8. Sensationalism and "Gigantomania"	286
9. The Emergence of a Modern, Professional Sports Structure	287

Chapter Nine. Non-Competitive Cycling in the 1890s ... 291

Epilogue
- 1. A Period of Intensive Technological Change and Sport Development ... 309
- 2. Reviewing the Dynamics of Social and Technological Change ... 314
  - A. Agents of change within the sport and industry ... 314
  - B. The spectacular growth of the bicycle industry and the class penetration of cycling ... 315
  - C. Global expansion ... 316
  - D. Speed and modernity ... 318
- 3. Sport as Moral/Physical Crusade and Sport as Business ... 321

Chapter Notes ... 323

Bibliography ... 364

Index ... 373

Preface

Early Bicycles and the Quest for Speed is a social and technical history of the development of bicycle racing and bicycle technology between about 1868 and 1903, in Britain, France and the United States. It follows the earliest "velocipedes" from 1869 into the 1880s, the period of the classic high-wheel bicycle, and then into the "boom" era of the safety bicycle and the pneumatic tire of the mid–1890s, and the rise of modern, international road and track racing, including the first Olympic Games. It also explores cycling as recreational, touring and utility riding in the same period.

It is not an economic or an industrial history per se, but a broader social account that argues that there was a symbiotic relationship between the growth of the sport and the extraordinary expansion of the bicycle industry itself. Each needed the other as design ideas, technological needs and customer tastes changed. Product reviews and the correspondence columns of the specialized cycling press give ample evidence of this exchange of ideas, as did the discussion in the general press. The new bicycle was constantly in the news.

The bicycle trade created an annual consumer marketing pattern, where novelties were first introduced at the spring shows. Ultimately, when records and championships were at stake, effectively achieved and constantly sustained speed was the most important criteria of success, under varied road and track conditions. Racing and setting place-to-place records between towns or other landmarks were crucial parts of the evolution of man-powered machines right from the beginning. At first the horse, or the speed of horse and carriage, were the standards to be met. The railways were of course faster, but were also expensive.

The book is crammed full of documents, technical information, details of the formation of clubs and national and international governing bodies, the origins of national and world championships, insights into the role of the press, and the biographies of bicycle racers and the most significant personalities from the sport, the industry and the press. It also raises questions about understanding the evolution of bicycle technology, and examines changing styles and fashions. From a technological viewpoint, the account in this book situates the rise of the bicycle industry as a precursor to modern automobile transportation. It is directed at anyone who seeks to understand the foundations of modern cycling in the late 19th century, and the early development of what is still an underresearched modern sport.

* * *

I researched and wrote a short history of cycling called *King of the Road*, published in 1975. This was my first encounter with the extensive literature of the history of cycling. It was in the days of what came to be known as the first modern bike boom, of Tom Cuthbertson's *Anybody's Bike Book* and the first Bell helmets. An oil shortage stimulated the 1970s revival of the European 10-speed bicycle in the United States, and at the Missing Link in Berkeley, where I worked for a time, Suntour alloy rear derailleurs—Japanese—were being fitted in place of the plastic Simplex ones, made in France, which broke much too easily.

The European manufacturers with a foothold in the American market were being challenged by the Japanese and Taiwanese, and mountain bikes—which would quickly revolutionize the bicycle industry—were being invented in Marin County, California. We didn't recognize it from a historical perspective at that moment, but we were at a turning point, the beginning of what was to become a global cycling revolution. American manufacturers would play a vastly increased role in the world bicycle market.

I started cycling in about 1960, as a teenager, riding in South London and in the Kent and Surrey lanes. I was to discover later that since the 1880s south London had been a hotbed of cycling, and there were still dozens of clubs and specialist bike shops in the 1960s.

King of the Road can still be found for a few dollars. All in all, it's worn reasonably well, but in places the text is quite dated. I did much of the research in the old circular British Museum Reading Room and at the Cyclists Touring Club Library, then in Godalming, Surrey. It was my first exploration of the cycling press and the wider literature of cycling as a sport, a leisure pursuit and a developing technology. When I first approached the late Derek Roberts, the founder and editor of *The Boneshaker*—which has since become the leading journal of serious cycling history—for guidance, he gave me a short lecture about bad bicycle history books and the need for historical accuracy, which was his quest. As a message, this stayed with me. It's served me well in exploring and using the cycling literature of the last 150 years.

In retrospect, *King of the Road* turns out to have been a respectably accurate book in making sense of the essential historical and technological developments. However, *King of the Road* had the limitation of being a somewhat Anglo-centric account, and somewhat weak on the 1890s and on American and French cycling. Given the now large and wide scope of the issues covered by the umbrella description cycling history, it wasn't surprising that the book ran out of breath and space. In 2011, I self-published the hardcover *Quest for Speed: A History of Early Bicycle Racing, 1868–1905*, an earlier version of this book.

* * *

More recent cycling history has expanded considerably in the period since 1975, and has now become one of the subdisciplines of sport, social and transportation studies. Social history, history of technology, economic history, the sociology of institutions ... it is all there in the story of the bicycle, an unarguably interdisciplinary field. And yet, cycling history has something in addition, which sets it apart from other more easily defined fields of historical study. From its beginnings, cycling, as a competitive sport, a recreation and a means of useful transportation (for many cyclists, all three categories apply), has been defined by a kind of defiant enthusiasm—the mark of the fanatic, the rebel, the individualist.

The development of the bicycle and its constantly changing use and meaning is a challenging entry point. And changes in materials technology and fashion go on happening. The recent "fixie" and "urban bike" movement is an astonishing manifestation, a brand-new take on the old theme of function and style, as profound in its way as the invasion of Japanese products in the 1970s and the rise of the mountain bike in the 1980s.

Certainly, as a cycling historian who has gone through a Ph.D. program, I have been encouraged to broaden my intellectual horizons and to become less of a bike freak and more of a sport historian. That involved developing an approach towards understanding the history of broader sport, social and technological movements. Why and how does a technology change precisely in the ways that it does? Who were the authors and instigators of change? Who were the important players affecting that change? A cycling historian needs to become a sociologist and an economic historian, too, and has to understand the workings of a large and complex industry and something about the marketing of consumer products. The history of cycling has a truly bewildering variety of aspects to it. And it continues to expand with our exciting access to digitally searchable newspapers and magazines.

Also, we have now had more than twenty years of the annual International Cycle History Conferences, and the publication of the Conference's annual *Proceedings*, which have become an important repository of articles on many and varied aspects of cycling history. In many ways, cycling history, having been for many years somewhat inadequately researched and written about, is now at the point of becoming a global reference point for green and alternative technologies. It doesn't include just sport history, but also leisure/recreation history and utility/transportation history. The pressure to prepare and justify a historical point of view for the purposes of arguing the approach and method of my dissertation was tricky, but beneficial in the end. Illustrations, especially photographs and advertising copy, are a valuable and legitimate contribution to cycling history. The illustrations are a crucial part of this book, often revealing the deeper meaning of the text.

Early Bicycles and the Quest for Speed does give limited information about the role of women in the early history of cycling (please consult the Index), but it is not enough. I have been justifiably criticized for not giving them an entire chapter, and it was a mistake not to have recognized and documented more fully the genuine athletic feats of the female pioneers of the sport in the 19th and early 20th centuries. In London and Paris in the mid–1890s a cultural awakening of women's assertiveness and independence focused on the use of the bicycle. In the mid–1890s, Paris was the scene of an extraordinary festival of women's fashion, advertising and racing—in particular the café-concerts at the two popular velodromes. A hectic debate was conducted in the American and European general and cycling press about women's role as "the new woman." Was it acceptable for women to take part in public athletic performances? And what was the appropriate and convenient dress for cycling and other physical activities? Cycling, especially because of the delicate issue of the saddle and the need to free women's legs of the encumbrance of skirts and petticoats, was a huge contributor to women's emancipation

Though women were denied access to the high-wheel bicycle, in the 1880s there were strong women prepared to flout respectable convention and participate in entertainment competition, races which were undoubtedly sensationalized, but were nevertheless genuine tests of skill, speed and stamina. With the accessibility for women of the pneumatic-tired safety bicycle, women's inclusion was enabled although it did not become a formal sport for them as yet, on a par with the men's sport. It is now agreed that the growing popularity of women's cycling in the 1890s, by giving women greater independence and mobility, was a significant contributor to their emancipation. There was also more athletic women's riding and racing in the 1890s than is generally recognized. It is a fascinating and challenging story waiting to be further explored.

SUPPLEMENT TO "CYCLING," MAY 23rd, 1891.

ROAD-RIDERS OF 1890.
No. 4.

EDMUND DANGERFIELD,

Winner of both the 100 Miles Open Scratch Road Races, held last year, by the Bath Road and North Road Cycling Clubs

This illustration by George Moore depicts Edmund Dangerfield, who the caption states was the winner in 1890 of two 100-mile road races sponsored by important English clubs, the Bath Road C.C. and the North Road C.C. Dangerfield was also one of the founding editors of *Cycling* in January 1891 (see Armstrong's *Bouverie Street to Bowling Green Lane*, 1946). The illustration was published in *Cycling*, 23 May 1891, and typifies the image of the "scorcher," who was feared on the roads of England as a disruptive troublemaker (see Chapter 6 and elsewhere). It is reproduced here exactly as it was printed in *Cycling*. Was the image reversed by mistake to show the drive mechanism on the "wrong" side of the bicycle, or was there a period when a left-hand drive-chain was being constructed? Apparently, the latter is the correct answer.

Introduction: Sport, Speed, Technology and Modernity

SET IN A HISTORICAL context of a growing interest in sport and intense technological development, cycling has now been evolving for more than 150 years. Competitive bicycle racing is among the oldest and most celebrated of modern international sports. It joins athletics (track and field), cricket, golf, baseball, soccer, rugby, rowing and skiing as one of the modern sports that emerged in the second half of the 19th century, the products of intense social, economic, and technological change.

Today, cycling is popular worldwide, a competitive sport and recreational activity with a deep and complex history. It continues to expand internationally, outside its European and American roots. Unofficial "world championships" in cycling first took place between England and France in the early 1870s.[1] Cycling's earliest national governing bodies, the Bicycle Union (for racing) and the Bicycle Touring Club (for touring), were founded in England in 1878, the League of American Wheelmen followed in the United States in 1880, and France's Union Vélocipédique in 1881. Official World Championships were first held in 1893, promoted by the newly constituted International Cyclists' Association, and cycling was among the small number of sports included in the first modern Olympic Games in 1896.[2] The Tour de France, founded in 1903 and since then held annually except during two World Wars, wasn't organized until the sport was nearly forty years old.

At the beginning, bicycle racing was a brand-new sport in the sense that it didn't develop from a previous, less-developed prototype, as did soccer, rugby, baseball, skiing or sailing. It sprang into existence, "primitive" but fully formed, at the moment of the first velocipede craze of the mid/late 1860s. Chapter One describes how bicycle entertainment in the late 1860s borrowed from various other kinds of indoor and outdoor sporting activity. The key innovation was, of course, the machine itself—the bicycle.

The sport relied on an expensive, sophisticated, high-quality tool, with which it had a complex technological relationship. Bicycle racing can be defined as a modern sport in the sense that it depended on the industrial manufacture and consumption of specialized equipment dedicated uniquely to that sport, and on developing an efficient and comfortable relationship between athlete and machine. The sport was defined from the start by a mutually beneficial relationship with bicycle manufacturers, who needed it to test and improve many technological and practical aspects of their design and production process.

The origins of bicycle racing can be traced back to the creation of the modern bicycle in

Paris, and its subsequent speedy diffusion into Britain and America, in the late 1860s.[3] An 1869 illustration of the "forge" and "paint shop" of the Compagnie Parisienne in Paris shows that the production of the earliest bicycles involved a technologically advanced level of industrial activity, on a much larger scale than any previous velocipede manufacturing. Aspects of traditional blacksmith and carriage making technology were diversified into the mass-production and marketing of the earliest bicycles used in the new sport. The sport needed its essential tool, which could only be popularized through this complex manufacturing process.

Cycling was thus the product of this industrial culture, an early and conspicuous example of the new sports which evolved within that culture. "As a general rule," writes Neil Tranter, "the more industrial and commercial the economy, the greater the extent of organized sport and the earlier its inception. It was no accident that Britain, the first country to industrialize, was also the first country to introduce a codified, institutionalized and highly commercialized sporting culture."[4]

A crucial argument of this book is that bicycle racing has always tested constantly changing and evolving ideas about the design, appropriateness and reliability of highly specialized equipment whose job it is to transform the muscular effort of the "human motor" into forward motion as efficiently as possible. Body and bicycle have always had to be seen as one unit in the realization of power and speed. In the last quarter of the 19th century, cycling sport was characterized by an obsessive interest in speed and long-distance endurance. The obsessive compulsion to surpass previous performances—to break records—drove forward the dramatic technological progress of the bicycle.

Sport and technology cross-fertilized each other, as they continue to do today. The relationship, however, was not always a comfortable one and there was often tension between them.[5] Bicycle racing depended on the development of an optimally efficient machine, but this mechanical function was not socially neutral, it didn't always develop according to a pre-determined, self-contained, technological logic, but was the product of both a social and a technological process.

Fig. Intro.1. By 1869, bicycle manufacture in France was already being undertaken on a modern industrial scale. [Source: *Le Journal Illustré*, 1869, date/month unknown]

Introduction

Throughout its history, bicycle racing has illustrated a constant examination of how the bicycle can harness the physical capabilities of the human body most efficiently.[6] The history of bicycle racing demonstrates an evolving symbiotic relationship between the sport and its specialized tool, the bicycle itself. The nature of technological change itself has even been examined using bicycle technology as a paradigm. Yet there has been a lack of critical examination of this developing historical relationship between the human body and the bicycle. Nor have we seen a serious historical study of the relationship between the athletes/practitioners—the racing cyclists themselves—and the industry responsible for the design and manufacture of bicycles. This book proposes to fill that historiographical gap.

As well as giving an accurate historical account of historical events and personalities here, one of the significant issues in exploring this relationship between the human body and the bicycle is an examination of the processes of technological change, particularly in the 19th century when bicycle design was so fluid and change so pervasive. Why and how does an object such as the bicycle evolve and change?—does a theory exist which proposes to explain this change? I have found the most relevant and useful debate in this connection is that advanced by the SCOT (Social Construction of Technology) approach.[7] Briefly, SCOT, as most prominently articulated by Trevor J. Pinch and Wiebe E. Bijker in a series of papers and books, proposes that technological artifacts, or objects, are embedded in social factors ("relevant social groups") and undergo a process which leads to "closure" or "stabilization," when a completed stage of the object is reached. An active debate still surrounds the SCOT approach to understanding and interpreting technological change, and although theoretical discussion of technological change is not a primary task of this book, nevertheless it is an underlying theme.

* * *

"The bicycle was inseparable from the idea of speed," asserts Kobayashi in his study of the early industry and bicycle racing in France from the end of 1867.[8] From the beginning of 1869, there is plenty of evidence of bicycle racing on road and track in Britain and America. By early 1869, the bicycle had penetrated as far as California and Australia. The appearance of the first two-wheeled "velocipedes" on the roads of Europe and America immediately invited the challenge of comparing their speed with the speed of a horse or a horse-and-carriage over known routes or specific distances on the road. Where the railway ran, it was, of course, faster. In England, in 1868–69, the earliest bicycles were introduced from France into a gymnastic and sport environment where physical fitness and athletic strength were the concerns of mostly middle- and upper-middle–class men, and bicycles were soon being manufactured in Coventry, Wolverhampton, Birmingham and London, as well as in Paris, Berlin, Prague and New York.

But during the same period the velocipede was also introduced into the working-class entertainment culture of the music-halls, circuses and novelty shows, where both male and female professional actors appeared. This juxtaposition of upper-middle class, formal competitive sport and professional popular entertainment was characteristic of the early days of the bicycle, and was continued into the 1880s and the "boom" of the 1890s, when track racing often combined the excitement of athletic speed with the show-business drama of the indoor arena.

The bicycle first became popular in England shortly after the foundation in 1866 by former university athletes, from Oxford and Cambridge Universities, of the Amateur Athletic Club. In 1867, this club added a membership clause excluding anyone who was "by trade or employment a mechanic, artisan or labourer" (i.e., a professional), thereby giving the earliest working definition of amateurism. Cycling found enthusiasts not only among the socially privileged student athletes of Oxford and Cambridge in the early 1870s, but also among a working-class "professional" class of riders. The formation of amateur cycling clubs proceeded at a brisk pace in the 1870s and 1880s, but early cycling was also rooted in popular recreation and entertainments—that is, with professional sport. So early cycling was not class-specific, and historian John Lowerson has identified it as "by far the most widespread 'growing pleasure for the middle classes,' relying on a club core with a wide periphery of individual pursuits and shifting over the whole pastime-athletic sport gamut."[9]

Bicycle racing was first essentially defined as a modern sport in England and France in the period from 1869 to about 1875, and became (as its influence radiated from its most developed state in those two key countries) predominantly a British, French, German, Italian, Belgian, Swiss, Dutch and American sport in the last quarter of the 19th century. Competitions between the leading national racers occurred from the earliest "championship matches" between England and France in the early 1870s. In the 1880s, international competitions between Britain, France, Germany and the United States were frequent, indeed unofficial international "championships" were held, and the sport became significantly more international in the "boom" of the 1890s, with the inclusion of Italian, Spanish, Australian, South African, Czech, Russian and Danish cyclists, culminating with the first official world championships in 1893.[10]

Cycling developed most energetically in those countries where there was industrial capacity, a well-developed road system, and a relatively affluent middle-class. Bicycle racing remained, at its professional and upper-amateur core, a predominantly British, French, Italian, German, Dutch, Belgian, Spanish and American sport through the first half of the 20th century, although Australian, Scandinavian, Russian and Japanese athletes had a small presence, and those countries tended to import machines while their own domestic bicycle industries were developing. Only in the last thirty years has the sport been profoundly transformed and further internationalized, particularly by the freeing of the former "pseudo-amateurs" of the Communist-bloc countries, since 1990 able to compete on the open market, and the addition of, for example, Australian, Mexican, Colombian, Kazakh and Japanese participants.

Bicycle racing has always been an extraordinarily demanding athletic activity. The sport is about speed, strength and endurance and tests those human capacities to their limits.[11] It is also about balance, judgment, style, courage and danger. In a long road-race, riders experience a profound relationship with the natural environment, ride in all weathers, climb high mountains and descend them at break-neck speeds. But cycling also takes place in the man-made environment of the track or velodrome, where specially prepared surfaces and banked corners ensure maximum speed and competition can be seen at close quarters by spectators. Bicycle racing tests the physical limits to which an athlete can be stretched in a variety of disciplines, and because of that extreme physical pressure, the negative consequences of the sport—the danger of injury from accidents, the temptation to use drugs and stimulants, have always been very much in evidence.

Fig. Intro.2. A popular 1869 Currier and Ives lithograph shows the new American velocipede taking on a horse and light cart: "We can beat the swiftest steed, With our new velocipede" read the caption. [Source: author's collection]

* * *

If formal racing has measured the competitive limits of cyclists as specialized athletes, and created constant experimentation to find the best machine for the job at hand, recreational riding, touring, and utility transportation have also always included an athletic element, what Lowerson calls "a very real sense of physical testing," with limits self-imposed by the individual participants, and also a similar kind of experimentation with the best machine for those tasks.[12]

I hesitated before including the discussion of recreational cycling in Chapter Nine, but decided in the end that too many issues were raised there which needed to be spelled out, and therefore it has been included in the book.

These three categories—racing, recreation, and utility—must all be taken into account and may be considered as SCOT categories ("relevant social groups") in the development of bicycle technology in the 19th century. Members of each group of users brought their particular interests to bear on the bicycle manufacturers, to make machines more appropriate to their needs. My main concern here is with the influence of the racing cyclists, who perhaps made the most intense demands on the industry, but the differing needs of recreational and utility riders also need to be borne in mind. The three groups, however, were not mutually exclusive, and interchange between them frequently occurred. The same person, for example, might compete on Saturday, go for a club run on Sunday and ride his bicycle to work on Monday, either on the same or on different machines. How can this person be categorized for the purposes of historical examination?[13]

It is difficult to know exactly how many cyclists made up each of these three loosely-defined and overlapping groups. A well-educated guess is that in the 1890s not more than about 5–10% of club members were active racers, though some specialized racing clubs had a much higher percentage of racers. The co-existence of these three groups of users—competitive, recreational and utility cyclists—has significant technological implications. How do these different kinds of users relate to the development of bicycle technology in the late 19th century?

I argue here that competitive sport—and the wider field of athletic cycling—was the engine that drove much of the innovation and technical change in the bicycle industry in the 1880s and 1890s.[14] There is also evidence that the competitive "mode" became a "style" or "fashion" among those who did not compete formally (just as it is today), and that utility and practicality may sometimes have been sacrificed to lightness and speed. Utility, in other words, did not at first exert as much influence as sport. It can plausibly be argued that only the introduction of the pneumatic tire in 1890–92—bringing increased comfort—began to attract significant numbers of serious utility riders, including women and older men, into cycling's orbit.[15]

By the early 1890s, the bicycle had become an industrial success story and a recreational and utilitarian fact of daily life in the developed world. Cycling had become a widespread social movement, and only a small minority were involved in competitive aspects. The social and economic significance of the bicycle was huge, and the "sport and pastime of cycling" was not confined in a narrow sense to competitive sport. Although only a small proportion of the bicycles produced were used in competitive sport *per se*, there was nevertheless a significant athletic element in recreational and even in utilitarian cycling.

Sport, recreation and

Fig. Intro.3. English professional champion Richard Howell typified the athletic nature of high-wheel bicycle racing in the mid-1880s. Illustration by George Moore. [Source: *Bicycling News*, 11 June 1887]

utility thus overlapped in various ways. Accounts of strenuous touring rides at home and abroad abound in the cycling press from the late 1870s on. With the advent of the "safety" bicycle and the pneumatic tire, cycling emerged as a popular leisure and recreational activity, as well as providing practical transportation and mobility. But other than the membership statistics of cycling organizations, and an occasional survey of bicycle usage in specific geographical locations, statistical information about 19th century utilitarian cycling is hard to locate.[16]

* * *

This book, then, in addition to exploring the history of early cycling competition, identifies sport as a key factor in the evolution of bicycle design, particularly in the three most significant large-scale changes in design: first, the evolution of the high-wheel bicycle (familiarly known as the "ordinary," or "penny-farthing') in the 1870s and 1880s; second, the development of the "safety" bicycle in the mid- to late 1880s; and, third, the invention and universal acceptance of the pneumatic tire in the early 1890s. It is argued here that the emergence of the high-wheel bicycle was driven primarily by sporting rather than utilitarian considerations. Its rise to exclusive popularity over a period of 12–13 years (say, from 1875 to about 1888) can only be explained through an understanding of the logic and imperatives of sport. Nevertheless, the popularity of the high-wheel bicycle as a sporting vehicle did result in the demand for better roads for utility cyclists through the 1880s and 1890s.

When the diamond-framed, solid-tired "Rover safety" bicycle emerged in the mid1880s, its speed was emphasized as much as its safety, and it was tested and recognized as a fast and efficient racing machine at the same time as it was promoted to the consumer for safer, practical transportation. Thus a discourse about sporting use and practical, functional efficiency was very evident in the discussion about and

Fig. Intro.4. *Bicycling News*, whose 801st issue from 1892 is pictured here, was founded in 1876 and described itself as "The Oldest Cycling Paper in the World." [Source: author's collection]

production of these rival designs. Starley and Sutton, makers of the Rover safety bicycle, in 1885 advertised their machine in the following way—"Have you seen the Rover safety? If not, do so at once—and try it. Pronounced by experts the Fastest Cycle ever yet made. One trial will prove this." One could argue that this moment was the point of "invention" of the modern racing bicycle.[17]

It was only with the arrival of the pneumatic-tired "safety" bicycle in the early 1890s that this radical re-definition of the bicycle, with its innovative design formula, brought recreational and practical mobility, as well as faster speeds, to a much wider public than had been able to use either the high-wheeler, the tricycle or the solid-tired "safety." Racing continued to enable evaluation of rival versions of the "safety" bicycle, and demonstrated the convincing superiority of the pneumatic tire in terms of both speed and comfort over the solid tire, on both road and track. This process is discussed in Chapter Five.

The realization of these two primary functions of the bicycle—speed and practical utility—was vividly demonstrated in long-distance place-to-place races which began with the first Bordeaux-Paris race in 1891, explored in Chapter Six. Although long-distance racing had been held since the early 1870s, these well-publicized road races promoted from the early 1890s onwards demonstrated the long-distance capabilities of the modern pneumatic-tired bicycle and were the foundation of the existing "classic" European bicycle racing calendar. These races were often sponsored by newspapers and embraced as publicity opportunities by bicycle and tire manufacturers. They demonstrated the athletic and technological possibilities of the bicycle as well as proving that racing could be used to sell bicycles, tires and sport-related newspapers to the general public. The bicycle industry continued to use the sport to publicize and market its products to the consumer, a trend that still typifies the relationship between consumers and the Tour de France, a huge annual event which tests new products and defines taste and fashion for competitive and recreational cyclists.

* * *

This book provides an historical account of the emergence of bicycle racing between the late 1860s and about 1903, focusing heavily on Britain, but also looking at France and the United States as the two other major international players. It outlines the social and institutional organization of cycling and the wider cultural, economic and technological context of the sport. In charting the early growth of cycling in Britain, France and the United States, the book attempts to provide a framework for understanding cycling's wider, contemporary international history. I have examined bicycle racing in the context of a large bicycle industry with important manufacturing centers in the English Midlands, France and the United States. I have approached the sport in the wider context of cultural and historical change, recognizing the huge impact of cycling upon habits of mobility and patterns of leisure and recreation.

I have been continually aware that actual competition is a relatively small, though crucial and extremely influential, part of cycling as a sport and recreation, and in Chapter Nine I discuss this issue in greater depth. Throughout, I have tried to recognize and explain the extent to which recreational, touring and utilitarian cycling intersected with, was influenced by, and reacted against the urge in the industry towards lightness and speed.

Finally, I introduce many of the principal actors involved in this early period of cycling—riders, trainers, journalists, bureaucrats, promoters, publishers, publicists, entrepreneurs and manufacturers—men whose modern careers helped to define new styles of athletic activity, new habits of leisure and recreation, and new ways of making and marketing consumer products for the sport and pastime of cycling.

Chapter One

The Origins of Bicycle Racing

1. The Earliest Bicycle Racing

MOST HISTORICAL ACCOUNTS of the beginnings of the bicycle in England, in the late 1860s and 1870s, have tended to focus on technological and manufacturing aspects, the evolution of design, and the brief flowering of what has been widely acknowledged as a "craze." The "two-wheeled velocipede" was a brand-new phenomenon.[1] During this early period, from 1868 to about 1872, the new word "bicycle" was used more and more frequently to distinguish the new "two-wheeled velocipede" from the 3- and 4-wheeled "velocipedes" already in existence.[2]

Later, more detailed, critical accounts of the earliest days of the commercial popularity of the bicycle note the appearance of a handful of contemporary publications on the subject in 1869–1870, mostly "how to" manuals, intended to give background information on velocipedes and bicycles, and to instruct new riders on how to choose a machine and how to ride it. The authors often added a brief, and mostly inaccurate, "history" of the velocipede, as if to give its arrival status and relevance. Two typical titles were, *The Velocipede, Its History and How to Use It* and *Velocipedes, Bicycles and Tricycles: How to Make and How to Use Them, with a sketch of their history, invention and progress.*[3]

The earliest competitive aspects of cycling have not, however, received much critical attention. This chapter therefore examines aspects of the origins and early evolution of the sport of bicycle racing in Britain, France and the United States. How much evidence is there of the earliest bicycle competitions and races? What kinds of events were they? What were the social, economic and technological stimuli behind them? Who organized them and where were they held? What sort of people competed and who were the spectators? Who made the bicycles and what kind of relationship did the bicycle makers have with the riders? What was the cultural context in which these competitions took place? Within this time period, 1869 and the early 1870s, how typical or untypical were bicycle races of athletic contests in general, and what were the main characteristics they shared with other contemporary sports events? From a social perspective, how were they perceived at the time and how should they now be viewed? To what extent were they class-specific?

* * *

The earliest years of the bicycle saw not only the manufacture of the machine itself, and its sale to men interested in the new athletic activity (women were only occasionally involved in "velocipeding'), but also the rapid development of an original sport. As soon as the machines existed, people began to race them. The first bicycle competitions took place in the context of existing athletic and social institutions before developing their own distinct characteristics. The well-documented "velocipede" movement which erupted in England in 1869 was as much concerned with sport and entertainment as it was with the potential of the new vehicle for utility and transportation. Recreation, sport and utilitarian transportation were three interconnected aspects of the technological and cultural movement of early cycling. The new sport of bicycle racing in England gave a powerful technological and economic stimulus to the young bicycle industry—racing and design improvements stimulated each other in the early development of the bicycle.

Bicycle racing began to be popular in England early in 1869, when English bicycle making was still an embryonic industry. It was stimulated by the sport that was already established in France and the United States.[4] From early 1869, a surge of velocipede activities occurred, with races, displays and competitions of various kinds held at public venues. Competitions were organized in various locations, on road and track, outdoors and indoors. They were held where a promoter could hope to make a profit, where a social festivity was occurring, or when a faster time over a known route might be achieved. Riders competed for money, for equipment, or for a valuable cup. Indoor racing was held in halls and gymnasiums, and outdoor racing on fields and prepared tracks. Bicycle racing was integrated into horticultural shows and into athletic meets which also included running, jumping, hammer-throwing and horse-riding. Race meets, which were mainly but not exclusively an urban phenomenon, often included exhibitions of bicycles organized by makers and costume competitions for the riders.[5]

Fig. 1.1. *Velocipedes, Bicycles and Tricycles: How to Make and How to Use Them* was typical of the books produced in the late 1860s. [Source: author's collection]

Professional athletics (running, walking, prize-fighting, and horse-racing, for example) was already well established in England in the 1860s, and organized amateur athletic activity was emerging in the new athleticism of the public schools and the old universities.[6] Some early bicycle racing occurred in a proletarian context similar to that of the older sport of professional pedestrianism (which included walking and running), in which races were

Fig. 1.2. "Athletics at Derby" depicted the general athletic context within which the earliest bicycle racing was staged. [Source: *The Illustrated Midland News,* 9 Oct. 1869]

held either on an enclosed track or place-to-place on the open road. An interesting account of pedestrianism in this period can be found in John Cumming's book, *Runners and Walkers, A Nineteenth Century Sports Chronicle* (1981). The high initial cost of a bicycle may well have restricted participation by working-class athletes, although clubs came into existence partly to overcome this difficulty. In other respects, indoor bicycle competitions were closer to circus or music-hall entertainment. Indeed, to the unaccustomed eye, balancing on a velocipede may well have appeared at first to have been a trick, like juggling or other gymnastic feats.

Early bicycle racing provides an excellent example of the emergence of a new mass-spectator sport in the mid–19th century and of the marketing and consumption of a novel spectacle. Bicycle makers attempted to ride an entrepreneurial wave, promoters saw the opportunity to make money, good riders sought other riders to compete against, and enough urban spectators had the leisure time and disposable income to attend events.[7] The sport emerged quickly and began to exert its own unique priorities and needs, the most important of which were smoother, faster surfaces and better, lighter bicycles.

By the mid–1870s, bicycles had improved enormously and cycling institutions and clubs had evolved. Cycling had become a well-established professional and amateur sport, supported and sustained by a flourishing manufacturing industry. From improvised beginnings, a network of amateur clubs and race meetings had emerged and national caliber professional "champions," such as James Moore, Fred Cooper, David Stanton and John Keen, had arrived on the scene, traveling widely to compete for substantial amounts of money in front of large crowds of spectators. International racing was also established between England and France, and national and "world" championships were organized. Within five years, bicycle racing had been established as a popular, and rapidly expanding, spectator sport.

Early bicycle racing should be viewed not only in a middle-class context, but in a wider context which included proletarian and lower middle-class milieus, where feats of strength, speed and endurance were admired and marketed in the mid–Victorian period. Many early competitors in London, the Midlands and the North were from the proletarian "mechanic" class (that is, wage-earners employed by manufacturing industries in manual trades), though middle-class—and even aristocratic—athletes did race bicycles as the amateur clubs grew. The bicycle, however, appears to have been socially "modern" in the sense that many of its devotees were from the emerging middle-class of wholesale and retail merchants and the urban professions.

It is more difficult to be precise and specific about the audience, the spectators, although contemporary reports provide many clues. What kinds of people went to early bicycle races? Undoubtedly, the kind of audience depended on the locality and cultural environment within which individual events were promoted. Whereas the crowd was frequently described, for example, as "select," or a report noted that "the greatest order prevailed" at a race, there are, not surprisingly, few reliable or detailed surveys of the social background of the spectators. Industrial Wolverhampton, for example, was predominantly a working-class city, and yet the *Wolverhampton Chronicle*, reporting a bicycle race in 1873, notes that the large crowd "represented all classes of the community":

> The view from the upper terraces was exceedingly beautiful, for, comingled with the husbands of the present and the future, the feminine element of our population largely patronised the scene, the varied colours of their costume and diverse style of bonnets, relieved the uniformity of male attire and afforded a study of the fashions which many of our Black Country lasses no doubt carefully treasured in their mind.

Such a report tends to contradict the assumption that the spectators at a bicycle race, in Wolverhampton in this example, would inevitably have been exclusively male and working-class, or of only one particular social class, and suggests that the humble "Black Country lasses" who attended were envious of the display of fashionable bonnets of the wealthier women.[8]

Women did not participate regularly in

Fig. 1.3. Mlle. Victoria, a vaudeville or circus performer, "Queen of the Lofty Wire," appeared in New York about 1870. [Source: Lorne Shields collection, Toronto, Canada]

the club formation and racing that constituted the early bicycle movement. The infrequent accounts of their participation describe evidently risqué, exploitative displays of gymnastic and athletic ability in the urban music-hall environment of European and American capital cities and occasional races in France. These, it can be argued, should be viewed as progressive, genuine athletic contests even though the main intention of the promoter was to be risqué and sensational. Performances involving women appear frequently to have been for salacious entertainment, rather than to showcase athletic prowess or exertion, although the fact that they occurred at all is significant.

Diarist Arthur Munby decided, after he had seen two women velocipede riders from the Paris Hippodrome perform in London in June 1869, that "there was nothing indecent in their performance, or in the girls' behavior, if once you grant that a woman may, like a man, wear breeches and sit astride in public."[9] The presence of women in this early bicycle entertainment milieu was the harbinger of their later increasing participation in cycling competitions in the 1880s and 1890s. Progress was still slow, however, and even as late as the 1920s in England it was still considered of questionable taste for a woman to compete, in public, on a bicycle.

2. The Beginning of Commercial Bicycle Production, 1865–69

The hobby horse, or "pedestrian accelerator," popularized in England in 1818–19 (and slightly earlier, in Germany, as the Draisine), was the first commercially produced "bicycle" which enabled a rider to balance and steer on two wheels. Some historians claim it as the first genuine bicycle. But it was not, because although it could be balanced and steered, it had no drive mechanism and was powered only by the legs pushing alternately against flat ground, or by gravity on a downhill slope.[10]

The Bicycle of 1869.

Between 1820 and 1860 there was well-documented, intermittent experimentation in three- and four-wheeled velocipedes, and the construction of various treadle-and-crank-driven two-wheeled velocipedes by Scottish artisan-mechanics, Kirkpatrick Macmillan and Gavin Dalzell, and others, who shared and passed around the design in an example of a

Fig. 1.4. Illustrations of "the bicycle of 1869" and "the racing bicycle of 1874" showed the design changes in a 5-year period. [Source: N. Salamon, *Bicycling: Its Rise and Development*]

The Racing Bicycle of 1874.

craft-based technology. A strong argument can be advanced that these were the earliest "bicycles"—they were two-wheeled machines that could be balanced and steered at the same time, as well as being propelled continuously forward.[11]

Although there is evidence of hobby-horse races in 1819 and occasional three- or four-wheeled velocipede speed trials later, the vast majority of these "transitional" machines did not progress beyond a prototype stage, were never put into production, and consequently could not effectively enter any organized competition. The first front-wheel driven bicycles were produced in Paris between 1865 and 1868 by Michaux, Olivier, Lallement and others, and created a fashionable craze which included a considerable amount of racing. The United States followed closely behind France, while what was sometimes referred to as the velocipede "mania" in England appears to have begun in late 1868 and early 1869.[12]

The bicycles considered in this chapter were initially heavy machines with wooden, cast-iron or steel frames and wood-spoked wheels rimmed with a metal band. They were the product of an advanced carriage and blacksmith-shop technology, but were soon being mass-produced in larger numbers, using more sophisticated manufacturing processes. Bicycle technology developed rapidly, and by about 1874 the heavy early velocipede was transformed, with a light, tubular frame and wire-suspension wheels with solid rubber tires, typified by the bicycles of champion rider and manufacturer John Keen, which are more fully described in Chapter Two.

The most conspicuous design changes were the enlargement of the front wheel to cover more ground with each pedal stroke—hence making greater speed possible—and the reduction in the size of the rear wheel. From reports and discussions in the press documentation of the period, it is clear that racing events were the crucial factor in this evolution of the velocipede into the early high-wheel bicycle. Competition brought together the latest designs and technological developments in a conspicuous public testing ground, and demonstrated clearly the weaknesses of the old and the merits of new approaches to the nascent sport.

3. Velocipede Developments in France and the United States, 1867–69: Their Influence on the British Sport

An energetic young industry, with an associated velocipede sport, similar in many respects to the British sport which is the main focus of this chapter, emerged in France and America *before* it emerged in Britain. The British industry and sport was stimulated from abroad. An ongoing interest in 3- and 4-wheeled velocipedes in Britain ensured the willing reception there of the new two-wheeled velocipede. But, in the light of this well-documented interest in multi-wheel velocipedes, and also the British passion for sport and indoor entertainments, it has not been convincingly explained why Britain lagged behind French and American developments.

With a rapidly developing velocipede manufacturing base, the French sport quickly reached a sophisticated level from 1867 to 1870, and outdoor road and track races were held, as well as the fashionably sumptuous indoor practice sessions depicted in Fig. 1.6. The

One. The Origins of Bicycle Racing in England, France and America 21

velocipede was enthusiastically embraced, and a Parisian and regional club structure was quickly organized. American velocipede sporting events, which increased in 1868 and 1869, appear to have emphasized indoor entertainment, although American spectators did also enjoy outdoor track racing. In France, the Franco-Prussian War of 1870–71 interrupted manufacturing processes and disrupted sporting activity, and in the United States what was a brief but intense athletic and entertainment fad appears to have lost its appeal quickly. In Britain in the early 1870s, however, manufacturers took advantage of what they had learned from French technological advances and an energetic sports culture embraced the new velocipede. With the arrival of the velocipede in Britain in late 1868 and early 1869, the British sport immediately took off and was subsequently firmly embraced and developed throughout the 1870s in an unbroken cultural, manufacturing and organizational continuity.

The earliest French bicycle racing has been documented by Keizo Kobayashi.[13] Kobayashi has found that races were held as early as 1867 and were popular throughout France in 1868, when at least 21 race meetings occurred. Reports in *Le Vélocipède Illustré* and Parisian and provincial newspapers provide extensive documentation of racing in 1869 (180 races or race meetings), and in 1870 (77 events), until the outbreak of war with Prussia in August.

Races were initially organized by velocipede makers (including the prominent Parisian maker, Michaux) and existing athletic organizations, and later promoted by velocipede clubs and "fête" committees. The majority of races were short-distance track races, but place-to-place road races were also held, often between prominent locations, from the

Fig. 1.5. Velocipede racing for women occurred in Bordeaux as early as 1868. [Source: *Le Monde Illustré*, 21 Nov. 1868]

Champs-Élysées to Versailles, for example, or from Paris to Rouen. It is clear that athletic use of the velocipede was responsible for popularizing and developing it: "Velocipedes have become a rage. Everybody talks of them," wrote the Paris correspondent of a London paper, *Orchestra*: "Athletes and gymnasts led the way, and now you see them in the hands of old, young, serious and gay."[14]

Clubs were formed specifically to encourage and organize velocipede racing. There were two clubs in Paris and Rouen, and various clubs in Marseille, Avignon, Beauvais, Bordeaux, Chartres, Nantes, Rennes, Le Havre, Lyon and Versailles. By 1870, there were about 40 clubs in France, although no central organizing body had been created.[15]

Many of these races are well-documented, providing lists of starters, the name of the manufacturers of the bicycles ridden, and details of the prizes awarded. Several "stars," such as Hippolyte Moret, André Castera and James Moore, emerged from this period of French racing; they won races all over France and became well-known internationally.[16] Kobayashi documents at least twenty examples of women's velocipede racing in France and Belgium. Women's races often occurred on the same occasion as men's racing and included an emerging group of women performers identified by their first names or by nicknames, i.e., "Miss Olga," or "Miss America."[17]

The most significant French road race in this early period was the Paris-Rouen race, sponsored on 7 November 1869 by René Olivier, owner of the velocipede company Compagnie Parisienne, and Richard Lesclide, editor of *Le Vélocipède Illustré*, who wanted to

Fig. 1.6. The "grand manège" of the Compagnie Parisienne in Paris in June 1869. [Source: *L'Illustration*, 12 June 1869]

stimulate business and encourage riding by proving that "on the Bicycle it is possible to cover considerable distances, with much less fatigue than walking, and in a much shorter time," and offered 1,000 francs as first prize. The industry would be stimulated by the competition and by demonstrating the practical utility of the bicycle. There were no limitations of design or size of wheel, the rules stipulating only that machines had to be driven by muscle-power and that no outside help was allowed. The winner was the English rider James Moore.[18]

All this activity across the Channel did not go unnoticed in England. In August 1867, *The Field* wrote of "the mania for velocipedes at present existing in Paris," and reprinted an account from *Le Sport*:

> From nine to eleven in the forenoon the space about the Cascade is crowded by the amateurs and spectators of these races.... Many of these have become so skilful as to go 24 kilo-metres (15 miles) an hour without the least fatigue. Some grand races during the autumn are at present being organized, the course to be gone over extending from the Rond-point of the Champs Élysées to Saint-Cloud.... In fact, some considerable bets were made on that occasion. These gentlemen are about to form a velocipede club to be devoted to the new sport.[19]

It is clear from this and other accounts which appeared in the British press, including *The Times, The Mechanic* and *The English Mechanic*, that Parisian velocipede activities were widely reported and stimulated interest in the new sport in Britain.

In February 1869, an article in the London *Times* asked, "How long before the velocipedestrian mania attacks young England? France revived the obsolete machine and gave interest and excitement to its use.... From our neighbours across the Channel the furore migrated to our brethren across the Atlantic, passing over us."[20] The interesting phrase—"France revived the obsolete machine"— indicates that the writer of *The Times* article was certainly aware of the pre-history of hobby-horses and other later velocipedes.

Reports of the Parisian velocipede craze also appeared in American newspapers, and racing undoubtedly began in the United States shortly before it occurred in Britain.[21] The Paris correspondent of the *New York Times* reported to its readers in August 1867 that: "the experts in this new and cheap mode of locomotion make twelve miles an hour, and a higher speed will be

Fig. 1.7. James Moore and the Michaux velocipede on which he won the race from Paris to Rouen in November 1869, in Hampstead, London, in 1930. [Source: *Coureur, Sporting Cyclist*, April 1968]

attained.... The young men of leisure are said to be organizing a club for racing, which of course will only embrace "gentleman riders."'22

By August 1868, a shipment of French velocipedes was reported to have arrived in New York, and in September a French-style velocipede was introduced by its maker, Pickering. By November 1868, the *New York Times* commented prophetically:

> We plainly foresee another "field-sport" about to be added to our slender American catalogue, or at least another athletic game. The Paris velocipede is now so firmly naturalized here that we have simultaneously a local report of regular two-wheelers racing in Central Park and one of a race in Boston.... We presume that "velocipede clubs' will now be formed, and velocipede contests waged; then of course will follow velocipede matches for the "Velocipede Championship of the United States" and then international matches for the "Championship of the World"'23

The prediction of the *New York Times* was accurate: the business and sport of velocipeding quickly became fashionable in New York, Boston, Indianapolis, Chicago, and even San Francisco, out on the West Coast. The American press, including the prestigious *Scientific American*, printed copious reports of the craze, including its diffusion outside the original centers. *Scientific American* reported that, "The velocipede fever is raging in Massachusetts ... the Cincinnati Velocipede Club have given a series of races," and that, "It is amusing to notice how rapidly this fresh idea has germinated, budded, and bloomed, and is actually bearing fruit in the way of active action. There are trials and competitions on the Common and in other convenient locations.... It is certainly the source of innocent amusement, and promotes muscular development."24

Fig. 1.8. A brochure issued by Wood Brothers, on Broadway, New York, offers French velocipedes to the American market. [Source: John L. Weiss collection]

Velocipede entertainment and sport traveled as far as California, which was isolated geographically from the East Coast and from Europe, but was connected culturally through the constant incoming stream of immigrants since the 1849 Gold Rush. The railway link to the west coast from St. Louis was not completed until May 1869, so that imported velocipedes had at first to come laboriously overland or round the Horn on cargo ships. Velocipeding in San Francisco quickly became very popular, a testimony to the attractions of the new sport and the influence of the media in popularizing new ideas, particularly where handsome profits could be made in entertainment.

In January 1869, when a San Francisco manufacturer, Palmer, Knox

Fig. 1.9. "Scene in a Riding-school, New York City" depicts the indoor environment in which much early bicycle sport took place in Europe and America. [Source: *Harper's Weekly*, 13 Feb. 1869]

and Co., was already making a "greatly improved" velocipede, the *San Francisco Morning Chronicle* printed a front-page article entitled "Velocipedes—The Greatest Mania of the Age," which spoke of "the restless desire of the Parisians," which had created "the wonder of the age, the velocipede."[25] The exaggerated language—"mania of the age," "wonder of the age"—suggests an aspect of popular culture, of modern life, which was promoted, briefly bloomed, and could perhaps be expected to fade out just as quickly. It was the fad of the moment.

After late 1869, the American bicycle appears to have declined in popularity, and optimistic forecasts for the sport's future in the United States proved wrong. Karl Kron wrote in the mid–1880s of the "wildly impetuous and frenziedly hopeful beginnings" and the "sudden and ignominious ending" of the velocipede movement: "The American carriage-makers all dropped the veloce in a hurry, with a feeling of contempt for their own folly in having interrupted their proper business in behalf of such a deceptive toy," he wrote, "But the less excitable Englishmen kept pegging away at it, both on the road and in the machine shop, until the modern bicycle was evolved. Velocipeding never entirely ceased in that country."[26]

Thus, French and American bicycle racing began earlier than it did in Britain. British accounts reported the more developed state of things abroad, even as Britain's own velocipede "craze" was getting under way. The international nature of this early velocipede industry and sport raises interesting questions about the transmission of a new sport and sporting equipment from country to country in the late 1860s, and highlights the crucial role of the press in the dissemination of trends and new ideas. Particularly interesting is the wide geographical range, and the speedy communication of machine designs, manufacturing expertise, and the sport itself.[27]

The velocipede seems to have spread initially from France to the East Coast of the United States, while Britain was slow, at first, in taking it up. In America, the fad spread quickly from the East Coast to the Midwest and as far as California, a remarkable fact considering the distances involved, and the fact that the pioneering transcontinental railroad had only recently been completed.[28] Amazingly, there seems to have been bicycle racing in San Francisco even earlier than in London! Meanwhile, both manufacturing expertise and bicycle racing styles appear to have filtered from France and the United States back to England, where they were enthusiastically embraced.

Fig. 1.10. The short American velocipede rage is beautifully captured in this line engraving of Pickering's velocipede in New York. [Source: *Harper's Weekly*, 19 Dec. 1868]

It seems reasonable, therefore, to assert that the widespread enthusiasm in France and America for the new bicycling "craze" had a significant impact on the British and certainly helped both to ensure its speedy assimilation in Britain and the rapid development of machines and facilities. The evidence supports an early 1869 date for the beginning of widespread commercial activity in selling bicycles in England and the beginnings of the sport. An article in *The Times* (19 Nov. 1868) stated:

> Anybody who has visited Paris within the last few months cannot have failed to notice the large number of velocipedes going to and fro.... The cost of the best velocipedes in France is about £12, but they will probably be manufactured at a much lower price in England if they come into extensive use as is not unlikely, considering that they afford opportunities for vigourous exercise, in addition to the facility with which long journeys may be made on them.

Was it the availability of skilled manufacturing labor in the English Midlands which enabled such a rapid growth of the bicycle industry? Or was it the English attraction to sports of all kinds? An article in *The Times* (1 Feb. 1869) asked: "How long before the velocipedestrian mania attacks young England? ... From our neighbours across the Channel the furore migrated to our brethren across the Atlantic, passing us over.... Our turn may come yet." Another article, from January 1869, in an industrial trade journal, gave the following chronological perspective:

One. The Origins of Bicycle Racing in England, France and America 27

Fig. 1.11. Velocipede riders, on imported and locally made machines, outside the Mechanics' Pavilion in San Francisco, probably early 1869. Photograph by Edward Muybridge. [Source: Lorne Shields collection, Toronto, Canada]

The mere fact that we have not yet experienced the furore that has accompanied the introduction of the iron horse into France, constitutes no evidence that it will not be equally popular in this country.... It is to be borne in mind that up to the present time the English public here has not been tempted by any supply of the two-wheeled vehicles, French and American requirements fully occupying their several manufacturers; but we already hear of measures being taken to reproduce in this country, under arrangements with the several patentees, the best descriptions of this machine.... We may take it, therefore, for granted, that the velocipede so strongly recommended by the practice of our neighbours, and the praise of which is wafted to us across the Atlantic, is destined not only to come largely into use in this country, but to be a permanent "institution."[29]

Later in February, the same publication commented": Sinceour last issue new evidences have been presented that although England has been slow to follow the movement in France and the United States, a general demand is springing up, so much so, indeed, that our velocipede manufacturers experience already the greatest difficulty in supplying orders. We hear of Sheffield and Birmingham houses being engaged to fulfil the orders of London manufacturers, whilst velocipedes are being daily imported from France."[30]

4. CHARLES SPENCER'S LONDON GYMNASIUM

A description of one of the earliest appearances of the bicycle in England shows vividly the links between the importing of French bicycles into England, manufacturing activity in the English Midlands, the pursuit of physical fitness as a leisure activity, and the sale of athletic supplies to the consumer. In an account published in 1875, John Mayall, Jr., the son of a well-known London photographer, describes how in the winter of 1868–69 he went to Charles Spencer's gymnasium in the City of London, "to look at some monster hollow dumb-bells that had just been made for a 'professional' to make a *sensation* with at a Music hall," when a box was unpacked, containing a French velocipede brought from Paris by Rowley Turner.

This was evidently Mayall and Spencer's first hands-on contact with the bicycle, although Turner, the agent in Paris for the Coventry Machinists' Company (which manufactured sewing machines), had already been exposed to the velocipede craze there. It was not the first appearance of the bicycle in England, but was certainly a significant event in our understanding of the origins of the English sport and the industry. Rowley Turner took this velocipede on to Coventry, to the Coventry Machinists' Company factory, where some of the earliest English bicycles were being manufactured during a period of economic slump for the sewing machine industry.[31] The connection thus established between velocipedes and sewing machines was not an coincidental one, for the industrial capacity—the precise machining of small metal parts—was a crucial requirement in both cases.

Fig. 1.12. Varieties of velocipede racing and riding were illustrated on the cover of the Recreation Supplement of the *Gentleman's Journal*, 1 April 1870. [Source: Lorne Shields collection Toronto, Canada]

A similar commercial dynamic can be seen in an account of how Thomas Humber first became involved with bicycles which is given by A.B. Demaus in his *The Humber Story, 1868-1932* (1989). Humber was employed by William Campion, who made hosiery machinery in Nottingham. While showing his own machines at the Paris Exhibition of 1867, Campion was impressed by the Michaux-style velocipedes he saw in the streets. He bought one, took it back to Humber in Nottingham, and asked him to make six sets of forgings based on it. Humber's first machines were made in a shed at the back of his house. But by 1872–73, Humber was making a "Spider Bicycle" with a much bigger front wheel which was the forerunner of the later high-wheel bicycle.

Charles Spencer was an

ex-champion gymnast and entrepreneur who manufactured and sold sporting goods. The bicycle was thus introduced into an athletic context, because Spencer's gymnasium was a center of physical fitness and gymnastic endeavor in London and velocipeding was at first very much an acrobatic activity, requiring the skill of balance, much of which took place indoors. Indeed, Mayall specifically recollected in his 1875 memoir that "the energy with which I went into velocipeding in its early days was essentially a part of my gymnastic tastes."

With his business partner, Snoxell, Spencer began to market the velocipede. In mid–February 1869, the *English Mechanic,* an important scientific and manufacturing journal, which catered to self-made artisans and small manufacturers, carried an advertisement publicizing the company as "Velocipede and Gymnastic Apparatus Manufacturers," who had "introduced the best Paris Model of the New Two-Wheel Velocipede, and having made several important improvements thereon, are now prepared to execute orders to any extent."[32]

Fig. 1.13. One of the earliest commercial bicycle advertisements was for Snoxell and Spencer's "new two-wheel velocipede." [Source: *English Mechanic,* 19 Feb. 1869]

These men who were involved in this indoor athletic and gymnastic innovation in London also took the bicycle out onto the road. They practiced riding in Regents Park, London and in February 1869 they rode to Brighton. "They had a preliminary run around Trafalgar Square, and then started off at the rate of eight miles an hour on roads which proved to be generally good, but against a very strong wind all the way." This event was intended to advertise and promote Spencer's business and the sale of velocipedes and was widely reported in *The Times* and other newspapers.[33] But it was also intended to demonstrate that the machine could be used to travel longer distances, that it had utilitarian potential.

By 1870, Spencer's business was no longer associated with Snoxell, and his catalogue advertized him as "Manufacturer of Gymnastic Apparatus, Velocipedes, and all Athletic and British Sport Requirements." He was also "Contractor for fitting up all the Military Gymnasia to Her Majesty's Government for Home and Foreign Stations." The catalogue included extensive gymnastic and weight-lifting products, as well as fencing, football, cricket, hockey and croquet supplies. He also supplied velocipedes "of first class manufacture only," one model "guaranteed for long journeys and hard wear," another "for ordinary use and racing." The catalogue also advertized his two books, *The Modern Gymnast* and *The Bicycle: Its Use and Action.*[34]

All of this was the start of Spencer's long involvement with the bicycle, as rider, journalist and publisher. In 1873, Spencer and three companions rode from London to John o'Groats, the northern-most tip of Scotland, a pioneering long-distance ride. And Spencer's *Bicycle Road Book*, which gives details of mileages and road conditions throughout Britain, went through many editions in the 1880s and was the prototype for the many route books published for cyclists in the 1890s.[35]

Although Spencer's gymnasium was especially significant in early bicycle manufacturing history because of the connection between Rowley Turner, Charles Spencer and the Coventry Machinists' Company in Coventry, it was just one of many sources of the spread of the new consumer fad and recreation. It was economically beneficial to manufacturing businesses that the bicycle be publicized, and that clubs be formed. Another company, the "French Velocipede Co.," owned by A. Davis, who called himself "Agent and Manufacturer" in the first commercial advertisement for bicycles published in England, was "prepared to give information to amateurs and inventors, clubs, schools, regiments, gymnasiums, etc.... Any gentlemen desirous to form Clubs in London or the country may have assistance in their primary organization from the Co., who will act as secretary, and find offices, etc, where necessary."[36] This was the earliest example of the offer of commercial sponsorship of cycling clubs in the history of the British sport.

5. Bicycle Competition as Athletic Novelty and Public Spectacle

As we have seen, the British public could have read accounts of velocipede racing in France as early as 1867. *The Sport* reported "the mania for velocipedes" in Paris, where racers included aristocrats, some of whom "have become so skilful as to go 24 kilometres (15 miles) an hour without the least fatigue.... These gentlemen are about to form a velocipede club, to be devoted to the new sport."[37] By late 1868, *The Mechanic* reported that Parisian velocipede races, already well developed and generally held on a "fete day," were "rather exciting affairs":

> The racing-ground is all marked out with flags, and there is certain to be a large cluster of banners flying at the starting place, near to which, in some reserved enclosure, scores of velocipedists are exercising their docile steeds. A certain number of them wear jockey caps and jackets of various coloured silks, and all appear to have their legs encased in high leather boots.
>
> The moment of starting arrives, and the competitors are duly drawn up abreast.... The fair sex mount on chairs and wave their little hands and flourish their pocket handkerchiefs, and laugh and almost scream with delight as at the grounding of the starter's flag their several favourites dart off, working their legs up and down...
>
> After the lapse of a few minutes, the crowd opens to allow of the passage of the victor, who drenched

in perspiration ... passes the winning post amidst the cheers and laughter of the crowd, who enjoy the sport more than they would the finest horse-race; and as soon as he has dismounted proceeds to dip his sun-burnt beak into a foaming glass of Strasburg beer.[38]

Racing on the novel velocipede was clearly excitingly "modern," a sport made possible by a machine created in a progressive, industrial, technological society. The many reports of the earliest bicycle competitions in Britain contain frequent expressions of wonderment, emphasizing the novelty of the new sport. Even the elementary fact that the machine could be balanced and propelled forward was at first seen as somewhat astonishing. Nevertheless, the settings in which competitions and displays took place tended to be traditional and familiar. The new "two-wheeled velocipede" was introduced in a variety of entertainment contexts, and promoters appear to have experimented to see what format would be most likely to attract a crowd and make money. There was clearly a strong "show-business" element at work, and velocipede competitions took their place among the many commercial entertainments available.

Events were also staged by amateur social and sporting gatherings and velocipede clubs. Participation demanded ownership of, or at least access to, the expensive new machine and rental arrangements for the general public and cooperative credit schemes for club members made bicycles more accessible to the less well-off. The sport of velocipeding, or "bicycling," as it very soon came to be known, evolved alongside these commercial entertainment activities. And, of course, some riders preferred just to ride on city streets, away from any competitive or commercial context. These riders, when they went out for the fun of it, or just to go somewhere, became the earliest recreational and utility cyclists.

Thus the sport struggled to express its young identity. A successful commercial sporting formula was not predictably or easily created, and an amateur sport structure for velocipede or bicycle racing did not yet exist. A London sporting journal was at first skeptical of the new sport: "The large hall at Islington seems governed by magic influence in its changes of attraction," *The Field* commented sarcastically on 19 June 1869:

> fat cattle, monster balls, popular concerts and horse shows have followed in rapid succession, and now a "bicycle race" is the object of public interest; indeed we are not sure that it is any longer the "Agricultural Hall" as the enterprising manager has named it anew the "Velocipede Cirque'... There is no doubt that the spectacle called a race was got up with a sole view to profit, and in all probability, so far as that was concerned, it answered excellently well ... but whether such an exhibition will prove a permanent source of profit we will not venture to predict.

On that occasion, *The Field* was disappointed with the poor quality of the racing in Islington, North London: "There is no doubt that as yet good riders are too scarce to make such contests interesting.... We have certainly seen many better workers of the bicycle on the road than the majority of those who competed for the silver cup," which was offered at this race.[39] Although the promoter in Islington spent a large amount of money installing a special floor and stands for the spectators, the event was still profitable, indicating that it did succeed in drawing a good audience. Perhaps the betting, which *The Field* regretted, helped to fill the promoter's pockets. But it was an unpredictable business. And together with the risk of loss went the possibility of fraud. The value of a cup could easily be inflated, the results could be fixed, and prizes left unpaid.

Nevertheless, the new sport arrived quite suddenly, and easily attracted and fascinated large crowds. Promoters were willing to take risks and were quick to capitalize on the new sensation. Well-publicized outdoor races and indoor displays were significant in creating a surge of popular interest in the new machine, as was the volume of press coverage which both reported and promoted the new sport. Many people saw the machine for the first time because they paid to see it.

But to be successful, such events demanded skilled riders within a recognizable entertainment formula. The promoters of the "Velocipede Derbys" at the famous Crystal Palace at Sydenham, South London experimented with their productions and refined their events. "The Crystal Palace Company, ever on the alert for novelties, were not likely to let the velocipede mania subside without duly utilizing it," commented *The Field* on 29 May 1869:

> The announcement of a velocipede race was sure to draw many hundreds of that faithful British public who, day after day, from year's end to year's end, go everywhere to see anything. They may be disappointed, but their faith remains unshaken.... Accordingly, young and old went down to the Palace on Thursday to enjoy this latest sensation. We wish we could add that they did enjoy it, but the weather was dreadful, and the contests were neither exciting nor well conducted.[40]

In spite of this disappointment, however, the Crystal Palace promoters quickly learned the lesson of successful promotion and staged many interesting and important races at the well-located South London venue through the summer of 1869.

Crowds did not only assemble in an indoor arena or around a grass or cinder track, although that was the easiest way for promoters to guarantee themselves a box-office fee. Road racing, which was a different, more strenuously athletic kind of test, also attracted audiences, and introduced another hugely significant component of the sport to England.

In April 1869, a "Great Bicycle Race" was held on the road between Chester and Liverpool, a distance of 13 miles. The road was already "laid with macadam, but some portions of it were complained of as detrimental to bicycle travelling, owing to numbers of loose stones being scattered on the surface." The *Liverpool Mercury* carried a long report of the race, noting that "the excitement caused by this singular race was something marvellous":

> A considerable gathering of spectators was expected, but scarcely anyone imagined that there would have been such an enormous crowd of persons assembled to see this novel contest. The competitors were announced to start from Chester about half past two o'clock, but long before that time thousands of people, rich and poor, thronged the Chester-road for miles, and up to four o'clock the thoroughfare from Birkenhead was dense with pedestrians. An immense number of well-dressed persons crossed the river from Liverpool and the Rock Ferry steamers alone, between one and four o'clock, carried over to Cheshire upwards of 3,000 passengers.
>
> Besides pedestrians, there were vehicles of all sorts and sizes—bicycles, velocipedes, carriages, cars, gigs, spring carts, donkey carts, etc. At some points from Rock Ferry to Bromborough the road was almost blocked up, and farmers and others who were returning home from Birkenhead had great difficulty in making a passage through the crowds of people. In many parts the hedges were also lined with spectators ... at all the villages on the route through which the bicycles passed there was a general turn-out of the inhabitants.[41]

It would have been fascinating to have seen this mixture of bicycles and velocipedes out on the road that day. The spectators were so dense, in fact, that they obstructed the competitors, who "had difficulty in winding their way through the crowd."[42] A good race could hardly be held under such conditions, and other road users had just cause to complain about the obstruction of their right of way, and of the unwanted disturbance of rural harmony by city-dwellers, an issue that continued to be a problem for organizers of events and for riders racing on public

One. The Origins of Bicycle Racing in England, France and America 33

Fig. 1.14. The Bicycle Tournament at Liverpool saw the velocipede used as public entertainment, with suggestions of medieval jousting. [Source: *Illustrated London News*, 1 May 1869]

roads through the 1880s and 1890s. In fact, the conflict between different categories of road users would be a decisive factor in determining the future character of the British sport.

Liverpool was an early hotbed of velocipede competition.[43] After the road race, the Liverpool Velocipede Club was obliged to stage an extra evening performance of its "Bicycle Tournament and Assault at Arms" at its Gymnasium, because "it was found utterly impossible to accommodate the whole of the people who applied for tickets for the first and the committee of the club was anxious to meet this popular demand." The Gymnasium program included members of the club "Tilting at the Ring, Throwing the Javelin and demonstrating general proficiency in the various modes of managing the Bicycle."

Just as it had been introduced earlier at Spencer's gymnasium within a gymnastic context, the velocipede was employed here in the "Tournament," a revamping of current gymnastic displays to capitalize on the entertainment potential of the new fad. In this curious example of a profit-making show-business event organized by a newly constituted club, the modernity of the bicycle and the newly acquired skill of the riders were set in an anachronistic and artificial context of medieval "jousting" and "tilting," though it was also noted that the bicycle had practical potential as "a safe and rapid means of locomotion."[44]

The potential of the bicycle as a tool for speed and modern sport was not fully realized yet, and bicycle racing was here promoted by reference to long-dead, festive, cultural traditions. The *Liverpool Weekly Courier* carried a glowing description of the jousting "Tournament":

the public, who have been accustomed lately to see this latest novelty in locomotion under the unskilful guidance of venturous youth wobbling about the streets in an apparently unmanageable manner, in peril of being run down by the cabs and other vehicles, would scarcely conceive the absolute control under which the machine is brought by successful practice. Though this forms no part of the curriculum of physical education received at the Gymnasium, the bicycle has found there a patronage and encouragement sufficiently liberal to have enabled a large number of its admirers to attain a remarkable degree of perfection in its management, so as to place beyond doubt the fact that it may be made a safe and rapid means of locomotion. The skill of the riders and the efficiency of the various kinds of these machines which have been introduced in rapid succession since they were brought, still recently, before the attention of the public, could not be more thoroughly demonstrated than by such tests as those to which they were put in the Tournament on Saturday.... The Gymnasium was thronged with eager spectators, the majority of whom were ladies, to whom the novelty of the joust afforded great diversion.[45]

In Liverpool, this "Bicycle Tournament," staged by men, was graced with the presence of many "ladies," whose presence validated it as a respectable social occasion. The crowd-pleasing potential of bicycle entertainment was also evident in London. For the already mentioned "Velocipede Derby" at the Crystal Palace in May 1869, a formula which was repeated at frequent intervals throughout the summer, "a large number of visitors was induced to go down to Sydenham with a view to witnessing the properties of a machine which has lately engaged so much public attention."[46] At the Agricultural Hall, Islington, where "Grand Bicycle Races" were held for several weeks in June and July, opening night attracted "about 1,500 persons," and on a subsequent Saturday night "there was a much larger assemblage of persons present than on any past occasion," allowing a reduction of the admission charge.[47]

Crowds of people continued to attend bicycle racing at popular venues in English cities as the sport expanded onto open-air tracks, and the initial craze appears to have solidified into a well-established sporting habit. On a Saturday afternoon in April 1870, 3,000 people were present at Aston Cross Grounds, Birmingham for "the championship of the Midlands.... The large space fronting the green, the great gallery, as well as the trees, were literally crammed, the green being reserved for the ladies, of whom a fair sprinkling were present."[48] One thousand people were reported at Vauxhall Gardens, Wolverhampton on Monday, 6 June 1870, to see "William Turner's All-England bicycle contest for amateurs who have never won any prize."[49] In August 1870, to watch races at Molineux Grounds, Wolverhampton between international caliber professional riders, John Keen, E. Shelton, James Moore, J.T. Johnson and others, "nearly 2,000 persons paid for admission on Saturday, and another 2,000 on Monday."[50]

Quite astonishingly—a fact that has gone unnoticed in the historical accounts to date—little more than a year after the sport had begun, 2,000 people were commonly counted attracks in the cycling centers of England when well-known riders were competing, and there was soon a small group of "champions" who could be marketed as stars in the important racing cities such as Birmingham, Sheffield, Liverpool, London, and especially Wolverhampton. An elite category of "champion" rider had quickly emerged within the new sport.

6. Links Between Manufacture and Sport

While there was no unifying organization working to promote the bicycle in these geographically scattered early exhibitions and racing events, the most interest in bicycle racing tended to be in those areas where the manufacturing and marketing of bicycles was most active, that is, in and around London, Wolverhampton, Manchester, Birmingham, Liverpool and Sheffield. Reporting on racing at the Molineux Grounds, Wolverhampton in June 1873, the *Wolverhampton Chronicle* suggested that: "Bicycle riding seems to have localized itself in Wolverhampton as an amusement no doubt owing, in a great measure, to the favourable nature of these grounds, but aided by the district being the principal seat of the manufacture of the two-wheelers."[51]

Especially in the larger cities, competitive events gave promoters and manufacturers an opportunity to stage exhibitions of machines as an additional attraction and source of income, a further indication that the sport was, from its very beginning, used in advertising and promoting the products of the bicycle industry. Such exhibitions typically took place in London, at the Crystal Palace, or at the Agricultural Hall, Islington. But even in one very rural location, racing was linked with an exhibition of the latest technical developments. At Studley Pleasure Grounds, Yorkshire, "within the shade of that famous and most beautiful of all monastic ruins, Fountains Abbey," as part of its "11th annual exhibition of plants, flowers and vegetables," the Ripon Horticultural and Floral Society organized a velocipede exhibition which historian, H.H. Griffin, wrote "brought together the finest display of cycles ever seen up to that date," held at a moment "which was very prolific in new ideas."[52]

The Wolverhampton Velocipede Club's *Rules*, from 1869, provide telling evidence of this connection between the sport and the industry in its earliest period. The Club was established to buy velocipedes for the use of members at the Club's "practice room." The rules included the provisions that "when the members are efficient in the use of the machines, excursions into the country will be arranged by the Committee," and that "all races between other Clubs, and meetings, etc., are to be first submitted to the Club for their approval, and the Committee shall decide on the terms of every such Race and meeting." Most significantly, the *Rules* carried an advertisement for "Forder and Traves, Manufacturers to the Wolverhampton Velocipede Club," a mid–Victorian model of the kind of sponsorship for supplying equipment that still exists throughout the sports world today, one that is integral to the structure of modern bicycle racing.[53]

A probably slightly earlier account, from the *Wolverhampton Chronicle*, suggests that this Wolverhampton Velocipede Club was originally conceived as the Wolverhampton and Staffordshire Velocipede Company or Association, and was formed "for the purpose of promoting velocipeding in the town and neighbourhood," whereby members would buy shares and be enabled to buy velocipedes, "by paying £10 in monthly instalments.... They would buy velocipedes, rent practice grounds, teach velocipeding and lend velocipedes to members." Alderman Bantock attended a Saturday evening meeting at the Agricultural Hall and "recommended the use of the velocipede as a means of pleasant relaxation and healthful enjoyment." At this meeting, Messrs. Forder and Traves demonstrated "the ease, rapidity and security of the bicycle" and subsequently "entered into an arrangement by virtue of which the new company will be appointed the sole agents for the sale of velocipedes in this town."[54]

At this early stage in the development of the sport, a technological and economic logic had developed in the relationship between riders and manufacturers, between the sport and the industry, which made it likely that riders would become makers and vice versa. An ordinary customer might ride a velocipede occasionally, tolerating deficiencies. But serious riders were more demanding and were acutely aware of discomfort, inefficiency, bad design, heavy weight, harsh suspension, or any other technical problems or difficulties. The key concern for racers was speed, but speed could only be achieved through a combination of mechanical efficiency, reliability and physical comfort. The addition of a rubber cushion or tire to prevent the early metal-ringed wheels from slipping was one example of technological improvement. The skill of the rider and the type of riding surface were also important. These aspects were debated constantly within racing and manufacturing circles, and tested in competition. Racers became the most critical and demanding of consumers, and gave the most valuable feedback to the manufacturers.[55]

The Londoner John Keen, who participated in many professional championships at various distances between 1870 and 1880, winning many of them, was the pre-eminent example of an outstanding champion who was also a distinguished manufacturer, widely credited with having played an important role in advancing early bicycle design and technology. Amateurs and professionals alike coveted a Keen machine for the state-of-the-art technical edge it gave them.

In November 1871, a writer to *The Field* reported "the greater efficiency of Keen's 'Spider' bicycle, the superiority of the 'rigid wheel,' the lightness, durability and rigidness.... No other maker has brought the bicycle to such luxurious excellence as he has." Another report in the same paper, in May 1872, commented that the Keen Brothers' "Spider" bicycle "has come to be extensively used ... on account of the prompt manner in which certain well-tested improvements have been adopted." The building of a strong, light wheel was a crucial design element in this early period, and Keen's wheels were among the best in the business, making it possible for the size of the wheel to increase to as much as 60 inches.[56]

A catalogue for the Keen bicycle from 1874 claimed that "the practical experience of its maker has enabled him, after much study and perseverance, to produce a machine which for durability, lightness and speed, cannot be rivalled." "Patent Anti-friction Bearings," and other improvements in frame and wheels constituted the "great superiority" of Keen's machines. There was "as great a contrast in riding on a well constructed bicycle and on an

Fig. 1.15. The only known photograph of bicycle pioneer Charles Spencer was published in 1909. [Source: *Cycle Times*, 1909]

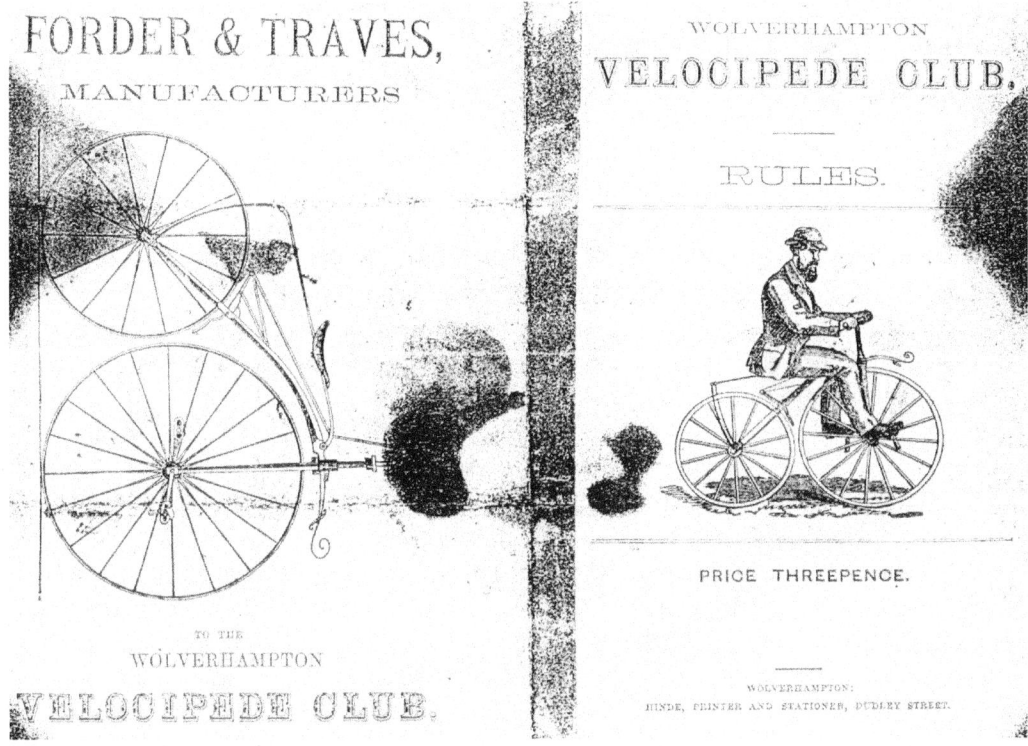

Fig. 1.16. The Wolverhampton Velocipede Club's 1869 "Rules" advertised a sponsorship arrangement with a local manufacturer, Forder and Traves. [Source: Lorne Shields collection, Toronto, Canada]

inferior one, as there is between riding in a light spring carriage and in a cart without springs."[57]

John Keen's outstanding early role was recognized in 1884, when a committee made up of prominent cycling personalities, including the rider Ion Keith-Falconer and editors George Lacy Hiller and Harry Etherington, was formed to collect money for a "testimonial" to him, to prove to him "that his life and doings have not gone unnoticed and unrewarded." In a letter circulated to *Wheeling* and *The Cyclist*, these luminaries called Keen "the pioneer of our sport," and attested that "beyond the manufacture of machines, the credit of first proving their use also falls to John Keen.... Not only did he once carry everything before him upon the racing path, but down to the present day he is undoubtedly the best and prettiest road rider we have." Such a statement lends powerful support to the assertion that competitive cycling was a crucial factor in the technological and economic development of the early bicycle industry. Keen's important role will be further discussed in Chapter Two.[58]

Briefly, there were many technical experiments in the early years of bicycle design, mostly aimed at increasing a rider's speed and comfort. Speed was greatly affected by the "gear," defined by the size of the pedaled front wheel of the bicycle and thus the distance covered with each pedal rotation. Attempts were made to "gear up" this wheel mechanically, but the easiest way to cover more ground with each rotation of the pedals was to enlarge the drive-wheel, resulting in a slight advantage for a taller rider, with longer legs, over his shorter rival, who could, however, overcome this disadvantage with a quicker pedalling technique. By about 1875, the high-wheel bicycle had emerged and would dominate bicycle design for the following ten years, continuing the strong athletic and acrobatic tendencies inherent in early velocipede displays.

Throughout the 1870s and into the first half of the 1880s, the high-wheel, or "ordinary," bicycle was the machine upon which athletic prowess was demonstrated on both road and track, whether it involved the greatest speed over short distances, or endurance over longer distances. Many riders proud of their skill on the high bicycle were at first scornful of the lower, chain-driven "safety" bicycle when it was first introduced in 1884–5. Nevertheless, the advantages of the "safety" were so obvious and undeniable, that even before the advent of the pneumatic tire, the high-wheel bicycle was quickly outmoded and for serious competitive purposes was more or less abandoned by 1890.

7. Varieties of Competitive Activity

It is clear from the many accounts that early bicycle competition took various forms. The French velocipede which arrived at Charles Spencer's gymnasium in London in January 1869 may well have been one of the earliest occurences of indoor riding in England. The cold and rainy climate tended to encourage indoor venues, and the crowded and dangerous state of the city streets, and the necessity of renting a machine to try it out, were also factors in the popularity of indoor arenas, most of which also doubled as velocipede schools. The velocipede rider who chose to ride outdoors, where he was often the object of ridicule, did not have an easy time on rough cobbles, amid hectic horse and carriage traffic. Demonstration riding thus led to indoor tournaments and racing.

In late April 1869, for example, as already mentioned, the Liverpool Velocipede Club promoted its "bicycle tournament, an entertainment of a most novel and completely modern character," according to the *Liverpool Mercury*. "Of course that which created the greatest interest and caused the most amusement was the exhibition of skill in the management of the bicycle under the most difficult circumstances, such as tilting, throwing the javelin and broadsword attacks."[59]

In May of the same year, *The Field* reported "a curious display" which took place at the Velocipede Riding School run by Snoxell and Spencer in London. A young French expert and acrobat, 17-year-old Henri Pascaud, was invited and pitted against John Mayall and others. "The leading English amateurs present displayed much excellence in the new art…. But Mr. Pascaud stands alone. The feats he accomplishes have never been approached in this country, and it was amusing to remark the utter amazement of the velocipede teachers and pupils."[60]

These small-scale beginnings eventually led to public performances by experts in locations where the public could also rent velocipedes, such as the Agricultural Hall, Islington, in London, where races were held from June onwards. "The arena, where the horses have been in the habit of displaying themselves, is boarded over as evenly as the floor of a dancing saloon," reported *The Field*: "At each corner of the inclosure a huge tub of flowers is placed, about six yards from the barricading, and the course was nine times round the arena between these tubs and the outside barricade." An improvised, indoor track tended to be slow and confining, however, and entertainment aspects, slow, trick and "fancy" riding, were frequently as important as racing, as described earlier at the Liverpool "Tournament." *The Field* reporter was disappointed: "A contest that partakes so much of the "show" element is not likely to be attractive to the muscular athlete who goes plodding down lanes and unfrequented streets," he wrote: "At least half the velocipedists who competed on Saturday were mere scramblers on their bicycles, and could not even sit them when going a perfectly straight course; and it was this want of proficiency that rendered the contests less interesting than they might otherwise have been."[61]

However, the teething troubles of such events did not prevent the crowds from flocking to them. The price of a ticket in Islington was reduced on Saturdays, and the *North London News* reported that there was "no diminution in the rage for velocipedestrianism, if one may judge by the daily increasing patronage bestowed upon that excellent arena for practice, the Agricultural Hall." 1,200 people paid admission the following Saturday.[62]

Place-to-place rides on the road created a good deal of "noise" in the press. Although they were not always actual races, they were important athletic displays and demonstrated that a strong velocipede rider could rival a horse or the coach. In February 1869, as described earlier, Charles Spencer, John Mayall and Rowley Turner stage-managed a 60-mile ride to Brighton, arranging to have a reporter from *The Times* accompany them in a horse-drawn carriage. As a publicity stunt, the ride was evidently successful, for it was widely reported in the press and credited with popularizing the velocipede.[63]

Journalist H.H. Griffin wrote later that "to these three riders fairly belongs the honour of introducing and popularizing, by proving its practical utility, the use of the bicycle in this country."[64] At the end of March, two members of the Liverpool Velocipede Club rode from Liverpool to London in four days. "This is stated to be the longest bicycle tour yet made in this country, and the riders are of the opinion that they could have accomplished the distance in much less time," reported the *Liverpool Mercury*. But such pioneers encountered the surprised and sometimes hostile reactions of the rural public:

Fig. 1.17. Mr. Kilbourne Billings, velocipedist, smartly dressed in a flat-top hat, poses for a portrait in a photographic studio, enthused with the pride of ownership. [Source: John L. Weiss collection]

> Their bicycles caused no little astonishment on the way, and ... at some of the villages, the boys clustered round the machines, and when they could, caught hold of them and ran behind till they were tired out. Many inquiries were made as to the name of "them queer horses," some calling them "whirligigs," "menageries"' and "valaparaisos." Between Wolverhampton and Birmingham attempts were made to upset the riders by throwing stones.[65]

Strong, adventurous riders were prepared to take on the challenges of empty roads, hostile natives, and unpredictable conditions, however, and newspapers happily reported the longer place-to-place rides. In August 1869, a Mr. Klamrath rode from Edinburgh to London in 5 days,[66] while in October, Edwin Goddard, an employee of Soper's Engineering Works, Vauxhall, London, rode 60 miles from London to Newbury "on a bicycle of his own make.... Goddard's physical powers are good, and he completed the journey without the slightest inconvenience to himself."[67]

In June 1873, Charles Spencer, with three other members of the Middlesex Bicycle Club, George Hunt, William Wood and Charles Leaver, rode from London to John o'Groats, covering 800 miles in fourteen days in a ride sponsored by Thomas Sparrow, the London agent for the Coventry Machinists' Company. It was, thought Spencer himself, "a really important exemplification of the practical purposes to which a bicycle might be put."[68] The *Daily Telegraph* thought that:

> a more extraordinary journey, prepared under more extraordinary conditions, has been seldom recorded. A distance of 800 miles has been covered in 14 days, at a rate of 60 miles a day. To say that the work would tire a horse is a feeble description of it. The strongest horse would break down under such a journey.... As an example of what a bicycle enables a man to do, the bare fact of a journey so made is full of interest.[69]

This journey dramatically demonstrated, for the first time, that it was possible for a man to go from one end of the country to the other on a bicycle, a feat of both athletic and utilitarian significance.

These individual, long-distance, place-to-place rides, although not competitions, tested the athletic ability of riders and established time standards which would be attacked by later record-breakers. They laid the foundations of a style of racing which would become more and more important in the sport later in the 19th century. Place-to-place record rides between prominent cities, or over easily identifiable distances (100 miles, for example), were to become one of the most visible and publicized kinds of events in bicycle racing in England and France in the 1890s, providing crucial publicity opportunities for the bicycle and tire manufacturers who sponsored them.

Velocipedes were also raced on public roads, usually where smoother, well maintained, stretches could be found, around large cities like London and Liverpool. Both *The Field* and *The Daily News* reported a very early two mile race in Dulwich, South London in January 1869, "in which four gentlemen travelled over 2 miles of ground

Fig. 1.18. John Mayall, Jr., the hero of "An Extraordinary Velocipede Feat" in Feb. 1869. [Source: photo by John Mayall, Senior, *Cyclist Yearbook and Annual for 1893*]

for a sweepstake of £20," won by a Mr. Waloski.[70] The Liverpool road race already described was held in April 1869, on a macadamed road, "perhaps a thoroughfare better adapted for the purpose could not have been fixed upon in this locality, as it is tolerably level and straight the whole length." There were 19 entries, though only 12 started, and they were handicapped according to the size of their driving wheels. Those with bigger wheels started later, since the bigger wheel was considered to give riders an advantage. The winner, Henry Eaton, a member of the Liverpool Velocipede Club, rode a "Miss Julia" machine and covered the distance of 13 miles in 1 hour 27 minutes "under very unfavourable circumstances—a strong head wind and a crowded road. When Eaton reached the winning post he appeared to be greatly exhausted, and was carried from his bicycle into a garden … where he was supplied with a little brandy, which soon rallied him. He was enthusiastically cheered by the spectators."[71]

Newspaper reports of this Liverpool race included a starting list of riders, probably the earliest documented start-card in British bicycle racing, which identified the manufacturers or the names of the bicycles ridden. The *Liverpool Weekly Courier* provided information about the origins of some of the bicycles involved: "Several of the bicycles were manufactured by Messrs Brown, of Liverpool," it said, "but there were several of French make, of which the second in the race was one." Henry Eaton won "a handsome silver bicycle" for his afternoon's work, "the gift of Mr. W. H. Brown, bicycle manufacturer."[72] Once again, a manufacturer was involved in the sponsorship of a race by providing a substantial prize, the obvious implication of the newspaper report being that the Liverpool-produced bicycle was in competition with the imported French models.

A bicycle race could also be held in almost any good-sized field, or on the grounds of a tavern. This was where outdoor track racing began, and such an event was often promoted by a tavern owner to encourage business. One such owner was Jack Warner, who held the licence of the Old Welsh Harp Inn, in rural

Fig. 1.19. A poster advertising the Molineux Pleasure Ground, Wolverhampton, in the early 1870s. Bicycle racing is taking place on the track in the foreground. [Source: author's collection]

Hendon, on the outskirts of north London, where he provided skating, swimming, boxing and wrestling matches, hunting, shooting and fishing for a London clientele. It has been suggested in various historical accounts that Warner organized the earliest bicycle race in England at his inn. Primary documentation of the event is lacking, but one source claimed that the race took place on Whit Monday, 1 June 1868, and that it was won by Arthur Markham. The truth is probably that for the "1868" of many accounts we should substitute 1869.[73]

More reliable documentation exists for the activities of another tavern owner and promoter, O.E. McGregor,[74] the proprietor of the Molineux Arms and Gardens in Wolverhampton, who started promoting bicycle races, probably in 1870, after seeing the success of the first Wolverhampton races organized by manufacturers Forder and Traves at the Vauxhall Gardens. McGregor was responsible for building his inn into probably the most important venue in the country in the early 1870s, turning Wolverhampton into England's bicycle racing Mecca.

Reviewing the racing season of 1870, the *Wolverhampton Chronicle* published glowing accounts of the bicycle contests that had taken place at the Molineux Grounds during the year, "both as regards the number of visitors and the quality of the riding. They have not been confined to Wolverhampton and the district, but have been open to All-England, and have, therefore, brought together some of the best riders in the kingdom." Prizes were good: a substantial first prize was offered by the "Sun Bicycle Association" (perhaps organized or owned by O.E. McGregor himself) at the final races of the season. "In the evening, about fifty of the members and friends of the Association sat down to an excellent dinner provided by Mr. McGregor, the proprietor of the grounds."[75] Perhaps this generosity was one of the secrets of McGregor's financial success!

Racing was also promoted as a component part of larger, not specifically sporting, social events. The 1869 Crystal Palace "Velocipede Derbys" were a prominent showcase for English manufacturers and for the young sport, held at a famous, centrally located, international exhibition site,

GREAT BICYCLE RACE
BETWEEN CHESTER & ROCK FERRY.

This novel event, which was anticipated with great interest by velocipedists and others during the last two or three weeks, came off on Saturday afternoon last, the prize contested for being a handsome silver model bicycle, presented by Mr. W. H. Brown, bicycle manufacturer, Sir Thomas's-buildings. The model has for some time back been exhibited in the window of Mr. Mayer, silversmith, Lord-street. The road selected for the race was between Chester and Rock Ferry—a distance of about 13 miles—and perhaps a thoroughfare better adapted for the purpose could not have been fixed upon in this locality, as it is tolerably level and straight the whole length. At Backford, between three and four miles from Chester, there is a short hill, but after that the ground presents almost a level surface till reaching Bromborough bridge, from which place there is a slight ascent as far as the New Ferry tollbar.

At first there were 19 entries for the race, but only eleven persons started, besides Mr. Brown, who accompanied the competitors the whole way on a bicycle. The following were the entries, with the names of the bicycles and the colour worn by each driver:—

RIDER.	COLOUR OF CAP.	NAME OF BICYCLE.
George Ball	Blue and pink	Knight of the Garter.
A. L. Lane	White, with blue stars	Firefly.
J. Moss Bennett	Red and blue	Knight Templar.
W. E. Potter	Violet	Centaur.
G. M. Jones	Pink	Mandarin.
R. W. Leyland	Yellow and black	Pegasus.
W. Long	Green	Hermit.
J. S. de Wolfe, jun.	Magenta	Maccaroni.
W. H. de Wolfe	Blue, with white stripe	Gladiateur.
George Scott	Chocolate	Parisian.
H. Brown	White and blue	Doctor.
William Hope	Red	Aurora.
L. Notara	Black	Comet.
Henry W. Eaton	Light blue	Miss Julia.
C. Haldon	Red and white	Menzikoff.
A. S. Pearson	White	Britannia.
J. C. Cannon	Dark blue	Jupiter.
F. A. Macdona		Chester.
G. H. Wilson	Light blue	Eclipse.

Fig. 1.20. The report of the "Great Bicycle Race between Chester and Rock Ferry" included a "start list" including entries, names of the bicycles and the colors worn by each rider. [Source: *Liverpool Mercury*, 5 April 1869]

which attracted large audiences to many different kinds of cultural events. Bicycle races began in May and continued throughout the summer, and French professionals were brought over to challenge the home-grown amateurs.

Late in May, Monsieur Biot "was easily recognized by his white cords and hot boots," reported the *Sydenham Times*, and easily beat his opponents in "an excellent race." It was "a day to be remembered in the annals of the bicycle, notwithstanding the drenching showers."[76] French expertise was a great advantage: "It was very plain that Biot is much superior to any of the other competitors," reported *The Field*, "and, so far as we could see, his advantage was principally owing to his position on his bicycle. He sat well back, and thrust the cranks forward instead of sitting over them and treading them down, as many of the English competitors did." But *The Field* was critical of the organization of the races and the sharp turning point of the course, which in one heat caused all the competitors "to come to grief together."[77]

Fig. 1.21. This slouching, cycling "character" from the early 1870s posed with a transitional high-wheeler. [Source: author's collection]

The Crystal Palace's role in publicizing the velocipede during the "craze" of the summer of 1869 culminated in the autumn with a month of almost continuous racing and the promotion of the "International Velocipede and Loco-machine Exhibition." The speculative and commercial nature of this exhibition was expressed in a publicity advertisement where it was stated that the purpose of the Exhibition was "to hold conferences having for their object to examine the possible application of velocipedes to practical business purposes and to discuss their scientific construction."[78] Entertainment was mixed with exhibitions and theoretical and "scientific" meetings. Dr. Thomas Clarke, of Cheshire, read a paper to the Conference entitled "Scientific principles which should guide in the construction of velocipedes."[79] The Exhibition attracted 200 machines, representing more than 70 companies, and was certainly the scene of stimulating commercial, technical and social exchanges. Advertisements, run in many daily papers, spoke of:

> a great Velocipede Contest and Competition which will take place daily, forming an afternoon's amusement of the most popular character. These exciting and interesting Velocipede displays, in which all

Fig. 1.22. Early bicycle racing was promoted by landlord McGregor in the grounds of the Molineux Arms, Wolverhampton, c. 1870. [Source: Wolverhampton Public Library]

the latest improvements in bicycles are exhibited, must be seen to be appreciated. They have interested those who have already seen them to an unusual degree.

Once again, continental riders were brought in, including "Mons. Moret and Mons. Michaux, of Paris and Mons. J. Johnson, the Belgian champion." There were races nearly every day in the "Velocipede Circus." A show business atmosphere prevailed, and the bicycling events were intermixed with opera and the sensational Blondin on his tightrope.[80]

At the already-mentioned Ripon Horticultural and Floral Society's Fête at Studley Pleasure Grounds, bicycle racing was incorporated into a traditional community festival. "Cheap trips were run from Leeds, Halifax, Bradford, Manchester and other places," and on the grounds there were "fruits from the hot house of the Earl, the conservatory of the squire, the greenhouse of the amateur and the garden of the cottager. Every available space was occupied with good plants, flowers, fruits or vegetables. Ingledew's celebrated Leeds model band played a choice selection of music, and attendance during the afternoon was of a highly select and fashionable character." And surprisingly for this rural location, "the south side of the field was occupied by a numerous array of bicycles and tricycles of various kinds of workmanship, which were to be judged by Mr. Dunnington, a joiner, and Mr. Mountain, coach builder and coach proprietor," showing that the making of bicycles and tricycles was still very much rooted in the carpentry and carriage trades. The "novelty of the velocipede races," run around the lake, took place on Saturday, near Fountains Abbey. The Abbey green was crowded with spectators, who were in general disappointed because there were organizational difficulties, particularly concerning the hill on the course: "The race in the case of the bicycle was not with the strongest man, but the man who was an expert in mounting his machine after ascending the hill; if he could do this quickly he was soon far ahead of his opponents."[81]

The momentary popularity, the athletic novelty, of the new velocipede tempted many organizers of sporting events to feature it, and it was in the context of other athletic events that "bicycle races" were accepted as a novel addition to a varied repertoire of sport.[82] In May 1869, for example, Nottingham Football Club's "Athletic Sports" at Trent Bridge Ground included a "Velocipede or Bicycle Race," contested by six riders. In October 1869, Richmond Cricket Club's "Athletic Sports" at the Old Deer Park, Richmond included a "Half Mile Bicycle Race" also contested by six riders, one of whom was "J. Keen," whose club was given as "Surbiton Amateur." The same club's April 1870 "Athletic Sports" included an "Open 1 mile Bicycle Race," contested in two heats with a final. In July 1870, Bradford Cricket Club included a 1-mile "Bicycle Race" in its "Athletic Festival," and a week later the "Knutsford Annual Athletic Festival" included a "Velocipede Race."[83] In September 1869, the Licensed Victuallers Asylum sponsored a "Grand Gala Fête, Bicycle and other Races, as well as a Cricket match," at Lord's Cricket Ground.[84]

The earliest amateur bicycle championships, held under the umbrella of the Amateur Athletic Club from 1871 to 1874, were similarly included in existing athletic events, usually at the same time that "pedestrian" (that is running and walking) events were held. The differing needs of the bicyclists, however, their increasing specialization, the expansion of the sport and the need to include many different categories of bicycling events, soon made it essential that separate bicycle championship events be promoted.

8. AN ELITE EMERGES: MATCH RACING AND CHAMPIONSHIPS

Match racing was the most sophisticated form of early bicycle racing, in which pure athletic skills—speed, strength, experience and tactical finesse—were put to the test in races between just a few experienced rivals.

An elite group of international-calibre riders emerged, competing against each other at the highest level. At first, these top-level riders were all British or French and included James Moore, Hippolyte Moret, Camille Thuillet, André Castera, John Keen, David Stanton, J.T. Johnson, J. Palmer, T. Shelton, Rowley Turner, Fred Wood, George Waller and A. Forder.[85]

The most important races between leading champions quickly became *de facto* national and world "championships" and were advertised and reported as such. From 1870–71 onwards professional and amateur "world championship" honours were contested between members of this elite group, usually in London or Wolverhampton.[86] Traditional wagers between contestants, managed by a promoter such as Wolverhampton's McGregor, with the stakes usually held by an impartial outside body, for example, a sporting newspaper such as *Bell's Life, Sporting Life* or *The Field*, were the basis for most professional challenges and "championships" from 1870 onwards.[87] The 1871 "professional championship" was held at Aston Cross Grounds, Birmingham. The prize was considerable, "for which half a dozen of the best performers in the kingdom contended, the conditions of the competition giving the winner the title of champion of England." The winner was J.T. Johnson over J. Palmer, with James Moore coming in third.[88] And, through a working relationship created between the southern clubs and the Amateur Athletic Club, amateur bicycle "championships" were held under A.A.C. jurisdiction from 1871 until the formation of the Bicycle Union in 1878–

79, although there was an overlap in both 1878 and 1879, when both organizations held their "championships."

There is plenty of evidence of substantial growth in competitive bicycle racing in the contemporary press accounts, although the reports of huge crowds at events should be treated with some scepticism. In June 1870, the *Wolverhampton Chronicle* reported that "upwards of 1,000 people" were at the Vauxhall Gardens, Wolverhampton, for the "All-England amateur bicycle contest," where despite the event's announced national aspirations, most of the riders were local. In August 1870, the *Chronicle* reported "champion bicycle contests," including "the All-comers Champion Cup race of one mile" for a £30 cup and a "first-class amateur race" for a £5 silver cup and "a handsome wine flask." There was a prize for "the wearer of the neatest costume," which was divided between Shelton and Turner, Shelton being "attired in a rich mazarine blue jacket, with white sash," and Turner in "an emerald green jacket, and white breeches." The "championship" on this occasion, contested in a number of heats, was won by the Parisian James Moore, who rode a state of the art 43" French "Spider" bicycle made by Eugene Meyer, beating England's John Keen. It was claimed that McGregor's two-day promotion attracted 2,000 spectators on Saturday and the same number the following Monday.[89]

Further examination of this August 1870 racing season reveals the importance of these early

Fig. 1.23. "Frederick Hanlon, the distinguished acrobat, seems to have transferred all his gymnastic and flying trapeze skill to the véloce, and has justly earned the name of Champion Velocipedist of the world." [Source: *The Velocipedist*, Feb. 1869]

Fig. 1.24. Thomas Humber's "Spider Bicycle," from 1873, was an early and influential example of the radical enlargement of the front wheel. [Source: *The Humber Story*]

"championship" races in the technological evolution of the high-wheel bicycle. They were occasions when both state-of-the-art manufacture and bicycling technique could be demonstrated. James Moore, who won the championship race, later wrote: "I myself won the Paris championship on a tension wheel of Meyer's make in 1870, and raced at Molineux Park, Wolverhampton, in the early summer of 1870. I was riding a 43" Meyer tension-wheel bicycle and used toe-pedals, whilst my opponents were yet pedalling from the instep on Phantom 36" wheels." On 21 Sept. 1870, the *Wolverhampton Chronicle* reported that at a race between progressive builder, John Keen, and a rider called Wallace, from Aberdeen, "the latter, whose machine, though of fine build, was somewhat antiquated for these days of "phantom" and "spider" wheels, for a long time refused to strip, averring that he had no chance; at length, however, he came on the course."[90]

Wheel size was a crucial factor in competition between 1869 and 1871. This is underlined by the fact that wheel dimensions were frequently listed in newspaper reports and were also made the basis for handicapping riders. A letter to the *English Mechanic* in December 1870 stated, "The machine of the present day is a very different affair from the old clumsy articles which were in vogue two years ago. We thought then that we were doing well when we covered a mile in 7 minutes and a 36" driving wheel was the maximum size. Now the time for a mile run on a course is 3+ minutes, and the driving wheels are from 48–50" in diameter. What has enabled us to obtain such good results is the introduction of the "spider" wheel."[91]

At this point, many bicycle races were already being billed as for either amateur or professional riders, although "all-comers" races were open to both classes. Professionals were those who earned their livings as athletes, or worked in the industry, and those to whom the "mechanic, artisan and labourer clause," as defined by the Amateur Athletic Club, would apply. A competitor who was an actual maker or an employee of a manufacturer, that is a "mechanic," exactly fulfilled the gentleman amateur's conception of a "professional."

Amateurs were all those others who could not obviously be defined as professionals. The "mechanic, artisan and labourer clause" was an essentially class-oriented measure, designed to exclude working and lower-class competitors from amateur competition. Muscular "mechanics and artisans" were considered to have a physical advantage over the softer-living "gentlemen," and were in fact excluded from the amateur sport because the

Fig. 1.25. The masthead of *Le Vélocipède Illustré* in 1869 showed a woman rider who signified and epitomized an image of progress. [Source: *Le Vélocipède Illustré* throughout 1869]

"better class" of athletes did not want to have to rub shoulders with their social inferiors, or risk being beaten by them.

The circumstances surrounding the first official amateur championship, promoted by the Amateur Athletic Club at Lillie Bridge Grounds, Fulham, London on 12 August 1871, throw into vivid perspective the practical results of the imposition of the "mechanic and artisan clause" in competition, and provide evidence of the social and class divisions within the early sport. The championship race was a 4-mile event, and according to historian H.H. Griffin: "Out of about twenty entries, seventeen were ruled out, and protests were lodged against two of the three starters, and it was almost a walk-over for H.P. Whiting, a public-school man."[92]

It was hardly surprising, therefore, when contemporary chronicler, Nahum Salomon, reported that "Mr. Whiting, though opposed by one or two other competitors, had not the slightest difficulty in winning." The result might have been very different had Whiting confronted the best of the tough Midlands professionals that year, although the fact that he went on to win three further amateur championships, from 1873 to 1875, shows that Whiting wasn't an inferior rider.[93] It was predictable, too, that the "professional" bicyclists who had been excluded from this event may well have decided in the future not to enter Amateur Athletic Club events, and preferred to define themselves as professionals.

So this 1871 championship exclusion may well have been significant in influencing the future direction of the sport, and emphasized the divisive social and class distinctions between amateur and professional riders which would in the future have such a profound impact on the structure and organization of competitive cycling.

* * *

The historical evidence thus demonstrates that the earliest bicycle racing was stimulated by the need of makers and agents to publicize their machines, and built on an already existing enthusiasm for sport of many different kinds, during a period of heightened speculative commercial activity.

Perhaps the most remarkable characteristic associated with the early sport of cycling was the suddenness of its arrival as an athletic activity and the speed of its development. In this sense, it was perceived as "the latest thing," and its adoption and practice was considered modern, a sign of progress. A telling sporting image was used on the front cover of *Le Vélocipède Illustré* throughout 1869, which shows a woman wearing tights and a divided skirt, carrying time's arrow, to which is attached a banner labelled "Progrès." The woman is riding a velocipede that is projecting the rays of a bright light conspicuously forward.[94]

The earliest indoor competitions were embryonic velodrome races. The speed of bicycle racers in the brief "velocipede" era was relatively slow, particularly on the road, and was judged by comparison with walking or horse-riding. Except for the rare macadamed surfaces on the outskirts of large cities, road and track surfaces were bad.

Contemporary commentators appear to have been most impressed by long-distance place-to-place rides, where stamina over hard roads was the most admired quality. As bicycle technology improved, however, speeds increased, reaching a sustained 20 mph on a good track by the early 1880s, although road speeds were, of course, much slower.[95]

By 1873, there were seven bicycle clubs in London and twenty-two others "in the provinces."[96] Alfred Howard, the Secretary of the Surrey Bicycle Club, wrote in 1874 that "of all the pastimes and athletic exercises with which we are acquainted, none has so rapidly come into public favour, and retained its hold thereon so firmly, as the art of bicycle riding."[97] In the same year, Nahum Salamon corroborated Howard's opinion and wrote that "during the last 3 years, the Bicycle movement has rapidly advanced in public favour."[98]

By 1876, an editorial in a national newspaper called bicycling "a great national pastime which has become not only a popular but a fashionable amusement,"[99] and Alfred Howard wrote that "the year of grace, 1876, will form an important period in the history of bicycle riding, for the pastime has increased rapidly and surely amongst all classes, and in place of being looked at with derision and curiosity is regarded and recognized as a useful and healthy exercise, and a valuable addition to the means of locomotion."[100]

Thus cycling, according to the views of this evidently partisan insider, had by 1876 gained credibility both as a sport and as a means of transportation.

Fig. 1.26. Harry Hewitt Griffin, later to become a prominent journalist and commentator on British cycling, in 1873, mounted on a bicycle built by Underwood, of Newport, Shropshire. [Source: Griffin, *Cycles and Cycling*, 1903]

Chapter Two

Expansion of Bicycling in Britain

1. A Cutting-Edge, Modern, Technological Sport

IN CONTRAST TO THE NOW popular view of the "penny-farthing" bicycle as a quaint machine, bicycle racing in the high-wheel period (from about 1874 to the later 1880s) was in actuality a highly technological, modern, competitive activity, on the absolute cutting edge of sport. In addition, it was dangerous on road and track for serious racing cyclists and for those who rode merely for exercise and pleasure. There are many accounts of accidents on the racing track, and of nasty "headers"—cyclists who fell forward from their bicycles—on the unpredictable roads of the period. Cycling was at first seen as eccentric, but energetic young men from various class backgrounds welcomed the novel opportunity it gave for exercise and adventure. Cyclists formed themselves into clubs to organize rides, races and social events, quickly giving an organized social structure to their new-found enthusiasm. Racing and recreational riding became rooted in a club structure.

Bicycle riding and racing attracted participants and spectators because nothing like it had ever been seen or tried before. Soon after the sport was established in 1869, large crowds were reported at races in London and the Midlands. As the sport grew, a number of "stars" emerged, such as John Keen and David Stanton, who attracted large crowds.

The early sport was promoted as a profit-making business and there was an energetic professional scene. However, amateur championships were also held as early as 1871 under the auspices of the Amateur Athletic Club, where the exclusionary "mechanic, artisan or labourer clause" was applied. The growth of the amateur sport received fresh impetus from its acceptance into the thriving athletic milieu at Oxford and Cambridge universities from 1873 on.[1] The polarization of professional and amateur racing cyclists accelerated in the mid–1870s, the result of ongoing tension in society about the role of sport. As cycling grew in popularity, the need for national organizations became apparent, and both the Bicycle Union (for racing and club cyclists) and the Bicycle Touring Club (for touring and recreational cyclists) were created in 1878 to promote these two different aspects of cycling. The Bicycle Union established systematic regulations for bicycle racing, and sponsored annual championships over courses of varying distances.

An energetic specialist press emerged to report on the activities of competitive and recreational cyclists, to promote the bicycle manufacturing industry and to act as an advertising channel for its products. *The Bicyclist*, a monthly first published in London at the end of 1875, was the first British periodical devoted exclusively to cycling. *Bicycling News*, first published in January 1876, was the first weekly newspaper devoted to the sport, followed soon after by *The Bicycle Journal*, edited by Alfred Howard, advertised in *The Bicycle for*

1877 as "the largest and most influential publication wholly devoted to bicycling." Both *Bicycling News* and *The Bicycle Journal* were published on Fridays, timed to advertise weekend club rides. They carried reports of club life, events and races, as well as many pages of advertising. They also commented on the sport's impact on the general public and reported on the efforts to have the sport organized on a national level. This was the beginning of a period of rapid growth for the cycling press which continued through the 1880s and 1890s. "No sport can compare with cycling in the variety and completeness of the records kept, and ... this fact undoubtedly accounts for the vitality which it possesses and the enthusiasm it creates," wrote George Lacy Hillier in 1889. In 1896, at the peak of the bicycle "boom," journalist Harry Griffin wrote that "cycling, the world over, is by far the most richly endowed of any sport whatsoever by newspapers."[2]

Fig. 2.1. Sanders Sellers winning a National Cyclists' Union championship race at Aston, Birmingham, 13 June 1885. Illustration by George Moore. [Source: A.J. Wilson, *The Pleasures, Objects and Advantages of Cycling*, 1887]

At the end of 1874, Nahum Salamon, the agent for the Coventry Machinists' Company in London, published his *Bicycling: Its Rise and Development,* which contained one of the earliest published histories of the sport. He wrote that "during the last three years the Bicycle movement has rapidly advanced in public favour.... The newspapers have fully recognized the importance of the movement, and duly record the achievements of its votaries. Ten thousand persons have assembled at one time to witness a Bicycle contest.... The records of matches and feats are sufficiently full to furnish material for a history of Bicycling."[3]

Salamon was right: the growth of the sport was meticulously documented. A good deal of attention was given in the press to long bicycle rides, because endurance rides were particularly dramatic in showing the new-found capabilities of both riders and machines, and in redefining the speeds and distances an athlete could achieve under his own muscular power. Individual riders tackled many place-to-place rides over difficult roads. In June 1873, for example, Charles Spencer and three other cyclists from the Middlesex Bicycle Club rode about 700 miles from London to John o'Groats in 15 days, and in March 1874,

Fig. 2.2. The technological and commercial development of the bicycle, and the growth of the sport, were linked with the rapid emergence of a specialist cycling press. [Source: *Bicycling Journal*, 29 Dec. 1876]

William Cann and Henry Wilson raced between Sheffield and Plymouth for a prize of £50, a contest reported in both the *Sheffield Daily Telegraph* and the *Western Morning News* (Plymouth), whose offices were the race's arrival point, which suggests that newspapers were using the ride for publicity purposes.[4] Track racing became increasingly popular.

The organized professional sport expanded quickly in some areas. On Boxing Day (December 26th), 1875, in the middle of winter, at the Molineux Grounds in Wolverhampton, which had become the Mecca of English bicycle racing under the enterprising management of proprietor O.E. McGregor, a huge crowd gathered to watch "championship" races between leading professionals Fred Cooper, James Moore, John Keen and David Stanton, although invited French star Camille Thuillet had been prevented from crossing the Channel by bad weather. "The fact that bicycling is an extremely popular sport in Wolverhampton has been frequently shown ... but it was scarcely to be expected, however, at this season of the year, that nearly 18,000 spectators should gather together to see four bicyclists run, but the quality of the four made up for their deficiency in quantity," reported the *Wolverhampton Chronicle*. The essential economic rule of sport promotion had been well understood—stars draw crowds, crowds help to create stars. The people at the Grounds "covered the green hill like a swarm of locusts," and the entrance gates were "a veritable pass of fear. The crush could not have been greater on the occasion of a Drury Lane pantomine first night and many ladies were quite afraid to encounter such a very unloving 'squeeze' as they would have been subjected to."[5] *The Bicyclist* thought that "the monster attendance of between 15,000 and 16,000 people" was "a great proof of the immensely increasing popularity of bicycling." The weather was "dull and dispiriting, and accompanied by a fine Scotch mist," but the event was still "one of the largest gatherings ever known in this district to witness an athletic performance of any description."[6]

Top: Fig. 2.3. Crowds of spectators were depicted at bicycle races in illustrated magazines from the mid–1870s. This race, showing a rider "coming a cropper," was in London, at the Kennington Oval. [Source: *Pictorial World*, 13 June 1874] *Bottom:* Fig. 2.4. shows a 25-mile race at Lillie Bridge, London, between Ion Keith-Falconer and A.P. Whiting. [Source: *Pictorial World*, 6 Feb. 1875]

A year later, the same Christmas event still drew a large crowd, even though "the weather was unfavourable in the extreme, as there was both frost and snow to keep the bicyclists company." *The Bicycle Journal* reported, however, that "the people of Wolverhampton are too fond of this particular sport to be frightened away by bad weather, and accordingly, considering the circumstances, there was a large number of spectators— between two and three thousand." The course was "heavy-going" and "the sport was not up to the Wolverhampton level." The weather was so bad, in fact, that the heats could not be completed on the 26th of December, and the organizers announced that the second day's admission would be free, "and placarded the town to that effect, a solid fact, which speaks volumes of their desire to stand well with the public." Champion John Keen was once again victorious in the final race, winning "amidst a burst of cheering."[7]

Whereas five years earlier velocipede sport had been a rudimentary form of entertainment, it had matured considerably by the mid–1870s. Bicycles had improved enormously. They were being manufactured by a rapidly expanding industry based in London and the Midlands. A club and competitive structure supported the enthusiasm of young men for their new sport, and promoters made a profitable business of racing where they could. By 1883, Charles Spencer expressed surprise at the "excellence, elegance and usefulness" attained by the bicycle. He had not foreseen, he wrote, "how universally popular would become an exercise which was at first regarded simply as a professional sport, and not likely to be taken up by the general public."[8] In the 1870s, cycling was going through an industrial and athletic expansion and transformation that would have an impact on a national level. By the end of the decade, it had become a prominent sporting, social and economic institution with its own governing bodies, a large network of clubs, an extensive, well-established racing calendar, specialized industrial production, and its own specialized press.

2. Technological Innovation at the Birth of Cycle Sport

It would be a mistake, however, to suggest that the sport evolved smoothly between the period of diverse competitive and entertainment activities described in Chapter One and the more developed later–1870s stage discussed here. On the contrary, the fledgling sport grew fitfully as the bicycle itself underwent a technologically experimental and geographically scattered development.

Charles Spencer, from his well-connected vantage point in the athletic goods and bicycle business in London, remembered that the velocipede "craze" of 1869 had been followed by a slump of a year or two: "Great was the disappointment of those who had anticipated making a harvest out of the pastime. Quite suddenly the game came to an end, and hundreds of machines were thrown on the hands of their makers, who up to this time had found it impossible to turn them out quickly enough." However, Spencer continued in a revealing passage, an inner circle of dedicated enthusiasts, "a few faithful devotees," remained, "who liked the exercise for its own, and not for fashion's sake; and for these sober and sedate persons it was worth the while of the best manufacturers to continue the business. Accordingly, some of them turned their attention seriously to the capabilities of the machine for improvement." And it was these technical improvements, asserts Spencer, that "attracted the more serious attention of active and athletic men."⁹

The improvement of the bicycle and the growth of the sport were thus propelled forward by the collaboration and cooperation between riders and manufacturers, who together constituted "a few faithful devotees." Significantly, among references to "exercise" and "active and athletic men," Spencer does not mention practical utility as a priority for these "devotees," which suggests that utility—the development of the bicycle for practical transportation—was not initially the dominating impulse behind early cycling.

George Lacy Hillier, the winner of four amateur championships in 1881, journalist, editor and historian, cycling bureaucrat and outspoken proponent of amateurism, later echoed Spencer's view. "There is no doubt that cycling owes much of its success to the racing man," Hillier wrote in his authoritative Badminton *Cycling* volume, first published in 1887; "He is in fact largely responsible for its phenomenal development: a development which is far in advance of any parallel growth of a sport in this country." Racing cyclists, he continued:

> very soon decided that it was necessary to demand from the manufacturers an improved vehicle.... The result of considerable labour was a vehicle which was then considered a marvel of lightness and strength. The existence of a demand very soon created a supply. The makers vied with each other in their attempts to meet the requirements of their customers, and in due course produced the thirty-five pound machine of 1879... Once having discovered the advantages derivable from a saving in the weight of a machine, the racing men incessantly clamoured for further reduction and obtained it.

But Hillier was also emphatic in recognizing that the technological advances demanded by the small racing community would also benefit the general consumer:

> We venture to credit the comparatively small section of racing men with being the "original cause" of the rapid improvement which has been made in both classes of velocipedes [that is bicycles *and* tricycles]. Possibly the manufacturers would tell us that the racing men gave them more trouble, and were more difficult to please, than any other section of their customers, and doubtless this would be quite true; but it is particularly this fact which has brought about a desire on the part of the manufacturers to meet these particular gentlemen, and in that endeavour they have vastly improved the

Fig. 2.5. Design changes illustrating the technological evolution of the bicycle: from about 1869, the mid–1870s, and 1886. [Source: A.J. Wilson, *The Pleasures, Objects and Advantages of Cycling*, 1887]

machines they manufacture, not only for the small class of racing men, but for the much larger body of general riders.[10]

The nature of the technological improvements involved an increase in the size of the front wheel made possible by a suspension system and tangent spokes, the making of a light, hollow frame, the universal adoption of ball-bearings for front and rear wheels, and more effective rims and rubber tires. Leading early manufacturers included John Keen, Thomas Sparrow, the Coventry Machinists' Co., Haynes and Jefferis and Thomas Humber. Experience in the sport was almost a prerequisite for manufacturing expertise. In a catalogue from about 1879 in which he described himself as "The First Champion Bicyclist," small manufacturer Arthur Markham wrote: "My experience both as a Rider, and a Trainer of Bicycle Riders, has given me that knowledge of the Bicycle, so much required in a manufacturer, having myself won upwards of 20 matches … and having trained D. Stanton in his successful matches against Keen."[11]

Advertisements for bicycles that were being developed and marketed by the mid–1870s illustrated this quest for technological improvement, phrased in the hyperbole of advertizing. The manufacturers were concerned with reduced weight, speed, reliability and strength, all of which can also be seen as athletic priorities, but those concerns had to be combined in a practical, marketable product. At the high end of the market, "champion Bicyclist" John Keen in 1877 offered his "Eclipse" bicycle which "still retains its position as the BEST BICYCLE FOR ALL PURPOSES. Being made of the BEST MATERIAL, combined with superior workmanship and the great practical experience of the maker … these Machines have accomplished all the

Fig. 2.6. Advertising for the racing bicycle of the mid–1870s emphasized the virtues of lightness, speed, durability, and strength. [Source: A. Howard, *The Bicycle for 1877*]

FASTEST TIMES at all distances, also the LONGEST JOURNEYS ever ridden. For Speed, Durability, Safety and Elegance they cannot be equalled. Testimonials from all the best riders in the world" (capitals as in original text). Stephen Simpson, Mansfield, advertised his "Defiance" bicycle as offering "Strength, Lightness, Elegance, Durability," and claimed it as "the STRONGEST, LIGHTEST and most serviceable roadster of the day." His roadster weighed 34 lb; a racing model was available at to 28 lb. W.G. Lewis of Romford, Essex, offered "The Suspension Bicycle," with "Patent Rigid Wheels and Anti-friction Roller Bearings—The Best Rigid Wheel ever invented," while the Surrey Machinists' Company in south-east London offered "The Invincible" bicycle, "constructed with our Patent Parallel and Anti-friction Roller-bearings, Double Lever Brake, Improved Leg Rest, Steel V Rims, Light Steel Back bone, Indestructible Red India-Rubber Tires, and the Latest Improvements."

Thomas Sparrow, a maker with a showroom on Piccadilly in the heart of London, claimed his bicycles as "the strongest, best and lightest of their day, every improvement is adapted as soon as produced." Hydes and Wigfull, of Sheffield, advertised the "Stanley Racer" bicycle, which "is admitted to be the lightest, swiftest, and strongest Machine in the market, and is in great demand for racing purposes.... The riders of this very elegant and handsome Machine have taken Prizes at all the principal contests during the past year."[12]

Looking at the hectic, geographically dispersed manufacturing activity, the technological improvements and the energetic creation of new sporting institutions in the mid–1870s, it is hard to discern the dominance of one trend over another. The new sport and the young industry, to make the point again, were fused into a symbiotic relationship, and new social and commercial institutions were rapidly emerging out of that relationship. Both riders and makers focused their attention on mechanical excellence, strength, lightness, speed and up-to-date technology, and the bicycle came to be on the cutting edge of industrial production for the athletic consumer. One example of a collaboration between rider and manufacturer was that between ex-professional Frederick Cooper and Thomas Humber of Nottingham. And John Keen, as a manufacturer, had an ongoing relationship with many of the leading riders. In March 1877, manufacturer W.H.J. Grout, then producing the "Tension" bicycle in north London, wrote to the *Bicycle Journal* suggesting a union of makers and riders: "I wish to state as an unattached bicycle maker, that I am willing to join and assist in the formation of a master bicycle maker's club, considering that all bicycle riders should be united, thereby keeping the sport under due self-control."[13]

While these design and manufacturing improvements were making the bicycle lighter, faster, more practical and effective, there was a parallel development in cycling's social institutions. Small, community-based clubs were organized first, during the initial velocipede "rage." The Liverpool Velocipede Club appears to have been organized by January 1869, and was "making arrangement for a tournament on bicycles to be held in the Gymnasium."[14] By April 1869, the Wolverhampton Velocipede Club was organized; it bought velocipedes and hired an instructor "who shall have power to prevent any member from using the new machines, whom he does not think can ride sufficiently well to be entrusted with the charge of a new one."[15] A correspondent complained to the *English Mechanic* in September 1869 that there was as yet no "veloce club" in London. It was time, he said, that "the young men of London made a step forward, the world is in advance of us." Three weeks later, another correspondent replied that, indeed, there was "a veloce club" in Hackney, London called the St. Katherine Club, and he had no doubt that there were "several clubs on foot in the suburbs." He urged "a more extended endeavour to bring the importance of veloce clubs more prominently before the public, for the cultivation of an exercise as healthy as it is pleasurable."[16]

In London, the Surrey Bicycle Club (formed in Kennington, London), the Pick-wick (Stoke Newington, London), the Middlesex (Kensington, London) and the Amateur Bicycle Club (London) had all been created by 1870. The Amateur Bicycle Club took its members from the staff of the Middlesex Hospital, the Skating Club and the London Rowing Club and was described as "a club in which gentlemen may seek their recreation and enjoyment."[17] By 1873, according to Charles Spencer, there were seven bicycle clubs in London and twenty-two outside the city. Perhaps all these clubs might be said to have been created by the "few faithful devotees, who liked the exercise for its own, and not for fashion's sake," as described above by Charles Spencer. The formation of the London clubs appears to have reinforced the distinction between the amateur and the professional sport, between the more heavily professional and proletarian Midlands and North and the increasingly amateur South. The distinction was based largely along class lines, the majority of the leading professionals being working-class, while the amateurs were more likely to be from the middle or upper classes.

In 1874, the first combined "meet" of many clubs took place at Hampton Court, Surrey, demonstrating the organizational capabilities of the bicycle movement. 50 riders participated. But one year later, there were nearly 500 riders.[18] By 1874, *The Field*, the *Country Gentleman's Newspaper*, a sporting paper which catered to an upper-class and upper-middle-class readership, was regularly publishing a bicycling "Fixtures" column which advertised at least five club runs organized in the greater London area every Saturday. In 1877, Alfred Howard's *The Bicycle for 1877* listed 23 clubs in London and more than 100 in the rest of Britain, while his review of the 1876 racing season consisted of more than sixty pages of results, covering races that began in early January and

Fig. 2.7. Maker W.H.J. Grout (1839–1915) with a road bicycle of his own manufacture from the mid–1870s. [Source: author's collection]

continued until the end of December.[19] The impact of this energetic, cycling club formation was clearly recognized. Reviewing the season of 1876, Alfred Howard wrote:

> The year that has just passed away leaves our pastime in a flourishing, but above all, in a progressive condition. Its roots, imbued with their native soundness, have taken firm hold on the soil, and grow stronger daily, while above a young but vigorous tree is sending branches out in all directions, that derive fresh sustenance from the air around, and thus react upon their parent stem.[20]

The press of that time also reported on the public awareness of the growing influence and impact of the new recreation and sport, and on the advantages it provided as a practical means of transportation, at least for the energetic. At a debate held in March 1877 at the headquarters of the influential Stanley Bicycle Club in Camden Town, north London on the subject "Bicycling, and public objections thereto," Mr. Sargent spoke of:

> young men who were not long in seeing that they had within their reach a means of healthful recreation just suited to their requirements ... containing a considerable element of utility. The result is that bicycling has become a most popular sport, a new industry has been created, a large number of clubs have sprung up ... newspapers have been started in the interests of bicycling, and it is in great measure owing to the able manner in which they have been conducted that we are indebted for the position we as bicyclists now enjoy. Amateur riders on the road have performed feats which put all other modes of travelling into the shade; the distance from London to York in 22½ hours, a journey which used to occupy three days in the times of fast coaching, and required the services of about eighty horses.[21]

3. Amateurism and Professionalism in the 1870s

The Wolverhampton, Sheffield and Leicester areas became important centers of professional bicycle racing in the 1870s. The combination of energetic promoters, such as Molineux's McGregor, who were prepared to put time, energy and money into creating good tracks, and local manufacturers who were also interested in promoting the new sport, was essential to its expansion. It is probable that the existing, working-class athletic culture, with its enthusiasm for pedestrianism, football and boxing, was equally enthusiastic and receptive to the new sport. But the huge crowds reported at the Wolverhampton races at Christmas, 1875 suggests that it was the novelty of cycling—a new, modern, well-promoted sport—which attracted the crowds, as opposed to the more traditional formats of the older sports. Amateur competitions took place, as we have already seen, within the context of other, established athletic club events, or as cycling became more popular, in events promoted by cycling clubs.[22]

In *The Bicycle for 1874*, Alfred Howard published a list of the race sheld in Britain during 1874 which he called "an authentic record of the bicycling of the year."[23] Included in the list is a total of 92 racing events of various kinds broken down by amateur and professional events. The list provides a valuable account of the structure, organization and geographical location of the races.

It should be noted that this table refers only to the number of particular categories of events that were held, and gives no indication of the size of an event or the number of competitors. An amateur track meeting, for instance, held in the context of another athletic event, might consist of just one bicycle race, whereas a professional meeting sometimes lasted for two days, and involved several different categories of events, some of which had

Table 2 A. Occurrence of different categories of races, listed in order of frequency, as recorded by Howard in *The Bicycle for 1874*.	
Amateur track meetings	46
(in context of another athletic event—	36)
(exclusively cycling events—	10)
Professional track meetings	16
Amateur road races	12
Professional track "matches"	10
Professional road races	3
Mixed professional and amateur track meetings	2
Professional time trial on road	1
Professional time trial on track	1
Professional bicycle versus horse	1
Total	92

dozens of heats. Of the 92 events listed, there were 26 professional track meetings and "matches" and 46 amateur track meetings. The professional track events consisted of 16 full-scale meetings and 10 "matches" of various distances between individuals, while the amateur track meetings consisted of 10 events devoted exclusively to cycling (promoted, for example, by the Dark Blue Bicycle Club, of Oxford University or the Surrey Bicycle Club) and 36 where bicycle racing took place in the context of other athletic activities (organized by the Halifax Amateur Athletic Society, for example, the North of Ireland Cricket Club Sports, or the Eccles Gymnastic and Athletic Festival). There were only two meetings where both professional and amateur events occurred on the same program, a strong indication of the polarized nature of the sport at this early date.

Professional "matches" were races between already well-known "champions," ridden over a specific distance, involving a wager held by a respected, independent referee.[24] At Molineux Grounds, Wolverhampton, for example, on 4 May 1874, James Moore and John Keen were matched over 1 mile, for £25 a side (winner takes all), with "Mr. J. Vandy, of Bell's Life" as the referee. Similarly, on 30 Nov. 1874, Keen met David Stanton at the same venue for a 50-mile match, for £25 a side, with "Messrs. J. Vandy and W.H. Leverell as Judges and Timekeepers." Professional meetings usually consisted of short-distance races, frequently of 1 or 2 miles, often run as handicaps, with a series of heats leading to a second and third round and ultimately to a final. These heats were frequently run off over a two-day period. On 6/7 April 1874, for example, at the Molineux Grounds, Wolverhampton, in a race described as a "One Mile Handicap. Professional," 45 riders contested 16 heats in the first round, 7 heats were run in the second round, 2 in the third, producing 4 riders to compete in the final, which was won by a Wolverhampton rider, J.T. Williams. At the same meeting, a race described as a "One Mile Championship. Open to the World" was run with only three riders, the well-known professional champions, James Moore, John Keen and E. Shelton.

Howard lists the riders' home towns in many cases, providing ample evidence of the preponderance of local, probably working-class, Midlands riders in these early professional events. At the 6–7 April event mentioned above, for example, of the 45 riders listed as having started in the 1-mile handicap event, 17 were from Wolverhampton, 17 from Birmingham, 3 from Newcastle, and the remainder from Derby, Gateshead and Surbiton (London). At a meeting held at Bramhall Lane, Sheffield on 25 and 27 April, out of 33 riders who competed in the 19 heats of the first round, 14 were from Sheffield, 7 from Wolverhampton, 7 from Birmingham and the remainder from Nottingham and nearby Mansfield. The vast majority of the professional meetings and matches in 1874 took place either in Wolverhampton (Molineux Grounds) or Sheffield (Bramhall Lane Cricket Ground, Queen's Ground or Newhall Grounds), but professional events also took place in Newcastle (Fenham

Park Grounds), Derby (Arboretum), Portsmouth and in London (Lillie Bridge Grounds, Fulham and Star Grounds, Fulham). Although this happened infrequently, on three occasions amateur clubs did sponsor professional events: on 25 July, the Derbyshire Athletic Club sponsored a professional event at the Arboretum, Derby; on 23 Sept. the Mansfield Bicycle Club included a professional event in its meeting at Rawson's Cricket Ground, while St. George's Bicycle Club sponsored a mixed professional and amateur event in London at Lillie Bridge, Fulham.

In compiling his "authentic record of the bicycling of the year," Howard showed a keen awareness of the difference between amateur and professional status and warned his readers not to confuse the two. Amateurs, he wrote, should "take care not to compete in open races, and never to run for money, or knowingly against a professional." "Open" races are described in various ways; for instance, "Open to all comers," "Open to all England," or "Open to the world." "It cannot be too well known that such are professional races," wrote Howard, "although the prize may not be in money; and that if any amateur compete, he is disqualified, and virtually becomes a professional." Where Howard describes an event as a "championship race," it is usually an indication that the race was for the highest caliber, "champion" riders only, probably by invitation, rather than a "championship" according to our current, annual-event definition of the word.

In 1876, in another edition of his annual, the number of racing events had increased from 92 to 317, and Howard commented: "The races have swollen out much beyond our expectations, therefore space compels us to curtail accounts of them." The number of clubs listed had increased from 33 to more than 130, indicating the extraordinarily rapid expansion of the amateur sport. Indeed, Howard confirmed the fact that there had been "a much greater increase of amateur than of professional riders."[25]

Fig. 2.8. Cambridge University Bicycle Club members, with Ion Keith-Falconer left center (in white, without cap), at the Club's own new track in the city in the late 1870s. [Source: Cambridge Public Library]

4. Cycling at Oxford and Cambridge Universities

The popularity of bicycling and of bicycle racing at Oxford and Cambridge universities in the mid–1870s marked a significant stage in cycling's penetration into British society and in the emergence and growth of the amateur sport.

By 1876, the Cambridge University Bicycle Club had about 120 members, and 242 by the end of 1877.[26] The energetic members funded the construction of a small racing track in the city, one of the earliest purpose-built cycling tracks constructed anywhere. When the track opened, *Bell's Life* commented that "amongst the many interesting spots at Cambridge on which the muscular Christians of the University may exercise their powers, there are none which promise to be more popular than the new bicycle ground."[27]

The more prominent of the Club's members went on to play a significant role in cycling at a national level. Cambridge undergraduate Ion Keith-Falconer (1857–87) was widely praised as one of the best amateur riders of his time, and Gerard Cobb (1857–1904), the Club's young president, was an influential political advocate for cycling at a moment when local and national government legislation threatened to repress and limit it. Cobb also became the president of the Bicycle Union, the first national governing body of British cycling.

In June 1874, *The Field, the Country Gentleman's Newspaper* reported that "at Oxford a bicycle club has existed longer than at the sister University.... During the present term

Fig. 2.9. Cambridge University Bicycle Club, in the late 1870s. [Source: Cambridge Public Library]

bicycling has been indulged in as an amusement to a considerable extent at both Universities, 'meets' occurring once at least in each week, when some fifteen or twenty have taken a run of twenty or thirty miles together."[28] Writing in 1883, Charles Spencer comments further on the acceptance of cycling at the two oldest Universities, with their strong interest in athletic sports, and on this process by which the bicycle gained in social prestige:

> The practice extended to the Universities, where it became popular, but to the word "velocipede" there seemed to be attached a soupçon of vulgarity little to the taste of the Oxford or Cambridge undergraduate. To indulge in a sport which had become ridiculous by its popularity with the "hoi polloi," to take up with a toy just discarded by the outside vulgar, was not to be thought of.

Technical advances, however, and the growing prominence of "the bicycle" in the press, had changed its social profile, and the word "velocipede" had been thoroughly rejected in favor of "bicycle": "The machine had undergone a change in appearance, and had become altogether superior to the low 'velocipede' of the past."[29] The bicycle, in other words, had become acceptable; it was considered worthy of athletic endeavor, and was thus taken out of a heavily proletarian context and accepted among other respectable, bourgeois sports.

The Dark Blue Bicycle Club (Oxford University) was formed in 1873 and the Cambridge University Bicycle Club in 1874; inter–Varsity matches were held from 1874 onwards. At the beginning of May 1874, "a challenge was sent to Oxford and immediately accepted," and a road race over the 85 miles between Oxford and Cambridge was arranged, with each University fielding three competitors.[30] According to Nahum Salamon, the 1874 road race between the two famous universities was "one of the most celebrated amateur matches that has ever yet been ridden."[31] *The Field* spoke of "a somewhat novel proceeding, a bicycle race

Fig. 2.10. Cambridge University Bicycle Club members at the start of a race at their track in Cambridge, with onlookers in the stands. [Source: Cambridge Public Library]

Fig. 2.11. In 1875, Keith-Falconer was the winner of the second inter-university road race. Presumably a post-race photo. The time for 52 miles from Cambridge to Oxford was 4h. 9m. [Source: *The Cyclist Year Book*, 1891]

between members of Oxford and Cambridge Universities," and emphasized the sophistication of the "splendid" racing machines ridden by the affluent competitors:

> By some persons the art of bicycling may be thought to have degenerated, but thanks to the recent vast improvements which have been made in machines, this mode of locomotion appears to be fast gaining popularity, as to a certain extent evidenced by the race in question.... At Oxford only a few persons were present to witness the start, but at Cambridge the greatest enthusiasm prevailed, for nearly the whole town turned out at 5 o'clock to witness the finish. The road from Trumpington to Cambridge, a distance of two miles, was lined with people the whole way, most of them on foot, but some on horseback–some in cabs and traps of all descriptions, and not a few on locally-built bicycles, which contrasted very unfavourably with the splendid machines used by the competitors. In fact, there must have been at least five thousand persons present at the close of the match.[32]

The race was won by Cambridge, with E. St John Mildmay of Trinity College first, and the Hon. J.W. Plunkett, also of Trinity College, second. The winners were "loudly cheered by the numerous spectators present, Mr Mildmay being carried to his rooms by some enthusiastic artisan class." The 85 miles were covered in 8h 5m, "a very tolerable time considering the bad state of the roads and the adverse north-easter which blew all the way."

In May 1874, the Hon. Ion Keith-Falconer, an aristocratic member of the Cambridge University Bicycle Club, rode from Bournemouth to Hitchin, a distance of 135 miles, and sent a report of the ride to *The Field*. On a bicycle made by Thomas Sparrow of Knightsbridge, London ("these machines are very strong, and especially adapted for long distances"), Keith-Falconer covered the 135 miles in 19¼ hours (about 16 hours riding time, "excluding stoppages"), for an average speed of just under 9 mph. The road was good in general, although at a certain point, "it became so excessively sandy and loose that every now and then I was obliged to dismount and walk." Keith-Falconer had to contend with the summer heat and reported that he "should have got sunstroke if I had not worn one of Tress and Co.'s pith and felt solar hats, which I strongly recommend to bicycle riders for summer use." Thus we already see the beginnings of modern commercial endorsement of consumer products by an athlete![33] Writer and editor George Lacy Hillier, a strong proponent of amateurism, remembered the report of this ride as "one of the earliest extended notices which was given to our sport," and had "little doubt that Mr. Keith-Falconer's name had much to do with popularizing cycle riding. It is a matter of curiosity and interest to note how often this particular ride ... is referred to in contemporary papers as a very fine performance, and as giving great assistance to the sport, illustrating emphatically the manner in which one good name, such as his, assists the development of a sport."[34]

Keith-Falconer's ride was undoubtedly long and difficult. Like other long road rides recorded in the press, it was an isolated ride, an individual achievement, significant in that it demonstrated that a long distance could be covered in a day by a strong, determined rider on the challenging, unpredictable roads of the period.[35] Because he was well-connected socially and had a "good name," Keith-Falconer's ride was amply publicized, and clearly it lent credibility and respectability to cycling within bourgeois society, as did the activities of the University clubs in general. Lacy Hillier's comments, however, apply primarily to the increased interest in the amateur sport in the south of England. It is unlikely that Keith-Falconer's "good name" had much impact on the professional riders of London, Wolverhampton, Sheffield and Birmingham, or on the working-class crowds who watched them race. The activities of these participants and spectators were also "popularizing cycle riding," though in a different social context.

The Cambridge University Bicycle Club's *Rules and Bye-laws* from "October Term, 1876" filled a 20-page booklet and illustrate the processes of codification and bureaucratization of amateur cycling. New "traditions" were created in the nascent sport *within* a bastion of cultural tradition and privilege. The very existence of the "rule book" was evidence of the absence of earlier traditions. Members of the club, taking part in club races, for example, "are required to wear the Club Race-cap, or the straw hat with Club ribbon, as uniform, and are requested to do so when taking part in races elsewhere." A code of behavior and signals was recommended for Club rides on the road, when "bugling is too elaborate a method of signaling to be recommended, and on the public road is unnecessarily obtrusive." It was necessary to pay attention to the "rules and courtesies of the road," especially in dealing with horses, as the bad behavior of some bicyclists had "caused great annoyance to the public, and created prejudice against bicycling very difficult to eradicate."[36] Upper-middle-class cyclists, a new category in the public arena of sport, had an obligation to uphold respectable standards of behavior, and not to behave in any way that would cause others to be critical of their activities.

5. "Muscular Christianity": the Cycling Career of Ion Keith-Falconer

The outstanding amateur racing career of Ion Keith-Falconer (1857–87), a member of the Cambridge University Bicycle Club, illustrates the class distinction that existed in the early sport between the "gentleman amateur" and the professional cyclist. But it was not always easy to differentiate the professional from the amateur in early cycling, and class stratification was less rigid than is sometimes suggested.

During the 1870s, in England, cycling appears to have been an exception to the already established sports such as running ("athletics'), rowing, cricket or boxing in that it challenged the prevailing notion that amateur and professional competitors ought to be segregated, and consequently was seen as something of a trouble-maker. The influential Gerard Cobb, president of the Cambridge University club and of the Bicycle Union, argued for a more liberal interpretation of the distinction between amateur and professional than was allowed by the Amateur Athletic Club, which sought to exclude all "mechanics, artisans and labourers" from the amateur ranks.

An aristocratic Cambridge University student when he took up cycling seriously in 1874 at the age of 17, the Honourable Ion Grant Neville Keith-Falconer was the son of the 9th Earl of Kintore, of a noble Scottish family. His high social status was in marked contrast to that of the working-class athletes and bicycle industry "mechanics" who crowded the rough tracks of London, Wolverhampton and Sheffield in the 1870s, out of whose ranks leading professionals, such as John Keen, David Stanton, E. Shelton, Fred Cooper, Richard Howell, Fred Wood and Tom Battensby, emerged.

Keith-Falconer, "a very tall man, well put together, with broad shoulders, and extremely powerful lower extremities,"[37] rode and raced the high-wheel bicycle for eight years from 1874 until 1882, a year when he broke the record for a ride from Land's End to John o'Groats in 13 days and contested two national championships, winning the 50-mile championship and beating the record by nearly 7 minutes. He competed in matches between Oxford and Cambridge from 1874 to 1878, contested Bicycle Union amateur championships from 1876 to 1882 and established several long-distance road records.[38] Breaking out of his strictly amateur status, he contested several high-profile matches with the leading professional John Keen, for which a special permission from the Bicycle Union was required. He was president of the Cambridge University Bicycle Club, president of the London Bicycle Club from 1877 to 1886 and participated in the formation of the Bicycle Union in 1878.[39]

Retiring suddenly and completely from his athletic career, Keith-Falconer, an Arabic scholar, linguist and fervent Christian, became a missionary in Aden in 1883 and died there in

Fig. 2.12. The Hon. Ion Keith-Falconer was widely praised for his athletic achievements after his death. [Source: *Cyclist Annual and Year Book*]

1887 from a tropical fever at the age of thirty. His sudden, premature death was mourned by the cycling community.

In 1888, his theology tutor, the Rev. Robert Sinker, Librarian of Trinity College, Cambridge, published a biographical account, *Memorials of the Hon. Ion Keith-Falconer*, which documented a privileged life rooted in classical scholarship and religion and deeply imbued with the ideologies of amateur athleticism and muscular Christianity.[40] According to Sinker, cycling was the only sport in which Keith-Falconer "habitually indulged," a "secondary interest which served him for relaxation of mind and body." A letter given to Sinker by E.E. Bowen, one of Keith-Falconer's school teachers at Harrow School, provides a telling vignette of his achievements and attitudes:

> I saw him often when he was in Cambridge, and was happy enough to retain his friendship 'til the last. His bicycling feats were one subject of common interest between us. Bicycles were just coming into fashion when he went to the University; he was an enthusiast in the use of them, and an admirable performer; and when he appeared in riding costume in Harrow, with his tall figure mounted on the enormous machine that he rode, it was a sight to see. He kept up the amusement for many years: for two or more he was certainly the best bicyclist in England, and his delight in success only shewed in more than common relief the charming modesty with which he carried his honours. He had a real delight in feats of strength and endurance for their own sake. He seemed to have found the same quality in one of the professional bicyclists with whom he became acquainted; and again and again he would tell me how John Keen was a man whose soul was above prizes—a man to be made a friend of.[41]

The Keith-Falconer Bowen describes was an ideal, prototypical "gentleman amateur" and "muscular Christian." He participates in an "amusement" rather than a sport, he "carries his honours with charming modesty" and he "delights in feats of strength and endurance for their own sake." Not only does he possess those admirable qualities, but as a morally pure amateur, he is seen as having shared those values with his rival John Keen, a highly successful professional athlete. It is suggested that a professional and an amateur would not be expected to share common attitudes towards the value of "feats of strength and endurance," but that Keith-Falconer made a magnanimous exception in Keen's case. Keen, a manufacturer and rider, was certainly interested in cash prizes, depending on them for his livelihood. But from Keith Falconer's assumed viewpoint, Keen was someone he *was* willing to race against and whose friendship he was not ashamed to cultivate. This biographical detail gives a glimpse of the subtle realities of the cultural distinctions between "amateur" and "professional" in cycling at the time.[42]

Keith-Falconer had considerable athletic ability, and he was widely praised for his accomplishments. However, Lacy Hillier suggested that there was a conflict between Keith-Falconer's athletic and academic commitments:

> Keith-Falconer, despite his splendid record, was an unreliable rider. Just when he was fittest and most expected to score, he either declined the contest or gave up; thus, after training for several weeks in 1883 for the 50 miles Championship, he left the track for Brighton on the morning of the race and did not compete. On the memorable occasion when, after many efforts to bring them together, he at length met the late H.L. Cortis, that redoubtable rider ran him off his legs at seven miles, to the intense disgust of the Cantab's [i.e.—from Cambridge University] friends. Keith-Falconer was a very effective rider on the path. His style was excellent, though perhaps too upright for latter-day ideas. He sat close up to the head of his machine, and being a tall man (over six feet) he looked remarkably well, and rode with skill, his win in the Fifty Miles Championship of 1882 being accomplished by good judgement and with consummate ease.[43]

In another account, Lacy Hillier mentions some of Keith-Falconer's limitations at the time:

> When he went down at Surbiton before Cortis in their 10-mile match, he was beaten as much by want of judgement as anything else.... He was so much superior to his contemporaries at the Universities that he had very little opportunity of developing that "head" or judgement in cycle racing which would have enabled him, when pitted against men who were as good as himself, to use his immense physical powers to their best advantage."[44]

Later, in his *Amateur Cycling*, an 1893 publication, Hillier discusses the question of strength and height, the physical attributes necessary for a cycling champion:

> Now, in the old days of ordinary racing, a man had to possess many qualifications before he was a champion. He not only had to possess the necessary qualifications other than physical, but he had also to possess certain physical developments, as for example: height, and a long reach, so as to ride with ease a big wheel, and thus secure an advantage over the smaller men, who could not bestride a wheel of such diameter. Nearly all the notable champions of the past, from Keith-Falconer and Cortis, onward, were big men—the two or three exceptions simply proving the rule.... Thus it came about that cycling produced several champions whose merits were unquestionable ... and the public loved to see them ride, and cheered them to the echo, and cycle racing took the public fancy and became a very popular branch of athletic sport.[45]

The late HON. ION KEITH FALCONER
(the first amateur record-breaker).
Shewing the racing machine of the period.

Fig. 2.13. Keith-Falconer, a tall man, pushed his ability to ride a large wheel to his advantage in riding against smaller men. [Source: *The Cyclist Year Book*, 1890]

A tall man did indeed have a longer reach, making it possible for him to ride a larger wheel, and thus for it to be geared higher. But Hillier's comments show subtle evidence of class bias. A smaller man could indeed be a champion, as John Keen demonstrated, and exceptions *disprove* the rule Hillier was attempting to make. What a rider lost in leg-length [and a slightly lower "gear'], he could make up for with a quicker pedaling technique and other athletic qualities–strength, staying power, suppleness and tactical skill.[46] As a socially biased observer and historian, Hillier favored amateur champions such as Keith-Falconer and H.L. Cortis (whose father was a doctor) over the working-class and lower-middle-class professionals, whose athletic abilities he appeared unwilling or unable to

Fig. 2.14. Bicycle versus Horse: a race at Alexandra Palace, London between Stanton and Mr. Macdonald's "Lady Flora." [Source: *Pictorial World*, 24 July 1875]

evaluate fairly. Hillier rarely praised the professional riders in print or recognized their achievements, and the careers of these early professionals are now much harder for the historian to document than those of the prominent amateurs.

6. "Gentlemen, Not Players": The Establishment of the Bicycle Union, 1877–78

Of the two contrasting social groups that were participating in the new sport–the proletarian professionals in Wolverhampton and Sheffield, and the "gentlemen" and upper-middle-class amateurs of London, Oxford and Cambridge–it is not surprising that it was the latter group who spearheaded the movement to organize and institutionalize the developing sport at a national level, and to remove it from the control of the Amateur Athletic Club. Lacy Hillier later described cycling at that moment (1876–78) as "so wide-spread, so valuable from a health-giving and economic point of view, so distinct from all the minor branches of athletics, which have their Alpha and Omega in the competitions on the cinder path, and moreover, so easily applicable to the stern business of life" that it "was not likely to remain for any length of time under feeble control."[47]

In the late 1870s, the question of who should control cycling, and who should control which aspects of cycling, was the subject of intense discussion and negotiation. There were squabbles and rivalries within the cycling community that needed to be resolved. But there was also opposition and a legislative threat to the new sport from the outside, from other road-users and the police, which had to be confronted and dealt with, for much of cycling took place on public roads. Thus, "sharing the road" was already an issue early on in the history of cycling.

Amateur championships on the track—usually on cinder or grass surfaces used primarily for running—had been organized under the auspices of the Amateur Athletic Club since 1871, but such events had become increasingly inadequate to the specialized demands of cyclists. An editorial in the *Bicycle Journal* from late 1876 complained of the continued inadequacy of the Amateur Athletic Club's bicycle championship:

> The race for the amateur championship should most certainly be in the hands of the bicycle clubs, and it is an anomaly only to be found in bicycling, that such is not the case. For three years now one club or another have been holding race meetings in London, but so far, none have ventured to institute a championship.[48]

The efficient organization of track racing was thus one pressing issue. But, perhaps more important, the much broader category of road riders, only some of whom were club members, had no organization to represent their interests and rights as users of the public roads. A series of well-publicized altercations between cyclists and horse riders and horse-driven carriages, and several serious assaults on cyclists, left the riders of the high-wheel feeling vulnerable and discriminated against.[49] The bicycle was not as yet legally recognized as a vehicle, and there were various central government and local legislative threats in 1878 to restrict and regulate cycling, which created a sense of urgency among cyclists and galvanized the Bicycle Union's founding members into action.[50] In many respects, cycling had to confront issues that "on location" sports such as cricket, running, tennis or golf, for example, had never had to contend with.

Both racing cyclists and club riders felt the need to organize in order to protect themselves and to give the sport its own institutional identity and independence. They were thus "determined to create a governing body elected by cyclists to rule cycling."[51] The essential question, negotiated in many club committee meetings from 1876 to 1878, was exactly how a national organization should oversee racing, as well what its involvements should be in other aspects of cycling. Except for track racing, cycling was not easily defined by a specific competitive arena, but involved all the various ways in which sporting cyclists interacted with society, as road racers, as recreational travelers and tourists, as utilitarian users of the roads and railways, and as patrons of roadside hotels and businesses.

The outcome of many meetings was the creation in 1878 of two parallel but independent bodies, the Bicycle Union (later the National Cyclists' Union) and the Bicycle Touring Club (later the Cyclists Touring Club). From the outset, the Bicycle Union controlled racing and dealt with legal matters, and the Bicycle Touring Club was concerned with actual road conditions, accommodations for cyclists while traveling, and the provision of maps and road signs.

The establishment of the two separate bodies in the same year was thus a significant indication of the dual nature of the sport of cycling, which on the one hand embraced serious racing and, on the other, promoted touring and recreational riding. The existence of the two parallel bodies was itself controversial: "There are not wanting cyclists who think that, had an association been formed combining the C.T.C. and N.C.U., the result would have been for the benefit of the sport," wrote Lacy Hillier in 1885, "whilst another section cling to the belief that the healthy rivalry which existed between our two great associations in their youthful days was the reason of their splendid development, as shown at present by the power and prestige which both undoubtedly possess."[52]

Various preliminary meetings were held in 1876 and 1877 between members of leading London clubs. The Temple, the Wanderers, the London, the Pickwick and the Surrey Bicycle Clubs, as well as the Oxford and Cambridge University Cycling Clubs, were all actively involved. The influential Temple Bicycle Club, for example, held a public debate on 19 March 1877 at its headquarters in the City of London to discuss "the advisability of forming a general association of bicyclists," to make decisions about championships, the definition of amateurism, and the settlement of racing disputes "on a basis acceptable to the general body of cyclists."[53] Sub-committee followed sub-committee, resulting in a report containing a resolution to create a Union. Ion Keith-Falconer was among those invited to attend a meeting in London, on November 17th, 1877, chaired by Gerard Cobb, also of the Cambridge club, at which it was unanimously resolved: "That a Prospectus of the Bicycle Union be published in all the bicycle journals, and a copy of it sent to the secretary of every bicycle club in the United Kingdom." Lacy Hillier suggested that this was an open, democratic process, that "its origin was brought about at an open and honest meeting in which all who cared to be represented could take part, and thus the opinions of all who had any right to speak were obtained." The reality appears to have been that the northern clubs, as a result of distance or lack of interest, were effectively excluded at this stage, as were professional riders.[54]

Fig. 2.15. "Waiting for the Pistol": bicycle racing was from the start the object of satirical attention. [Source: Badminton *Cycling*, 1889 edition]

The Bicycle Union, Britain's first national cycling organization, was formally established at a meeting in the Guildhall Tavern, London on 16 February 1878, when its constitution was debated and approved under the chairmanship of Gerard Cobb, the young president of the Cambridge University Bicycle Club. One of the pressing priorities of the Union was to make its representatives' voices heard by Parliament in Westminster, particularly with regard to the threatening provisions of an amended Highways Bill then in the process of being drafted. In July 1878, Gerard Cobb (Chairman), C.R. Hutchings (solicitor to the Bicycle Union) and Nahum Salamon (chairman of the Coventry Machinists' Company), met in Whitehall with the President of the Local Government Board, Mr. Scater-Booth, "to ask that the Highways Bill should be so framed as not to make its operation toward bicycle riders oppressive, and to get the bicycle declared a carriage within the purview of the new Act." The representatives stressed that cyclists formed "a sufficiently large and important body to render any hasty or ill-conceived legislation with regard to them most undesirable."[55] The economic benefits of the expanding bicycle industry were also emphasized. Salamon, speaking for the Bicycle Union, told Sclater-Booth that:

> five years ago the bicycling industry was represented by the Coventry Machinists Co. alone, making 5 bicycles a week; now there are 14 makers in Coventry, and some 120 scattered throughout different towns. The present weekly wages paid to makers of bicycles in Coventry ranged from £1,500–2,000. The amount of capital invested in plant and machinery may be estimated at about £1 million, and the value of bicycles throughout the country at between £600,000 and £800,000. In London there were upwards of 10,000 bicycles; in the country, 50,000.[56]

The Union's purpose was not only to look after the legal and legislative interests and rights of cyclists in a broad sense, but also "to examine the question of racing in general, and to frame definitions and recommend rules on the subject. To arrange for annual race meetings, at which the amateur championship shall be decided." At that moment, the Bicycle Union declared itself open to both amateur and professional riders, but in practice it was, and remained, heavily biased towards amateurism, and was rarely involved in the affairs of professionals.

Keith-Falconer was chairman of the Racing Committee which, on 4 April 1878, made a report to the Council attempting to define precisely what "amateur" and "professional" meant in the new sport of cycling. It was under pressure to do so because the Bicycle Union was planning to promote its first official Amateur Championships that year. After "lengthened discussion," it was resolved that the following definition of professional and amateur should be accepted: "A Professional Bicyclist is one who has ridden a Bicycle in public for money. An Amateur Bicyclist is one who has never done so, and who has never competed with a Professional Bicyclist in public (except at a meeting specially arranged by the Bicycle Union), and who has never publicly engaged in any other athletic exercise for money."[57] Another meeting, on 11 May, elaborated slightly on this brief definition, declaring that:

> a professional bicyclist is one who has ridden a bicycle in public for money, or who has engaged, taught or assisted in bicycling or any other athletic exercise for money, and that a bicyclist who shall have competed with a professional bicyclist for a prize knowingly and without protest (except at a meeting specially sanctioned by the Union), shall also be considered a professional bicyclist. Any person not included in the above definition shall be considered an amateur bicyclist.[58]

The definition that was finally agreed upon at a subsequent meeting (June 13) was essentially the same, but somewhat more concise in its wording, with an explanatory coda which attempted to define the ways in which a competitor might move over the imprecise boundary between amateurism and professionalism:

1. A Professional Bicyclist is one who has ridden a bicycle in public for money, or who has engaged, taught, or assisted in bicycling or any other athletic exercise for money.
2. A Bicyclist who shall have competed with a professional bicyclist in public or for a prize, knowingly without protest (except at a Meeting specially sanctioned by the Bicycle Union), shall also be considered a professional Bicyclist.
3. Any person not included in the above definitions shall be considered an Amateur Bicyclist. To prevent misunderstanding in reading the above, a majority of the Committee propose that the following explanations of its terms should be published with the definition: A bicyclist forfeits his right to compete as an amateur, and thereby becomes a professional bicyclist, by:
    a. Pursuing the art of riding the bicycle or any other athletic exercise as a means of gaining a livelihood.
    b. Riding the bicycle or engaging in any athletic exercise for a money prize or for gate money.
    c. Accepting remuneration for riding the bicycle or for engaging in any athletic exercise.
    d. Accepting payment for training or coaching others for bicycle racing or for any athletic exercise.
    e. Receiving payment for services personally rendered in teaching bicycle riding.
    f. Competing with a professional bicyclist in public for a prize according to paragraph 2 of the definition. Bicycle manufacturers and agents are cautioned, that to personally teach bicycle riding, as a means to effect the sale of a machine, will be taken as an infringement of clause e.[59]

The Bicycle Union here specifically rejected use of the Amateur Athletic Club's conservative, exclusionary and socially divisive "mechanic, artisan and labourer" clause, which had been framed in 1866 to reflect, maintain and reinforce class distinction within the sport, and had been rigorously imposed at the first amateur cycling championships in 1871, when seventeen out of twenty competitors were excluded as "professionals." Rather than excluding all working-class riders from amateur status, the Bicycle Union's definition, with its looser, modernized language, suggested that "professionalism" ought to be assigned only to those who earned their livings in the sport as full-time competitors or instructors.

The Bicycle Union's definition was controversial and broke new ground. It threatened to create a rift with other amateur athletic institutions. Two of the leading London cycling clubs, the Wanderers B.C. and the Temple B.C., initially withdrew their support of the new Union in protest. Lacy Hillier wrote that the Bicycle Union's definition, "ignoring as it did the social qualification as regards the amateur athlete, gave rise to an immense amount of discussion, and the cyclists were threatened with ostracism by some of the older followers of sport ... threats of protest being heard on all sides against the cycling division, who had thus taken this bold step in advance of the older branches of athletic sport."[60] One editorial spoke of the Bicycle Union as "fighting in the vanguard for a pure republic of sport."[61]

The Times, in a prominent and progressive April 1880 editorial, was:

glad that some body of athletes or quasi-athletes has been found bold enough to incur the risk with which the bicyclists are now threatened. We only wish they had been rebellious at more points, and had disregarded absolutely the vexatious rules which most other clubs have passed on their own account or have submitted to at the dictation of the rest. The fact is that the distinction between an amateur and a professional is becoming more and more an arbitrary one.[62]

The Bicycle Union demonstrated its determination to follow its own line with its decision to withdraw its championships from under the umbrella of the Amateur Athletic Club and to promote its own events. Within bicycle racing, progressive elements were thus striving to promote a more liberal, democratic, socially inclusive approach to competition, although it was also clear that deeply-rooted class distinctions could not easily be overcome.

The amateur/professional issue was compulsively discussed in the cycling press over the next twenty years, and was a constant source of tension within the new sport. If the new Bicycle Union was formed to give identity and independence to cycling as a whole, in reality it had little relevance to the working-class professionals, whose business affairs were handled by promoters and trainers with close ties to the bicycle industry.

Alfred Howard, in an editorial in the *Bicycling Journal* of June 1877, initially took a somewhat conservative stance in defense of the existing amateur "law." He was "afraid that there is a general wrong impression as to who is an amateur, and who is not ... many think that so long as they have never competed for money or against professionals they are entitled to rank as amateurs." But, Howard pointed out, although "it may be hard, unfair, or unjust," rules are rules: "the "mechanic, artisan or labourer clause" is the rule, or definition, and as such must be observed. No bicyclist therefore who is a "mechanic, artisan or labourer" can claim to be an amateur, or a member of an amateur club." But it was clear that shifting occupational and social definitions were making such perceived social and class categories within sport questionable:

> There is—especially in London—a great wish to be an amateur, and very few care to be called professionals, and partly for this reason also we presume that many small clubs are being established, some of which admit riders who would be refused entrance into existing amateur clubs. The would-be-amateurs trust by this means to get over the line, but of course whenever the unpleasant question of vocation comes to be asked the result is disqualification. It would, we think, be by far preferable if certain classes of riders would accept their position.[63]

The opinions and activities of Cambridge's Gerard Cobb, president of the Bicycle Union, were influential and significant in the debate at this particular moment. As a prominent sports institution within a bastion of cultural privilege, the Cambridge club might well have taken a hard line on the question of professional athletic exclusion. Its actions between 1877 and 1879, however, show Cobb's club, under his leadership, as questioning and challenging a narrow, traditional view of amateurism. In September 1877, the club invited H.P. Whiting, the Amateur Athletic Club champion in 1871, 1873, 1874 and 1875, who had been expelled from the A.A.C. for having compromised his amateur status by competing against professionals, to compete in an "open" amateur race in November.[64] Alfred Howard now welcomed this new departure in the *Bicycling Journal*:

> We are informed that the committee of the Cambridge University club in electing the competitors do not profess to be guided by the definition of "gentleman amateur." We are glad that such is the case and we think the example set may well be followed by other clubs, and this undefinable term laid aside for good ... we have all along held that the definition of an amateur is ill adapted to bicycling, and not in accordance with the spirit of the age.

The Cambridge University club, Howard went on to say, was "a large association, and contains some of the best riders of the day," but "they are little known beyond their own racing circle." The London clubs, he thought, were under more pressure to rule on the amateur question since they "compete all over the country. These are the clubs which really ought to re-arrange the amateur question, as it concerns them the most. The feeling that something ought to be done is daily getting stronger; perhaps now the C.U.B.C. has opened the ball the vexed question may soon be settled; until this happens we are sorry to say that we do not see how any amateurs can safely run against Mr. H.P. Whiting."[65] Such expressions of opinion on the question emphasize how shifting and tentative the definition of amateurism actually was.

Gerard Cobb continued to be provocative. In a letter to *Bicycling News* in August 1877, he outlined his position on "The Amateur Question." Amateurs and professionals should not be prevented from competing against each other and an amateur who raced against a professional for a trophy, "to test and stimulate his strength and skill," should not forfeit his amateur status, he argued. The most convincing reason to encourage competition between amateurs and professionals was "the development of the art" of bicycling, to stimulate the creation of "the perfect machine and the perfect rider."[66] There was "something radically wrong in any rule or definition which tends to limit the scope of competition, and thereby jeopardises progress in an invention destined to be so widely and beneficially employed as the bicycle." The current amateur rule was "unreasonable, unusual and detrimental."[67] The influential journal *The Field* agreed: "bicycle racing is a new form of sport—the growth of the last few years—and its exponents must be allowed to make their own rules," and suggested only that an amateur should not race against a professional for money.[68]

Fig. 2.16. John Keen at speed. [Source: author's collection]

The Cambridge Club and the Bicycle Union tested their convictions by promoting a series of amateur versus professional races in 1878 and 1879, with the official sanction of the newly created Union, in which amateurs Keith-Falconer (Cambridge University B.C.) and H.L. Cortis (Wanderers B.C.) and professionals John Keen (London), W. Phillips (Coventry) and Fred Cooper participated.

The first races were held in Cambridge in October 1878, and in a 5-mile event Keith-Falconer defied most expectations by beating Keen by 5 yards, and in the process broke the record for that distance, from 16m 1½s to 15m 13⅗s. "No race that has yet been run has created more interest than that of Amateur versus Professional which took place at Cambridge last week," commented *Bicycling Times*, "Prior to the existence of the Bicycle Union such a contest would have been impossible without the disqualification of the amateur ensuing.... It reflects the greatest credit on John Keen that in his desire for sport he ran without reward, and acted throughout as a thorough sportsman."[69]

In May 1879, Keith-Falconer, Cortis, Keen and Cooper raced over 2 miles in Cambridge, and then in October, Cortis and Keen participated in races at three distances for a 25 guinea cup, over 20 miles in Wolverhampton, and then in London at Stamford Bridge over 1 mile and 5 miles, where they "excited an enormous amount of interest, the Stamford Bridge grounds have seldom since their opening seen such an assemblage of spectators. There must have been six or seven thousand persons present, parts of the ground being inconveniently crowded."[70] Cortis was victorious over the long distance, but Keen won both the shorter races, to take the cup.

Tactical issues, the rider's position on the bicycle, and especially the question of "pacing," or drafting—riding in a leader's slip-stream—proved to be of crucial importance in these three "amateur versus professional" races between Cortis and Keen. The riders contested their experience and their competitive intelligence, and not only were the riders' strength and speed at stake, but so, too, their tactical finesse. In the 20-mile race at Wolverhampton, Cortis led from the start, with Keen "quite content to be in the rear of his rival." In the last lap, "Keen made strenuous efforts to overtake the amateur, but it was of no avail and Cortis responded to every spurt," winning by two yards.[71] Accepting Cortis' fast pace at the front in the 1-mile race a week later in London, Keen rode:

> an unvarying length in the rear, maintaining his favourite position.... When the bell rang as they entered the last lap, Cortis seemed to improve the pace slightly; but Keen made no attempt to pass until they approached the final straight. As they rounded the corner he came out, judged the distance and pace to a nicety, and coming away in splendid style, won on a spurt by half a yard.[72]

Clearly, the tactical technique of "pacing," the realization that a second-placed rider gained considerable benefit in the slip-stream of his rival, and that a winner could make use of his opponent's pace until the very last moment of a race, was thoroughly understood and practiced in high-wheel bicycle racing. Cortis and Keen, top-level amateur and professional athletes, were closely matched, shared identical tactical concerns and made use of this knowledge in competition.

In promoting these professional versus amateur races, the Bicycle Union thus came into conflict with the Amateur Athletic Club, whose effective control of amateur cycling had been taken from it by the new organization. Voicing approval of the Union's independent stance, *Bicycling Times* adopted an assertive "I told you so" attitude in its comments, and described:

> such an assemblage at Stamford Bridge to witness bicycle races *only* as has never yet been brought together in connection with athletic sport in London.... Persons who were preaching about the heinousness of allowing the best professional of the year to compete with the best gentleman amateur, and the dreadful effect it would have on all bicyclists who rode under Union rules will sooner or later realize the fact that bicycling is a sport which can stand by itself.[73]

7. JOHN KEEN (1849–1902)

The career of Ion Keith-Falconer, the quintessential "gentleman amateur" cyclist, has already been described. By comparison, the life and career of John Keen, his professional opponent in the "open" races, who "ran without reward in his desire for sport" and was "a thorough sportsman in these unusual matches," was also of huge significance, a monument of the early sport.

The unassuming London athlete and bicycle maker, John Keen (1849–1902), has received little wider historical recognition, but was a towering presence in English cycling for two decades, as racing champion and manufacturer. A prominent article in *Wheel World* in 1885 called him "perhaps the best known bicyclist, professional or amateur, in the world," and the fact that he had been racing since the very earliest days of the sport put him "in the first rank of cycling celebrities," and he could still claim to be "the fastest man in existence on the road."[74] He gained international fame as a champion cyclist and was praised for his engaging personality.[75] Keen started to race in the very earliest days of the sport in 1869, and in 1870 was already described as "a celebrity who brought a large company together" whenever he appeared at races.[76]

As a racer, Keen dominated English professional championships during the 1870s and 1880s, with an unrivaled record of victories in 1873, 1875, 1876, 1878 and 1879, and as runner-up in 1870, 1872 and 1874 (though with several "championship-level" races, it was difficult to know which was *the* championship, in modern-day terms).

In the mid–1880s, Keen was still winning races. He was a huge attraction and an extraordinarily consistent performer at the regularly scheduled events in the centers of professionalism—Wolverhampton, Sheffield, Birmingham, Leicester and London. As a professional "champion" working in the show-business environment of early professional cycling, Keen issued challenges to other professional riders and often raced against horses and runners under varied conditions, for wagers, particularly at the end of his career. Keen also traveled to America at least three times, where with Harry Etherington and David Stanton he pioneered top-level professional racing.[77]

But Keen was also widely recognized at the time as perhaps the most important and innovative small manufacturer of racing bicycles, and epitomized the close connection between manufacturers and the sport. During his entire career, Keen rode on high-wheel bicycles of his own manufacture and provided the best machines for many of the leading amateurs and professionals. He won the 1875 1-mile championship in Sheffield on a 56-inch machine with ball bearings on the front wheel. This was typical of his technologically innovative machines, which provided a standard by which other makers judged their own products, and many of these innovations (which were not systematically patented) were later consistently incorporated by other manufacturers into their machines.[78] *Bicycling Times* wrote that: "His reputation as being *the* man has enabled him to secure an immense number of patrons for his make of bicycle, known as the "Eclipse," and richly he deserves it."[79]

But it was the breadth and range of his knowledge, and experience of the sport and the industry, that earned Keen the most praise. In 1877, *Bicycling News* said Keen "has from the birth of bicycling been one of its principal stays." It called Keen "probably the best known bicyclist in the world.... Possessing a marvellous staying power, he has also a splendid style of going, and a turn of speed which is probably unsurpassed by any amateur or professional.... From the very first, he has been a fine example of straightforward riding, admired not only by amateurs, but also by the professional world, including those whom he has vanquished, and is spoken of as uniformly pleasant and courteous to those with whom he comes in contact."[80] *Bicycling World* interviewed him in Boston in 1879 and thought he was "unquestionably the most interesting bicycling character who has visited us from abroad." The paper praised "his graceful and effective style of riding, his frank and honourable deportment, which gain him friends everywhere," and found him "a gentlemanly, practical man, who knows the art and business of bicycling in all their phases, and is ready in imparting his knowledge to others."[81]

Fig. 2.17. John Keen, 1849–1902. [Source: *Wheel World*, author's collection.]

Keen's comportment apparently was in contrast to the coarser standards of behavior of many other professionals. Most of the leading amateurs of the 1870s were coached by Keen, including Cortis and Keith-Falconer, his opponents in the professional-amateur matches. His prominence in the early sport was recognized when an appeal for funds was launched on his behalf in 1884, and quickly raised a considerable amount of money. Keen had concentrated on his racing and bicycle-building activities to the neglect of his business affairs:

> Keen may be said to have given that push to cycling that has enabled it not only to creep up ... but to equal, if not excel, any other of our national sports. For a man to have been the instigator of such a success is undoubtedly worthy of every recognition, particularly as the foundation of the sport has given rise to an industry finding constant occupation for thousands of skilled mechanics. Beyond the manufacture of machines, the credit of first proving their use also falls to John Keen.[82]

8. A New Athletic Liberalism

The tendency towards a new athletic liberalism, and an attempt to redefine or limit the amateur/professional stratification within the sport of cycling, gained significant momentum. In between the contrasting social poles of the privileged Oxford, Cambridge and London clubs and the proletarian professionals, cycling appealed heavily to young, middle-class men who were perhaps less inclined as a group to respect established social distinctions. They were interested, in an objective sense, in developing the bicycle technologically and in comparing the athletic talents of leading amateurs and professionals. In order to ride a bicycle, join a club, and to buy equipment and a uniform, disposable income was needed, and those who rode on the weekend or competed in races were a younger gen-

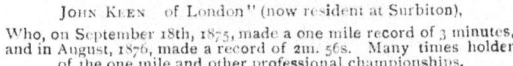

Left: Fig. 2.18. John Keen. [Source: *The Cyclist Annual and Year Book*] *Right:* Fig. 2.19. John Keen. "Keen is probably the best known bicyclist in the world, and there is seldom a race meeting of importance at which the face of Happy Jack is not seen." [Source: *Bicycling News*, 9 Nov. 1877]

eration of men who tended to be unencumbered by family or agricultural responsibilities. Club uniforms were introduced to create an image of middle-class respectability, to encourage the social acceptance of cycling. But of course, not every rider joined a club.

Cyclists made up a new social grouping, outside the respectability of, for example, the hunt or the steeple-chase, the cricket ground, the tennis court, or the golf course. Cycling on the road occurred in the public space, rather than in a restricted, private environment; riders were exposed indiscriminately to other categories of road users. Both the recreational rider and the racer encountered the unexpected—in the towns, crowded streets crammed with horses and carts; in the country, unpredictable road conditions, a flock of sheep, a hunt party, or slow-moving horses pulling a coach or wagon. Out on the road, riders had to be their own mechanics and repair their machines. The danger and the dirty road conditions meant that cycling could never be a genteel sport. Cyclists braved the elements, and a social leveling was implicit in this.

Serious cycling on the road initiated participants into a fraternity, a shared democracy of tough, athletic activity. Clubs organized amateur rides on the road, while a professional might undertake a place-to-place road ride for a wager. But racing on the track was more formally structured and it was there that the need for a distinction between amateurs and professionals became most pressing. And the distinction between amateur and professional cyclists would continue to be hotly contested through the 1880s and 1890s: it was the source of constant debate and organizational controversy.

Thus a social tension existed within cycling from the earliest days of the sport. The inherent democracy of cycling as a challenging physical activity, as exemplified by the working-class professionals on the track and the uncouth "scorchers" on the road, came up against the efforts of amateur proponents such as George Lacy Hillier and the members of the Bicycle Touring Club who were attempting to direct the sport upwards socially and maintain an image of amateur respectability. The Bicycle Union (renamed the National Cyclists' Union in 1883) struggled to legislate relationships between competitors of different social classes and cultural backgrounds, as well as to deal with a complex and affluent industry for the next twenty years. The Bicycle Union was centered primarily in London and the surrounding counties, and did not at first include Midlands and Northern clubs. In spite of the creation of local chapters in an attempt to overcome this emphasis on London clubs, such a London-based national institution did not represent or benefit all regions equally. Its attempts to regulate a wide variety of sporting and economic interests related to club life, racing and the industry were seen as an unwelcome bureaucratic intrusion by those who had little interest in centralized control. Lacy Hillier wrote optimistically that "the Union then as now was so constituted as to admit professionals to membership, and thus secure a body representing not merely a section but the whole sport," but he added cryptically that the proposal to form the Union "attracted but little attention in the provinces, where things were scarcely ripe for the new departure."[83]

In fact, the sport of cycling was much too diverse, geographically and socially, to be represented by one single body. Hillier commented that Gerard Cobb's influence was "recognized throughout, in the very wide and liberal lines" on which the first proposal for the Union were drawn up, but one of the Bicycle Union's most pressing tasks was "to examine the question of bicycle racing in general, and to frame definitions and recommend rules on the subject," and it was "soon evident that the first question which the Union would have to take in hand was that of the amateur definition."[84] The amateur/professional issue was not to be resolved easily.[85]

9. THE BICYCLE TOURING CLUB, 1878

The adventurous and pioneering spirit of early high-wheel bicycling on the roads of Britain when the Bicycle Touring Club was founded in 1878, as well as its predominantly urban roots, is conveyed perfectly by James Lightwood in *The Romance of the Cyclists' Touring Club*:

> No sooner had the bicycle become recognized as a new means of progress in this country than those who possessed them experienced a longing to get away from towns and streets and explore the countryside. This joy of the open road was a new experience, giving all the charm of novelty mingled with a spice of adventure and a modicum of risk, as riders soon found to their cost. Roads were bad, maps indifferent good, sign-posts frequently illegible or misleading, wayside inns and country hotels were rarely prepared to receive guests—and such guests, too, with a day's dust or mud thick upon them. Route-books, or road-books, such as we know them now scarcely existed then.... But those were the days of great adventure, and the first impulse of those who mastered the art of riding the bicycle was to go forth on voyages of discovery into the Great Unknown.[86]

"The Great Unknown" beckoned the majority of club and unattached riders into non-competitive, place-to-place rides, either one day jaunts, or more extended multi-day touring rides. With more members in the North than in London, and founded to offer support and information to riders on the road, the Bicycle Touring Club embodied ideals of community and mutual aid rather than competition. It was known as a "league or brotherhood," indicative of its exclusively male membership. But if the Bicycle Union at first nominally allowed professionals to become members, the Bicycle Touring Club was from the start exclusively amateur. It was founded on the conviction that the serious recreational cyclist—part athlete, part tourist, part utilitarian traveler, part record setter—also had interests that needed to be protected and needs that had to be met.

Tourists, as Lightwood recognized, needed food, accommodations, and the means to clean themselves after a day on the dusty roads. They needed travel information, directions, and better roads. They had inherited a well demarcated, ancient road system which had been very much neglected since the 1840s, when the much faster railways had succeeded in luring travelers away.

Fig. 2.20. Three anonymous club riders from the early period showed the wear and tear of hard-riding cyclists. [Source: Lorne Shields collection, Toronto, Canada]

Fig. 2.21. The "shared democracy of the road" included physical danger, especially in the urban environment, as illustrated by George Moore. [Source: author's collection]

Many Bicycle Touring Club members were also members of smaller clubs. But one of the Club's primary objectives was to assist the many bicyclists who did not have a local club to join, and who benefited from belonging to a national club which soon had branches and representatives all over the country. The idea for the Bicycle Touring Club was originally suggested in the pages of *Bicycling News* in 1876, and the "league or brotherhood" was founded at the North of England Meet held at Harrogate, Yorkshire, on 5 August 1878 by three young enthusiasts: Stanley Cotterell (Mid-Lothian Bicycle Club, Edinburgh), S.H. Ineson (Bradford Bicycle Club), and T.H. Holding (Banbury Bicycle Club). The aims of the organization were: "To encourage and facilitate touring in all parts of the world. To protect its members against unprovoked assaults. To provide riding or touring companions. To secure and appoint at fixed and reduced rates hotel headquarters in all parts of the country. To enlist the co-operation of a leading wheelman, who should act as a Consul in every town, and who should render to his fellow members local information of every description."

The Club's headquarters moved, along with its different presidents, from Edinburgh to Newcastle to Bradford, and then finally to London in 1883. By 1884, the Cyclists' Touring Club, as it was by then named (the Club had undergone a name-change in 1882–83 to accommodate the growing number of tricyclists) advertised itself as "the Success of the Age in the Athletic World," and not only basked in its status as the largest bicycling organization in Britain, but claimed to be the largest athletic organization in the world, with 11,000 members, a total which had grown to more than 20,000 by 1889.[87]

This large membership, which had grown within only a few years, offers convincing proof of the extraordinary growth and popularity of bicycling as a sport and pastime. However, although such a large membership might seem to indicate a social leveling, the Bicycle Touring Club in fact appears at first to have encouraged an image of social exclusivity. There was no actual competition included in the Club's activities, but membership was "strictly confined to Amateur Cyclists," indicating that a code of social decorum and gentlemanly behavior was expected of the members. A candidate who was already a member of "a recognized Amateur Cycling Club" was automatically admitted. An unattached candidate needed either a reference from two other members, or "must give reasonable and satisfactory proof of his respectability and position to any of the Representative Councillors of the Division in which he resides, or to the Chief Consul." Club publicity from 1884 stated that one of the advantages of membership was that:

It is par excellence the club for professional men. It not only includes in its roll many of the nobility and gentry in all parts of the land, it is supported by some of the highest dignitaries of the church, by members of the legal, medical, military, and naval professions, and indeed by amateur riders ... who produce credentials showing that they belong to a respectable station in life.[88]

Although it was at first conservative in its attempt to promote middle-class respectabil-

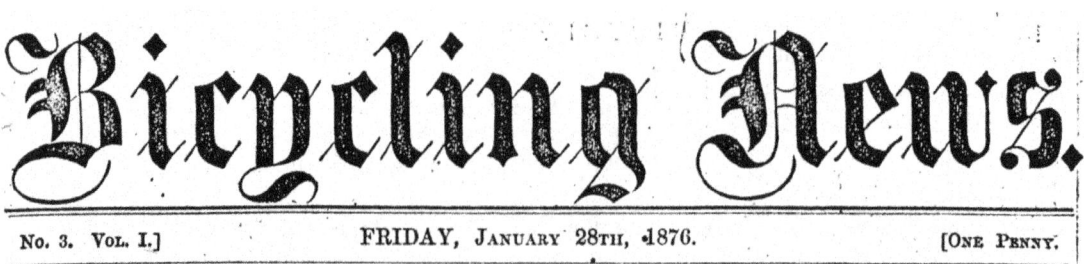

Fig. 2.22. *Bicycling News* was first published in 1876. [Source: author's collection.]

ity, the Cyclists' Touring Club nevertheless appears to have quickly expanded its membership base across class and gender distinctions and was certainly progressive in welcoming "Ladies" as members; this was the first formal acceptance of women members by a cycling organization. The Cyclists Touring Club thus encouraged the expansion of the sport of cycling outside the narrow confines of formal competition and opened recreational cycling to a wider, broader membership.[89]

10. Public Recognition of Bicycling

Road racing and riding, track racing, widespread club formation at a local and national level, a booming industry and trade, the creation of a specialized cycling press, and an increase in recreational touring—by 1877/78, a critical mass of cycling activity, a conspicuous commercial and cultural movement, had occurred in Britain, creating a prominent sport and pastime that generated a great deal of interest in the national press. Cycling on the high-wheel bicycle was recognized as a serious athletic activity—from hesitant beginnings, cycling had become a permanent part of sports culture.

In an editorial in the first issue of his new *Bicycle Journal* (18 Aug. 1876), Alfred Howard commented that bicycle racing had "made great strides." Athletic clubs had "scouted the idea of introducing a bicycle race in their programmes," and had found that "the bicycle contest created more enthusiasm and excitement than all the 100 yards, quarter, and mile races put together." The cyclists had "succeeded in setting the fair sex in such a flutter and fluster" that the runners had been unable "to raise a solitary cheer." In 1875, there had been "between fifty and sixty athletic meetings at which bicycle contests were held"; in 1876 that number had already increased to about ninety by August, when the editorial was written. The number of bicycle racers in the country had "nearly doubled" in the previous year, and the expansion had been especially great in the "northern and midland counties," where "fresh men have come out with great abundance. Here the promoters of athletic meetings have been quicker in perceiving that a Bicycle race helps to make a good gate, and constitutes an important feature in their sports." Howard regretted that some of the courses used were terrible, but hoped that "with the increase of racing will come better paths and less risks to the rider."[90]

A *Daily News* editorial, also from August 1876,

Fig. 2.23. Smartly dressed, middle-class club cyclists were increasingly seen on the roads of Britain in the late 1870s. [Source: John L. Weiss collection]

said that the bicycle "ought to be regarded not as a mere plaything of the hour, but as a substantial addition to the conveniences of life."[91]

At the second annual race meeting of the West Kent Bicycle Club, held at Crystal Palace in late September 1877, where a variety of races were run in many heats and professional John Keen performed an exhibition ride, the prizes were presented by the club's president, Member of Parliament Robert Lowe, who addressed the assembled crowd and congratulated them for "the very pleasant, and I will say rational manner in which we have spent the afternoon." It had been "a contest of very fine young men, all doing their very best, but only disposing of their own strength and energy." Lowe had been "from the first a very strong advocate for the bicycle … not only because I thought it would be an amusement, but because I saw in it a great many advantages. I thought it was a fine employment and exercise for young men, and would keep them out of a great deal of mischief." Lowe asked the West Kent cyclists to behave well on the road, to be "under the same control and self-imposed regulations as in riding a horse," since "nothing could be more injurious to the spread of bicycling than that there should be accidents or serious cause of complaint."

Commenting upon Lowe's speech in the *Bicycle Journal*, Alfred Howard congratulated bicycling for having a spokesman like him, "whose word will be of greater weight with the generality of people than that of all other bicyclists put together":

> Now that Mr. Lowe has spoken on our behalf, it is satisfactory to note an improvement in public opinion towards us, and that the well-chosen remarks uttered at the Crystal Palace have attracted almost universal attention, and have been favourably commented upon in several quarters. Even those who were avowedly hostile before, and decried bicycling as a novelty dangerous and delusive, have been forced to admit its utility as well as its stability.... The result is that we have a status admitted to us, which, though undefined, is none the less real and existent.[92]

The use of the word "undefined" here to describe cycling's status should perhaps be interpreted as confirmation of the sport's tendency to challenge existing social groupings. Howard again celebrated the health of the sport of bicycling in a February 1878 *Bicycle Journal* editorial. "Bicyclists in this country may be pardoned if they congratulate themselves on the spread of their pastime," he wrote; "Favoured, perhaps, in some measure by circumstances—as, for instance, the general excellence of our roads and the superiority of English mechanical arts and appliances—bicycling has taken firm hold on the youth of Great Britain; and we regard it as a convincing proof of the practical nature of the English character to have made such good use of the opportunity."[93]

Gerard Cobb's mission as president of the Bicycle Union was to crusade for better understanding and toleration of the new sport and for recognition of cycling's utility.[94] In two long letters entitled "Bicycling and the Public," which he sent to the *Daily News* in July 1878 and which were also published in the cycling press, Cobb countered many of the objections which had been raised against cycling and spelled out its benefits and advantages. The letters carried significant weight, as they came from a Fellow of Trinity College, Cambridge who was also the president of the cycling club of that prestigious university.

In the first letter, Cobb argues that "it is a matter of national importance" that cycling "should receive full and fair consideration." Cycling, he argued, was primarily "of commercial importance"; second, cycling was "of real practical and professional service" and third, "as a pastime it has strong physical, moral and intellectual recommendations." Cycling was "a pursuit which enabled a certain class of young men more or less connected with the desk or counter to substitute fresh air, bracing exercise, and the sight of the country, for a City youth's usual evening programme." The bicycle was also of practical benefit:

> the ease with which a bicycle can be driven, the distance it enables its riders to cover, its speed ... added to its durability and comparative cheapness, render it by far the best form of road-locomotion for all to whom economy, whether of time or money, is an object. As such its use is daily extending among professional men of all classes, especially clergymen and doctors; whilst as the prices of bicycles in second-hand markets gradually get lower, working men are getting more and more to use them for their daily transit to and from work.

As "a pastime rather than a professional necessity," bicycling was "enormously on the increase," and one out of every five of Cobb's Cambridge students possessed a bicycle. Physically, cycling had much to recommend it, since it required good balance and enabled the rider "to get a thorough change of air as he passes over many different soils and local conditions of climate, in the course of his ride. It will be readily understood that to students a form of exercise which confers this benefit must be of peculiar value." Cobb especially notes the "nerve and pluck" required to ride the tricky, dangerous high-wheeler:

> Among the moral characteristics which have made us as a nation what we are, few have played so important a part as nerve and pluck, and it is this very need of their exercise which makes bicycling so popular with us, and has apparently prevented its taking root on the Continent. It would be nothing short of a national disaster if a pastime which tends to develop these important facets of character, and which is now rapidly assuming national proportions, should be placed at the mercy of repressive local legislation.[95]

In his second letter to the *Daily News*, Cobb deals with specific issues in order to reassure the public that they should not feel threatened by cyclists. Considering that there were about 60,000 cyclists on the roads, he argues, the number of accidents was small and "hardly justifies the recent outcry." As far as timid horses were concerned, they should be treated with consideration, and they would get used to bicycles; "in neighborhoods where bicycling made an early start, it is the greatest rarity in the world to find a horse shy at a bicycle." The penalties against "furious and dangerous riding" should be strictly enforced. Unfortunately, the public needed to be protected from "the thoughtlessness, or the ill-bred selfishness ... of a very small portion of the bicycling community." Rules of good behavior had been issued by the Bicycle Union, "and their essential features are almost universally observed by "club" men and the better classes of the "unattached." But unfortunately, all bicyclists are not amenable to the same regulations, nor sufficiently imbued with a proper spirit of consideration for others." It was necessary, therefore, to insert a clause in the Highways Bill under consideration by Parliament to "regulate the use of bicycles on roads," but there needed to be uniformity in the laws that applied to cyclists. Acceptable bye-laws were those that ordered cyclists to carry a bell or whistle to signal their approach, to use a lamp after dark, and to obey speed restrictions within town and city limits.[96]

Giving conspicuous recognition to the national debate about cycling, and the extent to which the sport and recreation had impacted everyday life, *The Times* published a leading article in September 1878. "A curious question is coming on," it announced, "The bicycle has come to the front and is fighting for existence ... the bicycle has now surmounted the difficulties of construction, and adapted itself to human capabilities.... Bicyclists are become a power." *The Times* marveled at the progress cyclists had achieved while at the same time acknowledging the need for fair and unprejudiced legislative restraints. On the plus side,

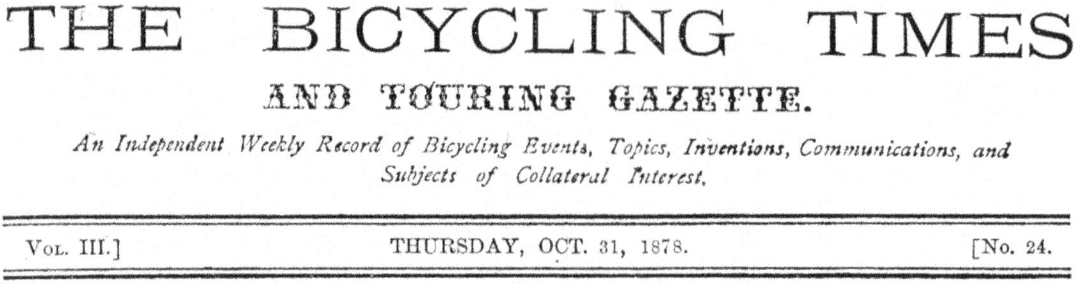

THE BICYCLING TIMES
AND TOURING GAZETTE.

An Independent Weekly Record of Bicycling Events, Topics, Inventions, Communications, and Subjects of Collateral Interest.

Vol. III.]   THURSDAY, OCT. 31, 1878.   [No. 24.

Fig. 2.24. Masthead of *Bicycling Times*. [Source: author's collection.]

it recognized that the bicycle "augments at least three-fold the locomotive power of an ordinary man. A bicyclist can perform a journey of a hundred miles in one day with less fatigue than he could walk thirty." But on the negative side, "the bicyclist will have to submit to the same rules as all others enjoying some advantage over foot passengers. He will have to use bells when required…. He will have to use his eyes. Above all, he will have to bear in mind that in every thoroughfare, at almost any hour of the day, there will be a large proportion of stupid people, and a not very small proportion of people a little the worse for drink."

Gerard Cobb and the Bicycle Union had won a significant victory over public opinion. *The Times* greeted the arrival of the bicycle with an appeal for common sense and an ironical reflection on the many sources of frustration on the roads. The bicycle was criticized because it was fast and quiet, but "for all practical purposes, noise is a much greater nuisance than silence, and slowness a much greater nuisance than speed. The vehicles that make streets intolerable … are heavy vans, huge omnibuses, tradesmen's carts, costermongers proclaiming their wares." Society "used to be divided into the equestrian and the pedestrian orders," but cyclists "have found a third rank."[97]

* * *

In the short span of less than ten years, bicycling had evolved in Britain from an embryonic show-business entertainment into a formally constituted and recognized sport and pastime. Thousands of cyclists were seen on the roads, and thousands of spectators

No. 81. New Series Vol. 1.]   FRIDAY, MARCH 1, 1878.   [ONE PENNY.

Fig. 2.25. Masthead of the *Bicycle Journal*. [Source: author's collection]

attended bicycle race meetings. Cycling had become a cultural institution. It had two national organizations and a well-defined structure of clubs, championships, record-keeping and record-breaking. It was recognized as a specialized athletic activity, with specific training priorities and needs. The sport was supported by an important manufacturing industry and had its own specialized weekly and monthly press. It sent lobbyists to Westminster to represent its interests, and was sufficiently conspicuous and controversial for editors to take note and write about it in prominent daily newspapers such as *The Times* and the *Daily News*.

Cyclists could be divided into two groups of obsessively enthusiastic athletes: first, the small group of professionals that had emerged from the earliest entertainment context, and second, a much larger group of amateur racers and recreational cyclists. There was also a diverse group of manufacturers, businessmen, promoters and journalists who supported the sport and who epitomized a new kind of middle-class entrepreneur, organizing and selling sport, recreation and mobility to many thousands of riders.[98]

Although the bicycle could and did provide useful transportation, in the 1870s and early 1880s utility was a primary motivation only for those cyclists who were energetic enough to master the dangerous bicycle, a mastery that involved considerable athletic skill and experience.

Chapter Three

The Beginnings of Bicycle Racing in the United States

1. American Cycling in the late 1870s

AS WE'VE SEEN, American enthusiasm for the velocipede acted as a stimulus to the British sport in the late 1860s. But in the late 1870s, influences flowed in the opposite direction. The same conditions that led to the expansion of cycling in Britain—technological innovation and the popularity of sport among young, urban, middle-class men, as well as the university contingent—existed in the United States, and from 1876 onwards there was a surge of interest in the high-wheel bicycle there.

Culturally, New England identified with Britain, sharing a language and similar sporting interests with the British; and indeed, Anglo-Americans played a prominent role in the foundation of the American sport. One report spoke of "such a fraternity as that of the wheelmen of America and England," which "will do noble work in cementing the ties already existing in their common blood and friendship."[1]

Both professional and amateur sports were already firmly established in the United States, providing a fertile ground for the introduction of the new sport of bicycling, which fit easily into a sporting context that included running, walking and rowing competitions. International exchanges between British and American professional runners and walkers were frequently promoted from 1840 to 1870.[2] The New York Athletic Club was founded in 1866, modeled on the London Athletic Club, and held its first official meet in 1868. English-style amateurism was upheld within the American collegiate and athletic club scenes. In 1872, William B. Curtis, co-founder of the New York Athletic Club, and John Watson, of the Schuylkill Navy Athletic Club of Philadelphia, following a dispute about participation in rowing competitions, published pamphlets arguing for the differentiation of amateur athletes from those seeking cash prizes. In 1878, William Curtis became the influential new editor of *Spirit of the Times*, "The American Gentleman's Magazine," and in that capacity no longer covered professional pedestrianism. In 1879, the National Association of Amateur Athletes of America was founded, leading in 1888 to the formation of the Amateur Athletic Union. S.W. Pope writes that:

> Nineteenth century amateurism was an "invented tradition." As the rallying cry of late nineteenth century institutionalized sport, amateurism represented an attempt to draw class lines against the masses and to develop a new bourgeois leisure lifestyle as a badge of middle and upper-class identity. The amateur ethos was, moreover, an ideological reaction to a well-established professional sporting tradition in the United States.... Between the 1870s and early 1890s, amateurists honed their message about the meanings of amateurism in the media, collegiate circles and public debate, and developed organizations like the Amateur Athletic union to legitimize their message within collegiate circles and wider society.[3]

Developments within cycling were consistent with these wider movements in American sport and in fact provide excellent illustrations of them. Cycling was introduced into the United States in the late 1860s primarily as a professional sport, but by the time it underwent a second wave of popularity (in the late 1870s) it was embraced both professionally and in the rapidly expanding amateur sport world.

From 1877, amateur cycling clubs were formed throughout the United States, following the example of the British clubs. English promoter Harry Etherington's 1879 tour was significant in promoting professional racing in America. In an attempt to bridge the Atlantic, Etherington sought to popularize the high-wheel sport in the U.S., to make money himself and to help create a strong base for the British bicycle industry. Etherington, an editor, journalist and promoter of a series of indoor, long-distance track races in London which had generated a lot of publicity in 1878 and 1879, persuaded four of the top European professionals to go with him to the United States to take part in a series of "Six Day" and demonstration races. His promotional visit was an attempt to market the already well-developed British sport as a spectator enterprise in America, and provides a colorful vignette of the state of American cycling in 1879/80.[4]

Charles Pratt, Frank L. Weston and others in the Boston area, key players in the early promotion of amateur bicycling in the United States, were active in that city in this period. "In the use of the bicycle, Boston has led the rest of the country thus far. Four gentlemen—a journalist, an architect, a lawyer and a merchant—were the first to introduce the bicycle," reported the *Boston Globe*, suggesting that there was already "bicycle fever in this country."[5] A series of well-documented events marked the beginnings of the amateur sport in Boston: the first clubs were formed, rides and excursions were held, cycling publications were sold and bicycles became available.

English bicycles were first imported into the United States by the firm of Cunningham, Heath and Co. in 1877. They had attracted attention initially when they were exhibited at the Centennial Exhibition in Philadelphia from May to November 1876. A late 1877 report notes the dual potential of the bicycle as a "means of locomotion for useful work, as well as exhilarating sport":

> The surprising machines displayed by English makers ... attracted much admiring attention from many visitors, and a considerable number of the curious vehicles have since been sold in various directions. They have given so much satisfaction that the call for them has increased of late, and they are now for sale in all our principal cities.... There is a strong probability that the bicycle, in its vastly improved construction, will come into extensive use in our country; not, as in former years, to run an ephemeral career as a novel toy, but to become a staple addition to our means of locomotion for useful work as well as exhilarating sport. There are many among our readers who will take to them as a fish does to water. Among the same ... may also be found the champion rider, and the American mechanic, to still further improve the machine.[6]

The *American Bicycling Journal* was founded in December 1877 by Frank W. Weston, a partner in Cunningham, Heath and Co. An editorial in its first issue describes the bicycle as "perfect in its mechanical principles, the acme of graceful strength combined with delicate construction, affording to its rider a maximum of speed in return for a minimum of effort and exertion." It was "a means both practical and enjoyable of rapid locomotion." Lovers of the bicycle could "benefit themselves and posterity morally, mentally, and physically, by sparing a portion of their time for healthful exercise in the open air, expanding their chests and their hearts."[7] The Boston Bicycle Club, the first American cycling club, was founded

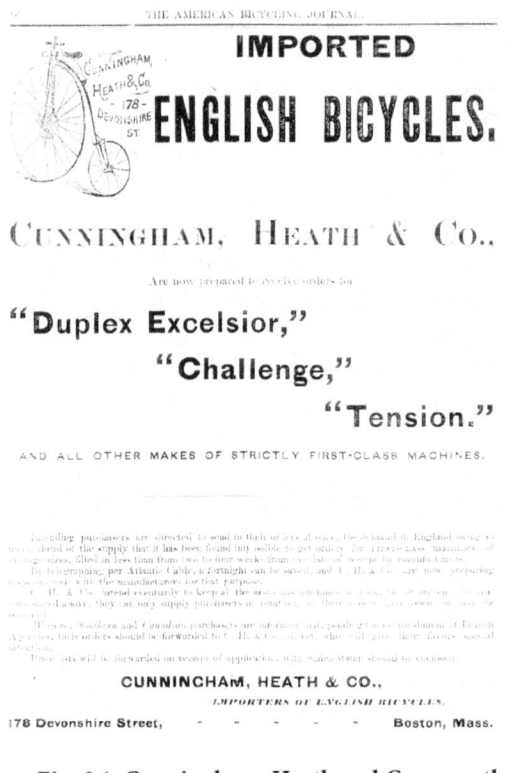

Fig. 3.1. Cunningham, Heath and Co. were the first company to import English bicycles into the United States. [Source: *American Bicycling Journal*, 22 Dec. 1877.]

Fig. 3.2. An early high-wheel rider in New York City, about 1875. This was advertising for the Martel family, perhaps a visiting French circus act. The bicycle is French, perhaps an Olivier. [Source: author's collection]

in February 1878, and others quickly followed. News of Etherington's London promotions, and other bicycle racing activity, reached the United States by means of reports in the *American Bicycling Journal*, and the expanding American cycling scene quickly became a sport entrepreneur's fertile ground.

At stake, looking at the commercial context of Etherington's visit, was obtaining a share of the potentially large American market. Colonel Pope of the Pope Manufacturing Company was also attracted to the machines he had seen at the Philadelphia Exhibition. The brief cooperation between Pope and the British soon evaporated with Pope's aggressive manufacturing and marketing and his assertive legal maneuvering that made it as difficult as possible for the British industry to gain a competitive foothold in the United States. Pope appears not to have been interested in using professional, indoor racing as an advertising medium to sell his bicycles, and preferred to use amateur, club channels for his advertising campaigns.

The emerging American sport of cycling in the late 1870s owed much to its British model, yet eventually became distinctively American. Etherington's professional tour played a significant role in raising awareness of competitive cycling, and a broader group of enthu-

Three. The Beginnings of Bicycle Racing in the United States

siasts participated in the subsequent foundation of the amateur League of American Wheelmen. In many ways, this chapter can be seen as a case-study of various aspects of the relationship that linked Britain and the United States in the expansion of both a major late 19th century sport and an important manufacturing industry.[8]

2. THE FOUNDATIONS OF AMERICAN CYCLING

American bicycle racing was much less advanced than was the British sport in the first half of the 1870s. The American velocipede "craze" of 1868–69, according to an account from December 1877, "died out in this country as rapidly as it arose, until their use seemed to be quite given over to an exceptional youngster here and there on his two wheels."[9] Such indoor racing as occurred was apparently infrequent, and may not have involved just American racers—a photograph from the mid–1870s taken in New York appears to advertise the services of a French performing or racing group, the [missing text, see PDF]

On 18 April 1876, the *New York Times* reported an "Exciting Bicycle Match" at the American Institute Building on 63rd Street between Mr. McClellan, "the American champion," and Mr. Stanton, "the English long-distance champion." On 11 May, Stanton was still in New York, where he raced William Butler of Kentucky over 50 miles, when "the spectators, notwithstanding the inclement weather, were numerous."[10] And in November 1876, William Du Noille raced the same William McClellan "for the championship of America" in another indoor professional meet. Du Noille, "who rode a machine with a wheel of 55 in. diameter, appeared on the track attired in white breeches, with red and white stockings,

Fig. 3.3. The first issue of the *American Bicycling Journal*. [Source: author's collection]

flesh-colored flannel shirt and a green cap. His opponent rode a machine with a wheel of 52 in. diameter, and wore flesh-colored tights, a loose-fitting white frilled shirt and a white cap."[11] An indoor "championship"-level professional sport had thus emerged by the mid-1870s. In January 1878, the *Boston Herald* called English immigrant Charles Booth: "the champion velocipede rider of the world ... prepared to defend his title against all comers." Booth was a typical show-business professional cyclist who had raced in England and France before settling in America.[12]

What Boston attorney, journalist and cycling promoter, Charles Pratt, called "the revival of velocipeding, the advent of the modern bicycle" in the United States occurred in the second half of 1877. A group of solidly middle-class, business-oriented enthusiasts, who were to be of supreme importance in the business and sport of cycling in America, began to ride in and around Boston.

This group formed the nucleus for the foundation of the League of American Wheelmen in 1880.[13] The *American Bicycling Journal*, the first American periodical devoted exclusively to cycling, was launched in Boston by Frank Weston on 22 December 1877. It contains comprehensive documentation of the beginnings of cycling in America. A keen interest in the English sport was communicated through this publication and through the many English periodicals that made their way to America. Cunningham, Heath and Co., of Boston, began importing bicycles in November 1877 and the first issue of the *American Bicycling Journal* ran advertisements for "Imported English Bicycles," which were in hot demand: "Intending purchasers are directed to send in their orders at once, the demand in England being so much ahead of supply that it has been found impossible to get orders for first-class machines filled in less than from two to four weeks. By telegraphing per Atlantic Cable, a fortnight can be saved, and C.H. and Co are now preparing a special code with the manufacturers for that purpose." The company also organized a riding school to accommodate novice riders.[14]

Fig. 3.4. The first two-day bicycle run in America, organized by the Boston Bicycle Club, 11–12th Sept. 1879, stopped in Pine Grove, Readville, Mass. The group includes Charles Pratt (sitting middle row, star on cap), Albert Pope (standing left, hand on bicycle) and Frank Weston (standing, hand on bicycle, fourth from right). [Source: author's collection]

The Boston Bicycle Club, which became the model for dozens of American amateur clubs, was formally constituted on 11 February 1878 with 14 members. Its "code of rules" consisted of seventeen "Articles," one of which, "Article 12—Bicycle Meetings, and Club Riding Upon the Roads," consisted of fifteen extensive sections, indicating that public perception of its activities was of great importance. The purpose of the club was stated in these "Articles" as being:

1. The mutual enjoyment of its members in the pursuit of Bicycling as a pastime; to which end club-meets, tours, excursions, races, etc. shall be arranged and carried out.
2. The promotion (by force of example) of the use of the Bicycle as a practicable and enjoyable aid to locomotion, by the general public.

"Clubs runs, tours and excursions" were governed by an elaborate set of "Road Rules ... the basis of which can be found in the justly celebrated Road Rules adopted by the Cambridge University Bicycle Club of England." A code of conduct was recommended for dealing with horses and other road-users, for example: "A horse should never be passed on both sides at once," and "A led horse should always be passed on the same side as the man who is leading it."[15]

The Boston B.C. (frequently known as the "Boston Bi. C.," to distinguish it from the Boston Baseball Club) had its own club-room, in the same building as Cunningham, Heath and Co, and the *American Bicycling Journal*, and consisted mostly of middle-class urban professionals. Among its founding members in 1878 were "six merchants, four salesmen, four students, three lawyers, three clerks, two officers of corporations, one architect, one litterateur and one physician." The oldest member was "about fifty years of age," the youngest "about seventeen," while the average age was "about thirty." By 1880, it had 44 members and by 1882 more than 100.[16]

Fig. 3.5. Known as "The Wheel Around the Hub," this 11–12th Sept. 1879 group ride united many of the significant and influential players in the nascent American cycling scene, including Charles Pratt and Albert Pope (first two from left). [Source: author's collection]

The solidly pro-amateur orientation of the club was debated and emphasized from the start, and was "settled" in May 1879, when there was "a free expression of opinion from nearly all the members," and "the president expressed what appeared to be the unanimous view of those present, that the object of the sought-for definition was to eliminate the money-making element from amateur athletics." This "amateur rule," according to Pratt, "was taken up widely by other clubs, and has substantially prevailed ever since." Forty clubs, organized along essentially identical lines, had come into existence by the end of 1879.[17]

The club's statement of purpose asserted its role in promoting the bicycle for both utilitarian as well as a sporting purposes, but its political activity was also implied. Charles Pratt wrote that "the Boston Bicycle Club has been often foremost, and its members have been often at the front, in all the various movements of defense and developments which affect the complex interests of bicycling in this country." The members of the club were "a band of active pioneers in almost all that relates to the multifarious interests of wheelmen" who "began to make the conversion of the world one of its aims."

Its prime object was "the pursuit of Bicycling as a manly and healthful pastime," but club life, social life, was also considered extremely important:

> In the revival of bicycling it was to be restored to a habitation, a name, a realm. There were fewer charms in solitude. Unity was strength, and concert of action was necessary to conquest. Moreover, there was then the ever-present conflict between the club spirit and the non-club spirit; and the mission of the Boston Bi. Club was to promote and extend the former.... Club-life, in our modern society, is, apparently, a necessary element. It is sure to be found by the majority somewhere.

Clubs were seen as "a practical example of the old adage that "Union is Strength.""[18] But Charles Pratt, a precise and articulate historian of these early days, estimated that one year after the founding of the Boston Bicycle Club, there were still only 242 "bicyclers" in the United States (of whom about 40 were members of the Boston B.C.), a small club coterie limited geographically to Boston and the New England states, and racing was limited to a few inter-club events, or a single bicycle race included in an athletic club program.[19]

Cyclists demonstrated club spirit and pride in the new sport during club runs, the first of which was held on 9 March 1878. As in England, club runs were a prominent demonstration of club activity and attracted a great deal of attention. Pratt remembered "the novelty and the mystery of those early manifestations of collective bicycling":

> The meets were usually on the wide macadam before Trinity Church and the Art Museum, where the open triangular "square" ... afforded a small circuit for formation and fine road-surface for a fair start. The riders, of almost every age and stature, in motley costumes, and on mounts as various in style and construction, wheeled up there, dismounted and oiled up—the oiling process was then a most prominent and important part of the programme.

Hundreds, sometimes thousands, of spectators gathered on these Saturday afternoons to watch the start of the runs, until "the sidewalks were almost impassable, the streets were impeded, and carriages waited."[20] On the road, cyclists were encouraged to ride in pairs, with an almost military precision; orders to start and stop were sounded with a bugle. Club members were highly aware of the impression they made on the public. F.W. Weston wrote in the minutes of a club meeting that his friends had reported that the club "presented a most interesting and gratifying spectacle." Even so, in retrospect, they were then "raw recruits," and were much less experienced than "the well-disciplined clubs of today as they appear on any stated occasions."[21]

Members considered a club uniform desirable because it expressed group solidarity and respectability, and the appropriate cut and color was vigorously debated. "Having bought your Bicycle, your next requirement will be an Appropriate and Becoming Costume to Wear When Riding It," announced an advertisement in early 1878: "All the latest patterns and styles of bicycling uniforms can be obtained at Oak Hall."[22]

The first Boston B. C. uniform chosen was not successful ("the club was costumed like tramps for more than a year"), and was changed first to "a seal-brown corduroy jacket and breeches, and helmet cap, with seal-brown stockings," and then in December 1880 to a dark green color, "which has become so well known,

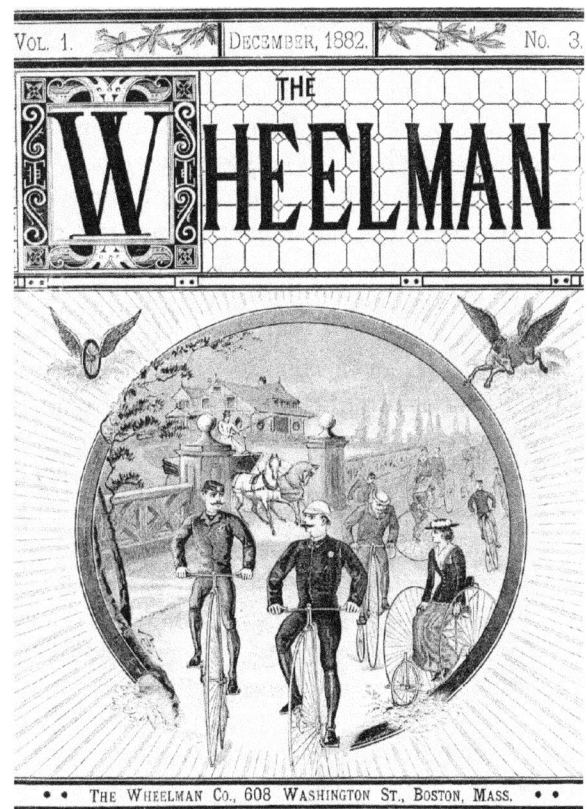

Fig. 3.6. *The Wheelman*, heavily subsidized by Pope, was a literary cycling periodical, published in the 1880s. [Source: author's collection]

Fig. 3.7. The second two-day bicycle run was made by the Boston and Massachusetts Bicycle Clubs to Springfield, Mass. in Oct. 1879. Photo taken at Wellesley, Mass. Seated on the ground are members of Harry Etherington's racing group then touring the U.S., including l-r Charles Terront (bowler hat), Etherington (club cap) and W. Cann (bowler hat). Among those standing is Charles Pratt (center, star on cap). [Source: author's collection]

admired and copied."[23] Good behavior and well-organized formation riding was recommended when riders were in public, or taking part in formal parades, and as the "Rules and Regulations" of the Boston Bicycle Club made clear, racing was discouraged on club runs: "The object of Club excursions is not to ride against time, still less to encourage any competition between individual members."[24]

Subsequently, cycling in the United States developed rapidly and its growth can be charted by the great number of clubs that continued to be formed, which implied the existence of a core group of dedicated enthusiasts, although of course not every rider joined a club.[25] According to C.E. Hawley, writing in the first issue of *The Wheel-man* in 1882, the cycling club, in addition to its obvious emphasis on sport, had a social and moral agenda: "it becomes a centre for social meetings, where many, otherwise friendless, find society and a refuge from ennui and loneliness, and from temptation to seek objectionable distractions." Clubs "exercise restraints upon the individual in many ways, teaching him self-control and submission to discipline."[26]

The *American Bicycling Journal* listed 17 clubs in August 1879 and 23 by October.[27] By March 1880, according to Pratt, there were about 50 clubs nationwide.[28] *Bicycling World*, in December 1880, reported 100 clubs, with "an aggregate membership of about 2,000 ... probably near one third of the active wheelmen owning wheels on this side of the Atlantic." The clubs were composed of "gentlemen in the good American sense of the word ... every profession and business and trade is represented in their ranks."[29]

The *Cyclist and Wheel World Annual for 1882* (a London publication) listed 101 American clubs (certainly an under-estimate by then), including clubs in the mid-western cities of Cincinnati, Cleveland, Grand Rapids, Louisville, Milwaukee, Minneapolis, Springfield (Ohio), St. Louis and Toledo, and Oakland and San Francisco in California. By way of comparison, the same source listed 187 clubs in the London area alone and 339 outside the capital city.[30] *Bicycling World* for January 1883 listed a total of 207 clubs in the United States and Canada, with 52 in Massachusetts, 27 in New York, 19 in Ohio and 16 in Pennsylvania.[31] Clearly this was a period of rapid expansion in the social popularity of the sport of cycling.

College clubs were also established, at Columbia University (November 1879), Harvard (April 1879) and Princeton (October 1879). "The American colleges ... are following in the footsteps of Oxford and Cambridge universities in boating and athletic sports," reported the *American Bicycling Journal*: "It is suggested that the colleges should now introduce bicycle riding ... bicycle contests for the championship would create just as much interest as the recent foot-ball match between Princeton and Yale."[32]

In Cambridge, Massachusetts, in January 1879, the "annual field sports of the Harvard Athletic Association" were held, but the track, "though in capital condition for other sports, was much too soft for bicycle racing ... another proof of the necessity which exists for a good cinder path, to enable us to exhibit any such record of speed as is found on the other side of the water.... It is to be hoped that Harvard will organize its bicycle club without unnecessary delay."[33] The club was formed in April 1879, when "a number of men assembled in Holden Chapel, Harvard College, for the purpose of forming an association of all members of the university interested in bicycling. Theretofore, though many students rode, they had done so singly, without feeling any stronger bond of union than that by which all riders on the steely steed are drawn together."[34]

In October 1879, "an athletic exhibition, under the auspices of the Brown University

Athletic Association and the Providence Bicycle Club took place at the Park Garden," where "there was a good attendance of collegians." Harry Etherington, and two of his professional companions, Charles Terront and David Stanton, took part in demonstration races.[35] By the end of 1880, the Harvard club had more than 90 members, clubs had been formed at Amherst, the University of Michigan, the Massachusetts Agricultural College and the Pennsylvania Military Academy, while at the University of Pennsylvania, Dartmouth, Williams, Brown University, the University of Virginia, Rochester University and "several other colleges, there are already devoted wheel-men, composing part of the active membership of other clubs."

Charles Pratt, who, as editor of *Bicycling World*, noted this popularity of college cycling, wrote that "there can be no question ... that the bicycle is best adapted ... for recreative exercise by students. As a branch of college athletics, it is gentlemanly and elegant, and one that excites great interest. The university races in England, held year after year with increasing success, afford good examples for illustration."[36]

Many spectators first encountered the sport when bicycle races were held during state Agricultural Fairs. In 1878, races were held in Framingham, Bridgewater, Concord and Taunton, Massachusetts and Portland, Maine and had "practically become an established institution ... the novel spectacle of bicycle racing proved a great attraction to the rural population, who thronged the grounds and manifested the utmost enthusiasm." The tracks, however, were "heavy and unsuitable."[37]

In early January 1879, a 2-mile bicycle race was held during the New York Athletic Club's winter meeting, but the track was "not at all in good condition for the bicycle," again demonstrating the need for "a proper cinder path laid for the purpose."[38] The bad condition of public roads, especially in the winter, was an impediment to competitive bicycling. Boston roads were as good as London suburban roads in good weather, sometimes better, but in winter "it is only semi-occasionally that a run is enjoyable or even practicable."[39]

Thus cinder tracks were needed if there was to be serious competition

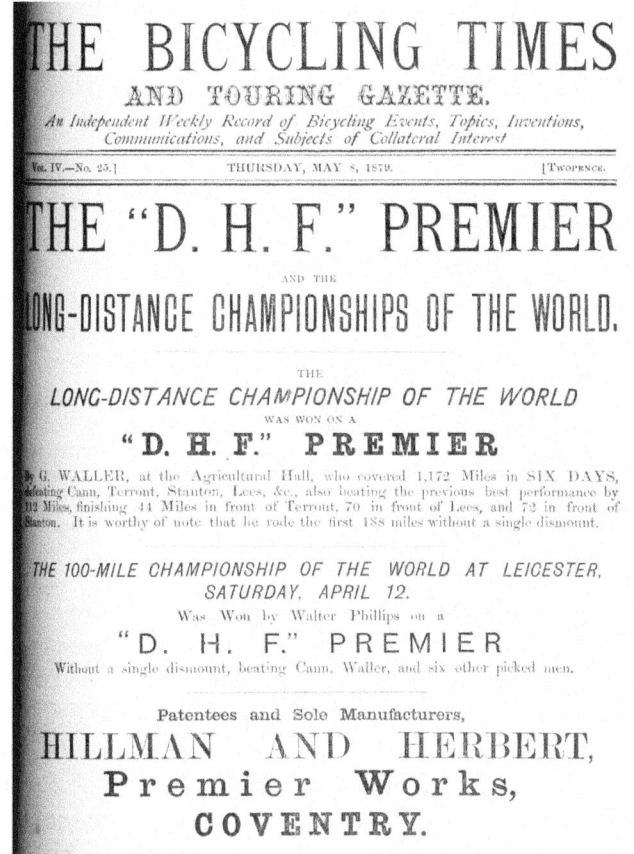

Fig. 3.8. By 1879 high-wheel bicycle racing had become sufficiently established for "world championships" to be promoted in London and Leicester. [Source: John L. Weiss collection]

in front of spectators. The Boston Bicycle Club overcame the problem of poor road and track surfaces by laying out a measured half-mile on the "hard, smooth" Boston city streets for July 4th celebrations, and held four races which were "the first 'official' acknowledgment of the existence and importance of the Bicycle and its riders, and of the claims of Bicycle racing to a position among other national and common sports and pastimes."[40]

The summer of 1879 appears to have been the season in which bicycle racing first became a recognized athletic event in the United States, was promoted in special events by bicycle clubs, and in which the first formal U.S. "championship" was held. At "Bicycle Races" held on Huntington Avenue, Boston on 4th July 1879 (with Albert A. Pope as one of the Judges), a list of "Rules and Regulations" included a prominent definition of professionalism.[41] And at a meeting of the National Association of Amateur Athletes on the grounds of the New York Athletic Club, four cyclists competed for the first official amateur 2-mile bicycle championship of America, with L. H. Johnson of the Essex Bicycle Club (Newark, New Jersey) winning the "proud distinction."[42]

The way cycling was organized and institutionalized in New England, and from there throughout the rest of the country, based on the already established British model, has an almost colonial feel about it, adopting habits and customs transplanted from across the Atlantic. Indeed, there was frequent discussion in the American cycling press of the sport's British origins. American cyclists, including businessman Colonel Pope, himself a club member, visited England to tour and inspect the Coventry bicycle factories. The *American Bicycling Journal* frequently reprinted articles taken from the British cycling press, further indicating that the Americans were imitating a sport that was already flourishing elsewhere.

Of the Boston Bicycle Club, Charles Pratt wrote that "when it started nearly everything was English, except its membership, and part of that was; and its traditions and proclivities are still, as sometimes remarked, decidedly British."[43] For one writer, the bicycle united America and England in a brotherhood of physical and moral superiority:

> The bicyclers of England and America are a superior class of men, as is evident from the fact of their being drawn to an exercise which taxes their vigor and their manhood.... The wheel tends to keep sound both body and mind, and makes men energetic and often daring.... Its benefits are great to every man who rides, and thousands owe to it restored health and prolonged life.[44]

* * *

Amid this expansive amateurism, speculative professional racing continued. In May 1879, a 500-mile "bicycle match," a type of indoor endurance test that was very much in vogue at that time in professional pedestrianism and bicycling on both sides of the Atlantic, was held at the American Institute Fair in New York City. William De Noielle took first prize, with his son, Charles De Noielle, close behind. The *New York Times* published a report of alleged cheating, typical of disreputable professional sporting events, the kind of low-class show-business chicanery that amateur organizations sought to purge from sport: "There was some complaint among the riders that they did not receive fair play.... The judges and scorers were unknown persons of no particular responsibility, who seemed all to be friends of the De Noielles." One competitor, William Rutland, was listed as "the champion of England," and another, Daniel Belard, as "champion of France," although both were unknown in Europe. Although this questionable race was "very meagerly patronized," still

Three. The Beginnings of Bicycle Racing in the United States 99

Fig. 3.9. As the high-wheel bicycle craze increased in the United States, clubmen in uniform could be seen around the larger cities and towns, here an unidentified club probably on the East Coast, circa 1887. [Source: Lorne Shields collection, Toronto, Canada]

the newspaper thought "it was one of the most pleasing exhibitions of endurance ever given in this City. Nothing could be more graceful than the easy, rapid motion of the bicycles, as they rolled almost noiselessly over the smooth floor of the Rink." The spectator response seemed less enthusiastic. Near the end of the race, there were only about 500 spectators in the building, while the competitors "seemed pretty well used up."[45]

This particular race may have been disreputable but it brought attention to bicycling. The day after the race, the *New York Times* published an editorial entitled "Personal Rapid Transit," affirming that the race at the American Institute "has not only furnished a pleasing variation on the monotony of walking matches, but has called attention, in this City, to the possibilities of the bicycle":

> Writers talk of the age of steam, the age of the telegraph, the mail-coach age, but no philosopher has yet been prescient enough to describe the era of the bicycle. Certain it is, nevertheless, that this instrument is the only contribution of importance that the inventive genius of all the centuries has made to what may be styled the problem of personal locomotion.... In the momentous matter of a more rapid personal motor than his unaided legs for the individual man, a motor wholly under his own control, thus far the only praiseworthy advance has been achieved by the bicycle.... It is not, however, until we note the feats that have been performed on this machine that we feel it to be a power of the future–an element in the suburban problem of rapid transit. The speed achieved by the first four of the riders in the American Institute is most suggestive.

The *New York Times* article went on to refer to "the far more startling performances which have been recorded for short distances–the distances that would represent ordinary daily use of the bicycle," and noted "a wonderful race held in England only a short time since" in which the winner had covered 1060 miles in six days, a race that was in fact one of Harry Etherington's promotions:

> In England bicyclism is as much a mania as pedestrianism has lately been here. The clubs are numbered by the hundreds, and the "horsemen" by tens of thousands; while, as to the steeds, it is alleged that 60,000 bicycles were made and sold in England last year. In America there has been no such bicyclical furor as yet; but at some points, and queerly enough at the geographical extremes of Boston and San

Francisco, bicyclism has strongholds. New York has been, to a remarkable degree, free from the fever, but it would not be difficult to predict that the late contest at the American Institute will give it a start.[46]

It was indeed surprising, as the *New York Times* commented, that the bicycle had quickly become so popular in San Francisco, at the extreme geographical edge of the country, a week-long railway journey across the United States. It would have been more logical for cycling to have taken off in other East Coast cities at this early date. Yet, the San Francisco Bicycle Club, founded Dec 1878, was the third cycling club founded in the United States, following the Boston (February 1878) and the Suffolk, also in Boston (April 1878).[47] San Francisco had witnessed an energetic velocipede "craze" in 1869, and the *Daily Morning Chronicle* had reported in May 1869 that "the velocipede is just at present quite the rage in this community."[48] Possibly it was the strong British emigré community there that encouraged and stimulated bicycling, as well as the "mild climate, with its snowless winters and rainless summers," which "excites the envy of bicyclists of a more severe climate."[49]

The *American Bicycling Journal* reported in mid–1879 that "the first bicycle race on the Pacific Coast took place on the 22nd of February last, under the auspices of the Occident Cricket Club, and formed one of the most interesting of a long series of Athletic competitions, in which the Caledonian, the Olympic and the Oakland Athletic Clubs took part.... A large concourse of spectators, to most of whom the English Bicycle was a novelty, witnessed the race and expressed the most unbounded enthusiasm at the result. More bicycle races will doubtless follow."[50] The1-mile bicycle race was mixed with running, high jump, long jump, hammer-throwing, hurdling and base-ball throwing, and R. Searle won some "bronze dogs" for coming in first. "The arrangements of the Club were perfect in every particular, reflecting great credit on the Secretary and other officers of the Club."[51]

Of primary importance to cycling enthusiasts was their equipment. One San Francisco cyclist, in a letter to *Bicycling World* of May 1880, described how bicycles arrived on the West Coast. One was "imported direct from Paris in August, 1876, by Mr. R. de Clairmont, and in June, 1878, he imported a Coventry Machinist's roadster.... Mr. G.L. Cunningham received a Duplex Excelsior from Cunningham and Co., of Boston." Others did the same, and "by December we found that we were sufficiently numerous to organize a club, which was done during that month," there being ten or eleven charter members. The writer went on to say that "it has taken a year and a half to build up any degree of confidence in the machine. The present year promises to show great accessions to our ranks, and much more interest in the sport than during the previous time." The club made an effort to have "the obnoxious ordinance in Oakland amended," legislation that had been introduced to control the excesses of the velocipede fever of 1869, "as the streets and roads in and about that city are by far the best riding we have."

Yet, despite the milder climate, the California roads still presented as much of a challenge as did those in the East, for:

> during the winter the country roads are as deep in mud as a western prairie, and the long, dry summers reduce such roads as have much traffic to a condition of dust better imagined than described ... in the fall, after the first rains have laid the dust, and in the spring after the heavy rains have ceased, the sport may be enjoyed in its best form."[52]

In November 1879, scarcely two weeks after the first race of Etherington's tour in Boston, a professional "three-day's bicycle contest" was promoted at the Mechanic's Pavilion in San Francisco. However, it was not until the end of 1880 that inter-club amateur races took place in San Francisco between the San Francisco and Oakland Bicycle Clubs, when "the wheelmen and their friends gathered in large numbers," and the riders were "now getting somewhere near the point of fast riding." On a Sunday in November 1880, professional indoor racing was again organized at the Mechanics' Pavilion, "on a track eight feet wide and seven laps to the mile." Between four and five hundred people attended, but Sunday was not "the proper day for public sporting, and gentlemen ought not to promote such infractions of good taste."[53]

Thus, by late 1879, the time of the Etherington tour, although British manufacturers and Boston importers had already been doing business for two years, American cycling was still in its early, speculative stages of popularity. Etherington aimed to expand the "box-office" profile of the sport and create a popular, profit-making, professional spectator sport in Boston and Chicago, and to promote it throughout the country. The time was ripe, he calculated, for such a potentially lucrative business endeavor.

3. HARRY ETHERINGTON: BICYCLING ENTREPRENEUR AND PROMOTER OF ENDURANCE SPECTACLES

"To give even a brief outline of Mr. Etherington's career," said a contemporary account, "would be to write the history of the sport of cycling." Harry Etherington was involved in the sport and industry as promoter, journalist and publisher. Above all, he was an entrepreneur, selling the quickly growing sport of cycling to the general public. Etherington was born in Sittingbourne, Kent in 1855, and was only twenty-four at the time of his 1879 trip to the United States. He had begun to ride the velocipede in 1868 and took up the bicycle in 1875. He was a member of the Surrey B.C., which he called "the crack amateur racing club of London," and later secretary of the Temple B.C., which "under his secretarial administration became the largest bicycle club in London," with 150 members. He was a tourist rather than a racer, though he promoted the Temple B.C.'s financially successful 1877 club races, which had 72 entries.[54]

By the end of 1878, Etherington was involved with *Bicycling Times* as owner and editor

Fig. 3.10. Harry Etherington wearing the club-cap of the Temple Bicycle Club of London in 1877. [Source: *Bicycling News*, 29 June 1877]

and it was there that he published a two-page supplement called "Etherington and Co's Bicyclists' Directory, Exchange and Guide," in which he described himself as "Advertising Agent," with an office in Whitefriars Street, in the City of London.[55] In 1879 Etherington published *The Sporting Annual, or Sportsman's Guide and Athlete's Companion for 1879* (subtitled, "A complete and comprehensive record of every sporting and athletic feat"), and *The Bicycle Annual for 1879* ("the only book of its kind issued"). Etherington's business activities were clearly growing at a rapid pace.[56] By the time a full-page advertisement for his publications appeared in *Icycles, Wheel World Christmas Annual, 1880*, of which he was joint-editor, Etherington had a publishing business in Fleet Street and was actively involved in selling the sport of bicycling to consumers. *Wheel World*, he claimed, was: "The recognized medium of advertisers to get their specialities and manufactures before the right people and into the proper channel."[57] Later, Etherington was joint-editor, from 1884 on, of the very successful *Wheeling* whose offices were also in Fleet St.[58]

Etherington was a shrewd and perceptive innovator. He understood how indoor, long-distance sporting events would draw spectators in the winter, and he was a pioneer in the promotion of cycling events in London, hiring the best professional riders available. His first "Six Days" bicycle race was held in the Agricultural Hall, Islington in November 1878 and was won by William Cann with a total of 1060½ miles.[59] A similar race was held at the same venue between 28 April and 4 May 1879 and George Waller came in first, with a total of 1172 miles.

A September 1–6, 1879 "Six Days Race," also at the Agricultural Hall, was promoted as the "Long Distance Championship of the World," and pitted Waller ("the holder of the belt"), Frenchman Charles Terront, Higham and William Cann, the leading exponents of this kind of racing, against each other. This race "proved from beginning to end to be of the most absorbing interest to the immense crowds of spectators…. Almost from the word go the lead was maintained by Waller, closely pressed by the other riders, especially Terront."

On the 5th day, Waller rode from 6 a.m. to 12 midnight without a single stop or dismount, covering 220 miles, "a performance which speaks volumes both for the endurance of the rider and perfection of the machine which he bestrode, and which was not treated to one drop of oil during the whole." In total, Waller covered 1404 miles and Terront 1390 miles. Such a performance demonstrated both the extraordinary athletic ability of the riders and the increasing efficiency and reliability of their machines.[60] *The Referee* commented that "the palm must be given to Waller—or rather to his machine, for there is little doubt that the rapid improvement shewn in Bicycling performances is duequite as much, if not more, to the superiority of the machines, as to the ability of the riders."[61]

Champion John Keen was pragmatic in his criticism of Six Day races, however. He told an interviewer, "I don't believe in six-day contests. It spoils your speed. If a man runs [i.e. rides] fifty miles as hard as he can go, he can show plenty of staying power in that."[62] The evidently exploitative commercial nature of the Six Day race caused some to accuse promoters of cruelty towards athletes and provoked objections from amateur circles. Gerard Cobb told a meeting of the executive of the Bicycle Union that "to ride round and round some 250 yards of deal board … can serve no possible purpose but to gratify the peculiar tastes of those who seem to discover pastime in the grotesque struggles of penultimate exhaustion."[63]

Fig. 3.11. Manufacturers Hillman and Herbert used the athletic feats of George Waller and others to advertise their bicycles in 1879. [Source: *The Cyclist*, 29 Oct. 1879]

Etherington responded to such criticisms from amateurs in a disdainful editorial in *Bicycling Times*: "A feeble endeavour is being made to detract from Waller's performance by suggesting that it was not sport," he wrote. In response, he raised the question:

> What is sport? The only reply that can be made to such a question is "Any contest of skill or endurance, or both, is sport." The least cruel of any sports are those where a man is a free agent and "takes it out" of his own physique, and does not act to the injury or detriment of any dumb animal. That bicycle racing has done more than anything else to improve machines no sane man who has studied the question will deny. That the wonder produced in the minds of non-riders by such marvellous performances as that of Waller must tend to increase the public interest in and respect for bicycling is certain. That there is any cruelty in such necessarily fatiguing, exhausting feats, is absurd, as the contest is quite voluntary.... Men have from the earliest records generously admired feats of pluck and endurance ... great feats of strength and endurance will always be considered in many thousands of men's minds to be sport par excellence.[64]

Indoor races such as these during the winter months were not only profitable commercial entertainments, but they were also, of course, an important opportunity to advertise and sell bicycles. At the November 1878 race "an exhibition of bicycles and sundries thereto pertaining, was held in the same building. Thirty-five different makers exhibited more than one hundred bicycles."[65] On the same occasion, *Bicycling News* published an advertisement for a "Monster Exhibition of Bicycles, Tricycles and Bicycling Appliances," which also touted the event as the "Great Six Days" Bicycle Race for the Championship of the World."[66] Professional bicycle racing was already inextricably interlinked with the commerce of cycling.

In some respects Etherington was an innovator, and in other ways an imitator. His idea of staging six-day cycling events in England and then exporting them to the United States showed more enterprise than originality. Indoor long-distance racing was already a popular form of sport entertainment at the time; it first appeared with pedestrianism earlier in the 19th century, and had become hugely popular on both sides of the Atlantic in the 1870s. Long-distance walking or running races outside on the road were hard to measure and regulate, and no admission fee could be charged. It made more sense for a promoter to stage a long-distance pedestrian contest indoors on a track or in an arena, where money could more easily be collected. The 1,000-mile mark, a familiar walking objective, took many days and racing could not acceptably be held on Sundays. Hence the "Six Day" Race.[67]

Etherington's originality as a promoter, then, was that he took advantage of the established popularity of super-endurance events and capitalized on it with the new sport of bicycle racing. He went to the United States aware of the hunger for endurance events and with the hope that he might be able to cash in on them.[68]

An article entitled "Trans-Atlantic Bicycling," published in *Bicycling Times* in October 1879, revealed the unapologetically promotional ambitions that lay behind this American tour. It boasted of Etherington's "untiring zeal and unflagging energy in anything concerning his favourite sport," and suggested that the names of the members of "the English Bicycling Team" were "as familiar as household words." Waller's 1404mile ride in Etherington's September 1879 Six Day race was praised as "one of the most magnificent exhibitions of manly courage on record." The article affirmed the role of long-distance racing and exhibitions in publicizing the industry and the sport and told of the surprise expressed at the time at the distances accomplished in these endurance events:

> It is an established fact that the great success which has been attained by Bicycling in England is mainly due to its having been prominently brought before the public by means of racing; and it is equally certain that this rapid increase in the popularity of the sport is due to the untiring zeal and energy of Messrs. H. Etherington and C.J. Fox, Jun. of the Bicycling Times, who have promoted the four grandest competitions in the annals of the sport, they having started the idea and undertaken the necessary pecuniary risk. The events we have alluded to are the three great Six days' contests for the Long Distance Championship of the World, and the Twenty-six hours Championship of the World, competed for at the Agricultural Hall. At each of these contests, the immense and extraordinary distances accomplished were first demonstrated, each competition far exceeding in the distance ridden, the expectation of the most sanguine of our sport—it never having appeared possible to the promoters of the scheme, for a single moment, that such a grand performance as 1404 miles would ever in 108 hours be accomplished...
>
> In connection with competitions, the Bicycle Exhibitions promoted by Messrs. Etherington and Co. have materially assisted the development of our sport; for while the racing has interested and delighted hundreds of thousands of spectators, the latter have stimulated in a surprising manner the efforts of various firms of Bicycle makers throughout the country.
>
> Where for instance shall we see such a magnificent sight as that witnessed during the last great race for the championship of the world; the barriers were hardly strong enough to restrain the wild excitement and almost mad enthusiasm of the surging mass which crammed the great Agricultural Hall in London to witness one of the most magnificent exhibitions of manly courage on record. As the competitors, who were racing as though their very lives depended on their efforts, tore around the course the enthusiasm would be raised to fever pitch by the smallest incident as the men flew onwards to the coveted goal. As mile after mile was knocked off, shouts of delight would rise from the excited spectators as one or other of the men would gain by an effort almost superhuman an advantage of a few yards.
>
> Many of those who have witnessed these efforts have for the first time realized a feeling of respect

for the skilful riders of the novel vehicle, the great utility of our iron horse. That any single man should by his strength alone be able to accomplish 1404 miles in six days, is a feat, which in itself would a few years ago have been deemed impossible.[69]

The racing achievements of the four "champions" Etherington managed and promoted confirm that he had engaged four of the biggest names in international bicycle racing, men who would "win for themselves fresh victories, coupled with the respect and admiration of the American nation." Charles Terront, William Cann, John Keen and David Stanton were experienced, seasoned professionals, deeply involved with the sport and the bicycle industry.[70]

4. ETHERINGTON'S 1879 "ANGLO-FRENCH" TOUR OF AMERICA AND ITS REPERCUSSIONS

An editorial in the *American Bicycling Journal* gave a frank assessment of the state of the sport in America at the moment of Etherington's arrival:

> In the present not wholly developed stage which bicycling has arrived at in this country, lacking as we do a single track to compare with those which the visiting riders have left behind them, and lacking too the sustaining universal public interest which assures the success of bicycle contests on the mother shore, we cannot but consider their visit in the light of an undertaking requiring more than a usual amount of pluck and devotion to the sport.... In a private letter from Mr. Etherington, he explains that the visit is more of a private pleasure trip than a business enterprise ... though of course, his riders "will not disdain to engage in any fair contest which can be devised."[71]

Despite the inadequate facilities and uncertain public reception, the Tour attracted a lot of attention in both the general and the cycling press, and Etherington produced a regular column for his paper, *Bicycling Times*. Events were thus documented from both the British and American points of view.

Cann, Terront and Etherington sailed out on the steamship "Montana" on the 4th of October, arriving in New York on the 15th, followed by Keen and Stanton on the "Adriatic" early in November. Etherington, originally intending to go to Boston, had been told to try New York, only to find that Madison Square Garden could not be booked, "the New Yorkers evidently not being fully alive to the pleasure and excitement of a sharp bicycle race." Changing their plan of action, the group went up to Boston, "the American bicycling metropolis," where they set up their headquarters with the Pope Manufacturing Company at 87, Summer Street.[72] Etherington lost no time in challenging American professional riders. On 27 October, he announced a 100-mile handicap race for 1 November, with a $200 first prize and a 10-mile start given to the American riders. He also announced a Six Day Race, with a $1,000 first prize, a 100-mile start to be given. On 28 October, he sent a second letter to the *American Bicycling Journal*

> I will match my team, either collectively or individually, against any team that can be organized, in this big country, to compete in a race at any distance, from 1 mile to 2 or 3,000... To give our cousins an equal chance, I will handicap my team to give all comers starts from 75, 100 to 150 or 200 miles in a 6 days race, the races to be contested for in any large city in the United States where a suitable building and good track can be found. Or I will match my team against any one or two riders upon horses, number of horses to be determined upon according to distance or duration of race.[73]

The European riders, then, appeared to have had no competition arranged in advance, but Etherington's challenge was quickly answered by J.H. Mack of Brooklyn, who agreed to furnish a team.

The same issue of *American Bicycling Journal* also contained an editorial, "Professional Bicycling," which was in essence a plea for honest professionalism:

> The minor contests which have hitherto taken place here are not, strictly, speaking, entitled to the term professional. Professional bicycling, as such, will really receive its first exposition in this city today, and the enlarging of the field of professional athletes which the Anglo-French bicycle contest must certainly result in, is fraught with not a little importance to the future of the bicycle throughout the country.
>
> Where contests for supremacy are carried out with manly fairness, their results can but be creditable both to the contestants themselves and the cause in which their efforts are made. More particularly is this the case in athletics, and the jealous care with which the amateur seeks to guard his title is the direct outcome of that spirit of honor, which should be distinctive of all who engage in athletic sports. The professional element, however, is unfortunately not so generally credited with that eager desire for absolute fairness which should outweigh all other considerations.

Evidently concerned with the bad reputation of professional sport, this editorial argued that the Americans "are fortunate in being able to profit by the experience and mistakes of the mother land. The dividing line between amateur and professional, while it should be most strictly defined, should not be observed in a way to exclude one class from interest in the other." In these "contests for supremacy carried out with manly fairness," the hope was that the racing would "prove to the public at large that there is at all events one sport in which they can repose the utmost confidence."[74] Another account, however, maintained that the "comparatively small professional element" was "remarkably respectable."[75]

While they were waiting for the American professionals to organize themselves, the visitors went on at least two rides with members of the Boston and Massachusetts Bicycle Clubs.[76] They "were looked up to by the riders of that day as to a superior race of beings."[77] On 29 October, they participated in the Providence (Rhode Island) Athletic Club Sports, where Etherington himself made an exhibition mile in a near gale-force wind.

The Six Day race, the exciting contest "for the

Fig. 3.12. A newspaper advertisement boosted the Six-Day race contested by Etherington's Anglo-French team in Boston. [Source: *Boston Globe*, 3 Nov. 1879]

Bicycular Championship of the Universe," in which "England and France Bid Defiance to the World!" took place before two of the star attractions, Keen and Stanton, had even arrived in America, even though their names were used in publicity for the event.[78] The American challengers included Gus Murphy, Thomas Harrison, George Harrison, Prof. Rollinson and Walter Lowder. The track, erected inside a huge tent, was banked at both ends, allowing for faster turns. The American riders did not have much experience on such a track and caused several crashes, and Terront and Cann were soon comfortably in the lead. The *Boston Globe* provided a vivid report of Terront in action:

> His appearance when riding is as though he belongs to and is part of his machine, so mechanically does he work and forge ahead. He is dressed in a pair of white flannel knee breeches, blue stockings and a light grey woollen guernsey, with a silk handkerchief tied loosely around his neck.... His body is slightly curved and leaned forward, thus bringing his weight immediately over the centre of his front wheel and so avoiding the labor of dragging his weight from behind. When bent upon going at an extra rate of speed, he leans still further ahead and works, as it were, all over, and in a thorough business-like manner, and those little legs of his going up and down at a rate of 135 to 140 a minute. His friends speak of him as being a great favorite with every lady he comes in contact with.

Cann, like Terront, was "but a sparse-built young man, thin and truly full of muscle and wiriness, and equal to any amount of strain and fatigue." Etherington confided to the *Globe* reporter that he attributed the failure of the Americans "to the fact of their want of knowledge as to how to proceed upon so long a journey, their partaking of food and drinks not being calculated to take them to the winning post." The final evening's racing and attendance was "all that could be desired by the managers." Terront won, with 660 miles, well below what he was capable of, had he been pressed. It seemed, thought the *Globe*, that he had "just been playing with his rivals."[79]

Bicycling World, reporting this Boston Six Day race, said that as it was "the first professional race in this country when men of any note were entered, it was looked forward to with great interest by all friends of bicycling." The paper was happy that "on Saturday evening the tent was fairly filled, and it was a noticeable fact that quite a large number of ladies were present." But the paper was critical of the result: "The sport has hardly attained growth enough in this country to enable us to name professionals to compete successfully with our English cousins, but it is hoped that before long America will be able to name men of equal endurance and speed."[80]

The second week's racing consisted mostly of fiercely contested exhibition matches among Etherington's four riders. The language of the newspaper advertisements suggested the extent to which these events were being speculatively promoted. In spite of cold weather and a small number of spectators, "lovers of the bicycle who were not there missed a grand treat as all the contestants were in fine trim, and gave the best exhibition of the speed of the iron horse that has ever been given in this country."[81] Emphasizing Colonel Pope's personal interest in the racing, the Pope Manufacturing Company presented a handsome gold medal and Etherington decided to put it up for a 50-mile race between Keen and Stanton.

Etherington's tour did run into some unwelcome obstacles along the way. Chicago was not a success. The amount of money being offered as the stake for a race, $4,000, was so large that it led to accusations that the racing was merely a "hippodrome," that is, a faked race with unrealistically large prizes advertised, designed to attract unwitting spectators. The *Chicago Tribune* reported that "people did not take to it even with the flagging zeal

THE NEW BICYCLE FEVER.—THE FOUR DAYS' BICYCLE CONTEST FOR THE CHAMPIONSHIP OF THE WORLD, RECENTLY HELD IN BOSTON.

Fig. 3.13. The "New Bicycle Fever" was promoted in a tent in Boston. Though obviously temporary, the scene is strikingly similar to a Six Day race in a modern velodrome. [Source: *Frank Leslie's Boys' and Girls' Weekly*, 20 Dec. 1879]

which they manifest toward pedestrian hippodromes." The event led to accusations challenging Etherington's honesty, which he resolutely defended in the British and American press.[82]

* * *

The most immediate repercussion of all the publicity surrounding Etherington's visit was that it inspired a great deal of imitation. Within a month, a "three-day's bicycle contest" was promoted at the Mechanics' Pavilion in San Francisco, indicating the impact of the press in the rapid communication of fads and fashions around the vast country. The *San Francisco Chronicle* noted that "the recent bicycle tournaments in the East have generated an enthusiasm far superior to that of the pedestrian matches, and contests have been patronized by the best citizens of New York, Boston and Chicago."[83]

The *Chronicle* reported that "the verdict of all those who have witnessed any of the riding is that it is sure to become a most popular amusement":

> Bicycle riding possesses all the charms of and many more than pedestrianism, and is without any of the disagreeable features of the latter amusement. It is neat and clean. The contestants use their muscles without any unpleasant effects being visible. Skill is required to ride at all, and the greater the skill

required, the more graceful, finished and rapid the riding becomes. Whatever their real condition may be, the riders always look fresh and pleasant, and the machines are never anything but glittering, clean-cut and attractive to view. Added to these advantages possessed by the bicycle, are those of speed and novelty. Rapid motion alone is attractive, and when in a contest the more rapid the more attractive.[84]

To this reporter, the bicycle thus exemplified cultural and technological modernity: "glittering," "clean-cut," "speed" and "novelty" were key words used to describe the event. "Rapid motion" had an intrinsic attraction. But perhaps most novel of all was the inclusion of two hours of women's bicycle racing each evening, at which time "the number of spectators was swelled to about 1500." Miss Lizzie Baymer, Miss Ada Lee and Mrs. Martin were:

> the most attractive feature of the exhibition.... Miss Lee appeared all resplendent in a green silk page's suit, trimmed with gold, and with cardinal stockings clocked with navy blue. Her wealth of natural black hair is hidden under a coquettish blonde wig of the short-curl style.... Lizzie Baymer appears much more to advantage as a bicyclist than she did as a pedestrienne. She was gorgeous in a Turkish vest, jockey cap, French tights of a flesh color, American bathing trunks and a button-hole bouquet of faultless construction. She rides well; she has muscular limbs, confidence and a serene smile—all that any bicyclist could ask for.[85]

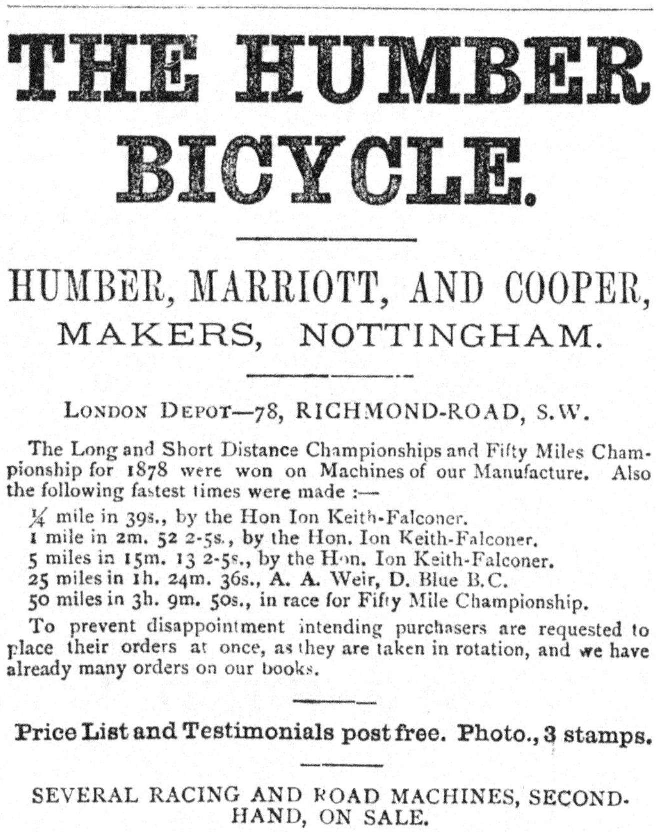

Fig. 3.14. While Stanton was in the United States, he attempted to introduce the successful English "Humber" bicycle into the American market. [Source: John L. Weiss collection]

This event, however, was a somewhat risqué, exploitative commercial spectacle along the lines of those that had been staged during the early days of the velocipede in the late 1860s, rather than a meaningful athletic event for women cyclists. The novel sporting enterprise was perhaps more linked with old-fashioned show-business in a promoter's search for profit than with genuine competition, but to have women competing at all was unusual and progressive for 1879.

Thus, with its impact on San Francisco, Etherington's modestly successful tour to promote bicycling in the United States appears to have been influential beyond Boston and Chicago. Promoting a brand-new sport, without a proven record, particularly in the middle of winter, was a risky endeavor. Charles Terront, talking to French journalist Baudry de Saunier twelve years later, did not have positive memories of the trip. The 200 meter track in Chicago was so small that it made him seasick, he recalled. Etherington agreed to divide the entire take (after expenses) into seven parts, two for himself and one each for the riders and his assistant, promising each rider not less than 10,000 francs. Spectators paid high prices, Terront said, but because of unforseen expenses, the riders only received enough to cover their passage back to Europe.[86]

But the Etherington tour was a significant part of the continuing flurry of commercial activity in the young sport and bicycle industry in the United States. An advertising flyer preserved in the United States National Archives confirms that Etherington's rider, David Stanton, was not only racing on this trip but was also acting as an agent for Rudge's "Humber" bicycle in America. His advertisement announced that "David Stanton, Fifty and One Hundred Mile Bicycle Champion of the World, being now on a tour in this country, and being desirous of giving American Bicyclists the opportunity of purchasing the celebrated 'Humber' Bicycle, which are used by all first-class riders in England, and acknowledged to be far superior to any other ever made," would take orders in New York City.[87]

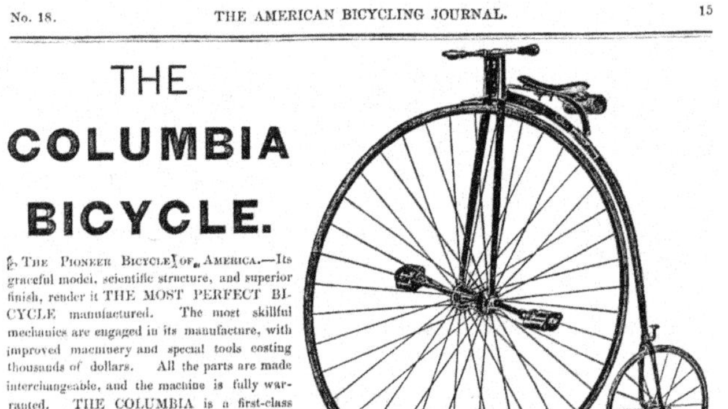

No. 18. THE AMERICAN BICYCLING JOURNAL. 15

THE COLUMBIA BICYCLE.

THE PIONEER BICYCLE OF AMERICA.—Its graceful model, scientific structure, and superior finish, render it THE MOST PERFECT BICYCLE manufactured. The most skillful mechanics are engaged in its manufacture, with improved machinery and special tools costing thousands of dollars. All the parts are made interchangeable, and the machine is fully warranted. THE COLUMBIA is a first-class roadster, equal in strength and workmanship to any English Bicycle, and superior to nearly all in finish. Any one wanting a good serviceable Bicycle for road riding will find the Columbia all that is claimed for it.

—A complete assortment of—

Alarm Bells, Saddle and Multum-in-Parvo Bags, Cyclometers, Lamps, Leggings, Stockings, Bicycle Shoes, Bicycle Stands,

And all other sundries used by Bicyclists constantly on hand. The following are the Principal Agents for the Columbia Bicycle:

LOCALITY.	NAME.	P. O. ADDRESS.
New York, N Y	Western Toy Co	58 Murray Street
Worcester, Mass	Hill & Tolman,	425 Main Street
San Francisco, Cal,	G L Cunningham,	206 Sansome Street
Denver, Col,	E A Rickard,	383 Larimer Street
Washington, D C,	H S Owen,	813 10th St. N W
Pittsburgh, Pa,	H B Thompson,	78 Fourth Ave
Detroit, Mich,	W W Seymour,	Hilsendegan Block
Philadelphia, Pa,	H B Hart,	813 Arch Street
Chicago, Ill,	John M Fairfield,	279 State Street
Amherst, Mass,	George F Fiske,	Amherst, Mass
Biddeford, Me,	R A Fairfield,	Biddeford, Me
Lowell, Mass,	Fred A Fielding,	128 Centre Street
Fitchburg, Mass,	W W Clark,	Fitchburg, Mass
Providence, R I,	E J Churchill,	No 1 P & W Depot
Trenton, N J,	J Y Clark,	Trenton House
Baltimore, Md,	T W Lawford,	10 So Holliday St
Herkimer, N Y,	H M Quackenbush,	Herkimer N Y
Haverhill, Mass,	Bridgman & Gay,	26 Merrimac St
Minneapolis, Minn,	Slafter & Clement,	26 Wash Ave S
New Haven, Conn,	J C Thompson,	93 Orange Street
St Louis, Mo,	Simmons Hardware Co	9th St & Wash Ave
Indianapolis, Ind,	J L Hunt,	126 South Penn St
Cincinnati, Ohio,	Wagoner & Bentley,	139 Longworth St
Cleveland, Ohio	T B Stevens & Bro	Cor Super & Bank
Springfield, Ohio,	Jas Leffell & Co	Springfield, Ohio
Yonkers, N Y	Elliot Mason,	27 South Broadway
Buffalo, N Y,	Geo R Bidwell & Co,	587 Main St
Johnstown, Pa,	Wm C Rhodes,	Iron St
Louisville, Ky,	O W Thomas, Jr,	61 West Main St

Send 3c. stamp for 24 page Illustrated Catalogue with price list testimonials and full information.

Commodious, Riding School

With competent instructors constantly in attendance.

THE POPE MANFG. Co,

87 SUMMER STREET,

BOSTON, MASS.

Fig. 3.15. The Pope Manufacturing Co. moved energetically into the American bicycle market, opening many regional distribution outlets as listed here, and supporting the growth of the sport. [Source: *American Bicycling Journal*, 1 Nov. 1879]

A second advertising flyer issued by the Pope Manufacturing Co., which appears to date from the second half of 1878, confirms that Stanton was competing in a market in which Pope was already actively committed.[88] Entitled "English Bicycles," the flyer announces:

> Having satisfied ourselves that the modern Bicycle, used by the English people, is a practical road machine of great utility; and learning from the best authorities that 60,000 of them were manufactured and sold in England last year, we have undertaken to introduce them into this country, and will keep constantly on hand, at our warerooms, a full line of Duplex Excelsior Bicycles, manufactured by Messrs Bayliss, Thomas and Co., of Coventry, England; also sample machines from all the best English manufacturers; and will take orders for any machine made in England, at as low a price as they can be purchased elsewhere."[89]

As an importer of English bicycles and maker of the first American bicycles—thus revealing an aggressive commercial ambition that

Fig. 3.16. The scale of Pope's operations is emphasized in this illustration of his bicycle storeroom. [Source: *Bicycling World*, 1 April 1881]

would typify his future business activities in the United States—Pope objected to Stanton's enterprise and in March 1880, on behalf of the Pope Manufacturing Company and its licensees, took out an injunction to restrain him, on the grounds of infringement of patent rights which Pope claimed to have acquired for the United States. Pope's claims were grandiose:

> I have for the past two years and a half made this subject a special study and have obtained copies of every patent that has ever been issued in this country or relating to this subject, more than three hundred in number, and have given them a careful and exhaustive study comparing their mechanical features and mode of operation. I have been to Europe for the express purpose of studying this art and on a previous visit spent much time in investigating same.

The grounds for Pope's accusation against Stanton were in line with his attempts to secure sweeping patent and distribution rights to the bicycle: "there are no unlicensed or infringing bicycles in this country save those that are about to be introduced and which are offered for sale by this defendant; that this defendant has no regular place of business, and has no commercial standing or reputation; that if he is not restrained by order of this Court from selling his 'Humber' bicycles, this complainant and its licensees will be greatly injured."[90]

The broader commercial context for Etherington's American racing tour thus became a competition for the American bicycle market. The Six Day races were important because they publicized bicycles. Pope used ownership of patents to try to prevent open competition in the U.S. bicycle market, and Stanton was a potential competitor among the English makers and importers whom Pope was determined to brush out of his way. Simply stated, Pope wanted American cyclists to ride American bicycles, made by the Pope Manufacturing Company. The bicycle was seen as a patentable, licenceable product, and Pope, with aggressive lawyers including Charles Pratt working for him, won many victories until his final defeat in a lawsuit against Gormully and Jeffrey of Chicago, which effectively declared the concept of the bicycle itself unpatentable.[91]

An article in *Bicycling World* of April 1881 described the Pope Manufacturing Co. as "A Great American Manufacture," with agencies in two hundred cities and towns, which had "expended thousands of dollars a year in systematic and judicious advertising." Pope had not tried "to construct an entirely new style of machine, or to invent something more excellent," but had "adopted the more prudent course of taking a good standard model already tried and popular." In other words, he had copied existing, successful English machines. The enterprise was one "which might be ventured upon by a competent businessman ... an undertaking in which not only the article is to be manufactured, but the demand is to be manufactured for it." Pope had taken up the industry "when there was scarcely a perceptible demand for their product," and had "spurred the demand by teaching the American people, by patronizing and encouraging the literature of bicycling, and favoring clubs and associations formed to promote its spirit and enjoyment." The article was likely written by Charles Pratt.

By 1881, in Hartford, Connecticut, Pope had created "the largest and best appointed bicycle factory in the world," capable of producing 1,200 bicycles a month. Illustrations showed the workshops which mass-produced the bicycles "from the rough material," and storerooms full of the finished product.[92] This was assembly-line production of a consumer product on a large and modern scale.

"The sport of Bicycling is one that has come into rapid favor in this country since the advent of the English riders, who have accomplished a thousand miles a week," reported *Whittacker's Handbook of Summer Athletic Sports* in 1880: "the only drawback to its universal adoption is the first cost of the machines. When that is reduced, as it will be, to about fifty dollars, payable in instalments like sewing machines, the bicycle will become a favorite with the whole American population as it is in England with the majority of middle class young men." The "fever" was spreading thanks to the efforts of Mr. Wentworth Rollins, "the present king of bicyclists in America," and "the pioneers of bicycling in the United States were the Pope Manufacturing Company, who started factories and schools in the cities of Boston and San Francisco, where the fever started almost at the same time, but since that period bicycling has spread to most of the large cities."[93]

Charles Pratt thought that Etherington's tour had "waked up the racing interest throughout the country."[94] The overall influence of Etherington's first racing tour was significant. It was the first of many 19th century bicycle racing exchanges between England and the United States, a rivalry that continued throughout the 1880s and 1890s, producing heated debates in the press as to the relative value of British and American performances.

In his article, "Entrepreneurs, Organizations and the Sports Marketplace," Stephen Hardy suggests that: "If historians are to uncover the development of the sport industry as a special, perhaps unique, system and structure, it will be necessary to outline the key moments of innovation and the key innovators in any given segment or activity."[95] From the evidence of the 1879 tour described here, and his subsequent visits to the United States,

Harry Etherington was clearly an important international figure in the promotion and development of bicycle racing spectacles and other consumer sports events. *St. Stephen's Review* thought that he occupied "a particularly prominent place in the annals of national and industrial exhibitions." It praised Etherington's "great powers of originality and organization ... in his attempts to bring cycling into favourable repute." The consensus appears to have been that Etherington was enthusiastic, honest and fair. "Throughout the American continent, no Englishman connected with sport and the sporting press is better known or more generally liked than Mr. Harry Etherington, whose visits with the conquering teams of English cyclists have ever been warmly welcomed, while his peculiar dash and smartness have made the Yankees almost consider him as one of themselves."[96]

5. THE FOUNDING OF THE LEAGUE OF AMERICAN WHEELMEN

Like its British counterparts, the Bicycle Union and the Bicycle Touring Club, the League of American Wheelmen was founded to validate, define and promote concepts of sport associated with honorable amateurism, and a code of behavior rooted in middle-class respectability.

The League was founded for the legal and physical protection of bicycle riders and to promote and encourage racing and recreational riding. Like the New York Athletic Club (founded 1866) and the National Association of Amateur Athletes of America (founded 1879), it was an institutional expression of the new importance of organized amateur sport and recreation in American society.[97] Charles Pratt described it as "a wheelmen's protective league, which should combine the best points of the B.U. and the B.T.C."[98] It was developed directly from the foundations laid down by Boston and New York cycling clubs, and was organized by Charles Pratt, then editor of *Bicycling World* and President of the Boston Bicycle Club, and Kirk Monroe, President of the New York Bicycle Club.

Fig. 3.17. The Overman Wheel Co. advertised endurance records and the victories of both "amateurs" and professionals in the cycling press. [Source: *Bicycling World*, 16 Oct. 1885]

The inaugural meeting of the League was held in Newport, Rhode Island, in May 1880. It already had more than 500 members when its constitution was drawn up at a New York meeting in September 1880. A March 1880 list of American bicycle clubs showed 49 independent clubs, all formed within the previous two years, with a total membership of about 850, although the total number of bicycle riders was estimated at about 3,500.[99] The League grew rapidly, and by September 1886 its membership was nearly 10,000.[100] Annual club "Meets" were held in different locations, where races were also held, and the parades of hundreds of bicyclists through city streets appear to have attracted as many spectators as did the racing itself. From 1881 onwards, annual League race meetings were also held for League championships, although the first such event, at the Polo Grounds, New York, was described as "the dreariest and deadest occasion of a sporting sort."[101]

The earliest club road racing in the United States was either distance-based, or place-to-place and the races were in general small affairs. In 1883, *Bicycling World* reported that "the first 100 mile road race ever held in this country," organized by the Boston Bicycle Club, had only 10 contestants, and that "the riders attracted little attention on the highway. Few who saw them would think them more than tourists on a pleasure trip."[102] The winner's time was a slow 9h 47m, but road conditions in the early 1880s were appalling. Many "high-wheel" bicycle records were set and reported in the cycling press, though guaranteeing accurate results was always difficult. In the 1880s, the League of American Wheelmen was involved in sanctioning races and approving road records; only later did a debate begin within the L.A.W. over the image of road racing, which continued into the 1890s, just as it did in Britain.

Road racing was limited by the bad condition of country roads, and the most pressing problem even for off-road racing was to find a suitable surface, since most available tracks were grass horse-trotting courses. Pratt recommended the "cinder-path" as "the only really suitable track for bicycle racing.... With the increasing interest in the sport, it is probable the like will

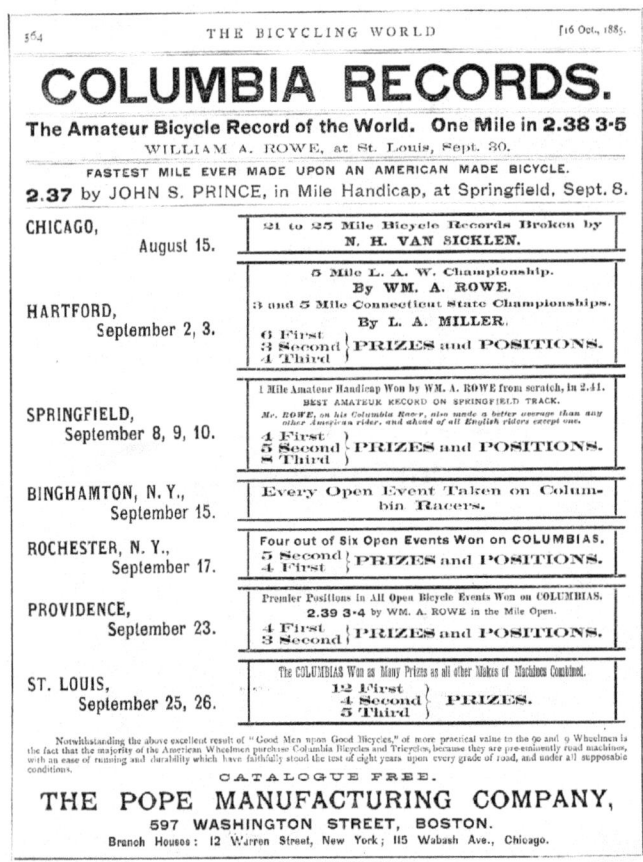

Fig. 3.18. Although most of the racing results listed here in 1885 were for amateur events, the Pope Manufacturing Co. openly made use of them to advertise its products. [Source: *Bicycling World*, 16 Oct. 1885]

be laid in many places, especially in connection with race-courses where it can be laid inside the trotting-track pretty satisfactorily. Next to this a good rolled grassy sod or a smooth gravel road is desirable."[103]

The League of American Wheelmen's *Handbook* described it as an organization to promote the general interests of cycling; to ascertain, defend, and protect the rights of wheelmen (which are those of any driver of horse and wagon), to encourage and facilitate touring, and to regulate the government of all amateur sports connected with the use of the wheel."[104] Thus, from its inception, the L.A.W. brought a political awareness and activism to its role as a sporting organization. Charles Pratt wrote in 1880 of "favorable editorials and generous news columns of the daily and weekly papers," which had brought about "a quite remarkable recognition of the rights of the bicycler throughout the country."

Pratt also noted the development of a symbiotic relationship between the sport and the bicycle industry as cycling evolved, and the significant role of the Pope Manufacturing Company in making and distributing bicycles: "At the bottom of all progress lies the commercial and manufacturing industry which bicycling has stimulated, and which in turn has stimulated bicycling."[105] A threat from the state of Ohio to suppress bicycle riding there caused the 1883 L.A.W. President Bates to write:

> No doubt most members of the L.A.W. are generally unconscious that the organization possesses any political power, since the League was not organized for the purpose of exercizing any political power, and has never exercized any such power directly and consciously.... The fact that we possess political power is our shield; the fact that we are ready to use it when attacked will double the strength of our shield. We trespass upon the rights of no man; let us make it plainly understood that no man will be permitted to trespass upon our rights with impunity."[106]

Bates went on to remind readers of *Outing* that the League was, in 1883, already more than 3,000 members strong, and that "these members are men and voters, not boys, men of business and political and social influence—gentlemen, including lawyers, editors, businessmen, clergyman, doctors—men possessed of both brains and money, who know their rights, and are thoroughly and very widely organized to maintain them." As Bates strongly asserts here, the vast majority of bicycle riders in

Fig. 3.19. The Coventry Machinists' Co. stressed here that it didn't pay riders who broke records, but machines and equipment were frequently supplied to "amateurs." [Source: *Bicycling World*, 11 Sept. 1885]

the United States were from the relatively affluent urban middle-classes, and had good legal advice from their friends in Boston, New York and Washington, D.C.[107] They were predominantly touring riders, and consequently the cycling clubs and the L.A.W. immediately became outspoken and effective promoters of road maintenance and repair, leading to what was subsequently known as the "Good Roads Movement."[108] The League became a federation, each state being eligible to have its State Division, with most activities organized on a state by state basis.

Racing affairs were concentrated in the hands of the Racing Board which "shall have charge of all matters pertaining to racing and the championships." The American definition of amateurism in cycling was identical to that spelled out by the English Bicycle Union, the National Association of Amateur Athletes of America and the New York Athletic Club, and professionals were excluded from membership.[109] L.A.W. rules specified that "an amateur is one who has never engaged in, nor assisted in, nor taught any recognized athletic exercise for money or other remuneration, nor knowingly competed against a professional for a prize."[110]

"Maker's amateurs" quickly became an issue, however, as American manufacturers used racing to push their machines into the public eye and to rival British records. In 1885, the Racing Board collected evidence that "almost every prominent prize-winner known to American wheeling had accepted pay from some bicycle-maker,"[111] and there was a rash of suspensions of alleged "professionals," causing them to become *de facto* professionals.

But it was clear that the Racing Board could not itself control the deals that went on between riders and manufacturers, and could not prevent clubs from offering financial incentives to leading amateur riders to enter races at their events. Chairman of the Racing Board, Abbot Bassett, told a general meeting of the League in June 1886 that "When a body such as ours proceeds to institute an inquiry into the relations between dealer and rider, it will find itself defeated at every point." He also regretted that "no work that the League

Fig. 3.20. Winona, Minnesota, south-east of Minneapolis, on the Mississippi river across from Wisconsin, witnessed the westward reach of bicycle racing out onto the American frontier in the 1880s. [Source: photographer Charles Tenney, Winona; author's collection]

delegates to its committees is more arduous than that which goes to the Racing Board, and no work is less pleasant in its nature."[112] It was a widely recognized fact that star riders boosted box-office receipts and ensured successful events and that old-fashioned, part-time amateurism did not easily breed champion material.

Competition between British and American makers for the American bicycle market was intense in the 1880s. Gormully and Jeffery of Chicago advertised their "American Champion" bicycle as "The greatest triumph of cycling manufacture in America. Entirely manufactured in America, with our own plant, and on our own premises, and with every care to suit the TASTE and NEEDS of an AMERICAN WHEELMAN."[113] While there was honest amateurism at the club level, at the top level of the sport amateur championship winners such as George Hendee, W.A. Rowe and George E. Weber were invariably supported with equipment and expenses, and manufacturers, including the Pope Manufacturing Co., openly advertised the victories of both "amateurs" and genuine professionals on its machines in the cycling press. The Coventry Machinists' Co. declared that it had used "No Paid Racing Men" in establishing American records in 1885, but top amateurs were under intense pressure to accept "gifts" from manufacturers and to slip into legitimate professionalism. In 1886, President Bates told *Bicycling World*:

> If bicycling wants to captivate the American people, it has got to parade the fliers. If the League wants to spread the glory of the wheel, it has got to beat the British records, and breed the faster fliers in the world.... Fliers have to be carefully cultivated from the hardiest stock. Somebody has got to pay for their cultivation.... Unless somebody foots the bills, you don't have fliers. Whether the club, or a manufacturer, or a wealthy promoter of the sport, pays the expenses, makes no difference with the result.[114]

Could there be a more "modern" statement of the exigencies of developing top-class talent in sport? There was thus a tension within the League of American Wheelmen between the controversial racing issues that concerned a minority of L.A.W. members and the recreational and touring issues which were the interests of the majority.

As the American sport grew, the huge annual "Meets" of the League of American Wheelmen and the Springfield Bicycle Club attracted the leading American riders and the cream of British cyclists. The Springfield Tournaments (which are discussed in greater detail in Chapter Four) grew in national and international importance, to such an extent that in 1886 the Springfield Bicycle Club advertised a "Grand One-Mile Race for the Bicycle Championship of the World!" to be held in September.[115] The ambitious promotions of the Springfield club's Henry E. Ducker, the son of British immigrants, raised the Springfield Tournaments to an unprecedented level of extravagance and success. At the first event, in 1882, 12,000 people attended. It cost more than $3,000 to stage, and earned a profit of more than $700. In 1883, $10,000 was spent on the event.[116]

While the influence of the annual Tournaments increased through the 1880s, Ducker's events became models of excellence for the new sport, putting particular emphasis on attracting the participation of top-level English riders and on establishing and breaking records. Both amateurs and professionals (in separate categories) were included in the programs, even though the Springfield B.C. was an "amateur" club.

"No man has ever given such an impetus to any recreative sport as Henry E. Ducker has given to cycling," said *Outing*: "Almost wholly by individual efforts, he has brought cycling to the foremost position it now holds in America."[117] Harry Etherington himself

Fig. 3.21. Two illustrations showed both the pleasures and the dangers of riding in the early high-wheel days. [Source: *The Wheelman*, Dec. 1882]

returned several times to the United States and went at least once to Springfield as a reporter for *Sporting Life*.

Top-level American riders found they could win cups as amateurs in the U.S. and make money as professionals in both England and France. The distinction between amateurism and professionalism in America was perhaps not surrounded by as precise a class demarcation as it was in Britain, thereby making the transition easier. World records were hotly contested on both sides of the Atlantic. In fact, there was hardly a world class or championship event through the 1880s which did not pit European against American cyclists. In the early 1890s, Arthur Zimmerman was one of a substantial number of world-class American cyclists who drew large audiences and were financially successful in Europe.

* * *

Reporting the speech of Member of Parliament Robert Lowe at a racing event promoted in 1878 by the West Kent Cycling Club at the Crystal Palace, London, the *American Bicycling Journal* commented that at these races:

> no less than sixteen representatives of as many London papers were present and furnished reports. This will show some of the still skeptical Bostonians the importance of the bicycling interest in England, and also the public interest in the new form of locomotion. We confidently expect the same interest to be exhibited in America, and that having the benefit arising from all the experiments and experience of the English and French pioneers, the progress of the movement in this country will be even more rapid than it has been with our English cousins.[118]

The confident predictions of the first American cycling newspaper were soon fulfilled. Because of its strong cultural connections with the "Old Country," Boston became the first business and organizational center of American cycling, although other cities—New York, Buffalo, Philadelphia and Chicago, for example, quickly became prominent in their own right. Like their British counterparts, American cyclists were predominantly middle-class and participated in well-organized club runs, venturing out onto unexplored roads. Group solidarity and respectability were established by wearing a prescribed uniform and, indeed, club activity had a slightly militaristic feel to it. College clubs were formed, emphasizing the role of cycling as one of the many sports practiced in the wider athletic movement of the early 1880s.

There was certainly a professional, show-business element in American bicycle racing in its earliest days, typified by the events of Etherington's tour, but the sport developed most energetically as an amateur and club-based activity in the late 1870s and early 1880s, expressing the novel social and sporting aspirations of educated, middle-class, urban participants. The organizational and cultural model was the already developed British sport, but the social level of American cycling clubs appears to have included more upper-middle

Fig. 3.22. A highly unusual action photo of high-wheel racing on an American track in the 1880s. [Lorne Shields collection, Toronto, Canada]

class members, and to have had fewer working-class members than London or north of England clubs.

The most prominent American clubs maintained elegant club houses where members could meet socially and where they could also store their bicycles. Certainly there is abundant evidence of ideological amateurism in the stated aims and agendas of the prominent East Coast and Mid-Western clubs. These aims were expressed institutionally in the founding of the League of American Wheelmen, an organization which became the watchdog of cyclists' interests, and was the controlling body of bicycle racing in the United States. The first official American championships were held under the jurisdiction of the National Association of Amateur Athletes of America in 1879, but State championships were organized soon after the L.A.W.'s foundation in 1880, and national championships were subsequently held on an annual basis. From its inception, the L.A.W. was involved in efforts to remedy the neglected state of public roads in America, and exerted varied influence as a recreational, sporting and political organization.

Emphasizing the commercial link between the sport and the bicycle industry, it is important to note the growth of the manufacturing activity which was essential for the expansion of the sport in America. Writing in 1890, E.P. Prial, the editor of *The Wheel and Cycling Trade Review*, noted:

> In a history of the sport it is but just to say that of the early makers and importers the Pope Company had the best conception of the business, and apparently took a broader view of the future of the sport than any of their contemporaries. They sank capital in manufacture and experiment, constantly improved their wheels, and nursed the sport. They helped clubs, and established a magazine to promulgate the doctrine of the wheel, on which they spent $70,000 in four years.[119]

In the United States in the late 1870s, cycling as a sport co-existed with, and was dependent upon, the industry which manufactured its essential tool. The sport and the industry sprang into existence contemporaneously, building on the example of the existing English sport, which was adapted to an American context.

Chapter Four

Expansion of the High-Wheel Sport

1. The New Sport Expands and Matures

> Since bicycling in its modern development has obtained in Great Britain, no season has seen such a rapid and general advance as the season of 1880, now drawing to a close. Not only has an active proselytising from all other athletic sports gone on, but a distinctly consolidating and solidifying force has also been at work. A glance at our club directory will shew an immense increase in the number of these associations.[1]

THERE ARE MANY SUCH contemporary comments attesting to the rapid expansion of the new sport, particularly in the annual trade reviews of the 1870s and 1880s which optimistically charted its progress. While businesses in Britain on the whole were not immune to cyclical economic instability, the bicycle industry—and the consequent growth of a sport, of recreation, of a new-found mobility—was nevertheless creating an unexpected economic boom in Coventry, Birmingham, Wolverhampton, Sheffield and in the other centers of the trade. In 1878, in a major trade journal, H.H. Griffin wrote:

> Having just returned from an extended tour through the bicycle manufacturing district ... we are very happy in being able to state the trade was never in a more healthy or vigorous state. It is, indeed, pleasant to be able to chronicle in these days of depression in business, wars and rumours of wars, strikes and failures, that there is at least one branch of national industry left us whose position is beyond being affected by the Eastern Question, or tightness of the money market. To show the numerical state of the bicycle trade we may incidentally say that the Coventry Machinists' Co. have made over 10,000 bicycles, Singer and Co. about 7,000, Haynes and Jefferis between the two. We thus get 25,000 from three makes.[2]

In another account from the previous year, Griffin reported "a vast increase on all sides of the bicycle trade ... the manner in which the leading and other firms have prospered is wonderful; in one case where eighteen months ago barely twenty men found employment, now nearly five times that number are kept busy." He estimated that there were in 1877 "about 100 makers in the trade," with the three largest of the nine manufacturers in Coventry (Coventry Machinists' Co., Singer, Haynes and Jefferis) employing a total of 400 workers.[3] In 1877, one estimate suggested there were about 40,000 cyclists in the United Kingdom.[4] By 1885, another well-informed source wrote that:

> reliable figures are not readily available, but from information I have been able to gather it may be taken as a fair approximation that between 300,000–400,000 persons are to be found among the ranks of habitual cyclists ... the number of machines placed on the market in the last ten years cannot be less than 300,000.[5]

As these figures indicate, cycling experienced remarkable growth in the late 1870s and

Fig. 4.1. On the Upper Richmond Road, Putney, a south-west London cycling club demonstrated exemplary behavior, with all of its members wearing the prescribed uniform. [Source: author's collection]

1880s. The bicycle industry expanded rapidly in a symbiotic relationship with the athletic and recreational consumers who tried and tested its products. Industry and consumers were engaged in a mutually advantageous experiment. Outside the bustling industrial machine-shops of the manufacturers, the developing institutional aspect of the sport in Britain could be seen in the growth of the two national cycling organizations, the National Cyclists' Union and the Bicycle (Cyclists') Touring Club, the formation of hundreds of cycling clubs under the umbrella of the N.C.U. and the expansion of a regular nation-wide program of amateur and professional race meetings.

Britain clearly dominated, both in the practical expansion of the bicycle industry and promoting the development of the sport. In continental Europe, particularly in France, but also to a lesser extent in Germany, Belgium, Holland, Italy, Austria and Bohemia, cycling grew along similar lines, although its evolution varied from country to country, and it generally developed at a slower pace than it did in Britain. In all these European countries, British bicycles were at first in great demand, and British cycling was the model, although national industries also sprang up in response to demand.

In the United States, the growth of the industry occurred with the Pope Manufacturing Co. as the leading manufacturer and the League of American Wheelmen, founded in 1880, as the governing institution of the sport. In 1881, the Pope Manufacturing Co. was described as "the largest and best appointed bicycle factory in the world," capable of making 1,200 bicycles a month.[6]

In Britain, the *Cyclist and Wheel World Annual* for 1882 listed 189 "Metropolitan clubs" in Greater London, including a "Press Bicycle Association—strictly confined to members of the Press," and 355 "provincial clubs" in the rest of the country, as well as 8 newly formed "tricycle clubs."[7] By 1889, the Cyclists' Touring Club was called "the largest athletic association in the world," with a paid membership of more than 20,000 cyclists. The same source estimated that in 1885 there were "not far from 400,000" cyclists in Britain, although it admitted that the figure "is a rough one."[8] Although only a small proportion of these cyclists rode competitively, such a large number of individual clubs and the large membership in two national organizations is further evidence of the overall growth and popularity of the sport at the time.

Racing enthusiasts, who were athletes and competitors, trained and "scorched" on the open road. Others preferred the more relaxed recreational and social aspects of cycling.[9] Individual tourists explored the extensive network of roads in Britain, whereas club cyclists were gregarious, and summer club runs and races were interspersed with social events. In the off-season there were dances, music-hall performances and concerts. "It is not a little surprising how gregarious are the manners and customs of the average amateur sportsman," commented a later editorial in *Bicycling* News; "It is hardly too much to say that clubdom is absolutely essential to cycling, and that its wonderful popularity today may be to a very great extent ascribed to this cause."[10]

Joining a club gave social cohesion and a social context to the new athletic and recreational activity. Club members displayed their pride in owning a new bicycle, a pride that is illustrated in the many studio photographs of man and machine taken during that period. Cycling was an intrinsically public sport; wearing a club uniform was encouraged as a way for club cyclists to demonstrate their respectability and their group solidarity in the face of criticism and resistance from other road-users.

Riding the high-wheel bicycle, far from being a quaint or romantic activity (as it is compulsively portrayed in retrospect), was for the riders of the 1880s an expression of modernity and mobility, an energetic exercise and recreation that offered the added spice of physical risk and the ability to travel to new places. The best amateur riders, who were driven by their pride as "gentlemen cyclists," tried their luck in formal competition, and a few—the professional athletic elite—attempted to earn a living by competing. The high-wheel bicycle was rarely promoted for strictly utilitarian purposes, but it was used in touring for both recreation and as a means of transportation. Bicycle track racing was firmly established as both an amateur and a professional sport, with thousands of followers, a regular schedule of meetings and championships, a tightly organized structure, and an increasingly international elite level of competition. Grueling long-distance road races and time trials tested the strength and endurance of the toughest road competitors.

While bicycle racing on the road and track was dominated by the high-wheel bicycle in the 1880s, cycling continued to evolve and change during that period. With the introduction first of the tricycle, then later of the "geared up ordinaries" and the "safety" bicycle, the latest innovative machines expanded the scope of racing and also competed for the consumer's attention, offering greater possibilities for recreation and practical transportation. Bicycles of different designs were pitted against each other in tests of speed and efficiency; manufacturers staged promotional races to demonstrate the technological advantages of various bicycle and tricycle designs. With the introduction of the "safety" bicycle in the late 1880s, road racing became increasingly popular, especially long-distance races which caught the imagination of the public.

Fig. 4.2. In this unidentified photograph from about 1889, uniformed club cyclists proudly pose with ordinary bicycles, Star-type bicycles [small wheels in front] and tricycles in about 1889. [Source: Lorne Shields collection, Toronto, Canada]

* * *

It is important to bear in mind that throughout the 1880s high-wheel bicycle and tricycle racing remained a high-tech, "cutting edge" sport. There was nothing "primitive" about early bicycle technology, which advanced with intense technological logic and precision. Racing bicycles for the track were light and stripped of every unnecessary component, while those used for serious road riding were more robust, but still as light as possible. The technological challenge was to make a machine that was both light and strong in order to maximize the power and speed of the rider. The journalist A.J. Wilson commented in 1887 that:

> For racing purposes, specially constructed bicycles and tricycles are used. These are identical in design with the ordinary roadsters, but have no brakes to check the momentum, and their every part is made as light as possible, the thinnest gauge of steel tube being used; with very fine spokes; the lightest of bearings and forgings; and, in fact, with every part reduced in weight as far as is consistent with the strength requisite to withstand the strains of racing on smooth and level paths. Such machines, of course, would soon go to pieces if used on rough roads, and even on the path their life is but short; yet, when we look at the immense strain put upon a bicycle or tricycle by a powerful athlete, it is truly astonishing that they can be made so light and yet so strong.[11]

This more than one century-old comment about technological modernity might easily have been taken from an advertisement from a page of a contemporary cycling magazine!

Technical improvements that were initially made with the racer in mind—hollow steel tubing, ball bearings, steering mechanisms, lightweight chains and efficient tensioned rim-and-spoke construction, for example—were often passed on to the recreational and utilitarian consumer. The commercial nature of modern sport is prefigured here—the bicycle industry was producing specialized sporting equipment which was tested by expert racers, who then advertised and promoted its products to the public. The competitive sport and the recreational sport both played a key role in multi-million pound/dollar businesses, and this economic relationship between competitors/users and the industry was an ever-present source of debate and controversy. There was constant tension and organizational wrangling between the "pure," unsullied amateurism advocated by an activist such as George Lacy Hillier—who sought to distance the industry from the sport, and to keep money as much as possible out of competition—and a more realistic, pragmatic approach, which recognized the reality of "maker's amateurs" and of sponsorship and full professionalism following the French model.[12]

The 1880s were also marked by a struggle for the control of bicycle racing in Britain by the National Cyclists Union since other organizations, such as the Amateur Athletic Association, still claimed the right to promote bicycle racing. There was also argument about which activities were likely to result in the expansion of the sport, or to demean it in the eyes of the general public.[13] Track racing, usually promoted by cycling clubs, continued as the mainstay of the sport. But concern about negative public reaction to bicycle racing on public roads, which could be ruled illegal if it was thought to constitute "furious riding," caused the N.C.U. to declare that road racing should be discouraged, eliciting a strong reaction from those clubs whose members preferred road riding and racing, and didn't much like the N.C.U.'s control. Thus in 1888, a new organization, the Road Records Association, was founded to promote individual place-to-place and long-distance record-breaking of individual riders on the road, outside the jurisdiction of the N.C.U.[14]

The influence of the specialized cycling media continued to be a crucial factor in the growth of the sport and the industry, with editors playing an activist role. At the same time, championship-level racing between British riders and riders from other countries created a greater international character within the sport at its highest level.

2. BICYCLE RACING INFRASTRUCTURE: ROAD CONDITIONS AND TRACK CONSTRUCTION

Despite the well-established and impressive network of major and minor roads in Britain, road surfaces were nevertheless often neglected, rough, and always unpredictable for cyclists on solid-tired bicycles. The riding and racing that occurred on public roads was always subject to adverse conditions, especially in the winter and during bad weather. Road riding was legitimately regarded as a very real test of strength, speed and endurance, and athletic road performances were judged alongside other modes of transportation, such as the horse-drawn coach and the steam locomotive. In England, in particular, clubs held local competitions on the roads. Long-distance place-to-place rides and 12-hour and 24-hour rides became recognized tests of stamina and riding ability. Stretches of well-maintained road, like the Great North, the Bath and the Portsmouth Roads out of London, were used frequently for breaking speed records in the summer months, and feature prominently in the record books.[15]

Since there was a great deal of opposition to racing on the public roads, especially to races involving group riding, club promotions and contests of pure speed were more effectively run, under more easily controlled conditions, on an enclosed track where spectators could watch, and where the racing surface was better prepared. "Racing on high bicycles began to attract the attention of the public when proper cycling tracks commenced to appear in various parts of the kingdom. Previous to the construction of cinder tracks some racing had taken place on grass running tracks."[16] The growth of bicycle racing as a spectator sport was thus initially dependent upon having appropriate venues in which to hold races, which involved an investment of capital. Those venues evolved from providing grass or cinder tracks, to offering surfaces of specially laid wood and cement. In these cases, cycling was among the first sports to offer a custom-made arena within which the sport could be presented.

In the United States, stretches of relatively good surface could be found on the outskirts of big cities, but further out, the condition of the roads was almost universally described as appalling.[17] One of the outstanding documents of early bicycle travel in America, Thomas Stevens' *Around the World on a Bicycle*, describes road conditions in the mid–1880s that were so bad that he had to walk for many miles, even in the East.[18] Bad road conditions, however, not only did not discourage the most athletic cyclists, but may indeed have served as an additional incentive to perform newsworthy athletic feats. Century (100-mile) rides by club members were documented in detail in the New England states, Washington, D.C., Cleveland, San Francisco—wherever clubs had sprung up. Typical speeds for a century on the road were between 7 and 10 m.p.h. Accidents were common and sandy roads sometimes necessitated miles of walking.[19]

This general neglect of American roads led in the 1880s to the rise of the "Good Roads Movement" within the League of American Wheelmen, and the formation in 1888 of a National Committee for the Improvement of Highways.

Fig. 4.3. Trans-continental traveler Thomas Stevens was welcomed by Oakland cyclists upon his return to the United States in January 1887. [Source: John L. Weiss collection]

As early as 1881, Lewis Bates (president of the Michigan Division of the League and editor of the *Detroit Post and Tribune*) spoke about the need for road improvement at the annual L.A.W. meeting in Boston. The bicycle, he said, was "one of the great benefits bestowed on this country in that it educated young men to know the difference between a good road and a bad one."[20] In 1887, *Harper's Magazine* noted that "the League of American Wheelmen members are everywhere serving the general public as well as themselves in striving with all their might to improve the conditions of American roads, and to keep them from the well-merited reproach of being the worst of those in use by civilized nations."[21]

In Britain, a Roads Improvement As sociation appealed to cyclists in the cycling press, although the activities of this group don't appear to have been very significant. The Cyclists' Touring Club was also constantly active in keeping an eye on road conditions, and its "Danger Boards" became a prominent feature of the roadscape. Britain was a much smaller country than the United States, and parishes had for a long time worked on rural roads to keep them passable for local and long-distance traffic.

In France, major roads were in general well maintained, which may partly explain why fewer tracks were built and why early racing was concentrated on the road. Thomas Stevens, arriving in Normandy from England in May 1885, found the roads "magnificent":

> A few days ago I called the English roads perfect ... but the Normandy roads are even superior.... There is not a loose stone, a rut, or depression anywhere on these roads, and it is little exaggeration to call them veritable billiard-tables for smoothness of surface. As one bowls smoothly along over them he is constantly wondering how they can possibly keep them in such condition.[22]

A French visitor to London told an interviewer from *Wheeling* in 1887 that racing was growing, especially in the Bordeaux region of south-west France, "but the great fault is the want of tracks, the only three in France being at Bordeaux, Pau and Dax":

> "Then what do you do when you want to give a race meeting?"
>
> "The club giving the meeting has to

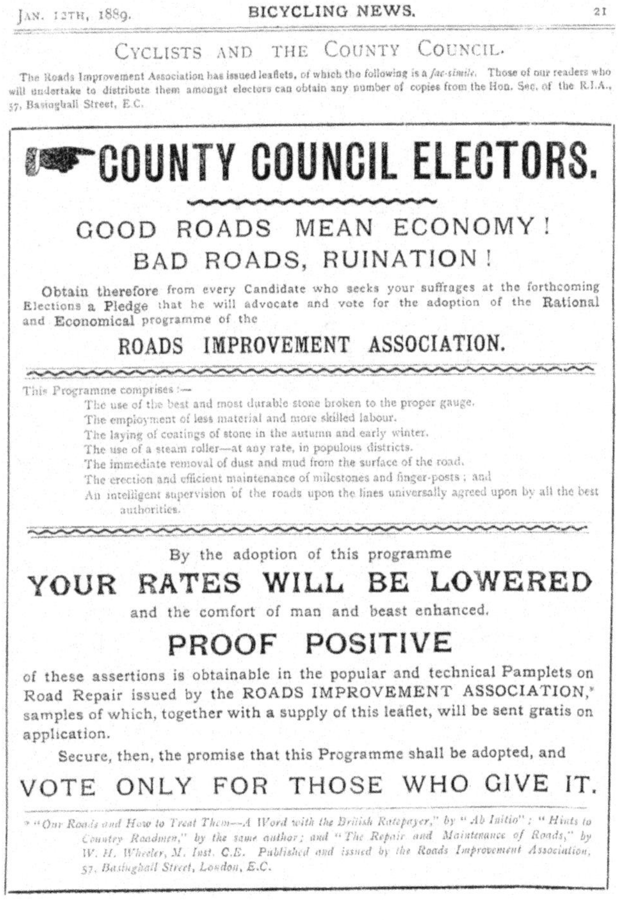

JAN. 12TH, 1889. BICYCLING NEWS. 21

CYCLISTS AND THE COUNTY COUNCIL.

The Roads Improvement Association has issued leaflets, of which the following is a *fac-simile*. Those of our readers who will undertake to distribute them amongst electors can obtain any number of copies from the Hon. Sec. of the R.I.A., 57, Basinghall Street, E.C.

COUNTY COUNCIL ELECTORS.

GOOD ROADS MEAN ECONOMY!

BAD ROADS, RUINATION!

Obtain therefore from every Candidate who seeks your suffrages at the forthcoming Elections a Pledge that he will advocate and vote for the adoption of the Rational and Economical programme of the

ROADS IMPROVEMENT ASSOCIATION.

This Programme comprises:—

The use of the best and most durable stone broken to the proper gauge.
The employment of less material and more skilled labour.
The laying of coatings of stone in the autumn and early winter.
The use of a steam roller—at any rate, in populous districts.
The immediate removal of dust and mud from the surface of the road.
The erection and efficient maintenance of milestones and finger-posts; and
An intelligent supervision of the roads upon the lines universally agreed upon by all the best authorities.

By the adoption of this programme

YOUR RATES WILL BE LOWERED

and the comfort of man and beast enhanced.

PROOF POSITIVE

of these assertions is obtainable in the popular and technical Pamplets on Road Repair issued by the ROADS IMPROVEMENT ASSOCIATION,* samples of which, together with a supply of this leaflet, will be sent gratis on application.

Secure, then, the promise that this Programme shall be adopted, and

VOTE ONLY FOR THOSE WHO GIVE IT.

* "*Our Roads and How to Treat Them—A Word with the British Ratepayer,*" by "*Ab Initio*"; "*Hints to Country Roadmen,*" by the same author; and "*The Repair and Maintenance of Roads,*" by *W. H. Wheeler, M. Inst. C.E. Published and issued by the Roads Improvement Association, 57, Basinghall Street, London, E.C.*

Fig. 4.4. In 1889, the British Roads Improvement Association appealed for cyclists' support in the cycling press. [Source: *Bicycling News*, 12 Jan. 1889]

Fig. 4.5. "Danger boards" were erected in Britain by the C.T.C. in the 1880s and 1890s. [Source: Badminton *Cycling*]

get permission from the Town Council to enclose an avenue or road, and the expense of enclosing a place for one day is so great that the entries and gate-money do not cover the expense."

"What do you think of our English tracks and roads as compared to the French?"

"There is simply no comparison; the English racing paths are as much superior to ours, as our roads are to the English ones."[23]

While attempting to promote the 1885 French championships in which champions De Civry, Médinger, Terront, H.O. Duncan and Garrard competed, the Véloce Club Bordelais struggled valiantly with less than adequate facilities. On 31 May, 15,000 spectators paid to see the racing, although "the track was in an awful state, and after a few races, the surface cut up and made loose gravel holes all over the ground especially at the corners, where riding was indeed dangerous." A few days later, however, at an evening "fête vélocipédique" illuminated by electric light and attended by about 20,000 people:

> the arrangements were perfect and the illuminations magnificent, about two thousand coloured lamps, and as many Venetian lanterns, were strung over the track, from pole to pole, in a very pretty fashion, and gave a scene of splendour to the surrounding decorations of drapery, flags and banners of every country and colour. Chalk was strewn all over the track, and the electric lights shone brilliantly as daylight upon this white surface, making matters less dangerous for the racing division.[24]

In Agen, near Bordeaux, "the Vélodrome du Gravier presented a very gay aspect, it being exceedingly well arranged.... The track was in excellent condition, and up to the present day can rank as the best track in the country." The track had a "smooth surface," and was "well arranged and in excellent condition—although the corners were sharp, they were easy to negotiate." About 10,000 spectators were present, and "the toilettes of the fair sex were exceptionally well to the fore, and gave an aristocratic appearance to the now popular sport." As at Bordeaux, the night race meeting at Agen was lit by electric lighting which was "upon a very large and gigantic scale; no less than 16 large globes of electric light were placed around the track to show the riders their way."[25]

Such a progressive, exceptionally innovative way of staging bicycle races appears to have been rare in France in 1885.[26] The Bordeaux track was the first permanent cycling facility to be constructed in France, and in 1892 it was reported that "its example has been followed by several other cities. Some other tracks have already been constructed and others are proposed ... but none of these are equal in size and in their quality of construction to those abroad."[27] With the building of at least three large new tracks in Paris in the early 1890s, however, France ensured that its facilities were world-class.

In Germany—where a British enthusiast, T.H.S. Walker, was editor of *Der Radfahrer* and President of the Berlin Racing Association, an organization to promote bicycle racing—there were about thirty tracks, some of which had cost as much as £1,000, which were "the property of the clubs in the different towns" and "are quite on a level with the leading clubs in England." The Berlin track cost £700 and the four-lap to a mile Leipzig track had been built "at great expense." German racing was almost exclusively amateur in the 1880s: "Professionalism simply does not exist here ... no money prizes are given."[28]

In Britain, the Molineux track, with its ambitious promoter McGregor, certainly helped to encourage racing in Wolverhampton from the earliest days of the sport. In 1877, addressing an issue that was discussed throughout the century, Alfred Howard wrote: "The want of good racing paths is severely felt in various parts of the country, and causes much road racing, which we are afraid is likely to bring bicycling into disrepute. A race course ... invariably fosters and encourages bicycling more than anything else. As proof of our assertion we point to Wolverhampton, where bicycling is popular amongst all classes."[29] The two principal kinds of racing that occurred are deftly identified here: track racing demanded as smooth a surface as possible, which had to be carefully prepared at great expense, while road racing used existing roads, but had to cope with whatever conditions were encountered, and risked alienating other road users, and thereby giving cyclists in general a bad name.

Clearly, the quality of high-wheel bicycle track racing in the 1880s depended increasingly, both for competitors and spectators, on the condition of the track where the races were held, and the improvement of existing tracks and the construction of new facilities were essential in the development of the sport. If good racing and high speeds (with the possibility of records being broken) were to be achieved, an improvised cinder or grass track normally used for horse-racing or other athletic events was unsatisfactory and dangerous. A track built specifically for bicycle racing, preferably banked, was much better suited for the sport.

* * *

When, in September 1880, English champion H.L. Cortis attempted "the unparalleled feat of riding 20 miles in an hour," he chose the Surbiton Recreation Grounds Bicycle Track, "acknowledged by all bicyclists to be the fastest in England." Not only was there a hard, compacted surface ideal for the actual racing, but there were also changing rooms for the cyclists and facilities for spectators, including a grandstand, seating, railings and a refreshment booth. Building a good track was a very expensive undertaking. It required investors, club backing, and a well-managed organizational structure that would guarantee regular use of the new facility. Such an expensive sports enterprise was a high-risk proposition. To succeed as a business venture, the track also had to be accessible to public transportation, and was most likely to be located either within or close to more densely populated areas. The construction of dedicated cycling tracks in urban areas in the 1880s was an indication of the expansion and popularity of the sport. And it also reveals the growth of an effective management and financial infrastructure.[30]

Regarding the track surface, what was necessary in the 1880s was "a firm, hard and smooth surface, not liable to get loose in dry, nor sodden in wet, weather. A first-class track for cycling must be used for no other purpose, even running or walking races being detrimental to the surface by reason of the spiked shoes worn by pedestrians."[31] By the mid–1880s, there were a number of good tracks in the London area: Crystal Palace, Surbiton, Herne Hill and Alexander Park were the best, while Lillie Bridge and Stamford Bridge were considered less desirable because of inferior bankings. According to A.J. Wilson, writing in 1887, "almost every city of size in England possesses some sort of a cycling track," and the same was true by then of most of the other major European cycling countries, as well as the United States, although the French appear to have been late in constructing good tracks. In his account of his professional cycling career from 1880 to 1887, H.O. Duncan described racing not only at prominent British locations (London, Wolverhampton, Aberdeen, Edinburgh, Newcastle, Leicester) but also in France (Angers, Grenoble, Agen, Bordeaux, Toulouse, Pau, Montpellier, Narbonne), Italy (Turin), Germany (Berlin, Frankfurt, Munich, Bremen, Mannheim, Nuremberg, Augsburg) and Austria (Vienna, Linz).[32]

Fig. 4.6. H.L. Cortis, the first cyclist to ride 20 miles in an hour, emigrated to Australia, where he died soon after. [Source: *The Cyclist Annual and Year Book*, 1893]

With the later boom in cycling's popularity in the 1890s, the inadequacies of older tracks were often addressed and remedied, and new, state-of-the-art tracks were frequently built. Builders experimented with different surfaces, choosing wooden boards and cement, for example, instead of compacted gravel.[33] The promoter H.O. Duncan, who was involved in building the cement-surfaced Vélodrome Buffalo in Paris (opened in June 1892), later engaged in a vituperative journalistic debate with Lacy Hillier (never one to avoid a good controversy), who had chosen a wooden board surface for the track at Herne Hill, over the relative merits of the two surfaces. Subsequently, it was almost universally agreed that cement was the preferred material for outdoor tracks.[34]

* * *

American tracks were soon renowned for their size and quality. As early as March 1883, the official publication of the League of American Wheelmen, *Bicycling World*, published an extensive discussion of the intricacies of track measurements, emphasizing the necessity of standardization in measurement procedures in order to guarantee the authenticity of record-setting rides.[35] When a group of English cyclists arrived in the United States in September 1884 for a series of important races promoted by the Connecticut and Springfield Bicycle Clubs, they were impressed by the quality of the tracks in Hartford and Springfield (Massachusetts). In Hartford, "by days of rolling and planing" the track "had been made as hard and smooth as a floor. It was a revelation to the English wheelmen."[36] In 1885, "after many practical experiments had been made," a track of "one-half clay and one-half gravel, thoroughly screened and mixed" was laid in Springfield. The track was again "superb ... the grandest racing surface in the world," and it was reported that "many towns in the States are making tracks upon the same plan."[37]

Fig. 4.7. In establishing new speed records on the high-wheel bicycle in 1880, H.L. Cortis used one of the best London tracks available to him. [Source: copy of poster in author's collection]

"For big things in the way of cycling tracks we must look to America," commented A.J. Wilson in 1887, "where a specially-built track of half-a-mile in circuit exists at Springfield, in the State of Massachusetts, a city boasting of a cycling club so enthusiastic in the promotion of cycle races as to have achieved world-wide notoriety. Here, every autumn, an immense three-days meeting takes place, at which British as well as American riders compete for valuable prizes." Wilson pointed out that several big meetings took place annually in the United States, "which attract enormous numbers of spectators," but added that in England there was "an uninterrupted series of Saturday afternoon meetings from May to September, it being no uncommon thing for two or three meetings in the London area to clash."[38]

In fact, the number of excellent track facilities in the United States increased rapidly in the 1880s, especially in New England, where they were managed by local clubs and supported by city councils and chambers of commerce. In Lynn, Massachusetts, the Lynn Cycle Club held a "Grand Opening Tournament" for its new track on Memorial Day, 31 May 1886. "Although it is the centre of bicycling, Eastern Massachusetts has not heretofore possessed a complete and modern cycle track," read an advertisement for the event: "The necessity for such led to the formation of the Lynn Cycle Club Track Association, which with commendable energy and dispatch has evolved the finest bicycle racing track to be found in the world, being a dead level, three-lap track, of perfect design. The opening tournament will include the fastest men in America, and extraordinary time is expected."[39] A similar advertisement for "The Third International Tournament" of the Connecticut Bicycle Club at Hartford in August 1886 explained that "Charter Oak Park has been greatly improved during the past year, and is now faster than ever."[40] The cost of such improvements obviously had to be justified, and both amateur and professional cyclists had to prove their worth by generating box-office revenue from spectators.

The results of outstanding distance rides on the road were widely reported and recorded, but such races were by their nature more difficult to time and compare accurately and convincingly. Since speed on a bicycle was so clearly related to the riding surface, with the improvement of tracks there was an increase in speed and this stimulated record-breaking attempts and the establishment of national and world records. In the early 1880s international bicycle racing results began to be consistently recorded, discussed and compared. Carefully measured tracks meant that distances as short as ¼ mile or as long as 100 miles could be accurately calibrated, and thus competition among English, French and American riders could be carefully documented, and international records established and compared. This also sometimes led to disputes. For example, the world record times allegedly achieved at the 1885 Springfield Tournament led to an intense and acrimonious debate about the accuracy of timing methods.[41]

The entire question of track construction—the size of a track, its banking, and its surface—was subjected to increasingly scientific examination. This was particularly true as the high-wheel bicycle was succeeded by the safety bicycle, the solid tire gave way to the pneumatic tire, and speeds greatly increased in the early 1890s. The track had to be banked to enable riders to maintain a constant speed, and to eliminate the obstacle of difficult, dangerous corners.

Only on a well-designed, well-built track could fast speeds be maintained and skillful tactics be employed. Since the purpose of the sport was "to allow talent and speed to shine through," wrote one French commentator, "cycling tracks should be arranged as perfectly as possible, to ensure interesting and consistent results." The subsoil needed to be properly compacted, and the surface neither too soft nor too hard. The surface had to be "affected as little as possible by rain, heat or ice; water should not remain on the surface, but run off it so that it dries quickly. These necessary conditions have to be especially studied and the engineers who have the responsibility of constructing cycling tracks have to understand them."[42] Whereas a rider on the road had to face all the vagaries of weather and geography, the purpose of the track was to eliminate as many variables in racing conditions as possible.

3. Competition in Britain: Amateurism and Professionalism in the Late 1870s and 1880s

Recapping the 1877 racing season, Alfred Howard wrote that "the bicycle races which have taken place during 1877 are almost innumerable.... In the Midlands and the North there have been very few athletic meetings at which a bicycle race has not been the most attractive feature of the program. To bicyclists the most noteworthy facts are the increase of the race meetings of bicycle clubs."[43] Charles Spencer wrote in 1883 that it was "a proof of the high estimation in which the sport of bicycle racing is held by its votaries" that in 1881 225 bicycle race meetings, consisting of considerably more than 1,000 separate races, as well as 30 tricycle meetings, had been held in Britain.[44] Through the 1880s, this number increased and race results were routinely published in the cycling and local newspapers. However, there was not yet any centralized bureaucratic control over this expansive sporting activity. In the early 1880s, when racing on the "high wheel" bicycle was firmly established, a network of cycling clubs was doing much of the race promotion, and a good deal of the racing was still being promoted by other athletic and social organizations, and publications as well, rather than under the jurisdiction of the Bicycle Union.

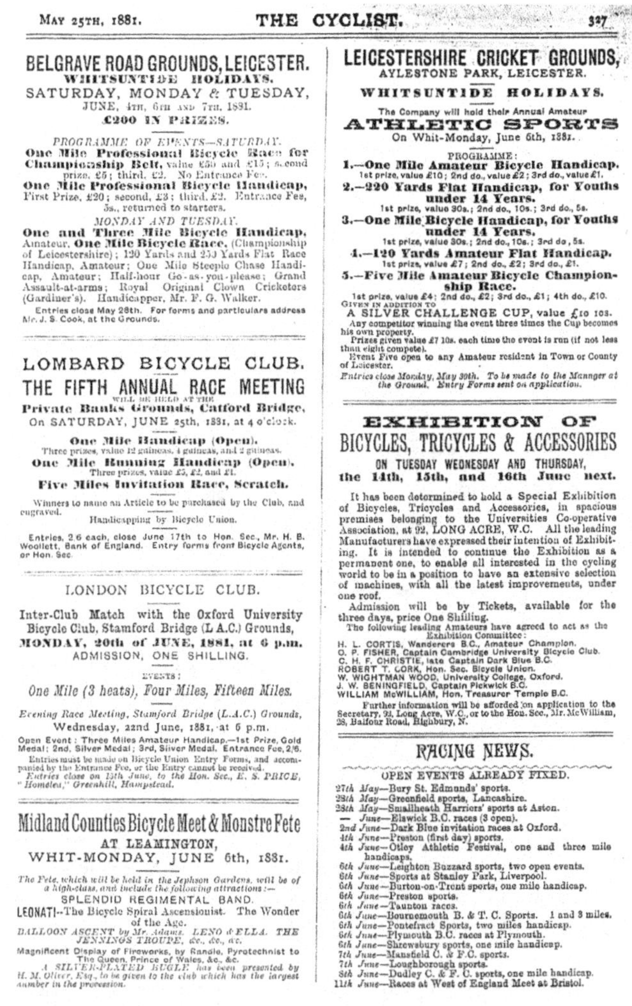

MAY 25TH, 1881. THE CYCLIST. 327

BELGRAVE ROAD GROUNDS, LEICESTER.
WHITSUNTIDE HOLIDAYS.
SATURDAY, MONDAY & TUESDAY,
JUNE, 4TH, 6TH AND 7TH, 1881.
£200 IN PRIZES.

PROGRAMME OF EVENTS—SATURDAY.
One Mile Professional Bicycle Race for Championship Belt, value £50 and £15; second prize, £5; third, £2. No Entrance Fee.
One Mile Professional Bicycle Handicap, First Prize, £20; second, £3; third, £2. Entrance Fee, 5s., returned to starters.
MONDAY AND TUESDAY.
One and Three Mile Bicycle Handicap, Amateur. **One Mile Bicycle Race,** (Championship of Leicestershire); 120 Yards and 250 Yards Flat Race Handicap, Amateur; One Mile Steeple Chase Handicap, Amateur; Half-hour Go-as-you-please; Grand Assault-at-arms; Royal Original Clown Cricketers (Gardiner's). Handicapper, Mr. F. G. Walker.
Entries close May 28th. For forms and particulars address Mr. J. S. Cook, at the Grounds.

LOMBARD BICYCLE CLUB.
THE FIFTH ANNUAL RACE MEETING
WILL BE HELD AT THE
Private Banks Grounds, Catford Bridge,
On SATURDAY, JUNE 25th, 1881, at 4 o'clock.
One Mile Handicap (Open).
Three prizes, value 12 guineas, 4 guineas, and 2 guineas.
One Mile Running Handicap (Open).
Three prizes, value £5, £2, and £1.
Five Miles Invitation Race, Scratch.
Winners to name an Article to be purchased by the Club, and engraved.
Handicapping by Bicycle Union.
Entries, 2/6 each, close June 17th to Hon. Sec., Mr. H. B. Woollett, Bank of England. Entry forms from Bicycle Agents, or Hon. Sec.

LONDON BICYCLE CLUB.
Inter-Club Match with the Oxford University Bicycle Club, Stamford Bridge (L.A.C.) Grounds,
MONDAY, 20th of JUNE, 1881, at 6 p.m.
ADMISSION, ONE SHILLING.
EVENTS:
One Mile (3 heats), Four Miles, Fifteen Miles.
Evening Race Meeting, Stamford Bridge (L.A.C.) Grounds,
Wednesday, 22nd June, 1881, at 6 p.m.
Open Event: Three Miles Amateur Handicap.—1st Prize, Gold Medal; 2nd, Silver Medal; 3rd, Silver Medal. Entrance Fee, 2/6.
Entries must be made on Bicycle Union Entry Forms, and accompanied by the Entrance Fee, or the Entry cannot be received.
Entries close on 13th June, to the Hon. Sec., E. S. PRICE, "Homelea," Greenhill, Hampstead.

Midland Counties Bicycle Meet & Monstre Fete
AT LEAMINGTON,
WHIT-MONDAY, JUNE 6th, 1881.
The Fete, which will be held in the Jephson Gardens, will be of a high-class, and include the following attractions:—
SPLENDID REGIMENTAL BAND.
LEONATI—The Bicycle Spiral Ascensionist. The Wonder of the Age.
BALLOON ASCENT by Mr. Adams. LENO & ELLA. THE JENNINGS TROUPE, &c., &c., &c.
Magnificent Display of Fireworks, by Randle, Pyrotechnist to The Queen, Prince of Wales, &c., &c.
A SILVER-PLATED BUGLE has been presented by H. M. Oliver, Esq., to be given to the club which has the largest number in the procession.

LEICESTERSHIRE CRICKET GROUNDS,
AYLESTONE PARK, LEICESTER.
WHITSUNTIDE HOLIDAYS.
The Company will hold their Annual Amateur
ATHLETIC SPORTS
On Whit-Monday, June 6th, 1881.
PROGRAMME:
1.—One Mile Amateur Bicycle Handicap.
1st prize, value £10; 2nd do., value £2; 3rd do., value £1.
2.—220 Yards Flat Handicap, for Youths under 14 Years.
1st prize, value 30s.; 2nd do., 10s.; 3rd do., 5s.
3.—One Mile Bicycle Handicap, for Youths under 14 Years.
1st prize, value 30s.; 2nd do., 10s.; 3rd do., 5s.
4.—120 Yards Amateur Flat Handicap.
1st prize, value £7; 2nd do., £2; 3rd do., £1.
5.—Five Mile Amateur Bicycle Championship Race.
1st prize, value £4; 2nd do., £2; 3rd do., £1; 4th do., £10.
GIVEN IN ADDITION TO
A SILVER CHALLENGE CUP, value £10 10s.
Any competitor winning the event three times the Cup becomes his own property.
Prizes given value £7 10s. each time the event is run (if not less than eight compete).
Event Five open to any Amateur resident in Town or County of Leicester.
Entries close Monday, May 30th. To be made to the Manager at the Ground. Entry Forms sent on application.

EXHIBITION OF
BICYCLES, TRICYCLES & ACCESSORIES
ON TUESDAY WEDNESDAY AND THURSDAY,
the 14th, 15th, and 16th June next.
It has been determined to hold a Special Exhibition of Bicycles, Tricycles and Accessories, in spacious premises belonging to the Universities Co-operative Association, at 92, LONG ACRE, W.C. All the leading Manufacturers have expressed their intention of Exhibiting. It is intended to continue the Exhibition as a permanent one, to enable all interested in the cycling world to be in a position to have an extensive selection of machines, with all the latest improvements, under one roof.
Admission will be by Tickets, available for the three days, price One Shilling.
The following leading Amateurs have agreed to act as the Exhibition Committee:
H. L. CORTIS, Wanderers B.C., Amateur Champion.
O. P. FISHER, Captain Cambridge University Bicycle Club.
C. H. F. CHRISTIE, late Captain Dark Blue B.C.
ROBERT T. CORK, Hon. Sec. Bicycle Union.
W. WIGHTMAN WOOD, University College, Oxford.
J. W. BENINGFIELD, Captain Pickwick B.C.
WILLIAM McWILLIAM, Hon. Treasurer Temple B.C.
Further information will be afforded on application to the Secretary, 92, Long Acre, W.C., or to the Hon. Sec., Mr. McWilliam, 28, Balfour Road, Highbury, N.

RACING NEWS.
OPEN EVENTS ALREADY FIXED.
27th May—Bury St. Edmunds' sports.
28th May—Greenfield sports, Lancashire.
28th May—Smallheath Harriers' sports at Aston.
— *June*—Elswick B.C. races (3 open).
2nd June—Dark Blue invitation races at Oxford.
4th June—Preston (first day) sports.
4th June—Otley Athletic Festival, one and three mile handicaps.
6th June—Leighton Buzzard sports, two open events.
6th June—Sports at Stanley Park, Liverpool.
6th June—Burton-on-Trent sports, one mile handicap.
6th June—Preston sports.
6th June—Taunton races.
6th June—Bournemouth B. & T. C. Sports. 1 and 3 miles.
6th June—Pontefract Sports, two miles handicap.
6th June—Plymouth B.C. races at Plymouth.
6th June—Shrewsbury sports, one mile handicap.
7th June—Mansfield C. & F.C. sports.
7th June—Loughborough sports.
8th June—Dudley C. & F. C. sports, one mile handicap.
11th June—Races at West of England Meet at Bristol.

Fig. 4.8. A variety of different types of forthcoming bicycle races was advertised in a prominent journal in 1881. [Source: *The Cyclist*, 25 May 1881]

One of the principal voices of the sport, *The Cyclist*, for example, on 25 May 1881 advertised a total of twelve upcoming race meetings for bicycles (and also tricycles, which were just beginning to be featured in racing), many of them scheduled for the Whitsun Bank Holidays on Monday and Tuesday, 6–7 June (see Fig.4.8). The Sutton Bicycle Club, the Stanley Bicycle Club, the North Kent Bicycle Club, the Lombard Bicycle Club and the London Bicycle Club all advertised bicycle racing, some specifying that the racing would be "Under the Rules of the Bicycle Union, and open to Amateurs as defined by the Bicycle

PREVIOUS WINNERS OF THE UNION CHAMPIONSHIPS.

	Name.	Club.	h. m. sec.	Date.	Place.
1878.					
2 Miles Bicycle	Hon. Ion K. Falconer	C.U.Bi.C.	0 6 29	May 11	Stanford Bridge.
25 Miles Bicycle	A. A. Wier	O.U.Bi.C.	1 27 47 2-5ths	May 11	,, ,,
1879.					
1 Mile Bicycle	H. L. Cortis	Wanderers	0 2 59 1-5th	June 12	,, ,,
5 Miles Bicycle	H. L. Cortis	,,	0 15 27 3-5ths	June 19	,, ,,
25 Miles Bicycle	H. L. Cortis	,,	1 24 4	June 26	,, ,,
50 Miles Bicycle	H. L. Cortis	,,	2 56 1 4-5ths	July 11	,, ,,
1880.					
1 Mile Bicycle	C. E. Liles	L.A.C.	0 2 55 1-5th	June 24	,, ,,
5 Miles Bicycle	H. L. Cortis	Wanderers	0 15 10 3-5ths	June 24	,, ,,
25 Miles Bicycle	H. L. Cortis	,,	1 22 15 2-5ths	July 1	,, ,,
50 Miles Bicycle	H. L. Cortis	,,	2 56 11 2-5ths	July 8	,, ,,
1881					
1 Mile Bicycle	G. Lacy Hillier	Stanley	0 3 11 3-5ths	July 16	Belgrave Grounds, Leicester.
5 Miles Bicycle	G. Lacy Hillier	,,	0 15 39 4-5ths	July 6	Surbiton.
25 Miles Bicycle	G. Lacy Hillier	,,	1 27 43 3-5ths	July 16	Belgrave Grounds, Leicester.
50 Miles Bicycle	G. Lacy Hillier	,,	2 50 50 2-5ths	July 27	Surbiton.
1882.					
1 Mile Bicycle	F. Moore	Warstone	0 2 47 2-5ths	July 8	Aston Lower Grounds, Birmingham.
5 Miles Bicycle	J. S. Whatton	C.U.Bi.C.	0 15 12 4-5ths	July 22	Crystal Palace.
25 Miles Bicycle	F. Moore	Warstone	1 25 8 1-5th	July 8	Aston Lower Grounds, Birmingham.
50 Miles Bicycle	Hon. Ion K. Falconer	C.U.Bi.C.	2 43 58 3-5ths	July 29	Crystal Palace.
5 Miles Tricycle	C. E. Liles	L.A.C.	0 19 39 2-5ths	Oct. 14	,, ,,
1883.					
1 Mile Bicycle	H. W. Gaskell	Ranelagh H.	0 2 55 2-5ths	July 14	,, ,,
5 Miles Bicycle	F. Sutton	Edgbaston H.	0 16 42 2-5ths	July 7	Aston Lower Grounds, Birmingham.
25 Miles Bicycle	C. E. Liles	L.A.C.	1 22 42 3-5ths	Aug. 2	Taunton.
50 Miles Bicycle	H. F. Wilson	Surrey	2 46 26 3-5ths	July 21	Crystal Palace.
1 Mile Tricycle	C. E. Liles	L.A.C.	0 3 18 1-5th	July 7	Aston Lower Grounds Birmingham.
10 Miles Tricycle	C. E. Liles	L.A.C.	0 33 45	July 14	Crystal Palace.
1884.					
1 Mile Bicycle	H. A. Speechly	Chelsea	0 3 30 4-5ths	June 21	Lillie Bridge Grounds.
5 Miles Bicycle	R. Chambers	Speedwell	0 15 36 4-5ths	June 28	Cardiff.
25 Miles Bicycle				July 26	N'castle-on-Tyne.
50 Miles Bicycle	F. R. Fry	Clifton	2 51 16 3-5ths	July 19	Crystal Palace.
1 Mile Tricycle	C. E. Liles	L.A.C.	0 3 29 1-5th	July 12	,, ,,
5 Miles Tricycle	C. E. Liles	L.A.C.	0 17 30 1-5th	July 12	,, ,,
25 Miles Tricycle	C. E. Liles	L.A.C.	1 28 58	June 21	Lillie Bridge Grounds.

Fig. 4.9. An N.C.U. race program from 1884 gave official legitimacy to previous championships by listing them since the foundation of the Bicycle Union in 1878. [Source: N.C.U. program, 26 July 1884, author's collection]

Union." The Belgrave Road Grounds, Leicester, advertised three continuous days of professional and amateur bicycle racing, including the "1 mile professional race for championship belt," a "1 mile Bicycle Race for the Championship of Leicester," as well as a steeplechase, a "Grand Assault at Arms," a "half-hour go-as-you-please," and the "Royal Original Clown Cricketers." The "Sixth Annual West of England Bicycle Race Meet" at Bristol was also advertised, as were the "Athletic Sports" to be held in Liverpool and at Loughborough. The Coventry Independent Order of Odd Fellows were holding "A Grand Fete and Amateur Athletic Sports," which included running, sack racing and hurdles, a bicycle exhibition, and "grand theatrical entertainment," as well as bicycle and tricycle racing, while at Leamington there was to be the "Midland Counties Bicycle Meet and Monster Fete," including "Leonati, the Bicycle Spiral Ascensionist, the Wonder of the Age," and "a balloon ascent by Mr. Adams." The Leicestershire Cricket Ground would be holding its "Annual Amateur Athletic Sports," including cycling and running races, and the Tricycle Association advertised its "Amateur Championship 50 mile Road Ride."[45]

Clearly, although the sport had evolved significantly since the early 1870s, and there was a well-developed and widespread institutional structure by 1881, there were still many similarities with earlier racing in, for example, the integration of amateur bicycle racing into a wider program of athletic, recreational and entertainment events. Perhaps the most conspicuous feature of these 1881 events was the preponderance of amateur racing over professional. Indeed, the promoters at the Belgrave Road Grounds, Leicester were the only organizers advertising professional racing and cash prizes, with "£200 in prizes" in May 1881. This may have been indicative of a decline in the popularity of professional racing as amateur competition increased. Alfred Howard's comment in 1877 that "contrasted with professional, amateur bicycling has not made equal progress in the way of fast or sensational times, although there has been a much greater increase of amateur than of professional riders" tends to support this view.[46] One might also suggest that the growing number of amateur competitors would have increased local interest and spectatorship, and that those same amateur competitors would most likely have been among the spectators eager to watch on the occasions when leading professionals did compete.[47]

A race program from only three years later illustrates how the amateur sport had developed its own championship level of competition by the mid-1880s. In July 1884, the "25 miles Amateur Championship Race Meeting" was held at Gateshead-on-Tyne (near Newcastle, in north-east England) as one of the National Cyclists' Union championship series. It was held under the jurisdiction of the N. C. U.'s local Newcastle center, which appointed a distinguished team of officials, including George Lacy Hillier (judge), Harry Etherington and Henry Sturmey (umpires). There was a total of eight umpires, a timekeeper, a handicapper, a starter, six clerks of the course, and four lap-takers. Fourteen riders competed in the 25-mile bicycle championship. In the program, the results of the N.C.U. amateur cycling championships were listed since 1878, classified according to distance, name of rider, club, time, date, place and category of event, thereby confirming the legitimacy and status of the Championships (see Fig. 4.9). In 1878, there had been

OFFICIALS.

JUDGE:
G. LACY HILLIER (Stanley and N.C.U.—"Tricyclist," –Amateur Bicycle and Tricycle Champion at all distances, 1881.)
Gold Ribbon.

UMPIRES:
MAJOR-GENERAL L. R. CHRISTOPHER (Uxbridge and Dist. and N.C.U.); M. D. RUCKER (London and N.C.U.); J. S. WHATTON (Cambridge and N.C.U.); ROBERT TODD (London and N.C.U.); H. C. WANSBOROUGH (Weston S. Mare and Bristol L.C.N.C.U.); W. TATTERSFIELD (Leamington and S.W.B.C.); J. WESTON BLAND (Speedwell); H. STURMEY, (Coventry C.C.—"Cyclist"); THOS. COX (Speedwell); H. Etherington ("Wheeling"); F. A. BIRD (Speedwell); C. A. PALMER (Dragon C.C.)
Pink Ribbons.

OFFICIAL TIMEKEEPER TO THE N.C.U.:   **ASSISTANT TIMEKEEPER.**
G. PEMBROKE COLEMAN (London & N.C.U.)   E. R. SHIPTON (London & N.C.U.)
Grey Ribbons.

STARTER: **HANDICAPPER:**
J. M. HUBBARD (B.A.C.)   W. W. ALEXANDER, (N.C.U.—"Athletic Star.")
Purple Ribbon.   Brown Ribbon.

TELEGRAPH STEWARDS:
F. HOWARD WARNER (Redditch and Dist. C.C.); E. G. WARDEN (Islington W.C.C.); G. A. SHREAD (Handsworth C.C.); G. HOGG (Rugby C.C.)
Navy Blue Ribbons.

STARTERS' STEWARDS:
W. E. ADLARD (N.W.B.C.); H. R. FRANKLIN (Forward B.C.); W. B. BROWN (N.W.B.C.); H. MARSON (Edgbaston C.C.)
Pale Blue Ribbons.

COMPETITOR'S STEWARDS:
J. D. WHITTLES (Leek C.C.); G. W. DAWES (S.B.C.); C. LAMSDALE (Heathfield T.C.); H. M. LORD (Wolverhampton C.C.)
Olive Green Ribbon.

PROGRAMME STEWARDS:
T. S. MAYES (Birchfield B.C.); E. C. SKINNER (Warstone B.C.)
Dark Green Ribbons.

LAP TAKERS:
ALGERNON PROUT (Hornsey and N.C.U.); J. PEARCE DERRINGTON (N.W.B.C.); A. J. LEESON (B.B.C.); H. J. LEAKE (Cheylesmore C.C.); C. DAVIS (Leamington C.C.); W. BROOKE CLARKE (Manchester Southern C.C. and Manchester L.C. N.C.U.); LAWRENCE FLETCHER (Anfield B.C. and Liverpool L.C. N.C.U.); J. MAIDEN (Burslem C.C.)
Light Green Ribbon.

CLERKS OF THE COURSE:
W. J. JENKS (Wolverhampton C.C.); J. D. PRIOR (Birmingham T.C.); F. W. WARWICK (B.B.C.); H. H. FOX (R.M.B. & T.C.); F. C. MOSEDALE (Dragon C.C.); E. DEAKIN (Edgbaston F.C.); J. SIMMS (Forward B.C.), A. H. WOODWARD (Centaur C.C.)
Orange Ribbons.

ENCLOSURE STEWARDS:
J. E. SPINK (Adderley B. & T.C.); J. W. ROBERTS (Dudley C.C.); REV. RANKEN (Malvern C.C.); MARTINEAU (Solihull); A. CHAPMAN (South Suburban); E. EVANS (Small Heath C.C.); W. T. EADES (Centaur C.C.); H. MORLEY (Birmingham T.C.); H T. BROUGH (B.B.C.); R. PRICE TAYLOR (Handsworth B.C.); W. T. COOK (Leek C.C.); C. H. JOLLY (Wolverhampton T.C.); J. WILSON (Centaur C.C.); E. H. ELKINGTON (Leamington C.C.)
Maize Ribbons

Fig. 4.10. A list from an N.C.U. championship event in Birmingham in 1885 shows the large number of officials considered necessary to legitimize it. [Source: race program from 13 June 1885, author's collection]

only two categories of N.C.U. championship events (2-mile and 25-mile bicycle), but by 1884, there were seven categories listed (1-mile, 5-mile, 25-mile and 50-mile bicycle, 1-mile, 5-mile and 25-mile tricycle). The cover of this program included an advertisement for Humber bicycles, although nearly all of the riders mentioned there were amateurs and were not supposed to endorse bicycles made by a specific manufacturer.[48] (see Fig. 4.11)

A year later, a program for national championship races in Birmingham in June printed an even more elaborate list illustrating the structure of National Cyclists' Union officials for the event (see Fig. 4.10).[49] In an undated photograph from the same period, officials can be seen gathered to the right of the competitors at the start of a race. Bicycle racing

NATIONAL CYCLISTS' UNION.

25 MILES AMATEUR
CHAMPIONSHIP RACE MEETING,
North Durham Track, Gateshead-on-Tyne,
SATURDAY, JULY 26, 1884.

Official Programme, 2d.

THE BICYCLE OF THE SEASON.

THE HUMBER, as ridden by R. H. ENGLISH, 5 and 10 miles Amateur Champion of the North.
THE HUMBER, as ridden by E. J. WILKINSON.
THE HUMBER, as ridden by D. DODDS.
THE HUMBER, as ridden by F. WOOD, Champion of the World.
THE HUMBER, as ridden by T. BATTENSBY, Ex-Champion of the World.
AND MOST OF OUR NOTED RIDERS.

SOLE AGENTS FOR HUMBER BICYCLES AND TRICYCLES,
W. NEWTON & Co.,
165, Westgate Road, Newcastle-upon-Tyne, and Prudhoe Street, North Shields.

had thus quickly become a structured, codified, bureaucratized, and systematized sport. The development of bicycle racing is an excellent example of how sport in general evolved during the period—an evolution typified by an increase in bureaucratic and organizational control.

Where as amateur racing was thus increasingly controlled by the National Cyclists' Union and its affiliated clubs in the 1880s, professional racing remained largely outside its jurisdiction (except when amateur versus professional events were specifically sanctioned by the N.C.U.). Professional racing depended upon the available pool of talent, the energy of promoters, and the varying regional enthusiasm of local populations for novel and dramatic sporting events

Above: Fig. 4.11. The cover of the same program from 1884 advertises Humber bicycles, although most of the riders named were amateurs. [Source: N.C.U. program, author's collection] *Below:* Fig. 4.12. Track officials can be seen gathered beside competitors in this undated photograph, probably at the start of an N.C.U. championship event from 1885 or 1886. G.L. Hillier in white, probably H.O. Duncan in black with black bowler, to his right. [Source: author's collection]

featuring "star" performers. Contracts were drawn up and purses held by trusted outsiders often associated with the sporting press.

The dominance of Wolverhampton in the early professional sport in England led to the emergence of a riders' code referred to as "the Wolverhampton rules" which governed conduct during competition and attempted to ensure fair play on the track. These rules stipulated, for instance, that: "Riders must pass each other on the outside, and be a clear length of the bicycle in front before taking the inside; and the inside man must allow room for his competitor to pass." In an attempt to keep the racing honest, the rules also included the stipulation that: "If the judge is convinced that two riders arrange for the winner to divide any prize, they shall be disqualified, and the prize given for a race at the next meeting."[50]

Professional racing was concentrated primarily in industrial, heavily working-class urban areas such as London, Wolverhampton, Sheffield, Leicester and Newcastle, although leading riders certainly travelled outside their home bases to compete. Further, the popularity of the professional sport varied from place to place. An American account from 1884 maintained, though not entirely accurately, that "professional racing ... is entirely confined to the Leicester and Newcastle districts, amateurism holding sole sway elsewhere."[51] Another account spoke of a proposed tournament in North Shields, near Newcastle, a town which was "situated in the midst of a racing community. We have within six or eight miles four tracks and two are in the course of construction. The public of our district have made cycling their chief sport."[52] The question arises, of course, as to whether this local writer was accurate at the time in claiming that cycling exceeded other sports (soccer or boxing, for example) in popularity and importance, and it is worth examining Newcastle and its local cycling champion, George Waller, to determine the significance of professional cycling there.

Fig. 4.13. Fred Wood, a world champion professional cyclist, wearing his championship belt in 1879. [Source: Lorne Shields collection, Toronto, Canada]

4. Two professionals: George Waller (c. 1855–1900) and H.O. Duncan (1862–1945)

George Waller (c. 1855–1900) was one of the most experienced and best-known of the small group of leading professional high-wheel cyclists in the late 1870s and 1880s.[53] His obituary said that "it was as a cyclist that he made his name famous" and that "as an athlete … he astonished all the world by his wonderful endurance."[54] Waller was apprenticed as a stone mason and had worked as a diver, "repairing the Tyne docks under water,"[55] but was competing in Wolverhampton as early as 1876. At a very young age he worked as a professional for the Coventry manufacturers, Hill-man, Herbert and Cooper, whose bicycles he used in competition and thus advertised for the company.[56]

In April/May 1879, Waller won Etherington's Six Day race at the Agricultural Hall, London, with a total of 1,172 miles, and in September of the same year he exceeded that distance in the "Long Distance Championship of the World," with a ride of 1,404 miles, a previously unimaginable distance for a bicycle rider, beating the French rider Charles Terront by only 12 miles. This sensational record-breaking endurance ride was widely reported in the press, even in the United States. Returning to Newcastle, "he made quite a triumphal procession. At many of the railway stations on the route, crowds of people awaited the arrival of the train and cheered him. The Central Station in Newcastle was crowded by thousands of people."[57] In short, Waller found that the London race had made him a local hero.

After this athletic and "show business" success, which unexpectedly thrust the 24-year-old into the limelight, Waller decided to invest in bicycle racing in the north of England, competing in and promoting cycling events. He acquired land to build the Bicycle Ground in Byker, Newcastle, where he promoted racing, and at the same time bought a large tent 200 yards long (similar to and probably inspired by the one used by Etherington on his American tour) within which he could promote racing using a temporary wooden track. He toured the north of England with this installation, producing a show which was a combination of athletic contests and a carnival or circus, with slow and trick riding, a brass band and other attractions. Other "star" riders, John Keen, H.O. Duncan, William Cann and Tom Battensby, were hired to appear. After the Bicycle Ground failed and the cycling "circus" was destroyed in a ferocious storm, Waller became a successful builder before suffering a fatal head injury in a pony-trap accident at the age of 45.

Waller's career ambitions in the world of cycling, like those of Harry Etherington and other young men who were seized with enthusiasm for the bicycle at a young age, were inspired by the novel recreational and business opportunities that the new sport presented. With the money he earned during his career, Waller appears to have speculated by taking the professional sport into the local community.[58]

* * *

H.O. Duncan (1862–1945). The class and social distinctions between "gentleman" amateurs and the predominantly working-class professionals in Britain is described further in H.O. Duncan's autobiographical account, *The World on Wheels*, which also contains many observations on the differences between the sport in England and France.[59] Following his racing career in Britain and France, which lasted from about 1880 to 1887, Duncan became the Paris agent for the Humber Company (1887–92) and later represented the Rudge Company there. He became one of the most important and innovative promoters and managers of continental bicycle racing, a role he was able to fulfill because of his early experiences in professional racing, and he gained international fame managing French record-breaker, Charles Terront. Making use of his own early experience in bicycle racing, he pioneered the practice of creating and promoting record-breaking "sensations" for commercial publicity purposes.

Herbert Osbaldeston Duncan (1862–1945) came from an established Leicestershire family, and his grandfather was "owner of the best stable of race-horses in England."[60] According to his own account, Duncan did not need to race bicycles to earn his living, and in this respect, and in his upper-class background, he was definitely not a typical professional cyclist of the era. He began

Fig. 4.14. H.O. Duncan, a leading international professional high-wheel champion, who moved to France to escape British class attitudes. [Source: John L. Weiss collection]

his career as an amateur in England, became a professional in 1880, and was one of the first English cyclists to race in France. He "gave up all thought of a business career to gain sporting laurels in England, France, Italy, Germany and Austria."[61] His most successful years as a competitor were from 1884 to 1886. He was the professional "world champion" in the 50-mile race in 1885 and 1886, and a runner-up in various other short-distance championships in 1885 and 1886.[62]

Duncan's arrival among the professionals in 1880, he remembered, "created quite a sensation in England. It was the first time that a young man of a family so honorably known had joined this class of racer." He was:

> perfectly disgusted at being obliged to mix with the "pro element" of those days. I did not realize what it really meant, whether it was the black atmosphere of Wolverhampton, the horrible dressing rooms or the men who were taking part in the handicap. Something strange had entered into this new sporting

life for me and I tried to ascribe it to the fact that the spectators at Wolverhampton were different from those I had appeared before at Windsor or in London. I realized that the professional racing bicyclists were a class of men difficult to mix with and, as I have already hinted, the dressing rooms were filthy, barren and unfit for use. The first thing I did at Wolverhampton was to ask the proprietor of the grounds for a suitable room in his hotel in which to dress for the various heats during the three days of the mile handicap.[63]

Duncan described "a striking example of how professionals were pictured in the minds of everybody in England in the early days," an incident which "proved that the English professionals were not held in very high esteem." He and French champion Baron Frédéric de Civry (who was living in England at the time) were scheduled to compete on "a very excellent gravel-laid bicycle track in the Sale Botanical Gardens near Manchester." They were offered accommodations at a hotel owned by the promoter, who, when they arrived at the hotel, appeared flustered and invited them into the bar to wait while their rooms were prepared. Later, over a glass of wine, the promoter "confessed his astonishment at our appearance on our arrival. 'I expected to see two strongly-built men with scarves around their necks—in fact, two pros of the type I am accustomed to meeting,' he said.… Arrangements had been made for two quite ordinary rooms, but when he found himself in the presence of two 'welldressed' men, he had given instructions that we should be given the choicest rooms in the hotel."

Duncan wrote that he was so affected by his social alienation from the English professional scene that he "decided not to race again as a professional in England, and during the whole of 1881, I refused to race anywhere in the country." Having inherited a fortune from his family at the age of twenty-one, he "felt completely independent of this professional stigma which had practically poisoned my sporting career," and preferred to live and compete in France from then on.

Duncan's contact with what he considered the more rational, "open" French sporting scene confirmed his dislike of its class-bound British professional equivalent. In France he "found there was practically no such division between amateurs and professionals and the regulations only made a distinction between juniors and seniors. Cash and objets d'art, medals etc were offered as prizes by the bicycle clubs who organized the races." He concluded that:

> the cash prize system and the payment of expenses in an open honest manner is the real solution of the progress of international sport.… Because a few gentlemen desire to retain their status purely as amateurs, the National Cyclists' Union has drawn up drastic regulations to govern these few towards maintaining their select seclusion to the detriment of the whole sport in general and the "professionals" in particular.… The world "professional" should be entirely discarded and abolished forever and some suitable designation invented to cover all other racing cyclists under a proper classification.[64]

Duncan's atypical position with regard to the English cycling scene emphasizes the deeply-rooted class distinctions that characterized it, in particular its tendency to encourage, exalt and codify amateurism as a superior, desirable kind of athletic activity and to look down upon professionalism. Because Duncan was not a stereotypical professional, he found the stratified British sport hard to accept. His rejection of the amateur/professional dichotomy, his espousal of cash prizes in sport and his innovative approach towards the promotion of cycling, which is discussed later, gave him an unusual status and was indicative of an attitude that anticipated the much later "open" structure of sport organization.

5. Competition in France[65]: the Tendency towards an "Open" Sport

In spite of its early prominence in velocipede development, the French industry and sport was severely disrupted by the Franco-Prussian War of 1870–71. Although the duration and geographical extent of this disruption is difficult to determine, it appears to have been most severe in Paris and in the industrial north-east, but had less of an impact in the provinces, particularly in the Bordeaux area and in the south-east. The non-essential young bicycle industry was interrupted by the manufacturing needs of the war in France, and everyday social and recreational activities were limited in the war zones.

Most contemporary British accounts of cycling in the 1870s asserted the superiority of the English bicycle industry and the dominance of British athletes, but this assumption was, of course, challenged by the French, creating a long-standing sporting rivalry. One of the leading "French" competitors, James Moore, who won important races in France and was featured in unofficial "world championships" (using technologically advanced bicycles by French maker Meyer and Paris-based English maker Charles Garrard), was in fact an English expatriot based in Paris. Between 1870 and 1877 Moore won four of these "championships" (1870, 1874, 1875 and 1877).[66]

In 1874, following races for a "championship cup" between French and English riders in Wolverhampton, where James Moore, John Keen and E. Shelton won the first three places, *Le Vélocipède Illustré* asked: "For how much longer will the English riders go on outwitting the French on the bicycle? Who will come forward to beat these racers from the other side of the Channel?"[67] In 1878, an editorial in the *Bicycle Journal* explained that "the superiority of English mechanical arts and appliances" and "the practical nature of the English character" was responsible for "the spread of their pastime." In France, cycling "seems to live a mere lingering existence; probably it was nipped in the bud by the Franco-German war; the absence too of a love of out-door exercise has doubtless tended to keep the sport at a low ebb in spite of the splendid climate."[68]

While this kind of chauvinism (which was expressed in editorials on either side of the Channel) might now have influence on our objective evaluation of the importance of sport in each country, it is clear that whereas there was indeed a disruption of opportunities for recreation in France, the enthusiasm for cycling in England did not flag in the 1870s, and that an experienced English champion, such as John Keen, was always very hard to beat. As far as machines were concerned, English bicycles were very much in demand in France and were sold through agents in Paris.[69]

In the late 1870s and early 1880s, clubs were formed in Paris and in French provincial cities. There was plenty of racing activity on both road and track, and a lively specialist press was created. According to H.O. Duncan's account of the period, however, there were few tracks built specifically for cycling in France, and races were held "upon the public promenades, gardens or military grounds. A long public walk or promenade was staked off with wooden railings and gaily decorated with national flags, coloured-paper lamps, ribbons and flowers." We have already seen that at least in one location—Bordeaux—very modern means were used to stage bicycle races, including the use of electric lights for night-time meetings. Race meetings were organized by the local bicycle club, civic dignitaries were involved, and the races "formed part of the annual fêtes subscribed to by the leading trades people and the town itself and were held with luxurious surroundings. Many of the bicycle clubs throughout the country were exceedingly chic, rich and prosperous," particularly the leading Paris clubs, such as the Vélo-Sport de Paris.[70] In this sense, as outlined by Duncan, French bicycle racing appears to have developed differently from the British sport, with athletic cycling events occurring within local civic or religious (feast day) celebrations, rather than in the wider context of other athletic events.[71]

The sport of cycling seems to have had a lesser impact in France in this early period than it did in England. Fewer people participated in the sport, and it was slower to gain in popularity. One French source, from 1892, remarked that "it is only in the last ten years that the cycling movement has really taken off ... we are well behind our neighbours, the English, in this respect."[72] The Union Vélocipédique Parisienne was founded in 1876 and the French governing body, the Union Vélocipédique de France (U.V.F.), in 1881. The U.V.F. began with nine clubs as members and by 1892 had grown to 60 member clubs, then in a spurt of growth to 179 member clubs and about 2,500 individual members by 1893.[73] A prominent publication from 1891 lists 270 French cycling clubs, with 18 in Paris, 5 in Rouen and Toulouse, 4 in Grenoble and Marseille and 3 in Bordeaux—few towns had more than one or two clubs.[74] Another, from 1892, agreed, listing 260 clubs in all with 15 in Paris. That same source, however, emphasized that England had more than 1,000 cycling clubs, with more than 280 in London alone.[75]

In the late 1870s, several outstanding French cyclists emerged who became contenders in fiercely contested professional "world championship" competitions between England and France. These included James Moore, Laumaillé, Camille Thuillet, Frédéric de Civry, Paul Médinger, H.O. Duncan, Charles Terront and Jules Dubois. These professionals trav-

Fig. 4.15. An organized "Meet" of club cyclists and tricyclists at Dunster Castle, near Minehead, Somerset, the home of the Luttrells (presumably family at center). These "Meets" occurred in the late 1870s and early 1880s. [Source: author's collection]

elled widely within Europe to race, including to Britain, France, Italy, Austria and Germany. Following a racing tour in Germany and Austria in 1887 (encouraged by T.H.S. Walker, the English editor of the leading German cycling paper, *Der Radfahrer*), Duncan stayed in Berlin for three months to train amateur members of Berlin cycling clubs.[76]

In spite of the expansion of the professional sport, however, and the energetic racing activity within France, French and British cyclists were prevented from participating as equals in international amateur competitions due to the differing structures of competition in the two countries. British amateurs could not race in France without threatening their amateur status, and French riders (who were categorized only as "seniors" and juniors," all of whom could win cash prizes) could race in Britain only as "professionals." According to a correspondent who wrote to *Wheeling* in 1892, "the U. V. F. has thrown overboard all legislation of every kind upon the amateur question.... For years past the amateur-professional difficulty has been the burning question in French cycling circles, never settled, always temporized with, until now amateurs and professionals are all one in a state of utter chaos."[77] The irony of the situation, though, was that the best French riders were as good as the English professionals, where as many of the English "amateurs" ("makers" amateurs") were in fact as "professional" as the French. Only bureaucratic definitions kept them from competing against each other.

6. British "Meets," the Springfield Tournaments and the Growth of International Competition

From the mid–1870s on, a significant feature of British cycling were annual "Meets," which were attended by club members and other enthusiasts, and were an organized expression of the solidarity of cycling as an athletic and recreational activity. The first of these was held at Hampton Court, near London, in April 1874, when "some fifty well-mounted bicyclists rode in procession ... amidst the applause of several hundred spectators."[78] The event attracted more and more participants and became increasingly important. In 1876, 289 riders from 16 clubs, as well as about a hundred cyclists "not enrolled in any club," attended. "Vast crowds of people assembled to witness the spectacle, which was imposing in point of numbers and unparalleled in its novelty." Further "Meets" were held that year at Leamington, Bristol and Crystal Palace, London.[79]

The following year at Hampton Court, 41 London clubs and 20 provincial clubs totaling 1,028 riders gathered with about 200 "unattached" riders, while in 1879, 73 London clubs and 23 provincial clubs gathered for a procession "which pleased an immense concourse of orderly and well-managed spectators."[80] From 1877 to 1880, similar "Meets" were held in Scotland, in Edinburgh, Glasgow, and elsewhere.[81] The 1880 Hampton Court event attracted a total of 100 London clubs and 37 "country" clubs, with 49 participants from the Temple Bicycle Club (secretary, Harry Etherington) and a total of 1,745 riders taking part in the procession.[82] Charles Spencer reported that in 1882, "no less than 2,500 defiled before an assembly so numerous that it was impossible even to form an approximate estimate of their number,"—132 London clubs and 53 provincial clubs were represented.[83]

Fig. 4.16. Many of the pioneers of British cycling and founding members of the Cyclists' Touring Club assembled at the "Meets" in the late 1870s. [Source: Lorne Shields collection, Toronto, Canada]

Another well-attended annual "Meet" was held at Harrogate, Yorkshire from 1877 onwards, organized by the Bradford Cycling Club, where parades, races and games were held over a period of three or four days at a temporary cycling camp and cyclists slept in tents, like Boy Scouts. At these events, the sport of cycling drew people away from their everyday concerns, and participants and spectators were united in a celebration of health, fitness and club-based good fellowship, as well as a shared enthusiasm for the technological modernity of the bicycle. The events were also demonstrations of group solidarity in sport. Riders were encouraged to take pride in representing their clubs by wearing uniforms and processions were choreographed to have an impressive effect upon the spectators. At a "Meet of Bicyclists and Tricyclists" held in connection with the Leicester Bicycle and Athletic Sports in June 1884, the committee presented a silver bugle "to the club most largely represented and presenting the neatest turn-out."[84]

The idea of a "meet," or "camp," a celebration of riding, competition, display and socializing rooted in club life, was a British practice that was soon incorporated into the American sport. "Among all the outdoor sports, which, from their nature, call for a certain amount of communion among their followers, perhaps the one which appeals most to the spirit of good fellowship, developing generally into close friendship, is cycling," wrote a contributor to *Outing* in 1884.[85] From 1880 onwards, the League of American Wheelmen held an annual

Fig. 4.17. British multi-club "Meets" in the early 1880s resembled a Boy Scout camp, accompanied by serious experimentation with technology. [Source: Lorne Shields collection, Toronto, Canada]

"Meet" where racing and social events were combined in a week of activity.[86] These L.A.W. events and also the Springfield Tournaments, organized by the Springfield Bicycle Club at Hampden Park, Springfield, Massachusetts beginning in 1882, epitomized the growing energy of American high-wheel bicycle racing. The Springfield Tournaments showcased the best United States and British riders (enabling their times to be compared) and became the most important annual events where the highest level of international competition could be witnessed. Springfield was also the place where many American and world records were set between 1883 and 1886.

An editorial in *The Wheel* called the first Springfield Tournament in September 1882 "the largest and most successful bicycle race meeting that this country has ever seen," and congratulated the Springfield Bicycle Club for "undertaking such an enormous scheme, that will naturally advance the growing cause of bicycling."[87] At the Tournament, George Hendee, a member of the Springfield Bicycle Club, broke the American ½-mile record. The 16-year-old Hendee was "an early-to-bed and early-to-rise young man, temperate in habits, neither smoking, chewing nor drinking. He was always foremost in athletic sports, and was one of the leaders of Springfield high school in long and high jumping."[88]

The 1883 Tournament, another 3-day affair, included both amateur and professional events, and was advertised as "The Monarch of all, the Grandest, Greatest and most glorious Bicycle Camp, Meet and Tournament." A $1,500 gold cup (the Columbia Bicycle Prize Cup)

for the 20-mile amateur championship of the United States was awarded by the Pope Manufacturing Co., but "it will probably not be so offensive to amateurs, or so conspicuous a piece of advertising, as to deter any wheelman from desiring to possess it, or any amateur racing man from competing for it."[89] In the 10-mile event, "ten of the foremost riders of the day were entered," making it "without doubt the most exciting race ever witnessed."[90] The ninth mile was decisive; "the crowd saw that the real struggle had begun, and every man, woman, and child got up and yelled for all they were worth" as Hendee "set a fast pace, and came to the finish

Left: Fig. 4.18. George Hendee, the first amateur, League of American Wheelmen, champion of the United States. [Source: John L. Weiss collection] *Below*: Fig. 4.19. The Springfield Tournament, held Sept. 1883, was hailed as "the greatest sporting event of the year." [Source: poster, John L. Weiss collection]

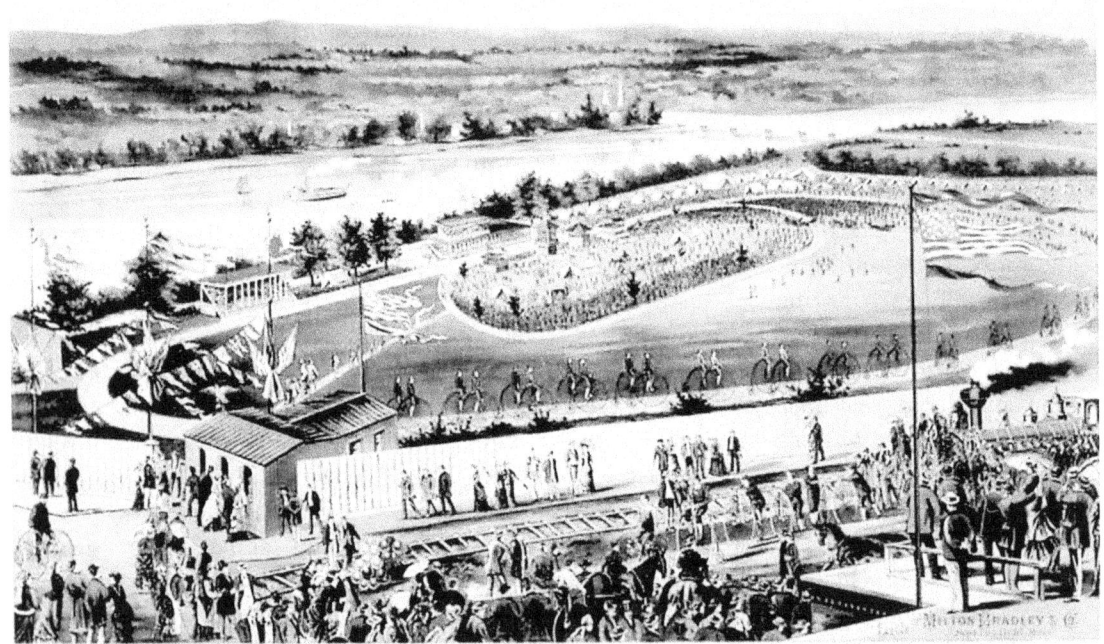

ten yards in front of the plucky young Englishman, "Doodle" Robinson." There was great excitement: "Hats, canes, and parasols flew up in the grand stand; old and young men jumped up and down, shook hands, hurrahed and cheered with all their lungs. Hendee, who bore his honors most becomingly, was carried off by his friends. Prize, a $300 gold medal."

By the end of 1883, Hendee had won 28 first prizes and 3 second prizes, worth $2,600, held several world records, and was "the acknowledged pet and pride of Springfield" and one of the best-known cyclists in America.[91] The 1883 Springfield meet was "distinctly a triumph of American cycling," said *Bicycling World*, which "proved that we are able to promote and carry out in this country a race meeting which will vie with any ever held in the older countries."[92]

The 3rd Springfield Tournament, a 4-day event in 1884, was ambitiously advertised: "The Springfield Bicycle Club will spare neither pains nor expense to make this the Great Cycling Event of the World for 1884." $8,000 in prizes were offered and $20,000 spent for the promotion. The Club boosted the event: 50,000 people, it was claimed, had attended the 1883 Tournament, and even more would attend "the greatest sporting event of the year."[93] Professional riders were invited to compete for substantial cash prizes in both 1883 and 1884, and the amateurs were rewarded with bicycle hardware and huge, elaborately decorated cups. "The use of the cup as a prize for victors in contests of skill and strength dates back to the old Olympic games in Greece," explained *The Springfield Wheelmen's Gazette*:

> In the early Olympiads, the prizes were simply laurel wreaths, and the winners returning from the games were welcomed as greater heroes than even warlike conquerors. In later years, after the Greeks had acquired from conquered nations great stores of the precious metals, elaborate articles of gold and silver took the place of the laurel wreath. These trophies were most often in the form of exquisite design and delicate workmanship, and ever since the cup has been an approved reward in all athletic contests.[94]

This 1884 Springfield Tournament was a huge athletic event, and the "throng" that gathered was "cosmopolitan, with wheelmen present from all over the United States, Canada and England," including professionals Richard Howell (Manchester) and Robert James (Birmingham), and amateurs Sanders Sellers (Preston), R. Chambers (Birmingham), G.H. Illston (Birmingham) and H.W. Gaskell (Birmingham), and "they came to ride, not to disgust people with swaggering remarks, as some of the Britons did last year."[95] On Thursday, 18 September, approximately 15,000 people attended the event. Total attendance for the four-day event was 40,000, earning the Springfield Bicycle Club $7,000.

The 21-year-old Sellers, who had just set a new 1-mile world record of 2m 39s at Hartford, broke several other world records at Springfield and won every race in which he started, including a win over the reigning American short-distance champion, George Hendee. This was described as "the smashing of a local idol, a catastrophe which the worshippers seemed to take more to heart than the idol did." For his efforts in America, Sellers won "a $100 dollar diamond stud, a $100 Colt shot-gun, the Springfield club cup, a silver tea-service, a $50 marble clock, a pottery umbrella-rack and a $100 cup," while Richard Howell, a professional from Manchester, won $740 and a gold watch.[96]

The *Springfield Wheelmen's Gazette* reported that at the event, all track records from ¼-mile to 10 miles were broken, as were eight world records. The paper compiled "a very complete and perfect report of the meeting.... The timing is accurate, two men timing the first man, and one each the second and the third.... The races were run on the new half-mile track, which is pronounced by racing men to be the most perfect track in the world."[97] Praise for the event was hyperbolic; it was:

> undoubtedly the most notable occasion of the sort yet held in the world. The number, fame, and skill of the contestants, the excellence of the track, the completeness of the arrangements, the magnitude and character of the crowds witnessing the sport, and the results of the races, combine to make the occasion unique and memorable.[98]

There was rivalry among clubs in the promotion of prominent American events. In September 1884, the New Haven Bicycle Club sponsored a tournament at Hamilton Park, Connecticut: "The New Haven Club is noted for its world-wide hospitality and the generous manner in which it entertains its guests.... Racing men will find Hamilton Park to be one of the fastest half-mile tracks in the U.S."[99] Earlier in the season, there were major tournaments at Pittsfield (Mass.), Cleveland (Ohio), Hartford (Conn.), Albany (N.Y.), a Pennsylvania L.A.W. division meet at Philadelphia and Germantown, and then the Springfield and New Haven Tournaments. But Springfield, heavily promoted, was the leading American cycling event, which "was regarded in England as a matter of international importance.... Springfield is known where it never was known before for any reason, as the great cycling center of America.... In matters pertaining to the wheel, Springfield undoubtedly leads the world."[100]

The 1885 Springfield Tournament marked an increase in competition between Britain and the United States. Comparative records of British and American cyclists' times were published in cycling journals on both sides of the Atlantic, and the September event was advertised as "the one and only Great International Meeting for the Year," indicating the organizers' desire to promote a world-class event.[101] The Springfield Bicycle Club invited "all the riders in the world, professional and amateur, to visit Springfield and contest in friendly rivalry for supremacy and honor." The track had been improved and was expected to be "at

Fig. 4.20. The "Fifth Grand International Tournament" of the Springfield bicycle Club, 14–17 Sept. 1886, advertised its 1-mile race as the "Bicycle Championship of the World." [Source: *The L.A.W. Bulletin*, 6 Aug. 1886]

least 4 seconds faster, so that it will be possible for our racing men to go below 2m 35s for the mile," while improvements in management, "and particularly in the matter of timing," had been made.[102]

The British "invasion" of 1885, to compete at the Hartford and Springfield Tournaments, was led by Harry Etherington, cycling promoter and editor of *Wheeling*. Fourteen championship-level amateur and professional riders (including English title-holders Richard Howell and Fred Wood) crossed the Atlantic.[103] All the amateur and professional American and world records were broken, suggesting that up to that time, "most of our races have been simply a procession of wheelmen riding at a fair pace."[104] Most dramatic was William A. Rowe's lowering of the amateur 1-mile world record to 2m 35⅖s, as well as his breaking the 3-and 20-mile records, feats which "stamped him without a doubt the fastest amateur bicycle rider in the world today.... To the credit of America, it can be said that he is an American and rides an American (Columbia) wheel."[105]

Fig. 4.21. George Lacy Hillier, editor of *The Cyclist* in the 1880s, was N.C.U. high-wheel champion at all distances in 1881. [Source: *The Cyclist Annual and Yearbook*, 1893]

In England, *The Cyclist* published an article written by Lacy Hillier ("A Burning Question—The Records! What Are They Worth?") which publicly questioned the accuracy of the world-record times achieved at Springfield, accusing American timekeepers of incompetence and their watches of inaccuracy, and suggesting that it was in the interests of the Springfield Bicycle Club, at their "big business meeting," to fabricate the fast speeds and that Harry Etherington was in some way complicit.[106] The article suggested that the fast times tended to favor the American competitors (even though British riders had won many of the prizes), and that American officials were dishonest in their measuring, timing and judging. The American press was incensed. "Who is Mr. Hillier that he sets himself up as the great and only infallible cycler of this earthly planet, the god to whom all cyclists in America must bow in reverence?" asked Henry Ducker, editor of the *Springfield Wheelmen's Gazette*. *Cycling Times* felt "considerable disgust at the manner in which some of the English cycling papers have expressed themselves."[107]

What annoyed Americans most about Hillier's suspicions and accusations was "the aspersion upon the honor of the wheelmen of America and particularly the L.A.W.... It is for that body to judge whether the times made at Springfield are correct or not ... to doubt them is uncourteous and insulting in the extreme and unworthy of a member of the British press." The year 1885 had also been marked by the well-publicized completion of Thomas Stevens' journey by bicycle across America.[108] The *Springfield Wheelmen's Gazette* was proud to editorialize that "as the year 1885 is about to close, America holds all the important records ... all accomplished by the energy, enthusiasm, and enterprise that are born of the American people, and are found in an equal degree nowhere else on the face of our globe."[109]

Fig. 4.22. George Lacy Hillier, controversial editor of *The Cyclist*, caused an international dispute by publicly questioning the accuracy of American timing at the Springfield Tournament of 1885. [Source: *The Cyclist Annual and Yearbook*, 1893]

National aspirations and rivalries, and the associated jingoistic journalistic posturing, were thus carried into the public arena through the medium of athletic competition. Such expressions of chauvinistic athletic pride were expressed from both sides of the Atlantic within the new sport of bicycle racing. The Americans were seriously challenging the British cyclists for the first time in a series of well-organized, annual international meetings. The fast times at Springfield were the result of a splendid track and heated competition among well-trained athletes. "Our American racing men are only just beginning to find out what they are capable of doing on the bicycle when thoroughly trained and carefully fitted for contests of speed and endurance. So far the Englishmen have beaten them at the shorter distances, but Yankee muscle and pluck are not going to be kept in the background for any length of time," said the *Mirror of American Sports*.[110]

Amid the international controversy over fast times, after spending the summer in Springfield, William Rowe was welcomed home to Lynn, Mass., where "the platform at the depot was packed with humanity as the train approached," and thousands of people had gathered to greet him in Central Square.[111] The contested Springfield times were allowed to stand, and American manufacturers, particularly the Pope Manufacturing Co., advertised their victories in the cycling press.

The unprecedented success of the Springfield Tournaments was attributed largely to the entrepreneurial skill and energy of Henry E. Ducker, one of the original members of the Springfield Bicycle Club, president of the club from 1882 to 1887, and founder of the *Springfield Wheelmen's Gazette*: "In his own town he has raised an obscure club to a position

Left: **Fig. 4.23. W.A. Rhodes.** *Right:* **Fig. 4.24. W.F. Knapp. [Source, both photographs: John L. Weiss collection]**

of such prominence as to be almost without a rival in the whole country." Ducker spent over $60,000 promoting bicycle racing during his presidency, and made a profit for his club. In 1883, Ducker "raised the Springfield people to such a pitch of enthusiasm that, on the second day of the tournament, all the banks and principal manufactures, many of the stores, and even the public schools, were closed." Ducker understood the importance of efficient promotion, financing and organization:

> Mr. Ducker is essentially an originator. Whatever tends to make a successful race meeting when traced back, nine times out of ten, will be found to have its impetus from him. The arranging of programs, track building, timing, scoring, novelty races, all bear his stamp.
> Everybody concedes that the Springfield tournaments were models; everything was managed with clockwork precision, and rarely was there a hitch in the program.[112]

In 1886, Ducker ambitiously proposed that the next Springfield Tournament be considered a "recognized championship of the world," which would "establish beyond dispute who is entitled to the championship of the world, believing that these contests ... will prove a means of introducing a friendship among wheelmen unknown to any other sport." Early that year, Ducker wrote to Abbott Bassett, Chairman of the Racing Board of the League of American Wheelmen, promising that:

Fig. 4.25. H.G. Crocker. This is one of a series of portraits of American high-wheel racers, illustrating their fitness and muscular power. Fig. 4.26. James Frederick Dingley. [Source, both photographs: John L. Weiss collection]

> the Springfield Bicycle Club will do all in its power to assist the N.C.U. and the L.A.W. in uniting upon a plan to establish a recognized championship race of the world. The Springfield Bicycle Club hereby extends to the legislative bodies of the world a cordial invitation to send representatives to the fifth annual meeting of the club to be holden at Springfield, Mass ... in the month of September 1886, and there to enter into a friendly competition for the championship of the world on such conditions as may be mutually agreed upon.[113]

Riders were invited from other countries, and their expenses in the United States were paid by the promoters. At the 1886 Springfield Tournament, the races were advertised as "World Championships," although the lack of a world governing body prevented formal recognition of the title, and there was always the considerable problem of enticing top riders to cross the Atlantic. There was also the persistent issue of defining "amateurism." A new category, "promateur," was introduced for "maker's amateurs," into which stars such as Hendee and Rowe could be put, and bicycle manufacturers continued to put pressure on event organizers, challenging the concept of "pure" amateurism. An editorial in the *Springfield Wheelmen's Gazette* from April 1887 maintained:

> Mr. Ducker well knows, as does any man who has ever had dealings with the racing men, that the word amateur is a FARCE of the biggest kind. Take a tournament of the size of the Springfield Tournament, and we can name one in which sixty-three different men were entered as amateurs, and only TWO (2)

owned their wheels; the entire balance, sixty-one men, had their machines furnished by the manufacturers ... neither Mr. Ducker nor the Springfield Club is to blame.[114]

The "makers' amateur" problem was just as much of an issue in England at the same moment, as can be seen in an American report from 1888:

> Many first-class men have been removed from the amateur ranks by the suspensions of the N.C.U. "Makers' amateurism" was their crime, and though many sympathize with them ... still they were wittingly breaking the Union rules, and it was imperative—if amateurism were to exist—that they should be suspended. Most of them have accepted their sentence and turned professionals.[115]

In 1888, Ducker continued his push to claim "world" status for American cycling events by promoting a three-day "Annual World's Cycling Tournament" under the auspices of the Buffalo International Fair Association.[116] But in spite of attracting thousands of spectators to Buffalo, this event fell disappointingly short of "world championship" status, since only two English professionals and one French cyclist attended. The track was not ready, the weather was terrible and many contractual and financial disputes erupted. According to professional manager W.J. Morgan, "Henry Ducker's reputation for veracity and management has received a shattering blow which will take years to regain."[117] However, Henry Sturmey, the editor of *The Cyclist*, always the optimist, thought the event gave hope for the future:

> The interest which this Buffalo Tournament engenders once more turns our thoughts to that day in the dim and distant future when some universally recognized system of International contests may be arranged, when International championships shall be held in the different cycling centres of the world in rotation, and when each country shall be represented by a specially selected team of both amateurs and professionals.[118]

Both Springfield and New Haven, perhaps more so than the comparable British tournaments, exuded an air of middle-class respectability, as a large proportion of both competitors and spectators were from the urban professional classes, and came from Boston, New York, Philadelphia, Pittsburgh, Buffalo and the old university towns of New England. At the same time, a new, wide-ranging social democracy was implied by the presence of competitors from Chicago, Denver, St. Louis, Minneapolis and other western and midwestern locations. On the East Coast, bicycling was certainly not viewed as a proletarian activity, and there were hardly enough professionals for them to have been considered a socially threatening presence, although amateur sportsmen were consistently suspicious of the "maker's amateur." The *Providence Journal* praised bicycle exercise in the following expressive way, emphasizing its following among the educated classes: "It brings into play every muscle, expands the chest and fills out the unused air cells in the lungs, steadies the nerves and brings them into harmonious action with the muscles, purifies the blood and sends it tingling along the flaccid limbs, improves the digestion, increases the appetite, and gives a new tone and fresh vigor to all the vital parts. One of the keenest delights about the whole exercise is the after-glow."[119] This almost spiritual appreciation of the benefits of the bicycle was a far cry from the more mundane materialism of professional athletes.

At the Springfield Tournaments, guidelines insisted "that the men who enter for the tournament races should make a respectable and decent appearance as regards costume," and on one occasion it was remarked that "without exception the amateurs were neatly dressed." The Springfield Tournaments were attended not only by "the most respectable and refined female society of Springfield," but "many ladies came from a distance and expect to witness a contest of gentlemen of good taste, who know how to demean themselves in good society ... the Springfield Club purposes to keep that good character if possible, and proposes that those who enter the races shall be properly dressed." Bare legs were discouraged, as were "fancy circus tights." Proper attire included "a loose woolen shirt, and drawers and stockings of the same material, elastic, comfortable and cool, entirely unobjectionable in every respect."[120]

Held between 1882 and 1886, the Springfield Tournaments, expensive, elaborately choreographed, international, athletic events, may be considered both from their organizational intent and their spirit of competitive "friendship" among nations (and indeed from the often-expressed chauvinism and nationalism) as precursors of the first official world cycling championships in 1893 and the first Olympic Games in 1896.[121] In 1884, a writer in *Outing and The Wheelman* noted that a Springfield clergyman "remarked that he knew of nothing so nearly resembling the old Olympic games as a modern bicycling tournament," and suggested: "Perhaps there may be some lessons for us in our modern tournaments. We may, perhaps, gain some hints of high and beautiful motives with which to invest our innocent and healthful recreations." He went onto explore the history, the significance and the positive moral values of the ancient Olympics.[122]

Fig. 4.27. James Starley, the "father" of the tricycle, in 1875. [Source: *Bartleet's Bicycle Book*]

The Springfield Tournaments, under the direction of Henry Ducker, were international events that actively sought "world championship" status. The Rudge company advertised the 1885 1-mile event as having been "The Bicycle Championship of the World," and in 1886 the tournament was again advertised as the "5th Grand International Tournament" of the Springfield Bicycle Club, with a "Grand One-Mile Race for the Bicycle Championship of the World."[123] Whereas the many other events at the 1886 Tournament were specifically designated as either "amateur" or "professional," on this occasion Ducker challenged the prevailing tendency to separate amateur and professional categories by giving the "World's Championship" a "promateur" category, that is one open to "maker's amateurs,"

Fig. 4.28. Affluent tricyclists outside the White House, Washington, D.C. [Source: Lorne Shields collection, Toronto, Canada]

that is, amateurs whose true status was questionable. In other words, Ducker wanted to create "open" competition. In the "world championship" race, George Hendee was defeated by William Rowe, but the 1886 event was not as exciting as the fiercely contested 1885 races since many of the leading English amateurs were advised to stay away due to the risk to their status in participating in the "promateur" events.

In their promotion of international competition and in their "world championship" status, the Springfield Tournaments were typical of a global sport phenomenon that was perhaps more progressively advanced within cycling than in any other sport in the late 1880s.[124] This was the apogee of the high-wheel era in global competition. In 1885, the Springfield races were advertised in England as "The Great International Races" and in 1886, the German Cyclists' Union announced "Great National and International Races" in Berlin.[125] In April 1888, "International Races" were held in Leicester and Jarrow-on-Tyne. In May 1888, a "Munich International Tournament" was held. In June the same year, "Great International Races" in Berlin and a "Glasgow International Exhibition and Grand Amateur Athletic and Cycling Meeting" were held. In August, a "National and International Two Days' Meeting" was held in Scheveningen, Holland, while in Birmingham, England a "Grand International Cycling Tournament—England versus the World" was promoted by *Sport and Play*.[126] In September, as already noted, the "International Tournament" was held in Buffalo. Clearly, the sport of cycling was becoming increasingly popular, at its most intense international competitive level.

7. New Departures: Tricycle Racing and Recreational Tricycling

In addition to the bicycle, the tricycle played a significant role in cycling sport and recreation, and should not be forgotten. The tricycle proved to be a crucial testing ground for many aspects of subsequent transportation technology. While energetic, athletic men mastered the high-wheel bicycle and spectators flocked to see the novel sport, tricycles were manufactured and marketed in Britain beginning in 1876, went through an intense technological development throughout the 1880s, and had a significant impact on the growth of the sport.

Tricycles carved out a parallel niche in the cycling marketplace and broadened and diversified the range of those who were interested in the sport. Tricycles moved cycling more in the direction of recreation and useful, practical transportation, and made it possible for women (who were excluded from high-wheel cycling, with a handful of professional exceptions) to participate at least on a limited basis. Bicycle makers were faced with the same challenge that had confronted velocipede makers of the 1850s and 1860s: to make a workable, efficient, 3- or 4-wheeled human-powered vehicle. But by the late 1870s, makers were able to benefit from the technological gains achieved by several years of improvements in high-wheel bicycle technology.[127]

Light, strong, all-metal wheels and ball-bearing systems were particularly beneficial to tricycle makers, as were, of course, the by then well-established, well equipped bicycle factories with their experienced, skilled workers, their wide variety of machine-tools, and their marketing and advertising departments. Perhaps the most significant new technological factor in bicycle and tricycle design by the mid–1880s was the widespread use of chains to connect crank system to driving wheels and rapid improvements in strength and flexibility of these chains, which were to be crucial for the subsequent development of the "safety" bicycle.

In 1880s, an annual review of the sport reported that "tricycling has been making rapid

Fig. 4.29. Start of the N.C.U. 1-mile tricycle championship at Crystal Palace track, 11 July 1885, won by P. Furnivall on the right. [Source: Lorne Shields collection, Toronto, Canada]

strides, and is fast becoming a very important branch of the wheel sport... In and around Coventry it is quite a commonplace thing to see ladies and young girls on these neat machines, for which the City of Spires is celebrated."[128] In 1884, when Henry Sturmey published the 4th Edition of his *Tricyclists' Indispensable Annual and Handbook*, he documented more than 100 manufacturers of tricycles in Britain, with the majority in Coventry (20 makers, 120 varieties), Birmingham (12 makers), Wolverhampton (9 makers, 25–30 varieties) and London (12 makers, 30 varieties).

These makers had, for about three years, he wrote, "given almost their entire attention to the improvement of the once-despised machine, with a result which has not only astonished themselves, but opened up a healthy, invigorating, and economical pastime to thousands of men who would never have taken the trouble to learn to ride the bicycle, as well as to the fair sex, to whom the bicycle was, of course, a sealed book."

Fig.4.30. Charles Edgar Liles, of the London Athletic Club, set a 1 hour tricycle record of 16 miles 1,685 yards on 21 June 1884. [Source: *The Cyclist Year Book* for 1891]

Use of the tricycle had "spread throughout the length and breadth of the land," and was "destined to effect a practical and social revolution, having a considerable and lasting effect on the physical constitution of the people." Tricycling was now "one of the leading pastimes of all classes, sexes and ages, and the heavy lumbering vehicle of yesterday has given place to dozens of varieties of light, airy, handsome structures, the outcome of the best mechanical skill in the country." The greatly improved tricycle had "opened up a new method of progression, a new sport, and a new branch of manufacturing industry, all of which tend in their own small ways to the elaboration and completion of the civilization of the world, and of England in particular."

The improvements in the tricycle widened the possibilities for recreation and sport:

> Many of the crowned heads of Europe are now possessors of the new vehicle for occasional use ... and a large number of the English aristocracy not only possess them for occasional use in private, but appreciate the pastime to the full, and put them to the legitimate use of exploring the country by their means. Retired military and naval men in hundreds patronize the new form of wheels, and professional and business men of all classes find the possession of a tricycle not only lessens their own labours and expedites their work, but affords them the means of pleasurable and health-giving recreation in their

spare hours, whilst the ladies in great numbers already find in the new pastime an exercise that puts rinking and lawn tennis in the shade by its greater usefulness, greater variety, and more health-giving properties.[129]

Tricycling, in other words, had vastly expanded the possibilities of cycling. Sturmey, who perhaps did more for the tricycle than any other contemporary player, discusses the general advantages and disadvantages of the tricycle for various uses. On the positive side, it was more stable, more comfortable, less dangerous and "of more universal utility" than the bicycle. On the negative side, it was heavier, slower, giving "more frictional resistance by reason of a larger number of bearings and greater road resistance," and more difficult to store. In terms of comparative speed, a stripped down tricycle ridden by a strong, experienced rider was only marginally slower than a bicycle. The tricycle was more adaptable for appropriate gearing, and introduced many of the issues involving pedaling rate and wheel rotation which were to be of crucial importance in the rapid development of the "safety" bicycle, including multiple gearing. The growth in the popularity of the tricycle marked a huge expansion of both racing and of recreational cycling, as well as of the industry in general.[130]

Early tricycle sport and

Top: Fig. 4.31. Thomas Humber, founder of the famous bicycle and tricycle company, on one of his own machines, c. 1886. [Source: author's collection] *Bottom:* Fig. 4.32. Edward B. Turner, Ripley Road Club, holder of 1-hour solid-tired tricycle record, about 1890. [Source: *The Cyclist Year Book,* 1891]

recreation were also crucial factors in influencing technical and manufacturing decisions, and the tricycle was quickly integrated into competition, thereby testing out technological innovations. "In England there has been a rapid increase in the use of the tricycle within the past year or so, and this use has been stimulated in every possible way by manufacturers and others interested," wrote Charles Pratt, editor of *Bicycling World*; "An esprit du corps has been developed among the devotees

Fig. 4.33. As women were tempted to ride the expensive new tricycles, the need for a more rational dress was readily apparent. [Source: author's collection]

of this new favorite."¹³¹ This "esprit du corps" was partly a reflection of the need some tricyclists felt, as a superior class, to distinguish themselves from the bicycle-riding *hoi polloi*. "Tricyclists will generally be of a better class than bicyclists, and will seldom consist of mere beardless youths, but men of position and experience, and above all, by the fair sex," wrote a correspondent to *Bicycling News*.¹³²

In 1880, a letter was sent to tricyclist members of the Bicycle Touring Club: "It is desired by most Tricyclists to separate themselves entirely from the Bicyclists, who are a disgrace to the pastime, while Tricycling includes Princes, Princesses, Dukes, Earls, etc. There are none of the upper circle who ride bicycles."¹³³ With the enthusiasm for the creation of clubs so characteristic of the bicycle movement, a separate Tricycle Association was formed in 1882, "for the purpose of carrying out the Annual Meet and Championship Road Ride from year to year … and generally to advance the interests of tricycling," only to be quickly re-absorbed into the Bicycle Union, which was newly named the National Cyclists' Union in 1883.¹³⁴

The energetic introduction of tricycles thus expanded the market for cycles of all sorts to include younger women, children and older men, all of whom could for the first time enjoy the recreational sport safely, respectably and comfortably. The tricycle provided women with the opportunity to participate alongside men in recreational club activity. "Health is in fashion. Girls no longer pride themselves upon painfully pinched feet or spider-like waists," wrote a contributor to *Outing and The Wheelman* in 1884: "Every form of exercise that takes girls and women out of doors is a direct power in making the health and happiness of the world. The growing use of the tricycle is a very good thing. There is no doubt that a woman's right to a healthy body is on the way to full recognition."[135]

The "sociable" tricycle, which seated the woman rider beside her companion (and later the tandem bicycle, which at first put the woman in front of the man and then later behind him), became popular and was frequently illustrated in the press. "Cycling provides a healthy, invigorating, and entirely novel form of exercise for ladies, and if not overdone is of marked benefit to the majority, who obtain a breath of fresh air combined with a certain amount of healthy exercise and mild excitement," wrote Lacy Hillier:

> By far the larger number of our lady riders began their cycling experiences upon sociables or tandems, with their husbands and brothers, and thus gained by degrees the experience and confidence necessary for the fullest enjoyment of a cruise upon wheels, eventually attaining the self-reliance necessary for a trip upon a single tricycle. It is perhaps upon a tandem with a gentleman companion that the lady rider looks most at home, and when, clad in a well-fitting and becoming costume, she flits by on the front seat of one of these light and speedy machines, the most sceptical observer is converted to the same view.[136]

Women were still constrained, however, by their long skirts—"the voluminous divided skirt has proved singularly ill-adapted for the work"—and the influential "rational dress" movement for women cyclists began with women tricycle riders in the 1880s. With the advent of the tricycle, new technology, expanded possibilities for recreational sport, and provocative social mobility came inextricably together. Experience upon the tricycle provided an opportunity for women to move, later, to the even more independent "safety" bicycle.

The advantages and disadvantages of various tricycle designs were tested in races in England. In 1882, the National Cyclists' Union instituted an official 5-mile tricycle championship on the track, and by 1884, there were competitions for 1, 5 and 25-mile races. Records were quickly established, and as quickly broken, in the new field of tricycle racing. In July 1883, the London Tricycle Club held a 24-hour race for tricyclists in which 67 competitors took part, and the race was won by Tom. R. Marriott, captain of the Nottingham Tricycle Club, with a total of 218¾ miles.[137] In 1885, Marriott set a tricycle record of 6 days 15h 22m for the ride from Land's End to John o'Groats, which was actually faster than the standing bicycle record (James Lennox, July 1885, with 6 days 16h 7m). But this record was beaten a year later, when G.P. Mills rode a Beeston Cripper tricycle over 881 miles from Land's End to John o'Groats in 5 days 10h, beating Marriott by 29 hours.[138]

Because of the great number of different tricycle designs (both single and tandem), records were set on many different kinds of machines, and races were used to evaluate the merits of rival design concepts. As with the bicycle, records continued to be compulsively attacked and beaten. For road riding, the tricycle was in one important respect superior to the high-wheel bicycle—because it was usually geared lower, it could be ridden uphill more efficiently. "Bicyclists of fair skill are astonished to find that tricyclists can hold their own upon the road, and even beat them at hill work," wrote Lacy Hillier:

> When tricyclists can cover 150 or 180 miles within 24 consecutive hours; when many men, no longer young, can be found able to cover 70, 80, 90 or even 100 miles in a day; when members of the softer sex are able to cover similar distances, and surmount hills which are considered a fair test for the

bicyclist's skill, it cannot be denied that the tricycle can claim an equal place with its two-wheeled rival.[139]

* * *

The "classic" period of high-wheel bicycle racing—the late 1870s and 1880s—can thus be seen to have diversified as it expanded. Tricycle racing introduced another layer of complexity into the sport, because tricyclists demanded their own events and added categories of speed and distance events for which championships could be awarded and records set. Tricycling also provided a whole variety of new recreational opportunities for a broader range of enthusiasts. And the tricycle provided another opportunity for testing rival makes and designs.

Thus, the high-wheel bicycle was not the only source of cycling sport in the mid–1880s, for the development of tricycles created a boom in technological experimentation and was responsible for a huge expansion within the bicycle industry. At the annual Stanley Show in London in 1883, 289 different tricycle models were exhibited, whereas there were only 233 bicycles models on display.[140] By the later 1880s, different models of the "safety" bicycle had appeared alongside the "ordinary" bicycle, the "geared-up ordinaries" and the various kinds of tricycles, and races were held between all these different categories of cycles on both road and track. Consequently, the number and variety of events and records increased.

By 1885, the "safeties" were already the fastest on the road, where they could be ridden recklessly in competition. But it was only towards the end of the 1880s that the "safety" bicycle emerged definitively as the fastest bicycle, whose basic design won universal acceptance into the 1890s, leading to an unprecedented boom in the sport. In 1888, Harry Hewitt Griffin, in one of the leading annual surveys of the bicycle industry, wrote: "Taking the average through the trade, at least six dwarf safeties are now

Fig. 4.34. "The wretch rides like the very demon—if we relax a minute, we are lost!" Scorching on the tricycle by George Moore. [Source: *Wheel World*, 1885]

made to one ordinary, some makers having only one order in fifty for an ordinary. We have devoted fully four-fifths of our space to what is undoubtedly the most popular machine of the day," by which he meant the "safety" bicycle.[141]

As the sport of cycling expanded and took root in Britain, France, Germany and the United States in the 1880s, international competition became more attractive, viable and potentially profitable as a spectator experience. Nationalist and chauvinist sentiments were encouraged and promoted, to intensify emotions during international exchanges. But international competition also lifted the sport to a new, higher level of intensity. Athletes were pushed to their limits, and specialization became inevitable. Professionalism expanded as manufacturers sought new and exciting ways to bring their products to the attention of the spectators, and top amateurs were increasingly tempted into the professional ranks.

Cycling was truly evolving into a thoroughly modern sporting activity.[142]

Chapter Five

Sport, Speed and Safety, 1885–93

1. Design and Technological Ferment within the Bicycle Industry and the Sport

THE MID– TO LATE 1880s was an extraordinary period of experimental activity in the evolution of bicycle technology. Technological experimentation to produce the most efficient and appropriate designs both for sport and for utilitarian transportation was accelerated. An extraordinary *variety* in the range and number of solutions was developed to answer crucial questions about speed and utility in human-powered transportation. Innovators within the bicycle industry experimented with complex and far-reaching technological and design elements, relying on constant practical input from those most actively involved in the sport. Such cooperation proved crucial to the future of the bicycle. Coventry, in the English Midlands, with its tradition of small-scale machining and its skilled work force, was the geographical crucible within which much of this ferment of design and manufacturing took place.[1] But Birmingham, London, Nottingham, Wolverhampton and Leicester also played their parts.

Until the mid–1880s, bicycle racing was centered around the high-wheel bicycle. But the later 1880s was a time of diversification and innovation, when many radical redesigns of the machines used for racing and club riding were tried out. The energy put into developing new designs of tricycles was especially significant. A hugely important printed work was Henry Sturmey's 1883 magnum opus—the third edition of *The Tricyclists' Indispensable Annual and Handbook*, so much sought after that it changed hands for double or triple the cover price. The roads around Coventry and London were full of unusual machines! Safety and comfort were the new watchwords, as well as speed. The future possibilities of recreational and utilitarian cycling and tricycling were beginning to be seriously appreciated and implemented. It was a period of intense and extraordinary industrial design and production.[2] Much of the technological and manufacturing foundations of the future automobile industry were laid during this period.

The advertising pages of the cycling press were crowded with manufacturers' proud and frequently exaggerated boasts of the superiority of their products, measured in terms of design, speed, strength and reliability. Successful championship and record rides were systematically used to create positive publicity, and collaboration between makers and winning riders was carried into the arena of retail marketing, in a way similar to endorsement advertising today.

In Britain, in addition to the regular program of club races and National Cyclists'

Union-sponsored championships on the track, organized road racing became increasingly popular and prominent in the 1880s, and clubs such as the North Road Cycling Club, the Catford Cycling Club and the Anfield Bicycle Club began to specialize in this branch of the sport. The N.C.U. itself did not, however, promote or encourage road racing, and the growing resistance to racing on the public roads presented the national organization with a serious public relations problem. Some races were organized by manufacturers themselves to test their products with the specific intention of garnering publicity, raising further official objections within the cycling community. Amateur purists within the N.C.U. objected that true amateurs should not take part in such commerce-driven races. But Harry Etherington, the editor of *Wheeling*, like others, argued in favor of them:

> What is the difference between a prize given by a club or by a firm of manufacturers ... are they in any respect detrimental to the sport? Far from it. In our opinion it is quite the reverse.... Nothing can bring out the good points of a machine like a trial over 100 miles of straight-away road embracing surfaces varying from the roughest macadam to the smoothest gravel, and yet we are told that these races or rides do no good to the sport.... The public are thus shown what the powers of a machine really are, and are not slow to profit by it.[3]

Fig. 5.1. The "Facile" was the first of the "dwarf" safety bicycles to break records and gain acceptance for the "safety" bicycle, both in racing and recreational use. [Source: *Wheeling*, 11 June 1884]

The increasing popularity of road racing in Britain, particularly road racing with commercial backing, became a divisive political issue within the N.C.U. and a challenge to its authority. The resulting tension led in 1888 to the creation of the Road Records Association, a new, breakaway organization, outside the jurisdiction of the N.C.U., devoted to the promotion of racing and record-breaking in Britain. In France and the United States, the increase in road racing was not greeted with such vocal, organized opposition as it was in Britain, and from about 1890 onwards there was a shift in European racing emphasis, with French road competition becoming increasingly prominent.

As well as the tricycle innovations, radical changes in bicycle design in the mid–1880s included the development of solid-tired "safety" bicycles like the "Xtraordinary" (a lever-driven high-wheel bicycle), the "Facile" and the "Kangaroo," with smaller front wheels driven by levers or chains, and ultimately the development of the rear-driven "safety" bicycle.[4] In this creative ferment, the industry began to produce, *simultaneously*, high-wheel bicycles, tricycles of various types, and increasingly, different versions of experimental safeties. Racing remained a priority of the industry, a trial-and-error method of testing machines for mechanical feasibility, strength, efficiency, reliability, comfort and speed, qualities that were also relevant to a machine's marketability and user-friendliness for the wider consuming public.

It should be emphasized that this wider market for utility cycling had still hardly been tapped by the end of the 1880s, and that cycling remained largely a sport and recreation for young, athletic men, with racing largely a club activity. While racing and riding in the club scene continued to be dominated by the high-wheeler, tricycles were also raced, and various safeties were a serious challenge in record-breaking. Whereas races on the track were by then familiar tests of pure speed and endurance, rides on the road added the less controllable elements of terrain, weather and road conditions. They were tests not only of the speed and endurance of the athlete, but of the mechanical reliability and especially of the hill-climbing and descending capabilities of the various novel bicycle designs.

Fig. 5.2. The "Kangaroo" (behind) was a chain-driven, small-wheeled ordinary bicycle, seen here racing against a Rover "safety," drawn by George Moore. [Source: *Wheel World*, Nov. 1885]

In the early 1890s, very soon after the "safety" bicycle had become the almost universally accepted substitute for the soon-outmoded high-wheel bicycle, the pneumatic tire was introduced and took the place of the solid tire, which had become an outmoded technology by the end of 1891.

2. Alternative Designs: the "Facile" and the "Kangaroo"

Long-distance rides in Britain of around 100 miles and of 24 hours in duration were established tests of endurance and mechanical reliability. In the fall of 1883, J.H. Adams established a record road ride of 242½ miles in 24 hours on Ellis and Co's "Facile" bicycle, a "dwarf" ordinary bicycle with a treadle-driven, indirect front-wheel-drive mechanism, allowing a lower center of gravity.

In May 1884, Adams, of the Lewisham Bicycle Club, set another important record on a 46-inch "Facile" safety bicycle made by London manufacturer Ellis. Adams rode the full distance of more than 900 miles from Land's End in the extreme south-west of England to John O'Groats in the far north-east of Scotland in 6days 23h 45m. He set off on 17 May and arrived in John O'Groats on 24 May, accompanied by Tom Moore, of *Bicycling News*, who used the train and a bicycle to keep up with him. On this "End-to-End" ride, Adams' consecutive daily mileage totals were 123, 111, 112, 92, 144, 134 and 204 miles, for a total distance of 924 miles, and he was paced over parts of the route. On the seventh day, "despite the fact that he had 200 miles of ground still to cover, over an unknown road and against a choppy wind, Adams announced his intention to reach John O'Groats that day or perish in the attempt." The Ellis company used Adams' record in publicity for their machine.[5]

Adams beat the previous record, 9 days 4h 40m, set by James Lennox in 1883, by the huge margin of more than two days. *Wheeling* thought the ride was "by far the biggest thing ever done in the history of cycling, and proves Mr. Adams the best road rider in the world. The Facile bicycle, his mount, must also be awarded every praise.... The Scotch roads were remarkable, as being much superior to the English, and beautifully engineered through the hills." The ride was considered sufficiently important for "a perfect portrait and biography of Adams" to be published by Harry Etherington's publications *Wheeling* and the *Sporting Mirror*. In October 1884, "the indomitable Adams" again broke the all-day (24 hour) record on the "Facile," increasing it to 266½ miles. "The firm of Ellis and Co. have every reason to be most thoroughly satisfied with this grand performance," reported *Wheeling*, "which stamp the "Facile" to be quite the machine of the road."[6]

While the "Facile" was one experimental new safety bicycle, another was the "Kangaroo," designed by William Hillman and first introduced commercially by the firm of Hillman, Herbert and Cooper in 1884. The "Kangaroo" differed from the "Facile" in one important respect. While the cranks of the "Facile" were connected to the front driving wheel by levers, the "Kangaroo" was chain-driven. Chains were increasingly being used for the heavier, more cumbersome tricycles, but had not yet been used in a commercially produced safety bicycle. Irish journalist R.J. Mecredy wrote that the "Kangaroo" was "not generally used until comparatively recently," one of the possible reasons being "that chains had not been got to work really well when these machines were first proposed." Mecredy notes that in about 1885 "came the great Kangaroo rage. From being a totally unknown machine it suddenly jumped into popularity, largely owing to a number of road records which were made on it."[7]

Chain technology, which helped to free bicycle design from the limiting front-wheel direct-drive, was being rapidly developed in the mid–1880s, primarily for drive mechanisms on tricycles, and inventors were beginning to recognize its practical significance in thinking about "safety" bicycles and subjected it to minute examination.

Without tricycle innovations, it is safe to say that the safety bicycle would not have been possible:

> Just as the modern tricycle owes its success to the development of the bicycle, so in turn the modern safety bicycle is indebted to the tricycle for its possibility; for until the tricycle had enabled manufacturers to grasp the chain-gearing principle thoroughly it was impossible to properly construct a chain-geared bicycle, and until the tricycle had so far familiarized the public with the lowly position of its rider that vulgar derision was silenced, nobody would look with favour upon the insignificant dwarf bicycle.[8]

A highly significant ride took place on 27 Sept 1884, when George Smith, of the Merry Rovers Tricycle Club, established a new, paced 100-mile bicycle road record of 7h 11m 10s on the "Kangaroo," breaking the ordinary record which had been standing since 1878 (7h 15m 18s; F. Appleyard, of the London Bicycle Club, in a race from Bath to London). This new record was established in a race organized by Hillman, Herbert and Cooper, the Coventry manufacturers of well-known "Premier" bicycles and tricycles, specifically "for the purpose of giving a public trial to their new safety bicycle, the Kangaroo." According to *Wheeling*:

> that trial has succeeded beyond their most sanguine expectations. Even those who were most conversant with the merits of the little machine could not have believed that a 36 inch wheel could be driven for 100 miles along an undulating, and in many places rough and loose, road at an average rate of 14 miles an hour.... The good people of Maidenhead had evidently got wind of the affair, as the streets were thronged, and murmurs of astonishment were heard on all sides at the marvellous rate at which the men were travelling.[9]

Other reports of riders of the "Kangaroo" were equally positive. "We regard the Kangaroo as being a thoroughly sound and reliable little mount," reported the *Cyclists' Touring Club Gazette*, "likely to win its way more and more into popular favour, particularly among those who value their necks too highly to risk them upon the ordinary bicycle." A correspondent wrote that he had "ridden it since the end of January, often riding down hills at night in a most reckless manner, and I have not had one tumble.... I think I should have quite come to grief on an ordinary machine."[10]

These races were the scene not only of technological experimentation, but of athletic achievement and an ostentatiously Bohemian life-style, although riders had to be well supported to have a chance of excelling on the road. Participants appear either to have been middle-class young men, able to free themselves of other responsibilities, or men who

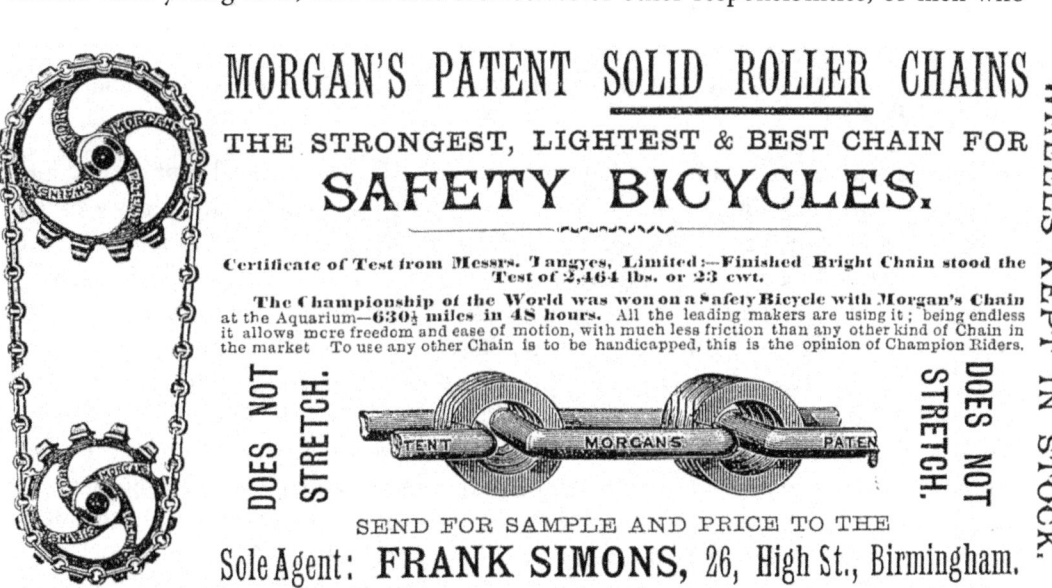

Fig. 5.3. Chain technology, allowing "gearing up" in the transmission, was the key ingredient in manufacturing successful tricycles and in the emergence of "dwarf"—and "Rover"—type "safety" bicycles. [Source: *The Cyclist*, 19 Aug. 1885]

STANLEY SHOW, 1887.   STAND 102.

THE ACME OF INVENTION.

SOLID LINK.   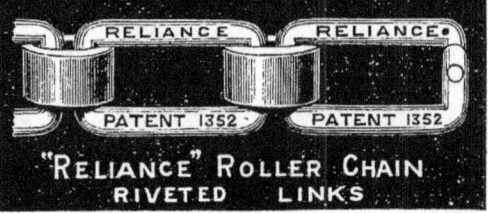   **SOLID ROLLER.**

Officially tested   to 2,800 lbs.

NO JOINT OR RIVET THAT WILL OPEN OR BEND.

APPLEBY'S

PATENT ADJUSTABLE STEEL CHAIN.

Links are made of Solid Steel. For simplicity, adjustability and strength, cannot be excelled.

PERRY & CO., LIMITED, BIRMINGHAM.

Fig. 5.4. The "roller" chain was a significant technological advance for transmissions. [Source: *The Cyclist*, 2 Feb. 1887]

arranged in one way or another (either openly or secretly) for financial support and gifts of equipment from the bicycle industry. Good weather was crucial as fast times were out of the question following a heavy rain. For J.H. Adams' long Land's End to John O'Groats ride in 1884, Tom Moore of *Bicycling News* agreed "to act during the trip as guide, philosopher and friend, taking business arrangements of the affair entirely in his hands."[11] At the 24-hour race for riders of Rudge's "Coventry Rotary" tricycle in 1885, the arrangements were "the most complete, generous and perfect on record in connection with any such competition," and "a capital supper was enjoyed by competitors and officials." The winner, J.H. Adams, after riding more than 200 miles, reached Norman's Cross Hotel, near Peterborough, "in very sorry order, having to be lifted from his machine."[12] Respectable behavior was also important, however, in order not to attract negative attention, particularly from the police. At the 1884 "Kangaroo" record ride mentioned above, "the route was kept as secret as possible in order to prevent any interference on the part of the authorities," and at the North Road Cycling Club's 24-hour race in 1887, "at Biggleswade the cavalcade was reported to be led by two bicyclists with bare legs, who would have been disqualified if they had been identified."[13]

3. The Rear-Driven "Rover Safety" and the First "Safety" Races

The "Kangaroo," first introduced in 1884, was a short-lived and somewhat successful attempt to overcome the limitations and dangers of the high-wheel bicycle. According to Mecredy, writing in 1890, the popularity of the "Kangaroo":

> lasted for about a year and then, when all the makers were turning out large numbers, the "Rover" type of safety burst on the public, and its popularity waned rapidly; indeed, it is hardly ridden at all now, and its manufacture has been quite discontinued, whereas the rear-driving type of safety has been found to be so speedy, as well as safe from liability to headers, that it has almost monopolized the public taste, successive improvements having resulted in the manufacture and use of this type far exceeding that of the "ordinary" or tall bicycle.[14]

"Many novelties are again introduced," reported the *Cyclists' Touring Club Gazette* at the Stanley trade show, in February 1885, but "the most observable speciality is the safety bicycle, which every maker worthy of the name now considers it a religious duty to add to his stock." The safety bicycles exhibited there were largely of the "Kangaroo" type, but among the novelties was Starley and Sutton's "Rover," which was introduced to the public for the first time.[15] In April 1885, Starley and Sutton were advertising their "Rover" as being "as safe as any Tricycle and a better Hill-climber than any Bicycle or Tricycle yet made."[16]

Starley himself confirmed that the design of the "Rover" would enable better mechanical efficiency for the athlete, a better application of power resulting in greater speed, as well as improved safety:

> The Rover is absolutely the outcome of a determination to obtain advantage previously unknown in a bicycle. We felt confident that a large percentage of unused power could be utilized if the rider were properly placed, particularly with regard to hill-climbing. In this we were not mistaken, as the enormous success of the Rover undoubtedly proves. Being a very safe bicycle, we were induced to call it the Rover Safety, and have debated the matter on many occasions as to the advisability of dropping the word, which we usually have done in our advertisements.[17]

In another passage, addressing a meeting of the Society of Arts much later, Starley said of the "Rover":

> The main principles which guided me in making this machine were to place the rider at the proper distance from the ground; to connect the cranks with the driving wheel in such a way that the gearing could be varied as desired; to place the seat in the right position in relation to the pedals, and constructed so that the saddle could be either laterally or vertically adjusted at will; to place the handles in such a position in relation to the seat that the rider could exert the greatest force upon the pedals with the least amount of fatigue; and to make them adjustable also.[18]

"The "Rover" was indeed a phenomenon. It was with this machine, and with others like it that followed it quickly onto the market, that the design and configuration of the modern rear-driven bicycle first became thoroughly evident. Racing was used to demonstrate the "Rover"'s capabilities and potential, and successful results were used to advertise it. On 26 Sept 1885, George Smith broke his previous "Kangaroo" record on the "Rover" by only about 6 minutes, riding 100 miles in 7h 5m 16s, in a race specifically "promoted by Messrs. Starley and Sutton to advertise their speedy "Rover Safety" bicycle.... Though fine, the day was hardly very favourable, the men receiving no assistance from the wind, while the roads for a good part of the distance were certainly not first class."

STARLEY & SUTTON'S "Rover" Safety

NOW HOLDS THE 50 & 100 MILES WORLD'S ROAD RECORDS FOR EVERY KIND OF CYCLE.

IF YOU HAVE NOT TRIED ONE DO SO AT ONCE.

50 Miles in 3h. 5m. 34s.   100 Miles in 7h. 5m. 16s.

THE BUTTS, COVENTRY, SEPTEMBER 28TH, 1885.

DEAR SIRS,—I am very pleased with the running of the "Rover" Safety, and although I have ridden nearly all the other types of Safeties, I am sure the "Rover" is the fastest machine I have been on. So much so, indeed, am I impressed with this opinion that had it not been for my spring breaking in the recent race I feel sure I should have lowered the record to six and a half hours.

Yours truly, S. GOLDER,
Coventry C.C. and Leamington and S.W. B.C.

Illustrated Price Lists with Testimonials free on application.

STARLEY & SUTTON, METEOR WORKS, WEST ORCHARD, COVENTRY.

Fig. 5.5. Starley and Sutton's "Rover" safety bicycle quickly established itself as an alternative, both in terms of safety and speed, to the high-wheel bicycle. [Source: *The Cyclist*, 21 Oct. 1885]

Road record rides were critically dependent on good conditions; recent rain producing muddy roads would slow riders considerably. The first prize was a gold watch worth 50 guineas, the second a racing "Rover," while gold and silver medals went to all those finishing within 8 and 9 hours respectively. Although garnering publicity was the specific aim of the race, because so many people opposed road racing, "the route had been studiously kept secret, so that there was no crowd at either the start or the finish."[19]

H.O. Duncan wrote that "taking due advantage of this success, Starley's firm availed itself of every opportunity of launching the machine upon the market, and the "Rover" became a wonderful commercial proposition."[20] Many other accounts confirm the dramatic impact of Starley and Sutton's "Rover safety":

> Even in their wildest flights of fancy Messrs Starley and Sutton could not have imagined the effect their Dwarf Safety—the Rover—would have upon the trade when they exhibited it at the Stanley Show of 1885. At that time riders were firmly wedded to the Kangaroo type, but the progress of the Rover in 1885, more particularly in the 100 miles Road Race, quickly turned the tide in its favour, and last year nearly every maker began making it. The natural outcome followed, an all-round improvement in this class of machine, and today it is the most popular in the market.... An entire revision of the speed rates may be confidently looked for in the coming season, more particularly in dwarf bicycles. The marvellously light and highly-finished machines of today are the best part of 100 yards in a mile faster than the machines of last year.[21]

Fig. 5.6. The "Rover" quickly went through a series of design improvements. [Source: *The Cyclist*, 10 March 1886]

The "Rover" competed with other rival designs of safety, particularly the Rudge "Bicyclette."[22] Duncan, a distinguished high-wheel athlete and championship winner, one of the most active competitors on the European scene and an agent in France for the Rudge company, played a crucial role in using and publicizing the new Rudge "Bicyclette safety" bicycle in France. At the end of 1885, "he entered successfully into negotiations for the agency and received a sample machine at Montpellier," which he used in March 1886 to set a road record from Montpellier to Paris.

Wheeling reported that this 700-mile, 6-day ride was "to show the wheeling division, and the public generally in France what a "steely steed" is really capable of, from a practical point of view."[23] In St. Etienne, en route, the machine was seen by "a clever young cycle engineer named Gauthier" who promptly "constructed a similar machine in his workshop," evidently the first such safety machine made in France.[24] Duncan's account suggests that the subsequent development of the safety in France was as rapid there as it was in Britain, with French makers quickly supplying the home market and St. Etienne becoming an important bicycle manufacturing center.

In the summer of 1886, at international races at Auch, Toulouse and Mont de Marsan (all in the south of France), leading high-wheel cyclists Duncan, De Civry and Terront complained about a Belgian competitor, Eole, using a Rudge "Bicyclette." Judges initially found in favor of Eole's participation, but in a number of races the competitors on high-wheel bicycles refused to compete against the safety. Their objections were directed not so much at the speed of the new machine as the practical danger of the two very different styles and heights of machines being included in the same race. A "Union" of professional riders was also discussed. The professional riders out on the lucrative European circuit wanted to defend their professional reputations, and their very considerable investment in equipment (and the high-wheel style of racing), against the new "safety."[25] Subsequently the Union Vélocipédique de France ruled that high bicycles, safeties and tricycles should not compete together. This separation in competition on the track certainly bought some time for the high-wheel bicycle, whose competitive life was thereby prolonged by about three years, until 1889. Duncan later wrote that "this decision was a happy one for the high bicycle as it practically gave this machine a new lease of life which was maintained until the introduction of the Dunlop pneumatic tyre."[26]

Starley and Sutton advertised the "Rover" in 1885 and emphasized its speed as much as its safety. "The Rover safety holds the World's Road Records for 50 and 100 miles—The

Fig. 5 7. In Starley and Sutton's advertising, the Rover safety is depicted as riding away from other current designs of bicycles at a race meeting; drawing by George Moore. [Source: *Wheeling*, 5 May 1886]

Fastest and Safest Machine ever made," claimed the company in November 1885.[27] Other advertisements in 1885 asked the public, "Have you tried the 'Rover Safety'? If not, do so at once. Pronounced by experts the FASTEST CYCLE ever yet made." Following his record ride, George Smith praised not only the safety of the "Rover" but also its speed: "I am now thoroughly convinced the "Rover Safety" is the fastest machine ever made.... I am also convinced that all track records will be lowered upon it; nothing can live with it either upon the road or path." Another racer, George Gatehouse, asserted that "the pace to be got out of it is extraordinary, and I have no hesitation in saying that it is the fastest 'safety' I have tried, and faster than an ordinary bicycle on the road."

In an attempt to convince buyers that the speed of their new bicycle was a significant selling point, Starley and Sutton published an illustration of a confident "Rover" rider beating all other bicycle designs in a sprint.[28] However, manufacturers' energetic sponsorship of promotional races and their advertising of the results was criticized by advocates of pure amateurism. The races were considered to be "under the cloud of trade promotion," to have "the taint of maker's amateurism," and were "a scandal to the sport."[29] Since the primary motivation behind the development of the "Rover safety" was the search for a safer machine, the superior speed of the new design was at the time clearly a surprise.

George Smith's new "Rover" record lasted only a month and on 20 October was again broken, in another grueling race promoted by Hillman, Herbert and Cooper. Edward Hale (Gainsboro' Cycling Club) rode 100 miles on a "Kangaroo" in 6h 39m 5s, an improvement of 25 minutes. According to the *Wheeling* report, "nearly all the competitors (of whom there were eleven) rode light racing Kangaroos, highly geared and averaging in weight about 33 lbs apiece. The Kangaroo Safety bicycle, in once more topping the record at 100 miles in such a decided fashion, has regained its lost laurels."[30] However, this was almost the end for the "Kangaroo," which then disappeared from the record lists. Like nearly every other manufacturer, Hillman, Herbert and Cooper, the makers of the "Kangaroo," also launched a rear-driven safety bicycle in 1886:

> While contending that no form of safety bicycle can equal the "Kangaroo," Messrs. Hillman and Co. recognize the existence of

Fig. 5.8. Rival designs were tested in competition on the road in England: a "Kangaroo" 100-mile road record set by Edward Hale in October 1885 was soon beaten by a Rover safety. [Source: *The Cyclist*, 28 Oct. 1885]

a demand for rear-driving safety bicycles of the "Rover" type, and have accordingly perfected a machine ... the "Premier" safety ... a fast at the same time as a safe bicycle.[31]

Thus, as rival versions of the safety bicycle entered the market place, the leading contenders attempted to get an edge over their competitors with slightly differing designs promising greater speed. But the superiority of the rear-wheel chain-driven, safety bicycle with equal-sized wheels was powerfully asserted over the ordinary bicycle, and proven in practice in competitive sport. A humorous advertisement from January 1887 shows a club rider successfully navigating mud and snow on his "Rover" safety while a high-wheel rider falls off and a tricycle rider lags behind.[32]

This may have been an imagined scenario, but the truth of it had been experienced by many riders. And evidence from that time demonstrates that the potential of the "Rover safety" bicycle design was evaluated not only in terms of safety, but in terms of other advantages it might hold for athletes: speed, comfort, vibration, and hill-climbing ability.

In Henry Sturmey's 1885 *Indispensable Handbook to the Safety Bicycle*, the "Rover" was described as follows:

> by the use of two large wheels, and the placing of the rider between them, vibration over rough roads is saved, and by placing the rider over and almost in front of his work, the machine is made to go with great ease, and climb hills well. It is both fast and safe, and when used to the steering, possesses quite a number of before unseen merits.

In fact, increased vibration under certain road conditions was the only significant negative factor widely experienced with the Rover, which riders commented upon, a fact that encouraged the search both for suspension and for softer, "cushion" tires. Reflecting on the competition within the industry for a successful safety bicycle, Henry Sturmey added:

> Whether the present rage for safety bicycles will last or no I cannot say, but I am inclined to think that it will be in a few seasons a case of "the survival of the fittest"—that one or two makes which in the course of time prove themselves to be good, and to possess the best combination of real safety, with speed, ease and elegance, will remain, and good business be done; but that very many of those hastily flung together to catch the market at present will disappear rapidly.[33]

Two years later, in another edition of Sturmey's *Indispensable Handbook* series, the "Rover" is referred to as "the pioneer of this now universally popular style of machine. It led the way and others followed, and the makers have the benefit of a longer experience than any other. It is a thoroughly reliable and very strong roadster, and will be built to order either as a light roadster or racer at the same price." Henry Sturmey recognized the profound technological shift that had occurred, although at that moment he was reluctant to admit that it would become permanently popular among "the young and active," and could not have foreseen how quickly the ordinary bicycle would be outmoded in the racing world:

> Since the appearance of the last edition, the modern safety has arisen and taken a firm hold on the popular fancy as being a happy medium between the bicycle and the more cumbersome tricycle. The front-driven dwarf machine, or Kangaroo-pattern, has come and very nearly gone.... Its success was phenomenal, and it served its purpose well by preparing the popular mind for the reception of the rear-driver, which now holds premier position in popularity. The sudden and surprising demand for these machines has caused many to exclaim that the days of the ordinary bicycle are numbered, but in this opinion I cannot concur. The ordinary bicycle for the young and active is the most delightful form of cycle to possess.[34]

Five. Sport, Speed and Safety, 1885–93

The "ROVER" SAFETY. Inventors and Sole Makers—STARLEY & SUTTON, Meteor Works, COVENTRY.

A list of all types of bicycles and tricycles shown by manufacturers at the London Stanley Show in February 1887 showed 313 different tricycles and 320 different bicycles. Of the 320 bicycles, the breakdown of types is described as follows: "Ordinary, 148; Rovers, 108; other rear drivers, 5; Kangaroos, 22; other front drivers, 29; children's, 4; Dicycles, 4." Starley and Sutton were the leading makers of the "Rover" type with 11 models, followed by Hillman, Herbert and Cooper, with 6 models.[35]

* * *

Above: Fig. 5.9. An advertisement from Jan. 1887 showed a club rider successfully navigating mud and snow, while the high-wheel rider falls and a tricycle rider lags behind. [Source: *The Cyclist*, 26 Jan. 1897] *Right:* Fig. 5.10. The "Star" bicycle, designed and built only in the United States; late 1880s, unknown location. [Source: unknown, author's collection]

The essential, original development of the safety bicycle alternative to the ordinary appears to have taken place almost exclusively in Great Britain. Both French and American manufacturers borrowed British models, which had been tested in competition on road and track, as their inspiration. In the United States, the *Springfield Wheelmen's Gazette* reported the "Kangaroo" and "Rover" safety races of 1884 and 1885.[36] The "Rover safety" was being advertised by a Boston distributor in March 1886, and the "Kangaroo," "the Original Perfect Safety Bicycle, Faster than any Bicycle, Safer than a Tricycle," was on sale from A.G. Spalding by May 1886. In July 1886, Starley and Sutton themselves advertised the "Rover," which had "proved itself the fastest cycle in the world," in the *League of American Wheelmen Bulletin*.[37]

Races in which safeties competed against ordinaries to contest their superiority do not appear to have taken place in the United States, although the American industry was quick to react to the design impetus from England, producing safety bicycles of American make, of various designs. The life of the high-wheel bicycle seems to have been extended in America by the introduction of an alternative design of high-wheel safety which was never sold, or gained popularity, in Britain. This was the "Star" or "Eagle" design, which reversed the standard large front wheel and small trailing wheel, putting the small wheel at the front, thereby reducing the possibility of a header. The "Star" design was popular for a short time, and was made famous by the fact that the American champion, Arthur Zimmerman, began his career on one. But soon high-wheel and Rover competitors were forced to race separately. At an international race meet in Buffalo in October 1888, five races were specifically designated for Rover riders only.[38]

4. The Rise of Road Racing

The road racing and attempts at record-breaking on British roads, staged specifically to test rival designs of the safety bicycle, were described as "a mania" in the mid–1880s. A variety of routes were used for record attempts, but certain roads, such as the Great North Road out of London, a long stretch of road in good condition where fast times were more likely to be recorded than anywhere else in Britain, were particularly favored. One stretch was described as having "a splendid smooth gravel surface," another as "eleven miles of the best road in the world."[39]

A.J. Wilson, a journalist and fan of long-distance road riding, wrote revealingly that "the manufacture, and fracture, of cycling road records is a decidedly modern, and almost exclusively English, species of sport." Wilson made a distinction between track cyclists, "who are delicately-trained men, so highly strung as to be susceptible to all manner of trifling influences which upset their form," and "the road-riding crack" who:

> does very little "training" in the athlete's acceptance of the term, his regimen consisting of hard riding, and plenty of it ... the hardening and inuring of his frame to fatigues and prolonged efforts, and the cultivation of the dogged pluck necessary to persevere against and combat the almost overpowering tendencies to stop and rest, or fall asleep, on a long journey.[40]

Road racing, the exclusive domain of the high-wheel bicycle at the beginning of the 1880s, became in the mid–1880s the ideal testing ground for rival designs of bicycles and tricycles. They were more appropriately and thoroughly evaluated under varied road con-

Fig. 5.11. The New Inn, Ham Common, Surrey, the kind of pub favored by hard-nosed road riders and record-breakers in the late 1880s. [Source: author's collection]

ditions than on the track. The high-wheel bicycle was a notoriously poor hill-climber and the improvements made in different alternative machines (geared-up ordinaries, tricycles and safety bicycles), enabling them to climb hills well, was very important in road riding. 50-mile, 100-mile, 12-hour and 24-hour road races were mechanical and athletic challenges, and a true test of long-distance road riders. Even longer rides, culminating in the ultimate British endurance event, the Land's End to John-o-Groats "End-to-End" ride, became athletic objectives for road racers.

Shorter races were at first paced, massed-start events, but the public frequently objected to groups of fast-moving cyclists on the road, their numbers often increased by the presence of pacers. These objections created a public relations problem for the sport. Individual attempts to break records were less conspicuous. To be officially recognized, records on both track and road had to be submitted to the Records Committee of the National Cyclists' Union, which had the power "to decline to accept any claim where they consider that the interests of the sport would not be promoted." The Committee was at first useful in insisting on rigorous standards of proof for the timing and supervision of road record attempts, whereas earlier records had sometimes been uncritically accepted (on the basis, for example, of postcards mailed from locations along a route). Such records were described as having "grotesque looseness" by A.J. Wilson, who thought "the new order of things was infinitely preferable to the old."[41] But the N.C.U. did not agree to sanction road records for long.

In reaction to this official resistance to road racing within the N.C.U., the North Road Cycling Club was formed in October 1885, under the impetus of A.J. Wilson, specifically for the purpose of "encouraging and facilitating fast and long-distance riding" (condition of membership was that a rider had to have ridden 100 miles in a day), and its first official run was in February 1886.[42] The members of the club "form the bulk of the habitual sojourners at the various hostelries along the route," among which was the Salisbury Arms, Hatfield, "a coffee-tavern considerably favored by London clubmen," and the Ongley Arms, Biggleswade, run by bicycle-maker Dan Albone, "whose cheery nature is proverbial, and who understands the Bohemian and unconventional habits of the record-breaker, and is never so happy as when laying himself out to plan routes and arrange for timekeeping, checking and pace-making."[43]

To break a long-distance record, a rider had to count on the right combination of well-organized authentication, pacing assistance, mechanical help, food and changes of clothes, a well-chosen route and good weather conditions. Autumn, for example, was "recognized as the best time of the year for road riding ... because the weather is cooler and the roads usually less dusty than in summer time." For a 24-hour ride, a full or near-full moon was desirable for fast night-riding, although "the roads are always lonely during the night, save when an occasional stray horse is startled out of the road, or a night policeman glances up at the silent cyclist flashing past."

No other factor was so important in record-breaking, however, as the assistance of good pace-makers, who gave shelter from the wind, picked a good course on the road, guided the record-breaker through towns, and "will be ready to run ahead to obtain refreshments, to open railway gates, to send telegrams, to oil up the machine while the rider is feeding, and in every imaginable manner to aid in saving time and increasing mileage."[44]

During 1886 and 1887, 18-year-old George P. Mills, of Liverpool's Anfield Bicycle Club, undertook a series of grueling road rides and set new records at many distances on different kinds of machines. Mills became, in fact, a prominent "maker's amateur," and the Anfield club riders gained a "reputation for endurance and dogged perseverance by the establishment of a stupendous list of diurnal records." Mills' performances "have probably received more attention at the hands of the daily press and the public generally than has ever been awarded to anything in cycling of recent years." His record rides in 1886 were described as "without doubt the most wonderful feats ever accomplished on cycles,

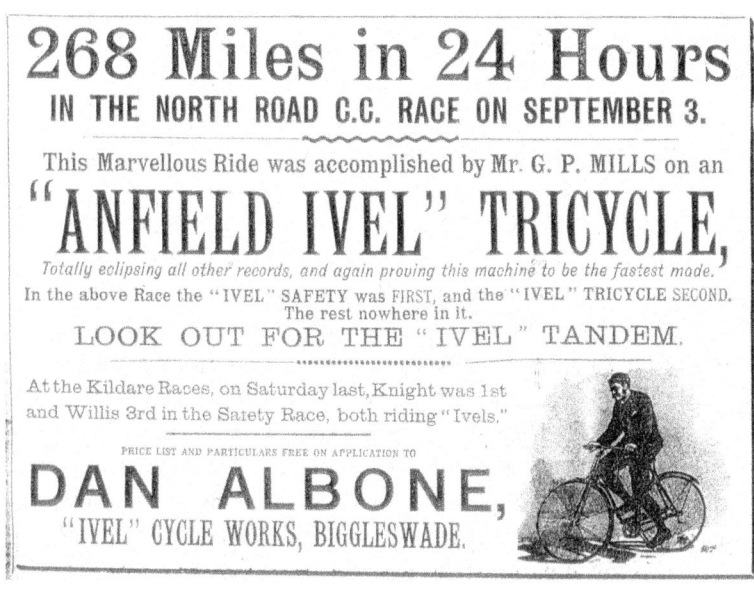

Fig. 5.12. G.P. Mills was an outstanding English long-distance road rider, who tested the performances of various designs of safeties and tricycles in races in the late 1880s and early 1890s. [Source: *Wheeling*, 21 Sept. 1887]

and as an exhibition of human endurance and physical strength, it is doubtful if they have ever been excelled."[45] "G.P. Mills has proved himself to be, beyond doubt, far and away the best road rider England, and perhaps the world, has ever seen," commented *Wheel World* at the end of the season: "Such rides would have been pronounced impossible a couple or three years ago."[46]

The second North Road Club "All-Day Race" in 1887 attracted 37 riders on a variety of machines (5 ordinary bicycles, 20 safeties, 10 tricycles and 1 tandem tricycle), including the promoting club's G.P. Mills and S.F. Edge (Anerley B.C.) on tricycles. The route went out of London on the Great North Road to Peterborough, headed east to Norwich and returned to a circular finishing circuit in Biggleswade. Rain had left the roads "excessively sticky," and competitors who rode out to the start from London "arrived in a fearfully splashed condition." At the start, "the stables were filled to overflowing with a magnificent show of cycles, safeties predominating," while the athletes feasted on "Brobdignagian supplies of rump steak and tomatoes."

Starting together at midnight in a group, the riders raced through the night, later encountering better conditions, with "the full moon shining brightly in a cloudless sky." The following day the riders were allowed to be paced, and "pacemakers galore were about," though they were not helped by rain which continued to fall throughout the day. When the 24 hours ran out at midnight on Saturday night, winner G.P. Mills, on a tricycle, once more had a new record, with 268 miles to his credit. Dan Albone, the maker of Mills' "Ivel" tricycle advertized this ride as "again proving this machine to be the fastest made."[47]

The increased intensity of racing on the roads, however, and the publicity surrounding these record rides, did not come without a price. At a National Cyclists' Union Council meeting in December 1886, a resolution was passed by 22 to 12 that "the Council of the N.C.U. expresses its disapproval of the growing practice of racing on the public roads, and directs the Executive to do its utmost to discourage road racing." The recent flurry of industry-sponsored safety record-setting races described above was evidently fresh in their minds, for one member called them "scandals" and regretted that "road records were becoming much more valuable than path records. They were so to makers."[48] Once again, in September 1887, the Council emphasized that the N.C.U. did not sanction road racing:

> It should be pointed out that by a resolution of the Council strong disapproval was expressed at the practice of racing on the public highways, and in view of the action which it is extremely probable the authorities may take in the immediate future, the policy of the Union cannot be too widely known. As the matter now stands the rights and privileges of thousands of road riders are jeopardised by the inconsiderate action of a very limited number.[49]

In October 1887, a little-known club called the West Roads Cycling Club organized a 25-mile "open" handicap race with a field of more than 70 riders plus pace-makers in a prominent cycling location, the Ripley Road, which "showed a great want of common sense on the part of the officials," and resulted in "over 70 cyclists at a time tearing through country villages." The race, "one of the worst managed races it has ever been our fate to witness," brought attention from the police, and a harsh editorial reaction from *Wheeling*:

> The time has come for a change. Road racing is a danger to every good interest of cycling. It is ruining path racing, it is annihilating the old club gatherings, it is changing the spirit of the road, it is infuriating public opinion, and finally it is paving the way for restrictive legislation, which will press hardly upon thousands of cyclists who never competed in a race of any sort in their lives.... We are not so bigoted

or narrow-minded as not to see the charm of road racing. We should like well to take part in it ourselves, but the sentiment is purely selfish. No reasonable man can doubt that the practice is unfair to the public ... the greatest happiness of the greatest number demands the suppression of road racing.[50]

The road races that critics principally objected to were the commercially-driven events described above, and *Wheeling* suggested a penalty of the forfeiture of amateur status for riders taking part in them.

Both Harry Etherington and Lacy Hillier ("We are at last agreed on one subject!") presented a motion before the N.C.U. suggesting that any rider taking part in a road race of less than 100 miles would risk suspension. The N.C.U., effectively powerless to actually ban road racing, issued further warnings during 1887 and decided that it would no longer recognize road records of any kind, which it had started to do in 1885; only track records would be recognized.

This was a serious and contentious rift within the bicycle racing community, which would have far-reaching repercussions. The immediate result was the foundation in April/May 1888 of a new organization, the Road Records Association, following a meeting called by A.J. Wilson of the North Road Cycling Club. The stated aims of the Road Records Association were "to check and verify the genuineness of claims to best performances on record accomplished by cyclists on the road, and to prevent the publication of fictitious or unchecked records."[51] This organization still exists.

The foundation of the Road Records Association, the third national body created in early British cycling, was thus in a sense a secession from the N.C.U., although A.J. Wilson stressed that the new organization would not be hostile to the older national body and it agreed to accept N.C.U. road records established and recognized between 1885 and 1888. The creation of the new organization, on the other hand, did allow the N.C.U. to distance itself strategically from a racing activity which had become a public relations problem.

The Road Records Association was also progressive in the important sense that its events were "open," and records could in fact be supported by the industry, in effect condoning professionalism. But the withdrawal of N.C.U. support for road racing, which can be seen as a failure to present a united front in defense of an important, expanding aspect of bicycle racing, also had profound, and unfortunate, consequences for the future of the sport in Britain.

The absence of any organized opposition to racing on public roads in France, Belgium, Italy and Germany led in the early 1890s to the first well-publicized massed-start "classics" of bicycle racing—the beginnings of the modern European sport. The promoters of road racing in Britain, however, were obliged to stage events differently, holding inconspicuous early morning time trials and individual place-to-place record attempts in order to avoid public criticism and police interference. In France and Belgium, on the other hand, road racing was presented to the public as an epic sporting battle, played out on terrain well known to spectators, with heroic contestants worthy of admiration who spectators could easily identify with. A working-class victor was all the more celebrated on account of his humble origins.

British officials, in contrast, appear to have been fearful that the conspicuous presence of the "rough" lower middle-class and working-class riders in bicycle racing would reflect badly on the sport and provoke hostility towards non-racing cyclists. Other popular sports such as golf, tennis, rowing or cricket were easily integrated into and preserved within the middle-class life-style and expectations of behavior, but from its earliest days competitive cycling attracted a considerable number of working-class riders. Again, the public nature of a sport that took place in public spaces, and in which strangers "scorched" through towns and villages, meant there was much greater potential for inter-class friction and disputes over the rights of different categories of road-users and local residents.[52]

5. Competition and the Invention of the Revolutionary Pneumatic Tire

The advantages of the rear-driven safety bicycle could be seen equally in racing, in recreational road riding, and in utility riding. They could be summarized as follows:

Fig. 5.13. A mid–1890 advertisement for The Pneumatic Tyre and Booth's Cycle Agency emphasized the speed and record potential of the pneumatic tire. [Source: Mecredy and Wilson, *The Art and Pastime of Cycling*, 2nd ed., 1890]

1. The safety bicycle had a lower center of gravity. It was safer because it couldn't tilt forward, and more practical because the foot could be put to the ground for starting and stopping.
2. The riding position was at the same time comfortable and efficient. It overcame the inherent problem of the high-wheel bicycle, of both pedaling and steering the front wheel, which involved contradictory efforts.
3. The weight of the rider was better distributed between the two wheels, which was better for hill-climbing and for descending.
4. With the chain-drive a machine could be geared up or down to suit the rider's needs; the design opened the possibility of variable gearing.

The only really serious disadvantage of the safety on rough and stony roads was the increased vibration from the nearly equal-sized wheels, which were smaller than the big driving wheel of the ordinary and equipped with solid rubber tires. This issue immediately focused attention on the tires and inspired experimentation with various kinds of sprung frames, the best-known of which was the Linley and Biggs' "Whippet." Various kinds of "suspension," "cushion" and hollow tires (non-pneumatic) were experimented with, and the introduction of the first pneumatic tires followed quickly. The pneumatic tire became the key factor in the bicycle racing and recreational cycling boom of the 1890s and was crucial in the subsequent development of motor-driven vehicles.[53] Perhaps no other previous advance within bicycle technology had such a wide-ranging impact and underwent such explosive growth as the invention and general adoption of the pneumatic tire. The repercussions for the nascent rubber industry were gigantic.

How exactly should we seek to explain the close chronological proximity of the rise of the safety bicycle and the subsequent introduction of the pneumatic tire? What is the precise social and technological relationship between these two landmarks of bicycle technology? Should it be explained simply as a logical chronological progression—the success of the "Rover" safety and subsequent designs of many safety bicycles creating a new problem (vibration) which immediately stimulated the search for its solution? Certainly the intense inventive developments, rival patents and litigation within the pneumatic tire industry provide a fascinating example of socio-technological evolution in the 1890–1893 period. Once the pneumatic principle had been demonstrated as superior and accepted, many details of the design and fixing of the detachable tire, rim and valve remained to be worked out and put onto the market. And the test-market was, of course, the hundreds of thousands of racing and recreational cyclists—consumers who were using the tires on their bicycles.[54]

In the 1890 edition of *The Art and Pastime of Cycling*, Irish journalist Richard Mecredy summarized the impact and the advantages of the pneumatic tire:

> Perhaps nothing in the history of cycling has created such a revolutionary sensation as the Pneumatic Tyre. Invented late in 1888, it was tested quietly for nearly a twelvemonth in and about Belfast, before being launched upon the British and foreign cycle markets; and its success in 1889–1890 was so phenomenal that it must be regarded as a distinctive feature of this age.... The advantages which the Pneumatic Tyre have been proved to possess are many. Comfort to the rider, perhaps, ranks first in importance.... Increased speed is another advantage which appeals to every cyclist. Both on road and path, on macadam and gravel, on cinders and grass, Pneumatic tyred machines have been proved to be faster than solid tyred. Personally we estimate the difference to be from half a mile to three miles an hour, according to the nature of the road. The rougher the road the greater the advantage.

And the pneumatic tire had the huge advantage of helping to eliminate vibration:

> Few people have any conception of the wearying effect of vibration.... Pneumatic tyres almost double the powers of the average tourist on bad roads. As the roads get better the advantage becomes less, until on a surface like that of the Great North road, it is at its minimum.[55]

An advertisement from the same book, for The Pneumatic Tyre and Booth's Cycle Agency (Dunlop), in Dublin, proclaimed: "It is now an acknowledged fact that no Solid or Cushion Tyred Machine can compete with a Pneumatic for speed." The advertisement also quoted a significant passage from *Scottish Sport*: "It is clear that before a year the solid tyre will no longer be fitted to racing machines." So great were the proven advantages of the pneumatic tire for racing that less than two years after its introduction, the disadvantages of the solid tire had made it unacceptable. Only a very few racing men attempted to hold onto the high-wheel bicycle principle by fitting pneumatics to specially adapted wheels, but their "retro" optimism was short-lived!

In the 1893 (third) edition of the same book, Mecredy confirmed the optimistic predictions he had made in 1890:

In the second edition of this work, we concluded the present chapter with the remark that the pneumatic tyre (then a complete novelty) "promises to effect wonders," and it is scarcely needful to say how abundantly that prophecy has been fulfilled. The pneumatic tyre has thoroughly revolutionized the cycling trade within two seasons; and bearing in mind this invention alone, he would be a bold man who would essay to prognosticate what evolution is in store for cycling. At the present time, it may be safely said that all classes of cycles have attained to a pitch of perfection not surpassed in any other department of mechanical science.[56]

Fig. 5.14. John Boyd Dunlop and his son Johnny with a new spring-frame safety in October 1890. Apparently, this did not meet with success. [Source: *The Irish Cyclist*, 29 Oct. 1890]

There is evidently a strong element of self-interested pride in bicycle industry achievements in this passage, but it serves to illustrate how one person centrally involved in progressive bicycle technology viewed his participation in these historic developments. Richard Mecredy, whose brother Alexander Mecredy was a bicycle manufacturer in Dublin, and who was himself a record-setting amateur road cyclist, was editor of the *Irish Cyclist* in Dublin, the initial center of the extraordinary technological and economic developments around the young pneumatic tire industry. Richard Mecredy's perception of the bicycle industry as being on the cutting edge of technological change was therefore that of an experienced insider. Perhaps he already had a sense of the radical global impact pneumatic tire technology would have in the future.

W.J. Grew, in *The Cycle Industry*, published in 1921, also wrote of the impact the first pneumatic tires had on the industry and on racing, and of Mecredy's proximity to the crucial events:

> I saw one of the first of these very crude tyres made by the Dunlop Tyre and Booth's Cycle Agency, Dublin, on a tricycle ridden to Coventry by Mr. R.J. Mecredy, the editor of the Irish cycling and motoring papers.... The tyres were quite unknown, and when the tricycle was left outside a hotel (not in the centre of the city) for ten minutes, a crowd of 400 or 500 people were found pushing each other to obtain a sight of it.... Within a few months everybody in the city knew all about pneumatic tyres. The Du Cros brothers, an athletic family of Dublin, commenced to race on bicycles fitted with them, and very soon handicappers had to give racing cyclists on solid tyres a considerable start if riders of pneumatic tyred machines were entered. Within a year of the commencement of the serious manufacture of pneumatic tyres no racing man of any pretensions troubled to compete on anything else.[57]

The essential history of the invention of the pneumatic tire in 1887–88 by John Boyd Dunlop, a Belfast veterinary surgeon of Scottish origin, is reliably documented in a number of different places.[58] The most unusual feature of Dunlop's early involvement was, perhaps, that he initially had no contact with the bicycle industry, and that pneumatic tire experiments did not begin within the industry; they were not conducted, for example, by the manufacturers of solid tires, as might have been expected. Dunlop, who was not even a cyclist, fitted the first embryonic pneumatic tires to his son's tricycle, and soon after had experimental bicycles built by Belfast bicycle agents and makers, R.W. Edlin and Finlay Sinclair. Dunlop took out his first patent on the idea on 23 July 1888 and it was registered on 7 December 1888.[59] Early in 1889, Edlin and Dunlop ordered new, large bicycle frame castings, necessary for the new, wide tires, from a Glasgow castings company. These were used to make twelve pneumatic-tired bicycles and six tricycles. Mecredy reported that he saw these bicycles in the process of being assembled at the Edlin works in February 1889.[60]

No sooner were the first pneumatic-tired bicycles completed than they began to be used in local competitions. Enter into the story the extraordinary athletes of the large Du Cros family. The first appearance of a bicycle fitted with pneumatic tires at a race occurred on 18 May 1889. W. Hume (Belfast Cruisers Cycling Club) appeared on an Edlin safety bicycle weighing only 23 lbs, fitted with the new tires, at a Queen's College, Belfast, Sports Day, where he won all four races in which he competed, beating Alfred, Willie and Harvey du Cros, Jr., who were all riding solid-tired ordinary bicycles. This race was also the first occasion on which J.B. Dunlop met Harvey du Cros, the father of the beaten Du Cros brothers. Hume's convincing victories had immediate repercussions. The Du Cros brothers, realizing that they didn't stand a chance against Hume, didn't wait until the conclusion of the race meeting and returned immediately to Dublin with their father. Another brother, Arthur du Cros, who had already abandoned the ordinary bicycle and was racing on a solid-tired safety, was pitted against Hume on 1 June 1889, in the 5-mile Championship of Ireland, held at the North of Ireland Cricket Club Sports, and on that occasion won on

Fig. 5.15. The Du Cros family from Dublin epitomized the rise of the "gentleman amateur" in racing. They were pioneers in proving the pneumatic tire in competition. Seen here (top to bottom, left to right): George, Arthur, Harvey (Jr.), William, Alfred, Harvey (Sr.), and Fred du Cros. [Source: author's collection]

Fig. 5.16. These photos of very early pneumatic races were at a Dublin University Bicycle Club meeting, in which R.J. Mecredy, Stadnicki and the Du Cros brothers scored victories. [Source: *The Irish Cyclist*, 16 July 1890, author's collection]

solid tires, with Hume, on pneumatics, coming in second. Soon after, Arthur du Cros borrowed a pneumatic-tired bicycle from Dunlop himself, and on 5 September 1889, in Cork, won all four races in which he competed.[61]

W. Hume was the first Irish rider to compete in England on pneumatics. He appeared at the Liverpool Police Sports on 20 July 1889, where he won the 1 and 3-mile handicaps. "To say that the tyres caused a sensation is to put it mildly," wrote H.W. Bartleet; "a majority of the public simply roared with laughter, and only a few of the experts realized the possibilities of the air tyre." The pneumatic tires were, of course, much bigger and fatter than the usual solid tires. Bartleet quotes from the reminiscence of a spectator of the races, who confirmed that "the first appearance of Hume created contemptuous laughter, which was turned to amazement and then to applause when he made common hacks of his opponents."

Hume himself remembered that "the spectators at Liverpool were very hard to keep away from my machine; everyone wanted to see the old Irish home-made bicycle. Even the handicapper, when he saw it first, said that if he had known I was going to ride a machine like that he would have put me on a longer mark: he changed his mind before the day was finished."

Bartleet recounts that Hume's bicycle was displayed in the window of a bicycle shop in Lime Street, Liverpool, and "attracted such a crowd of curious sightseers that they overflowed the pavement on to the roadway and had to be moved on by the police."[62] The "Irish Brigade" (B.W. Pigott, Arthur du Cros, K.N. Stadnicki, R.J. Mecredy, Harvey du Cros, Jr., and F.F. MacCabe) visited England in 1890 and won a large numbers of races on Dunlop tires. Most impressively, Mecredy pulled off a clean sweep of the four N.C.U. national championships at the Paddington, London track, at 1-mile, 5-mile, 25-mile and 50-mile distances, as well as establishing new

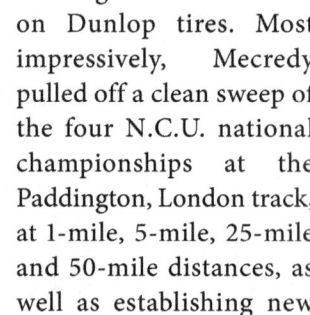

Top: Fig. 5.17. Arthur du Cros, one of "The Irish Brigade." [Source: *The Irish Cyclist*, 1890] *Bottom:* Fig. 5.18. Three of "The Irish Brigade"—Arthur du Cros, R.J. Mecredy and Harvey Du Cros—with the earliest pneumatic-tired bicycles, in a photograph published in *The Irish Cyclist*. [Source: *The Irish Cyclist*, 20 Aug. 1890]

competition records at five distances, the ¼-mile, 1-mile, 5-mile and 10-mile records (set by Mecredy), and the ½-mile (set by Arthur du Cros).[63]

During September and October 1889, the first Dunlop company, known as The Pneumatic Tyre and Booth's Cycle Agency, Ltd., which incorporated the Edlin company, was created in Dublin. The first board meeting was held in Dublin on 30 November 1889, with Harvey du Cros as chairman. The other board members were J.B. Dunlop; Richard Booth of Booth's Brothers; Richard Mecredy, editor of the *Irish Cyclist*; Frederick W. Wood, and John Griffiths, of Booth's Brothers. And there were subsequent legal challenges to the validity of the pneumatic patent taken out by Dunlop's original company. In January 1891, highlighting the quickly expanding commercial impact of the pneumatic tire on the international market, Harvey du Cros traveled to Chicago to set up a branch of Dunlop tire. A Coventry Dunlop factory and a London retail outlet, managed by A.J. Wilson, were also established in 1891. In 1894, the Pneumatic Tyre and Booth's Cycle Agency became the Pneumatic Tyre Co., and this in turn became the Dunlop Pneumatic Tyre Co. in September 1895, though Dunlop himself had resigned from the company in May of the same year.

The foundations of the Dunlop commercial empire were thus laid in a few short years entirely within the bicycle industry, and Dunlop was heavily dependent on bicycle racing to advertize the viability and superiority of its products, and the recreational demand increased quickly. Other companies, notable among which were the North British Rubber

Fig. 5.19. *The Irish Cyclist* honored "The Irish Brigade" with a photo supplement, left to right, B.W. Pigott, Arthur Du Cros, Count Stadnicki, R.J. Mecredy, Harvey Du Cros, F.F. MacCabe. [Source: *The Irish Cyclist*, 1 Oct. 1890]

Company, the Macintosh Company, the Preston Davies Tyre and Valve Company, Smith's Company, the Palmer Tyre and others, engaged in fierce competition to develop viable tires for this huge new market, putting a sudden demand on the import of high quality rubber from colonial outposts abroad.[64]

Not all new tires were pneumatics, however, and for a brief period "cushion" tires (tires with a hollow, springy, though not inflated interior) were put on the market. Tire manufacturers rapidly became as important as bicycle makers in the sponsorship of record rides, and from 1891 onwards, the pages of the cycling press were crammed with advertisements touting the superiority of different makes of tires, tested in competition, over their rivals. The ambitions of tire makers to sign up leading champions to break records in order to publicize their products led to the increased professionalization within the sport.

The enormous impact of the introduction of the pneumatic tire into bicycle racing and recreational riding is hard to over-exaggerate, as are the contributions which competition made to the testing, development and perfecting of the tire manufacturers' emerging technologies. An article by Harry Hewitt Griffin in *Cycling* in 1891, which reported a lecture given at the Stanley Show by E.R. Shipton, Secretary of the Cyclists' Touring Club, gave many hints of the unfolding technical complexities involved in the new tire technology when the need for a light pneumatic tire for track racing was the issue:

> Happily, racing cyclists are mostly men to whom expense is a mere nothing, therefore those who are anxious to bring down the bicycle record ... will doubtless go in for something as follows: (a) a much lighter frame than at present. (b) a large but very thin skin bladder. (c) light silk covering instead of heavy canvas. (d) much lighter outer rubber, exceedingly thin except the point of contact with the ground. Built thus, a safety might well be got well inside 20 lbs, and an immense improvement in speed rates would be certain.... Thanks to the rapid development of the tyre question, we now feel competent to forecast what is wanted and what conditions must be fulfilled by tyres if they are to be of practical use. Only inflated tyres need serious consideration in connection with anything approaching the perfect cycle. With these, imperative conditions are demanded (sic). They may be roughly summarized as:
>
> 1. Simplicity of construction.
> 2. Ease of repair.
> 3. Readily inflated and leakage reduced to a minimum.
> 4. Quick means of releasing air, so as to be kept slack when not in use.
> 5. Reliable, proof as far as possible against cuts, punctures, etc.
> 6. Cheapness.
> 7. Ample supply by the trade and manufacturers.
>
> Any type or types of tire fulfilling these requirements will be in universal demand, and ere long anything else will be considered antiquated.[65]

Thus, the same issues that had had to be addressed in the manufacture of racing bicycles in the 1880s—strength, reliability, lightness, efficiency, simplicity, all of which were aspects of athletic performance, and contributed towards athletic success—had once again to be taken into consideration in the development of the pneumatic tire in 1891.

6. The Cycling Revolution, 1888–93

The days of the ordinary, the high-wheel bicycle, once the best tool to achieve maximum speed in racing, were numbered. "An ordinary bicycle race is certainly one of the prettiest contests that a sports-loving crowd can witness," wrote the editor of *Cycling* in May 1891, but:

> the ordinary is the machine of the past, and the safety is the machine of the present time.... The safety bicycle is essentially a speed machine, and the still greater qualifying advantage it possesses lies in its adaptability to all sizes of riders. The absolute necessity to a speedy ordinaryist is height, and consequently a fast wheel; but a safetyist may be short and sturdy, or tall and slim, as nature may have moulded him, and he can still find in the dwarf a machine quite plastic to his requirements, upon which he may accomplish speed performances that he could never approach upon the necessarily small-wheeled ordinary he must ride'[66]

Another crucial advantage of the Rover safety design is identified here. The gearing-up capability of the safety introduced a leveling effect among competitors of different heights, so that its adaptability (saddle and handlebar height could be adjusted easily) became one of its crucial merits. Through the later 1880s, the British, Continental and American national track championships and road races were still dominated by the high-wheel bicycle, but it became increasingly apparent that the safety was faster and that the dissimilar machines could not be safely raced against each other side by side, even though their relative speed under similar conditions was still compulsively compared. The difference in speed between the solid-tired ordinary and the solid-tired safety was dramatically emphasized when the safety bicycle was fitted with pneumatic tires, in spite of the initial scepticism and hilarity which greeted the earliest fat pneumatics. The increased comfort of the pneumatic tire was a benefit that was easily demonstrated in competition and one that the recreational and utility rider could also enjoy. Thus, a group of advantages marked the decisive socio-technological "victory" of the safety over the ordinary bicycle.

From 1890 to 1892, a short period of competitive overlap, the National Cyclists' Union ran concurrent ordinary and safety championships on the track. In 1890, as already mentioned, Richard Mecredy (Dublin University Bicycle Club) swept the 1, 5, 25 and 50 mile safety championships using pneumatic tires, while F.J. Osmond (Brixton Ramblers) won all the ordinary races at the same distances, clinging to the older machine with solid tires. In 1892, with the pneumatic tire firmly established and visiting American Arthur Zimmerman winning three of the four amateur safety championships, J.H. Adams (Speedwell Bicycle Club) won all the ordinary championships. In spite of the abortive attempts to rescue the high-wheel bicycle from competitive extinction by fitting it with pneumatic tires, from the early 1890s onwards the outmoded high-wheel bicycle was no longer in serious competitive contention and by 1893 official N.C.U. ordinary bicycle championships on the track had been abandoned.

Thus, the introduction of the safety bicycle, closely followed by the appearance of the pneumatic tire and the associated improvements in pneumatic technology (detachable, repairable tires, efficient valves), had a dramatic impact on bicycle racing, as well as on recreational and utilitarian cycling. Racing tested and proved the technological changes that were subsequently introduced into the wider consumer market. At first unreliable, the pneumatic tire was rapidly improved and it led to increased speed in all areas of the sport—on road and track, in championship events and in competition aimed at setting world records—as well as to an expansion of the scope and popularity of recreational and utilitarian cycling.

This constant improvement in times and distances led to a kind of euphoria within the sport and industry, the result of accelerating change and seemingly limitless competitive possibilities. "In the sport of cycling no feature is so marked as the rapid progress in lowering previous bests on record ... there is practically no limit to the improvement and future development of the cycle," wrote the editors in the first issue of *Cycling* in 1891:

> The hollow tyre has opened up a wide field of future possibilities in record breaking. A year ago when the big tyres made their initial appearance before the English cycling public, the wiseacres sagely shook their heads, and even if they had some slight belief in their utility for road riding or for rough grass courses, they never imagined for a moment that on the fastest tracks in the world the riders of hollow-tyred machines would carry all before them, and pulverise every existing record.[67]

Four years later, in a review of the Stanley Show of 1895, where a record number of 2,690 different bicycles and tricycles was shown by 212 manufacturers, the always precise chronicler of technical information, H.H. Griffin, wrote that:

> after the chaos brought about by the safety form of bicycle ... the 20 pneumatic bicycles shown in 1890 acted as a torch of enlightenment, and set alight the conflagration which has practically consumed every other type of tyre. From all solids in 1889, and .064 cushions in 1890, cushions jumped to 54% in 1891, pneumatics being only 14%, and it was not until the autumn show of 1891 that the pneumatic asserted itself—39¾% to 32½% cushions; by 1893 pneumatics were 85%, cushions 8%, and solids 1%.

Griffin went on to express his opinion that "the concentration of taste and attention upon the rear driver is at last universal. Since 1891 only 5 ordinaries have been shown, not one since 1893, and geared ordinaries have been extinct for the same time." Reviewing the 1896 Stanley Show, Griffin wrote that "in no other form of manufacture has so vast a revolution swept over the country."[68]

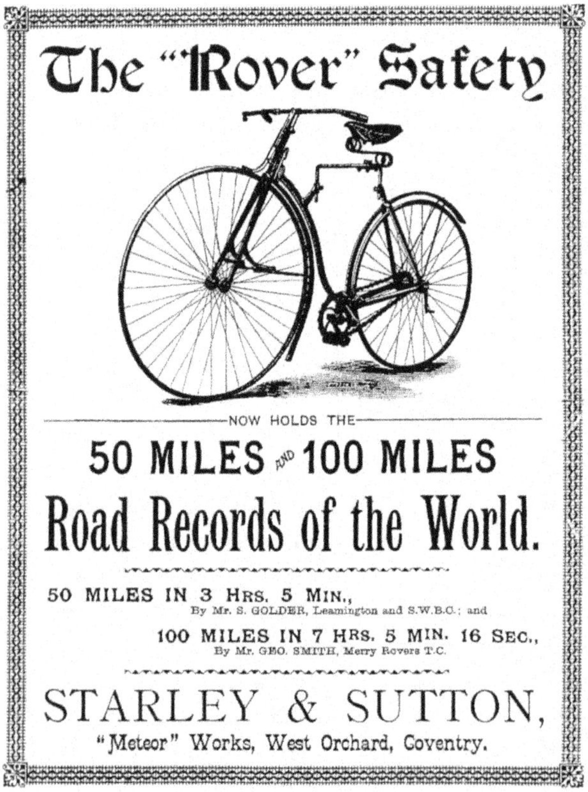

Another persistent and accurate chronicler of technological developments, Henry Sturmey, noted the expanded business opportunities presented by the safety bicycle and the pneumatic tire, "which in the course of one or two seasons drove the high machine out of the market." But he noted that the concentration on the pneumatic safety also impacted further improvement of the tricycle, "the makers' attention being entirely devoted to the improvement of the safety, to the utter neglect of the till then much considered tricycle, that form of machine too, despite its many advantages, lost its hold on popular favour, and left the rear-driven safety of today complete master of the field for the time being."

The principle reasons for the

Fig. 5.20. The "Rover" safety bicycle established road records in 1885, marking it decisively as not only safer than the ordinary, but also faster. [Source: author's collection]

Table 5 A. Comparison of selected "ordinary" and "safety" bicycle competition records on the track recognized by the National Cyclists' Union between 1885 and 1893, compiled from *Wheeling*, 21 Oct. 1885; *The Wheel*, 28 June 1889; *The Wheel*, 26 Aug. 1890; *Cycling*, 19 Nov. 1892, and *Cycling*, 18 Nov. 1893. Some of the later records were paced.

	1 mile	5 miles	25 miles	50 miles	100 miles
1885					
Ordinary bicycle	2m 39²⁄₅s	14m 18s	1h 16m 41³⁄₅s	2h 43m 58³⁄₅s	
Safety bicycle	2m 55²⁄₅s	No race	No race	No race	
1889	1 mile	5 miles	25 miles	50 miles	
Ordinary bicycle	2m 31⁴⁄₅s	13m 55s	1h 13m 49³⁄₅s	2h 40m 33²⁄₅s	
Safety bicycle	2m 37s	13m 58⁴⁄₅s	No race	No race	
1890	1 mile	5 miles	25 miles	50 miles	
Ordinary bicycle	2m 28⁴⁄₅s	13m 55s	1h 13 49³⁄₅s	2h 33m 05²⁄₅s	
Safety bicycle—Solid tires	2m 34⁴⁄₅s	13m 43³⁄₅s	1h 14m 37¹⁄₅s	2h 41m 47s	
Safety bicycle—pneumatic	2m 26⁴⁄₅s	13m 16²⁄₅s	No race	No race	
1892	1 mile	5 miles	25 miles	50 miles	100 miles
Ordinary bicycle	2m 28⁴⁄₅s	13m 44¹⁄₅s	1h 12m 48³⁄₅s	2h 33m 37²⁄₅s	5h 50m 5²⁄₅s
Safety bicycle—pneumatic	2m 12³⁄₅s	12m 16¹⁄₅s	1h 5m 55²⁄₅s	2h 17m 1⁴⁄₅s	5h 4m 18¹⁄₅s
1893	1 mile	5 miles	25 miles	50 miles	100 miles
Ordinary bicycle	2m 28⁴⁄₅s	13m 44¹⁄₅s	1h 12m 48³⁄₅s	2h 33m 37²⁄₅s	5h 50m 5²⁄₅s
Safety bicycle—pneumatic	2m 4¹⁄₅s	11m 33¹⁄₅s	59m 6⅘s	2h 5m 45⁴⁄₅s	4h 29m 39¹⁄₅s

decline in the use of tricycles may certainly have been their unwieldiness, their weight and their size (very difficult to store in small houses with narrow front doors), but Sturmey's suggestion here is that the technological changes successfully implemented in the safety bicycle had also become expressions of fashion and taste.[69]

Although it is of course impossible to draw precise chronological boundaries, the unrelenting changes in the industry and sport in the years 1888 to 1893 marked the end of what might be termed the era of "early" cycling for many inter-related reasons. First, the safety bicycle had successfully pushed aside the high-wheeler as it proved itself superior in safety, speed, efficiency and adaptability. Second, the pneumatic tire had effected a technological revolution in sweeping aside the solid tire. And third, the tricycle had declined almost to the point of non-participation as a serious racing machine. Finally, due to the increase over the years in international competition and the need for commonly agreed upon competitive standards, the first international governing body, the International

Table 5 B. World records on the track at all distances, established on pneumatic-tired safety bicycles during the 1893 season, recognized by the National Cyclists' Union and the League of American Wheelmen. *All* world records had been established on pneumatics. [Source: *Cycling*, 18 Nov. 1893]

Record	Time/Distance	Holder	Place	Date
¼ mile (flying start)	24²⁄₅s	J.S. Johnson	Independence, Iowa	1 Nov. 1893
¼ mile	28s	Ditto	Ditto	Ditto
½ mile	59²⁄₅s	Ditto	Ditto	Ditto
¾ mile	1m 30³⁄₅s	H.C. Tyler	Springfield, Mass.	5 Oct. 1893
1 mile	2m 0²⁄₅s	Ditto	Ditto	11 Oct. 1893
5 miles	11m 6¹⁄₅s	L.S. Meintjes	Ditto	11 Sept. 1893
10 miles	23m 4³⁄₅s	L.S. Meintjes	Ditto	14 Sept. 1893
25 miles	57m 40³⁄₅s	L.S. Meintjes	Ditto	Ditto
50 miles	2h 5m 45⁴⁄₅s	J.W. Stocks	Herne Hill	30 Aug. 1893
100 miles	4h 29m 39¹⁄₅s	A.V. Linton	Ditto	21 Oct. 1893
1 hour	26 miles 107 yds	L.S. Meintjes	Springfield, Mass.	14 Sept. 1893
6 hours	127 miles 130 yds	H. Desgrange	Buffalo, Paris	3 Oct. 1893
12 hours	240 miles 690 yds	C.W. Wridgeway	Herne Hill	7 Oct. 1893
24 hours	426 miles 440 yds	F.W. Shorland	Ditto	21–22 July 1893

Cyclists' Association, was founded in 1892 by European and American national cycling bodies, and the first formally organized amateur World Championships were held in Chicago in 1893, a recognition of America's importance as one of the leaders in cycling and of the global reach of cycling as a sport.

In all these respects, the sport had arrived at an identifiable point of maturity and "modernity." The technological revolution had brought the bicycle to the verge of a commercial "boom" that would profoundly affect all aspects of cycling—competitive, recreational and utilitarian.

The modern bicycle had been born.

Chapter Six

The Foundations of Modern Road Racing

1. Road Competition in Britain and France

THE FACT THAT BRITAIN was so close to France was conducive to international competition between 1869 and the early 1890s. But differing cultural approaches and competitive standards, particularly concerning the interpretation of the amateur rule, limited regular meetings between the two European countries with the biggest bicycle industries and the greatest enthusiasm for cycling as a sport.[1]

The Union Vélocipédique de France did not make a strict distinction between amateur and professional cyclists, and in France, as in most other European countries, it was considered normal and acceptable to race for cash prizes. No barrier existed in France, therefore, to exchanges between British and French professionals. But a British amateur who raced in France risked his amateur status at home and could be declared a professional by the National Cyclists' Union because he had raced against other "professionals." It was safer for a British amateur to stay at home. Similarly, a French rider who wanted to compete in England was automatically suspect there and likely to be excluded from amateur events.[2]

The Union Vélocipédique de France was founded in February 1881, "to promote all forms of cycling," and French track racing in the 1880s produced champions such as Frédéric de Civry, Paul Médinger, Georges Cassignard, Jules Dubois, H.O. Duncan, Henri Fournier, Charles Terront and others. In this large, still mostly agricultural country, racing was most popular in Paris and the north-east, and in the south-west, with Bordeaux and its club, the Véloce Club Bordelais, an active center of cycling activity.

Baron Frédéric De Civry (1861–93), ex-champion high-wheel rider, died in Paris on 15 March 1893 at the age of 32. He was widely mourned in the cycling press. De Civry, born into an impoverished aristocratic family, earned his living as a cyclist on French tracks in the 1880s, and then relied on his connections and business acumen to do what would now be called "marketing" in Paris, first for Rudge and then for Adolphe Clément, who was still his employer at the time of his death. He had been ill with tuberculosis for some time, reported Maurice Martin in *Véloce-Sport*, but that had not prevented him from being involved with racing almost to the end. De Civry was involved organizationally with the first surge of commercialized road racing in France. In 1891, he supervised second-placed finisher Jiel-Laval's training for the first Paris-Brest-Paris race, and looked after the long-distance rider, Stéphane, during his 24hour record ride at the Velodrome Buffalo in September 1892. De Civry's career, wrote Martin, was "one of the most active and most original a man could have had."[3]

De Civry was born in 1861, and had his most successful period as a cyclist between 1880 and 1887, when he was the most popular French champion, a rival and companion of Howell, Terront, Médinger and Duncan. In 1881, he won 33 of the 35 races he entered in France and all of the races he entered in England. Of 331 races in which he competed during his 8-year career, he won 290 places (211 first, 61 second and 27 third). He was several times French champion at both short and long distances, and his most outstanding ride was cited as his 50-mile professional World Championship in Leicester, in 1883. De Civry was buried in style in March 1893. The wreaths on his coffin were from many of the important names in the cycling world, including his employer Adolphe Clément and the Dunlop Company. De Civry's death was symbolic of the passing of an era. He represented the democratic aspect of French sport, a poor Baron successfully earning his living in bicycle racing, but without class stigma being attached to his professionalism.

Road racing became increasingly popular in France, England and the United States in the late 1880s and early 1890s, and first emerged during those years as a distinct, increasingly specialized branch of the sport. The most difficult aspect of road racing was that racers encountered the challenges of the natural environment: hills, wind, rain, heat, cold and often appalling roads. They needed extraordinary strength and stamina and suffered an unprecedented level of fatigue. The most controversial aspect was that racing took place in public space, and had to share that space with other road users, but that also brought the riders into intimate contact with the population of the towns and villages through which they passed, and created opportunities for a new kind of publicity. Road and track racing were not mutually exclusive, but whereas track riders tended to train for relatively short distances (20 miles was considered a long-distance race on the track until the mid–1890s), road riders were endurance athletes.

Because of the different social conditions in England and France, however, road racing developed differently in those countries. A French journalist, writing in 1885, frankly admitted the superior strength and numbers of the English riders: "The English are strongest in the sheer numbers of their outstanding champions; compared with the four or five first-class racers we have, they could easily have about twenty at the starting line."[4] In England road racing was organized by clubs, with an emphasis on long-distance time trials such as the ones promoted on the Great North Road by the North Road Cycling Club (founded in October 1885) or the Anfield Bicycle Club. But the National Cyclists' Union did not promote or sanction road events or championships.[5]

Over a period of many years, the English road sport was opposed by the general public and by certain factions within the cycling community. Questions were raised about its public image and its respectability. But in France road racing in the early 1890s appears to have expanded without objections about its propriety and image, and even with the support of local civic leaders and the open financial backing of the press and the bicycle industry, both of which, of course, profited from it.[6]

Bicycle racing in Britain confronted a major turning point in the early 1890s. While French enthusiasm for racing in centers such as Paris and Bordeaux was growing, British road racing was going through a period of public criticism and self-examination. Strong opinions were expressed about organized "scorching" on public roads. It tended to give cycling a bad name. Some people thought it should be severely restricted, or even banned altogether. Public complaints and direct intervention by the police were realities which promoting clubs had to contend with. There was constant pressure from within the National Cyclists' Union to preserve what many N.C.U. officials saw as the integrity and respectability of British amateurism. This meant discouraging the direct involvement and financial support of the bicycle industry.

In the United States, road racing enjoyed a surge of popularity in the 1880s and 1890s in and around major cities, but the peak of the enthusiasm of the mid– and later 1890s appears to have been short-lived.[7] Around major cities, such as New York, Boston and Chicago, road racing was promoted by clubs and local newspapers and races were held on the relatively good urban and suburban roads, such as, for example, the Chicago and Pullman races (Chicago), the Martin (Buffalo) and the Irvington-Millburn (New Jersey), which were held annually and referred to as "classics."[8]

Fig. 6.1. Frederick John Osmond, one of the leading English road riders of the early pneumatic period, adopted a position still closely related to that of high-wheel riders. [Source: *Cycling*, 1 Aug. 1891.]

A small group of long-distance riders, affiliated with the Century Road Club of America, established city-to-city records between, for example, Chicago and New York, Boston and New York, and other cities. While commercial interests and competition between the many clubs in a large city like Chicago may have generated enthusiasm for local road races, city-to-city rides were discouraged by the long distances involved and the bad rural roads. Opposition to the use of public roads for racing was also a significant factor. In the United States, as in England, there was often tension between proponents and opponents of road racing on public highways. Commercial sponsorship was therefore directed more profitably into track racing, where the action and excitement for spectators was contained within an accessible arena and gate money could more easily be collected. Thus, for a variety of reasons, popular place-to-place road races in the United States were not easily established as a permanent part of the sporting calendar, as they were in continental Europe.

2. The Foundations of Modern Professional Road Racing in France: Sport as Business and Athletic Celebration

Nowhere can the emergence of modern continental road racing be seen better than in the heated contests that took place over the well-maintained 580 kilometers between

Bordeaux and Paris, a race that became one of the most important events of the French cycling season during the 1890s. The date of the first of these marathon single-day races has been widely recognized in French accounts as marking the beginning of modern road racing.[9] The recent introduction of the pneumatic tire, and the associated general expansion of the bicycle industry, was a powerful stimulus to the growth of road racing at that moment. The first Bordeaux-Paris road race, promoted by the well-established cycling paper *Véloce-Sport*, which had offices in both cities, and the Véloce Club Bordelais, was held on 23/24 May 1891. It was advertised as an amateur event specifically to encourage the participation of British amateurs, and was reported in the English paper *Cycling* as "nothing less than an International Road Championship of a most unmistakeable order."

The race resulted in the conspicuous defeat of their French rivals by a group of British long-distance road riders who had tested their strength and experience in 12-hour and 24-hour time trials on English roads, particularly those held on the Great North Road. G.P. Mills (1st in 26h 35m), M.A. Holbein (2nd in 27h 50m), S.F. Edge (3rd in 30h 13m) and J.E.L. Bates (4th in 30h 13m) all finished ahead of the best-placed French riders, Jiel-Laval (5th in 32h 15m) and Coulliboef (6th in 35h 18m). According to the editors of *Cycling*, "never in the whole history of cycling has so much excitement been created as by the marvelous performance of the British contingent."[10]

Twenty-eight riders started the race, with twenty-five of them riding on pneumatic safety bicycles. Georges Thomas, president of the Union Vélocipédique de France, and

Fig. 6.2. Competitors in the 1891 Bordeaux-Paris road race line up for the early morning start at the Gare de la Bastide in Bordeaux. [Source: engraving from a photograph, author's collection]

Hubert Delisle, president of the Véloce Club Bordelais, officiated at the starting-line. The British riders excelled over the superb roads, with their long, rolling hills. Totally unexpectedly, they rode non-stop through the night, ignoring a scheduled overnight rest stop at a hotel, arriving in Paris early the following morning. Lacy Hillier, editor of *Bicycling News*, wrote that the British success "gave a very great stimulus to this class of sport since it afforded French bicyclists a standard, whereby they could judge of their own quality. They were then hopelessly out of the race, and the experience showed that they had much to do before they could expect to successfully compete with English bicyclists."[11]

Crowds gathered along the route and in the towns through which the race passed, a clear indication of the power of cycling competitions on the road to attract and excite the general public. French journalist Victor Breyer recollected much later that: "This race was an eye-opener for the masses. The press, which previous to the event had hardly given it a notice, came out with big headlines after the event, Mills and his comrades being lionized and hallowed as heroes. That human beings had been capable of riding nearly 400 miles on their frail machines, almost without a dismount, filled everybody with admiration. It came as a tremendous revelation."[12]

The race was also a test of the strength and efficiency of the competing machines and

Fig. 6.3. The British riders who scored a resounding victory over the French in the 1891 Bordeaux-Paris road race. [Source: George Moore, *Cycling*, 30 May 1891]

pneumatic tires, whose manufacturers and agents were keenly interested in the results.[13] H.O. Duncan, the agent for the Humber Co. in France, wrote that "to successfully manage a cycle business at this period, one had to be a journalist and a sportsman as well as a business man. As the best method of advertising was the winning of important races, I selected quite a 'stable' of the best French amateur and professional riders." Duncan added that "in order to persuade the English champions to come over to compete, the contest was open to amateurs only," an official nicety necessary to prevent their getting into trouble with the N.C.U. for having competed in France in a race involving "professionals."[14] However, these "amateur" riders did not compete without financial and logistical support from the industry, and in fact were typical of the controversial category of "maker's amateurs." Mills was riding a Humber bicycle and was managed by Duncan, and his victory was clearly a publicity coup, for "in every town and village vast crowds blocked the way, and pacemakers had to dismount from their machines and fairly fight their way through." Duncan was also involved in supporting and feeding Holbein, as a backup for Mills.

The pacing for the British contingent was minutely organized, "plans of campaign were earnestly discussed and drawn up, pacemakers allotted their respective stretches." Mills was met at Vendôme at 11:25 p.m. by professional Charles Terront, "the old crusted veteran, who accompanied him to the finish, Fournier (ex-French high-wheel champion) bringing Holbein along an hour later." Mills was "taken along," as *Cycling* put it, over the entire course by a total of at least eight pace-makers. Terront, who could not compete himself because he was a well-known professional, in fact paced Mills for about 90 miles, a huge help from such a strong rider, and a significant factor in Mills' victory. Bordeaux-Paris second-placed Holbein was also paced by at least twelve riders, including the strong and experienced Frank Shorland. All this support was organized by the canny Duncan, who knew the continental cycling scene better than any of his British contemporaries. The experience gained by riders, pacers and other helpers at Bordeaux-Paris in May was extremely valuable for the next major road competition, Paris-Brest-Paris, which took place in September.[15]

Cyclists who excelled in such early long-distance road competition could do so only with direction and logistical support from a "manager." In this respect, Duncan was a pioneer in the role of the modern *directeur sportif*, directing, planning and executing the victories of his athletes, as well as the post-victory publicity. In 1897, Duncan wrote of "the managers, that is to say directors or administrators who had in the last few years come to the fore and seemed sure to occupy an important role in the sport." He described them as "a new kind of man."[16] As agent in Paris for the English Humber bicycle company, Duncan managed his riders to gain maximum publicity from their victories, which were advertised in the press as demonstrations of the superior quality of the bicycles and tires used in competition.

Duncan later described his concern that his employers in London, the Humber company, might question the heavy costs he had incurred to ensure Terront's win in Paris-Brest-Paris, and the volatile nature of the manager's job was underlined when Duncan switched his allegiance from Humber to the Rudge Cycle Company, taking his star rider, Charles Terront, with him. But Duncan's pioneering promotional methods were soon adopted by others, and became a crucial component of the rapid commercial expansion of the sport in the 1890s. Outstanding athletic achievements, record times and distances, sensational rides, were increasingly exploited as effective advertising tools for the bicycle industry. In addition, races were often sponsored and reported by newspapers to stimulate their circulation: cycling sold papers and also brought advertising revenue from manufacturers.

"From a cycling trade point of view," wrote Duncan, "perhaps the most important bicycle race ever organized was the first great road race from Paris to Brest and back, a distance of 1,200 kilometres.... This wonderful contest was announced on the front page in leading articles and aroused considerable interest not only in France but throughout the world. It practically meant a fortune for the cycle firm who should be successful."

The race was promoted by Pierre Giffard, editor of *Le Petit Journal*, one of the leading French daily newspapers. Duncan chose veteran professional Charles Terront as his most-favored competitor.[17] Terront's ride, in which he covered 1,200 kilometers in 72 hours with hardly a break, was widely reported and made him famous instantly. He overcame fatigue and lack of sleep and fought an

Fig. 6.4. G.P. Mills, of the Anfield Bicycle Club and North Road Cycling Club, winner of the 1891 Bordeaux-Paris road race. [Source: George Moore, *Cycling*, 6 June 1891]

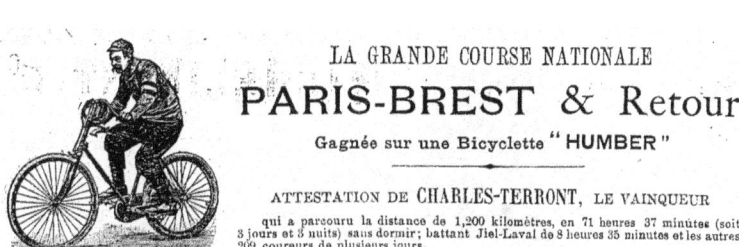

Fig. 6.5. H.O. Duncan managed the victory of his star rider, Charles Terront, in Paris-Brest-Paris to publicize the Humber bicycle he rode. [Source: *La Bicyclette*, 22 May 1892]

epic battle with second-placed Jiel-Laval, who was forced to take a sleeping break near Paris while Terront rode surreptitiously by him. As the two leading riders approached Paris, thousands lined the roads to greet them. The story of this race, which Terront described as "one of the most fantastic adventures of my entire life," was told in his *Mémoires*, hastily ghostwritten by journalist Baudry de Saunier and published in 1893: "I was invited to eighteen banquets after this. My portrait was published in nearly every French newspaper, and it was because of this widely publicized event that I became so well-known in France."[18]

Terront, a 34-year-old veteran, was "in his prime for such terrible trials of endurance," reported *Cycling*. He rode a Humber bicycle with "pneumatic tyres of a French make" (Michelins), fitted with Harrison Carter's gear-casing, "now indispensable to long-distance riders" for the protection it gave against the dust and mud of the rural roads. *Cycling* described the competitors leaving Paris for Brest as "a pantomime … we verily do not believe there were more than half-a-dozen riders who knew exactly the task they had in hand, the majority taking matters in the most easy fashion…. Were such a crew to appear at the starting-point of the North Road Hundred, we believe the Britishers would forthwith go and bury themselves in shame. We looked upon the whole procession in disgust." *Cycling* also complained about the fact that there was a regulation restricting riders to the use of only one machine, which was inspected and approved (the French word "poinçonné"—"stamped"—was used), and had to be repaired in the case of puncture, breakdown or accident rather than being substituted. "Instead of it being a race of men," said *Cycling* sarcastically, "it is a race of machines."[19] But the offices of the sponsor *Le Petit Journal* were surrounded all day by thousands of people, and "the contest will undoubtedly be a splendid thing for the cycle trade in France next year."[20]

Fig. 6.6. Terront's non-stop ride of 653 km in his 1,000 km match against Jean Corre in Paris in 1893 was typical of the dramatic feats of endurance promoted in the 1890s. [Source: *Véloce-Sport*, 16 March 1893]

While its report on the Paris-Brest-Paris race highlighted a superlative performance by Terront, *Cycling* did not discuss Duncan's role as manager or comment on his relationship with the industry that had made Terront's victory possible. The paper did, however, publish an editorial complaining about bicycle races which involved "unreasonable physical exertion. It has ever been our opinion that such unnatural strains on the human frame should cease to be tolerated, and that a race should be limited to somewhere about 200 miles. This is quite as much as most men can stand without passing through periods when they are ghastly to behold." Longer distances were bound to cause injury, either mental or physical, or both, thought *Cycling*, a criticism of endurance events which pinpointed exactly why they were successful publicity vehicles. Because such dramatic events set new standards and broke new athletic ground, they elicited either wild acclamation or negative criticism, but were never ignored.[21]

Searching for ever more sensational challenges, in March 1893 Duncan capitalized on Terront's fame by pitting him against Jean Corre in a 1,000-km race on the track at the Palais des Machines in Paris. Terront rode a Rudge bicycle, again equipped with Michelin tires, covering 653 km in the first 25 hours without stopping, and finishing the 1,000 km in 41 h 58 m 52⅘ s, at an average speed of 23.819 km/h, with Corre only 9 km behind him. Once again, the race was the focus of intense publicity. *Véloce-Sport* wrote that the French press had given the event "attention unknown until now in our sport," and the public mobbed the Paris office of *Véloce-Sport* for the results of the race.[22]

Later in 1893, Duncan organized Terront's ride from St. Petersburg to Paris, a distance of 3,000 km in 14 days, which was reported as having been accomplished on Clincher tires without a single repair. The difficulty of coordinating this dramatic ride was described in a hastily published book—*En Suivant Terront de St. Petersbourg à Paris* (published in 1894), and Duncan circulated a publicity photograph of himself as the suave, all-knowing manager/promoter of Terront's athletic feats.

Arriving in Paris from Russia, Terront was immediately challenged by Cody ("the King of the Cowboys of the Wild West") to a horse-versus-bicycle match, but was unable to compete due to his wife's ill health. Duncan, however, accepted the challenge on behalf of the Danish rider Charles Meyer, in Terront's place.[23] Soon after, Duncan presided over another highly publicized Terront performance, a ride from Rome to Paris. As promoters of such dramatic endurance feats that created a great deal of "noise" in the press, Duncan and Terront were an unrivaled team at the time. Indeed, as was suggested by an image from Rudge publicity in 1894 showing Terront riding around the world, their exploits had global implications.

* * *

Eighteen ninety-one was the first year of such prominent place-to-place races, much-publicized endurance events that were sponsored by publicity-conscious newspapers and used as testing grounds by bicycle and tire manufacturers. 1891 was also the first year in which pneumatic-tired bicycles appeared on the market, adding about 25 percent to the cost of a bicycle, a huge profit-making opportunity for the industry. A second Bordeaux-Paris race was run in 1892 without any British competitors, and Terront and Jiel-Laval declined to participate. Conditions were ideal, with warm, sunny weather and a friendly tail-wind pushing the fifty-four riders who left Bordeaux towards Paris. "The proprietors of *Le Véloce-Sport* had done everything they possibly could to attend to the requirements of the competitors, and these latter had profited by their experience of last year in providing themselves with plenty of pacemakers and efficient aid in case of accident."[24] The winner, Stéphane, finished in 25h 37m, beating G.P. Mills' 1891 time by 58 minutes, at an average speed of 14 mph for 572 km (357½ miles), with Vigneaux second. The victory was used to advertise Clément bicycles and Dunlop tires.

At the 1893 Bordeaux-Paris race, although no distinction was made between amateur and professional, a distinction was made between one category of riders, "coureurs de vitesse" (speed riders), who wore white jerseys, and a second category, "routiers" (road men), who wore black. Riders placed themselves in either category based on their own personal expectations, their age, experience and athletic abilities. The brand names of the bicycles and the tires of all the competitors were listed on the start sheet. The contest was "a Homeric struggle" between two men, Cottereau and Stéphane, neither of whom could drop the other, the race being declared a dead heat (after an appeal) because of confusion caused by crowds of riders and pace-makers at the finish and the inexact marking of the finishing line.[25]

By 1897, the Bordeaux-Paris race had become "a firm annual fixture in the cycling world, and may be said to constitute the cyclist's blue riband.... No other event excites so much interest on the part of the general public, while each machine and tire maker strives to have his particular representative well to the front." The 1897 race was a match between Gaston Rivierre and the Dutch long-distance rider, Cordang, and was won in record time by Rivierre, riding a Humber bicycle with a Simpson lever chain. Cordang had two pacing tandems or triplets with him at all times and a total of 180 men "to help him along the road," while Rivierre had 60 pace-makers and Frederic (in third place) had 150. Rivierre was also assisted and paced by automobiles which introduced a problematic new element—whether to allow pacing by motor-vehicles (still relatively unreliable) in long-distance bicycle races.[26]

Many other long-distance place-to-place bicycle races were initiated in the mid1890s, tests of the strength and stamina of a new kind of super-endurance athlete and of the speed and reliability of the newly developed pneumatic-tired bicycles. Tire manufacturers participated aggressively in these contests. In the 1892 Paris-Clermont Ferrand race, the Michelin brothers "themselves scattered thousands of nails on the road, with the specific intention of causing punctures to their pneumatics and thus to prove that they could be easily repaired. The Clément company, whose riders Stéphane and Vigneaux

Fig. 6.7. A widely circulated photograph illustrated the modern relationship in sport, between manager/promoter, rider and machine, created by Duncan and Terront to market Rudge bicycles to the consumer. [Source: *En Suivant Terront de St. Petersbourg à Paris*, 1894]

were on Dunlop pneumatics, claimed that the nails had been scattered to puncture their Dunlops."[27]

Another prominent, much-publicized event was the Paris-Brussels race, held in August 1893 in accordance with "the international amateur rules of the National Cyclists' Union" and sponsored by *La Bicyclette*. Pierre de Coubertin, the founder of the Olympic Games in 1896, was one of the presidents of its organizing committee. It was won by Henri André, who covered the more than 400 km in just under 20 hours. The race was endorsed by the King of Belgium, Leopold the Second, who donated a special prize to the winner.[28]

Special arrangements were made at the Franco-Belgian frontier to allow the race to pass through without interruption. The French and Belgian people, said *La Bicyclette*, were united "in the same love of sport" and the event had "done more for the good relations between the two countries than the best efforts of twenty diplomats." The road race was planned to coincide with a track racing festival at the Brussels Velodrome and all the events were timed implicitly to be the European alternative to the American-centered International Cyclists' Association's World Championships taking place at the same time in Chicago (see Chapter Seven). "Can it be said that French amateurism only includes shy and incapable people in its ranks," asked *La Bicyclette*, "that, in contrast to what occurs in our neighbors' country, professionalism in our country has drained away the vital forces, the vigor of our sports-loving young people?"[29] Twenty thousand people were reported to have been at the start in Paris, while 80,000 lined the roads at the finish in Brussels.

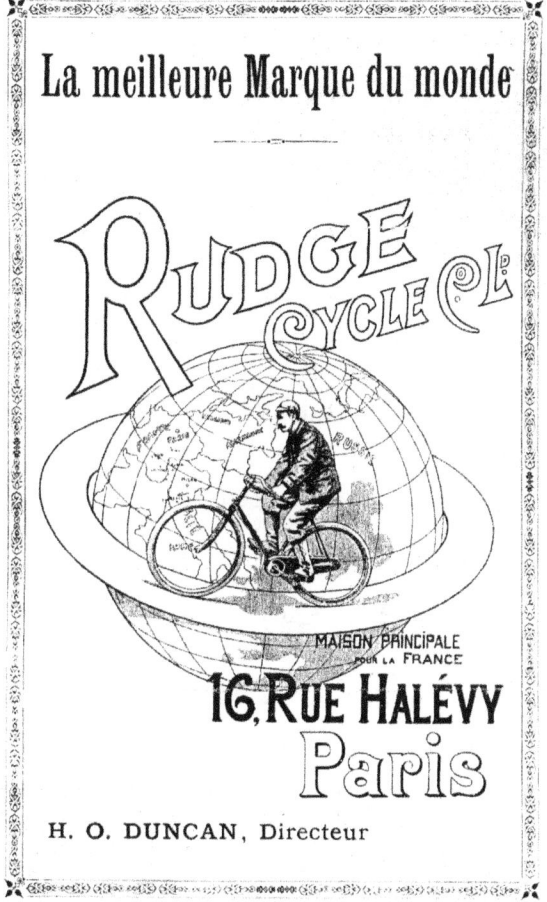

Fig. 6.8. Publicity put out by Rudge, represented in Paris by Duncan, suggested accurately that the new, pneumatic-tired bicycle would soon have a global impact. [Source: Duncan and Lafitte, *En Suivant Terront de St. Petersbourg à Paris*]

In August 1894, a "great road race from Lyons to Paris and back, distance 646 miles, resulted in an easy win for Rivierre, who covered the distance in 53h 17m 30s."[30] In 1896, two textile industrialists from Roubaix, Théo Vienne and Maurice Perez, collaborated with *Le Vélo* in Paris to organize a race from Paris to Roubaix across the rough roads of northeastern France, a race that has continued until today as the oldest and most prestigious on the European cycling calendar. The 1896 race was won by German cyclist Josef Fischer, who had previously won races between Moscow and St. Petersburg (1893) and between Trieste and Vienna (1895).[31]

A table showing the expansion of European road races between 1891 and 1896 can be found in Table 6 B.[32]

The majority of these cycling competitions were sponsored either by the bicycle industry or by cycling or local newspapers, and were run from place-to-place in order to stimulate the interest of a local spectator audience. If a local rider could win in the destination city, as Maurice Garin did, for example, in the Paris-Roubaix race in 1897 and 1898, additional local publicity could be generated.[33]

Many of the races mentioned above were continued on an annual basis. Bordeaux-Paris, the most prominent road race on the calendar, became the showcase for dramatic annual increases in speed as the techniques of pacing a strong rider were better understood and put into practice. In 1897, 1898 and 1899, the race was paced by automobiles, resulting in the Constant Huret's extraordinary 1899 ride of 594 km in 16 h 35 m (35.79 km/h), before it subsequently reverted to the use only of human pacers. Leading riders in this race, Gaston Rivierre, Maurice Garin, Constant Huret, Josef Fischer, Lucien Lesna and Hippolyte Aucouturier were among those who rode in the first Tours de France beginning in 1903. For the sake of comparison, and to show the development of cycling speeds on the road, the winners of the first twelve years of the annual Bordeaux-Paris race are shown in Table 6 A.[34]

These early place-to-place races, promoted by newspapers and sponsored by equipment manufacturers, laid the promo-

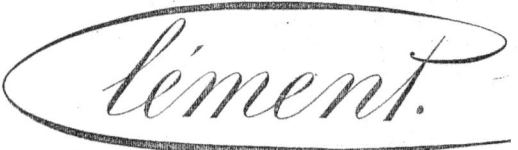

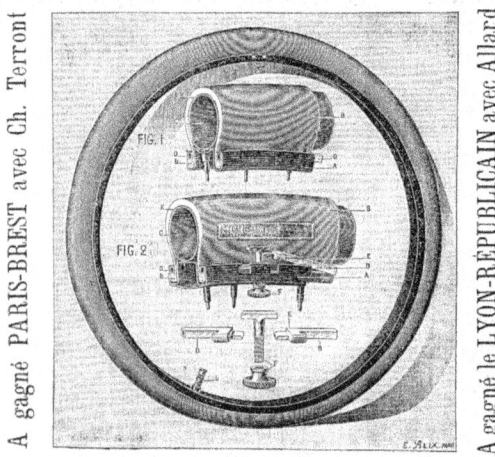

Top: Fig. 6.9. Stephane's win in the 1892 Bordeaux-Paris race was used to publicize both the Clement bicycle and the Dunlop tires used. [Source: *La Bicyclette*, 22 May 1892] *Bottom:* Fig. 6.10. Tire and bicycle manufacturers were equally aggressive in using the results of road races to publicize the superiority of their products. [Source: *La Bicyclette*, 7 Aug. 1892]

tional and organizational foundations for the later development of the Tour de France, which began in 1903 and quickly became the most challenging of all road races. The writer and critic Baudry de Saunier, who attended many of the prominent Parisian races and reported on them, was one of the most perceptive critics of the expanding bicycle racing scene in France. In 1892 he wrote: "I did not exaggerate when I suggested earlier that cycling constitutes a revolution in human locomotion. A revolution in social relationships, a revolution in habits, a revolution in business—cycling, which some short-sighted people still make fun of, will create all these upheavals."[35]

In his *L'Art de la Bicyclette*, published in 1896, reflecting on recent developments in France, journalist Baudry de Saunier stressed the point that bicycle racing was the primary testing ground for bicycle technology, a fact that can easily be seen in the advertising issued throughout Europe following an international ride such as Terront's St. Petersburg-Paris marathon. De Saunier's comments are particularly relevant to the increasing demand for pneumatic tires and the participation of tire manufacturers in bicycle racing in the early 1890s:

> Since the very beginning of cycling, racing has had the important function of showing, through remarkable performances, the economy, the ease and speed of a new type of transportation. Racing has always been, and still is, the best school of instruction for bicycle makers.... What is certainly true is that all the improvements which have been made in bicycles in the last ten years have come from racing. Without the racing and the riders, it is a pretty good bet that the stiff, light machines, cushioned so well with the pneumatic tires we use today, would still have been much more like the primitive and heavy machines of 1880. Makers had the most to gain in making efforts for the sake of the racers, and even today improvements can only really be tried, adopted or rejected, by the people who do the most cycling, the racers themselves. One could very well claim that the velodromes are the universities of cycling. We all benefit from the mechanical research and speed tests which are being carried out on a daily basis[36] [author's translation].

3. Opposition to Organized Road Racing in Britain

The extraordinary technological promise of the safety bicycle and the pneumatic tire inspired manufacturers to test them and prove their strengths under real road conditions. The commercial pressure to promote long-distance road racing, and subsequently the public appetite for it, increased. Testing the limits of human endurance and the mechanical strength and reliability of machines on road and track had long been a priority in bicycle racing, as we have seen in the early Six Day Races organized in the late 1870s by Harry Etherington, and in the trials of various safety bicycles in the mid–1880s. The more extraordinary the performance, the greater its publicity value. Riders liked the challenge and the surprises of a long road race on the generally little-traveled roads of the period. "Road racing is so free, so unartificial, it has the ring of reality about it," wrote the editors of *Cycling* in 1894. Road racing was "the most liked and enjoyed of all forms of cycling sport, in spite of an opposition that few sports have ever had to undergo."[37]

But because the sport was on prominent display in the public arena, road racing in Britain was opposed and became controversial. The problematic nature of sporting events organized to take place in a shared public space was later summarized by Lacy Hillier in an essay called "Cycle Racing," published in 1911. Speaking of the races held over the Great North Road and other roads in the early 1890s, Hillier wrote:

> The attention attracted by these contests, and the very full reports published by the sporting as well as the cycling press, caused the popularity of this phase of the pastime to grow exceedingly. The winner of a big road race not only secured great credit to himself, but gave a widespread advertisement to the machine he rode, and as a natural consequence the trade appeared upon the scene, the friendly character of the assemblies gradually disappeared, things became more business-like, pacing was supplied, tandems and often larger multi-cycles swooped down in shoals upon the highways, and some riders unquestionably allowed themselves to be subsidised by the makers of the machines they rode.[38]

In short, commercial pressures challenged Hillier and other critics' conception of the amateur ideal and amateur cycling interests had a public relations problem on their hands in England. In spite of the bicycle industry's long history of promoting racing, the advocates of "pure" amateurism, with Hillier as a kind of ring-leader, wanted to disassociate themselves as much as possible from the commercial and publicity aspects of cycling, a project that was an uphill battle given the economic realities of the bicycle industry.

On the continent, as we have already seen, the public appears to have accepted bicycle racing as a commercial spectacle without much objection, whereas the more class-conscious British road users—cyclists and others—and residents viewed racing on public roads as a lower-class activity that gave other cyclists a bad name and created danger and conflict with horses and other vehicles.

British roads tended to be more crowded than French roads and residential and industrial areas were more densely populated. This perhaps explains why people reacted more negatively than in predominantly rural France. Public opinion in Britain hinted at a stricter regulation of cyclists in general. *Cycling* commented in 1892 that "the general opinion of the pedestrian section seems to be that the wheelman should be taxed and placed under strict restraint, especially in large towns.... Should such restrictions be made, they will have been caused by the imbecility and reckless disregard for propriety shown by the rowdy few."[39]

The relationship between cyclists, particularly racing cyclists, and other categories of road-users had always been problematic, and since about 1887 the more controversial question of organized road racing had been aired from time to time in the cycling and the general press, particularly in Lacy Hillier's editorials in *Bicycling News* which invariably reflected his articulate, pro-amateur perspective, and were intense reflections of the public's negative reactions to the sport. Cyclists racing on the road came into direct contact with the general public and had to deal with whatever conditions they met on the roads. They might encounter sympathetic spectators willing to applaud them, or just as likely, a shepherd driving a flock of sheep or an aristocratic carriage-driver impatiently navigating a narrow country lane. An 1887 Lacy Hillier editorial issued a warning against the possible prosecution of cyclists following a Catford Cycling Club open road race:

> We once again raise our voice in emphatic protest against this style of competition, which is absolutely certain, sooner or later, to bring us into serious trouble with the authorities. A member of the Gainsborough C.C. told us that he saw four police-constables on the look-out on the road near Horley, and we once again reiterate our words of warning.... When seventy or eighty cyclists are summoned for furious driving, and the authorities seek to put checks upon our speed upon the road, the main body of wheelmen will regret that individual clubs should have been permitted to inflict such injury upon the sport as a whole.[40]

Fig. 6.11. Riders from the North Road Cycling Club at the start of a race, probably 1892–93. [Source: North Road Cycling Club, author's collection]

In December 1887, the National Cyclists' Union adopted a motion which expressed "disapproval of the growing practice of racing on the public roads," and directed the Executive Council "to do its utmost to discourage road racing."[41] At a special meeting in March 1888, the Council of the N.C.U. voted to no longer recognize road records officially.[42] The controversy continued throughout 1888 and the break-away Road Records Association was constituted by May. Its "Regulations" focused on the recognition of individual record-breaking attempts rather than encouraging massed-start racing. Even though the new organization was founded in opposition to the National Cyclists' Union policies, the wording of its first byelaw shows that the R.R.A., too, was keenly aware of the potentially negative impact road racing could have upon public opinion:

> The Road Records Association will adjudicate upon cycling road records claimed by amateurs eligible to compete under N.C.U. rules, and also upon cycling road records claimed by professionals, but it shall be in the discretion of the committee to decline to accept any claim where they consider that the interests of the sport would not be promoted thereby.[43]

Tension between cyclists and the police remained high. An editorial in *The Cyclist* (probably written by Henry Sturmey) stated that: "From all sides our correspondents report activity on the part of the police." It expressed the fear that compulsory measures would be taken, "to enforce that respect for the wishes, comfort, and safety of the rest of the community which the advocates of road racing refused on their own accord to concede ... if cyclists don't regulate their road riding themselves it will be done for them, and that, too, in a manner at once unpleasant to those immediately interested and detrimental to the pastime at large." "Furious driving," it was pointed out, was illegal, but "a properly conducted affair over a route blessed with little traffic, and through no towns or populous villages, would, if properly introduced, receive the sanction of the authorities." But such a race would, of course, be deprived of most of its potential audience—those who lived along the route.[44]

Editorials and opinion pieces continued in the English cycling press throughout 1889. "It seems advisable to check the present craze for road-races," wrote Hillier in *Bicycling News*:

> for the magnitude of the evil must soon cause the authorities to take action, and that action will be stringent.... Personally, we think a road-race a most interesting affair, and were it possible to promote such contests without infringing the rights of other citizens we should be just as warm in support of, as we are now in opposition to, this form of the sport. The roads were not made for cycle-racing, or for the use of cyclists alone, and the comfort and convenience of other users of the highways must be considered.[45]

Cyclists were threatened with the possibility that they might have to proceed at 6 mph with a red warning flag in front of them, and suffer imprisonment for "furious riding." Lacy Hillier's argument was that racing, the recreational cyclist road-user and the bicycle industry would all suffer if the sport did not regulate itself: "We address ourselves to the road-rider as opposed to the road-racers, to the tourists, to the steady users of the cycle for health and business; we invite their cooperation, and we also invite the cooperation of the C.T.C., whose interests must be seriously menaced by any prospect of official restrictive legislation."[46]

A.J. Wilson, President of the North Road Cycling Club, which promoted a 24-hour road competition, one of the most prominent road races in Britain, disagreed with Lacy Hillier. He responded that:

> it is possible to promote road-races without infringing the rights of other citizens, and my club has repeatedly proved the possibility by organizing road-races at which not a breath of complaint has been possible. I challenge you to refer to a solitary instance in which the rights of any citizens have been interfered with by any of the open road-races promoted by the North Road Cycling Club.... We go far away into secluded parts of the country, where we know that there is no danger; and we fix our routes so as to avoid the possibility of endangering or scandalizing the inhabitants of towns.[47]

Lacy Hillier was adamant, however: "We conceive it to be our duty to the sport, and to all concerned in its welfare and prosperity, to continue to warn the cycling world at large of the dangers to which a certain section are exposing the steady users of the wheel. We have long foreseen the trouble ahead, and we shall go on warning all concerned until the action of the ruling body of our sport—or the outside authorities—do away with road-racing altogether."[48] Hillier seemed unable to conceive of well promoted, properly planned and publicized road racing, supported perhaps by the industry (with which he was unwilling to cooperate), as a public sporting spectacle presented for the general public's enjoyment.

* * *

Thus, while French road racing expanded in the early 1890s both in terms of organization and of popularity (indeed, it became a public celebration of a new kind of athletic prowess and endurance), the attitude towards road racing in Britain became increasingly hostile. Why would a promoter put energy and money into organizing a big public cycling spectacle, a massed-start Edinburgh to London road race on the model of Bordeaux-Paris, for example, if it would most likely be opposed by certain members of the press and by certain editors and officials within the sport? Without careful prior arrangements, such a race might well have been stopped by the police in one of the cities through which it passed, hardly making the event a sound financial or marketing investment.

And there was the ever-present issue of class divisions in Britain. In spite of a few influential and articulate aristocratic and upper middle-class representatives at the top levels of cycling's governing bodies and club institutions, leading newspapers in general recognized bicycle racing as a predominantly middle-class and working-class sport and appear not to have understood the potential value of bicycle racing as a vehicle for publicity.

This was very different from the enthusiasm with which the French and other continental newspapers promoted and reported road racing.

4. GEORGE LACY HILLIER: AMATEURISM VERSUS THE "NEW PROFESSIONALISM"

The ongoing ideological conflict between amateurism and professionalism continued to play a crucial role in this decisive phase of road racing in Britain, isolating British riders from freely developing continental professionalism. British "amateurs" (most of whom were de facto professionals!) had not been penalized for competing against the French in the first Bordeaux-Paris race in 1891 because it had been officially announced as an amateur event. But the French "amateur," according to an editorial by Lacy Hillier in *Bicycling News*, was "a sort of hybrid creation, and though he would scorn to make a living by his prowess, he would not object to make a money bet upon his skill, or to accept money as the prize in a race." The N.C.U., according to Hillier, could not and would not accept the Union Vélocipédique's definitions because:

> they would only weaken their own ... they would practically recognize an element of professionalism in the amateur ranks.... Under any circumstances, the condition of racing in France would disqualify the majority of amateurs from running in that capacity in England.... The Union Vélocipédique de France can only do one thing, and that is to remodel their rules upon those of the N.C.U.[49]

The imperious position of Hillier—his bigoted assertion that only *his* definition of the sport was that which should govern international competition—is extraordinary. The *Irish Cycling News* characterized Hillier in the following terms:

> Always heard before he is seen, Mr. H. discourses on every topic, and lays down the law in tones rather suggestive of bombast; he speaks to no one in particular but at everybody in general. Mr. George Lacy Hillier is a man of good physique; a fine, athletic, well-knit figure, topped by a face of rather Mephistophelian cast. The moustachios have an aspect of soldatesque ferocity; they are waxed furiously, and stick out in a bold, defiant way, as becomes an integral portion of the amateur champion of 1881... But with all his peculiarities, Mr. Hillier has much to recommend him. He is almost an insanely enthusiastic sportsman; he believes himself to be the guardian angel of English cycling; he has done a good deal for it, and he ever strives according to his lights, to purify racing and lift it above suspicion.[50]

And in a later scathing attack on Hillier in *La Bicyclette*, Paul Hamelle asked, "What else is the theory of amateurism but a system of prejudice, born of error, supported by lies.... Blessed by the N.C.U., Hillier has made amateurism his credo, an article of faith outside of which there is only shame and misery for the obstinate sinner.... From the heights of his intolerant dogmatism, he goes on passing opinions on people and events, making judgments which the facts hasten to contradict, without questioning his serene belief in his infallibility." Hillier was "a high priest without any believers, who expends his substantial power blowing on dead ashes, a naïve supporter of lost causes who is inevitably opposed to any novelty ... barring the road to progress and crying out to anyone whom he sees from far off, "Halt! Who goes there? No entry!; Progress will pass through nevertheless. G. L. H. will at least have had the consolation of having sometimes stood in its way!"[51]

What exactly were those amateur ideals, which Hillier defended so passionately within the National Cyclists' Union and in the press, and for which he claimed the right to be a moral spokesman, showing an "almost insane enthusiasm?" In a *Bicycling News* editorial entitled simply "Sport," Hillier spelled out his beliefs:

> What is sport? ... Everything depends on the sportsman, is all the answer that can be given. Sport is amusement solely, but different amusements please different minds.... The essence of sport is relaxation. Sport is when we disport ourselves from labour and our usual daily work. Any pursuit followed regularly as a means of livelihood is no longer a sport ... the paid athlete is not a sportsman whether he be runner, cricketer or cyclist; these pursuits are trades for the professionals, not sports for them at all. They must be followed for pleasure to be sports.... The sportsman, then, is the man who has an amusement which may cost him something, but which must not bring him in anything, for an amusement which brings him in anything is not a sport but a business.... The best sport, then, is the one which gives the most amusement, affords the greatest relaxation, and enables us to carry ourselves away from labour and our usual daily work most readily. And in this last condition lies the secret of the supremacy of cycling. Most sports amuse us only at holiday time.... The cyclist can have his bit of fun at any time.[52]

Sport, then, was an amusement, a relaxation, and followed for pleasure; it was not to be a means of livelihood, a trade, or a business. The paid athlete was not a sportsman. Hillier's prominent editorial makes very clear the rift between his ideals and the economic reality of commercial bicycle racing interests at that time.[53]

During the winter of 1891–92, the N.C.U., asserting its ideological and bureaucratic control over the sport, voted to prohibit British amateurs from racing in France because the Union Vélocipédique de France would not yield to pressure to accept the N.C.U.'s definition of amateurism, as the governing bodies of Germany, Austria and Holland had already done. *Bicycling News* published a leading article from its Paris correspondent entitled "The Amateur Question in France," which examined the repercussions of the ruling. "More broad-minded" people involved in cycling were disappointed with the N.C.U., said the article, because:

> this prohibition will isolate completely the cyclists in France from their brethren elsewhere. No one can pretend that this will help forward the cause of sport upon that side of the Channel, for competition is the soul of cycling, as it is of business.... The fact that France has declined to accept the advances of the N.C.U. shows that there is a very big Chauvinist party who will suffer any inconvenience rather than submit to the masterful spirit of perfidious Albion.... The creation of a logical amateur standard would work wonders for cycling, which already has taken first rank in the sports of the country.[54]

Six. The Foundations of Modern Road Racing

This surge in the constant waves of argument about amateurism and professionalism came immediately prior to the 1892 formation of the first international governing body of the sport, the International Cyclists' Association. The I.C.A.'s rules and standards (further discussed in Chapter Seven) essentially confirmed the amateur definitions set forth by the National Cyclists' Union and the League of American Wheelmen. Its founding represented the bureaucratic and organizational victory of British, American and German conceptions of cycling competition—indeed, their wider conceptions of amateur sport in general—over French customs, leaving the Union Vélocipédique de France outside the newly-formed coalition. However, although the I.C.A. was attempting to exert its control over international amateur racing, the French certainly did not fall behind in the professional sport, or suffer very much from the exclusion of many of their amateurs from Anglo-American competition.

The early 1890s marked a turning point in the organization of British bicycle racing. From 1892 onwards, road races continued to be organized by the big road clubs, the North Road, the Bath Road, the Anerley and the Catford clubs, as well as the Road Records Association. These were large, active and popular clubs. But police presence and threats of action also increased. Incidents involving "scorchers" and other road-users were given high-profile coverage in the press, and the police were frequently reported watching cyclists on the road. At meetings of the National Cyclists' Union, Lacy Hillier and the anti-road racing faction continued their campaign. The issue was constantly debated in the cycling press. "Every week for the last month or so has made it more apparent that if road-racing is not absolutely doomed, it is in great danger," wrote the editor of *Wheeling* in September 1894.[55]

In the same month, *Cycling* reported that "with due deference to the police authority," and with regard "to the interest of all road riding cyclists," the leading Manchester clubs had either cancelled or transferred to the track their long-distance road championships.[56] Six weeks later, a *Cycling* editorial sided with the anti-road racing faction:

> Road racing in particular, and speed riding on the highway in general, are entirely responsible for the existing police tyranny, and at the present time all classes of the wheeling community are subject to stringent, unjust, and intolerant treatment at the hands of police and magistrates. Prejudice against cyclists is rampant and increasing, and the few who race on the road are almost entirely responsible for it. Road racing, when looked at from this point of view, can only be indulged in for the future by the most selfish and inconsiderate of wheelmen. The thoughtful and unselfish cyclist must see that the interests of a vast community are at stake, and he will set his behaviour right, moderate his pace on the highway, and generally endeavour to put himself right with the public.[57]

At an N.C.U. council meeting held in Manchester in June 1895, "the proposal for the suppression of road-racing made by Mr. Hickson (West Riding) was rejected."[58]

But two years later, the N.C.U. London meeting decided to support a proposition "to abolish road races and record time trials on the road by suspending all licensed riders taking part therein," which was voted on and carried at an N.C.U. quarterly meeting, where it was resolved "that no licensed rider may take part in any race or paced record attempt upon the road."[59]

The N.C.U.'s opposition to road racing thus extended roughly over a ten-year period beginning in the late 1880s, rather than being the result of one specific act of Union legislation. But the N.C.U., though influential, had no right to stop any races held outside its jurisdiction, and could exert actual control only through its refusal to promote road racing

Fig. 6.12. **Cyclists raced on country roads while the horsy set looked on disapprovingly.** [Source: *Badminton Cycling*, 1896]

and its ability to exclude offenders from its own sponsored track events and championships. The reaction from the road racing interests was predictably strong. *The Times* reported that "the stringent road-racing resolution recently passed by the National Cyclists' Union seems to have created much dissatisfaction among some of the big road clubs of the union, and there are rumours that such important clubs as the North Road, the Bath Road, and the Anerley, among others, contemplate immediate withdrawal from the union."[60]

At a general meeting of the North Road Club held in London a few weeks later, the club, by a large majority, withdrew from its affiliation with the N.C.U. and declared that "notwithstanding the recent legislation of the union on the subject of road-racing, the club do continue to pursue its present policy."[61] Not surprisingly, the sport of road racing in Britain suffered drastically. The N.C.U., as a result of its pushing through such radical opposition to a vibrant branch of the sport, became fragmented, especially as the national organization was already severely divided between southern and northern members.

The long-term effect of this protracted conflict within the sport in Britain was to change the nature of road racing and to push it increasingly underground. No large place-to-place competitions along the lines of the emerging French races were promoted; there are no British "classics" dating back to the 1890s, races such as, for example, Edinburgh-London or York-London, which would have become the British equivalent of Paris-Roubaix or Bordeaux-Paris. British professional road racing, which with its outstanding early champions certainly had the potential to become a popular national sport, was prevented from developing largely by N.C.U. officials who were primarily interested in protecting the amateur ideal. Their decisions were based on the compulsion to compartmentalize and limit, as a primary definition of athletic merit, the economic affiliations of leading competitive cyclists. Place-to-place routes were mostly tackled by single, unpaced, amateur cyclists riding under the auspices of the Road Records Association.[62] New regulations were drawn up mandating an acceptable, black costume for racing cyclists on public roads—no short trousers or short sleeves were to be worn. Road racing would subsequently take place surreptitiously, without spectators or advertising. Distance races, such as the Cuca Cocoa 24-hour Race which was promoted in London between 1892 and 1896 by Lacy Hillier's own club, the London County Cycling and Athletic Club, increasingly took place on the track.

The bicycle industry was not alone in understanding the marketing potential of bicycle racing to sell its products. The manufacturer of another popular British product, the Cuca Cocoa company, was the first general consumer product manufacturer to sponsor a long-distance race.[63] The "Cuca Cocoa Challenge" 24-hour track races in London (and the subsequent, similar Parisian "Bol d'Or" 24-hour race, sponsored by a newspaper) attracted thousands of spectators, and these paced, 24-hour world record attempts were grueling tests of endurance in cycling, more intense even than road rides, unrelenting in their speed and the physical demands they placed upon the riders. Teams of tandems, triplets and quadruplets were used to pace the individual competitors, who switched from one team to another to maintain their high pace. "It was in these historic contests," said *The Hub*, "that the art of pacemaking was first scientifically cultivated."[64] As night fell, the track was illuminated, bands played at intervals and food and drink were provided for both competitors and spectators.[65]

Holbein, Edge and Bates, competitors in the 1892 Bordeaux-Paris race, were on the starting line of the first, 1892, Cuca Challenge at Herne Hill track, a race won by Frank Shorland, with a record 413 miles 1615 yds in 24 hours.[66] Shorland went on to win two other Cuca Challenge races, setting a world record of 460 miles 1296 yards in 1894 at the Herne Hill track in London.[67] These long-distance competitions were novel and controversial and generated public debate about what limits, if any, should be set on sporting events. They were criticized by *Cycling* as "involving unreasonable physical exertion. It has ever been our opinion that such unnatural strains on the human frame should cease to be tolerated, and that a race should be limited to somewhere about 200 miles." Such "unnatural competitions" were "brutalizing" and "proportionately injurious." Even H.O. Duncan told the press, after directing his man Terront's win in the recent Paris-Brest-Paris race, that he "hoped never to take part in such a horrible affair again."[68]

During the 1893 Cuca Cocoa race in London, where he acted as Judge for the London County Cycling and Athletic Club (his own club, which promoted the event), Lacy Hillier was involved in an international controversy concerning timing.[69] When Frank Shorland asked him what the world record for 12 hours was (then held by French rider, Jules Dubois), Hillier replied within earshot of French riders and spectators that Shorland should pay no attention whatsoever to the record, that it was "a record timed with a cheap watch held by the maker of the bicycle" Dubois had been riding. Hillier had on previous occasions made similar comments about American records. If this was possibly Hillier's supercilious sense of humor, it was not appreciated. The important journal, *Véloce-Sport*, carried a leading article by Emile Mousset protesting Hillier's behavior. Mousset himself had directed the race when Dubois broke the record, he wrote, it had been timed by three independent time-keepers with first-rate watches, and the manufacturer had had absolutely nothing to do with the timing. French journalists had never questioned records set in England, he went on, and it was extremely disappointing to see an English figure who occupied one of the highest offices in the sport not extending the same courtesy to his French colleagues.[70]

Lacy Hillier was not easily persuaded to change his behavior. In a September 1894 article, "Timing and Timers. Comparative articles on timing at home and abroad," he once again questioned the professional integrity and honesty of non–British timekeepers:

> Why should we, in this country, be called upon to accept, without question, the records made upon foreign tracks, when we ourselves insist upon the most exhaustive tests and the most absolute precautions before the times are accepted? ... I know, as regards English records, made under N.C.U. rules, that the timekeepers are men of reputation, that their watches have undergone an exhaustive test, that the tracks upon which they are made are of standard measurements, and that, in all cases, every precaution is taken to ensure accuracy; and I prefer to accept these records and to stand by them rather than to accept records accomplished upon tracks of dubious measurement, clocked by excitable, not to say Chauvinistic, timekeepers with watches of doubtful accuracy.[71]

George Lacy Hillier was one of the leading figures in British cycling in the 1890s, a dominant, assertive and ambitious personality who was intimately involved in many of the social tensions and economic contradictions within the sport, and undoubtedly had considerable influence on the future direction of cycling. In addition to being president of the London County Cycling and Athletic Club, director of the Herne Hill track, and editor of one of the most influential weekly cycling papers, he played a significant role as a committee member of the National Cyclists' Union, and was instrumental in the formation of the International Cyclists' Association and the creation of the first official amateur World Championships. Yet Hillier remained resolutely committed to British-style amateurism as a moral crusade, and refused to show respect to the international cycling community which the expanding sport needed. In a speech at the fourth annual dinner of the London County Cycling and Athletic Club, held in London in March 1896, Lacy Hillier "dealt with the past season's work of the club and laid down their future policy. He strongly urged the cause of the true amateur. The London County Club were determined to uphold it in every sense." There was no positive mention of professionalism.[72]

Lacy Hillier, with his imperious and assertive presence, was a complex personality.[73] As a journalist, N.C.U. official and judge, club president, track director and stock broker, he had his fingers in many pies. Although he was the most outspoken advocate of amateurism, he himself had an economic interest in the bicycle industry. As a stockbroker, he participated in the financial launching of various bicycle companies during the "boom" of the mid–1890s, and he also promoted racing events for his club, the London County Cycling and Athletic Club Ltd., where profit was crucial. In his mind, there was no conflict of interest here, although an "amateur" rider who accepted equipment or funding from the bicycle trade might be suspended from competition fordoing so. In a letter published in *Wheeling* in 1894, the arch-professional H.O. Duncan suggested that Hillier, for all his protestations on behalf of "pure" amateurism, was far from pure himself: "I have witnessed many a cycle company's prospectus, with Mr. Hillier's name down as 'broker'; but I suppose this does not count, being in his business capacity—yet he cannot deny having made money out of the trade and sport...," a suggestion which Hillier later dismissed as "slanderous."[74]

The issue was again thoroughly aired in *Wheeling* with the publication of a challenging anonymous letter (from "Rational") entitled "Is Amateurism Possible?," to which Hillier responded: "Is Amateurism Possible?—Yes!"[75] Hillier was being challenged precisely on the dividing line he had set between the hypothetically "pure" amateur and a competitor who made some financial gain from some aspect or other of the bicycle trade and industry. In response to Duncan's challenge, Hillier responded that his business life was his own affair, and had nothing to do with his repeatedly expressed views about "pure amateurism" within the sport: "If 'Rational's' example is to be followed, and a man's private business is to be dragged in as he drags in mine, honorary officials will soon be as extinct as the dodo. Let 'Rational' seek the rules of amateurism ... and see if they deal with the financial officers of limited companies." Yet it was blatantly clear that it was also "a man's private business" which was being investigated when an N.C.U. committee investigated and ruled on an accused rider's "professionalism," for accepting equipment from a manufacturer, for instance. The question was a crucial one. Wasn't Hillier, a man who was paid 1 or 2 guineas to act as judge at race meetings, who promoted large, successful, commercially-backed events for his club, and earned his living working as a stock-broker in a firm which frequently handled bicycle industry accounts, in fact a "professional" to the same extent as were the "maker's amateurs" whose status Hillier was quick to question, whose private affairs were investigated, and who were suspended and sometimes expelled from the amateur ranks by the N.C.U.'s racing committee?

This debate between Duncan, Hillier and "Rational" brought to the forefront the two contrasting ideas about what constituted "sport" in the bicycle racing world in the mid–1890s. Which was preferable, traditional, club-based, non-business-oriented, amateur sport, or what was frequently referred to as "the New Professionalism," a modern, commercially-oriented, activity. Hillier's own success in July 1894 with the Cuca Cocoa 24-hour race promoted by his club demonstrated that, in the new realm of mass-spectator sports, excellent riders, good organization, good promotion and good business instincts were all necessary components for successful racing, and traditional concepts of amateur (and amateurish) events could no longer play a role. Hillier himself, although he clung tenaciously to his amateur ideals, was forced to provide an efficient, professionally-organized, modern event, and with the London

Fig. 6.13. Ex-high-wheel champion, author, journalist, newspaper owner, race director, committee man—Hillier had his finger in every pie of the cycling world in the 1880s and 1890s. [Source: *Cycling*, 20 Feb 1897]

County Cycling and Athletic Club Ltd., created a limited company to protect himself against personal liability, a far cry from the amateur clubs of ten years earlier.

Hillier's opposition to the "New Professionalism" sought to counteract the inevitable movement towards modern, commercial sport, and the pressures of the advertising money of bicycle and tire manufacturers. But "the trade" was always knocking at the door. Only a few weeks after the third Cuca Cocoa Cup race of July 1894, Herne Hill track opened its doors to an important professional meeting, organized by "the Buffalo Cycling Club of Paris," starring Americans Arthur Zimmerman, George Wheeler, George Banker and other European professionals who were touring in Britain. A *Wheeling* editorial commented that:

> the New Professionalism may be said to have been on its trial in England last week.... We think that professionalism has come well through the ordeal. We still believe that it is possible to have a school of honest, decent, professional riders.... The very fact that the proprietors of that track—who are keenly alive to the necessity of keeping it above reproach—saw no reason to shut their doors against professionals is proof that there is a vast difference between the old and new order of things ... professional racing has as good a right to claim public support as any amateurism that we have ever known. The advent of the professional at Herne Hill is a vindication of an article written by us some month's ago, in which we said that the proprietors of race tracks would ultimately agree with us.[76]

The same issue of *Wheeling* poked fun at Hillier, who had chosen not to be present for the professional racing at his own home base because he could not bear "to see the horrible scene at Burbage Road" (the location of Herne Hill Track, in south London), and "could not bring himself to look on his last and greatest love in the embrace of professionalism.... It was certainly hard lines on Hillier after all his solemn protestations that never would Herne Hill be profaned by the foot of the pro. Seeing that the current was too strong for him, he was wise to keep out of it."

Professional cyclists, stolidly proletarian in Britain, were initially discriminated against and without proper representation until the new professional class of managers, like H.O. Duncan and, later, "Choppy" Warburton, saw the new opportunities to manage and promote them. But Hillier would never openly recognize the inevitability or the integrity of professionalism, or the legitimacy of the participation of the bicycle industry in the sport.

5. Road Racing in the United States

In spite of reports of generally appalling road conditions in the United States, there were good roads on the outskirts of Eastern and Mid-Western cities such as Boston, New York, Buffalo, Chicago, Milwaukee, St. Louis, Toledo and Indianapolis, which made road racing an attractive possibility.[77]

Just as in Britain, road racing on the high-wheel bicycle in the States was a popular club-based activity by the late 1880s, one that attracted crowds of spectators and enthusiastic reports in the daily press. This interest continued to increase into the boom of the mid–1890s. Around Chicago, for example, there were good short-distance road racing possibilities, but place-to-place races were also held, over shorter and longer routes: Irvington-Millburn (New Jersey) and Buffalo-Erie (New York), for example. Wide open spaces and the flat terrain of the Mid-West meant that speeds could be very fast, given a good road surface.

But, just as in England, road racing on the outskirts of cities also provoked conflicts with other road-users and public opposition became a significant issue. In many locations, road racing was an ephemeral sensation that attracted large crowds and was both a new kind of athletic event and an opportunity to advertise and sell cycling-related products. Many reports in regional newspapers show that they used racing to promote sales, carrying advertisements from local bicycle retailers to stimulate sales. Although they were not races *per se*, the rides of individual cyclists, such as Thomas Stevens and George Nellis, also saw the vast distances in the United States as a challenge to be overcome, and the hazards and adventures of a trans-continental ride made good reading in published accounts.[78] Press accounts from the same period contain fairly frequent reports of lone coast-to-coast rides.

Road racing on the high-wheel bicycle was a tough and demanding sport, practised by youthful male club members in the 1880s.[79] A large number of high-wheel road records were set and reported in the press, although authenticating the results was always a difficult issue. The League of American Wheelmen initially did not hesitate to sanction road racing and approve records, and it was only later that a debate began within the L.A.W. over the image of road racing. "The Road Race is becoming a popular institution," wrote the editor of *Bicycling World* in 1885, "We do not ... get as good time, nor is there the excitement that there is in a

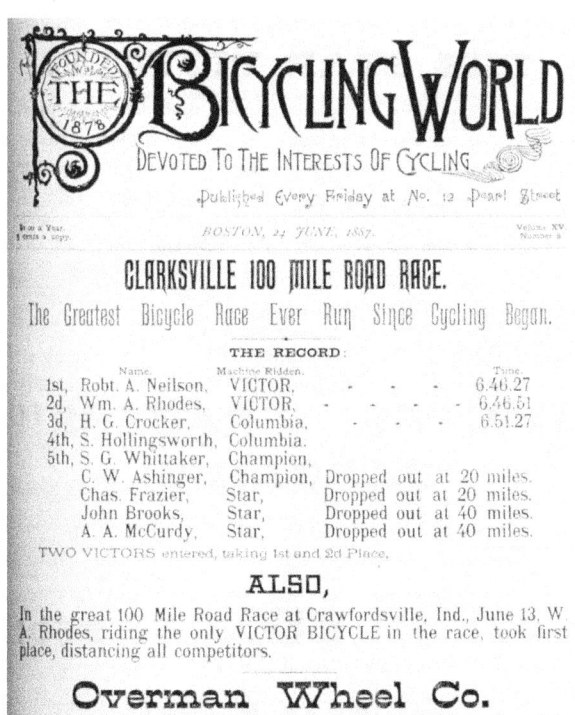

Top: Fig. 6.14. L.D. (Birdie) Munger set records on American roads in the mid–1880s. [Source: John L. Weiss collection] *Bottom:* Fig. 6.15. Prominent advertising to "boom" records set in road races appeared from the 1880s on in the United States, as in the case of the Clarkeville Road race, "the greatest bicycle race ever since cycling began." [Source: *Bicycling World*, 24 June 1887]

race where the riders are in sight the whole distance, but we get a test of machines built for service and under conditions that they are likely to meet with in ordinary use; and we get a test of the abilities of the riders on the roads." At the same time, the paper recognized that "the thing is in violation of the law and can only be pursued under the indulgence of the authorities," and that "in the hands of irresponsible men, a great deal of injury will be done."[80]

When L.D. (Birdie) Munger, a Detroit rider who was later to become Major Taylor's mentor and trainer, set a record of 211½ miles in 24 hours over New England roads in August 1885, he took great pains to establish its authenticity. "Pace-makers accompanied him the whole distance and he was never alone," reported *Bicycling World*, "The distance was measured by a Butcher cyclometer, which had previously been tested at the machine shop of the Butcher Cyclometer Co. Postals (i.e., postcards) were mailed by Munger from all the towns passed through to this office, and they substantiate the presence of Munger in each." Munger also mailed "postals" to Abbott Bassett, Chairman of the Racing Board of the L.A.W.[81] The level of competition that already existed in the mid–1880s is suggested by Munger's record-setting margin of only 4 miles over the previous holder, F.S. Cook, from California, with 207 miles.

Road conditions were variable, and at their worst, terrible. Munger had to contend with "rough and sandy stretches through Essex County," and "a heavy white mist which rose from the marshes and made it impossible to distinguish objects ten feet distant."[82] The New England roads were rougher and sandier than British roads at this time, which perhaps explains why Munger's record mileage was more than 50 miles short of the then current British record of 266 miles for 24 hours set by J.H. Adams on 4 October 1884, though the less developed competitive structure in the U.S. may also have been a factor. Early in 1886, Munger again attacked the 24 hour record, on that occasion riding 259¾ miles on an Apollo bicycle, a record that was broken by S.G. Whittaker in October 1886, with a ride of 300 miles.[83] Long-distance riding was, therefore, evolving rapidly and riders" speeds were constantly improving.

In 1887, the *Springfield Wheelmen's Gazette* thought that "road racing is by far the most genuine test of rider and wheel that could be devised," while it asserted that "the League will not touch it because it seems to be illegal." Public reaction was evidently a major concern by this time. The *Gazette* thought that:

> there may be something in that, yet road racing is not essentially criminal, and it can be done legally, if proper steps are taken. Pass a rule that, prior to any road race, a petition shall be circulated among the citizens in the vicinity of the course. Then let the petition be presented to the proper county commissioners, and permission obtained to have the race. Then carry out the race decently and in order.[84]

In June 1887, a St. Louis cycling paper, the *American Wheelman*, promoted "The Clarksville 100 Mile Road Race" which was touted as a race "for the Championship of the World"—somewhat ambitious, since no riders from outside the U.S. were invited or were present. It was "boomed" by the Overman Wheel Company following the triumph of its "Victor" bicycle as "The Greatest Bicycle Race Ever Run Since Cycling Began." A "World's Championship Cup, solid silver" and a light roadster bicycle, together worth $440, were offered as the first prize. Held in conjunction with the annual meet of the League of American Wheelmen in St. Louis, the promoters ferried riders out to Clarksville on the Mississippi River for the race back to St. Louis, while the St. Louis, Keokuk and Northwestern

Fig. 6.16. A League of American Wheelmen century ride in San Francisco gathered together an enthusiastic crowd of club cyclists in about 1890, a moment of transition between the high-wheel and the "safety" bicycle. [Source: author's collection]

Railway sold special tickets for the event. The winner, Robert Neilson, rode 100 miles in 6hrs 46m. The race was a display of many different designs of machine, for "there were bikes of every kind upon the road ... all the familiar makes were represented ... while tandems, tricycles, safeties, stars, extraordinaries and bicyclettes spun up and down."[85]

In discussing the public reaction to this race, and to road racing in general, the *American Wheelman* maintained that "the people not only favor the race, but are so anxious for it that they are willing to spend considerable money putting the road into condition. In fact, we think it will be found as a rule that the inhabitants of a district are much more interested in than opposed to a race." The solution to public opposition was to "select a locality where the people are favorably inclined, and do not infringe on the rights of the horsemen."[86] Such an approach was more open-minded, it seems, than the negative British attitudes expressed at the same moment.

The questionable legality of road racing clearly did not prevent its rise in popularity throughout the United States during the mid–1890s. Road races in Providence, Memphis, Wilmington, St. Louis, Denver, Buffalo, Louisville, Cleveland, Rochester and Brooklyn, as well as relay road races which pitted one club against another from Cleveland to Buffalo, from Chicago to New York, from Hamilton to Kingston (Ontario), from Chicago to Cincinnati and from Oakland to San Francisco around the San Francisco Bay, were all announced in the "Coming Events" section of an Indianapolis cycling paper for April 1892.[87]

Road racing was not an isolated phenomenon, but was linked to the general expansion of club cycling in urban and suburban areas throughout the United States. This indicated an interest in a modern technological sport that was accessible to spectators and could be promoted by local press and commercial concerns. Local races were typically short, 25 miles or so, frequently handicaps with riders sent off in small groups according to age and ability which took place on the good roads surrounding or radiating out from the center of older cities such as Boston, Chicago, Detroit or New York and smaller, expanding cities such as Indianapolis, Cleveland or Toledo. But longer races were also held. Many newspaper accounts from the period reported thousands of enthusiastic people mobbing the start and finish lines of road races, to such an extent that they impeded the competitors and made judging impossible. At the Chicago Road Race in June 1894, it was reported that:

> the crowd was the largest ever witnessed at an event of a sporting nature in this city. For nineteen miles the crowd lined each side of the road, in places from 10 to 20 deep. It is estimated that at least 100,000 people were in Lincoln Park, and probably three or four times that many lined the course its entire length. Throughout the country the crowd maintained perfect order without ropes. The course extends through many of the most populated suburbs of Chicago-Edgewater, Argyle, South Evanston, Rogers Park and Evanston—and apparently every resident of these places was on the streets, besides many who went out early in the morning from Chicago. Accounts of the race printed the names of manufacturers of the bicycles and tires ridden by the winners.[88]

A similar enthusiasm greeted the 128 competitors at the 1894 25-mile Martin Road Race in Buffalo, New York, where it was estimated that 20,000 people, "a pushing, seething mass of human beings" were at the finish, so that "it required the most strenuous efforts of the police officers to keep the course clear, so eager and determined were the spectators to see all they could see."[89] In May 1896, the *Worcester Telegram* estimated that 50,000 people, "the biggest crowd ever got together by day light in Worcester," had turned out to see the Telegram Trophy Race, "lining the course from start to finish, climbing the trees to get a better view, bringing the normal business of the town to a standstill."[90] In June 1896, the *Worcester Telegram* reported that "the wheelmen live in race fever."[91] In July 1894, 104 riders lined up for the start of the Atalanta Wheelmen's 100 mile handicap in Newark, New Jersey, although the course of the race had to be changed at the last minute because the authorities of nearby Cranford "would not allow the race to pass through the town as there was an ordinance prohibiting fast riding."[92] The newspapers of every sizeable American city contain such reports during the boom of the mid–1890s.

Road racing in Chicago, in fact, attracted particularly large, enthusiastic crowds, and experienced a remarkable, if short-lived, surge of interest as a popular sport, among both competitors and spectators. At the sixth annual Pullman Race in 1892, the *American Cyclist* reported that:

> every point of vantage along the entire course was occupied. Windows, balconies, doorsteps and housetops were crowded with sightseers, and hundreds of residents displayed the colors of the different cycling clubs represented in the race. Boys were perched in trees and on telegraph poles and lampposts ... the sidewalks were crowded with a surging mass of humanity.[93]

At the 1894 race, "there was no trouble about getting to Pullman to see the finish, for the Illinois Central Railroad ran World's Fair express trains through in a few moments."[94] In 1895, the *Indianapolis Sentinel* reported that:

> Road racing in Chicago has assumed proportions of wonderful magnitude the past year. Saturday afternoons is the accepted time for the running of 5 to 10 mile club events. It is not at all uncommon for a round dozen of these events to be run off in an afternoon. There are three or four accepted courses, which by silent consent of the authorities are monopolized every weekend. It is not uncommon to see several thousand people present at each of the different finishes.[95]

Some races, for instance the Chicago and Pullman Road Races (Chicago), the Martin (Buffalo, New York) and the Irvington-Millburn (New Jersey), which had already been

Fig. 6.17. The start of the *Worcester Telegram* (Massachusetts) road race in 1896, with a black rider prominently in the front row. [Source: author's collection]

established as small-scale events in the 1880s, and became increasingly popular in the 1890s, and were referred to as "classics." The Irvington-Millburn (promoted by the Metropolitan Association of Cycling Clubs)[96] attracted 155 entries in 1894, and the Chicago race more than 400 entries. Organizers of road racing, including American newspapers, knew what was happening in France and were aware of the publicity potential of such events. In 1894, the *New York World* launched an ambitious proposal to organize "a Great Road Race" from New York to San Francisco, with a prize of "at least $1,000," which did not, however, happen.[97]

In spite of this initial surge of popularity (indeed, perhaps partly *because* of it), road racing in America tended to alienate other road users and, just as in England, some cyclists also saw it as giving the sport a bad name. While public enthusiasm and crowds on Saturday afternoons were tolerated at first, they were less acceptable on a regular basis and resistance to the use of public spaces for private purposes became more vocal. There were accidents, horses were scared, normal activities on city streets were disrupted, and rural life was disturbed. As in the case of Cranford, New Jersey, some communities passed public safety ordinances prohibiting fast riding.

Although both the League of American Wheelmen and the National Cycling Association—a new professional organization—discouraged group road racing from the mid–1890s, the Century Road Club acknowledged place-to-place records by individual riders through the 1890s. In 1896, for example, its Road Records Committee recognized a record from Chicago to New York (5 days 17h 21m), with intermediate record times to Cleveland, Buffalo and Rochester.[98] But by the end of 1898, the *New York Evening Journal* wrote of "the downfall of road racing" in a report headlined, "Cycle Road Racing on the Wane. Too Many Difficulties Confront Those who Race on Thoroughfares":

ROAD RACING.

Fig. 6.18. In Britain, road racing was seen by people both inside and outside the sport as a threat to cycling, likely to increase legislation directed negatively at the recreational and utility cyclist. [Source: *Bicycling News*, 4 June 1892]

Road racing on bicycles no longer possesses the interest it once had.... In former years these contests over the public highways were exceedingly popular. Thousands flocked to the scene of the struggle. Riders entered by the hundreds, while manufacturers were eager to offer costly prizes for the publicity.... But this year the few road races held excited little rivalry.

The reasons given for the decline were that "the intense rivalry which prevailed among the clubs no longer exists," and that "those clubs which once supported racing men generously have abandoned the expensive luxury." But another factor was "the local ordinances against speeding over public thoroughfares" and "the dangerous accidents which have resulted."[99]

Public resistance to the dangers and inconveniences of road racing was, therefore, certainly a factor in limiting its ability to find a permanent place on the American sporting calendar, as was the waning of what had been a sporting fad or fashion. Promoters preferred to put their money and energy into staging track events, where spectators could be charged entry fees, crowds could be controlled and the racing was more efficiently and effectively organized. Track surfaces were smoother, distances and times for record-breaking attempts could be more easily and accurately measured on the track, and night-time racing could also be held under electric lights. The economic logic of promotion, the need to advertise new products, promoters' desire to create and market bicycle racing "stars"—these were the factors that caused the energy of cycling as a new American sport to be increasingly focused on the track rather than on the road in the 1890s.

6. Racing Bicycles on Public Roads: Danger or Celebration?

The different ways in which road racing evolved in England, continental Europe (principally France, Belgium and Germany) and the United States can be explained through a variety of inter-related social and economic factors. In all those countries, bicycle racing on public roads was likely to encounter a negative reaction from other categories of road users.[100]

The class-bound, amateur-dominated sport bureaucracy in England exerted a great deal of influence on the conditions under which road racing emerged. There was resistance to promotion by the bicycle industry and road racing was seen as a serious threat to the rights of all cyclists. Whereas in France, the Union Vélocipédique de France was positively disposed towards "open" racing, including sponsorship by bicycle and tire manufacturers, and the promotional participation of newspapers and the cycling press. The staging of road races in France was accepted, in fact, as a sort of public street theater, celebrated on religious festival days, with the start and finish choreographed and minutely organized, and municipal and cycling authorities conspicuously in attendance.

By 1888, a serious rift had already occurred within the National Cyclists' Union on the question of road racing, and an alternative body, the Road Records Association, had broken away from it to pursue sponsorship of road racing, although even the R.R.A. drew the line at encouraging massed-start races. The heavily pro-amateur structure and stance of the N.C.U., its constant hostility towards sponsorship by "the trade," and its refusal to endorse road racing or promote official road championships, effectively prevented the expansion of road racing in Britain as a popular modern sport. Road racing in general was depicted as a threat to the wider sport of recreational cycling. The largely working-class and lower middle-class "scorchers" were considered an intrusive presence on public roads; police interference was feared and sometimes occurred.

Fig. 6.19. The "scorcher" as threat: Edmund Dangerfield, the founder of *Cycling* in 1891, is depicted here by artist George Moore as winner of two important 100-mile road races, the Bath Road C.C. and North Road C.C. events. [Source: *Cycling*, 23 May 1891]

The R.R.A., consequently, was forced to adopt a low profile, and promoted races that emphasized individual endurance (time and distance trials), with inconspicuous athletes dressed in sombre clothes, rather than large, competitive group races. Promotion was muted, but it still enabled long-distance record-breaking rides to be held, which were subse-

Table 6 A. The first 12 years of the Bordeaux–Paris road race, with winners, times, average speeds, and interaction with pacers, including automobile pace between 1897 and 1899:		
1891	G.P. Mills (GB)	572 km in 26:34:37 (21.531 km/h) (human-paced)
1892	A. Stephane (F)	572 km in 25:37:00 (22.329 km/h) (human-paced)
1893	Louis Cottereau (F)	572 km in 26:04:52 (21.923 km/h) (human-paced)
1894	Lucien Lesna (F)	572 km in 25:11:07 (23.506 km/h) (human-paced)
1895	Charles Meyer (Dk)	592 km in 25:30:00 (23.216 km/h) (human-paced)
1896	Arthur Linton (GB) (tied) Gaston Rivierre (F)	592 km in 24:12:15 (27.809 km/h) (human-paced)
1897	Gaston Rivierre (F)	592 km in 20:36:46 (28.720 km/h) (automobile-paced)
1898	Gaston Rivierre (F)	592 km in 20:39:01 (28.688 km/h) (automobile-paced)
1899	Constant Huret (F)	594 km in 16:35:47 (35.791 km/h) (automobile-paced)
1900	Josef Fischer (D)	594 km in 21:57:57 (27.042 km/h) (human-paced)
1901	Lucien Lesna (F)	594 km in 21:53:40 (27.130 km/h) (human-paced)
1902	Edouard Wattelier (F) Maurice Garin (F)	575 km in 22:43:01 (25.312 km/h) (unpaced) 575 km in 18:41:20 (30.767 kph) (human-paced)
1903	Hippolyte Aucouturier (F)	575 km in 20:03:50 (28.658 kph) (human-paced)

quently boldly advertised in the press. The secrecy in which these kinds of races took place, however, meant that very few spectators saw them. And the avoidance of town centers, where racers were most likely to encounter police attention, discouraged the development of a sense of civic pride in the sporting event, or the possibility of public admiration for the athletes.

Bicycle racing on British roads, therefore, did not spread beyond the limited club coterie that practiced and enjoyed it, whereas in France and Belgium, where road racing was accepted and encouraged, spectators were engaged and riders rewarded. At a moment when professional bicycle racing on the roads of Britain might have been embraced, and various kinds of commercial promotion and municipal sponsorship encouraged, class-driven amateur idealism and the minimization of the influence of the industry were still the preferred priority of the ruling elites of the N.C.U.

The situation in France was dramatically different. With a barely developed concept of "amateurism" (which was viewed by the French as a peculiarly British obsession), and a tradition of racing for cash within an "open" structure, the U.V.F. welcomed the participation of the bicycle manufacturing industry. Manufacturers sponsored races and involved themselves in their promotion, while the names of the brands of bicycle ridden by competitors were openly advertised. Bicycles were inspected and stamped ("*poinçonné*") before races to guarantee that the same machine was used throughout, thus ensuring a stricter test of mechanical and technical capabilities. Newspapers and the cycling press promoted and reported races to their readership as a way of increasing circulation, presenting contests of personalities and demonstrations of speed, physical strength and endurance.

Road racing in France blossomed in the early 1890s, with the establishment of place-to-place road races between geographically important and symbolically resonant locations. Bicycle races were held between many of the European capitals and regarded as culturally and politically significant events. Spectators were invited to identify with the racers from their own home regions as they covered the long distance between Bordeaux and Paris, for example, or Paris and Brussels, and they could admire the dust-covered riders as they passed on the road or at the "controls" in town. Publicity and advertising were essential to

Table 6 B shows some of the principal place-to-place road races inaugurated between 1891 and 1896, with approximate distances, sponsorship (where known) and winners:

Date	Itinerary	Distance	Sponsor/Winner
May 1891	1st Bordeaux–Paris	587 km	Sponsored by *Véloce-Sport*
?1891	Angers–Tours–Angers	224 km	Won by Charron and Fournier
?1891	Paris–Dieppe–Paris	357 km	Won by Vigneux
Sept. 1891	1st Paris–Brest–Paris	1,200 km	Sponsored by *Le Petit Journal*
May 1892	2nd Bordeaux–Paris	587 km	Sponsored by *Véloce-Sport*
May 1892	Basle–Strasbourg		
?1892	Geneva–Berne		Won by Masi
June 1892	Paris–Clermont-Ferrand		Sponsored by Michelin, won by Henri Farman
June 1892	Liège–Bastogne–Liège	155 miles	Won by Léon Houa
?1892	Lyon–Montelimar–Lyon	525 km	Won by Marius Allard
July 1892	Paris–Nantes–Paris	1004 km	Sponsored by *La Revue des Sports*, won by Allard
May 1893	Paris–Beauvais–Paris		Sponsored by *La Bicyclette*
May 1893	Paris–Rouen		Sponsored by *La Bicyclette*
May 1893	Paris–Trouville		Sponsored by *La Bicyclette*
May 1893	3rd Bordeaux–Paris	587 km	Sponsored by *Véloce-Sport*, won by Cottereau
June 1893	2nd Liège–Bastogne–Liège	155 miles	Won by Léon Houa
June 1893	Vienna–Berlin	582 km	Sponsored by Opel and Michelin, won by Josef Fischer
July 1893	Paris–Ostend		Won by Dubois
July 1893	Paris–Bruxelles	404 km	Sponsored by *La Bicyclette*, won by André
Sept. 1893	Paris–Luchon	830 km	Sponsored by the Luchon Casino
Oct. 1893	Saint Petersburg–Paris	3,000 km	Terront, sponsored by Rudge and Clincher
May 1894	4th Bordeaux–Paris	587 km	Won by Lucien Lesna
May 1894	Rome–Paris		Won by Terront
? 1894	Milan–Turin	530 km	Won by Pavie
? 1894	Milan–Munich		Won by Fischer
?1894	Trieste–Vienna		Won by Fischer
Aug.1894	Lyons–Paris–Lyon	646 miles	Won by Rivierre
May 1895	5th Bordeaux–Paris		Won by Charles Meyer
April 1896	Paris–Roubaix	280 km	Sponsored by *Le Vélo*; won by Josef Fischer
May 1896	6th Bordeaux–Paris		Won by Linton and Rivierre

the success of the novel sport and the industry: publicity sold bicycles and tires, and bicycle racing sold newspapers. Companies such as Clément and De Dion-Bouton were quick to recognize this fact. Thus, road racing promised a modern, exciting, spectacle. The sport was presented as an epic battle, fought out on the same roads which the general public (still heavily agrarian) knew as their own, and the riders were "created" as popular, proletarian heros whose courage and tenacity the public could embrace. A new kind of athlete, embodied by cyclist Charles Terront, emerged and a new kind of sports manager, typified by H.O. Duncan, staging events and manipulating publicity and public opinion, was born.

In addition, there was a keen awareness of the technological novelty of bicycle racing, and an aesthetic appreciation of the actual process of competition, of the speed, endurance and athletic endeavor of cyclists as universal human qualities. That these qualities were supported by the financial sponsorship of the industry and the press was not regarded as diminishing or minimizing their athletic merit; rather athlete and manufacturer were regarded as participating in a shared enterprise. This was true of bicycle racing both on the road and on the track. The opening of a new track in Paris, the Velodrome Buffalo, caused *La Bicyclette* to comment on "new proposals for magnificent struggles and gripping matches." In quick succession, the paper noted, "24 hour records, international races, long-distance and sprint races follow each other, more and more of an attraction to people interested in cycling."[101]

In perhaps the most important critical and theoretical French text written in the early 1890s, a period of rapid sport expansion, journalist Baudry de Saunier hinted at the profound impact of cycling on public awareness and habits when he wrote:

I did not exaggerate at all when I suggested earlier that cycling constitutes a revolution in human locomotion. A revolution in social relationships, a revolution in habits and customs, a revolution in business cycling, which some short-sighted people still make fun of, will succeed in effecting some convulsive changes.... But ultimately cycling is more than a revolution of commerce and special products. In our age, when it is necessary to get through life on the basis of courage and will, the marvellous exercise teaches initiative, endurance and obstinacy. Its most wonderful quality, in the end, is a moral one.[102]

As De Saunier's analysis suggests, the roads of France, and to a lesser extent, perhaps, the velodromes, as well, became public spaces where sport was openly encouraged commercially but also had an idealistic social value. The races were an expression of the human and moral value of physical and athletic challenges. In the 1893 Bordeaux-Paris race, wrote Davin de Champlos in *La Bicyclette*, "The riders, both winners and losers, have given us a wonderful example of courage, endurance and tenacity."[103] The same values were expressed after 1903 in the annual Tour de France, where roads were completely closed to normal traffic while the race passed, as they still are today.[104] The roads of Britain, in marked contrast, were thought of as a territory to be defended against the dangers and risks of fast cycling in the interests of safety, propriety, class exclusivity, the non-cycling road-user, and those more sedate touring and utilitarian cyclists who did not want to be identified with the "scorchers."

Fig. 6.20. Long-distance cycling as record-breaking theater: Charles Terront, pacer Meyer, and manager H.O. Duncan after the St. Petersburg to Paris ride, 1893 [Source: *En Suivant Terront de St. Petersburg à Paris*]

Six. The Foundations of Modern Road Racing

* * *

[Some of the information in Table 6 B has been taken from Jean Durry, *La Véridique Histoire des Géants de la Route* (1973). Races held earlier in the high-wheel era show that place-to-place races were not a new idea in France, and had in fact been organized almost continuously since the 1869 Paris-Rouen race. Races held included Dijon-Besancon (1870), Paris-Versailles (1871), Lyon-Macon-Lyon (1872), Lyon-Chalons-Lyon and Marseille-Avignon-Marseille (1873). As early as 1876, a 224 km Angers-Tours-Angers race was won by Tissier, who repeated the victory in 1877. In 1879, an Angers-Le Mans-Angers race was won by Terront. Other races included Rennes-Dinan-Rennes (1880) and Paris-Blois-Tours (1881).]

Chapter Seven

International Competition

1. Bicycle Racing as a Global Sport

BY THE MID–1890s, there was a compulsive drive towards technological improvement, organizational systematization, and bureaucratic codification within British, French and American cycling, three characteristics that defined it as a decisively "modern" sport.[1] Little was now left to chance: the rules for competition were systematically spelled out, a "record" of times and distances was kept which became the standard by which future performances could be judged, and the races were meticulously documented in the press. The written "record" of the early sport is surprisingly complete; a handful of the very earliest races, perhaps, are not dated or fully described, although many are.[2]

"A complete history of cycle racing would fill a very bulky volume," wrote F.T. Bidlake in an 1896 book on cycling. Bidlake gives a brief resume of the British championships since the beginnings of the sport:

> The first amateur championships of the National Cyclists' Union were held in 1878; prior to that date, the Amateur Athletic Club having organized a four miles' championship from 1871. The Union was then called the Bicycle Union, and its championships were for ordinary bicycles. In 1882 a tricycle championship was added, and in the following year two such events were run; while from 1884 to 1888 inclusive, the set of championships was 1, 5, 25 and 50 miles for ordinaries, and 1, 5 and 25 miles for tricycles. In 1889, the first safety championships were held, and in 1890 they were all won by R.J. Mecredy on the then novel pneumatic tyre, F.J. Osmond securing the complete set of ordinary championships. The ordinary falling into disuse as a racing machine, the ordinary championships were abandoned in 1893, the 1892 races being practically uncontested, and the tricycle events reduced to 1 and 10 miles, and will probably also be abandoned.[3]

Clearly, the British cycling championships had a complex history, and their development reflected the technological evolution within the sport. As bicycles and tricycles changed, the nature of competition changed, and the different styles of machines were tested and validated within the annual championship process. Annual championships existed then, as they still do, to test the top performers in a given sporting discipline, under shared conditions. Bidlake was charting only the amateur championships, and merely hinted at the ongoing debate over amateurism and professionalism which continued to trouble national and international cycling affairs throughout the 1890s.

One of the most important tasks of the National Cyclists' Union was: "To examine the question of Amateur and Professional Bicycle and Tricycle Racing in general, and to frame definitions and recommend rules on the subject. To arrange for Annual Race Meetings at which the Amateur and Professional Championships of Bicycling and Tricycling shall be decided."[4]

But Bidlake thought that the results of this objective had "not been a success, for at the present day the question of amateurism in cycling is as troublesome as it was when the Union started to examine it." In another passage in his book, he was critical of the N.C.U.'s attempt to legislate an amateur/professional segregation, claiming that this had had divisive repercussions within the sport and had held back its development. Bidlake complained that:

> In the formation of rules for racing the Union has been very zealous, and has spent immense time and trouble in attempting to define an amateur, and to keep the class so defined pure, but the result has been a ludicrous failure, as sham amateurism and veiled professionalism have been rampant more than ever in the past few years, and the sorting process has been carried on in such a way that some of the worst offenders have been untouched, and not a few straight men have been unnecessarily interfered with. Consistency has not been observed throughout the country and a great deal of dissatisfaction has been manifest; in consequence the sport of England has not been encouraged as it might have been. In an endeavour to maintain amateurism, the Union has really degraded it...[5]

As competition intensified in the 1890s, and the bicycle industry continued to play an assertive role in using the sport to test and advertise its products, it became crucial to have a clear and functional definition of what "amateur" and "professional" really meant, but this was always difficult. While the bicycle industry was able to support an increasing number of full professionals, other cyclists, partially sponsored or supported with equipment or expenses, fell into a grey area that was neither fully professional nor completely amateur. And the bureaucrats of the N.C.U., in their zeal to defend amateurism, continued to be concerned with what many of them saw as the pernicious intrusion of "the trade" into the amateur sport.

This chapter examines national and international competition during the expansion of high-wheel racing in the 1880s and the bicycle boom of the 1890s. It describes how international competition developed at the elite level and how the professional class grew with bicycle industry sponsorship.

It looks at the growth of the European and American governing bodies of cycling and examines the foundation of the International Cyclists' Association (the first world governing body of the sport), the staging of the first official World Championships in Chicago in 1893 and the first Olympic Games of 1896. And it pays particular attention to the constant tensions within the sport between amateurism and professionalism, illustrated in the controversial events which surrounded the international career of Arthur Zimmerman.

Cycling had grown from a naïve set of indoor gymnastic exercises and jarring trips over cobbled city streets into a globally popular competitive and recreational sport, with national organizations and a world governing body, in less than 25 years.

2. National Championships, International Competition and Early "World Championships"

Professionalism in cycling (racing for cash prizes or for a share of the money put up as a wager) had existed from the earliest velocipede racing, and was similar in its organization to other wagered contests such as pedestrianism (walking and running), pugilism (boxing and wrestling) and horse-racing. At the highest level, riders such as James Moore, an English resident of Paris, and South Londoner, John Keen, traveled between London and the English Midlands and featured prominently in "championship" contests in the 1870s.[6]

Races at the Crystal Palace in South London in 1869 were promoted in the press as "International Velocipede Races," and the contestants were called "English and Continental Champions."[7] Professional racing became increasingly popular through the 1870s. Amateur bicycle racing, strongly attached to its athletic club connections through the 1870s and 1880s, continued to develop alongside the professional sport. The two categories were not totally segregated; amateurs and professionals occasionally appeared on the same program. But, in general, professional events were organized by autonomous, profit-making individual promoters while amateur events were held under the jurisdiction of athletic or cycling club organizations, or organized by the National Cyclists' Union.

Early professional events, held before the existence of any official governing body,

Fig. 7.1. An enormous crowd of cyclists gathered at the Meet of the New York Division of the L.A.W. in Buffalo in 1883. [Source: Lorne Shields collection, Toronto, Canada]

showed just how profitable bicycle racing could be at the box-office. Promoters needed stars and the habitual winners of important events were identified as "champions." Indoor professional races included both long-distance as well as short-distance events in the 1870s, because long events enabled the promoters to create a carnival-like atmosphere and longer periods during which they could sell tickets. Six-Day races, which began in the mid–1870s, were marketed as sensational, super-human endurance events. Huge crowds attended outdoor Six-Day races in the English Midlands in 1876.[8] The strongholds of professional cycling in England included Wolverhampton, Sheffield, Birmingham, Leicester and London. In Edinburgh, Newcastle, Liverpool and Manchester, areas with large working-class populations, professional racing was also popular.

Early rivalry between cyclists in neighbors England and France gave bicycle racing its first international contests. French and English riders contested the earliest "world championships," first held in 1870, in which the English were dominant. By 1874, the idea of world championships had been firmly implanted: the 1-mile event held at the Molineux Grounds, Wolverhampton in April 1874 was referred to variously as the "world's mile challenge champion cup," "the race for the championship cup," and the "course de Championnat du Monde." Howard's *The Bicycle for 1874* refers to it as a "One Mile Championship. Open to the World."[9]

In one of the earliest examples of trans–Atlantic cycling competition, English professional "crack" David Stanton made a trip to the United States in 1876, infusing life into the embryonic bicycle racing scene there.[10] When Charles Terront, David Stanton, John Keen and William Cann traveled to the United States in 1879—the trip promoted by Harry Etherington—their presence was an indication of a pattern of international exchanges to come. In 1882, *Bicycling World* conceded that:

> England is pre-eminently the home and paradise of bicycle racing, and when American cyclists hear the loud bayings of the celebrated British dog "Brag," we tremble on our pedals with despair, accept with resignation our ignominious inferiority, and complacently congratulate ourselves if we win an occasional and patronizing approval from over the water.[11]

But by the mid–1880s, British amateur and professional riders crossed the Atlantic to compete at the Springfield Tournaments and in the later–1880s, parties of American riders crossed the Atlantic to appear on the European scene, competing in England and France, and contributing to an intensified level of international competition.

A professional championship was not at first recognized under the auspices of the National Cyclists' Union. Although some of the amateur members of the earlier Bicycle Union wanted to exclude professionals from their membership, they were nonetheless very interested in the professionals' abilities and often went to see them perform. Deep-rooted class discrimination was responsible for whatever animosity existed, but a "liberal" attitude was certainly emerging in the new sport, manifested by the amateur-versus-professional races organized by Gerard Cobb and sanctioned by the Bicycle Union in 1878–79.

Some amateur riders at the time—particularly those in the North—perceived the national governing body as hostile to them and resented the intrusion of a central organization into regional affairs. The N.C.U., however, claimed to be looking after the interests of cyclists of both categories. A Committee for Promoting Professional Racing was formed, and its report presented at a council meeting of the N.C.U. on 3 February 1887. The report concluded that "the present obscure and unsatisfactory position of professional racing" was due to "the scarcity of opportunities for racing for money prizes ... and the social disabilities under which professionals now exist." The committee recommended that "regulations existing in most clubs excluding professionals be removed wherever possible, and the fact of a man riding for money be not made a bar to his becoming or remaining a member of a club, providing his social position in all other respects be sufficiently satisfactory." It was further recommended that a set of rules for governing professional racing be worked out, that professionals be allowed on teams selected for international representation. The N.C.U. was not an exclusively amateur body: this was "not sufficiently known and understood throughout the country," and professionals should be on its Council or Executive.

On the question of amateur versus professional racing, however, which the Executive still supported, they were "aware of the difficulties surrounding such a suggestion" and thought that such races "should be an exceptional occurrence, and be under the direct sanction and control of the Union."[12] By 1894, a motion, proposed by Henry Sturmey, was carried in the N.C.U. Executive that: "The Union shall hold, or permit to be held, at least one professional championship in each year," as well as an "open" championship, "open to all riders licensed by them, without the amateur rider losing his status."[13]

* * *

As we already know, the French saw things differently. They encouraged professional racing, exerted no pressure to separate amateurs from professionals either in track racing or in the early classic road races, where riders were distinguished more by how they were expected to perform, a distinction being made between athletic expectations, between "coureurs de vitesse" ("speed riders," more likely to be experienced, i.e., professional level) and "routiers" ("road-men," more likely to be of amateur level).

In France, winners were frequently paid in cash and were openly recognized as professionals. This difference became a problem only during international competition when the British insisted on amateur "purity." With British amateurs unable to compete in France without risk to their status upon their return, and French riders not being sure of their status when they competed in events in Britain, international competition was hindered. "A new complication has been brought into question by the fact that Frédéric de Civry, titular amateur champion of France, has been over in England racing with our professionals for money prizes," reported the *Wheel World Annual* in 1880.[14]

The French openly criticized what they saw as a British obsession with trying to classify bicycle racers. They pointed at the apparent hypocrisy of certain N.C.U. officials who were willing to declare that some French and American riders were "professionals" and therefore ineligible to compete internationally as amateurs, while at the same time turning a blind eye to their own questionable amateurs. In 1892, an unsuccessful attempt was made to create a uniquely amateur body in France, in the face of opposition from the Union Vélocipédique de France. A *Cycling* editorial reported that English observers had "assisted in the inauguration of amateur racing in France," and described amateurism in France as being "in its earliest infancy," and that "across the Channel the conditions under which cycle racing is carried on are clearly unfavourable to the growth of true amateurism."[15] Such attitudes clearly demonstrated the status of amateurism as a moral ideology which its adherents attempted to construct and define within cycling: "amateurism" and "professionalism" were two sides of the same coin, each struggling to define the essence of the sport, or offering rival versions of it.

According to the rules governing most amateur clubs, "professionals" were specifically denied membership, and the N.C.U. and the League of American Wheelmen had an uncomfortable, ambivalent relationship with them. First, there was the problem of framing definitions to identify who was a professional and who was an amateur. Second, what exactly did the distinction between the two categories mean in practical terms in actual competition? When *could* they compete against each other? Third, what kind of sanctions could be brought to bear on competitors who infringed official regulations?

No other issue was as troublesome for the promoters of early bicycle racing, and the need to clarify these distinctions led to various licensing and classification schemes and to riders being subjected to intrusive questioning by various governing bodies. The cause of many disputes in the 1880s and 1890s, growing out of cycling's intimate economic relationship with the bicycle and tire manufacturers, were the "maker's amateurs," or semi-professionals, who accepted equipment from manufacturers or expenses from promoters, but held on for as long as they could to their official amateur status. They were hard to regulate, and a thorn in the side of officialdom.

At the beginning of the 1870s the concept of a "world championship" was still in an embryonic form, and didn't really mature for another twenty years. Until the International Cyclists' Association's first amateur championships in 1893, there was no officially recognized cycling "world championship." The character of unofficial world championships within the sport during this twenty-year period changed considerably.

In the early period, a promoter could advertise a world championship based on a personal challenge that one rider had issued to another, using the term partly as a marketing ploy, and also as a real recognition of the elite level of competition. In the 1870s and 1880s, most "world championships" consisted of matches between the leading English riders, or between English and French riders—the American, Belgian and German contenders arrived on the scene a little later. On the basis of his many international victories, John Keen was often referred to as "world champion" in the 1870s.

A rider could also claim the "world championship" by setting a new world-record time. When, for example, English amateur Sanders Sellers broke the 1-mile amateur world record at a meeting of the Connecticut Bicycle Club in Hartford, Connecticut in September 1884, he was reported in *Outing and The Wheelman*, as having won "the world's championship." Sellers and the reigning English professional champion, Richard Howell (then holder of the world professional 1-mile record, in 2m 40⅘s), were members of a British contingent of riders who had traveled to America including Robert James, R. Chambers, G.H. Illston and H.W. Gaskell.[16] Amateur Sellers broke Howell's professional record on 9 September, with a ride of 2m 39s. The result of the race "made the audience almost wild with excitement," and Sellers was "pronounced the world's champion." Howell immediately tried to retake his record, but failed. On 17 September, however, at the Springfield Tournament, American professional John S. Prince was successful in again breaking Howell's professional record, equalling Seller's time, with a ride that elicited "a mighty cheer from the 12,000 spectators." It was reported that "he had wrested the world's professional championship from Howell in 2m 39s."[17]

In this case, amateurs and professionals competed for the same record at the same

```
              THE BICYCLING WORLD          [12 September, 1884

                    GRAND
              INTERNATIONAL
           BICYCLE TOURNAMENT!
                    OF THE
           SPRINGFIELD BICYCLE CLUB,
                 HAMPDEN PARK,
         SPRINGFIELD, MASS., SEPT. 16, 17, 18 and 19, 1884.

           $8,000.00 * IN * PRIZES!

                REMEMBER THE DATES.
              Tuesday, September 16.
                Wednesday, September 17.
                  Thursday, September 18.
                    Friday, September 19.

           GRAND PARADE, WEDNESDAY, SEPT. 17.
         Grand Display of Fireworks, Thursday, Sept. 18.
              NINE GRAND AND EXCITING RACES EACH DAY.
```

Fig. 7.2. The Springfield Bicycle Club succeeded in internationalizing its annual race meetings, attracting British riders in spite of the distance from European competition. [Source: *Bicycling World*, 12 Sept. 1884]

race meeting. It was evident that the mile record was what mattered, and that amateurs and professionals were evenly matched. The athletic quality of these races as "world championships" was unquestionable, and their promotion by the Springfield and Connecticut Bicycle Clubs, two of the most important American clubs, with the approval of the Table 7 A. A chronology of the establishment of national governing bodies of bicycle racing and touring, showing the expansion of cycling organizations in the late 1870s and 1880s, the high-wheel era.[18]

League of American Wheelmen, gave them prestige and credibility. But they still lacked official international recognition by a world governing body to establish their authenticity as true "world championships."

In February 1886, Henry Sturmey published an editorial in his paper, *The Cyclist*, entitled "International Championships." He was practical and down to earth, as usual, as well as perceptive. The English championships, he wrote, no longer had "the right to practically claim the title of world's champion for any of our riders without a contest of the same," and it was "high time systematic arrangements were made for the regulation and holding of world's championships at truly international meetings." Sturmey added that "cyclists in other countries have been making rapid progress," particularly in the United States, Germany, France and Australia, and that "until now the supremacy of British limbs and wheels has been undoubted, but as nation after nation increases in proficiency on the cycle, that position must be each year more open to doubt." He proposed the immediate formation of "a federation for the arrangement of an annual series of international contests for the supremacy of the world of wheels," the contests to circulate annually among the participating nations.[19]

The possibility of having the annual Springfield Tournaments recognized as official world championships obviously appealed to the affluent and well-organized American club, which eagerly took up Sturmey's suggestion. In April 1886, the president of the Springfield Bicycle Club, Henry Ducker, wrote to Abbott Bassett, Chairman of the Racing Board of the League of American Wheelmen, promising that:

> the Springfield Bicycle Club will do all in its power to assist the N.C.U. and the L.A.W. in uniting upon a plan to establish a recognized championship race of the world. The Springfield Bicycle Club hereby extends to the legislative bodies of the world a cordial invitation to send representatives to the fifth annual meeting of the club to be holden at Springfield, Mass ... in the month of September 1886, and

Seven. International Competition

Table 7 A. A chronology of the establishment of national governing bodies of bicycle racing and touring, showing the expansion of cycling organizations in the late-1870s and 1880s, the high-wheel era.18

1878	England	Bicycle Union
1878	England	Bicycle Touring Club (renamed Cyclists' Touring Club)
1880	United States	League of American Wheelmen
1880	France	Union Vélocipédique de France
1881	Denmark	Dansk Cycklie Club
1882	Germany	Deutsche und Deutsch-Österreichische Velocipedisten Bund (including Austria)
1882	Ireland	Irish Cyclists' Association
1882	Canada	Canadian Wheelmen's Association
1882	Australia	Australian Cyclists' Union
1883	Holland	Nederlandsche Vélocipédisten Bond (renamed 1884 as Algemene Nederlandsche Wielrijders Bond)
1883	Switzerland	Schweizerischer Radfahrer Bund
1883	Belgium	Fédération Vélocipédique Belge
1883	Bohemia	Bohemian Cyclists' Union (had Czech title)
1883	England	National Cyclists' Union (renaming of Bicycle Union)
1884	Germany	Deutscher Radfahrer Bund
1884	Russia	(Exact name of Russian federation uncertain)
1885	Italy	Unione Velocipedistica Italiana
1888	England	Road Records Association
1888/89	Scotland	Scottish Cyclists' Union
1890	France	Touring-Club de France

there to enter into a friendly competition for the championship of the world on such conditions as may be mutually agreed upon.20

The annual Springfield Tournaments, as we have already seen, were the scene of intense competition between American and British riders on American soil, and provoked heated chauvinistic debate about the athletic strength and speed of the riders, and about the measurement of distances and the timing of record events. The organizers of these prominent events had as early as 1884 already asserted the status of the races as an "International Tournament" and proudly announced a 1-mile race as a "Grand Race for the World's Championship!" in spite of the fact that competitors were drawn almost exclusively

Fig. 7.3. In 1886, the Springfield club ambitiously advertised its 1-mile race as a "Grand race for the World's Championship." [Source: *The Cycle*, 20 Aug. 1886]

from the English-speaking countries and did not attract French or German cyclists. In the absence of a world governing body, however, this attempt to designate the Springfield Tournaments as a formal world championship was unsuccessful.

In the world of international racing in the late 1880s and early 1890s, the National Cyclists' Union championships continued to be accepted widely as the most international, with a surprisingly large number of foreign riders winning various British championships between 1887 and 1896.[21] And the distance from Europe certainly did not strengthen the case for promoting an annual world championship in America.

As cycling became ever more international in scope, the question of who should represent substantial populations of athletes in areas of central Europe with divided, or ambiguous, national identities, became crucial, particularly within the Austro-Hungarian empire. Exactly what constituted Germany, for example? Should Austria be included, and where did German-speaking Sudetan Bohemia belong? How should multi-ethnic Switzerland be represented? Amid talk of "world" championships, regional cycling championships offered a more practical arrangement. French and other nation's athletic pride was asserted against what the Europeans tended to see as the hegemony of the English-speaking cycling governing bodies.[22]

Fig. 7.4. The American professional team was welcomed to Britain during the winter season of 1887–88. [Source: *Bicycling News*, 26 March 1887]

By the late 1880s, as the sport expanded and track facilities improved, high-wheel bicycle racing was enjoying its final moment of glory before it was replaced by the arrival of the safety bicycle and the pneumatic tire. Bicycle racing was becoming a more international sport, with ambitiously promoted race meetings, and foreign riders who were used as marketing incentives. The creation of better organized bicycle racing within national governing bodies, together with increased international competition at an elite level, were accompanied by a third tendency: a more systematic and successful promotion of competition within the professional ranks, and a growing number of professionals made possible by industry sponsorship.

At the end of 1887, *The Cyclist* wrote of "a strong and decided revival of professionalism" and later expressed the view that "the chief interest in racing this year will centre upon that amongst professionals.... On all sides, we find professionalism taking a decided advance."[23] By 1893, international professionalism had advanced to the extent that the Palmer Tyre company, of Birmingham, England, advertised its sponsorship of cyclists in England, America, Canada and South Africa.

Table 7 B. Races defined as "International" in the late 1880s	
10 April 1888	"International Race" between Richard Howell (GB) and W.A. Rowe (USA) at Leicester.[24]
10 May 1888	Munich International Tournament.
13–17 May 1888	Bohemian Championships, Prague.
21–23 May 1888	Sport and Play International Cycling Tournament, Birmingham.
June 1888	"Great International Races," Berlin.
June 1888	Glasgow International Exhibition "Grand Amateur Athletic and Cycling Meeting."
6–8 Aug.	"England versus the World," Grand International Cycling Tournament.
11–12 Aug. 1888	National and International Two Day's Meeting, Scheveningen, Holland.
26–27 Aug. 1888	"Great Race Meeting," Berlin.
Sept. 1888	Buffalo International Tournament, United States.
	Hartford International Tournament, United States

In 1888, a number of race meetings[25] in various countries were all promoted as being "international."

The promotional opportunities offered by well-choreographed and publicized international exchanges were well appreciated, for example, during the visit of a team of American professional riders to England in 1887/88. W.J. Morgan (often referred to as "Senator" Morgan) brought W.M. Woodside (Philadelphia) and Ralph Temple (Chicago) to compete against R.H. English (North Shields), Jack Lee (Clay Cross), Richard Howell (Coventry), A.H. Robb (Birmingham), Jules Dubois (France) and Charles Terront (France). The audiences attending the races were enormous.

Indoor races were promoted in Britain throughout the winter of 1887–88 in various locations (such as the Agricultural Hall, Waverley Market, Edinburgh; St. George's Drill Hall, Newcastle; Bingley Hall, Birmingham), reminiscent in many respects of Harry Etherington's sensational long-distance promotions of 1878–1880.

The show business elements were emphasized in a series of three "Cowboys versus Cyclists" events in London and Birm-

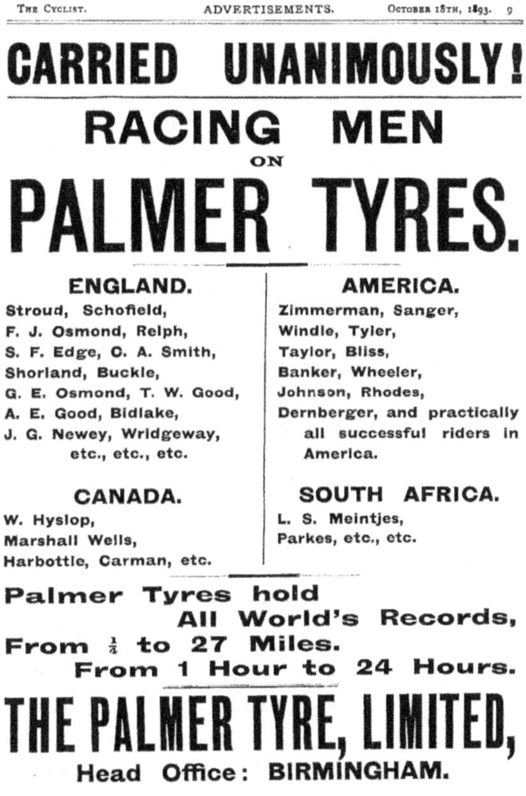

Fig. 7.5. By 1893, international professionalism within cycling had advanced to the extent that the Palmer Tyre company was sponsoring riders in four countries. [Source: *The Bearings*, 21 July 1893]

ingham, where Howell, Woodside and Terront raced against "cowboys" on horseback in a "six day's race, eight hours per day"; the race "went on day by day, enlivened by a programme of matches and trick-riding."[26] But serious racing was mixed with this show business entertainment. Thomas Battensby, backed by the manager of the Newcastle branch of the Rudge Cycle Co., issued a challenge to "any member" of the American team to ride "for six days, eight hours a day."[27]

At the same time the American team was visiting England, there was heated match competition for professional honors between English champions Richard Howell and "Billy" Wood (North Shields), who rode competing makes of bicycles, Howell on a Rudge and Wood on a Premier,[28] and between Howell and recently arrived American professional W.A. Rowe (Lynn, Massachusetts), who competed against each other in three matches, over 5 miles at Leicester, 1 mile at Wolverhampton and 10 miles at Coventry.[29] Rowe and Wood were also matched at Jarrow-on-Tyne.[30]

Fig. 7.6. The first official World Championships in Chicago in 1893 were advertised in Chicago as "America versus the World." [Source: *The Bearings*, 21 July 1893]

While Britain and the United States were staging these international events, there were also frequent international meetings on continental Europe, in Berlin, Vienna and Dresden.

3. THE INTERNATIONAL CYCLISTS' ASSOCIATION, 1892

The difficulties of defining and organizing a satisfactory, true "world championship" should not be underestimated. The British and American cyclists were active and energetic rivals—they argued about accurate measurement of time and distance and they challenged each other's claims to world records. British and French amateurs, as we know, did not routinely compete against each other because they could not agree on the definition of an "amateur." The European nations, Germany, Austria, Holland, Belgium, Switzerland and Italy, were inclined for practical reasons to think in terms of a European championship, and yet the often-claimed "superiority" of the British needed to be challenged. A definitive world championship was difficult to promote because rival nations were so far apart and it was logistically difficult to assemble all the best competitors in one place, at one time.

But above all, international agreement about a structure for true world championships was impossible without a world governing body of some kind, a federation of participating nations.

According to cycling historians René Jacobs and Hector Mahau, the secretary of the Unione Velocipedistica Italiana, Gustave Brignone, made an attempt to form an international body in Turin in May 1890, closely followed by another attempt by the president of the Deutsche Radfahrer Bund in June of the same year. In April 1892, the Union Vélocipédique Suisse issued invitations to an international congress in Berne, but that effort also did not meet with success.[31]

Perhaps because the organizational reach and influence of the National Cyclists' Union was more developed, the British succeeded where these continental initiatives had failed. The most active figure within this multi-lateral movement to create an official world governing body was Henry Sturmey, editor of *The Cyclist* and a powerful figure within the National Cyclists' Union, although the equally powerful George Lacy Hillier was also involved at the committee stage and in framing draft governing rules.[32] These rules were drawn up and circulated to all active national cycling bodies, and a convention called for November 1892, in London, during the important Stanley Show, the annual trade event at which manu-

Top: Fig. 7.7. Henry Sturmey. Writer, journalist, publisher, historian, inventor, and bureaucrat, Sturmey was a driving force behind the creation of the first International Cycling Association in 1892. [Source, *Wheel World*, Dec. 1883] *Bottom*: Fig. 7.8. Arthur Augustus Zimmerman, photographed in 1893, the year in which he won the first official 1-mile World Championship. [Source: author's collection]

facturers presented their new season's products. Delegates from England, France, Germany, Holland, Italy, Ireland, Belgium, Canada and the United States were present, and the Canadian delegate, Dr. Doolittle, was elected Chairman.[33]

The meeting had two related objectives, to "institute a universally recognized series of world championships," and to create an organization that would "tend towards the establishing of a common amateur definition." The first task was easily accomplished. Sturmey moved that: "In the opinion of this meeting it is desirable to combine for the purpose of holding organized championships of the world," and the motion was carried unanimously.[34] Amateur championships were to be held in 1893 in the United States under the auspices of the League of American Wheelmen, whose powerful chairman, Howard E. Raymond, was appointed the first president of the organization. The championships would coincide with the Chicago World Fair, with medals given for races of 1 mile, 10 km and 100 km paced.

The second task—to agree on a common definition of amateurism—was more problematic. Officially, the French amateur sport was represented at the convention by the Union des Sociétés Françaises de Sports Athlétiques, even though the Union Vélocipédique de France was the acknowledged governing body of French cycling. This was because the U.V.F. continued to pursue an independent course, flouting British/American definitions of amateurism by allowing all riders to compete together for cash, and resisting English attempts to segregate a "pure" amateur class. Chairman Doolittle ruled that the three U.V.F. representatives present could be heard, but could not vote. The U.V.F. was essentially told that it needed to fall into line with the majority definition of amateurism before it could become a full member of the new international organization.

The successful formation of the International Cyclists' Association in London was not an entirely democratic initiative, therefore, but an assertion of the dominant British and American ideal of segregated amateurism in sport—a power play from within the National Cyclists' Union and the League of American Wheel men to gain wider recognition for that ideal on an international basis, and to steer the recalcitrant French and Italians towards separating amateurs and professionals in competition. The possibility of "open" championships was rejected, and professionals were, at first, relegated to an ambivalent position outside the world governing body. The first clause of its initial set of bye-laws declared that, "The International Cyclists' Association of the recognized governing bodies of Amateur cycling sport throughout the world is formed expressly and solely for the holding of the "Amateur Cycling Championships of the World,' and for the proper conduct and carrying out thereof."[35]

The definition of amateurism accepted by the I.C.A. was strictly that framed and used by the Bicycle Union/National Cyclists' Union since its creation in 1878, and stated that:

> An amateur is one who has never engaged in, nor assisted in, nor taught any athletic exercise for money, or other remuneration, nor knowingly competed with or against a professional for a prize of any description, or in public (except at a meeting specially sanctioned in writing by the Union of the country in which he resides), or who is recognized as an amateur by the ruling body of his country.

The championships would rotate from country to country. The prizes would be gold medals. Significantly, national unions could pay the expenses of their amateur riders. All races were to be on the track and events such as sprinting, middle-and long-distance riding were to be recognized, but no road races were planned or sanctioned. An editorial in the *Scottish Cyclist* by J.R. Nisbet, who was at the convention in London, commented that:

For long the championships of the National Cyclists' Union have been regarded by all nations as World's Championships, though the N.C.U. never claimed to so entitle them. They were open to all who complied to the N.C.U. definition of an amateur, and riders of various nationalities have taken part in them. It is creditable to the N.C.U. that, though possessing the distinction of holding what were recognized as the championships of the world, it took the initiative of instituting an organization by means of which other countries would share, as they deserved to, in the honour.[36]

Another editorial in *Cycling* thought that the new International Cyclists' Association was "a most important progressive move" and would "give such a fillip to the sport as it has never had before, and will go far towards breaking down the anomalies of our present amateur definition." *Cycling* welcomed the decision to pay the expenses of amateur competitors in the championships.[37] The 1893 Championships were in Chicago, and the 1894 championships in Antwerp were contested on a brand-new track, especially built for the occasion.[38] In spite of the initial rejection of professionalism, professional championships were inaugurated in 1895, when a professional sprint race and a 100 km paced event were held in Cologne.

If there was optimism among the British and Americans about these first formal World Championships, the French, however, were unenthusiastic. In an editorial revealingly entitled "Paris versus Chicago" in the Paris—based paper *La Bicyclette*, Paul Hamelle protested strenuously about "the menacing, grimacing, ugly question of amateurism ... which blocks all of the pathways of cycling. This latest manifestation of its vitality is a real as well as an underhanded declaration of war on our country." The I.C.A. conference in London was a "farce" from which France, "one of the three most important sporting nations in Europe" had been excluded. It showed hostility towards France, which for a long time had had to put up with the prejudices and "tyrannical pretensions of their Majesties, the National Cyclists' Union."[39]

The unwillingness of some other European countries to accept the *fait accompli* of the I.C.A.'s World Championships was demonstrated when an amateur road race between Paris and Brussels was promoted by *La Bicyclette* with the endorsement of the Belgian King, Leopold II. The race was staged in August 1893, together with a "Grand Prix International" as part of a series of "Grandes Fêtes" at the Brussels Velodrome, and was timed to take place at precisely the same time as the I.C.A.-sponsored World Championships in Chicago, which did not include French riders.

A report of this Paris-Brussels road race in *La Bicyclette* spoke of the love of cycling as a sport which had united the French and Belgian peoples. It thought the race "had done more for the good relations between the two countries than all of the best efforts of twenty diplomats." The success of the race showed that France's obvious strength in professional cycling had not drained away the energy of its "jeunesse sportive," and that French amateurism, too, was ready "to take the place of honour in international sport which is its rightful due." This snub to the British-American World Championships was a blatant assertion of European pride and independence—the French simply would not attend the British-American party![40]

The first official amateur World Championships were held in Chicago in 1893. They were scheduled to coincide with the important International Exposition held in August in this important center of the American bicycle industry, with people coming from all over the world. The Chicago organizers advertised the races in terms of "America versus The

> BICYCLING NEWS.   ADVERTISEMENTS.   SEPTEMBER 9TH, 1893.
>
> # CHICAGO WORLD'S FAIR.
>
> One Mi'e International and Ten Kilometres (Six Miles) International, being the
>
> ## TWO GREAT EVENTS
>
> and Twelve other First Prizes won on the
>
> # "RALEIGH,"
>
> by A A. Zimmerman, N.Y.A.C.
>
> Get Zimmerman's book on Training with "Points for Cyclists," price 1/- from this office, or post free from ourselves for 1/2½.
>
> THE RALEIGH CYCLE CO., LTD., RUSSELL ST., NOTTINGHAM.

Fig. 7.9. The Raleigh company was the *de facto* sponsor of Zimmerman, although he was still officially an amateur in 1893. [Source: *Bicycling News*, 9 Sept. 1893]

World!" The National Cyclists' Union, which had instigated the championships, did not send any British riders because of "the inability of the English association to secure the requisite amount of funds necessary to defray the expense," as the *New York Times* coyly described the British lack of funding. Ironically, having pushed for these Championships, the British found themselves priced out of the international market.

The League of American Wheelmen, however, presided over a successful six-day event, at which American national, as well as the "International Championships" were decided. A party of more than a hundred cyclists from New York and New England left for Chicago on a special train and a crowd of fully 8,000 persons enjoyed the "hotly contested events" on the final day. Controversial star, Arthur Zimmerman, took the 1-mile sprint and the 10-km race, while a South African, L.S. Meintjes, won the 100-km title, validating the championships as a truly international event.[41]

But the World Championships did not, of course, resolve questions about cycling supremacy. The entry list was "the largest ever known for any bicycle meet in this country, and includes all the prominent racing men from the various States of America, while but few entries are in from foreign countries."[42]

After the Chicago championships, there was dissatisfaction on both sides of the Atlantic, from American critics because the English had not come, from the English because the races had, in effect, been a cake walk for the Americans. Subsequent Championships were held in Antwerp (1894), Cologne (1895), Copenhagen (1896), Glasgow (1897) and

Vienna (1898) before they returned across the Atlantic to Montreal (1899), a geographical reach that successfully emphasized their international character, and Championship winners were typically drawn from the dominant cycling nations.

A list of winners and their nationalities can be found in Table 7 C, which shows dates, locations, events and winners of official amateur and professional World Championships.

For the usual reasons of distance and expense, there were no American entries for the 1894 championships in Antwerp or the 1897 championships in Glasgow, which, said *Spalding's Official Bicycle Guide*, "is the only excuse offered for not having the world's championship medals in this country at the present time." But *Spalding's* hinted at the stimulus created by annual, official World Championships when it wrote of the future 1898 Vienna championships that "already preparations are being made to send a large and representative American team abroad to battle for the world's championship honors."[43]

Criticism regarding a lack of competition was also directed at Major Taylor, when he became world 1-mile professional champion in Montreal in 1899. A number of writers complained that the best of the European riders had simply not been there to challenge him, and that he was, therefore, a less than worthy world champion. It was partly for this reason

Table 7 C. World championships from 1893 to 1900, sponsored by the International Cyclists' Association. There were no professional Championships in 1893 and 1894.

Year	Location	Event	Winner
1893	Chicago	Am. Sprint	Arthur Zimmerman (USA)
		Am. 100 km	L.S. Meintjes (South Africa)
1894	Antwerp	Am. Sprint	August Lehr (Germany)
		Am. 100 km	Wilhelm Henie (Norway)
1895	Cologne	Am. Sprint	Jaap Eden (Holland)
		Am. 100 km	J. Cordang (Holland)
		Prof. Sprint contested	R. Protin (Fr.)/G. Banker (USA)
		Prof. 100 km	J. Michael (England)
1896	Copenhagen	Am. Sprint	Harry Reynolds (Ireland)
		Am. 100 km	M. Ponscarme (Fr.)
		Prof. Sprint	P. Bourrillon (Fr.)
		Prof. 100 km	A.A. Chase (England)
1897	Glasgow	Am. Sprint	E. Schaeder (Denmark)
		Am. 100 km	E. Gould (England)
		Prof. Sprint	W. Arend (Germany)
		Prof. 100 km	J.W. Stocks (England)
1898	Vienna	Am. Sprint	Paul Albert (Germany)
		Am. 100 km	A.J. Cherry (England)
		Prof. Sprint	George Banker (USA)
		Prof. 100 km	R. Palmer (England)
1899	Montreal	Am. Sprint	Tom Summersgill (Great Britain)
		Am. 100 km	John Nelson (USA)
		Prof. Sprint	Major Taylor (USA)
		Prof. 100 km	H. Gibson (Great Britain)
1900	Paris	Am. Sprint	A. Didier-Nauts (Fr.)
		Am 100 km	L. Bastien (F)
		Prof. Sprint	Edmond Jacquelin (Fr)
		Prof. 100 km	Constant Huret (Fr.)

that Major Taylor's 1901 European matches drew such large crowds—the European champions who had not been in Montreal in 1899 were eager to see how they measured up to him, and Taylor's most important rival in Paris was Jacquelin, the 1900 world sprint titleholder.[44]

Following these inaugural 1893 amateur championships, there was a strong movement to accept French-style professionalism in racing. Zimmerman and other successful American riders turned professional, attracted by the money in the professional ranks. The 1894 season in Europe, in Paris especially, was full of big professional matches on the track and energetic sponsorship of road racing. An accelerated acceptance of professionalism by riders and the general public, and the understanding that organized professionalism would inevitably be instituted as a permanent component of the sport, no doubt caused I.C.A. officials to vote in the first official professional world championships in Cologne in 1895. Robert Protin (Belgium) and George Banker (U.S.A.) became enmeshed in a series of appeals there following a muddled championship race, the results of which were never clearly determined.[45]

By the beginning of the 1897 season, the National Cyclists' Union's *Review and Official Record* reported that: "the most prominent feature in the racing side of the Union's work in 1896 was the great boom in professional racing.... About 300 riders were licensed by the N.C.U., and the establishment of a healthy class of professional racing is bound to have a good effect on the amateur side of the sport."[46]

* * *

The formation of the International Cyclists' Association could not, therefore, solve all the logistical problems of actually bringing national champions together. Just as the Europeans had not attended the Chicago event in 1893, so the Americans were absent from Antwerp in 1894, leading to a comment from the New York paper, *The Wheel*, that "it was not a world's championship because America was not represented. It is now certain that there is only one world's champion, and he is elected by public opinion. The champion of the world is Zimmerman." The British weekly *Wheeling* was incensed: "When these events were held on American soil, they were lauded to the skies.... When they were transferred to Europe, ridicule and contempt were heaped on them.... The ambition to establish real world's championships is a great and a laudable one, but we fear that it can never be realized."[47]

Far from resolving all questions of superiority within international cycling, the new I.C.A. championships became only another occasion—albeit an "official" one—when top competitors could challenge each other, and yet another occasion when national idiosyncrasies and the fairness of judging and timing could and would be debated in the press. Skirmishing for bureaucratic power within the international sphere continued, particularly as the French continued to resent and resist the I.C.A. as a British-dominated body. "At present the International Cyclists' Association seems to be little more than a nice little family party," alleged a columnist in *Bicycling News* in 1896, an accusation that brought a stinging response from Henry Sturmey, the N.C.U.'s representative on the I.C.A.:

> The International Cyclists Association is a federation of every recognized cycling Union in Europe, America and Africa, the countries forming the federation being America, Belgium, Canada, Denmark, England, France, Germany, Holland, Ireland, Italy, Norway, Scotland, South Africa and Switzerland.

Each one of the Unions governing cycle sport, both amateur and professional, in these countries has formally decided upon joining, and applied for and been elected to membership.[48]

But Sturmey's protestations did not calm the suspicions among the Europeans, particularly the French, Italians, Germans and Austrians (the Dutch and the Danes appear to have accepted the I.C.A. more easily) that the International Cyclists' Association's management by the influential English figure (it was in effect run from within the National Cyclists' Union) was "tyrannical, despotic and harmful."[49]

As Gherardo Bonini makes clear in an article on national identity in early cycling, the collapse of the I.C.A. in 1900 was brought about by an alliance between the French, the Germans and a new American national professional organization (the National Cyclists' Association), and resulted in the creation of a new, French-dominated organization, the Union Cycliste Internationale, which still governs the sport today.[50]

The decline of the influence of the British-dominated I.C.A. was also brought about by the reluctance of the amateur-orientated, conservative leaders, Sturmey and Hillier, to move with the times, to recognize the strength of the professional sport in continental Europe, and the power that resided with track owners and the commercial sponsorship of the sport.[51]

The vibrant international sport of road cycling which grew in the 1890s and still exists today was essentially a historical victory for professional sport and for massed-start road racing over the segregated amateurism preferred by the first International Cycling Association in the mid–1890s, and an international rejection of the resistance to road racing and the encouragement of discreet early-morning time trailing which became the official racing policy of the National Cyclists' Union.

4. World Champion: The International Career of Arthur Zimmerman

Of the many cycling careers well documented in the 1890s, that of Arthur Augustus Zimmerman (1869–1936) was one of the most prominent and meteoric.[52] It was certainly very representative of the preoccupations and controversies that existed at the highest level of the sport at the time, and Zimmerman exactly straddled the changeover from high-wheel to safety bicycle in competition. Zimmerman's active racing career lasted only from 1889 to about 1896, but as we've already seen this was a period of intense change within the sport.

Zimmerman began his cycling exploits as an amateur on the high-wheel bicycle, and his outstanding initial success led to national champion status, world records and international professional stardom. His athletic qualities and cycling abilities were highly rated at the time: in 1893 the *Wheelmen's Gazette* called him "the greatest cycle racer of the time," *The Wheel* said that he occupied "the most exalted position ever held by an athlete," and writer Gregory Bowden later called him "one of the most extraordinary superstars of the sport the world has known."[53] As a professional, he was sponsored by two of the largest, most important bicycle and tire manufacturing companies, Raleigh and Dunlop.

Zimmerman was born in Camden, New Jersey, the son of a wealthy real-estate owner, and as a teenager planned to go into business and the law. From an early age, however, he "showed great proficiency in athletic sports," winning prizes in running and jumping.[54] In 1889, he began to ride the solid-tired "Star" high-wheeler, driven by an unusual lever action, and by the end of the 1890 season, as a member of the New Jersey Athletic Club and Freehold Cyclers, he had won 45 first prizes, including a victory over Willie Windle, the reigning American sprint champion. For the 1891 season, as a member of the New York Athletic Club, Zimmerman made the transition from the high bicycle to the newly introduced pneumatic safety bicycle, and by the end of the season had amassed 52 first places, won the League of American Wheelmen national ½-mile championship and established several short-distance world records.

Early in 1892, after his speedy rise to the top of the amateur American sport, Zimmerman announced that he intended to race in England and George Lacy Hillier invited him to become a member of Hillier's own club, the newly formed London County Cycling and Athletic Club, and to train at the South London Herne Hill track, of which Hillier was also the director. As soon as he arrived in England, Zimmerman was invited to Nottingham and was presented with a state-of-the-art lightweight Raleigh bicycle and other equipment by Frank Bowden, the Chairman of the large and prosperous Raleigh company, whose bicycles had been ridden by winners of many national and international championships.

Zimmerman had already begun to ride a Raleigh in America that year, and although his amateur status had been questioned by the League of American Wheelmen, the League's "Class B" amateur rules did in fact allow him to accept some equipment from commercial sponsors. "One of the main reasons for the tremendous demand for Raleigh bicycles in the 1890s was that they were so very successful in racing all over the world," asserts a history of the company: "This was yet another aspect of Frank Bowden's business genius; from the moment he became chairman of the firm, he began to approach leading cycle champions of every nationality and encourage them to race on Raleighs. The combination of his infectious enthusiasm and the excellence of his machines proved irresistable and by 1892 Raleigh was leading the world in cycle sport successes."[55]

When he first started training in England, Zimmerman "was winning golden opinions

Fig. 7.10. Zimmerman (fourth from right) at the start of the 5-mile L.A.W. national championship, Chicago, 1893. [Source: *The Bearings*, 11 Aug. 1893].

Fig. 7.11. At the world championships, Zimmerman, on the Star bicycle, also took part in a "retro" 1-mile high-wheel championship race, one of the last to be held. [Source: *The Bearings*, 11 Aug. 1893].

everywhere by his unassuming manners, and the good tempered way in which he bore defeat with the same quiet smile as when afterwards victorious."[56] His amateur status, however, was questioned by *British Sport*, which, "without mincing its words about the matter, plainly demands that the N.C.U. should make inquiry into Zimmerman's financial resources.... In justice to the English riders, it should be ascertained who pays the piper for the Yankee."[57] The situation was complicated by the League of American Wheelmen's two-tier amateur class, "Class A" and "Class B," where the latter could accept certain expenses from promoters and some equipment from makers, and by the fact that Zimmerman had indeed been disqualified by the L.A.W. for a "technical violation of the Amateur rule" and then reinstated. A letter attesting to his amateur status was sent to the N.C.U. by the L.A.W. and read in Committee.[58]

As a member of the London County Cycling and Athletic Club, and a registered L.A.W. amateur, Zimmerman was eligible to compete in all four of the English amateur national championships. In the 25-mile race, "he fell through the crowded condition of the track," but in the 1-mile and the 5-mile, he "made common hacks of the best in England," while in the 50-mile race he beat Frank Shorland, one of England's best distance riders.[59] Zimmerman's performances in the two short-distance races in Leeds, reported the *Irish Cyclist*, marked him as "a champion of champions ... we never saw a man sprint as Zimmerman sprints, and sweep by men with such supreme ease. His pluck and quiet determination have excited our liveliest admiration from the first.... In Zimmerman, the Americans really have a rider to be proud of, one possessing the best qualities of a MAN first and of a racing crack afterwards."[60]

Zimmerman's relationship with Raleigh made him the most prominent of that controversial category of semi-professional cyclists, the "maker's amateurs." As an amateur, he was not supposed to be fully sponsored by a manufacturer. Bowden, of course, must have known this, and Hillier, whose own club profited from the large crowds that Zimmerman's presence generated, could not have been unaware of Zimmerman's relationship with

Raleigh. As an aggressive proponent of amateurism, Hillier had created a conflict of interest situation, in which his own club benefited from the attractions of the questionably "amateur" star.

The 1892 European tour was a resounding success. Zimmerman did not meet F.J. Osmond, England's best long-distance rider, but there was good sportsmanship on all sides, and Zimmerman was a popular star. The *American Cyclist* thought that "nothing could have been more graceful than the Englishmen's acknowledgement of the American representative's prowess."[61] *Wheeling* concluded that: "There is probably no man racing in England today more popular personally than Zimmerman."[62]

Zimmerman's victories in the English championships made him an even greater celebrity in the United States, where the press was effusive with its patriotism. "The American champion's visit to England excited greater attention and interest than any previous happening in the history of all cycledom," reported the *American Cyclist*:

> He went abroad to meet the English racing men solely from motives of personal curiosity and pleasure. He did not in any sense posture as a representative of America against England. But nothing on the face of the earth could have prevented the international aspect of the events in which he competed while on the other side. All American wheelmen have expanded with pride over Zimmerman's success with the English. They have appropriated everything connected therewith and have made Zimmerman's personal cause a cause of America *versus* England. The American eagle has flapped his wings and screamed himself hoarse. The champion was received back with such an ovation as was never before accorded to any living cyclist.[63]

At home, Zimmerman broke a world record at the Springfield Tournament, for which he won a carriage and a pair of horses worth $1,000, and took the New York state championship. The sum total of his 1892 season was, out of 100 starts, 75 first, 10 second and 5 third places, for a total value of $8,800. During that season, he was reported to have won "29 bicycles, several horses and carriages, half a dozen pianos, a house and a lot, household furniture of all descriptions, and enough silver plate, medals and jewelry to stock a jewelry store."[64]

Yet Zimmerman was still officially an amateur upon his second visit to England in 1893, where he intended to contest the English championships again. He raced and won in Ireland and France. But in June 1893, the N.C.U. stirred up international cycling relations by refusing to recognize him as an amateur. He was, reported the *New York Times*, "without having been given a proper hearing, told to change his wheel [i.e., his make of bicycle]; this he declined to do unless he was given time to get an American make of wheel.... Zimmerman said that he considered his treatment exceedingly unsportsmanlike and contrary to a spirit of fairness."[65] Later, challenged to reveal why it had acted in such a high-handed fashion towards the American star, the N.C.U. alleged that he had received shares of Raleigh stock, that he had published a book endorsing Raleigh, that Bowden had given him diamonds and that he continued to have a business relationship with the Raleigh company. Evidently, to combat this ongoing, high-profile sullying of the amateur ranks, the N.C.U. had decided to make a prominent example of Zimmerman.[66]

An exacerbating factor may have been Zimmerman's refusal, on this second visit, to be contractually bound to appear exclusively in meetings organized by Hillier and the London County Cycling and Athletic Club, and Hillier's seemingly hypocritical determination as a powerful official within the N.C.U. to exclude him from amateur competition completely if he could not have Zimmerman's crowd-pulling power in the palm of his hand. Upon his return to America, Zimmerman outlined the above explanation of the controversy to the *New York Times*, telling a reporter:

> It is not difficult to understand the position of Hillier's Association. Here they were in the position of standing by and seeing their championships go over the water again. I do not think I exaggerate when I say things looked that way. I had won the first twenty races I had started in, and the men whom the Englishmen had counted on to beat me were not track possibilities, having been protested off the track. Unless some charge was trumped up against me, what hope had they for their championships![67]

The long interview gives further interesting revelations of the hypocrisy and double-dealing within the power structures of English "shamateurism," and is particularly interesting on the role of Lacy Hillier and Zimmerman's reactions to him:

> Lacy Hillier, one of the cycling editors of the metropolis, has become quite an autocrat on racing matters. The first year I went over I placed myself under his guidance. He took me everywhere and got some credit, I can fairly say, out of my victories. Of course, when the season was nearly over, lovers of racing in various parts of the United Kingdom expressed themselves with some bitterness to me. They argued that I had no right to slight their cities, that I was a drawing card, that they had always been friends of mine, and that I had hurt honest sport by continuing my work to the limits set by Hillier. You see, most of my racing had been done under the direction of the London County Association [in fact, the London County Cycling and Athletic Club], a limited company which gives athletic tournaments. Mr. Hillier is financially interested in it. My presence at their meetings always meant a big gate for them, and of course they were interested in keeping me as much as possible under their wing. I don't boast when I talk thus of big gate receipts, for that was a fact based on the international character that I would give a meet.... I see all this more clearly now than I did then. I didn't appreciate then that I had made a mistake in not taking in the Irish and Scotch championships instead of confining myself so largely to London events.
>
> This year when I went over I decided that I would do a little of my own directing and race all over the kingdom. It is not going too far to say that this was not agreeable to the Hillier crowd, who would thus lose the monopoly of what was formerly a source of revenue and more or less reputation. I went to Scotland and to Paris on my own hook and won my races as before. I suppose that if I had allowed my name to be used for the exclusive advantage of the London County Association Limited, I might not have encountered such fierce opposition and found my amateur standing so bitterly protested. I believe that the Scotch and Irish racing men stand by me, as do those who are outside of London and are not under the influence of the London Association.

Véloce-Sport, the leading French cycling journal, understood the attitude of the National Cyclists' Union, but criticized it heavily; "It is logical, but it is also profoundly regrettable. Once more, we in France condemn this idiotic business of classifying riders, which deprives international competition of really good matches by excluding men of the same level. Above all, the English should at least be as strict with their own maker's amateurs as they are with Zimmerman."[68]

The American press exploded with impatience, hardly stopping to remember that Zimmerman's "amateurism" had also been questioned at home. The *New York Times* reported the affair with intense interest. *Bearings* called the N.C.U.'s actions "uncalled for and disgraceful ... not only unsportsmanlike, but cowardly and dishonorable."[69] An editorial, "The Treatment of Zimmerman," in the Indianapolis *Wheelmen's Gazette*, protested at the "insular pride and prejudice" of the N.C.U.:

> There is no doubt that in matters of sport England is exceedingly unfair. When the English think they are going to see something superior, they shut their eyes—and don't see it.... If the American is a second-class performer he is welcomed, if he is first-class and threatens to wrest a prize away from

Britain's sons he is given the cold cut…. The action of the National Cycling Union of England in withholding a licence from Zimmerman is a particularly aggravating instance of this British peculiarity. To refuse to recognize Zimmerman as an amateur is such a spiteful affront that the officials of the League of American Wheelmen are at a loss to understand its meaning. At least, so they say, but we doubt not that they thoroughly understand it. The action was due to a determination to prevent Zimmerman from reaping the benefit of his pluck and skill. He won the championship events last year and there was every reason to believe that he would repeat the achievement this year. So the wily Britons ruled him out.[70]

The N.C.U.'s actions against Zimmerman raised the possibility that the L.A.W. and even the International Cyclists' Association might also rule against him, and that he might have trouble qualifying as an amateur for the World Championships about to be held in Chicago. But the N.C.U., with all its power, could not claim jurisdiction over him in America. Having been excluded from N.C.U. competition, Zimmerman returned to America to win the first amateur World Championships.

These championship races were also ridden on a Raleigh, and Zimmerman subsequently appeared as official "Champion of the World" on an internationally distributed advertising poster for the Raleigh company (now frequently reproduced in various versions) where his image and fame were used openly to endorse and advertise the company's products.[71] No sooner had an "amateur" world cycling champion been created than he was immediately and thoroughly co-opted by the bicycle industry, and became a *de facto* professional! An altogether modern kind of advertising had been instituted, using a champion's racing victories to endorse and sell bicycles to the general public.

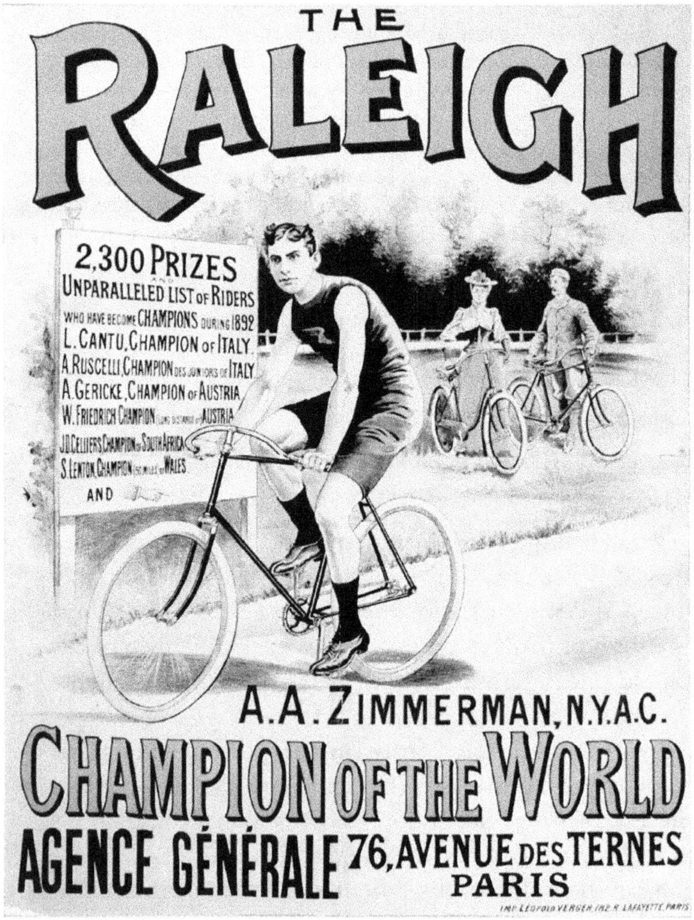

Zimmerman, in spite of his prominent success, was reported as a reluctant and reticent "star." In Indianapolis, in August 1893, where the young Major Taylor watched as Zimmerman won a gold cup worth $1,000 and set a new 1-mile world record, he:

Fig. 7.12. First official world sprint champion, Zimmerman's career straddled the worlds of both amateur and professional cycling in the mid–1890s. [Source: author's collection]

shot by the grandstand like a stone from a catapult.... He then dismounted and walked back with that awkward, gawky gait of his, looking neither to the right nor the left, as the cheers rent the air and hundreds of handkerchiefs were waved.... He received an ovation which would have caused most any man to have swelled visibly, but he paid no attention to it, and ambled along to his dressing room like some green, country boy who never seems to know where to put his hands.... When he is called upon to make a speech or respond to an address of presentation, he blushes and stammers and gets as nervous as a school girl, and yet he can go out on the track and whip the world riding.[72]

By the end of 1893, Zimmerman was a *de facto* Raleigh professional in every sense except his official, licensed status. Even friendly American commentators agreed that his amateurism was merely titular: "Those near him admit and even boast that the smiling Jersey-man has turned his racing abilities to more practical account than any other man on the path, either amateur or professional. But Zimmie never broke the rules blatantly. If he bartered his speed for coin of the realm, it was most diplomatically done."[73]

Full, formal professionalism appeared inevitable, and Zimmerman took out his professional licence at the beginning of the 1894 season. The editor of *The Wheel* expected Zimmerman to be "as smooth, level, imperturbable and honest" as a professional as he had been as an amateur, and "to prove that a man may be a professional crack-a-jack and continue to advance in those graces, talents and attributes which settle upon the right men as they grow into manhood."[74] Zimmerman went on to bring "glory, delight and prosperity to Raleigh by winning a total of 100 races that year in England, France, Germany and Ireland," against all the leading European riders.[75]

Zimmerman's decision to turn professional was made when Baduel, the director of the Velodrome Buffalo in Paris, made him an offer he could not refuse. Zimmerman's manager, Willis B. Troy, went to Paris early in 1894 and negotiated a contract worth about $10,000 cash, 30 percent of gates receipts and any prizes he won.[76] The press generally approved of his move. "Nothing has awakened so much interest in a long time as the desertion of the amateur ranks by Zimmerman," commented *Bearings*:

> it has been almost the sole topic of cyclists and the cycling press for the past few weeks.... What does it all mean? It means that we are coming nearer an era of professionalism; that, before long, professional bicycle racing will be as well established as horse racing. That time has already come in France, and it is bound to come in this country. The fact that the great Zimmerman has led the way will make it all the easier for others to follow.

Outing thought that "in these days of big purses for pugilists and expensive prizes for amateurs, the successful athlete despises the simple prizes which were given in the olden days when amateurs were really amateurs. The king of amateurs will become the king of professionals.... It is a question, however, whether Zimmerman can last longer than a season or two more."[77]

Others were tempted by generous offers from Raleigh, and Harry Wheeler (East Orange), George Banker (Pittsburg) and Austin Crooks (Buffalo) also joined the professional ranks to make up a Raleigh team in Europe, with Willis Troy as "diplomat, general manager, cashier and treasurer," and Harry Rue as trainer.[78] Troy, like H.O. Duncan, also represented a new kind of figure in the world of sport, the promoter/manager/trainer/agent, who began to play an increasingly important role in professional cycling in the mid–1890s. It was reported that Zimmerman expected to make as much as $30,000 during his trip.[79] J.M. Erwin, a Paris-based reporter who followed Zimmerman and Wheeler in Europe during the 1894 season, wrote of "the triumph of professionalism in Europe." The professionals were everywhere; only England held out as an amateur country, with its "severe and tortured" amateur definition. France was "a sort of apostle of the revolutionary professional movement," with its attractive velodromes and rich prizes. Belgium was a hybrid of professionalism and amateurism. Switzerland was much like France, and Italy went further still, with organized betting at its tracks.[80] Erwin was convinced that "next year will see professional racing in the ascendancy in England. The hide-bound sticklers for amateurism still hold out against it ... but the public wants the professional racing, and that means they will have it."[81]

Zimmerman himself was of the opinion that the amateur sport had been eclipsed by the high quality of the new professionals: "In Europe, amateurs who one could really call racers are now in such a minority that when they appear at race meetings it is an occasion for curiosity and amusement. This is true above all in France and Italy, where the racing is at such a high level that the other countries go there to take lessons."[82] But, after his experiences in Europe in 1894, Zimmerman was less sure of the future of professionalism in America. He complained of the readiness of American audiences to criticize and slur athletes' performances, suspecting them of dishonest practices: "Europeans take naturally to professional cycling. It is the style they have been mostly educated to like, and they accept defeats of idols philosophically, not with murky glances and whispered slurs. The outlook for professional racing in this country for this season is not bright. The very best men will be continually driven to the other side by these unjust criticisms."[83]

* * *

Zimmerman's 1894 season in Europe lasted from May to November. As a visiting American star, he was obsessively pursued by the press as he competed in 34 race meetings in France, England, Switzerland, Italy and Belgium. He was first 27 times, second twice and fourth once.

In Paris, he stayed at the best hotels and arrived for his training and racing at the famous Buffalo and Seine velodromes wearing a top hat and dress suit. In Belgium, he was beaten by Belgian champion, Houben, and in England, he raced in London, Birmingham, Leicester and Newcastle.

In Newcastle, "the boys who sold programmes on the street had 'Zimmerman' in large letters on their hats, and 'Zimmerman, Champion of Champions' could be seen on tramcars and omnibuses," while promoters Troy, Baduel and H.O. Duncan "watched the people pass through the gates, and the click of the turnstiles was sweet music to their ears." But the crowd was not happy at the doubling of the price of admission from the customary 6 pence to 1 shilling, and Troy was called "a damned thieving Frenchman."

In Leicester, Zimmerman made the mistake of throwing a few pennies to the street urchins, and quickly "boys in various stages of dirt or rags sprang up from the pavement.... They fought and rolled over in the dirt for every coin that jingled on the stones, and the people came in swarms to watch the fun."[84] Thus we can see the intensity of sport promotion in the mid–1890s, as professionalism expanded, and bicycle racing was marketed to an enthusiastic public.

"Why do Zimmerman, Wheeler, Lehr, and a host of other famous riders, prefer the Raleigh?" demanded the Raleigh Cycle Co. in an advertisement in *Cycling*, "Because they know it to be the Fastest Machine built. The Fastest Machine is that which is The Easiest-Running. This is what YOU want!"[85] "Zimmerman, Wheeler, Banker, the Great American Professionals who are beating all the European cracks, all ride the wonderful Dunlop Racing Tire. And that wonderful Dunlop Racing Tire Holds all World's Records from 110 to 460 miles," trumpeted the American Dunlop Tire Company.[86]

Interviewed by the press when he returned to the United States, Zimmerman was effusive in his praise of the European racing scene. "To the European the idea of amateur racing for clocks, prizes etc is ridiculous. The poor and the wealthy riders alike wish to race for money," he told *The Wheel*. And for the *New York Times*, he painted a glowing picture of Paris. He had, he said:

> never seen such splendid tracks as the Buffalo Velodrome in Paris and the track in Bordeaux. They are about perfect.... There were about 12,000 people at the Seine track, in Paris, one day when I was there. The French enjoy themselves at these races in great style. The events are twenty minutes to half an hour apart, and during these intervals the people sit around the grounds, drinking, smoking, and discussing the last race. In Paris the tracks, or rather the grounds about them, resembled a picnic. They do not have classes, as we do. All their racing men are professionals, and ride to advertise the firms whose wheels they use. Such clubs as we have are unknown, the men being unattached.... Paris is the best place in the world for bicycling. Nothing surprised me more at first than the great number of wheels used in Paris.[87]

Zimmerman underwent a rapid athletic decline after 1894, for reasons that are not altogether clear. He visited Australia in the winter of 1895–6, had a successful tour (27,000 people attended the opening meeting in Sydney),[88] but announced his retirement soon after that. He attempted a comeback in both 1897 and 1899, but his racing consisted of little more than a few "exhibitions." At the races of the Quill Club Wheel-men, Manhattan Beach, Zimmerman "was surrounded by old-timers, but from the new field of racing men he attracted no attention. The champion of the world of but a couple of seasons ago passed in front of the grandstand and not a cheer was heard from the people. Such was fame."[89] He invested in a short-lived company manufacturing the "Zimmy" bicycle and wrote a column for a New York newspaper. He debated whether or not to return to France in 1896, but finally did not return until 1902, and by then he was merely a symbol of his past excellence, well past his athletic prime. He ultimately become a hotel owner in Freehold, New Jersey, and lived in semi-retirement as a distinguished ex-champion.

* * *

Yet Zimmerman's career was highly significant in the context of the emerging mass-spectator bicycle racing in the late 1880s and 1890s. One of a handful of pioneering international champion cyclists, he participated at the highest level in taking the sport from the solid-tired, high-wheel bicycle period into the era of the pneumatic safety; from a somewhat limited, athletic coterie out into the mass-market, where he became a star with enormous public appeal. In the 1890s, bicycle racing on the track became an important mass-spectator sport, where modern sporting heroes were created and promoted.

In a review of the 1893 bicycle racing season, the Indianapolis *Wheelmen's Gazette* spoke of "an exceedingly profitable season, both for race meet promoters and the racers themselves.... The racing cracks have thriven wonderfully the past season. They have been the idols of the land, and the whole cycling world has bent knee to do them homage. Rival cycling clubs have fallen over themselves in their frantic efforts to secure the attendance of the stars." Zimmerman had been the biggest attraction, "the ideal racer. He has yet to meet his superior on the cycle track. He is certainly the greatest cycle racer of the time and bids fair to remain so. He is an honest and gentlemanly athlete; as much cannot truthfully be said of some of his rivals."

In a similar review the following year, the same publication concluded that:

> There is no question but that the cycle racing season of 1894 outshone in brilliancy all preceding seasons. Public interest in the sport took on an even more enthusiastic tinge than ever before. Many more meets were held than in 1893, and the love of the American people for this phenomenally popular youthful sport was largely increased.... The progress of racing is dumbfounding the false prophets. This comparatively new rival of the diamond and the turf is shaking the hold of both on the public heart.[90]

A revealing editorial from *The Wheel* spoke of the "enlightened folk of the nineteenth century, who love football, the prize ring and the race track," many of whom "have come to look upon the cycle and its lithe and sinewy rider as the best exponents of the modern idea of clean, enjoyable athletics.... We turn to the cyclist as the coming man. The season just ended has proved beyond a doubt that man has at last secured for himself the one thing for which he has longed so many centuries, namely, a self-driven vehicle which will bear him further and faster in a given time than any animal-drawn conveyance."[91]

In a relatively short career, Zimmerman had made the transition from amateur to professional during a period of tremendous growth and change in the organization and economy of the sport; he became a "modern" professional athlete, his celebrity created not only by his own athletic ability, but also by the commercial interests that promoted him and profited from his success. Zimmerman was one of the most prominent athletes to carry bicycle racing from a national to an international level, and was one of the first cycling champions to become a media celebrity outside his own country. His three tours in Europe (1892, 1893 and 1894), as well as his amateur World Championship in Chicago in 1893, put the United States firmly among the world's foremost cycling nations.

Although Zimmerman had only a short career as a professional, his decision to become a full professional demonstrated that a professional class in the United States, sponsored by the bicycle industry, and organized outside the pervasive amateurism of the League of American Wheelmen, could indeed thrive. Zimmerman's gentlemanly sporting conduct and demeanor as a professional challenged the entrenched idea that only amateurs could uphold high standards of behavior. Zimmerman set a trend, going to Europe to take on the European champions, and paved the way for other Americans, such as Major Taylor and Frank Kramer, in the future.

5. Amateurism, Professionalism and Licensing Schemes

While professionalism was expanding in Europe, the National Cyclists' Union continued to support the segregation of amateurs and professionals—they believed that the current trends in cycling were making it all the more necessary to do so. In 1893, the N.C.U. introduced its "Licensing Rules" which stated that: "On and after May 1893, no rider shall take part in any race held under N.C.U. rules ... unless at the date of such race he shall hold a licence permitting him to so compete."[92] The specific purpose of licences was to distinguish between amateurs and professionals, and the N.C.U.'s definition of amateurism and professionalism were as follows in 1896:

> An Amateur is one who has never engaged in, nor assisted in, nor taught any athletic exercise for money or other remuneration; nor knowingly competed with or against a Professional or person under sentence of suspension for a prize of any description, or in public (except at a meeting specially sanctioned by the Union).
> To prevent misunderstanding in interpreting the above, the Union draws attention to the following explanations:
> A cyclist ceases to be an Amateur, and becomes a Professional, by:
>
> a) Engaging in Cycling or any other athletic exercise, or personally teaching, training, or coaching any person therein, either as a means of obtaining a livelihood, or for a staked bet, a money prize or gate money.
> (Cycle manufacturers and agents, as such, are not to be considered as Professionals, but are cautioned that to personally teach Cycle riding as the means to effect the sale of a machine will be taken as an infringement of clause a.)
> b) Knowingly competing with, or pace-making for, a Professional or person under sentence of suspension, in public, or for a prize.
> c) Selling, realizing upon, or otherwise turning into cash, any prize won by him.
> d) Accepting, directly or indirectly, any remuneration, compensation, or expenses whatever from a cycle manufacturer, agent or other person interested in the trade or sport, for cycle riding.
> e) Offering, directly or indirectly, any remuneration, compensation, or expenses whatever for cycle riding, to any amateur as such.
>
> (The General Committee, or the Committee of the Centre, has the right to call upon any rider to remove by proof any circumstantial evidence of his infringing, or having infringed, the provisions of clause d), and the onus of disproving the charge brought against him shall in such case rest upon the persons charged, who, until he does clear himself to the satisfaction of the General Committee, or a Centre Committee, may be suspended. All sentences of suspension pro. tem. which have been, or may be, passed upon riders suspected of "makers' amateurism" may be turned by the General Committee, or a Centre Committee, into sentences of permanent disqualification in the case of riders who do not within two months from their suspen-

Fig. 7.13. The National Cyclists' Union is shown here as a ferocious flying angel with a sword, slashing at a cyclist sheltering on the shoulder of a goddess labeled "Sport." [Source: *Cycling*, 27 April 1895]

sion disprove the charges brought against them, or enter appeals which ultimately become successful.)[93]

Suspicion of any economic gain by those claiming to be amateurs led to an almost Draconian questioning of some of them by the N.C.U. A declaration of amateurism had to be made, and if the amateur worked in the cycling trade, he had to make an additional declaration that he had not been given special time off for training or racing, and did not receive any bonus for his wins. All applicants for a license were expected, in the mid–1890s, to fill out an application which contained the following questions:

> Name of applicant. Age last birthday. Have you been licensed before? If so, by which centre? Give number of license. Present employment? Name of employers, with address? Hours of employment? How many open races did you compete in last season? With what result? The names of the three race meetings at which you competed furthest from your residence? Have you ever been called before a Committee, any Centre, or the General Committee of the Union for breach of rules; if so, which Centre or Committee? For what offense? With what result? ... Name of machine or machines you raced upon last year. Name of tyres raced upon last year. Name of machine you intend racing on this year. Name of tyres you intend racing on this year. What period of the day do you devote to training? Do you employ a trainer, or are you assisted by anyone of that calling? If so, give names and addresses. Does he accompany you to the various race meetings or races at which you compete? Have you ever done any pace-making on the road? If so, for whom, between what places, for what event or events? Have you ever been paid for pace-making? If so, by whom?[94]

Small wonder that riders were upset by a list of questions that seemed more like an inquisition by a Communist Party committee than an invitation to sport!

The inner circles of cycling politics were highly turbulent, removed from much of the racing activity, but nevertheless had a significant impact on it. Amateur riders could be denied a licence, temporarily suspended, permanently disbarred or physically prevented from starting in an event for infringements of their amateur status. The minutes of the Council Meetings of the National Cyclists Union during 1893 and 1894 make compelling reading on the question. The general tenor of discussion was that amateurism should not be tainted by professionalism, but that the professionals had nevertheless to be acknowledged and somehow accommodated. Exactly how that should be done was exhaustively debated.

Avid proponents of amateurism like Lacy Hillier were ideologically opposed to professionalism and distrustful of the industry's support of the sport. Faced with a proposal within the Union late in 1893 to take the professionals under its wing by licensing them, Hillier reluctantly conceded that "professionalism today has got a chance of a revival," but that this would need "the countenance, approval and active assistance of the N.C.U."[95] The proposed N.C.U. licensing scheme was controversial, creating new tensions in 1893 and 1894 because it put the personal economic lives of riders under the microscope. A cartoon from *Cycling* hinted at what the general cycling public thought about the N.C.U. bureaucrats and their licensing plans. Playing on the adage that "Fools rush in where angels fear to tread," the cartoon depicts the N.C.U. as a ferocious flying angel with a sword, slashing at a cyclist seeking shelter on the shoulder of a laurel-wreathed goddess labelled "Sport."[96]

Who would organize professional racing and put up the prize money if it was to be controlled by the N.C.U., or the L.A.W.? As Dr. E.B. Turner put it in *Cycling*—"two wet days and consequent bad gates would spell bankruptcy" for the Union as promoter. According to Turner, the problem with professional racing was various offences, such as "cutting-up, roping, arrangements and ramping," which had to be stopped. "Every form of sport depending on individual competition has, up the present, come to grief in the hands of professionals," he thought. But Turner did at least recognize that, in France and the United States, there was "a class of professionals actually making their living by their speed," athletes who were "kept and subsidized by the makers of different machines, and held under agreement to race for them on machines of their manufacture as an advertisement."[97] And just such a structure, with the economic underpinning of the bicycle industry, rather than tight supervision and control by national cycling bureaucracies, would in fact become the foundation for professional cycling in the future.

The mid–1890s licensing scheme was intended to bring professionals within the fold of the N.C.U., but many of them refused to be corralled in this way, and Birmingham and Nottingham riders rebelled against it in June 1894.[98] A *Cycling* editorial expressed the opinion that there was "no other alternative but to form a Cycle Racing Association," an independent professional governing body with control over racing, and that "the meeting of the two classes should be frequently permitted, as is that of 'Gentlemen v. Players' in cricket. This, at once, overcomes the whole difficulty of international racing." The same writer hoped that cycling would separate itself completely from the Amateur Athletic Association, and that that organization would "recognize the uselessness of attempting to preserve amateurism in all its purity."[99] Ultimately, as we have seen, the forces of the market in Europe and the United States ushered in a golden decade of international professional racing, from about 1894 to well after the turn of the century, which the advocates of amateurism were powerless to control. As 1896 approached, Olympism would take up the challenge and fly the flag of amateurism for the following 70 years.

6. The 1896 Olympic Games

The formation of the International Cyclists' Association in 1892 and the holding of amateur world cycling championships in 1893 were a recognition of the world-wide status of the sport of cycling. And the creation of the first modern Olympic Games in 1896 was further evidence of the expansion and globalization of sport in general and of the continued strength of the movement to honor the amateur ideal in sport. There are many similarities in the successful founding and promotion of these two ambitious international sports organizations.

The formation of international sports institutions was one facet of the fashionable internationalism of the 1890s, the product of easier and faster international communications and travel. World's fairs and exhibitions were another aspect of this conspicuous historical trend, a self-conscious expression of modernity. In 1890, Pierre de Coubertin wrote that "since Ancient Greece has passed away, the Anglo-Saxon race is the only one that fully appreciates the moral influence of physical culture and gives to this branch of educational science the attention it deserves. But this "moral influence" was confined to amateurs, and specifically excluded professional sport.[100]

There was in fact a parallel movement among the English in the 1890s for the recreation of an "Anglo-Saxon Olympiad," or a "Pan-Britannic Gathering." And suggestions were made that the World's Exhibition in Chicago in 1893 in fact also be the site of a major international

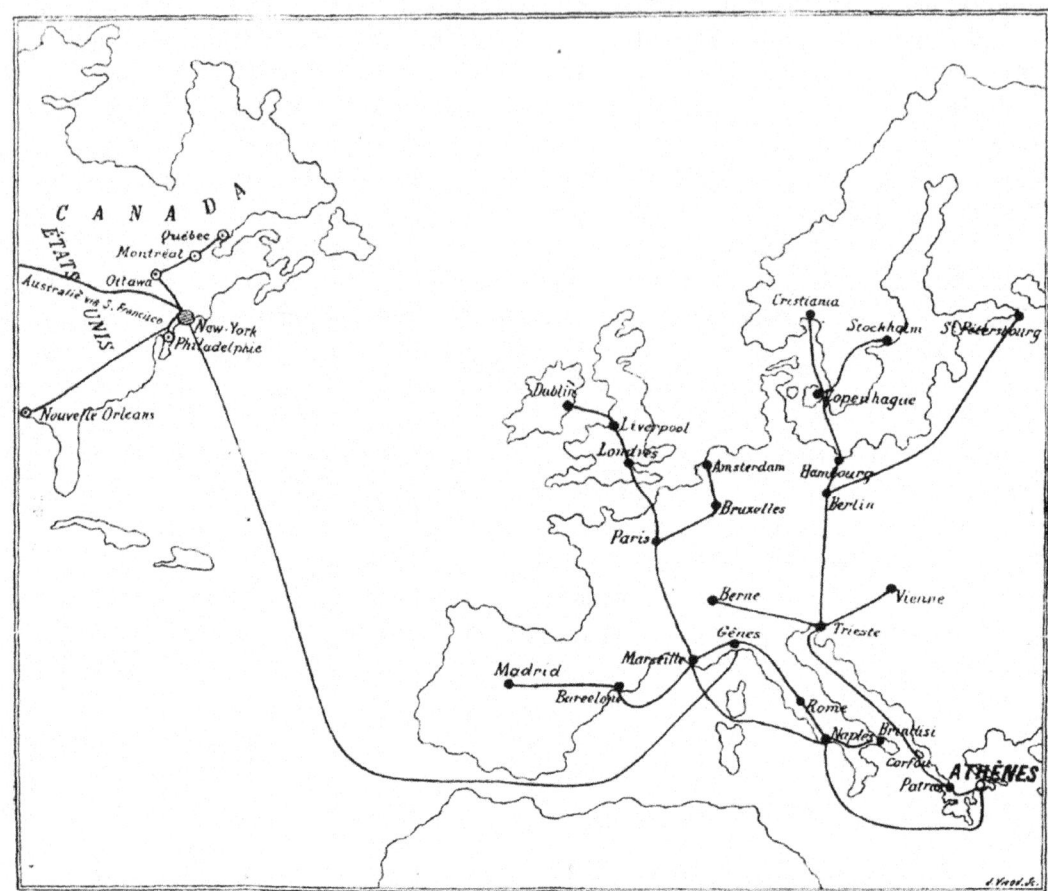

Fig. 7.14. The map released by Thomas Cook showing railway and steamship routes to the 1896 Olympic Games in Athens, for which special fares could be obtained. This map also represents the existing global reach of bicycle racing as a sport in 1896. [Source: *Bulletin du Comité International des Jeux Olympiques*, April 1895]

athletic festival. "If this matter of an International Athletic Festival to be held every three or four years is to be taken up seriously, what more auspicious year to inaugurate it than that of our World's Fair, when the eyes of the universe are upon us?" wrote an American correspondent to the magazine *Nineteenth Century* in 1892.[101]

As the amateur-oriented International Cyclists' Association was being formed in London, Pierre de Coubertin in Paris was trying to persuade French amateur sports organizations to join his Union des Sociétés Françaises des Sports Athlétiques, which in November 1892—although the organization was then only a couple of years old!—staged a "Jubilee" featuring a bicycle race and culminating with a closing meeting at the Sorbonne, where Coubertin announced his desire "to reestablish a great and magnificent institution, the Olympic Games." The creation of various kinds of "traditions" was a prominent aspect of national and international affairs at the end of the 19th century.[102]

Coubertin's evolving plans to bring together a prestigious group of international sports figures to plan the first modern Olympic Games were thus closely linked with the decision to hold the first official cycling World Championships in Chicago. Coubertin himself was involved in attempts to smooth over the conflict between the British National Cyclists' Union and French Union Vélocipédique de France over the definition of amateurism in cycling, which was also a problem in French-English rowing competitions. Coubertin was in fact an official French representative at the 1893 Chicago World's Exposition, during which the world cycling championships were held, and travelled extensively in the United States. Given his consuming interest in international competition, it is hard to imagine that he would have missed the cycling events.[103]

At the Congress of Paris, held in June 1894 to further the aims of Coubertin's Comité International des Jeux Olympiques, the Congress' President, Baron de Courcel, closed his opening remarks by reminding his audience that amid national tensions and hatred, with Europe "armed to the teeth":

> the chivalrous feelings of the fraternity of swordsmanship could ... limit the inevitable horrors of war. Let us hope that our international contests, if we do succeed in establishing them, will create such noble feelings among our contemporaries and in the future among the people of the 20th century. Let us gather all nations together for friendly sporting battles, and may the faithful observance of the rules that govern our games open their hearts to those feelings of mutual respect which are the most crucial foundation for ensuring peace between peoples.[104]

Compared with the dramatic and meticulously organized professional cycling spectacles audiences were served up with in London, Paris, Berlin and the United States, the 1896 Olympic cycling competitions in Athens were somewhat tame.[105] Events included a 1-lap (⅓ km) time trial, a 2-km match sprint, a 10-km track race, a 100-km long-distance track race, a 12-hour track race and an 87-km individual road time trial. The six events were thus a recognition of a wide range of cycling disciplines, though neither the increasingly popular massed-start road race or paced racing were included. Hardly any of the top amateur sprinters, distance riders or road-men were there. Most of the leading French riders did not qualify as amateurs, and the Games received scant attention in the European cycling press. The cycling events were not well organized, and the small number of competitors did not produce outstanding performances. In the 100-km track event, of ten starters only two remained at the finish; the one-lap, 2-km and 10-km races were all won by French rider Emile Masson; the 12-hour track endurance race saw only six entries, reduced to two riders at the finish who were unprepared physically for the demands of such an event. The 87-km road "marathon" also had only six starters and the bad road out of Athens "was lined with optimistic spectators in numbers out of all proportion to the quality of the cyclists and the organizers' preparation for such an event."[106]

Although the organization and performances at the 1896 Olympic cycling events left much to be desired, and though the event attracted little attention from cycling journalists who were more interested in the well-promoted and theatrical professional cycling events in Paris, London and Berlin, cycling's inclusion in the first modern Olympics has to be seen as a recognition of the sport's contemporary status and its broad international appeal. The map released by Thomas Cook showing railway and steamship routes over which special fares for the 1896 Olympic Games in Athens would apply, "both for competitors and interested people from all over the world," can also be seen as a diagram showing how far and wide bicycle racing as a sport had reached around the globe.[107]

Well-organized where cycling was most popular—Britain, France, Belgium, Italy, Germany and the United States—the national cycling bodies had already demonstrated their ability to organize themselves into an international body and had struggled successfully to formulate standards for international competition. There were similarities in the early ideological amateur agendas of the International Cyclists' Association and Coubertin's International Olympic Committee, although the unashamedly commercial nature of professional racing in London or Paris became a far cry from Olympic ideals.

And we should be careful not to view the 1896 Olympic Games, with a retrospective glow, as having had more influence over contemporary cycling affairs than they in fact had. Perhaps we should suggest, rather, that it was cycling that had an impact on the Olympic Games. Held only every four years, the Games were in their infancy, and could not compare in importance, size and frequency with the season-long cycling championships and professional race meetings in London and Paris, promoted by experienced entrepreneurs, supported by the affluent bicycle and tire manufacturers, and massively attended by the sport-loving general public.

7. Rival Philosophies of Cycling Competition and Sporting Excellence in the 1890s

From its beginnings in the late 1860s, through its high-wheel phase in the 1870s and 1880s, the sport of cycling had always had an international appeal. Skilled French riders entertained the audiences at the Crystal Palace in London in 1869, and early "world championships" were contested between the best French and English riders. Geographical proximity determined such international exchanges and there was always particular interest in a foreign star. The occasional visits of British cyclists to the United States, of American cyclists to Britain and of exchanges between France and England were an indication of the expanding reach of the sport, in which national pride sought out international competition to test and defend athletic prowess at the highest level.

But international competition also thrust differences of cultural habit and competitive structure into the forefront, particularly those between Britain and France. The track measurement and accuracy of timing were other areas of disagreement and friction. The need to convert times and distances between the European metric system and British and American systems was a constant headache. Thus, a coherent and consistent set of regulations and an organizational structure for international events needed to be created so that regular international competition could take place without acrimonious disagreements.

The mid–1890s was a period of intense organizational and institutional activity in cycling, as indeed it was within the structures of other developing sports.[108] The creation in 1892 of the International Cyclists' Association, the holding of the first official amateur World Championships in 1893 and the first Olympic Games in 1896 were events that elevated amateur track cycling to a new level of international significance and were part of the movement towards the increasingly global role of this modern sport during the decade. In the case of the first Olympic Games, a strong ideological connection was made between the ideals espoused by amateurism ("good sportsmanship," for example, and "playing the game") and ideals of international peace, brotherhood and harmony.

But at the same time, rivaling the ideological program of amateurism, the promotion of professional cycling on both road and track was pursued with great energy in France, Germany, Great Britain and the United States as a vehicle to advertise the bicycle industry's products, and as a dramatic, crowd-pleasing, modern spectacle. A power struggle within the membership of the I.C.A. resulted in the emergence, in 1900, of a new international governing body, the Union Cycliste Internationale, which marked a shift from British to French dominance of the bureaucracy of the sport, in effect marking the decline of old-fashioned amateurism.

Thus, two rival versions of competition and athletic excellence were being staged and promoted in cycling competition, one based on commercial expediency, profit and mass appeal, the other based on amateur ideals constructed around the honorable striving for excellence and the beauty of athletic performance. Because of the inherent conflict between these two visions of cycling, rival economic and social structures were created to espouse each of them, although as the sport expanded in the later 1890s, the economic costs of promoting either category of event demanded a similarly efficient organization. Bicycle racing, whether amateur or professional, had become big business.

The national cycling organizations, in the examples discussed here, were not only bodies that united bicycle enthusiasts, but were also manifestations of deeply-rooted class, ethnic and national tendencies and aspirations. International sporting events (particularly championships and professional "matches') often carried heavily-laden symbolic and/or nationalistic meaning for both the athletes and spectators.

Nowhere was this more true than in the emotionally charged environment of the velodrome, a confined space where nation was pitted against nation through the proxy of national athletes, and sport gave expression to—and could be an instigator of—national rivalries. In his three European tours, in 1892, 1893 and 1894, for example, Zimmerman was always, first and foremost, the "American" champion, and the fact that he won British championships in 1892 was seen as especially challenging and provocative.

In the case of the sprint contests between French champion Edmond Jacquelin and African American champion Major Taylor in Paris in 1901, which attracted extraordinary crowds of spectators, national rivalry was intensified by the unique racial component of the competition.[109] A "match" between two or three riders from different countries and backgrounds, especially when they had contrasting personalities, was a formula that was likely to be a successful promotion, and allowed the purely athletic rivalry to be embellished and exaggerated in the press.

* * *

As the daring high-wheel bicycle gave way to the pneumatic safety and cycling became an accepted part of everyday life in the early 1890s, the sheer numbers of cyclists, as Bonini has suggested, became "a factor of international visibility and social recognition," a significant social and political force. Competitive sport was a specialized aspect of cycling as a widespread international recreational and social phenomenon.

Major European cities such as London, Paris, Vienna, Berlin, Copenhagen, Rome, Stockholm, Prague, Frankfurt, Bordeaux and Milan all had more than 100,000 cyclists, but the smaller towns were also caught up in the cycling fever. The same was true in America, where New York, Boston, Chicago, Philadelphia, San Francisco, Milwaukee, Minneapolis and other major cities had thousands of cyclists.

Bonini calculates that "at least 2 million members were affiliated with European clubs, 1 million in Britain alone."[110] In Britain, the total membership of the National Cyclists' Union in 1897 was about 314,000, with 885 affiliated clubs (10,000 members in London alone, from 173 clubs), while that of the Cyclists' Touring Club in the same year was 44,500, figures that do not include those cyclists who preferred not to join a club.[111]

Membership in a local club, which was often affiliated to a national federation, had significant overtones of citizenship, nationalism and patriotism, and sporting events that gathered together large crowds of spectators could take on added social and political resonance as demonstrations of civic, regional and national identity and pride.

Chapter Eight

Bicycle Racing and Modernity

1. The Transformation of Bicycle Racing in the 1890s[1]

THE 1890s WERE THE HEYDAY of sprinting on the track, one of the most important disciplines in bicycle racing. One thousand metres, several laps on typical tracks, was the most common distance covered in these races. The racing took place in a velodrome, an enclosed arena around which spectators assembled, with the best and most expensive places in the grandstand along the finishing straight. The decisive factors in these races were tactics, surprise acceleration and pure bursts of speed over the last few hundred meters—the actual time of the entire race was relatively unimportant. Records were not set in sprint racing, but the races appealed to audiences that appreciated the subtleties of tactics between a number of evenly matched opponents, and the thrill of pure speed and a close, fast finish.

The sport had emerged in the 1870s and 1880s, the era of the high-wheel bicycle, when many of the stars of the 1890s had begun to race. By the 1890s, the "match race" between two or three rivals represented the classic form of sprinting. The stars of amateur and professional sprinting attracted huge crowds at tracks around the world. The American Arthur Zimmerman, for example, who won the first officially sanctioned world amateur sprint championship in Chicago in 1893, won more than 100 races in just one year—1892; the German champion Willi Arend collected 137 "Grand Prix" sprinting prizes between 1896 and 1903, and between 1896 and 1904 the African American sprinter Major Taylor raced in the United States, France, Belgium, Italy, Germany and Australia, earning a huge amount of money.[2] In hundreds of race meetings throughout Europe and America, short-distance sprint races provided the mainstay of amateur and professional bicycle racing.

However, as the sport broadened and diversified in the later 1890s and in the first years of the new century, the leading sprinters, the aristocrats of track cycling, began to lose their earlier pre-eminence. With the introduction of the safety bicycle and the pneumatic tire, the high-wheel bicycle quickly became outmoded. Through the 1890s, the years of the first consumer bicycle boom, bicycle racing underwent a transformation as improvements in equipment and pneumatic tire technology made racing bicycles faster and lighter. A new generation of banked and well-surfaced velodromes, built specifically to replace the often improvised tracks of the high-wheel period, effectively corralled paying audiences and provided the infrastructure for well-promoted events.

Better tracks contributed greatly to the remarkable increase in speeds achieved in the 1890s.[3] Gas and electric lighting made evening racing possible. There was increased interest in setting speed records over short distances and in amassing greater mileages in long distance races. An understanding of various pacing techniques, in which the cyclist was helped to overcome wind-resistance, helped to increase both speeds achieved and distances covered. Extreme long-distance events and performances on both road and track became increasingly popular.

It is important to note that all these changes took place in the context of, and driven forward by, the increasing commercialization and professionalization of the sport. Bicycle and tire manufacturers and newspaper owners became involved in sponsoring bicycle racing, and sponsorship was quickly seized upon as an ideal circulation-boosting and publicity vehicle. The bicycle racing that emerged in the 1890s—new, exciting and fashionably technological—had many of the characteristics of modern sport. Cycling increasingly became a business, with an accompanying growth of managers, agents and trainers. In addition, the organization and promotion of bicycle racing became more centralized, more efficient, more capable of encouraging high athletic standards. In the United States, for example, amateur and professional championships were fought out through the season on a "National Circuit," which took the leading contenders to the major cities, in an attempt to create a sport that was "national in the fullest sense of the word":

Fig. 8.1. Tom Cooper, a top-level American professional sprinter in the second half of the 1890s. [Source: John L. Weiss collection]

> It is the arena in which the pick and flower of American speedsters daily measure their relative standings in the racing world. It is the great cycle-racing university, to enter which is the fondest ambition of every young racer ... it enlists the cream of our racing talent ... to win its laurels is to attain the supreme pinnacle of racing fame. Without it, cycle racing would be sporadic and local in character and national fame would be well nigh impossible in racing circles.[4]

These new developments were a far cry from the more limited, club-based amateur events of the 1870s and 1880s. The new "professionalized" sport became less accessible, in its technical and athletic demands, to non-specialists, and top amateurs had highly accomplished, specialist professionals against whom to measure themselves.

* * *

The interest in promoting endurance events and in demonstrating extraordinary performances was found in many different sports. At a time of supreme human confidence in

Eight. Bicycle Racing and Modernity 265

Fig. 8.2. The huge crowd at this race in Adelaide, Australia, in 1904 shows the international reach of top-level racing at the turn of the century. Here Ellegaard (Denmark, 2nd from left) and Walter Rutt (Germany, 4th from left) take on Australian riders. [Source: *Sport-Album der Radwelt*, 1905]

knowledge, science and technology, improvements in athletic achievement appeared to be limitless. The suggestion, by extension, was that human abilities in general were without limits.[5] Technology, exemplified by the bicycle and the newly emerging internal combustion engine, served to enhance human physical capabilities. At the first official world cycling championships in Chicago, the two events contested were a 1,000 m sprint and a paced 100 km event. During the first Olympic Games in Athens in 1896, the first modern marathon was held. In the United States, there were six-day roller-skating races. The *Berliner Illustrirte Zeitung* reported a six-day race in New York City for the "Road-skuller," a rowing machine on wheels.[6] In 1892–93, long-distance races were promoted for cyclists, walkers and riders between Vienna and Berlin, and horse-back and long-distance events remained fashionable for many years.[7]

A new, "gigantic" form of bicycle racing emerged. Four categories of cycling events typified this new kind of racing: long-distance place-to-place races on the road; stage-races on the road; "stayer" or paced races on the track; and, lastly, Six-Day races on the track. Long-distance road races, several of which still survive today as the Classics of the professional cycling calendar, were organized over distances of as far as 500 or 600 km in the 1890s, often between major European cities, with Paris and Berlin featuring prominently in many of the events.[8] The first major international long-distance race from Bordeaux to Paris, held in 1891, was praised by the German Cyclists' Association as an example of "the bicycle race of the future" and as "the beginning of a new era for our sport."[9]

A new facet of the sport was introduced and emphasized, with the physiological and psychological stresses endured by athletes in events lasting longer than twenty-four hours. "Stayer" (that is, paced) races on cycling tracks were prolonged and extended from the 100 km distance (lasting only 2–3 hours) competed for in the first world championships of 1893 to 6-, 12-, 24-, 48- and even 72-hour races during the 1890s.

Soon, riding an uninterrupted 1,000 km had become a record-breaking objective. Six-Day races on the track and stage-races on the road spread over many days were introduced as even more extreme racing events. The demands of such racing placed extraordinary, hitherto unexplored, stresses and strains on the athletes. In no other sport did a machine enlarge and expand human potential to the extent that the bicycle did. The bicycle enabled an intensification, a maximization of human athletic effort, allowing previously unimagined, "gigantic," physical feats to be accomplished.

The desire to break records had been an intrinsic part of top-level bicycle racing since the beginning of the sport, and had posed an athletic challenge to leading riders throughout the high-wheel period. Racing had been crucial in stimulating the early technological development of the bicycle; it had been instrumental in defining the high-wheeler as the most appropriate and efficient kind of bicycle for the sport. Riders sought to improve times on certain roads, usually well-known place-to-place routes, and to achieve faster performances on the track. The two primary challenges to riders and equipment manufacturers were the race over 1 mile—or 1 km in continental Europe—and the race lasting 1 hour. The first rider to cover 20 miles in an hour, H. L. Cortis, had earned high praise and widespread publicity.[10]

A detailed and up-to-the-minute account of the best times on record, with comparisons of British, French and American athletes, became a regular feature of cycling periodicals and yearbooks from the mid–1870s on. In fact, documenting these "records" became an obsession within the sport. Timing procedures and standards for world records were vigorously debated in often chauvinistic exchanges in the press. There were genuine areas for confusion, such as, for example, exactly how the distance around a track should be measured (relative to a defined inside line), and how exactly the timing watch should be started and stopped relative to the pistol report. Authentification of times and distances on the road was always problematic. Thus, achieving faster times and racing over greater distances were objectives in all four of the "gigantic" events, and these objectives were characteristic of the sport through the turn-of-the-century.

These extreme cycling events, first established in the 1890s, have survived for more than a century, although the physical strains have now in general been reduced. Distances of more than 300 km in a day are now unusual in single-day professional races, as are stages of more than 200 km in professional stage-races. Paced races now usually last a maximum of one hour, and the actual daily racing time in Six-Day races is between 6 and 12 hours. However, the major stage-races—the Tour de France, the Giro d'Italia and the Vuelta d'Espana—are still of "gigantic" proportions, as is the recently introduced "Race Across America," during which about 3,000 miles are now covered in about 8 or 9 days by the fastest riders.

* * *

The four extreme types of racing discussed below may all be described as "gigantic." Such races developed similarly in the various countries that held them, although the specific developments occurred at different times from country to country. In England, Germany and France, for example, long-distance road races were first held in the early 1890s, followed by the extreme paced races around the mid–1890s. Six-Day races were not introduced in Germany until 1909 or stage-races until 1911, whereas the Tour de France, first held in 1903, preceded the first Six-Day race by ten years. In the United States, Six-Day races were popular from the early 1890s, and paced racing expanded rapidly in the mid–1890s, whereas long-distance road races were less popular.

2. Long-Distance Races on the Road

The idea of long-distance races was not new. Before long-distance cycling races there were long-distance horse-riding, running and walking races, where the objective was to cover a particular distance in as short a time as possible. In the late 1880s and early 1890s, long-distance road races were introduced in which there were no scheduled rest-breaks and "gigantic" demands were made on cyclists, who raced over distances of 500 or 600 km, or in English time-trials for 24 hours continuously). Road conditions were bad and bicycles unreliable, so where it took more than 24 hours to reach a destination, it was inevitable that the fastest riders would have to ride for at least one night without sleeping. Eating, resting, sleeping, coping with mechanical problems, organizing support, all become crucial parts of the competitive challenge.

The earliest international long-distance road race was the 577 km Bordeaux-Paris race, first promoted in 1891, which continued as one of the classic road races until it was abandoned in 1987. The cycling press showed a great deal of interest in this new event. Four British riders who had extensive experience with long-distance racing on English roads won the first four places, surprising the opposition by riding right through the night.[11] Bordeaux-Paris continued to be heavily publicized throughout the 1890s; in fact, the rival newspapers *Le Vélo* and *L'Auto* each promoted an event over this route in 1902. The patriotic feelings of the French were so hurt by the British sweep of the placings in the 1891 Bordeaux-Paris race that a second, even longer race, without British participation, was organized by Pierre Giffard, editor of *Le Petit Journal*, a leading French daily. More than two hundred cyclists participated in the first, 1196 km, Paris-Brest-Paris race, won by French rider Charles Terront, who rode for three days without sleep.[12]

This race, of unprecedented distance, demonstrated what a human being could endure and what it was possible to accomplish on a bicycle. The public could at first hardly make sense of the extraordinary performances of the winners of this race. At the turning point in Brest, the crowd watched with astonishment as Jiel-Laval, in the lead, ate a few pears and some beef soup, took a bath and then got on his bicycle to ride back to Paris. It was unprecedented for an athlete to ride 600 km in 33 hours without sleeping, and lack of sleep became the decisive factor in the race. With a lead of more than an hour on the road, Jiel-Laval took a sleeping break at Guingamp on the return journey while his manager, De Civry, posted guards to give warning of second-placed Terront's arrival. But spies reported Jiel-Laval's rest to Duncan, Terront's manager, who instructed his rider to make a detour through the back streets of the town, bypassing Jiel-Laval's hotel. Jiel-Laval awoke to learn that his rival was two hours ahead of him on the road. But Terront was also totally exhausted.

He fell off his bicycle and was only persuaded to continue after much urging by his brother. Ultimately, Terront arrived in Paris 8 hours ahead of Jiel-Laval after riding more or less non-stop for 71 hours 16 mins.[13]

Paris continues today to be the most prominent starting and finishing point for road-race cycling classics, including the now well-established arrival of the Tour de France onto the Champs-Élysées for the final sprint and victory celebrations. In the 1890s, the Germans also originated some long-distance races, most of which were, however, subsequently discontinued.[14] In 1891, a Leipzig-Berlin-Leipzig-Dresden-Leipzig race was held over 500 km, while others included Magdeburg-Cologne (1892, 457 km), Mannheim-Cologne (1892, 250 km) and Basel-Cleve (1893, 620 km).[15] The long-distance race from Vienna to Berlin organized in 1893 created favorable publicity for cycling in general and particularly for the utility and practicality of the bicycle.[16] The inspiration for this race was a long-distance ride by soldiers on horseback on the same route in 1892. The fastest horsemen covered the 580 kilometres in 71 hours 35 mins.[17]

Racing cyclists were intrigued by the possibility of measuring themselves against the military horsemen, demonstrating the viability of the bicycle for military purposes. From a field of 117 German and Austrian amateurs who participated in the race, Joseph Fischer was the first to reach Berlin, in 31 hours and 22 minutes.[18] He started on 29 June 1893 at 6:10 a.m. and arrived in Berlin on 30 June at 1:10 p.m.[19] Storms during the night created bad conditions for the cyclists, only 38 of whom arrived in Berlin within the prescribed time of 50 hours.[20] The event was a success for the sport of cycling, and the German bicycle industry experienced a strong surge in sales.

Several of the many European bicycle road races initiated in the 1890s still take place on a regular basis today. For example, there are Liège-Bastogne-Liège (first held 1890), Paris-Roubaix (since 1896), Paris-Tours (since 1896) and "Rund um Berlin" (since 1896, held today as an "open" race). The oldest amateur classic still held in Germany is the "Rund um Köln" race, first held in 1908. The enduring attraction of events

Fig. 8.3. Super-endurance rides between significant locations were undertaken, used in bicycle industry advertizing and popularized in accounts such as Robert Jefferson's *Awheel to Moscow and Back*, published in 1895. [Source: author's collection]

of this kind was proved by the fact that new long-distance races continued to be introduced until 1914, and those still held annually include the Tour of Lombardy (1905), Paris-Brussels (1907), Milan-San Remo (1907), the Tour of Flanders (1913) and the Championship of Zürich (1914).

3. STAGE-RIDING AND STAGE-RACES ON THE ROAD AND THE ORIGINS OF THE TOUR DE FRANCE

The concept of the stage-race can be traced to military movements, or to long overland coach journeys, where a stage was a designated location serving as an overnight stop for marching troops or travelers, allowing rest and the provision of fresh supplies. A stage-race in cycling is a race held over several or many days, consisting of separate daily races with aggregate finishing times. The idea of stage-racing for cyclists originated specifically with the long-distance rides undertaken by individual pioneers during the 1870s and 1880s. In the middle of the 1890s, stage-racing developed along with a kind of touring fever, in which cyclists undertook semi-competitive, long-distance rides that involved touring and record-setting, and which were frequently reported in the press.

Fig. 8.4. The first Tour de France, 1903, won by Maurice Garin, was a powerful demonstration of national pride, athletic endurance, and the skills of French makers. Garin covered the 2,428 km, over six days, in 94 hrs 33 mins, at an average speed of 25km/h, spending more than 15 hours a day in the saddle. [Source: *La Vie au Grand Air*, 4 August 1906]

In 1875, in a very early, pioneering demonstration of the potential of the bicycle in stage-rides, two French riders, Laumaillé and Richard, rode nearly 700 miles from Paris to Vienna in 12 days. With better weather, they might have made it in 9 or 10 days.[21] Thomas Stevens rode around the world on a high-wheel bicycle from 1884 to 1887, publishing an account of his travels in *Outing* as he went, and *Around the World on a Bicycle*, a two-volume book, when the trip was completed. In Britain, the record for the "End-to-End" ride, approximately 900 miles from Land's End to John o'Groats, was frequently challenged, with G.P. Mills' 1894 record of 3 days 5h 49m standing for many years. 12- and 24-hour rides on public roads were frequently organized by British clubs, and the distances covered in those times continued to increase.

Following his success in the Paris-Brest-Paris race, Charles Terront, supported by his manager H.O. Duncan, accompanied by pacers and sponsored by the Rudge bicycle company, the Clincher tyre company and the makers of Carter's gear-case, rode more than 3,000 km from St. Peterburg to Paris in 14 days 7 hours and 2 minutes. In his account of this ride, Duncan wrote that the ride had introduced the bicycle to a country "where it is almost completely unknown," that "man is still a powerful motor," and that "the word 'distance' is only a word."[22] As he arrived in Berlin, "cries of 'Bravo, Terront!' and 'Vive Terront!' were yelled from the hundreds of boys who tramped along behind the cyclists in the slippery muddy streets." In Hanover, Terront was escorted into the city by five hundred cyclists, while at the finish at the Velodrome Buffalo in Paris a crowd of 7,000 greeted him with "a colossal reception." The ride, thought *The Cyclist*, "was a great success, and one that has done no end of good to the sport and trade in Europe."[23]

Robert Louis Jefferson made bicycle trips to Constantinople, to Moscow and back, and a 6,574 mile ride from London to Irkutsk which was reported in his *Across Siberia on a Bicycle*, published in 1896.[24] In 1895, Théophile Joyeux and Jean Corre were rivals in undertaking separate tours of the whole of France; Joyeux covered 4,500 km at the rate of 225 km a day, while Corre rode 5,000 km in 25 days, at the rate of 200 km a day.[25] One of the companions who persuaded Joyeux to persist in his "tour" was Henri Desgrange, the founder of the Tour de France.

* * *

The first Tour de France in 1903 was a calculated publicity vehicle for Desgrange's sporting newspaper *L'Auto*, which was engaged in a circulation battle with its rival, Pierre Giffard's *Le Vélo*. The race, which consisted of six long-distance stages and passed through Lyon, Marseille, Toulouse, Bordeaux and Nantes before finishing in Paris, was intended to stimulate newspaper sales both in Paris and in the provincial stage cities. The readers were held in suspense as to the eventual outcome, and entertained with dramatic stories of the rivalries and ordeals of the stars. It was a well-orchestrated media event, centered in Paris, a capital city obsessed with sport, art and modern technology. In *L'Auto*, one of the first Tour's managers, Geo Lefèvre, writing from Bordeaux, reported: "I saw more than 10,000 peasants looking at their copies of L'Auto out in the fields today. Surely this proves that the Tour de France is the finest sporting creation of the century."[26]

In this first event, the race covered 2,428 km ridden in six one-day stages, with rest days between them. The winner, Maurice Garin, took a total of 93 hours 29 mins to ride the entire course. The riders spent an average of 15h 35m in the saddle during the six days of actual competition, so that the 60 competitors were on the road every racing day until nightfall. In the following years, the route, the overall distance and the number of stages were changed annually. Cyclists were faced with increasingly greater challenges: stages were shorter but there were more of them, so that actual competition occurred nearly every day for three full weeks. The maximum number of stages was in 1927, with 24 stages, and the longest distance covered, in 1926, was 5,745 km. The Tour quickly became—and still is—the most demanding sporting event in the world.

The amazing story of what happened to Eugène Christophe during the 1913 Tour de France illustrates the additional challenges riders had to face due to the severity of the Tour regulations; for example, repairs to their bicycles had to be done by the cyclists themselves. Christophe had gained a 20-minute lead on the favorite, Philippe Thys, on the Tourmalet mountain (a 2114 meter climb), but the fork on his bicycle broke during the descent. He then had to carry his bicycle 14 km to the nearest village blacksmith, repair it himself, and consequently reached the finish line with a four-hour deficit. In addition, the jury imposed a 15-minute penalty on him because a boy had operated the bellows in the smithy, which qualified as "outside help." Despite all this, Christophe managed to finish 7th overall. Such exploits helped to create the myth of the Tour de France as a race of heros engaged in a superhuman, "gigantic" endeavour.

However, strict regulations could not always guarantee honest results in stage and long-distance races. Because of the difficulty of supervising the riders during races, they were sometimes able to cheat by having themselves pulled by motorcars

Fig. 8.5. By 1906, the Tour de France had become an annual celebration of sport and French national and regional pride. The winner, René Pottier, was shown on the cover of a popular weekly sport magazine. [Source: *La Vie au Grand Air*, 4 Aug. 1906]

or by traveling part of the route by train. Rival bicycle manufacturers and managers not only organized support for their own riders but also arranged unpleasant surprises for other competitors, such as sabotaged bicycle frames or nails on the road—the strains on the cyclists were thus increased in many ways.[27] Some competitors even resorted to blockades of the road and physical attacks on rivals, as in the 1904 race, when passions ran high between competing teams supported by manufacturers La Française and Peugeot. Alleged infractions of the regulations caused the Union Vélocipédique Française to disqualify the first four riders, including winner Maurice Garin, against the wishes of the event's promoter, Henri Desgrange.

The idea of holding stage-races lasting as long as several weeks became very popular, both as athletic events and as successful vehicles for publicity. Exceptional strength and

Fig. 8.6. As the principles of pacing were understood and applied, individual riders were able to maintain high speeds behind teams of multi-cycles. Teams were expensively maintained by leading manufacturers, in this photo the Dunlop Company, who paced J. Platts-Betts to a record at London's Herne Hill track in 1898. [Source: author's collection]

stamina were demanded from the participants, while spectators and those following the race through accounts in the press enjoyed the daily thrills and sensational cycling feats. The heroic stature of rival contenders was carefully invented and nurtured. The successful formula of the Tour de France inspired other European countries to introduce their own national tours, and thus before the First World War, riders could compete for honors in the Tour of Belgium (1908), the Tour of Holland (1909), the Tour of Italy (1909), the Tour of Germany (1911) and the Tour of Catalonia (1911).

4. "Stayer" (Paced) Races

The phenomenon of "pacing"—a word used to describe the aerodynamic and athletic technique by which one cyclist benefits by riding in the slipstream either of another single cyclist, a multicycle or a motor-driven pacing machine—made it possible for cyclists to ride faster and further, and gave rise to the systematic organization of pacing to achieve record speeds and distances. Overcoming wind-resistance was understood very early on—even in the high-wheel days—to be a crucial factor in bicycle racing, and continues to this day to be the most fundamental technical and tactical aspect of the sport.[28]

The expression "pace-making" was probably initially derived from horse-racing, where the "pacemaker" ensured the desired speed. From the early 1890s, human-power—that is other cyclists taking turns—or tandems, triplets and even quadruplets and quintuplets (four and five-man bicycles) were deployed to pace an individual rider. Photographs from the mid–1890s show teams of cyclists riding multi-cycles. These riders were hired by Dunlop and other manufacturers to pace their sponsored riders, enabling them to set new speed and distance records. Skill and a precise technique were required from the solo rider in switching from a tiring pacing crew to a new, fresh crew, and the pacing process was frequently referred to in terms of "an art" or "a science." An article from October 1896, headlined "The Art of Pacemaking, which has revolutionized cycling contests," explained that:

> The pacing of the racing cyclist is at the present day not only a veritable science, but an extensively followed profession. Hundreds of men are earning their living as pacemakers; and the exhibitions of speed and skill given week by week on our faster tracks prove to what a high pitch of perfection the art has now been carried.... In most paced races, the riders go at absolutely top speed all through. Those who can "stick the pace" set them alone have a chance of success; the man who "cracks" is out of it.... With the increased speeds attained by the flying multi-cycle there comes a cry for more and still more "banking" on the bends of the tracks.[29]

Spaldings Official Bicycle Guide for 1898 commented that, "racing as an art has been practiced more regularly this year than ever before," making "the season just closed the most successful that has ever been known.... The star feature was the middle-distance match racing made popular in this country by the arrival of Jimmy Michael, a diminutive midget, who has revolutionized our races and set the racing and scientific world a-guessing.... Nothing of a sporting nature can begin to compare with a middle distance paced bicycle race for excitement and interest."[30]

Fig. 8.7. As the commercial pressure to break records increased, human pacing gave way to steam, electric and gasoline-powered pacing machines. Major Taylor established this 1-mile record in 1899. [Source: *Cycle Age and Trade Review*, 10 Aug. 1899]

Many reports in the press confirm that the sport was changing in the direction of more speed, more excitement, and longer races. "Revolution in cycle racing," headlined one American newspaper early in 1898, which predicted "almost a complete revolution in the methods, manner, style and quality of cycle racing in the United States," to the extent that "at the end of the coming year it is freely predicted that all unpaced events, from one mile to five miles, will have become practically obsolete." At the same moment, the *New York Times* headlined that "Innovations in cycle racing threaten to change the character of

Fig. 8.8. A dramatic shot from the top of the banking underlines the speed and danger as two paced riders compete in the 100 km world championship in Antwerp, 1905. [Source: *Sport-Album der Radwelt*, 1905]

the sport," and reported that "there is reason to believe that a year from hence cycle racing will be an altogether changed sport from that which America, England and the Continent have followed with interest hitherto ... short distance contests must sink to the level of introductory features, or fillers between the longer races." Half a dozen tracks had been built in the New York area, and "to secure a paying 'gate,' attractions of a high order must be presented at each track, and the result should be a continuous series of big matches, novel features, and assemblages of racing notables from all parts of the world."[31]

Electric and steam-powered pace-making machines succeeded human-powered multi-cycles, but were at first unreliable. Smooth, consistent power was needed to achieve higher speeds. Beginning in 1897, specially designed one- and two-seat, gasoline powered motor bikes proved to be most effective for pacing on velodromes, and they underwent a rapid technological development to enhance their capabilities. Record-breaker S. F. Edge told a reporter late in 1896: "Next year will see mechanical pacemakers at work.... Later on will come the most startling innovation, mechanical pacemakers fitted with wind-shields. The man going against time will ride, drawn along in the vacuum created behind the shield that is being propelled round the track before him."[32] An article in *Cycling* in early 1897 thought it "pretty evident that mechanical pace-making machines will soon be receiving attention from several quarters. No one who has watched recent developments in this direction can help seeing what possibilities are open to a tireless pacer that can keep up a perfectly even pace for an hour or so without flagging."[33] The article explored the various kinds of power available, and emphasized the one huge disadvantage of gasoline-powered pacing-machines, that they spewed out exhaust that the cyclist was forced to inhale.

Mechanical pacing-machines were systematically used to attack short-distance records, but the most impressive gains were realized over longer distances, where the prolonged advantage of efficient pacing was most dramatic. Photographs from the period show pacing-machines partially enclosed in leather fairings to reduce wind-resistance, and pacers sitting on their machines bolt upright to create the maximum shelter for their rider. The track races that used such pace-makers were called "stayer" races because they were held over longer distances and demanded a great deal of stamina or staying power. The pacing machines, built with increasingly powerful engines to achieve higher speeds, were a crucial link between bicycle racing and the emerging motorcycle, automobile and avia-

Top: Fig. 8.9. A heavily bandaged Thaddeus Robl, the best-paid German "stayer," looks as if he should be in a hospital, rather than about to start another race. [Source: *Sport-Album der Radwelt*, 1903] *Bottom:* Fig. 8.10. The "Renn-Bahn-Katastrophe" in Berlin in 1909, when a powerful pacing-machine left the track during a motor-paced race, resulted in nine deaths, fifty injuries, and a temporary ban on such racing in Germany. [Source: John L. Weiss collection]

tion technologies, all of which benefited from the knowledge, the skilled man-power and the economic base that had been developed within the bicycle industry.[34]

Such races were a dramatic new departure in a modern, machine age, a public demonstration of power and technological accomplishment. They were noisy, smelly and extremely dangerous events held within the confines of a banked, cement velodrome, with eager spectators surrounding the action. This was a significant form of "gigantic" bicycle racing, popular at the turn of the century, in which man and modern machine collaborated in a sporting endeavor. The spectacle of racing cyclists "towed" at high speed sometimes for hours on end by huge, gasoline-driven pacing-machines was an extremely potent and hazardous expression of technological and athletic modernity.

Speeds as high as 100 km/h, and the participants' willingness to take the consequent risks involved, characterized this new discipline as "gigantic," and these "stayer" race became hugely popular in France, Germany and the United States before the First World War, the element of danger adding drama to the sport. The enormous sums of money earned by the leading professionals—among whom American, Bobby Walthour, was one of the best-paid—ensured a constant stream of new talent prepared to accept these risks. Both the riders and the pace-making machines were generously sponsored by manufacturers who needed to subject their products to arduous tests and to publicize them. Tracks were more and more steeply banked to accommodate the high speeds, but serious accidents (caused most often by mechanical failure, or by a tire bursting) were frequent and numerous cyclists and several pacemakers died in them.

On 30 May 1903, 24-year-old international-level rider, American Harry Elkes, was competing on the opening day of the new Charles River Track in Cambridge, Massachusetts in front of a crowd of 10,000 people, who "realized that he was riding the fastest race of his life and cheered him to the echo," when he was run over and killed instantly by the heavy pacing-machine of one of his rivals. Elkes was leading comfortably in the 20-mile race against William Stinson, Bobby Walthour and James Moran, and had already covered 15 miles in world record speed, when his rear tire exploded and his back wheel collapsed. *Bicycling World* commented that it was "one of the most tragic and lamentable fatalities in the history of cycling.... It was a baptism of blood for the record-making course, and the bright, particular star of the record-breaking firmament was snuffed out while in the act of setting new figures for the emulation of the riders of the world." Elkes' short career was "one of the greatest careers ever known on the cycle paths in the world."[35]

A terrible accident at the Botanical Gardens in Berlin on 18th July 1909, in which a pacing-machine ran off a newly constructed board track and exploded in the crowd, killing nine spectators and injuring fifty-two, brought about a temporary ban, followed by strict new racing regulations, in Prussia.[36] The accident was a "terrible holocaust ... the worst accident that has ever taken place since the introduction of motor paced racing; it was of such an extremely startling character as to have a paralyzing effect upon those spectators who themselves were out of harm's way."[37]

"Gigantism" was exhibited not only in higher speeds, but also in the ever-increasing distances involved. Between 1886 and 1894, the record for a paced 24-hour ride on English roads increased from 227 miles (G.P. Mills) to 376 miles (C.C. Fontaine).[38] While long-distance races on the track had formerly been held over a maximum of 100 miles or 100 km, from the mid–1890s they were extended to a period of 24 hours, thereby increasing the distances covered. In the early 1890s, with human-powered pacing, riders rode enormous distances. The first "Cuca Cocoa Cup" 24-hour race was held on the Herne Hill Track in London in 1892, when amateur Frank Shorland covered nearly 414 miles. In 1894 he increased his total to 460 miles.[39] Also in 1894, in Paris, the first "Bol d'Or" all-day race was held, in which the winner, Constant Huret, covered 756 km in 24 hours behind tandem-pace, maintaining a speed of 30.706 km/h for the entire distance. The "Bol d'Or" subsequently became the pre-eminent annual, 24-hour, paced endurance race, in which, in front of huge crowds, world-record distances of 800 and 900 km (behind human-powered tandem pace) and, in 1899, 1,020 km (behind a gasoline-driven tandem) were accomplished.[40]

The dramatic increase in the speed of the bicycle over the previous thirty years was emphatically demonstrated in a chart published by the French newspaper *L'Auto* in 1909 on the occasion of the first hour record of more than 100 km/h set by French rider, Paul Guignard. On the high-wheel bicycle, by 1884, 32.707 km had been covered in the hour. On the solid-tired safety bicycle, by 1891 the distance had increased to 36.605 km. After 1892, with the introduction of the pneumatic tire and increasingly efficient pacing, the speed shot up quickly. By 1895, a rider had achieved 46.711 km/h; by 1900, 64.673 km/h; by 1905, 89.904 km/h, and by the date of publication of the list in *L'Auto*, Paul Guignard had just established his sensational record of 101.623 km/h, riding behind a powerful pacing-machine driven by German pace-maker Franz Hofmann on the Milbertshofen velodrome in Munich, a record which stood until 1924.[41]

As the "stayer" races were at the height of their popularity in the two decades preceding the First World War, the excessive stresses of such endurance races were often criticized. The *Berliner Illustrirte Zeitung* protested against a 24-hour race in Berlin in 1898, but nevertheless admitted afterwards that "the race has not completely justified our fears ... nobody fell off his bicycle from exhaustion, nobody suffered delusions and nobody went crazy."[42] Similar criticisms were directed at long-distance events in Britain, France and America. Even in the face of public criticism (perhaps, indeed, partly fueled by the controversy) this dramatic kind of bicycle racing continued to attract huge crowds, providing an ideal opportunity for manufacturers of bicycles, motorcycles and automobiles to advertise and market their products.

5. Six-Day Races

Six-Day races were indoor track races lasting for six days, in which either individuals or teams of two riders competed.[43] Athletic events were traditionally limited to six days in England due to Sunday religious observance laws; racing could begin at 12:01 a.m. Monday, but had to finish at midnight on Saturday. Six-Day bicycle racing began in the English Midlands in 1876 as a feat of endurance for a single rider. It was inspired by similar, long-distance pedestrian events that were popular at the time. At the Molyneux Grounds, Wolverhampton, "in the presence of 10,000 spectators, Camille Thuillet, of Paris, the champion bicyclist of France, ended his task of riding 650 miles in six consecutive days, a feat never before accomplished." At the same time, Frank White, of Wolverhampton, was riding 600 miles in six days at the Walsall Arboretum. It made perfect sense, therefore, for them to race against each other for six days later in the month.[44] Six-Day high-wheel bicycle races came to prominence in 1878–79 in a series of indoor events promoted at the Agricultural Hall, London by entrepreneur Harry Etherington. These races were widely reported in the press, and in the "Long-distance Championship of the World," from 1–6 September 1879, George Waller covered the extraordinary total of 1,404 miles. The race, reported the *American Bicycling Journal*, "proved from beginning to end to be of the most absorbing interest to the immense crowds of spectators." On the fifth day, Waller rode from 6 a.m. to 12 midnight without a single stop or dismount, covering 220 miles, "a performance which speaks volumes both for the endurance of the rider and the perfection of the machine which he bestrode."[45]

Etherington also introduced Six-Day bicycle racing to America in 1879. These early Six-Day races were literally round-the-clock, "gigantic" competitions, where sleep had to be snatched at the risk of slipping in the standings, whereas later races were held over six days with agreed upon rest-periods, but with at least 12 hours a day of actual racing. Throughout the 1880s, Six-Day races continued to be promoted as genuine athletic spectacles, and as entertaining and lucrative box-office attractions. In 1885, the *Deutsche Illustrirte Zeitung* commented that "simple competitions in the different sport disciplines do not seem to satisfy the English and the Americans any longer; now the competitions in walking, bicycle riding and ice skating, etc., are being extended to six days."[46] Two Six-Day races were held consecutively at the Royal Aquarium: a long distance walking competition with twelve "pedestrians" and a "bicycle tournament" on the 160 meter track with 8 hours of racing a day, which was won by Birt with a total of 630½ miles.

The first of a series of annual Six-Day races, ridden without formal breaks, took place at Madison Square Garden in New York City in 1891, with many of the riders imported from among the tough, experienced professionals from the north of England and Scotland. In 1892, riders competed for a $1,000 first prize. In December 1896, 40 cyclists from the United States and Great Britain competed, one of whom was the teenager Major Taylor, later to become American and World sprint champion.[47] The *New York Times* commented that the race was:

> by far the most interesting and by far the most successful test that has been furnished of combined speed and endurance on wheels.... It is interesting to note just how much greater for long distances is the speed of the wheel than that of the human animal unaided by any mechanical appliances.... An average of 14 miles an hour maintained for 100 hours by the propulsion of the human muscles is an astonishing performance.[48]

The 1896 race proved to be such a popular success that in 1897 another race was held, which was won by Charlie Miller with a total of 3,300 km.[49] Because of the considerable lead he gained, Miller could afford 7 hours of sleep in these six days, which meant that he spent 137 hours on his bicycle. On this occasion, the *New York Times* was much more critical of the excessive nature of the event, indeed, criticism of the negative aspects of this extreme form of sport had begun to be expressed, on medical and ethical grounds.[50] With these exceptional performances, a typically exploitative type of promotion began, including sensational press accounts designed to attract the crowds. Some newspapers reported that "the cyclists went crazy because of the strains, and they climbed up the columns of the hall, ate leaves or behaved like lunatics." In 1898, urged on by crafty promoters, Miller even got married in his racing jersey in the velodrome. Among the press comments were reasoned medical objections to the staging of such stressful athletic events.[51]

In these Six-Day races for individual participants, the fastest competitors might develop a substantial lead (several hundred miles was possible) which was almost impossible for lower-placed riders to recover on the small tracks, so that at the end there was very little suspense or tension in the racing. Hence, the New York race at Madison Square Garden in 1899 was raced with a team of two riders, only one of whom was on the track at a time, thus creating a faster, more exciting race. The race was won by Charlie Miller and George Waller with a total of 4,400 km. Even though the Six-Day "fever" spread in the United States from then on, the first modern race in Europe did not take place until 1909 in Berlin, and it was a great success. German promoters had first shown an interest when the German Walter Rütt was victorious in New York in 1907 and 1909.[52] Although the German press protested against the "mistreatment" of the riders, the trend was unstoppable.[53] Six-Day races were held in the German cities of Kiel, Bremen, Dresden, Hamburg, Mainz and Frankfurt before the neighboring countries, Belgium (Brussels 1912) and France (Paris 1913) followed. Other Six-Day races were held in Hanover (Germany), in the United States, Canada and Australia before the First World War.[54]

There are many reasons why Six-Day races were so popular and were such a permanent feature of turn-of-the-century bicycle racing, and have held such an enduring fascination to the present day. The length of the events provided steady box-office receipts over several days, and spectators were enthralled as the races pitted competitors against each other in a small arena, within a circus-like ambiance. But most important, the spectators witnessed

Fig. 8.11. Major Taylor (in front) was one of the highest-earning professional sprinters on European tracks for nearly ten years, 1900–1910. [Source: author's collection]

incredible physical and psychological performances by the cyclists. The audience's physical proximity with their idols, the feeling of sharing their suffering, accidents and injuries, added intensity to the atmosphere of the small indoor tracks. As the riders strove to gain time and win special evening prizes offered by the promoters, spectators filled the cheap seats after a day's work to cheer on the exhausted riders in their marathon ordeal.

6. Professionalization and Commercialization

These four "gigantic" cycling disciplines not only put intensive athletic demands on the cyclists, but also changed their way of life, their incomes and their social status. This "gigantism," and its compulsion to break records, had a clear connection with the growing professionalization and commercialization of the sport.

Professionalism—racing for cash prizes—was intrinsic to bicycle racing from the beginning of the sport in the late 1860s.[55] A winner riding a particular maker's machine provided a de facto endorsement of that product. Amateur clubs were formed as a reaction to the perceived moral undesirability of professionalism. Professionalism was traditional and already well established in other sports before the emergence of the first professional cyclists, the high-wheel sprinters. The construction and promotion of racing tracks was one of the principal factors leading to the later growth of professionalism in cycling. Promoters, backed by the advertising revenue of bicycle and tire manufacturers, were another key ingredient. They booked riders and were able to charge an admission fee for track events, which led the cyclists—the main actors in the racing drama—to demand their share to compete on a regular basis. By the early 1890s, bicycles and bicycle accessories were advertised extensively as the bicycle boomed and a sophisticated retail distribution system was established for this major consumer product. British, American, German and French cyclists, hired by bicycle and tire manufacturers to promote their products, found themselves in demand and were able to channel their athletic abilities into a well-paid sporting career.

According to German journalist and historian Fredy Budzinski, "The propaganda of action had a stronger impact than any of the claims made on paper about the quality of bicycles, and the German industry acted quickly and willingly to use this new promotional technique." The same was true in the bicycle industry world-wide.[56] The large advertising budgets of bicycle manufacturers enabled a large number of professional and semi-professional athletes to be employed in the 1890s. In 1899, the German Cyclists' Association listed 452 professional cyclists among its members. *Spaldings Bicycle Guide* reported in 1898 that "it is estimated that there are in the United States 1,000 professional racers." A year later, Albert Mott, the chairman of the racing board of the League of American Wheelmen, reported that "there are 621 professionals registered and over 20,000 wheelmen engaged in racing either as professionals or amateurs."[57]

By 1895, obvious changes in the sport had occurred due to this strong movement towards professionalization. Rintelen, writing in 1895, maintained that: "It is thanks to the professionalization in cycling brought about and sustained by the industry that we see today the enormous cycling achievements which have contributed so greatly to the popularity of cycling and of the sport of cycling."[58] Rintelen claims that it was the bicycle industry

Eight. Bicycle Racing and Modernity

that made professionalization possible, and that it was professionalism that enhanced the level of performances. This is partly true, but it does not fully explain the complexity of the situation. There was certainly a strong tendency for the best amateurs to get sucked into professionalism, and certainly professional cyclists could better adjust to the immense demands of the sport. But there were also amateurs who participated successfully in "gigantic" races.[59] It is also possible that at a time when society was enthralled with the current, expansive technological innovations constantly being introduced, there was an urge to push at the limits of what was humanly possible in sport. And as the limits of human abilities were thus being explored in bicycle racing, it was inevitable that such physically demanding and stressful work would be considered best done by full-time specialists.

The press also played a crucial role in the marketing and promotion of professional cycling. The print media showed a keen interest in the incredible accomplishments achieved; articles were sometimes euphoric, but sometimes critical. Advances in the sport were reported either as fascinating or as threatening and repulsive, and the heavy press coverage contributed to the popularization of professional cycling from the mid-1890s.[60]

It was not just the official, licensed professionals who took advantage of the financial

Fig. 8.12. At a time when shutter speeds were in general not fast enough to stop movement in sport, photographers began more often to catch the action and excitement of bicycle racing. Cologne, 1905. [Source: *Sport-Album der Radwelt*, 1905]

opportunities. So-called "maker's amateurs" also found ways to turn their prizes into cash and to be compensated for their expenses and their equipment. They were licensed to compete as amateurs, but functioned in most other ways as professionals. This trend towards the commercialization even of the amateur sport put the cycling associations in a predicament; "amateurs" were frequently suspended for taking money or racing against professionals. Perhaps in no other sport was there such a consistent history of disputes and controversy over the amateur/professional question. Among the prizes, worth more than $11,000, that American world champion Arthur Zimmerman was reported to have won as an amateur were: thirty-five diamond pins, rings and brooches, fifteen bicycles, twelve silver services, six grandfather clocks, eight pocket watches, seven medals, one piano, a building site, twelve bronze figures, a wardrobe, two carriages and many bicycle tyres.[61] But this list is an under-estimate. In fact, in 1893, his last official year as a "makers' amateur" (riding a Raleigh bicycle and Palmer and Dunlop tyres), during which he won more than a hundred races, Zimmerman was estimated to have won prizes worth $15,000.[62] It is understandable, therefore, that successful amateurs would routinely sell their prizes for cash or would simply become fully-fledged professionals.

A top professional's income during the boom of the 1890s was much greater than Zimmerman had been able to earn as an amateur. Total incomes are difficult to assess, since athletes earned money from a variety of sources, but the earning potential of professional cyclists (whose careers at the top of the sport were, of course, often short) can be outlined. *Cycling* reported in 1898 that "the earnings of a crack racing cyclist of today would make many a public man envious. Such men as Michael and Barden can safely rely on an annual income running into four figures, so long as their muscles hold out to the severe strain that modern cycle-racing undoubtedly entails." Jimmy Michael, the writer reported, had earned £3,000 in the States in 1897, while "next to America, Paris and Melbourne are the happy hunting-grounds of the professional racing cyclist."[63] The editor of the Chicago paper, *Bearings*, estimated that in 1897 the two best-paid French riders, Morin and Jacquelin, earned about $12–14,000 (between 60,000 and 70,000 francs), from "the fixed salary given by the manufacturers who engage them; the purses won in racing; the percentage allowed on said purses by the makers; and the allowance granted by the track managers in match events likely to draw a big crowd."[64] Less talented riders, however, earned their livings "pacing" the star performers, and were "attached to some firm in the tire or wheel business, at a fixed salary of from 100 to 150 francs per month," with a similar payment from the star who employed them "during training hours."

When the African American sprinter Major Taylor broke a series of paced short-distance world records (including the prestigious 1-mile record) in Philadelphia in November 1898 for his employer, the Sager Gear Company, the attempts cost "about $3,000 ... others have paid five times that amount ... and failed." The expenses were summarized as follows:

> In addition to the Major's salary, which is said to be $100 a week, and that of his manager which is less by $25, there is the salary of twenty pace-makers, rubbers [masseurs], an expert repairman, an attendant at the track, hotel bills of several members of the company whose gear the Major is riding, making in all a weekly salary list of close to $800. In addition to this, the Major gets $100 each for the kilometer, ¼, ½ and 2 mile records and $500 for the mile. The riders have been on the pay roll for three weeks ... the cost of the record trials will be any where from three to five thousand dollars.[65]

In 1900, as his drawing-power increased following his victory in the 1899 world professional sprint championship, Major Taylor was offered $10,000 to race in Europe for three months.[66] In 1905, the world's best "stayers" received 2–3,000 German marks as first prize in a major race.[67] On German tracks, world champion "stayer" Thaddeus Robl earned 26,430 marks in 1903, 39,500 marks in 1904, 27,450 marks in 1905 and 49,250 marks in 1906. Between 1895 and 1905, Robl earned a total of 200,000 marks at home and abroad, four times more than any other German "stayer." By comparison, on German tracks German sprinter Willi Arend earned 10,822 marks in 1903, only 5,655 marks in 1904 and 4,620 marks in 1905, emphasizing the increasing popularity of "stayer" races over sprinting in Germany. As a sprinter, Arend still made a lot of money outside Germany, however, for between 1895 and 1905, he earned a total of 125,918 marks; his compatriot sprinter Walter Rutt earned 23,964 marks at home and abroad in 1905.

These were the best-paid cyclists in their events, however, and most others made a great deal less. In a list of 66 professional cyclists (both "stayers" and sprinters) showing total earnings on German tracks between 1896 and 1903, only four earned more than 30,000 marks, four made more than 20,000 marks, 22 made more than 10,000 marks and the rest less than 10,000 marks.[68] World-class sprinters Ellegaard and Major Taylor reportedly had an annual income of about 100,000 marks at the turn of the century.[69] Contemporaries judged the highest of these incomes to be equivalent to those of Cabinet Ministers.[70] The total value of prizes awarded in Germany continued to increase more than tenfold between 1901 and 1907, from 99,956 marks to 1,101,803 marks.[71] A mid-level British professional, not employed by a bicycle manufacturer, told a reporter in 1896 that from 1893 to 1895, he

Fig. 8.13. In the search for speed, the multi-cycle pacing teams were an exciting interlude in the mid–1890s, of the spectacular track racing sport. This is A.A. Chase setting a record on Herne Hill track in 1895/6. [Source: R.W. Thomas, author's collection]

had made more than £700 annually, and that in 1896 he expected to make £1,200: "I am paid from the company whose tyre I ride, by the rim-makers, by the machine manufacturers, the people who supply the saddle, and I have just made a contract to use a certain make of shoe."[72]

In the United States, *Spaldings Official Bicycle Guide* agreed that "it would be hard indeed to estimate the amount of money won in prizes and salary by the average racing man, but it is fair to estimate that their winnings averaged $100 for each first, $75 for each second and $50 for each third, to which must be added their salary, as nearly all the professional riders are employed by makers of bicycles and their accessories."[73]

This growing commercialization was recognized and criticized at the time: "The heyday of the sport was in the 1890s, whereas today business pushes itself too much to the fore," commented *Bühne und Sport* in 1907.[74] The strong trend towards professionalization and commercialization, more and more apparent from about 1895 on, and "gigantism" in cycling complemented each other. The sensational performances by cyclists in the extreme disciplines—endurance racing on the road, stage-racing, "stayer" racing and Six-Day racing—were generously rewarded by their sponsors, a network of manufacturing and press interests, and by the general public who paid to see them race and enthusiastically embraced the often romanticized accounts of their exploits in the press.

7. "Gigantism" and the Pursuit of Records

Beginning as early as the 1880s, there was always a strong interest in breaking records in cycling, as evidenced by the large number of record lists that were published in the many cycling journals. "Gigantism" and the pursuit of superlative records occurred in both sport and the development of technology, especially around the turn of the century. Both phe-

Fig. 8.14. The palatial Friedenau track in Berlin is seen here, an arena with substantial speed advantages, but also danger for the paced riders. Here, in 1903, riders wait to be "picked up" by their pacing machines, waiting behind. [Source: *Sport-Album der Radwelt*, 1903]

nomena were fundamental expressions of an industrialized society, in which outstanding and hitherto unrealized achievements were the objective of all human endeavors. Such efforts and aspirations were evident, for example, in the building of the Eiffel Tower (1885–89), the undertaking of record-setting attempts in cars, motor-cycles, motor-boats and aeroplanes, as well as in the building of ever-larger warships and passenger steamers, to mention just a few examples. Record-setting Atlantic Ocean crossings to win the "Blue Riband" were widely publicized, and culminated in the hubris of the Titanic disaster. The trend extended to amusement parks as well: huge Ferris wheels from 62 to 110 meters high were erected in London, Chicago, Vienna and Paris between 1884 and 1900. The first skyscrapers also date from the 1880s. Thus, bicycle racing as a sport fit in very well with other contemporary trends and the spirit of the times. There was a belief in progress and the feasibility of everything man tried to achieve by means of technology and his own capabilities.

An article published in *Scientific American* in 1899 explored the phenomenon of the obsession with breaking records, and offered the following explanation of current developments:

> The craze for "breaking the record," whether it be on the train, the steamship, or the wheel, is prompted by something more than the mere love of the spectacular; for the world recognizes that every new performance is a further breaking away from that universal stag nation in which all matter lay before its present evolution began—a stagnation which it is the constant effort of our modern arts and sciences to overcome.[75]

A public euphoria with every new technological development and a desire to sweep away perceived barriers surely contributed to the flood of athletic records. The press and the public demanded records and gigantic achievements, and they wanted to witness them. Commercial ambition made this possible. In the process, cyclists were driven to make superhuman efforts, to struggle and suffer, and even to die. The first cyclists to achieve major feats were often themselves surprised to be capable of such performances, as in the case, for example, of Charles Terront and Jiel-Laval's three-day, 1,200 km, Paris-Brest-Paris ride in 1891.[76]

The new professionalization of sport, characterized by extreme achievements and record-breaking as a principal objective, appeared earlier and more prominently in bicycle racing than in any other sport. The fact was that bicycle racing was technologically-based, and the bicycle industry contributed significantly to racing trends. The obsession with record-breaking led to the excessive forms of competition we have seen, and also to a new assessment of the sport. In 1898, Karl Planck described sarcastically a negative trend which he saw expressed in professional cycling, in a sense the outcome that proponents of amateurism had always feared:

> The real sportsman does not care any more about naturalness of movement, or about beauty and dignity of appearance. The marvelous neck where the full chin contrasts with the finely curved line, is stretched out like an ugly goose's gullet, the upper part of the body is rolled up to look like a hedgehog, the legs compulsively working away at the pedals, in this way the cyclist is whizzing along, a "god on his machine." It doesn't matter that the legs and feet work in a way that is exactly the opposite of natural; that the muscles of the heart and lungs, strained to the maximum inside the compacted chest, finally fail and cause severe diseases of the heart and lungs, as long as the opponent is beaten by a fifth of a second! Because a victory has to be won, man becomes part of the machine.... All hail to the record! We don't give a damn about man! Nor do we give a damn whether human nobility can be seen in this

expression of power or when on other occasions—perhaps even to our liking—we recognize the ape in man.[77]

Even insiders involved with the sport fought against the excesses described above. Paul von Salvisberg, in an 1897 article headlined "Human torture," referred to the "nonsense of Six Day races" and reported that in the State of Illinois a bill had been introduced to legally limit the number of hours a cyclist could race in a day to twelve.[78] In 1898, the *Monatsschrift für das Turnwesen (Turning Monthly)*, which championed the ideal of a multifaceted, general physical education and was the mouthpiece for the German Gymnastics Association, quoted several newspapers which reported the deplorable physical condition of the cyclists at the end of a 72-hour race in Paris.[79] Examples were given of cyclists being taken to the hospital and of their going almost insane in long-distance races, and the demand for an "Association for the Protection of Humans" was voiced. Even before the first Six-Day race in Berlin was held, the *Sport-Album der Rad-Welt* for 1908–09 severely criticized contests of this kind. The Six-Day race was seen not as a sports event but as "a lucrative speculation which encourages the basest instincts of the masses who watch with brutal insensitivity as half-dead people try to chase their best friends to death."[80]

The opinions of critics outside the sport were similarly severe and more comprehensive. One condemned the "greed for speed," and professionalism and dependence on the industry as "degenerate."[81] Prof. Boruttau's writings were equally critical. He saw the professional cyclist as a modern "gladiator" who sacrificed his health and life "to thrill a brutalized public," and to satisfy "the commercial interests of the bicycle industry." This criticism applied in particular to endurance races such as the "6-days 24-hour races: in addition to the huge stress of the events themselves, there is the extreme risk which can be seen in the numerous fatal accidents that have occurred in such events, forming a blot on our culture."[82] Surrealist Alfred Jarry, using utopian fables, also denounced commercialization and doping among bicycle racers.[83]

In spite of emotional criticisms such as these, the advocates of unfettered progress and those who profited from this "gigantomania" prevailed at the time. Professional and commercial sports, with all of their excesses, continued almost unchanged until 1914. Only then was a real effort made to reduce the excessive stresses on cyclists. Thus, the sport of cycling pursued "gigantism" in its competitions in the dynamic period preceding the First World War. The four new "gigantic" events certainly helped to popularize bicycle racing, but they also led to a loss in the prestige of the sport, and were rejected by a significant, critical segment of the population.[84]

8. Sensationalism and "Gigantomania"

The bicycle was also used for other, more foolhardy tests of courage, which were not athletic events per se, but were spectacular events promoted for the amazement and entertainment of a paying audience. In 1869, Professor Jenkins, "the Canadian Blondin," wearing "white tights, black velvet knee-breeches, a crown-shaped hat, all profusely bedecked with tinsel and beads," rode "a velocipede" across Niagara Falls on a tight-rope.[85] Artistic trick-cycling was popular in Vaudeville theaters, at circus performances and during Six-Day races. Unusual cycling tracks were erected on stage. Cycling acrobats, for example, rode on circular tracks so small and so steeply banked that they were riding on an almost vertical wall.[86] The so-called "death slopes," looping tracks on which the cyclist had to perform an upside-down loop, became notorious. The biggest "death slopes," the so-called "looping the loop" tracks, could only be erected out-of-doors.[87] After a steep, fast descent, the cyclist performed a loop, riding for a short time upside-down. Cyclists jumped into water from ramps similar to those used by ski jumpers. In these sensational, daredevil performances, it was inevitable that accidents and fatalities occurred.

Satisfying the same "lust for sensation" and the obsession with breaking records, there were attempts to set bicycle speed records behind trains during the years 1896 to 1899. These pitted the human athlete against the most powerful, fastest vehicle on the land in an extreme example of pacing. Even the power of the train was harnessed to extend human athletic ability. In 1896, E. E. Anderson rode a mile in 1m 03s behind a train just outside St. Louis, Missouri, and a sextuplet raced against the famous Empire State Express on the New York Central Railway.[88]

But the most famous of these publicity-grabbing rides involving trains and cyclists was the record set in June 1899 by professional cyclist Charles "Mile-a-Minute" Murphy, who rode a measured mile in 57⅘ seconds behind a train on the Long Island railroad, an event reported in hundreds of American newspapers.[89] As he came almost to the end of the board track laid between several miles of rails, Murphy was plucked into the air by several assistants standing on a specially shaped platform built on the back of the train, escaping near-certain death by seconds.

This spectacularly dangerous ride was seen as a sensational athletic achievement which was both foolhardy and of scientific interest. *Scientific American* discussed the significance of Murphy's ride in an editorial, and commented that "without disparaging in any degree the persistence and pluck of the bicyclist, the most interesting feature of the ride is the impressive object lesson it affords as to the serious nature of atmospheric resistance on moving bodies." As a media star, Murphy enjoyed a brief moment of international fame.[90]

* * *

Cyclists thus made a significant contribution to "gigantomania" in spectacular events that emphasized the controversial image of bicycle racing as a sensational factor in modern life and mass entertainment. Although these events took place outside formal, sanctioned competition, the distinction between sport and entertainment was not scrupulously recognized by audiences.

And it was, of course, the spectators, hungry for sensation, who with their ticket purchases to a large extent financed both the legitimate "gigantic" racing achievements and the more unconventional, foolhardy exploits of athletes and performers.[91]

9. The Emergence of a Modern, Professional Sports Structure

The radical developments occurring within the sport of bicycle racing in the later 1890s were characterized at the highest athletic level by a compulsive search for speed, extraordinary feats of endurance and sensational public spectacles, and were driven forward by the economic interests of the bicycle industry. The industry was economically integral to the sport in all the technologically advanced countries and collaborated in the creation of new kinds of professional cycling stars, who were most advantageously presented to the public within state-of-the-art velodromes, but could also be admired on the public roads while competing in well-publicized road-races. The various cycling disciplines became increasingly specialized.

As bicycle racing became a more lucrative business, professionals increased in number, and in pursuing their vocations as specialists they tended to separate themselves from the top amateurs. Professional cycling teams were formed and supported by the leading manufacturers, and victorious riders and the machines and equipment they rode were featured in prominent advertisements in the press. A more scientific approach towards the achievement of greater speed was seen in the use of increasingly sophisticated techniques of pacing. Training methods, too, became more scientific. Presiding over this novel sports structure, and earning their livings within it, was a new generation of managers, promoters and journalists, whose job was to organize and present profitable sports events.

"Cycle racing is becoming a science," wrote Barry Hecla in the Chicago paper, *The Referee*, in 1894, in an article which gave an American perspective on contemporary changes within the sport:

> Only within the last four or five years has the racing team been developed on anything like scientific lines ... by far the greater proportion of the big teams of the path are organized and sent out by bicycle manufacturers who have learned, either from their own experience or that of their competitors, that a few first-class men doing brilliant work on one particular make of bicycle furnish one of the most effective advertisements for that bicycle that the fertile mind of the modern advertiser has yet devised.

According to this account, the role of sport in influencing the preferences of the public in the purchase of an expensive consumer item like a bicycle was well recognized:

> The general public has always cherished the idea that the wheel on which many victories are won on the path must be a stoutly built and thoroughly reliable machine; and of late years, the shrewdest makers have been taking more and more pains to encourage this

Fig. 8.15. Thaddeus Robl, victorious in a European championship in Leipzig in September 1904—a contrast to his appearance in Fig. 8.9. [Source: *Sport-Album der Radwelt*, 1904]

belief, each one at the same time striving to outdo his competitors in the number of victories won on his machine. Consequently, the racing men began to find their services more and more in demand. Manufacturers vied with each other in the attempt to secure the very best men available to ride their machines.

But such an arrangement demanded experienced managers: "The racing teams have become quite complicated and expensive affairs and form a very important item in a maker's list of expenditures." Consequently, there was a need for "competent men to take charge of the speed merchants on and off the track," with the result that "most teams of fast riders under thoroughly competent management have proven a profitable investment." "Thoroughly competent" managers, however, were scarce and could "easily be counted on the fingers of one hand."

Of course, the participation of the bigger, wealthier manufacturers put pressure on others to enter the promotional arena: "now that one or two firms have set the fashion, it is a matter of pride with every manufacturer to have his wheel represented on the path by the best possible riders obtainable, and few makers will be content to have their wheels unplaced in the struggle for racing honors."[92]

It was not only some brands of prominently advertised bicycles that attracted consumers, but also the racy style and image of the bicycle itself. In other words, amateur, recreational riders wanted to imitate the professionals. "The design of racing machines has in years gone by largely set the fashion for the construction of road bicycles," commented the American paper, *Cycle Age*, in 1900:

> Energized by the general enthusiasm in the new sport and pastime, practically every male convert to cycling developed an irrepressible ambition to emulate on the street and road the popular favorites of the race track, and as a consequence road racing models were demanded which resembled in every respect save in strength and weight, the track machines. Handlebar, tire, pedal, toe clip and gear styles were set for years by the racing men.[93]

As well as appealing to the desire of the male cyclist to have an athletic, sporty image, the bicycle racing presented to the public in the later 1890s in both Europe and America was thus more ambitious, athletically more demanding and commercially more sophisticated than in the early 1890s, when the pneumatic tire had first impacted the sport. It was also more speculative and risky, involving an investment and expenditure of larger amounts of money.

In 1897, the editor of *Bearings*, F.E. Spooner, wrote of the high cost of salaries and traveling expenses for the large groups of riders and managers on the National Circuit, "which averages very close to sixty people week after week and month after month throughout the season." He thought that the Circuit had cost more than $200,000 in riders' expenses, and that if "prize money" and "gate money" was included in the calculations, $1 million "will be found to be a very light estimate of the amount of money which is annually involved in this cycle racing game." Such a figure did not include track and grand-stand construction, which he estimated at a further $1 million.[94]

Spooner's figures were probably on the low side. At the beginning of the season of 1898, Albert Mott, Chairman of the Racing Board of the League of American Wheelmen, was reported in the *New York Times* as claiming that bicycle racing was the "most popular of sports," which "flourishes beyond any other method of entertainment in this country." As evidence, Mott offered the following statistics: in 1897, 8 million spectators "paid

$3,600,000 to attend 2,912 race meetings participated in by 9,000 men, who have won and received racing and pace-making prizes to the value of $1,645,020, giving the promoters a margin on the meets and incidentals of $1,089,180." He went on to describe the efficiency and sophistication of the promotions:

> One new feature that has improved bicycle racing during the past season is the entrance into it of capitalists and business men. Their meets are conducted in a business-like manner, and with system. Everything moves with precision, spectators are well cared for and better entertained, and the racing man is sure of the full value of the prizes he wins. It is not only in the large cities that these enterprises exist, or that the largest attendance is attracted. A track in a town of 200 inhabitants in the South drew over ten times its own population at one meet.[95]

Comparative figures for various sports showing the number of spectators, earned income, and overall expenditure are hard to come by, but it is frequently suggested that in the late 1890s, when bicycle racing was at its apogee of popularity and economic success, it rivaled baseball as the most popular spectator and participant sport in America.[96] The very success of the sport was an ongoing problem for the L.A.W., which represented itself as never having sought the responsibility for control of racing in the United States, especially coping with the exigencies of the new professionalism.

A new professional organization, the National Cycling Association, contested the control of professional racing with the L.A.W. between 1898 and 1900 and by enlisting the support of riders, promoters and track owners, succeeded in wresting control of the professional sport from the L.A.W. in 1900.[97] The L.A.W. was thus freed from the obligation to legislate the constantly troublesome distinction between amateur and professional competitors and enabled to "devote its energies to pushing side path and good roads work and its other legitimate work."[98]

This dynamic commercial activity and its impact on the character and organization of sport as outlined in the American analyses quoted above could be duplicated with many other accounts from the British and French press in the 1890s, and is reflected in the thousands of pages of advertising that can be found in the cycling and general press. More than a century before today's heavily commercialized sports industry, a strikingly modern organizational and promotional structure was evident within the sport of bicycle racing.[99]

Professional cycling, sponsored by bicycle makers, tire and accessory manufacturers, and the producers of other consumer products (newspapers, clothing, foods, drinks and stimulants), was used to adverstise those products to the general public, and such advertising heavily impacted the buying habits of recreational and utilitarian cyclists and set fashionable trends.

In the face of this successful specialized professionalism, the days of high-level, unadulterated amateurism became more difficult to maintain. Professional cycling, as in the case of French and Belgian road-racing, had become a firmly established and accepted modern sporting activity. Alongside it, the amateur sport thrived in the all-amateur Olympics and the widespread early Sunday morning time trialing in Britain, but the most intense racing was among the ranks of the professionals.

Chapter Nine

Non-Competitive Cycling in the 1890s

"Membership in a club gives a man a social standing in the bicycling world..."—Henry Sturmey (1879)

"...the bicycle is now used almost solely for utility..."—*Bicycling World* (21 Nov. 1903)

THIS BOOK HAS FOCUSED on the birth and growth of competitive cycling, and on the careers of those who took part in formal competition. However, it has always been difficult in this account to distinguish between the seriously competitive core of riders, and the many enthusiasts who were involved in cycling as an athletic recreation, and those for whom cycling was a means of practical transportation and not primarily a sporting activity.

This chapter, therefore, attempts to put the discussion of formal competition in the wider context of the recreational and utilitarian uses of the bicycle.

* * *

It is difficult to know exactly how many cyclists made up each of these three loosely-defined and overlapping groups. Various data sources, such as membership figures for the National Cyclists' Union, within which there were various kinds of club affiliation, and sometimes the need for some kind of a racing permit or licence, suggest strongly that the seriously competitive athletes (those who did need a permit to compete either as amateurs or professionals)—constituted a relatively small proportion of the entire body of active cyclists.

In 1894, when total British club membership approximated 80,000, a total of 2,682 licenses was issued by the N.C.U., indicating that about one person out of about 30 club members intended to race seriously.[1] If the total number of licenses issued in 1897 by the N.C.U. (2,626) is taken as a fraction of total membership of the N.C.U. that same year (31,397), then only one N.C.U. member in eleven requested a licence to compete that year.[2] Some riders, however, may well have raced outside any existing licencing rules. Based on such calculations, it appears that between 5 percent and 10 percent of club members in Britain were active racers, though some specialized racing clubs had a much higher percentage of racers as members.

The co-existence of these three groups of users—competitive, recreational and utility cyclists—had various social and technological implications. In the 1890s, for example, an individual cyclist might well ride a race on Saturday, tour with his wife on Sunday and then

Fig. 9.1. An ad hoc group of serious club cyclists, record-breakers, onlookers and the owners of the pub itself, the Misses Dibble, posed outside The Anchor, Ripley, Surrey, in April 1896. [Source: *Cycling World Illustrated*, 15 April; 1896]

ride to work on Monday, either on the same or on three different kinds of bicycles. How were these different uses related to the development of bicycle technology in the late 19th century?

It has been argued here that competitive sport (and the wider field of athletic cycling) was the engine that drove a great deal of the innovation and technical change within the bicycle industry in the 1880s and 1890s.[3] But there is also quite a lot of evidence that the competitive "look" itself became a style or fashion among those who did not in fact compete formally (very much as it still is today), and that utility and practicality may sometimes have been sacrificed to lightness and speed. And it can be plausibly argued that only the introduction of the pneumatic tire in 1890–92 began to attract significant numbers of serious utility riders, including women and older men, into cycling's orbit.[4]

* * *

This chapter examines the expansion and popularity of both recreational and utilitarian cycling alongside the specifically competitive aspects of the sport. Typical of many comments encountered in the 1880s, which recognized the recreational pleasures and advantages of the high-wheel bicycle, as opposed to the stresses and strains of racing, is this passage from a book—*Cassell's Complete Book of Sports and Pastimes*—which was directed at a popular audience:

> Amongst all manly and athletic pursuits bicycling holds a most prominent place, not only as a sport, but also as a really useful accomplishment.... The practice of bicycling is distinguished over all other sports by its independence. The adept, rising early in the morning, can encompass eighty or one hun-

Above: Fig. 9.2. A similar group of hard-riding road cyclists and tricyclists posed outside The Old Salisbury Arms, Barnet, in June 1896. These people were on the seriously athletic edge of club activities. Some raced, but some did not. [Source: *Cycling World Illustrated*, 17 June 1896] *Right:* Fig. 9.3. When the earliest bicycles built specifically for women came onto the market, women struggled in inappropriate long skirts, but still rode. [Source: *The Wheel and Cycling Trade Review*, 4 Oct. 1889]

dred miles with ease in the course of a holiday.... The toil-worn clerk can, by getting up an hour earlier than usual, take a quiet run amongst the green fields, and fill his lungs with fresh air before entering upon the labours of the day.... With care, bicycle-riding will be found most beneficial and health-giving.[5]

Later, as the bicycle's utility became more widely accepted, there was a conspicuous increase in the numbers of functional cycling trips in urban areas. In 1900, a source reported "the crowds a wheel, whose course is set during the rush hour of the morning towards the business center, and again in the evening as they seek the home."[6] And in 1903, *Bicycling World* noted that "the bicycle is now used almost solely for utility, which cuts demand down to a fraction of what fashion was able to produce."[7]

By the early 1890s, the bicycle had become an industrial success story and a recreational and utilitarian fact of daily life in the developed world. Cycling had become a widespread movement within which only a small minority of riders were involved in the competitive aspects of the sport. In 1897, the British journal *The Hub* offered the following statistics about the American industry: "In 1885, the United States had 6 cycle factories producing 11,000 machines. In 1890, 17 factories turned out 40,000 machines. In 1895, 500 factories produced 600,000 cycles and in 1896, over 700 factories manufactured 1 million bicycles, worth £12 million." Up until 1876, another issue of *The Hub* recorded, only about 300 bicycle patents had been issued; since then, 4,000 had been added, half of those since 1891.[8] At the turn of the century, *Leslie's* expressed great confidence in the usefulness, health benefits, and recreational possibilities of the bicycle:

> No review of the great inventions and remarkable achievements of the nineteenth century will be complete that does not give adequate space to the origination and wonderful development of the bicycle industry, that stands among the foremost in the amount of capital invested and the number of persons employed, and that ministers to the enjoyment and physical well-being of millions of people in all lands under the sun. And all this growth and development are covered by the history of hardly more than the last quarter of the century.[9]

Such statistics charting the expansion of the bicycle industry between 1870 and 1900 are impressive. Surely no other late-19th century sport and recreation witnessed the manufacture and consumption of such a vast quantity of equipment. Within the bicycle movement, there was a parallel development of sport, recreation and transportation, and the exponential increase in the number of bicycles produced both in Britain and the United States reflects this development.[10] Although only a small proportion of the bicycles produced may have been used in competitive sport *per se*, none of these bicycles were ridden without the use of muscular power

Fig. 9.4. By the "boom" of the mid–1890s, however, women had the choice of fashionably conservative dress, more practical "bifurcated" skirts, or the radical "bloomers" for their cycling activities. [Source: *Ladies' World*, July 1896]

and effort. Thus, there is clearly a significant athletic element in recreational and even in utilitarian cycling. A detailed examination of makers' catalogues and the kinds of machines advertised in the cycling press shows that clear distinctions were made between those machines that were intended for sport, for recreation and for utility, but that the dictates of fashion and practicality, as much as the specific intentions of the maker, meant that a "racing" machine was frequently used for recreational purposes, or that a substantial tour was done on a humble utility machine.

* * *

Many accounts confirm that the social and economic significance of the bicycle was wide and that cycling "sport and pastime" was not confined in a narrow sense to competitive sport. The enthusiasm for racing was not isolated from other uses of the bicycle. Interest in the "sport and pastime" extended beyond those who actually competed on bicycles. An institutional separation occurred early on in Britain (1878) between the Bicycle Union (mostly racing) and the Bicycle Touring Club (later the Cyclists' Touring Club, mostly touring). Competitive cycling's governing body in England, the National Cyclists' Union, struggled to accommodate the interests of its non-racing members and to answer the criticism that it was too heavily involved in racing. The *N.C.U. Review* reported that "the championships of 1886, instead of resulting in a handsome profit to the Union, as they have done in previous years ... have been the means of involving that body in a loss, equivalent to the annual subscriptions of 3,000 club-men."[11] In 1887, a committee member reported that:

Fig. 9.5. Situated with a perhaps new-found independence in ambiguous urban space, the cycling woman appeared to offer a provocative challenge to accustomed etiquette. [Source: author's collection]

an erroneous opinion evidently exists amongst cyclists ... that the N.C.U. is a racing association, pure and simple ... others condemn the Executive for giving too much of its time to racing matters, to the alleged prejudice of important work more essential to the interests of cyclists, and for which the Union professes to legislate.[12]

In 1887, Robert Todd, the Secretary of the N.C.U., admitted that "the racing constituents of the Union have for some time past absorbed more than their fair share of the time at the disposal of the Executive" and he proposed that the Executive would in future "devote much more of their time and efforts to matters which more generally interest and affect the large body of road-riding cyclists, who use cycling as a healthful means of recreation and rational enjoyment."[13]

Evidence of this wider interest was a struggle for the legal recognition of bicycles on the public highway in Britain, and the creation as early as 1887 of a Roads Improvement Association of the N.C.U. and the C.T.C.[14] In France, too, cycling had two principal organizations, the Union Vélocipédique de France (established 1880) and the Touring Club de France (established 1890). A similar dichotomy, and questioning of its essential purposes, confronted the League of American Wheelmen in the United States in trying to balance its control of racing with its role in touring, legal and transportation advocacy in what became known as the Good Roads Movement. At the end of the 1890s, the LAW essentially abandoned its involvement with racing in favor of support for recreational cycling.

Sport, recreation and utility thus overlapped in various ways. Many of the spectators at racing events, for example, were also recreational riders, and the emergence of the specialized cycling press helped to consolidate a network of non-racing, athletic, club-based enthusiasts. Accounts of strenuous touring rides at home and in foreign countries abound in the cycling press from the late 1870s on. The British, American and French cycling press underwent a huge expansion in the 1880s and

Fig. 9.6. Although racing for women was little developed in the 19th century, it did occur as a risqué high-wheel music-hall act in the 1880s, and in Paris in the late 1890s, Mlle Dutrieux was one of a handful of serious female competitors. [Source: H.O. Duncan, *Vingt Ans de Cyclisme Pratique*, 1897]

Fig. 9.7. Urban street conditions were typically quite difficult and potentially hazardous for women cyclists in the 1890s. The location is outside the George and Dragon, West Hill, Putney, on the western outskirts of London. [Source: author's collection]

1890s. As an illustration of this growth in France, Baudry de Saunier's *Le Cyclisme Théorique et Pratique*, published in 1892 in Paris, contained advertisements for fourteen weekly and monthly periodicals then available in France which either concentrated exclusively on cycling or featured it heavily.[15] Not advertised there was the Parisian *daily* cycling newspaper, *Le Vélo*, which first appeared in December 1892. Britain, at the same moment, had a similar number of cycling-related newspapers and journals. The publishers of these periodicals covering "the sport and pastime" of cycling were pioneers in demonstrating the viability of sport-specific print journalism. Earlier sport-related news items had been published in general interest publications such as *Bell's Life* and the *Bazaar, Exchange and Mart* in England, or the *National Police Gazette* and *The Spirit of the Times* in the United States.

By the 1890s, with the advent of the safety bicycle and the pneumatic tire, cycling had emerged as a widespread leisure and recreational activity, as well as providing practical transportation and mobility. But other than the membership statistics of cycling organizations, and an occasional survey of bicycle usage in specific geographical locations, statistical information about 19th century utilitarian cycling is hard to locate.[16] Even within an organization such as the Good Roads Movement, which was established within the League of American Wheelmen from 1880 to 1905, bicycle usage appears to have been such a self-evident fact that it was not much measured in statistical terms.[17]

Nevertheless, its importance was widely commented upon by contemporary observers. "The historian who will write the true history of the closing years of the 19th century will be compelled to say a great deal about the growth, influence and effects of the bicycle habit during that period," said *Harper's Weekly* in 1895: "The bicycle was taken up as an appliance for exercise and pleasure. These it has furnished to an extent not anticipated by its most enthusiastic devotees. In addition, it has passed beyond any limits of mere pleasure or exercise."[18] *Harper's* went on to list some of the facets of life impacted by the bicycle: its potential in war, its acceptance by "society," its promise as an alternative to the horse, its raising the question of better roads and its giving a new freedom of physical activity and dress styles to women:

> It is undoubtedly true that woman is riding to greater freedom, to a nearer equality with man, to the habit of taking care of herself, and to new views on the subject of clothes philosophy. The woman on the wheel is altogether a novelty, and is essentially a product of the last decade of the century.[19]

A close study of the expansion of the bicycle shows that women formed a small but significant proportion of the recreational and utilitarian users as the safety bicycle and pneumatic tires were introduced. At first, women riders in general labored in long skirts, but during the boom of the mid–1890s, cycling costumes became both a fashion and a statement of modern practicality, including "bifurcated skirts" and "bloomers." Only a tiny number of female cyclists became competitors, sufficiently small to attract a great deal of attention to themselves.

Harper's estimated that the American bicycle trade involved a total consumer expenditure of $50 million, that a half a million bicycles would be sold in 1895, and that a total of 1 million were in use in the United States. A further article in *Harper's* spoke of "the cheapness of bicycling as compared with horse-back riding.... A bicycle costs from $100–150, a horse costs from $200 to very much larger sums. The keep of a horse is at least $30 a month, including the charges of the farrier and veterinary; the cost of a bicycle for repairs ought not to be $3 a month."[20] By 1898, a good quality, brand new bicycle could be bought for between $25 and $50 in the United States, and a slightly outdated, used bicycle for much less. The bicycle had been diffused from its earlier, limited, specifically sport-oriented, athletic and competitive role, and become a practical tool for transport.

* * *

The progress and expansion of cycling and the bicycle industry between the late 1870s and the late 1890s were extensively documented by journalist and editor Henry Sturmey, who published a series of annual handbooks charting trends in the marketplace. His *Indispensable Handbook* and *Cyclist Annual and Year Book*, and other annuals listing and explaining the different models of bicycles and tricycles, were early examples of consumer product guides, where competing models and designs were rigorously examined and evaluated. Sturmey was also an active rider and clubman. "Membership in a club gives a man a social standing in the bicycling world which he could scarcely otherwise possess," he wrote in 1879, when he gave the following estimate of the number and size of British cycling clubs at that date, four or five years only into the active development of the high-wheel bicycle:

> There are at present time, upwards of 230 clubs in the United Kingdom, of which the Metropolis contains some 75. The number of club men in the kingdom is computed at between 8,000 and 9,000,

which gives an average of between 30 and 40 to each, although more than half number below 30. The largest of all is the Cambridge University Club, which numbers nearly 280, and has now been in existence five years.[21]

Sturmey's interest in documenting British cycling clubs continued in his annual *Cyclist Year Book*, a compendium of information about many aspects of the cycling trade and sport.[22] The lists of clubs and membership figures published there in the 1890s gives the opportunity for an analysis of Sturmey's data, and an example of the kind of data available for 1898 can be found in Tables 9A and 9B.

By 1899, as a National Cyclists' Union official and Secretary of the International Cyclists' Association, which had overseen world championships since 1892, Sturmey had become one of the most prominent figures in international cycling affairs. And in a characteristic display of late Victorian energy and thoroughness, Sturmey was still collecting and publishing data as a journalist. His 1899 *Cyclist's Indispensable Handbook and Year Book* is a historian's treasure-trove, including lists of new products, directories of manufacturers, national and world championships and records. It also contained a 50-page list of "The Cycling Clubs of 1898." As in previous editions, Sturmey had written to the secretaries of all the British clubs asking for details of membership. The result provides valuable

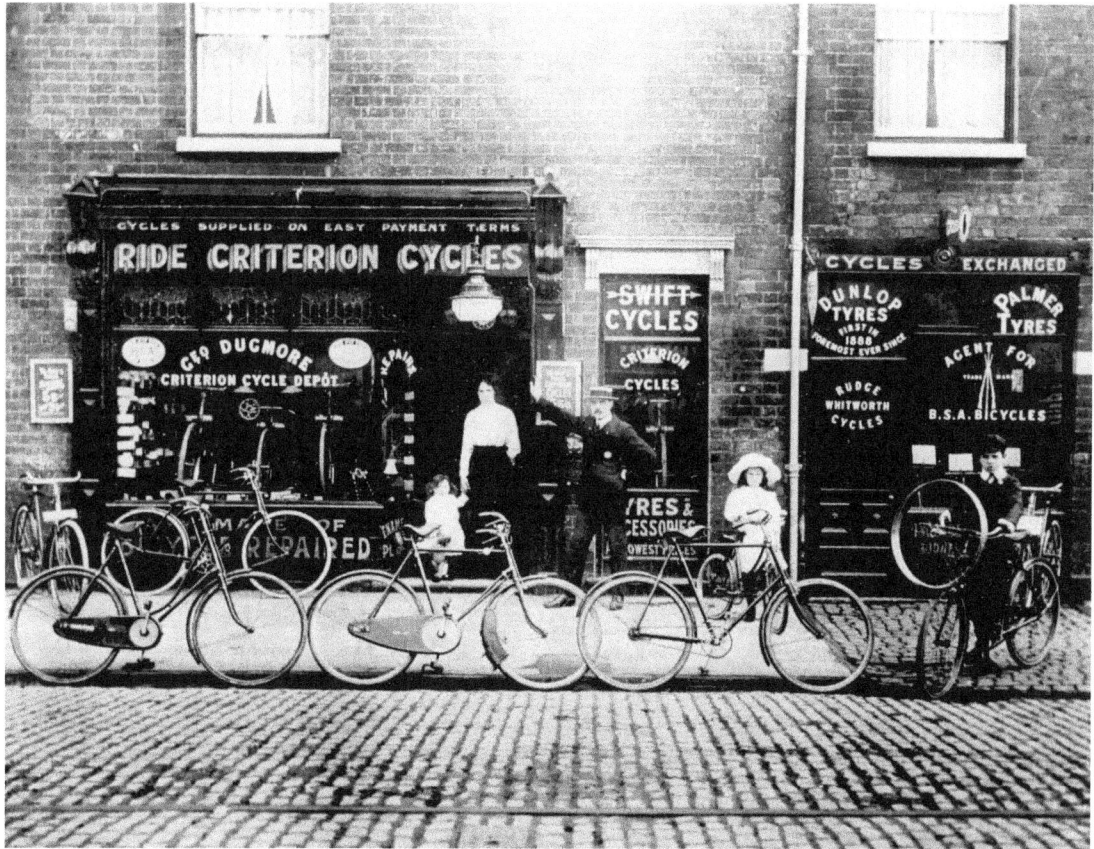

Fig. 9.8. A typical bicycle shop at the turn of the century period, probably in London, shows the penetration of purely utility cycling. [Source: author's collection]

evidence of the extraordinary penetration of sporting and recreational cycling, although it did not include any information on utility cycling. A logical approach to the club membership figures given here suggests that non-club-member recreational and utility cyclists must have constituted a large group of bicycle users, which was not accounted for in Sturmey's club lists.

This 1898 information has been included in Tables 9 A and 9 B, on page 303. In 1898, the total number of British cycling clubs listed by Sturmey was 1,816; England had 1,374, Scotland 250, Ireland 144 and Wales 44.[23] Of the English clubs, 256 were based in London, while several other major cities had 40 or more clubs. For example: Birmingham had 76, Manchester 49, Liverpool 47 and Edinburgh 44. If the 50 London clubs and approximately 200 provincial clubs whose secretaries did not respond to Sturmey's request for information are also counted, the total number of clubs in 1898 was about 2,050. The total nationwide membership of all the clubs listed by Sturmey was 128,936, with an average individual membership of 71 members. The 256 London clubs listed had a total of 20,597 members, with an average membership of about 80 people. The average membership of the clubs in the 14 provincial cities with the largest number of clubs was 66.

The size of individual clubs varied considerably. The largest were the well-established racing clubs, like the Catford C.C. (450 members), the Polytechnic C.C. (250 members), the Manchester Clarion C.C. (400 members) and the Belfast Cliftonville C.C. (650 members), certainly evidence that competition and serious "speed" cycling were strong motivating factors in club formation. But the "society" club, the Sheen House C.C. (whose

Fig. 9.9. The Catford Cycling Club in 1887, still in the solid-tired era, were clubmen, enthusiasts and, probably, but not necessarily, racers. [Source: author's collection]

Fig. 9.10. At the beginning of the pneumatic safety era, about 1890, the works cycling club of Rabbits and Son, in south London, was distinctly working class, and emphasized how organized sport had penetrated everyday life. [Source: author's collection]

members were more interested in fashion than in speed or distance) was also large, with about 1,100 members since 1896, while the smallest clubs listed had a mere12 or 15 members.

The names of the clubs listed by Sturmey confirm the penetration of cycling as a sport and recreation into many different kinds of social groupings.[24] Many of the big clubs, such as the North Road C.C., the London County Cycling and Athletic Club, the Catford C.C. or the Polytechnic C.C., existed primarily to race and "scorch" on the roads, to express an athletic and competitive sense of masculine identity rooted in physical strength, fitness and endurance.[25]

Most others, certainly the majority, were weekend riding and touring groups, with an active social calendar, particularly in the winter months. Some clubs were organized around a specific activity or social group, such as the Daily Press C.C. (London, 263 members), the Licenced Victuallers C.C. (London, 80 members), the London Scottish B.C. (70 members), the Vegetarian C.C. (London, 108 members), the Alington (Gloucester) Working Men's C.C. (12 members), the Hexham Congregational Church C.C. (31 members) or the Edinburgh Abstainers C.C. (65 members). Others were based in a specific working-class geographical area, like the Surrey Commercial Docks C.C. (42 members) or the Thames Ironworks C.C (150 members), or originated in one particular factory, such as the Humber C.C. (450 members) and the Rudge-Whitworth C.C. (200 members) in Coventry, or the Colchester Brewing Company C.C. Others, such as the nationally organized Clarion Cycling Clubs, or the Association of Conservative Clubs C.C. (London, 450 members), had an overt political agenda.[26]

Within and beyond this predominantly masculinist milieu, women too began to participate. Ladies' cycling clubs were increasingly common by the end of the 1890s (for example, the Lady Cyclists' Association, with 200 members), existing either independently or as the women's section of a male club, and women's participation in cycling was recognized with the development of a specialized press specifically directed at women.[27]

* * *

It is also useful to give some idea of membership totals for the National Cyclists' Union and the Cyclists' Touring Club, national umbrella organizations which consisted of a centralized government and local district committees, many of whose members were also members of local clubs. Table 9 C, on page 304, gives regional membership figures for the N.C.U. at the beginning of 1897.

The total estimated membership of more than 31,000 members of the N.C.U. shown in Table 9 C should be compared with Sturmey's projected total club membership for Britain of 128,936 in 1898 shown in Table 9 B, and indicates that only about a quarter of the cyclists who joined a local club availed themselves of the advantages of membership in the national organization, which gave legal advice and information about road conditions and published a handbook listing hotels and restaurants where members could get special rates. This suggests that club membership was a local, community-based matter and membership in the national organization was perhaps limited to the most active and enthusiastic. In 1897,

Fig. 9.11. Affluent tourists, experimenting with the latest in safety bicycle technology, at a railway station somewhere in Kent in about 1890. [Source: author's collection]

1898 City	Clubs	Total membership	Average membership
London	256	20,597	80.5
Birmingham	76	4,090	53.8
Bristol	35	2,295	65.6
Coventry	23	1,688	73.4
Hull	25	2,600	104
Leeds	33	2,160	65.5
Liverpool	47	2,524	53.7
Manchester	49	3,799	77.5
Newcastle	30	2,298	76.6
Nottingham	24	1,919	79.9
Sheffield	19	1,172	61.7
Edinburgh	44	1,869	42.5
Glasgow	38	2,220	58.4
Belfast	22	2,267	103
Dublin	27	1,598	59.2
Totals, without London		32,499 members	66.1—average membership
Totals, with London		53,096 members	71.0—average membership

[Table 9 A. Membership of cycling clubs in London and 14 other major British cities in 1898. Totals are for the listed cities only, not the whole country. Data compiled from Henry Sturmey, The Cyclists' Year Book for 1899.]

2,626 licences were issued by the N.C.U. (including amateurs and "trade" licenses, i.e., semi-professional) and this gives information about the numbers of cyclists who expected to race in formal competition as compared with those who rode for recreational and utility purposes. Expressed as a proportion of the total 1897 N.C.U. membership, license holders here made up less than 1 percent of the membership.[28] Another list of licenses

1898	
Total number of clubs in London	256
Total membership in London clubs	20,597
Average membership of London clubs	80.5
Total number of clubs in England, outside London	1,118
Total number of clubs in England, including London	1,374
Clubs in Wales	44
Clubs in Channel Islands, Isles of Man and Wight	4
Clubs in Scotland	250
Clubs in Ireland	144
Clubs not responding, or doubtful	No data
Total number of clubs in Great Britain	1,816
Average membership of 71.0 per club	128,936

[Table 9 B. Membership of British cycling clubs in 1898. Data compiled from Henry Sturmey, The Cyclist Year Book for 1899.]

issued in England and Wales in 1894 (Scotland is excluded) shows a similar total of 2,682 licenses (amateur: 2,207, "trade": 416, and professional: 59).[29] These deliberations further emphasize the difficulty of knowing with any degree of precision the proportion of active riders who actually raced in formal competition.

In 1892, the Cyclists' Touring Club advertised itself as "the largest athletic or quasi-athletic institution in the world! It is international in its character, and possesses over 20,000 members, which number is daily increasing."[30] The C.T.C. appointed Consuls abroad, as well as in all the British counties, thus recognizing the international aspects of bicycle touring and facilitating foreign touring rides by C.T.C. members. In 1899, the first Congress of the International League of Touring Associations was held in London in honor of the

	Total clubs affiliated	Membership paid	Class A licences (amateur)	Class B licences (semi-pro)	New clubs affiliated
London	173	6,725	725	48	29
Bristol	71	2,539	98	37	17
Birmingham	65	2,375	Not given	Not given	12
Liverpool	53	2,250	131	15	7
W. Riding Yorks	57	1,925	123	14	7
Manchester	61	1,875	195	23	5
Newcastle	70	1,864	97	10	4
N. Yorks	42	1,562	74	1	12
Southampton	37	1,608	126	27	3
N. Lancashire	36	1,425	125	26	10
E. Counties	37	1,090	87	19	11
E. Riding Yorks	25	1,050	68	8	7
Devon/Cornwall	30	1,029	36	12	Not given
S. Yorks	29	925	75	7	5
Northampton	32	875	141	23	13
Sussex	20	780	49	17	5
S. Wales	14	625	94	14	2
Leicester	20	550	28	5	4
Oxford/Berks	13	325	39	9	4
Nottingham	Not given	Not given	Not given	Not given	Not given
	885 clubs	31,397 Total paid	2,311	315	157

[Table 9 C. Membership in the National Cyclists' Union in March 1897, from *N.C.U. Review and Official Record*, March 1897.]

21st birthday of the C.T.C., founded in 1878. The League included 17 touring associations from 14 different countries.[31] Table 9 D illustrates the growth of the C.T.C. from its foundation in 1878 until 1898, and highlights the "truly phenomenal increase" which occurred during the bicycle boom years following 1894–5.[32]

In giving these various membership statistics, it should once again be emphasized that we do not have figures for active cyclists who were members neither of a local club nor of the N.C.U. or C.T.C., who rode primarily either for recreational or utility purposes and were content to be among "the unattached."

The League of American Wheelmen, the American national organization, also grew quickly. "I consider the act of joining the League of American Wheelmen one of the very first duties which every cycler in this country owes his fellows," wrote Karl Kron in 1887.[33] Founded in 1880, it had 527 members by the end of that year, and its subsequent growth is shown in Table 9 E, on page 305. It should be noticed here that the substantial fall in membership after 1898/99 obviously indicated a decline in interest in becoming a member of a cycling organization, but should not be taken as conclusive evidence of a decline in the numbers of recreational cyclists actually on the roads.

Mason notes that membership figures for the L.A.W. were "not an accurate measure of the strength of the League because they tend to underestimate its … power. There were several million bicycle riders in the United States in the 1890s and early 1900s who, for one reason or another, never joined the League." He goes on to argue that competition from the automobile was not a major cause of the decline of the League, for "membership in the

Year	Renewals	New members	Total paid
1878	—	144	144
1879	144	692	836
1880	616	2,740	3,356
1881	1,821	1,976	3,797
1882	2,676	4,029	6,705
1883	4,384	6,243	10,627
1884	8,134	8,491	16,625
1885	12,456	7,929	20,385
1886	15,099	7,217	22,316
1887	16,057	5,904	21,961
1888	15,881	6,103	21,984
1889	15,594	5,771	21,365
1890	15,074	5,357	20,431
1891	14,566	4,718	19,284
1892	13,058	4,263	17,321
1893	12,946	3,646	16,592
1894	10,897	3,269	14,166
1895	10,461	5,882	16,343
1896	13,312	21,343	34,655
1897	25,390	19,101	44,491
1898	33,128	21,208	54,336
1899	41,053	17,659	58,712

[Table 9 D. Annual membership in the Cyclists' Touring Club from its foundation in 1878 to 1899. Sources: C.T.C. Monthly Gazette, Sept. 1899 and Henry Sturmey, The Cyclists' Indispensable Handbook and Year Book for 1899]

Year	Total paid membership
1880	520
1881	1,654
1882	2,500
1883	2,131
1884	4,250
1885 (Dec.)	5,176
1886 (Dec.)	10,264
1887 (Dec.)	11,939
1888	11,948
1889 (April)	12,193
1890 (April)	12,703
1891 (Feb.)	18,504
1892	
1893	36,320
1895	38,477
1896	43,799
1897	102,636
1898	102,142
1899	75,045
1900	24,142
1905	"less than 3,000"

[Table 9 E. Annual membership of the League of American Wheelmen from 1880 to 1900. Source: Abbott Bassett (Secretary of the L.A.W.), "League of American Wheelmen—Items from Its History," in Luther H. Porter, Wheels and Wheeling (Wheelman Company, Boston, 1892)]

wheelmen's organization had declined considerably before the automobile received widespread public acceptance."[34] Once again, it can be inferred that the dramatic fall in membership after 1898, although giving strong evidence of a substantial decline in interest in recreational cycling, does not necessarily prove that a similar decline also occurred in utility cycling, for which appropriate figures are much harder to find.

These British and American organizations were not alone. France, Belgium, Holland, Germany, Italy, Canada and Australia also saw a similar growth and later decline of membership in cycling clubs. An exception was France, where growth in membership appears to have been consistently upwards. Since French clubs were obligated by law to register their existence with local municipal authorities, the statistics given in Alex Poyer's recent book appear to be solid. He gives the number of cycling clubs in France in 1880–82 as 52, in 1887–97, in 1891–308, in 1895–1390 and in 1909– 1834.[35] Obviously, "the unattached" were also present in large numbers in France too, and there was a distinct historical rift between "speed" and touring cyclists.[36]

* * *

All these umbrella social organizations, the huge National Cyclists' Union, the Cyclists' Touring Club, the League of American Wheelmen, the Union Vélocipédique de France, and also the diverse range of larger and smaller local clubs, shared certain aspects in common.

Their primary reason for existence centered on the possibilities of the bicycle, the speed and distance that could be achieved on it, the mobility it provided, the social interactions it cemented, the adventure, escape, release or education it mediated, the leisure and recreational time that it dominated and the political and organizational work which needed to be carried out, for instance in the Good Roads movement.

Obviously the existence of so many cycling clubs demonstrated a wide interest in cycling, but not only as a competitive sport. Indeed, those groups devoted to racing, and the proportion of the total membership of the National Cyclists' Union who raced, were certainly in a minority. Cycling clubs were a potent and popular means of organizing and giving focus to the leisure time and activities of a diverse range of special-interest social groups.

"Club Life of Today," an article published in *Cycling* at the end of 1901, attributed changes in the pattern of club activities to "the introduction of the safety, and especially of the lady's pattern; the restrictions in regard to road racing and a commendable effort to make the fixture lists more varied and enjoyable in character." The writer of the article emphasized the diverse athletic and social activities organized by different kinds of clubs:

> Many clubs have so widened their scope with the introduction of a more varied programme and the admission of lady members, that they have succeeded in retaining their old members and securing many new ones. I emphasize the social side because it may be thought that clubs exist solely for the fast rider whose only ambition is to "snork" club medals and "sew up" all other roads users.

A prospective club member "should join that particular club which caters for his tastes. It is as unsatisfactory for the "potterer" to join a club devoted to "speed runs" as it would be unwise for the "speedman" to join a "mixed" club, composed of both sexes and having a varied programme." Many clubs were purely social and undertook no hard riding whatsoever, "devoting attention solely, in the summer months, to ordinary club runs, picnics, river parties, etc., and during winter to dances, card parties, and of course to the new craze of today, Ping-pong."[37]

In the wider discussion of bicycle usage and club membership at the turn of the century, the problem of "the unattached" remains. The article discussed above does not mention cyclists who preferred to remain outside any organization, and simply ride by themselves, or with their friends, for pleasure or utility. From the perspective of those within the club community, these were "the unattached."

Thus we do have various useful sources of data about formal competition and club membership, as well as partial glimpses of utility usage. But the overall late 19th century picture of bicycle usage in competition, recreation and utility transportation remains complex and imprecisely measured. It has to be assumed that membership in cycling clubs was much smaller than the total numbers of cyclists on the roads, and that decline of membership in predominantly sporting and recreational organizations should not necessarily be taken as offering evidence about the status of utility cycling.

What we can say for certain is that outside the cycling club fraternity was a large group of anonymous cyclists frequently referred to as "the unattached," people whose numbers and identity we now know very little about except when they appear in fiction, in memoirs or photographs of the period, and among whom could be found the growing numbers of utility users.[38]

"The unattached" were a significant group of users, but essentially unknown in number. Was the female cyclist photographed in Fig. 9.5, on page 295, a club member? We just have no way of knowing.[39]

Epilogue

1. A Period of Intensive Technological Change and Sport Development

> "Few historians have noticed that modern sport has characteristics that are distinctive and that modern sport has its origins in precisely those social circumstances that fostered rationalized industrial production. For a while, industrial production and modern sport were uniquely regnant in England and both, subsequently, have spread over much of the world."
> —Richard Mandell, *Sport—A Cultural History* (1984)

THE STATEMENT ABOVE underlines the broad aspects of the character of the social, technological and sporting changes described in the book, which characterized the transformation of cycle sport from its beginnings in the late 1860s. What, then, are some of the conclusions which can be outlined?

Essentially, the story that has been told here is of the relationships between the sport, its social institutions and the bicycle industry. The book did not intend to be an economic history of the bicycle or of the bicycle industry, but it did set out to document the history of the sport in primary source material, and to set the sport in its wider social and economic settings. It has analyzed the relationship between the sport and the evolving bicycle, and the extent to which the sport contributed to bicycle design, and concluded that the influence of the sport was considerable.

The book has described how the velocipede "craze," which originated as a gymnastic entertainment, developed in the 1870s and 1880s into the serious, dangerous high-wheel sport contested by gentleman amateurs and tough professionals, and thereafter with the arrival of the "safety" bicycle and the pneumatic tire expanded as a competitive sport and also became a much wider recreational and utilitarian social activity. It has argued that the needs of the sport had a profound and continuous influence on the evolving designs of bicycles throughout the period.

Above all, the sport of cycling was enmeshed with and co-dependent upon the bicycle industry, which made the sport possible by creating its essential tool and also benefited from the sport by virtue of a continuous testing and experimenting process. However, this relationship of inter-dependence was often an uneasy one.

The commercial purposes and interests of manufacturers were not the same as the individuals within the governing bodies of the sport who preferred to espouse and protect amateur ideals, and the struggle between amateurism and professionalism was a characteristic and constant tension within the sport during the whole of the period.

The three modes of cycling—competition, recreation and utility—were inherent in cycling from the very earliest velocipeding activity. Within formal competitive sport, firstly, there was racing on road and track which this history has focused on particularly. Secondly, there was cycling as leisure and recreation providing physical exercise and certainly involving athletic ability. This recreational aspect merged into a third mode, cycling as a utilitarian activity.

The compulsion to go faster (competition), to explore unknown places (tourism), to develop better machines (technological ingenuity), to associate with others in competition and club life, to use the machine simply to go from here to there (utility), were all characteristics of the bicycle movement. The three modes were integral to the bicycle's broad-based social impact, and contributed to the varied "relevant social groups" which impacted its development.

However, in historical terms, the three categories are not easy to sharply differentiate. The word "sport" was not understood by the public to refer exclusively to competitive bicycle racing. Those who joined a club and rode for recreation and pleasure also saw themselves as participating in "sport."

Within cycling, tension existed between the racer and recreational and touring cyclists—a difference which became institutionalized in the different aims of the two British national organizations, the National Cyclists' Union and the Cyclists' Touring Club, and in the squabbles within the League of American Wheelmen. A similar rift emerged between the two French organizations, the Union Vélocipédique de France (formed in 1880, primarily interested in racing) and the Touring-Club de France (formed in 1890 to promote touring).[1] Paul de Vivie ("Velocio"), an ardent proponent of equipment innovations for touring, wrote in *Le Cycliste* that: "Sport and touring are not made to go together; they must follow parallel paths each with its own guides and chiefs."[2]

A significant demonstration of this tension was the opposition

Fig. Epilogue 1. High-wheel champion H.L. Cortis (here held by M.D. Rucker), riding a 59" bicycle on which he was the first to ride 20 miles in an hour in 1882, represented the acme of speed and power in the early 1880s. [Source: author's collection]

in Britain from the National Cyclists' Union and much of the cycling press to group road-racing in the late 1880s and early 1890s because of the widespread conviction that "scorching" by racing clubs on the public roads brought the general body of cyclists into disrepute. For many slower riders, racing and racing cyclists, who were referred to disparagingly as "scorchers," were anathema.[3] "We cannot too greatly emphasize the statement that records, the achievement of which has corrupted the whole tone of cycling as a sport, prove absolutely nothing," wrote Lacy Hillier, criticizing consumers who paid attention to manufacturer's claims for their machines based on speed records.[4]

It can be concluded that, throughout the 1880s and 1890s, the minority of racing cyclists were regarded as a somewhat undesirable fringe by the much larger numbers of more conventional club, touring and utility cyclists.

* * *

Quest for Speed has concentrated quite heavily on the British developments and explored the global impact of the British sport and industry between about 1868/9 and 1903. The United States was initially heavily influenced by these British developments, although an energetic American industry and sport was soon established which quickly became one of Britain's principal rivals. Taking account of the history of cycling in France has been more problematic, for French sources, especially in the early part of the period (1870–85), have been difficult to access and inadequately explored to date, and French sport historians have paid surprisingly little detailed attention to the early history of France's national sport—the period covered by this book.[5] The study of French sources for the 1880s and 1890s remains this writer's unfinished business.

In general, the relationship between Britain and France was of two neighbouring countries closely linked technologically, but pursuing independent directions in the organizational and social structuring of cycling as a sport. This relationship has been touched upon at many points in the narrative although it has not been a primary focus. The detailed international history of cycling as a sport in Italy, Spain, Belgium, Holland, Germany, Switzerland, Eastern Europe, Russia, Australia and South America has also in general been outside the scope of this book.

* * *

Quest for Speed has attempted to outline and examine the processes of social and technological change within the new sport and industry of cycling. The character and repercussions of the profound historical changes which occurred over the thirty-five year period examined here can be summarized as follows:

☐ First, cycling in its technical and social aspects represented a radical transformation, a new sport and recreation, with economic, organizational and social repercussions which led to profound changes in personal mobility, patterns of transportation, and in transportation and industrial technology. Cycling preceded and enabled the motorcycle, automobile and aviation industries. The developments in bicycle technology and cycle sport in the last thirty years of the 19th century should be recognized as part of a sporting and transportation continuum which led to the development of the motorcycle, the automobile and the airplane.

☐ Second, cycling was a radical change because it was an alternative to the horse for individual transportation over both short and long distances, and was independent, i.e., driven by human muscle-power, of other forms of transportation, the horse and carriage or the railway, and cheaper. Bicycle racing was about human-powered speed. In the 1880s there were frequent, well-publicized contests between bicycles and race-horses, to prove which was faster under a variety of circumstances. As bicycle speeds increased, the case was proven, and such contests gradually lost their interest.

☐ Third, the sport as it grew globally produced thousands of local clubs, national institutions and international bodies, including the first world governing body, the International Cyclists' Association, established in 1892. This growth was accompanied by an enormous expansion of the specialized cycling press, especially in Britain and France, catering both to the sport and the industry. This was the most prolific and heavily subscribed specialist press in any subject, and laid the foundations of subsequent specialized journalism in other sports.

☐ Fourth, the development of the sport and the new machine constituted a novelty in patterns of recreation and leisure. A minority engaged in formal competition. Either individually, or as members of clubs, cyclists ventured out of the crowded cities in a kind of sensual and athletic escapism. The bicycle redefined patterns of leisure and travel. Even for the majority of non-competitors, riding was an activity with a real sense of athletic challenge. "Sport" was not confined to competition.

☐ Fifth, there was an intense evolution within the sport as styles of machine evolved and as competition became more formalized and more specialized. Various styles of road and track racing evolved. Records were kept, styles and varieties of racing were experimented with, refined and organized. A similar progression occurred in other sports. The striking differences in cycling, with its heavily technology-dependent character, were that bicycles underwent profound design experimentation and speeds increased dramatically. They were also increasingly used for utilitarian purposes.

☐ Sixth, there was a prolonged struggle within cycling institutions (as within other sports), on behalf of ideological amateurism (love of sport for its own sake), which sought to keep money out of sport and to promote the idea that "true sport" had to be purged of the corrosive moral effects of advertising and competing for money. This was, in effect, a struggle between amateur ideals and the pragmatic interests of the bicycle industry and other sponsors. In England there was opposition to racing bicycles on public roads, whereas in France it was encouraged, and in the United States briefly tolerated. The promotion of track racing took the racing from contested public space into a private arena around whose perimeter a paying audience could be accommodated. Thus, in the developed cycling sport of the world cultural capitals of the 1890s—London, Paris, Berlin, Copenhagen, Brussels, New York, Boston and Chicago—the emergence of a modern professional spectator-sport can be seen, arguably the most developed flowering of a professional sport in the late–19th century.

☐ Seventh, as various recent studies of the social history of sport have argued, all these aspects of cycling as a new sport were related to a revolution in the economic well-being and purchasing capacity of an emerging urban middle-class, as well as new habits of work and leisure and expectations of recreation and pleasure. This is not to say that the upper class or the industrial proletariat did not participate, but that the majority of cycling enthusiasts came from this stratum.

☐ Eighth, all bicycles, whether used for competition or recreation, were also utility vehicles in enabling people to get from place to place.

☐ Lastly, what was crucially distinctive about the sport and recreation of cycling was the extent of its embeddedness in a massive manufacturing infrastructure—the bicycle industry. In no other late 19th century sport did technology and equipment play such a significant role. It is this relationship—in all its social and economic complexity—which this book has examined and sought to understand. It has been argued here that the sport had a profound influence on the industry, and deeply affected evolving bicycle design, throughout the period under examination.

* * *

The themes are by now familiar to the reader: the rise of the first velocipede races from a circus-like professional entertainment context; the rapid acceptance of the young, amateur sport into a club-based popularity; the three-mode nature of cycling as competition, recreation and utility; the links between the sport and the fast-growing industry; the popularity of the sport across class boundaries; the heavy involvement of the press; the increasing commercialization of racing; the creation of a new class of professional bicycle racing stars.

These have been the historical and social themes presented in *Quest for Speed*. Cycling shared many characteristics with other expanding sports of the last thirty years of the 19th century—its clubability, the formation of governing bodies with sets of rules, the organization of formal competitive structures and a system of championships and records, and

Fig. Epilogue 2. A well-designed, banked, wooden track in Paris in the mid–1890s, allowed a large crowd of spectators to watch fast, exciting bicycle racing. [Source: author's collection]

its growth as a mass-spectator sport in the 1880s and 1890s. "There is no doubt," writes Tranter, "that the period between the mid-nineteenth century and the outbreak of the First World War was characterized by a notable transformation in the scale and nature of Britain's sporting culture."[6]

Contemporary participants, looking back to the 1870s from the vantage point of the end of the century, documented an intense process of sporting, technological and transportational change which had occurred with the bicycle as its agent. Towards the end of the period covered by this book, this evolution was described as having been rapid and extraordinary. 1870 was seen as close chronologically, but distant in terms of the changes that had occurred. It was a past of primitive beginnings which could only be compared unfavorably with the present. The present was confident, full of technological mastery. Lacy Hillier, a dominant personality in this history, referred to the past as "the Dark Ages of Cycling."[7]

The bicycle industry had been built from the ground up, from blacksmith-shop beginnings, in about thirty years. By the late 1890s, bicycle technology was seen as so advanced that it was hard to even imagine what future improvements might consist of: "perfection" had been achieved.[8] The sport had been transformed, from the heavy metal-tired "boneshaker" of the very early sport, to the solid tired high-bicycle of the early 1880s raced on a dirt or gravel track, to the pneumatic-tired safety bicycle raced at tremendous speeds on a purpose-built, paved and banked velodrome, in front of thousands of paying spectators.

Motor-paced speeds of about 50 mph were maintained for long periods. In 1903, western Europe and the United States stood on the edge of a revolution in motorized personal transportation; aviation was just beginning. The bicycle industry had been essential in providing the technological advances and skills necessary for this next wave of mechanized mobility.

2. Reviewing the Dynamics of Social and Technological Change

A. Agents of change within the sport and industry

Conclusions about the dynamics of historical change in the period have been formed here from the wide-ranging original source material. They have also been informed by the biographies of contemporary participants who had first-hand experience of the sport and business of cycling and were themselves active in the process of historical change. In thinking about the "relevant social groups" which played their part in affecting the history of the period, it is evident that certain leading personalities can in effect be considered as representatives of those "relevant social groups," and particularly significant for that reason.

Many of these actors had carved out specialized, contemporary careers for themselves in the emerging sport and industry of cycling, with competition, manufacturing, marketing and journalism as key professions. Some, such as for example Keith-Falconer (amateur racer), John Keen (professional racer), George Lacy Hillier (amateur racer, journalist, editor, official), Harry Etherington (journalist, promoter, publisher), Henry Sturmey (journalist, editor), A.J. Wilson (journalist) and H.O. Duncan (professional racer, publicist, promoter), whose activities have been examined here, had defined new kinds of careers in sport. Their sport had become their business. As bicycle racers, they had started their involvement with cycling in their early teens and twenties, had ridden the high-wheel bicycle for about ten years or so, and were still only in their forties or fifties when our period closes. Other participants were non-specialist observers, journalists writing for leading newspapers and magazines. Many employees in the sport and industry of cycling changed gear in their careers around the turn of the century to work in the burgeoning motorcycle and automobile industries, which grew alongside the bicycle industry from about 1895 onwards. For engineers, mechanics and journalists, the transition was a logical and convenient one.[9]

The career of one participant, George Lacy Hillier, has been examined in depth here. Hillier was involved with almost every aspect of cycling, as high-wheel racer and championship winner, as journalist and editor, and as N.C.U. and club committee-man. He was a frequent judge at race meetings, a stock broker in the City of London and an international sports politician; he was an argumentative and passionate proponent of amateurism. Hillier wrote throughout the period, and his *Cycling*, written for the Badminton Library of Sports and Pastimes, is the most important work in English on the 19th century sport. *Cycling* was first published in 1887, and by 1896 had reached a 5th edition. In his 1887 Introduction, Hillier asserted that there was no sport "which has developed more rapidly in the last few years than cycling, nor is there any which has assumed a more assured position in popular favour."[10] By 1896, Hillier noted that his current historical chapter had been "carefully corrected and condensed" because the sport was "growing with such rapidity and spreading so widely." Since 1887, he wrote, "the Ordinary Bicycle has practically disappeared, and the Safety Bicycle reigns in its stead."[11] He thought that change was accelerating within the sport:

> A rapidly developing sport like cycling never stands still, its advance is constant; the records of today are but the average performances of tomorrow. Development follows development, existing standards are swept away, and others are erected in their place.... Machines are being invented, developed, remodeled, day by day; the apparently perfect contrivance is but the crude germ of some startling development.[12]

B. The spectacular growth of the bicycle industry and the class penetration of cycling

In the opinion of journalist and industry insider, Harry Hewitt Griffin, writing in 1892, cycling had made more spectacular progress than any other emerging sport. "The rise, development, and progress of cycling form one of the most interesting chapters in the history of British sport," he wrote; "In the annals of recreative pursuits there is no instance of a new pastime taking so quick and permanent a hold upon the people.... Great as has been the advance in athletics, and sports of every kind, cycling has beaten the field in the race for popularity."[13]

The "vast increase" of the bicycle trade, wrote Griffin elsewhere, "is almost unparalleled in British commerce." Griffin understood that the mid–1890s sport and industry was directly related to and had grown out of the earlier high-wheel sport:

> a restricted and rather dangerous sport has, thanks to the development of the safety, and the introduction of the pneumatic tyre, become the most widely followed and popular pastime in the world, and

added another to the industries of Great Britain, employing tens of thousands, and giving health, pleasure, and excitement to tens of hundreds of thousands: the 5,000,000 or thereabouts cyclists in the world.[14]

Significantly, in 1896, Griffin (like Sturmey in the 1899 *Handbook* discussed in Chapter Nine), chose not to mention practical utility as one of the primary achievements of the bicycle, referring only to "the most widely followed and popular pastime in the world."

In the Preface to the 4th edition of his *Cycles and Cycling*, published in 1903, Griffin did report the greatly increased social penetration of the bicycle, noting particularly the reduction of the price of popular models to about £10, even though he still did not emphasize utility cycling. "Cycling is everyone's pastime," he wrote, "Every rank in the social scale uses the cycle." Griffin estimated that there were about 1,200,000 cyclists in Britain, riding machines worth about £15 million; invested capital in the bicycle industry was at least £30 million; annual expenditure on bicycles and related items was between £15 and £20 million.

The comments from Griffin and Hillier came from two significant participants in British cycling who earned part of their livings as journalists. Other journalists, writing in the boom times of the 1890s, also expressed surprise at the wide-ranging social impact of the bicycle. An editorial in *The Times* in 1897 commented on "the extraordinary development of interest in all forms of athletic sports," including cycling, and noted particularly the crucial role that the press played in disseminating the enthusiasm among the middle-classes:

> Not only at the public schools and Universities and among the leisured classes generally, but in every stratum of middle-class society, cricket and football are among the most absorbing interests of life; while cycling matches, foot-racing, and other forms of athleticism count their devotees by hundreds of thousands. The growth of the newspaper press helps to stimulate and spread such interest ... every one reads a daily paper, every one can be familiar with the names and the doings of the heroes of sport.[15]

The expansion of sport into "every stratum of middle-class society" was especially remarked here. Class has been particularly considered here as an aspect of cycling, and once again it should be emphasized that although cycling had its educated, upper-middle-class bastions in the 1880s in London, Oxford and Cambridge and in Boston, Chicago and New York clubs, and the exclusionary class definitions of amateurism were at first applied, cycling was a sport which was easily entered by those further down the social scale, in fact appealed to all classes. The point is made by J.A. Mangan in a new book, that "the English middleclass was to be found in the vanguard of the Victorian and Edwardian "sports revolution" which in time had such extraordinary global consequences..." And a revolution was precisely what it was. It was wholly unlike anything that preceded it: "sport, in its modern, organized, commercialized and extensive form, was truly an "invention" of the Victorian and Edwardian age."[16]

C. Global expansion

These technological advances and the recreational revolution also occurred in the United States. In the developed world, cycling had become universal. The years 1894–98 were a period of an international bicycle boom, both in the industry and the sport. The *New York Tribune* quoted League of American Wheelmen Racing Board Chairman Mott as saying in an annual report that "there is no class of games, entertainment, recreation or sport in the civilized world that flourishes to the extent of that furnished by the wise, fostering care of the National Assembly of the Leagues of American Wheelmen." There had been "a wonderful growth of bicycle racing," which had become "the greatest and most popular of outdoor sports"; cycle racing had "reached a new era," and America "had become the Mecca of the cycle champions of the world."[17]

Mott gave the following statistics concerning the American sport: 8 million spectators had paid $3,600,000 to attend 2,912 bicycle race meetings in 1897; 17,316 individual races had been held, competed in by 9,000 cyclists who had won prizes totaling $1,645,020, and promoters had profited to the tune of $1,089,180. A year later, in a similar annual report, Mott reported that there were 621 professional cyclists in the United States, and that "20,000 wheelmen engaged in racing either as professionals or amateurs." Bicycle racing had "been a financial success for both promoters and racing men."[18]

From the bicycle factories of Coventry and Birmingham in England and St. Etienne in France, and the hundreds of clubs in those two countries, the sport and recreation of cycling was disseminated into the countries of the British Empire and into the technologically developed countries of Europe—Germany, Holland, Belgium, Denmark, Czechoslovakia. The American industry, centered in Chicago, Milwaukee, Cleveland, Indianapolis and other cities also exported its products and competed in Europe. "Sport had become extensively institutionalized, codified and commercialized," writes Tranter, "and had spread beyond a purely local or regional arena into national and even international competition."[19]

LES SPORTS. — STAYERS ET LEURS ENTRAINEURS
JEACK, *Stayer Suisse, entraîné par* ANDRE

Fig. Epilogue 3. In an extremely dangerous, but wildly popular, sport, the speeds of record-breaking cyclists were pushed up and up by powerful pacing machines. [Source: author's collection]

D. Speed and modernity

An essential element of cycling was speed. In 1892, cycling journalist Harry Griffin wrote:

> In this high-pressure age, speed in some form or another is the magnet which draws the attention of everyone ... the man, or machine, capable of doing the greatest amount of work in the shortest time is the most successful; even our pleasures must be supped swiftly. Cycling being the fastest form of competition, it draws in its train an army of admirers. The development of speed-rates forms the most interesting chapter in the history of cycling, as it marks the endless onward march of improvement in construction of cycles.

The lure of speed in the later 1890s, a sometimes fatal attraction in the case of motor-pacing experts, has been described in Chapter Eight. Speed and distance records were made only to be broken. This rapid pace of technological change also caused Griffin to question whether the constant breaking of cycling records necessarily meant that the quality of the current competitors was superior. Records were accurately timed and measured, he wrote, but:

> the ever-changing conditions prevent the progressive pace of cycle records from marking a commensurate improvement on the part of the riders. Cycles, tyres, and tracks are all getting faster and faster; and it is very doubtful whether the flyers of today are any better—as men—than those of long ago.[20]

Were riders who broke current records really better as athletes? Or was it simply that machines, facilities and track surfaces were better? The posing of the question was an indication of a modern, analytical approach towards sport, in which all aspects of performance were taken into consideration, especially the hardware.

The question is a legitimate one. Bicycle racing was a sport which was particularly influenced by extra-athletic technological factors—bicycle design, road or track conditions, and whether a race was paced or unpaced. Griffin's questions about the athletic quality of cyclists correctly recognized the impact that better bicycles, improved track surfaces, specialized training methods, increased professionalization and the large salaries of the top riders sponsored by the industry, had had on the sport by the end of the 1890s. Improving technology was harnessed in the service of increasingly specialized and highly trained athletes. Human athletic potential expressed through the agency of the evolving machine, and better facilities within which competition took place, were the two crucial elements which characterized the sport of cycling in the last quarter of the 19th century.[21] The pressure to excel also led to an increasingly scientific approach to training and diet, and also to early experiments with stimulants and doping, a complex subject which is outside the scope of *Quest for Speed*.

Table Epilogue A, showing world record times for specific distances on the track at five dates indicated (with speeds in mph). Many of these records were either human- or motor-paced. [Source: H.H. Griffin, *Cycles and Cycling*, 1903].

	1 mile	**50 miles**	**100 miles**
1880	2m $46\frac{2}{5}$s [21.63 mph]	2h 51m 35s [17.48 mph]	6h 37m 51s [15.08 mph]
1890	2m $20\frac{3}{5}$s [25.60 mph]	2h 25m $26\frac{2}{5}$s [20.63 mph]	5h 50m $5\frac{3}{5}$s [17.14 mph]
1893	1m $55\frac{3}{5}$s [31.14 mph]	2h 11m $6\frac{4}{5}$s [22.88 mph]	4h 29m $39\frac{1}{5}$s [22.25 mph]
1897	1m $35\frac{2}{5}$s [37.74 mph]	1h 34m $45\frac{4}{5}$s [31.66 mph]	3h 25m $21\frac{4}{5}$s [29.22 mph]
1903	1m $14\frac{4}{5}$s [48.13 mph]	1h 6m $42\frac{1}{5}$s [44.98 mph]	2h 33m $40\frac{4}{5}$s [39.04 mph]

It was this rationalized and technologized quality of the sport which allows us now to define it as a truly "modern" sport. These were ideas advanced by soci-

Fig. Epilogue 4. Sport begins with the spirit of play, and this German boys' club overcame supply problems with the ingenuity of their own hands. [Source: *Sport-Album der Radwelt*]

ologist Max Weber (1864–1920), whose life coincided with the rise of cycling. For Weber, "modernity" consisted of increasing specialization, increasing social division of labor, quantification, and in his special sense of the term, rationalization. Weber also discussed the relationship between man and the machine and the forces of mass-production, a relationship which was highlighted for spectators in the dramatic speed of bicycle competitions on the tracks of London, Paris, Berlin and New York in the 1890s, and in the grueling endurance of bicycle racing on the roads of Europe.[22]

Writing again in 1896 as an industry insider, Griffin identified the changes which had occurred in the sport of cycling as an expression of technological modernity, of scientific and industrial progress. "To compare racing of today with that of 1876 would be to compare modern warfare with the battles between the ancient Britons and the Danes," he wrote: "In the early stages of both, man had to do the work, science was almost

Table Epilogue B, showing world record distances covered within specific times on the track at five dates indicated (with speeds in mph). Many of these records were either human- or motor-paced. [Source: H.H. Griffin, *Cycles and Cycling*, 1903]

	1 hour	6 hours	24 hours
1880	19mi 1420yds [19.81 mph]	100 miles [16.67 mph]	218 miles [9.08 mph]
1890	22mi 620yds [22.35 mph]	100 miles [16.67 mph]	323 miles [13.46 mph]
1893	26mi 107yds [26.06 mph]	126mi 1560yds [21.15 mph]	426mi 440yds [17.76 mph]
1897	32mi 1086yds [32.62 mph]	165mi 1300yds [27.62 mph]	616mi 340yds [25.67 mph]
1903	48mi 862yds [48.49 mph]	222mi 1410yds [37.13 mph]	634mi 774yds [26.43 mph]

unknown." But today, "the bicycle racer has his low machine, high geared, air-bound wheels, cemented and banked tracks which have, combined, almost doubled the speed possibilities of a score of years ago."[23]

In his Preface to *Cycles and Cycling*, published in 1903, Griffin emphasized the "astounding" speed of bicycles, which "has developed in a wonderful manner—perfectly unbelievable a few years ago. No other sport in the world can show such marvellous progress."[24] To prove his point, Griffin published a chart showing world record speeds on the track for the years 1880, 1890, 1893, 1897 and 1903, which is included here as Tables Epilogue A and B, on pages 318–319. Particularly notable are the increases in average speeds: for the 1 mile distance from 21.63 mph in 1880 to 48.13 mph in 1903; for the 1 hour from 19.81 mph in 1880 to 48.49 mph in 1903; for the 24-hour distance from 9.08 mph in 1880 to 26.43 mph in 1903.

Significantly for an understanding of the technological nature of these athletic records, the most recent (1897 and 1903) of the increases in speeds and distances were achieved not by cyclists riding alone but with the assistance of pacing, which by 1903 had become routine, efficient and technically complex.[25]

By 1903, 634 miles had been covered in 24 hours by a rider behind motor-pace. Cyclist and machine worked together to go faster and farther than man had ever traveled before with his own muscle power. The desire to break records in cycling stimulated the production of larger and faster pacing-machines using powerful gasoline engines.

Pacing-machines were specialized racing motorcycles, and their progressively more powerful engines contributed to the development of automobile and aviation engine technology.

For spectators, the sight of the human athlete "glued" to the rear wheel of a noisy and smelly petrol-driven pacing-machine careening around a cement track at 60 mph had became, by the

Fig. Epilogue 5. The racing cyclist was depicted here, in 1891, as the epitome of modern speed, surrounded by other manifestations of modernity—the train, the steam yacht, the galloping horse, the skuller. [Source: *Cycling*, 5 Dec. 1891]

early 1900s, a potent symbol of the interconnectedness of sport and technology in modern life, and of the interest in speed and mechanical power which was characteristic of the 1890s.

3. Sport as Moral/Physical Crusade and Sport as Business

Much has been made here of the moral crusade of amateurism—the desire to keep sport free of the perceived degrading effect of money. This was a driving impulse of the relationship between the sport and the industry. The moral dimension of sport history in this respect differentiates it from the quantitative evaluations of economic history.

A book by the journalists R.J. Mecredy and A.J. Wilson, which went through several editions in the 1890s, held that cycling should be viewed as both "an art and a pastime." Its opening chapter, entitled "The Pleasures and Advantages of Cycling," proposed a wide definition of sport, based on the moral and practical virtues of health, strength and general physical well-being, with "the enjoyment of rapid locomotion" and contact with "the beauties of Nature" as additional attractions:

> The pleasures of cycling are so manifest that we hardly know where to begin. To be weak is miserable.... Cycling braces up the frame, and makes it strong, hardy and enduring. The rider rejoices in his strength, and exalts in the robust health which enables him to drive the revolving wheel with steady, sure, and unfailing strokes.... The faculty for enjoying rapid locomotion is one which is implanted in the human breast from earliest childhood, and the fact of one's unaided efforts being the active cause of this locomotion enhances the pleasure derived from it. But these pleasures, though keen in themselves, are subordinate to the concomitant ones derived from the use of the cycle as a vehicle to convey one from place to place for the purpose of beholding what is best and fairest in Nature...[26]

Fig. Epilogue 6. Looking to the future. Speed, power and relaxation on the bicycle are epitomized in this 1950 photo of Ferdi Kubler, the year he won the Tour de France. [Source: *Miroir-Sprint*, 8 Aug. 1950]

Sport, defined in this wider sense, was not restricted to the specialized athleticism of maximum speed or endurance, but was about strength, robust health, "keen, exquisite pleasure," and travel and discovery in Nature, ideals closely linked with the moral values held by proponents of amateurism.

Only for the minority of top amateur specialists and professional cyclists, therefore, was cycling about the compulsion to win races, the application of scientific training, tactical finesse and the strongest/lightest possible machine. In Chapter Eight we saw how the top levels of professional cyclists were pushed into the public eye and used for commercial advertising purposes in the 1890s. In the most intense marketing of mostly sport-related products ever undertaken up until that time, professional cyclists in the 1890s were used to advertise cycling and other products to the consuming public. In a strikingly prescient creation of the present-day commercial and social dynamics, the leading performers set "star" athletic standards.

The story of one professional star, Arthur Zimmerman, was told in Chapter Seven. By the end of the century, bicycle racing at its highest levels had become a truly "modern" spectator sport, with stars elevated to a heroic status and their athletic achievements challenged only by other dedicated professionals.

But thousands of amateur, recreational participants enjoyed the sport on a less demanding level as a test of their own, perhaps more humble, athletic abilities.

Chapter Notes

INTRODUCTION

1. Should the word "Britain" or "England" be used? "Britain" includes England, Scotland, Wales and Northern Ireland, and therefore any use of the term "Britain" or "British" implies the inclusion of all four countries. Nevertheless, the "British" sport and industry was centered to a large extent in England, and Scottish and Irish cycling had a distinct character and formed institutions that were often independent of those centered in England (in London or the industrial Midlands, for example). I most often use the terms "Britain" and "British" to include general aspects of social and cultural history, and the term "English" when it most appropriately excludes Scotland, Wales and Ireland.

2. The cycling events included a 1 lap (1/3 km) time trial, a 2 km match sprint, a 10 km track race, a 100 km track race, a 12 hour track race and an 87 km road time trial (see Chapter 7). The other sports included in the 1896 Olympics were: athletics/track and field (including 100 m, 400 m, 800 m, 1500 m running, 110m hurdles, high jump, pole vault, long jump, triple jump, marathon, discus), fencing and shooting. 245 men from 14 countries competed in 43 different events. See: David Wallechinsky, *The Complete Book of the Summer Olympics* (Boston, New York and London: Little, Brown, 1996).

3. I have purposefully avoided the use of the word "invented" here, since exploration of the moment of "invention" of the bicycle is too complex to undertake within the scope of this book. However, the athletic aspects of riding the Draisine or hobby horse in the 1818–1820 period, as well as various kinds of 3- and 4-wheeled human-powered velocipedes in the 1820–1860 period, should not be discounted. Although there were some earlier, experimental bicycle-like "velocipedes" which probably date to the 1840s, 1865–66 is now generally accepted as the date of the first manufacture of the "modern" bicycle in Paris, before its slightly later diffusion to the United States (1866–68) and Great Britain (1868–69). See Andrew Ritchie, *The Origins of the Bicycle: Kirkpatrick Macmillan, Gavin Dalzell, Alexandre Lefebvre—Documentation, memory, craft tradition and modern technology* (John Pinkerton Memorial Publishing Fund, 2009) and Andrew Ritchie, "The Velocipede of Alexandre Lefebvre and Problems of Historical Interpretation," *The Wheelmen*, No. 59, Nov. 2001, pp. 10–21 for a discussion of these pre-bicycle velocipedes.

4. Neil Tranter, *Sport, Economy and Society in Britain, 1750–1914* (1998), "The 'revolution' in sport," p. 29.

5. Two examples of this tension are: (1) the suspicions aroused in the 1880s and 1890s within amateur institutions of professionals supported by the bicycle industry, and (2) the control by the world governing body of the sport, the Union Cycliste Internationale, since the turn of the century, over precisely which bicycle designs should be allowed in competition for world records.

6. See Anson Rabinbach, *The Human Motor: Energy, Fatigue and the Origins of Modernity* (Berkeley: University of California Press, 1990).

7. The SCOT approach is broadly summarized as follows in "Common Themes in Sociological and Historical Studies of Technology," *The Social Construction of Technological Systems—New Directions in the Sociology and History of Technology*, p. 12: "The social environment ... shapes the technical characteristics of the artifact. With their emphasis on social shaping, Pinch and Bijker deny technological determinism. Borrowing and adapting from the sociology of knowledge, they argue that the social groups that constitute the social environment play a critical role in defining and solving the problems that arise during the development of an artifact... Pinch and Bijker point out that social groups give meaning to technology and that problems ... are defined within the context of the meaning assigned by a social group or a combination of social groups... Closure occurs in science when a consensus emerges that the 'truth' has been winnowed from the various interpretations; it occurs in technology when a consensus emerges that a problem arising during the development of technology has been solved."

If my examination and analysis of the relationship between cycling and the evolution of bicycle design in this book claims any principal guiding idea, it draws on the SCOT approach in proposing that the exigencies of the sport provided a broad and significant number and variety of "relevant social groups" which influenced the emergence of the many designs of bicycle in the 1870s and 1880s, leading in the 1890s towards at least a partial "closure" of bicycle design in the solid-tired and then the pneumatic-tired "safety" bicycle. See Trevor J. Pinch and Wiebe E. Bijker, "The Social Construction of Facts and Artifacts: Or How the Sociology of Science and the Sociology of Technology Might Benefit Each Other," Chapter 1 of *The Social Construction of Technological Systems—New Directions in the Sociology and History of Technology*. This account was later published in a revised form as "King of the Road: The Social Construction of the Safety Bicycle," in Wiebe J. Bijker, *Of Bicycles, Bakelites and Bulbs—Toward a Theory of Sociotechnical Change*. Stewart Russell criticizes Pinch and Bijker in "The Social Construction of Artifacts: A Response to Pinch and Bijker," and Pinch and Bijker respond with

"Science, Relativism and the New Sociology of Technology: Reply to Russell," both in *Social Studies of Science* (London, Beverly Hills and New Delhi, SAGE), Vol. 16, 1986. Trevor Pinch summarizes objections to SCOT in Robert Fox, ed., *Technological Change*, 1996, pp. 17–35. Nick Clayton reviews the historical accuracy of Pinch and Bijker's account of the bicycle in "Of Bicycles, Bijker, and Bunkum," *Cycle History 10—Proceedings of the 10th Cycle History Conference. Technology and Culture*, Vol. 42, No. 2 (April 2002, pp. 351–373), contains an exchange between Clayton ("SCOT: Does It Answer?") and Pinch and Bijker ("SCOT Answers, Other Questions. A Reply to Nick Clayton"), with a response from Bruce Epperson ("Does SCOT Answer? A Comment"). The most recent addition to this discussion is Paul Rosen, *Framing Production—Technology, Culture, and Change in the British Bicycle Industry* (Cambridge and London: MIT Press, 2002).

8. Keizo Kobayashi, *Histoire du Vélocipède de Drais à Michaux, 1817–1870* (Tokyo: Bicycle Culture Centre, 1993), pp. 237–239.

9. Lowerson argues that cycling "resists historians" attempts to identify class-specific attributes," and that cycling was by 1900 "more distinctly pan-class as a participatory recreation than any other late Victorian boom sport." (John Lowerson, *Sport and the English Middle Classes, 1870–1914*, pp. 116–17). Lowerson is not arguing here that cycling was not affected by class considerations, but that cycling was at different moments popular among all classes and social groups, especially in the maximum expansion of the "boom" years of the 1890s.

10. Recently published research has outlined the extent of the sport in Bohemia, where about 900 Kohout bicycles were manufactured in the 1880s. See Jan Kralik and Jaroslav Vozniak, "The History of Kohout High-Wheel Bicycles," *Proceedings of the 10th International Cycling History Conference*, pp. 25–31.

11. Bicycle racing, particularly in the later 1880s and 1890s, encouraged well-advertised, public tests of stamina. The hunger for long-distance events and superhuman feats of endurance and strength was a tradition reaching back into the 18th and 19th centuries, when marathon horse-riding and "pedestrian" (running and walking) tests had taken place, often on a place-to-place basis, frequently the result of a wager. See Don Watson, "Popular Athletics on Victorian Tyneside," *International Journal of the History of Sport*, Vol. 11, No. 3 (Dec. 1994), pp. 485–94; Walter Thom, *Pedestrianism; or, An Account of the Performances of Celebrated Pedestrians during the Last and Present Century; with a Full Narrative of Captain Barclay's Public and Private Matches; and an Essay on Training* (Aberdeen: Chalmers, 1813); Anon, *Memoirs of the Life and Exploits of George Wilson, the Celebrated Pedestrian, who Walked 750 Miles in 15 Days, etc* (London: Dean and Munday 1815); Thomas Elworth, *Sketches of Incidents and Adventures in the Life of Thomas Elworth, the American Pedestrian* (Boston, 1844); "Stonehenge," *British Rural Sports; Comprising Shooting, Hunting, Coursing, Fishing, Hawking, Racing, Boating, and Pedestrianism* (London: Warne and Co., many editions in 1870s and 1880s).

12. Lowerson, op. cit., p. 117.

13. A recent exemplary expression of this multiple nature and function of the bicycle can be seen in the development of the mountain bike in Northern California. The mountain bike, which originated in the 1970s as a cultish racing and recreational machine on the fire-trails of Marin County, was quickly and unexpectedly transformed into a globally popular and fashionable urban utility bicycle and seized upon by the bicycle industry. Mountain bike sales exploded, and its wider sporting potential was also quickly recognized. Off-road and downhill competition grew, sponsored by the industry, and within a few years had won Olympic recognition. A new style of utility bicycle and a new sport emerged almost at the same time. Informal sport fertilized technological innovation; innovation was then channeled into utility; and finally the exigencies of the consumer marketplace once again stimulated sport. One of the pioneers of the mountain bike has said of the early days of informal down-hill racing: "Races were a meeting place for the most innovative riders and builders because such events provide the most severe tests of performance available." Charles Kelly, quoted in *Cycling Weekly*, 1 January 2000; see also Frank Berto, *The Birth of Dirt—Origins of Mountain Biking* and Frank Berto, "Who invented the mountain bike?," *Cycle History 8, Proceedings of the 8th International Cycle History Conference*.

14. While recognizing this general dynamic—that competition had a strong affect on design—it is important to recognize that certain kinds of technological change certainly occurred with no need to be tested within competition. The introduction in the late 1880s of female-specific open frame design, for example (the woman's bicycle), was an innovation related to practical usage and was unrelated to speed. Similarly, the introduction of the luxury touring bicycle of the mid–1890s was directed specifically at the affluent recreational rider. But by the mid–1890s, bicycle design had solidified around the diamond-frame, which had by that time become the bicycle for all kinds of riding.

15. A valuable summary discussion on differences between American and French cycling patterns and on class and fashion elements in the development of recreational and utility cycling in those two countries is found in Thomas Burr, "French Expansion, American Collapse, 1890–1910," *Proceedings of the 16th International Cycling History Conference* (2006). This is expanded in Burr's doctoral dissertation, "Markets as Producers and Consumers: The French and U.S. national Bicycle Markets, 1875–1910" (unpublished Ph. D. in Sociology, U.C. Davis, 2005).

16. Exceptions include "Lawyer Won the Bet—2,836 Wheels Passed between Fourth and Walnut from 5.30 to 8.30 o'clock," *Louisville Courier-Journal*, 11 July 1897 (published in *The Boneshaker*, Summer 2001) and accounts of a census taken in Manchester, reported in the *Manchester Guardian*, 11 May 1896 and 17 May 1897 (published in *The Boneshaker*, Summer 2000). Burr (see Footnote 15) also mentions reports of widespread utility use in Minneapolis, and in Indianapolis there were "large bicycle storage rooms in the downtown district." A valuable contribution to the discussion of bicycle production and use statistics is Bruce Epperson, "How Many Bikes?," *Cycle History 11, Proceedings of the 11th Cycling History Conference* (San Francisco: Van der Plas, 2000).

17. *Wheeling*, 26 August 1885.

CHAPTER ONE

1. A good general account of the beginnings of the bicycle industry in Britain is Andrew Millward, "The Genesis of the British Cycle Industry, 1867–1872," *Proceedings of the 1st International Conference of Cycling History*, 1990. Another short account is Nick Clayton, "The Introduction of the Boneshaker into England," in Charles Spencer, *Bicycles and Tricycles: Past and Present* (reprinted by Cycling Classics, Oakland, California, 1996).

2. Throughout the 19th century the word "velocipede" had been used to denote a machine of any kind driven by human power. Thus the term "two-wheeled velocipede" was used simply to distinguish the new machine from 3- and 4-wheeled vehicles. Snoxell and Spencer's advertisement of 19 Feb. 1869 (*English Mechanic*) used the term "the new two-wheel velocipede," while a newspaper article of 5 April 1869 (*Liverpool Mercury*) used the headline "Great Bicycle Race," as well as describing riders as "velocipedists." For a brief period, the terms appear to have been used almost interchangeable. As "bicycle" came into increasing use from 1869 onwards, so "velocipede" was increasingly used to describe old-fashioned, out-of-date machines, usually with a pejorative meaning. The introduction of the word "bicycle" around 1869 merits further study.

3. About fifteen informational booklets on the earliest bicycles were printed in England. Some were in effect manufacturers' catalogues. Titles include: "Velox," *Velocipedes, Bicycles and Tricycles, How to make and how to use them, with a sketch of their history, invention and progress*"; "An Experienced Velocipedist," *The Velocipede, its history, and practical hints how to use it*"; "A Working Mechanic," *The Modern Velocipede: Its History and Construction*; J. Firth-Bottomley, *The Velocipede, its past, present and its future*.

4. For an account of the beginnings of the sport in France, see Keizo Kobayashi, *Histoire du Vélocipède de Drais à Michaux, 1817–1870*, Part IV, "Les Courses de Velocipedes," pp. 237–308. Kobayashi's interpretation is limited, however, by its failure to appreciate that the sport had its origins in popular entertainment. In categorizing his account of the early sport exclusively into "road" and "track" sections, he makes the mistake of seeing 1867–69 through the eyes of the later, "classic," development of bicycle racing, and neglects the popular entertainment aspects in France. The very early sport in the United States, beginning in 1868, which also had its origins in popular entertainment, has been extensively explored in Norman Dunham, "The Bicycle Era in American History" (unpublished Ph.D. thesis, Harvard University, 1956).

5. Were these costume competitions, with a prize awarded for the best-dressed competitor, in effect "fashion shows," to make the new sport more appealing, more respectable, or to mimic the fashionable French events? Reports of the races make frequent mention of the color and individual styles of riders' costumes. Bright costumes, of course, also helped to distinguish one competitor from another.

6. See J.A. Mangan, *Athleticism in the Victorian and Edwardian Public Schools* (Cass, London, 2000) and Peter Bailey, *Leisure and Class in Victorian England: Rational Recreation and the Contest for Control, 1830–1885* (London, 1978). Bailey writes (p. 124), "One of the more remarkable features of the expanding world of mid-Victorian leisure was the innovation of organized and codified athletic sports—a broad category of activities which comprised primarily the athletics of track and field events, as the term is understood today, together with a reconstructed version of football, and the previously reformed game of cricket."

7. The increase of leisure time included the invention of the "weekend" as a time for leisure rather than work. Spectators appear to have been drawn from various class levels, depending on the organizational context and geographical location of an event. Newspaper reports frequently made mention of the "respectability" of crowds and the presence of women.

8. *Wolverhampton Chronicle*, 4 June 1873.

9. Derek Hudson, *Munby, Man of Two Worlds* (Sphere Books, London, 1974), p. 271.

10. See Roger Street, *The Pedestrian Hobby-Horse at the Dawn of Cycling*. "The Pedestrian's Accelerator" was illustrated in *Imperial Magazine*, April 1819, with the comment that "the principle upon which this simple machine is constructed, seems to have been taken from the art of skating."

11. Andrew Ritchie, *King of the Road*, Chap. 2, "Amateur Mechanics," discusses the period 1820–60 extensively. See also Andrew Ritchie, *The Origins of the Bicycle: Kirkpatrick Macmillan, Gavin Dalzell, Alexandre Lefebvre—Documentation, memory, craft tradition and modern technology* (John Pinkerton Memorial Publishing Fund, 2009). The role and place of Kirkpatrick Macmillan in the 1840s is problematic and controversial. Can he justifiably be called the "inventor" of the bicycle? Current examinations of Macmillan's historical role tend to minimize his importance and to question the reliability of the documentary evidence and surviving machines. Recent accounts of Macmillan include, N.G. Clayton, "The First Bicycle," *The Boneshaker* 113, (Spring 1987) and Nicholas Oddy, "Kirkpatrick McMillan, The inventor of the pedal cycle or the invention of cycle history," *Proceedings of the 1st International Conference of Cycling History*. Another early rear-driven velocipede by Alexandre Lefebvre, in the museum at San Jose, California, can perhaps be dated to 1843, and is of a similar design and conception to the Macmillan-type velocipedes; see Andrew Ritchie, "The Velocipede of Alexandre Lefebvre and problems of historical interpretation," *The Wheelmen* No. 59, Nov. 2001.

12. The role of Pierre Lallement, who played a significant role in the transmission of velocipede ideas and design from France to the United States, should be mentioned briefly here (see David Herlihy, "Lallement vs. Michaux: Who Truly Invented the Bicycle?" *The Wheelmen*, No. 42, May 1993). Lallement later returned to Paris, where he began a company called Compagnie Vélocipédienne in April 1869, but he was not significant as a Parisian maker and was not producing bicycles in 1868 (see Kobayashi, op. cit.).

13. Keizo Kobayashi, *Histoire du Vélocipède de Drais à Michaux, 1817–1870—Mythes et Réalités*, Part Four, "Les Courses de Vélocipèdes, 1867–1870."

14. *Orchestra* quoted in *Scientific American*, 1 May 1869. On 8 December 1867, about one hundred "touristes vélocipédistes" raced from Paris to Versailles, the fastest covering the 17 km in about an hour (Kobayashi, op. cit.,

Le Petit Journal, 10 Dec. 1867). In May 1868, on the Feast of Pentecost, races were held at Saint-Cloud, where Englishman, James Moore, who lived in Paris, won a gold medal (Kobayashi, op. cit., *Le Petit Journal*, 2 June 1868). Races weren't confined to Paris, however, and were held for example in Cannes and Bordeaux. On 21 May 1868, Ascension Day, amateur races were held on the horse-racing track at La Réole (Bordeaux), organized by the "fete" committee with "a work of art" offered as first prize; velocipede racing was described as "si nouveau et si attrayant" (so new and so exciting) (Kobayashi, op. cit., *L'Union de la Réole*, 3 May 1868). Contemporary illustrations of these events show fashionably-dressed crowds of spectators, and a well-organized race structure, with uniformed riders and judges at the finishing line. The connection between velocipede racing and horse-racing is illustrated by the fact that velocipede races were held just before the horse-races at the Hippodrome de Paris, and that obstacles were introduced into one race (a kind of steeple-chase) which were held on horse-racing tracks. In addition, the adoption of brightly-colored dress for velocipedists was based on a jockey's uniform.

According to Kobayashi, the earliest French velocipede club was the Véloce Club de Valence, founded 12 March 1868, followed by the Véloce Club de Paris, in existence by 15 May 1868, at which time it already had sixty members (Kobayashi op. cit., p. 243). The Véloce Club de Paris was housed at the Pré-Catelan park, where a special track and grandstand were erected for its races. The Pré-Catelan was "made available by the City of Paris to promoters of fêtes and entertainments who hoped to attract large crowds there." The director of the Pré-Catalan, Monsieur de Saint-Félix, alert to novelties to attract spectators, included velocipede races on at least ten occasions in 1868 and 1869 (Kobayashi op. cit., *L'Univers Illustré*, 6 June 1868 and *Le Vélocipède Illustré*, 24 March 1870). Throughout France, velocipede races were closely associated with community and religious festivals, a fact which perhaps helps to explain the still rooted presence of bicycle racing in French society today.

15. See Alex Poyer, *Les Premiers Temps des Veloce-Clubs* (L'Harmattan, Paris, 2003). According to Christopher Thompson, "The Third Republic on Wheels," (Ph.D. thesis, New York University, pp. 136), the earliest French clubs were the Véloce Club de Paris and the Véloce Club de Toulouse, both formed in 1868. The Véloce Club Rouennais, the Véloce Club Rennais and the Thann Cycle Club were added in 1869. See also C. Petiton, *Histoire du Véloce-Club Rouennais: Son origine, son but, ses présidents, ses courses, ses travaux* (Cagniard, Rouen, 1896). The Union Vélocipedique de France was not formed until 1881. The racing and club activity were extensively reported in the leading journal of velocipeding, *Le Vélocipède Illustrée*, first published in Paris in April 1869, and this substantial weekly publication appears to have been the means by which the sport coordinated and organized itself nationally, though it did not usually promote racing, except for the Paris–Rouen road race. The statutes (or membership regulations) of the Véloce Club de Valence stipulated that "all discussions of a political or religious nature are specifically forbidden." Members of the clubs were in general young men in their twenties, and a typical club had 20 or 30 members, although that of Carcassonne listed 199 founding members. As well as promoting racing, the clubs also organized outings, usually on Sundays, where the wearing of a uniform was encouraged (Kobayashi, op. cit., pp. 244–45).

16. In racing, there was a clear yet debatable distinction between amateurs and "professeurs" of velocipedes and velocipede makers, who were excluded from amateur events, but a "Grand Prix" event was open to all categories of competitors, riding any size of wheel (Kobayashi, op. cit., p. 263). Most track races were short-distance, between 2 and 4 kilometres, and the fastest speeds over these short courses were about 27 km/h. Time trials were occasionally held.

17. Kobayashi, op. cit., pp. 267–69, "Les courses de dames." "Miss America," it seems, was the professional name adopted by the wife or girl-friend of R.B. Turner, who was working in Paris, and was responsible for taking the first French velocipedes to Coventry. In Bordeaux, on 1 November 1868, 3,000 people watched "Mlle Julie" beat "Mlle Louise" in a hotly contested race, and the crowd invaded the track to get a closer look at the "filles de l'air" (open-air girls) (Kobayashi, op. cit., *Le Bordelais*, 8 Nov. 1868). Women's racing was evidently a genuinely athletic contest, and the women velocipedists, like the men, sometimes crashed. Such racing was undoubtedly considered risqué and had the attraction of an unconventional, if not entirely respectable, new departure. At Carpentras, on 8 August 1869, for example, it was reported that—"for the first time women were seen taking part in these races and suffering in a kind of exercise which demands more lung-power and leg-power than grace." (Kobayashi, op. cit., p. 268). Prizes for women's races were generous and the few female competitors were much sought after for the popular, crowded race meetings, which often introduced the sport to the general public for the first time, and were a potent demonstration of "modern" ideas.

18. *Le Vélocipède Illustré*, 30 Sept. 1869. The race is described in detail in Kobayashi, op. cit., pp. 292–308. 120 contestants were sent on their way by Lesclide amid crowds of spectators. In terrible weather conditions; the race was won by James Moore, who covered the 123 km in 10h 40m (a speed of 11.53 km/h), and was followed fifteen minutes later by André Castera. Moore rode a bicycle built by Jules-Pierre Suriray, that incorporated wheels with ball-bearing hubs and rubber tyres attached to the rims. Suriray subsequently advertised himself in *Le Vélocipède Illustré* as a maker of "vélocipèdes de vitesse" (racing velocipedes), mentioning specifically Moore's victory in Paris–Rouen (*Le Vélocipède Illustré*, 21 Nov. 1869). Thirty-four competitors finished the race, including "Miss America," who arrived in Rouen at 6 a.m. the following day ("Course de Fonds de Paris B Rouen," *Le Vélocipède Illustré* No. 52, 11 Nov. 1869). The novel Paris–Rouen race was the stimulus for further road races through 1869 and 1870.

19. *The Field*, 10 Aug. 1867.

20. *The Times*, 1 Feb. 1869.

21. A comprehensive account of American velocipede developments, and the young sport in the United States, can be found in Norman L. Dunham, "The Bicycle Era in American History" (Ph. D. thesis, Harvard University, 1956); see Chapter 3, "The Parisian velocipede reaches America"; Chapter 4, "The velocipede craze of 1869," and Chapter 5, "The decline of the velocipede."

22. *New York Times*, 22 Aug. 1867.
23. *New York Times*, 25 Nov. 1868.
24. *Scientific American*, 6 Feb. 1869 and 20 Feb. 1869. Show business was frequently as much in evidence as athletic competition. In New York, at the Apollo Hall, "the tournament opened by the entrance upon the floor of twenty-five of the most expert young riders in the country, whose advent called forth immense applause, renewed as the graceful evolutions of the performers excited and delighted the admiring assembly. The affair was very select, and was attended by a large and fashionable concourse of ladies and gentlemen." (*Scientific American*, 24 April 1869). Riding-schools for beginners and "exercise halls" were the initial venues for the sport, but unfortunately some of the velocipede halls became "the resort of roughs who monopolize the floors." (*New York Times*, 28 July 1869).

In April 1869, races were "inaugurated at the Jersey City Velocipededrome," and there was "a grand race between two contestants there for a gold medal. Fred Hanlon, the noted gymnast, has challenged any velocipedist in the United States to race him for a thousand dollars and the championship of the country... The contest, when it does come off, will be an exciting one, and will attract thousands of spectators." (*New York Times*, 4 April 1869). In May 1869, there was a "Grand Velocipede Race" between A.P. Messinger, "the long-distance rider," and W.E. Harding, "the champion three-mile runner and noted pedestrian," at the Empire City Rink, New York; however, "little interest was manifested in the contest, not over a hundred people being present." (*New York Times*, 16 and 20 May 1869). In June, members of the American Velocipede Club, the American Bicycle Club, the Ivanhoe Velocipede Club and the Brooklyn Velocipede Club gathered to watch "a championship match" between Frank Swift and James Boyle at the Capitoline Ground (*New York Times*, 26 June 1869). The poor state of tracks often stood in the way of successful races, however. At the Union Course, Long Island in April 1869, "the great drawback to the success of the race was the condition of the track, the sandy dust on the main portion of it lying several inches thick, thus making the track hard for horses and still harder for the bicycle." (*Scientific American*, 29 May 1869). Consequently, there was discussion in the press of creating "a velocipede race course" in every large city, and of the necessity of separating velocipede racing from the trotting courses, where races were frequently held: "Let us have no more races on trotting courses. Velocipeding is now in respectable hands, and has a reputable status as a gentlemanly sport and exercise." (*New York Sun*, date unknown, quoted in *Scientific American*, 15 May 1869).

Gymnasts, runners, pedestrians, horsemen and oarsmen were among those who tried their hands at velocipede racing. Women, too, performed on velocipedes, but those who appeared at the Empire Rink in April 1869 did not please women spectators, for they were "two rough-faced women in flesh-colored tights nearly to their hips," and "lady spectators by dozens left in disgust," a display "which neither reflected credit on the management, nor added to the rink as a popular resort for the respectable class of velocipedists." (*New York Times*, 14 April 1869). When, however, "the popular lady velocipedists, Miss Katie Kavanagh, Miss Libbie Howard and Mlle Lottie" appeared in July at the Crosby Street Velocipede Academy, there were no complaints of impropriety (*New York Times*, 28 July 1869). Similarly, the skater Carrie Moore, the daughter of a Massachusetts Deputy Sheriff, took up velocipeding and became "undoubtedly the best lady velocipedist in the country, having acquired all the difficult movements done by our male experts," and travelled widely on the East Coast giving theatrical performances (*National Chronicle, Journal of American Sports and Amusements*, Boston, Mass., 27 March 1869). *Scientific American* reported that women exercised in gymnasiums "wearing the dress commonly used by them in calisthenic exercises," and thought that there was "no valid objection why ladies should not adopt a special dress for this sport, and enjoy it in the open air." (*Scientific American*, 20 March 1869).

25. *San Francisco Morning Chronicle*, 28 Jan. 1869. In an advertisement from the same date, Palmer and Knox state: "Parties having purchased previous to December 1st ult., will please return and exchange for our Improved Machines," indicating that manufacturing was already well under way late in 1868. By March 1869, a "Grand Velocipede Tournament," with twenty performers, was held at the Mechanics' Pavilion in San Francisco (*San Francisco Chronicle*, 21 March 1869). Ten thousand people could be seated in the Pavilion, and the event was highly organized: "Some of the races will be against time, and as there are some skilful performers whose time will be worthy of publishing, the greatest precautions should be taken to have all the conditions complied with—that is, a plainly marked out ring, which the velocipedists shall not cross; the ring to be carefully measured, and the number of feet contained in it stated to the audience. The mile can be made pretty close to five minutes by several of the performers." (*Daily Alta California*, 20 March 1869). Later, the Pavilion was the scene of a performance by "the daring young gymnast, Paul Martinetti," who "will make the transit of the entire length of the Great Pavilion, supported only on an Elevated Wire, and mounted on his Aerial Bicycle ... the Most Astonishing and Daring Feat ever witnessed in modern times." (*San Francisco Chronicle*, 14 May 1869). Indoor entertainments like this spread up the west coast to Portland, Oregon and Seattle, but velocipede competition does not seem to have become an outdoor or road sport, and after a momentary burst of activity, it was gone for at least a decade (see Frank Cameron, "The Pacific Coast Velocipede," *The Wheelmen*, Nov. 1987).

26. Karl Kron, *Ten Thousand Miles on a Bicycle*, Chapter XXVII, Boneshaker Days," p. 402. In 1875, Harding and Messinger (who was then described as "the champion long-distance rider of America") were still racing against each other. They contested a 26-hour race, which the *New York Times* referred to as "a velocipede championship," at the American Institute in New York. Messinger rode a 46" wheel and Harding a 41," still very small wheels for the date, suggesting that they were not in touch with the latest technical developments in England, where use of a much larger wheel was by then routine in competition (*New York Times*, 18 and 19 Dec. 1875). But the fact that the same two riders were still competing against each other across a time gap of six years suggests a continuity in the sport, which may well have been limited to certain urban localities. This is confirmed by a report in *Bicycle*

Journal in 1877, which spoke of McClellan, the American champion, "who has figured in bicycle contests for the last 6 years." (*Bicycle Journal*, 5 Jan. 1877). But further research is needed to ascertain exactly what occurred during the period between 1869 and 1878, when the high-wheel bicycle was reintroduced from England, and bicycle racing became an established part of American sport culture.

27. *The Times*, 1 Dec. 1869, in a report from Sydney, Australia, notes—"The velocipede is gaining ground here. They are not so commonly met with as at Melbourne, but I observe that races are got up at the Albert Cricket Ground." Thus, by the end of 1869, the new sport had become a global phenomenon.

28. The transcontinental railroad was completed at Promontary Point, Utah on 10 May 1869, and it is likely that up until that time, heavy, luxury items like velocipedes would have been sent to California from Paris or the East Coast around the Horn. It is not impossible, though, that they would have been sent by railway, bridging the gap by wagon. The difficulty of such transportation was an obvious stimulus to local makers in San Francisco to copy from imported models.

29. "Velocipedes," *The Ironmonger*, 30 Jan. 1869.

30. *The Ironmonger*, 27 Feb. 1869.

31. Mayall's account is entitled "Recollections of the first days of the bicycle," and was published in *Ixion*, Vol. 1, No. 1 (Jan. 1875). Accounts differ as to the exact date of this event, which is only of importance here in that it affects evaluation of the precise date when the earliest bicycle racing in England can be documented. Mayall dates it to "the early part of January 1869." Historian Bartleet, on the other hand, wrote that the machine was "brought to England by Rowley Turner in November 1868." Bartleet emphasized that this was not the first bicycle to arrive in England: "There is no doubt that a few bicycles were purchased by English visitors to the Exhibition, who brought them home and used them in England." (H.W. Bartleet, *Bartleet's Bicycle Book*.) The Exhibition referred to was the 1867 Paris Exhibition, when visitors saw velocipedes made by French maker Michaux on the streets (Michaux applied for space at the Exhibition, but there is no evidence his application was accepted), and where Rowley Turner also showed sewing machines made by the Coventry Machinists Company. *Coventry Herald and Free Press*, 27 Nov.1868, reported, "The sewing machine company ... have just received a novel order for a number of velocipedes from Paris, where these locomotives have lately been all the rage, and it is expected will soon be in general use in London." *Coventry Standard*, 1 April 1869, contains the first known advertisement for the Coventry Machinists Company's bicycles. Andrew Millward, "The Genesis of the British Cycle Industry 1867–72," *Proceedings of the First International Conference of Cycling History*, gives several instances of commercial manufacture of velocipedes by small makers and tentative importing of French and American velocipedes into England in 1868, though these are documented in secondary and therefore not thoroughly reliable sources. The period is problematic.

32. *English Mechanic*, 19 Feb. 1869.

33. *The Times*, 19 Feb. 1869.

34. The catalogue, dated 1870, is in the collection of Lorne Shields in Toronto, Canada.

35. Spencer's publications include *The Modern Gymnast* (1866); *The Bicycle: Its Use and Action* (1870); *The Modern Bicycle* (1876); *Bicycles and Tricycles Past and Present* (1883); *The Bicycle Road Book* (various editions from 1880 on). See also an article about Charles Spencer by H.H. Griffin, "Comments and Recollections: An 1869 Pioneer," in *Cycle Times*, 1909 (day and month unknown)."

36. *English Mechanic*, 12 Feb. 1869.

37. *The Field*, 10 Aug. 1867, quoting from *The Sport* (date unknown).

38. *The Mechanic*, 12 Dec. 1868, quoting from *London Society* (date unknown).

39. *The Field*, 19 June 1869.

40. *The Field*, 29 May 1869.

41. *Liverpool Mercury*, 5 April 1869.

42. *Liverpool Weekly Courier*, 10 April 1869.

43. Recent research indicates that the beginning of the importation of the Pickering velocipede from the United States into Liverpool should be dated to early in 1869, perhaps accounting for the rapid development of the sport there. In "The Genesis of the British Cycle Industry, 1867–72" (see Note 1), Andrew Millward gives several cases of manufacturing in 1868, but sources quoted are mostly secondary. In "The Introduction of the Boneshaker into England" (*The Boneshaker* No. 141, Summer 1996), Nick Clayton argues against 1868 as the earliest date for the arrival of French and American bicycles in England, and therefore also against the existence of racing pre–1869. The question of the alleged 1868 arrival of Pickering velocipedes in Liverpool is discussed and rejected by David Herlihy in "The Pickering Export Controversy: its Resolution and Some Pertinent Lessons" (*The Wheelmen*, November 1995). Herlihy's revision of the often-claimed 1868 date hinges on his assertion that a testimonial from John Shepherd, "Velocipede Instructor at the Liverpool Gymnasium, and to the Liverpool Velocipede Club," which was published in an advertising flyer for "Pickering's American Velocipede" issued by Liverpool agent Samuel and Peace and dated "March 10th, 1868" must have been wrongly dated. 1869 is a more plausible date, based on other documentary evidence. An article from *The Velocipedist* (March 1869) said, "The shipment of velocipedes from this country to England has commenced..." Another article from *The Albion* (U.S.), 3 April 1869 stated, "The introduction of the velocipede into Liverpool, though only of a recent date, is rapidly developing itself, and a very exciting eight mile race, for a prize of a silver cup, lately came off, the competitors being members of the Liverpool Velocipede Club." Herlihy thus concludes that Pickering velocipedes were not available until the autumn of 1868, and therefore could not have been available in England until the spring of 1869.

44. *Liverpool Mercury*, 24 and 26 April 1869.

45. *Liverpool Weekly Courier*, 1 May 1869.

46. *The Times*, 28 May 1869.

47. *North London News*, 19 June and 3 July 1869.

48. *Birmingham Daily Post*, 4 April 1869.

49. *Wolverhampton Chronicle*, 8 June 1870.

50. *Wolverhampton Chronicle*, 10 Aug. 1870.

51. *Wolverhampton Chronicle*, 4 June 1873.

52. *Ripon Gazette*, 1 July 1869; H.H. Griffin, *Cycles and Cycling*, p. 35.

53. Wolverhampton Velocipede Club *Rules*; Lorne Shields collection, Toronto, Canada. This pamphlet is not dated, but from further reference to the Club, can safely be dated to 1869.

54. *Wolverhampton Chronicle,* 21 April 1869.

55. Abundant evidence of the quest for a strong, light and fast machine can be found in manufacturers' advertisements from the mid–1870s. W.J. Boden of London claimed his machines "are made as light as possible, consistent with durability." John Keen, Surrey, "Champion Bicyclist," advertised "the most perfect machine of the day. For Speed, Durability, and Neatness of Design, it has no equal." John Dedicoat, Coventry, advertised that his bicycles had "Lightness, Strength, and Freedom from more than absolutely necessary Friction." (quoted from advertisements in *Ixion,* Jan–May 1875).

56. *The Field,* 18 November 1871 and 4 May 1872, quoted in Les Bowerman, "John Keen—The Life of a Cycling Pioneer," *Proceedings of the 4th International Cycle History Conference,* Boston, 1993.

57. "Keen's Bicycle," catalogue from 1874 in the Science Museum Library. Such claims made in promotional or advertizing context have as a matter of course to be treated with a certain amount of scepticism. Promotional material will always claim the superiority of the products advertised over rival products. In this case, Keen's own claims were supported by testimony from other sources, and by the use of his machines in competition.

58. *Wheeling,* 17 Dec. 1884 and *The Cyclist,* 24 Dec. 1884. The testimonial committee included Keith-Falconer (Cambridge University B. C.), Robert Todd (Secretary of the N.C.U.), Lacy Hillier (editor, *The Cyclist*), E.R. Shipton (Secretary of the C.T.C.) and Harry Etherington (editor, *Wheeling*).

59. *Liverpool Mercury,* 26 April 1869.

60. *The Field,* 8 May 1869.

61. *The Field,* 19 June 1869.

62. *North London News and Finsbury Gazette,* 19 June, 26 June and 3 July 1869. Indoor events on a better-organized scale later became a mainstay of winter bicycle racing, and occurred throughout the 1870s. Wooden tracks with banked turns were built especially for the races. The longer the race, the greater the amount of cash that could be collected at the box-office. Indoor cycling endurance events, the forerunners of later six-day racing, were sensational and were modeled on long-distance pedestrian races. The earliest English outdoor six-day cycling races were promoted in 1876 in Wolverhampton and Walsall, near Birmingham, and attracted large crowds. French champion Camille Thuillet (at the Molineux Grounds, Wolverhampton, in front of 10,000 spectators) and Frank White (at the Arboretum, Walsall) each rode alone for six days to establish records in September before they came together to compete against each other in October in the presence of "an immense assemblage of spectators." (*Athletic News,* Manchester, 30 Sept. and 21 Oct. 1876).

63. *The Times,* 19 Feb. 1869; according to an account by Rowley Turner published in *Bartlet's Bicycle Book* (Edward Burrow, London, 1931), this *Times* report was syndicated to and used by more than 300 local newspapers.

64. H. Griffin, *Cycles and Cycling* (1903 edition), p. 30.

65. *Liverpool Mercury,* 30 March 1869.

66. *Wolverhampton Chronicle,* 4 Aug. 1869.

67. *The Times,* 12 Oct. 1869.

68. Charles Spencer, *Bicycles and Tricycles.*

69. *Daily Telegraph,* exact date unknown, quoted in N. Salamon, *Bicycling: Its Rise and Development,* p. 14.

70. *The Field,* 30 Jan. 1869 and *Daily News,* 28 Jan. 1869; the appearance of this event in newspapers suggests that other velocipedes may already have arrived in England before the January 1869 events at Spencer's gymnasium. The race may have been a promotion intended to publicize the novel velocipedes just arriving in England.

71. *Liverpool Mercury,* 5 April 1869. The "Miss Julia" machine which was victorious in this race was gendered as female, an interesting example of men imputing femininity to an inanimate object.

72. *Liverpool Weekly Courier,* 10 April 1869. The "start list" for the race, published in the newspaper, is as shown in the table above. Many details of this race were interesting and significant: "the winning point was indicated by two flags placed on each side of the road"; "no passing on the footwalk was permitted"; "riders, if they chose, might dismount at the foot of a hill and trundle their machines along by hand instead of treadling by foot, but they were not to be assisted when they dismounted or remounted." Recognition was made that a larger wheel gave a speed advantage because the riders were "handicapped according to the diameter of the wheels of their bicycles. The strictest rules were enforced. Bicycles with wheels 37" in diameter and under were to start together; half-a-minute was to be allowed for every inch of wheel above 37 inches diameter up to 40 inches; and beyond that diameter a quarter of a minute was to be allowed for every inch."

Rider	Color of Cap	Name of Bicycle
George Ball	Blue and pink	Knight of the Garter
A.L. Lane	White, with blue stars	Firefly
J. Moes Bennett	Red and blue	Knight Templar
W.E. Potter	Violet	Centaur
G.M. Jones	Pink	Mandarin
R.W. Leyland	Yellow and black	Pegasus
W. Long	Green	Hermit
J.S. de Wolfe, jun.	Magenta	Maccaroni
W.H. de Wolfe	Blue, with white stripe	Gladiateur
George Scott	Chocolate	Parisian
H. Brown	White and blue	Doctor
William Hope	Red	Aurora
L. Notara	Black	Comet
Henry W. Eaton	Light blue	Miss Julia
C. Haddon	Red and white	Mensikoff
A.S. Pearson	White	Britannia
J.C. Cannon	Dark blue	Jupiter
F.A. Macdona		Chester
G.H. Wilson	Light blue	Eclipse

73. See H.W. Bartleet, "Half a Century of Speed," *Cycling*, 27 Feb. 1919. The claim is repeated in H.W. Bartleet, *Bartleet's Bicycle Book*: "This exhibit was purchased from Mr. Arthur Markham, who for many years carried on a cycle business at 345 Edgware Road, London, and who claimed to have won the first bicycle race ever held in England; this was run in a field near the Welsh Harp, Hendon, on Whit Monday, 1868 (before R.B. Turner came to England), the prize being a silver cup presented by a Mr. Warner, landlord of the Welsh Harp Hotel." A Hendon local history (unfortunately untitled when xeroxes were sent to me) provides further corroborating information about the Welsh Harp: "Its leisure potential was enthusiastically exploited by Jack Warner, who held the licence for 39 years from 1859. They provided a huge range of entertainments, including skating, swimming, boxing and wrestling matches, hunting, shooting and fishing, a concert hall, a menagerie and a skittle saloon... In 1870 the enormous Bank Holiday crowds persuaded the Midland Railway to open Welsh Harp station." The suggestion that it is not impossible for English racing to be occurring in mid–1868 is reinforced by a report in the *Cambridge Independent* as early as May 1868 describing the popularity of velocipedes in that city, where "there is talk of establishing a velocipede club (*Cambridge Independent*—exact date unknown, quoted in *Messager des Théatres*, Paris, 25 May 1868). However, no primary documentation of 1868 racing has been found.

74. I have been unable to discover "O.E. McGregor's" first name.

75. *Wolverhampton Chronicle*, 30 Nov. 1869.

76. *Sydenham Times*, 1 June 1869.

77. *The Field*, 29 May 1869.

78. *English Mechanic*, 6 Aug. 1869.

79. According to *English Mechanic*, 1 April 1870, which published a summary of it, the paper was subsequently published, but I have been unable to locate it.

80. *Morning Advertiser*, 27 Sept. 1869.

81. *Ripon Gazette*, 1 July 1869.

82. These events may well have been more widespread than has been recognized and cannot be accurately charted without a close examination of "Athletic Sports" meetings nationwide.

83. Programs of these events are illustrated in Anne Pallant, *A Sporting Century, 1863–1963* (self-published in 1997).

84. *Morning Advertiser*, 27 Sept. 1869.

85. For more complete details on the careers of these riders, see: "Camille Thuillet, the French champion," *Bicycle Journal*, 1 September 1876; "Cycling Celebrities. John Keen," *The Wheel World*, month? 1885; Nick Clayton, "The cycling career of James Moore," *The Boneshaker* 125, Spring 1991; Les Bowerman, "John Keen—The Life of a Cycling Pioneer," *Proceedings of the 4th International Cycle History Conference*, Boston, 1993.

86. See also Andrew Ritchie, "Professional World Championships, 1870–92," *The Boneshaker* No. 142, Winter 1996. The word "championship" is in quotation marks here to draw attention to the need to distinguish its early, less formally structured usage from current understanding of the word. The precise identification of early "world championships" is problematic since there was no governing body to give official status to events, and championship status was certainly used as an advertising tool. Realistically, however, only the best available riders could be featured in a "championship." "Championship contests" were often reported in the press and in cases where several "championships" were contested in one year, it appears to have been agreed in newspaper reports that the "world championship" designation be awarded to races with the largest, most international and highest-calibre field competing. Championship level events and the more important races in Britain were usually held at one of the following prominent locations: Star Grounds, Fulham, London; Lillie Bridge Grounds, Fulham, London; Tufnell Park, Holloway, London; Queen of England Grounds, Hammersmith, London; Aston Cross Grounds, Birmingham; Queen's Grounds, Sheffield; Bramhall Lane, Sheffield; Molineux Grounds, Wolverhampton; Vauxhall Gardens, Wolverhampton; Melbourne Grounds, Northampton; Powderhall Gardens, Edinburgh, Scotland.

87. Typical examples of wagering can be found in *Bell's Life* for 24 Sept. 1870, under the title "Velocipedism": "A Challenge to Velocipedists—Mr. W. Jackson of Pimlico, London, who has just arrived from Paris, is anxious to test the capabilities of his velocipedes, and will run his tricycle against any other three or four-wheeler of the same weight from London to Brighton, for £20 or £40 a side," and "Howard v. Johnson—The whole of the money, £50, for this interesting bicycle match of 12 miles has been staked with Mr. Whenman, the Bricklayers' Arms, Tonbridge Street, Euston Square, and the match takes place at the Star Grounds, Fulham, on Monday next. Both men are very fit, and a good race is anticipated."

88. *Birmingham Daily Post*, 30 May 1871.

89. *Wolverhampton Chronicle*, 8 June 1870 and 10 Aug. 1870. See also Nick Clayton, "Who Invented the Penny-Farthing?," *Proceedings of the 7th International Cycle History Conference*, Buffalo 1996.

90. The "Phantom" and the "spider" wheel were both emerging, new wheel systems making increasing use of metal spokes. See Nick Clayton, "Who Invented the Penny-Farthing?," op. cit. Moore's letter was written to F.T. Bidlake in 1931 and is quoted in *The Boneshaker*, 1958, No. 14, p. 7. Moore's championship rides are also discussed in H.O. Duncan, *The World on Wheels*, p. 293.

91. *English Mechanic*, 23 Dec. 1870.

92. H.H. Griffin, "Cycling under Three Heads. 2. The Sport," *Baily's Magazine*, June 1892.

93. Nahum Salamon, *Bicycling, Its Rise and Development, A Text Book for Riders* (2nd edition 1876), reprinted by David and Charles, 1970.

94. In Holland, the first bicycle clubs were given names which expressed this mood of modernity. In Deventer a club founded 22 Oct. 1871 was called the Velocipede Club "Immer Weiter" (which could be translated as "On and On," or "Always Further"); The Hague had a club called "Celeritas" (Speed), while Brummen (near Deventer) had a club called "Voorwaarts" (Forwards) and Apeldoorn one called "Vitesse" (Speed). See Theo Stevens, "The Elitist Character of Early Dutch Cycling," *Proceedings—12th International Cycling History Conference*.

95. After several unsuccessful attempts in 1880 on the much-coveted record of 20 miles in an hour, Herbert Liddell Cortis achieved it in 1882. On 27 July 1882, he rode 20 miles in 59m 31.8s at Crystal Palace; six days later, 2 August 1882, he set a new record in Surbiton, Surrey, of 59m 20.2s.

96. Charles Spencer, *Bicycles and Tricycles*, p. 68.

97. Alfred Howard, *The Bicycle for 1874: A Record of Bicycling for the Year*.

98. Nahum Salamon, op. cit.

99. *Daily News*, 23 August 1876. The distinction made here between "popular" and "fashionable" should be noted and examined. A "popular" pastime was one which would appeal to the masses, to the working classes; if it became "fashionable," it had gained acceptance further up the social scale, among the middle classes.

100. Alfred Howard, *The Bicycle for 1876: A Record of Bicycling for the Past Year*.

CHAPTER TWO

1. The Amateur Athletic Club (often called the Amateur Athletic Association) was formed in 1866 "to afford as completely as possible to all classes of Gentlemen Amateurs the means of practising and competing versus one another without being compelled to mix with professional runners." (H.F. Wilkinson, ed., *The Athletic Almanack*, 1868, quoted in Bailey, see below). It defined "amateur" as follows: "Any person who has never competed in an open competition, or for public money, or for admission money, or with professionals for a prize, public money or admission money, and who has never, at any period of his life, taught or assisted in the pursuit of athletic exercises as a means of livelihood, or is a mechanic, artisan or labourer." See Peter Bailey, *Leisure and Class in Victorian England: Rational Recreation and the Contest for Control, 1830–1885* (London, 1978).

2. G. Lacy Hillier, Badminton *Cycling* (1889 edition), p. 317; H.H. Griffin, "Cycling Twenty Years Ago," *The Cycle Magazine*, April 1896.

A note on the earliest bicycling periodicals follows. *The Bicyclist*, a monthly, was first published in Herne Hill, south London, in Nov. 1875. *Bicycling News*, a weekly, was first published 14 Jan. 1876. *The Bicycle Journal*, another weekly, was first published 18 Aug. 1876, and sometime between Feb. and Aug. 1878 changed its name to *The Bicycle Journal, Swimming and General Athletic and Pedestrian Recorder*, which suggests it was having problems surviving in the competitive cycling journalism marketplace. It went out of business with its issue of 27 Nov. 1878, promising to reappear the following spring. With editorial offices near Fleet Street, *Bicycle Journal* was printed in south London and distributed in 1876 to ten outlets in London and other major cities. From the offices of *Bicycle Journal*, editor Alfred Howard also published an annual review of the sport, a list of clubs and a road guide: *The Bicycle for 1877, A Record of Bicycling for the Past Year*, was his third such annual review. *The Bicycling Times* was first published in May 1877. *Bicycling—A Monthly Provincial Magazine and Country Club Gazette* was first published in Newcastle in Aug. 1878.

The successful growth of the cycling press was due overwhelmingly to one factor—the financial support provided by advertisers—manufacturers who needed to sell bicycles, equipment and accessories. "Cycling is much better situated in this respect than other sports," commented Lacy Hillier; "the maker of running shoes, or of swimming costumes alone, seldom spends much on advertisements, for it would take an immense sale of such articles to recoup a manufacturer for the considerable outlay which any serious amount of advertizing would necessitate." The bicycle, however, was an expensive item, much in demand: "It thus comes about that cycling is provided with a cheap, exhaustive, and essentially readable class press, which does much to popularize the sport and binds its votaries together," concluded Hillier, who added that "the cycling press is emphatically a practical class press." (Badminton *Cycling*, p. 314)

3. Nahum Salamon, *Bicycling, Its Rise and Development, A Text Book for Riders* (Preface, 2nd edition 1876). Salaman's book is a collection of various historical information and a guide book to English and Continental roads. In the Preface, Salaman writes: "During the existence of the wooden-wheeled velocipedes, and when in 1869–70, those vehicles showed some signs of vitality, several books appeared on the subject. When wooden-wheeled machines went out of use, these books became valueless, and now not a half-a-dozen lines in any of them would be found applicable to the Bicycle of today, and not a word in them would be of the least instruction to the Bicyclist… In the face of these facts, it must appear strange that there should not be in existence a single book of reference, or guidance on this subject. We have, therefore, ventured to supply the want with a brief volume, which will, we trust, be found practical, trustworthy, and instructive." Salamon was at first London agent for sewing machines for the Coventry Machinists' Company and in 1873 joined the board of the Coventry Machinists' Company as Managing Director, with an agreement to lend the company up to £5,000. By 1880, Salamon was Chairman of the company with a 21% holding. He later parted from the company and was involved in the Bicycle and Tricycle Supply Company (see *The Bazaar, Exchange and Mart.*, 8 July 1881). I am indebted to Nick Clayton for information about Salamon.

4. For an account of the John o'Groats ride, see G. Lacy Hillier, "A General Survey of Long-Distance Cycle Riding,": *Cyclist Annual and Year Book for 1893*. For the Cann v. Wilson race between Sheffield and Plymouth, see H.W. Bartleet, "Historic Rides, The First Long Road Race," *Cycling*, 14 July 1921. Some of the more prominent long road rides recorded in the press were listed by Nahum Salamon, *Bicycling, Its Rise and Development*, 1874 and 1876 editions:

- Sept. 1872; Charles Wheaton (Surrey B.C.) rode from London to Newcastle, 274 miles in 3 days.
- 2 June 1873; Charles Leaver, Geoffrey Hunt, Charles Spencer and William Wood (Middlesex Bicycle Club) rode to John o'Groats in the north of Scotland on bicycles built by T. Sparrow, 800 miles in 14 days (also reported in *Daily Telegraph*)
- August 1873; Surrey and Middlesex Bicycle Clubs raced from London to Brighton and back; 6 members from each club.
- 13 Sept. 1873; 2 members of Pickwick B.C. rode from London to Land's End in 58 hours.
- April 1874; Cann and Wilson raced from Sheffield to Plymouth.
- May 1874; Keith-Falconer rode from Bournemouth to Hitchin, 135 miles in 19 hours (reported in *The Field*, 20 June 1874)
- August 1874; race from Bath to London (106 miles) for the captaincy of the Middlesex Bicycle Club.

"Thomas Sparrow, who accompanied the race, started them and owing to the great number of people assembled, there was some difficulty in passing through the crowds."

5. *Wolverhampton Chronicle*, 29 Dec. 1875.

6. *The Bicyclist*, Feb. 1876.

7. *Bicycle Journal*, 29 Dec. 1876.

8. Charles Spencer, *Bicycles and Tricycles*, Preface. The use of the term "professional" here indicates a specialized, money-making performance, which an audience would pay to see, as distinct from a sport "likely to be taken up by the general public," that is, an "amateur" sport.

9. Charles Spencer, op. cit., p. 56.

10. Hillier quoted from Viscount Bury and G. Lacy Hillier, Badminton *Cycling* (1889 edition), pp. 176–79.

11. "Price List and Descriptive Catalogue of the "Champion" Long Distance Bicycle Manufactured Only by Arthur Markham, (The First Champion Bicyclist), Bicycle Manufacturer, 345, Edgeware Road, London, W.," date about 1879 (copy courtesy Nick Clayton).

12. All advertisements are quoted from Alfred Howard, *The Bicycle for 1877* and from *The Bicycle Journal*, 13 April 1877.

13. *Bicycle Journal*, 16 March 1877. An "unattached" rider was one who was not a member of a club, either because he chose not to be, or sometimes because he did not have the social standing or connections to be eligible for membership (see also "The Unattached," *Bicycle Journal*, 9 March 1876, p. 10–11). Grout's reference to "keeping the sport under due self-control" is a reference to discussion then currently going on to form a Bicycle Union, to keep cycling independent of the control of the Amateur Athletic Club, which sponsored cycling championships from 1871 to 1879.

14. "We hear that a number of gentlemen, members of the Liverpool Velocipede Club, are making arrangement for a tournament on bicycles to be held in the Gymnasium. The programme is to include tilting at the ring, throwing the javelin, broadsword contests, and engagement with lances. On Saturday evening it is intended to illustrate the power of the bicycle over obstacles, in other words to ride a steeplechase." (*Stockport Advertiser*, 29 Jan. 1869). This tournament appears to have been an earlier version of those reported later, in *Liverpool Mercury*, 24 and 26 April 1869 and *Liverpool Weekly Courier*, 1 May 1869 (see Chapter 1). The early existence of this Liverpool Velocipede Club suggests a precocious interest in the bicycle in that city. Both the Club and the Tournaments are probably best understood as promotional endeavors to encourage riding and to sell velocipedes, rather than as social activities organized by an already existing group of enthusiasts. The Liverpool Gymnasium, founded in 1864, had a subscription membership, an annual festival, ladies' classes and 2,000 members by 1866. Just as in London, at Spencer's Gymnasium the velocipede craze built on existing gymnastic foundations (see *Porcupine*, a Liverpool satirical weekly, 1864–1869). I am grateful to Nick Clayton for these citations.

15. Wolverhampton Velocipede Club *Rules*, see Chapter 1, note 54.

16. *English Mechanic*, 17 Sept. and 8 Oct. 1869.

17. Quoted in Nick Clayton, "Little and Often—The Records of the Amateur Bicycle Club," *Proceedings of the 5th International Cycle History Conference*.

18. Charles Spencer, *Bicycles and Tricycles*, pp. 62, 68 and 72–73.

19. Alfred Howard, *The Bicycle for 1877: A Record of Bicycling for the Past Year*.

20. *Bicycle Journal*, 5 Jan. 1877.

21. Ibid. 9 March 1877.

22. Discussions of professional or "primitive" (pre-rational) sport in the 1860–70 period include Don Watson, "Popular Athletics on Victorian Tyneside," *International Journal of the History of Sport*, Dec. 1994, pp. 487–494 and "Rational Recreation and the New Athleticism," Chap. 6 of Peter Bailey, *Leisure and Class in Victorian England*. Bailey makes a distinction (pp. 131–133) between "bourgeois" and "popular" culture, between "the new model athletic sports of the A.A.C." and "the sub rosa world of professional running and walking races," which were "eccentric and undisciplined." It is not easily apparent into which category the burgeoning professional cycling should be placed.

23. Alfred Howard, *The Bicycle for 1874. A Record of Bicycling for the Year*. Howard's section on "The Past and Present of the Bicycle" contains the following comment: "Of all the pastimes and athletic exercises with which we are acquainted, none has so rapidly come into public favour, and retained its hold thereon so firmly, as the art of bicycle riding… Combining as it does the chief advantages of the various athletic sports with a useful and agreeable method of swift and easy locomotion, it may be safely trusted to hold its own against all rivals… Bicycle racing is now fast becoming a national sport, and it far outrivals any other with which we are familiar… And especially in these days of luxurious indulgence and ease, when the youth of Great Britain are declared by the intellect of the age to be deteriorating fearfully, does bicycling come to our rescue, and by its fascination, once again induce our young men to restore the physical superiority of which Englishmen have always been so justly proud."

24. A similar pattern of professional wagering, with the stakes held by a trusted local figure such as a well-known pub-owner, occurred in early football in the 1840s and 1850s (see John Goulstone, "The Working-Class Origins of Modern Football," *International Journal of the History of Sport*, Vol. 17, No. 1, March 2000, pp. 135–143).

25. "Preface," Alfred Howard, *The Bicycle for 1877*, op. cit.

26. Of these approximately 120 members in 1876, more than 70 were members of Trinity College, including Gerard Cobb (President), Hon. J.W. Plunkett (Vice-President) and Hon. I.G.N. Keith-Falconer. Among the Trinity College members were three titled aristocrats, two Professors and two ministers. See "Cambridge University Bicycle Club, October Term 1876, Rules and Bye-Laws," contained in Add. 7628, boxes of documentation concerning the Cambridge University Bicycle Club in Cambridge University Library collection. *Bell's Life* (10 Nov. 1877) listed 373 members since the foundation of the Club, and 242 current members, an extraordinary increase in membership.

27. *Bell's Life*, 26 May 1877. Accounts for the building of this track also exist in Cambridge University Lib., Add. 7628.

28. *The Field*, 20 June 1874.

29. Spencer, *Bicycles and Tricycles*, op. cit., p. 56.

Notes—Chapter Two

30. *The Field*, op. cit.
31. H.M. Abrahams and J.B. Kerr, *Oxford v. Cambridge, A Record of Inter-University Contests from 1827–1930*; Nahum Salamon, op. cit. p. 13.
32. *The Field*, 20 June 1874.
33. *The Field*, 9 May 1874.
34. G. Lacy Hillier, "A General Survey of Long-Distance Cycle Riding." *Cyclist Annual and Year Book for 1893.*
35. See Note 4 for some of the more prominent long road rides listed by Nahum Salamon, *Bicycling, Its Rise and Development*, 1874 and 1876 editions.
36. See Cambridge University Bicycle Club "Rules and Bye-laws," as in Note 25.
37. G. Lacy Hillier, "A Brief and Critical Account of the One Mile Amateur Bicycle Path Record," *Cyclist Christmas Number*, 1891.
38. Keith-Falconer won the Amateur Athletic Club 4-mile bicycle championship in 1876, the Bicycle Union 2-mile championship in 1878 and the Bicycle Union 50-mile championship in 1882 (see Appendices A and C).
39. Rev. Robert Sinker, *Memorials of the Hon. Ion Keith-Falconer* (1888); James Robson, *Ion Keith-Falconer of Arabia* (Hodder and Stoughton, London, 1923); E.B. Parker, "The Honourable Ion Keith-Falconer," *The Boneshaker* No. 65, Winter 1971; Nick Clayton, "The Hon. Ion Keith-Falconer and the Cambridge University Bicycle Club," *The Boneshaker* No. 140, Spring 1996. Keith-Falconer's outstanding academic attainments set him apart from the Cambridge students who indulged in sport and not much else. See J.A. Mangan, *Athleticism in the Victorian and Edwardian Public School*, Chapter 6, "Oxbridge parents and imperialism," for accounts of Oxbridge memories, "idle years of cricket, fives, racquets and billiards, when work weighed lightly on the conscience and the river and games field engrossed many students."
40. "Muscular Christianity" is a term commonly used to identify and describe the particular combination of moral rectitude and passionate enthusiasm for sport and physical exertion which was found in the British public schools and universities from the mid–19th century onwards. See Mangan, *Athleticism in the Victorian and Edwardian Public School.*
41. Sinker, op. cit., p. 19.
42. All quotations from Sinker, op. cit.
43. G. Lacy Hillier, Badminton *Cycling* (1889 edition), p. 263.
44. G. Lacy Hillier, "A Brief and Critical Account of the One Mile Amateur Bicycle Path Record," *Cyclist Christmas Number*, 1891.
45. G. Lacy Hillier and W.G.H. Bramson, *Amateur Cycling* (1893), pp. 45–46.
46. For further discussion of issues of style and technique, see Note 70.
47. G. Lacy Hillier, Badminton *Cycling* (1889 edition), p. 277.
48. *Bicycle Journal*, 24 Nov. 1876, an editorial probably written by Alfred Howard.
49. One of the most widely publicized attacks occurred on 26 August 1876, when the driver of the St Albans coach attacked a cyclist with his whip, while his guard used an iron ball on a rope to drag the cyclist and his machine to the ground. Driver and guard were prosecuted and fined. See Hillier, Badminton *Cycling*, op. cit., p. 75.
50. G. Lacy Hillier, Badminton *Cycling* (1889 edition), p. 283. Some of the restrictive measures discussed included requiring bicycle riders to carry and ring a bell whenever they encountered a horse on the road, to dismount when encountering a horse, and prohibitions on riding in certain locations.
51. G. Lacy Hillier, Badminton *Cycling* (1889 edition), p. 277.
52. G. Lacy Hillier, Badminton *Cycling* (1889 edition), p. 278.
53. *Bicycle Journal*, 16 March 1877.
54. G. Lacy Hillier, Badminton *Cycling* (1889 edition), p. 278.
55. Gerard Cobb, letter to *The Field*, 18 Oct. 1878.
56. *Bicycling Times*, 25 July 1878
57. Bicycle Union Minutes, 4 April 1878.
58. G. Lacy Hillier, Badminton *Cycling* (1889 edition), p. 282.
59. *Minutes* of the Bicycle Union are housed at the Modern Records Centre, University of Warwick (Mss. 328/B/Temp). Later, an 1896 publication (F.T. Bidlake, *Cycling*, pp. 109 110) referred to the organization, which had been renamed the National Cyclists' Union in 1883, as "claiming to be the cycling parliament, or Jockey Club of the wheeling world." By then, its declared aims were more broadly summarized as follows:

1. To ensure a fair and equitable administration of justice as regards the rights of Cyclists on the Public Roads.
2. To watch and urge the action of the Road Authorities, with a view to the more efficient supervision and maintenance of the Roads throughout the United Kingdom.
3. To watch the course of any legislative proposals in Parliament, or elsewhere, affecting the interests of the Cycling Public, and to make such representations on the subject as the occasion may demand.
4. To consider the relation between Cyclists and the Railway Companies, with the view of securing, if possible, some modification of the present tariff for the carriage of Bicycles and Tricycles, and greater security in their conveyance.
5. To examine the question of Amateur and Professional Bicycle and Tricycle Racing in general, and to frame definitions and recommend rules on the subject. To arrange for Annual Race Meetings at which the Amateur and Professional Championships of Bicycling and Tricycling shall be decided.

60. G. Lacy Hillier, Badminton *Cycling* (1889 edition), p. 282.
61. "Modern Amateurism, or, Confusion Worse Confounded," *Wheel World*, No. 6 Vol. 1, Oct. 1880.
62. *The Times*, 26 April 1880. There is evidence in the C.U.B.C. papers mentioned above that Cobb attempted to gain wider acceptance in the amateur sporting world for amateur v. professional races, suggesting a desire to introduce "open" competition. In 1880, he attempted to organize the Cambridge University Athletic Club, the Dark Blue Bicycle Club (Oxford), the London Athletic Club and "the majority of the leading Metropolitan Bicycle Clubs" to oppose the strict amateur/professional segregation supported by the Amateur Athletic Union.

A draft resolution in Cobb's handwriting reads: "We are of the opinion that, Inasmuch as (1) The definition of an Amateur hitherto in force at our Athletic meetings was framed before Bicycling was known as a form of athletic sport, and had therefore no express reference to it, and (2) Experience has proved that such competitions under proper restrictions do really contribute to the advance of bicycling, the fact of having taken part in such competitions (as sanctioned by the Bicycle Union) ought not to disqualify a person who otherwise satisfies the prevailing definition of an Amateur from entering for any Bicycle Race or other Athletic contest open to Amateurs, and we hereby declare that all such entries will be received by us accordingly."

63. *Bicycle Journal*, 22 June 1877.

64. Whiting had won the Amateur Athletic Club's 1871 cycling championship after 17 "professionals" had been excluded, and had also won the Amateur Athletic Association's championships in 1873, 1874 and 1875. Whiting had then gone to France and become a member of a leading French club, Velosport de Paris, and in March 1875 he had competed against "professional" Camille Thuillet in Wolverhampton, thereby threatening his amateur status in England. The case highlighted the difference between the French and British definitions of professionalism, a disagreement that continued to plague international competition through the 1880s and 1890s.

65. *Bicycle Journal*, 7 Sept. 1877.

66. In a significant letter (Trinity College, 12 Feb. 1880) on the subject of the "amateur versus professional" racing, Cobb wrote: "The Council of the Union were mainly influenced in their opinion by the fact that bicycle racing does not *only* involve a trial of skill and strength between the competitors—as is the case with most other athletics—but also affords the greatest possible stimulus to Bicycle makers to develop and improve the machine. As the improvement of the bicycle is a matter of real practical importance to the general bicycling public, it was thought desirable to encourage the highest amount of competition possible, and that Amateurs and Professionals should be permitted to contend together in bicycling, as they have done under sanction of long custom in certain other branches of athletic pastime, such as cricket, tennis, etc." This statement emphasizes the central focus of this book, the symbiotic relationship between the bicycle racers and manufacturers in the ongoing improvement of the bicycle. (Cambridge University Lib., Add. 7628).

67. *Bicycling News*, 24 Aug. 1877. The holdings in the Cambridge University Library (Add. 7628) concerning the Cambridge University Bicycle Club and Gerard Cobb offer the opportunity to explore the subject in greater detail. The documentation includes scrapbooks kept by Cobb, minutes of the club activities, newspaper cuttings, posters and receipts from the building of the club's track.

68. *The Field*, 18 Oct. 1879.

69. "Editorial Notes," *Bicycling Times*, 31 Oct. 1878. In defeating Keen, Keith-Falconer challenged current opinion that "the professional champion was not to be touched by any of those who ride *con amore*." The contest proved that "when both men met they were about as nearly matched as possible." It also proved that "men's powers cannot be judged by their time performances, but that the only correct judgement can be arrived at by placing them alongside each other under the same circumstances as regards wind, weather and track."

70. *The Field*, 25 Oct. 1879. This report contained interesting comment on the contrasting styles of Cortis and Keen, and on technique and riding styles at the time. "As exhibitions of the art of riding, these two matches proved instructive to thousands of riders present, and thus served a useful purpose unthought of by the promoters. Nothing could be in greater contrast than the riding of these two accomplished bicyclists. Cortis, who is tall and of slender frame, never gets his leg straight even on his 60 in. machine, and being much given to leaning forward, his position appears cramped and painful, and by no means elegant. Keen, on the contrary, is a shorter man, with a powerful and well-knit frame, and riding a 56 in. wheel, his leg nearly straightens to the throw; no matter what is required of him he never leans forward, but sits quite erect, a slight swaying of the shoulders being the only indication of the way he concentrates the force of the whole body in an almost direct line upon the treadles. It is this economy of power which enables him to make such sudden bursts of speed, and with his perfect action, he drives his wheel with an accuracy which is universally admired. The prevalent style of riding amongst amateurs upon the path is to lean over till the back is nearly horizontal; this unsightly habit has caused numerous accidents, and the slight advantage obtained in escaping the wind must be all but counterbalanced by the compression of the lungs and consequent interference with breathing. If some riders would take Keen's riding for a pattern, we feel sure they would derive an advantage from it."

71. *The Field*, 18 Oct. 1879.

72. *The Field*, 25 Oct. 1879.

73. Editorial, "The Union Policy," *Bicycling Times*, 23 Oct. 1879.

74. "Cycling Celebrities," *Wheel World*, Feb. 1885.

75. Keen's life and career is documented in: Les Bowerman, "John Keen—The Life of a Cycling Pioneer," *Proceedings of the 4th International Cycling History Conference*, pp. 89–98; "Keen's Bicycle," a catalogue from 1874 in the Science Museum Library, London; "An Interview with John Keen," (conducted in Boston), *Bicycling World*, 29 Nov. and 13 Dec. 1879; "Cycling Celebrities—John Keen," *Wheel World*, Feb. 1885 (including extensive documentation of Keen's racing victories from 1869–1884); "A Chat with John Keen—Some Interesting Reminiscences," *Bicycling News*, 26 Feb. 1887. Obituaries were published in *Cycling*, 25 Jan. 1902 and *Surrey Comet*, 18 Jan. 1902.

76. *Sporting Life*, 26 Jan. 1870. I am indebted to Les Bowerman's research for many of these references to John Keen.

77. It is doubtful that Keen accompanied David Stanton to America in 1876, as is claimed by Michael Wells in "America and the Ordinary: In the Beginning, 1876," *The Wheelmen*, Nov. 1992. Pratt, *The American Bicycler*, 1880 edition, p. 152, does not include Keen among those who visited on that occasion.

78. Keen's innovations included: enlarging the size of the front wheel, which in effect was instrumental in the "invention" of the high-wheel bicycle; designing the "head" connecting the front forks to the backbone; the use of ball bearings in the wheel-hubs; the use of a v-shaped rim which secured a hard rubber tyre; screwing spokes directly into the hub; the use of a brake on the front wheel; the use of hollow forks; the use of "rat-trap"-style pedals and toe-clips.

79. "Trans-Atlantic Bicycling," *Bicycling Times*, 9 Oct. 1879.

80. *Bicycling News*, 9 Nov. 1877.

81. *Bicycling World*, op. cit., 29 Nov. and 13 Dec. 1879.

82. *Wheeling*, 17 Dec. 1884 and *The Cyclist*, 24 Dec. 1884. The appeal continued: "Unlike some fortunate people, Keen started at the bottom of the ladder, and consequently found that he had set himself a task calling for capital as well as labour. However, he kept steadily at work, preferring to go along in his own modest way rather than seek the responsibility of increasing his premises. To this reticence on the part of John Keen must be attributed the perfection machines have been brought to. Had he determined on money-making, his love for the work he had on hand would have fled; fortune might have favoured him, but it is very questionable if the sport would have developed to its present stage of popularity." The account of Keen in *Wheel World* (Feb. 1885) described the limitations of his situation: "…had he been aided by a sound business man as partner, with capital, John Keen and Co. would probably have been the name of one of the leading firms of the present day," but "he was unable to do two things well at the same time and could not, therefore, give full attention to business and racing too."

83. G. Lacy Hillier, Badminton *Cycling* (1889 edition), p. 281.

84. G. Lacy Hillier, Badminton *Cycling* (1889 edition), pp. 280–282).

85. The possibility of building an integrated, "open" sport was briefly hinted at by the "amateur versus professional" events specially sanctioned by the Bicycle Union, but a wider application of this novel approach to the organization of the new sport did not meet with general acceptance. Amateurs increasingly separated themselves from professionals and the two classes usually had their own segregated competitive arenas. The bicycle industry supported a strong professional class who were paid to advertize its products, and top amateurs could, if they were not extremely careful, slip into the suspect category of "maker's amateur" by accepting equipment and financial support from a manufacturer. But the vast majority of racers and recreational riders were amateurs who joined one of the new clubs. Cycling was not a team sport *per se*, but amateur clubs, with their uniforms and group regulations, approximated the "team spirit" of other team-based sports such as soccer or cricket. They were a part of a larger socially cohesive movement constructed within sport in general. As S.W. Pope has noted: "Nineteenth-century amateurism was an "invented tradition." As the rallying cry of late nineteenth century institutionalized sport, amateurism represented an attempt to draw class lines against the masses and to develop a new bourgeois leisure lifestyle as a badge of middle and upper-class identity… The rising bureaucrats of the movement used the amateur ethos as a mechanism for institutionalizing their social prejudices into resilient athletic structures… Even though the notion of original purity was largely a myth of their own creation, they sold a vision of an orderly, genteel, harmonious world of sport and healthful recreation, open to all classes, but under the benevolent governance of principled, manly, middle and upper-class men like themselves." (S.W. Pope, "Amateurism and American Sports Culture: The Invention of an Athletic Tradition in the United States, 1870–1900," *International Journal of the History of Sport*, Vol. 13, No. 3, Dec. 1996.).

86. J.T. Lightwood, *The Romance of the Cyclists' Touring Club*, p. 40.

87. G. Lacy Hillier, Badminton *Cycling* (1889 edition), p. 307.

88. R.E. Phillips, *Things a Cyclist Ought to Know*. The irony of the use of the term "professional" here should be pointed out. When it was applied to middle-class business men, "professional" indicated approval, but when used to describe working-class athletes, it became a pejorative! The word could thus be directed upwards or downwards on the social scale, depending on its context, although in all cases it meant people who were experienced at what they did and performed their jobs very well!

89. Women did not ride the high-wheeler, but the growth of tricycling, particularly of tandem tricycles, made it possible for women to join men on the road, and they were courted by the C.T.C. Women were urged to wear the club uniform, "made of an extremely neat and durable grey Cloth, which is woven in various thicknesses, and is thus suitable for Ladies' as well as Gentlemen's wear" (advertisement in Phillips, op. cit.). In an editorial entitled "Rationalism," in the Bicycle Touring Club's official *Monthly Gazette* of Oct. 1882 the author explained that the new grey cloth had been chosen to replace the previous "incongruous and unserviceable green" and came out solidly in favor of "rational" dress in allowing the participation of "the ladies" in cycling activities: "The solution of the difficulty in providing for our sisters, our wives, and our lady friends a uniform which shall admit of freedom of movement, and yet be indubitably free from ostentation, as well as innocent of the charge of being outré, lies, we are convinced, in the scheme advocated by the Rational Dress Society; a body whose raison d'être is essentially based upon rationalism, and with whose objects our readers are already familiar." It was "rationalism," also, which had helped to overcome the prejudices of those "who looked with horror upon the spectacle—now fortunately familiar in all parts of the land—of a lady on wheels enjoying a healthful recreation, who rambles far off into the country to visit scores of lovely nooks and glades, and pore over many a page in Nature's exhaustless volume." ("Rationalism," Editorial in *Bicycle Touring Club Monthly Gazette and Official Record*, Oct. 1882). Lacy Hillier commented that "the ladies' costume has proved very successful, and this is an especial boon to lady novices, who in the past were often sadly at a loss to know what to wear." (G. Lacy Hillier, Badminton *Cycling* (1889 edition), p. 311). Cycling's advocacy and acceptance of "rational" dress for women who wished to pursue athletic activity was extremely progressive for the time.

90. *Bicycle Journal*, 18 Aug. 1876.

91. *Daily News*, 23 Aug. 1876; quoted Hillier, Badminton *Cycling*, p. 74.

92. *Bicycle Journal*, 21 Sept. 1877.

93. *Bicycle Journal*, 8 Feb. 1878.

94. An obituary of Gerard Francis Cobb published in *The Cambridge Review*, 28 April 1904, showed the range of interests and accomplishments of this prototypical "muscular Christian," a Fellow of Trinity College. Cobb was born into an ecclesiastical family, studied theology

and classics and was a musician, organist and composer. His involvement with cycling was one of his many interests. "In his wide philanthropy and his ceaseless and undeclared generosity," said the obituary, "Mr. Cobb was a Christian of the highest type." (Thanks to John Green, Cambridge, for this citation).

95. Letter *to Daily News*, 30 July 1878, also printed in *Bicycling Times*, 1 Aug. 1878

96. Letter to *Daily News*, 3 August 1878, also printed in *Bicycling Times*, 8 Aug. 1878

97. *The Times*, 5 Sept. 1878.

98. See Stephen Hardy, "Entrepreneurs, Organizations and the Sports Marketplace," *Journal of Sport History* No. 13, 1986. "It is important to remember that the social history of sport does not constitute the totality of sport history... A number of important topics demand attention from perspectives that are closer to business and economic history. These topics require a shift in attention from the significance of consumption to the structures of production, from the broad sweep of social forces to the minute elements of decision-making. In general, they focus on the ways in which entrepreneurs have developed a special, perhaps singular, industry that has produced a particular part of the past." These comments certainly apply to the sport and industry of cycling.

Chapter Three

1. C.E. Hawley, "Uses of the Bicycle," *The Wheelman*, Vol. 1, No. 1, Oct. 1882, p. 25.

2. See John Cumming, *Runners and Walkers: A Nineteenth Century Sports Chronicle* (Chicago, Regnery Gateway, 1981).

3. S.W. Pope, "Amateurism and American Sports Culture: The Invention of an Athletic Tradition in the United States, 1870–1900," *International Journal of the History of Sport*, Dec. 1996, p. 291 and p. 298; Ted Vincent, *Mudville's Revenge—The Rise and Fall of American Sport* (Univ. of Nebraska, 1981), pp. 58–65.

4. The early history of American cycling has not been explored in great depth. In spite of the recent heightened profile of the sport, with the Tour de France victories of Greg Lemond and Lance Armstrong, the American cycling media shows minimal awareness of the importance of bicycle racing during the high-wheel period, or even in the 1890s. Cycling's history is generally seen as beginning in the post-World War II period, with the arrival of the European 10-speed bicycle in America. This chapter should be seen as an attempt to provide a profile of the richly documented—but neglected–early history rather than as a comprehensive account.

5. *Boston Globe*, 27 Jan. 1878, reprinted in *American Bicycling Journal*, 16 Feb, 1878, p. 7.

6. From the first issue of *American Bicycling Journal*, 22 Dec. 1877.

7. Editorial, "Salutatory," op. cit., 22 Dec. 1877, p. 1–2. Frank W. Weston, an Englishman living in Boston, was a central figure in establishing bicycling there. He was a partner in the importing firm of Cunningham, Heath and Co, a founder member and promoter of the Boston Bicycle Club, and founder of the *American Bicycling Journal*.

8. Hawley, in "The Uses of the Bicycle," *The Wheelman*, Oct. 1882, writes: "The manufacture of bicycles has necessarily been an integral part of their diffusion through the world. In the brief space of twelve years their number has rapidly increased, until more than one hundred and forty manufacturers in England, besides several in France and the United States, are actively engaged in the business. Several thousand men are employed, and fully six millions of dollars of capital are invested in this business. One firm alone, the Pope Manufacturing Company, has facilities for turning out twelve hundred bicycles per month." Stephen Hardy, "Entrepreneurs, Organizations and the Sports Marketplace," *Journal of Sport History* 13 (1986), is relevant here, as is an as yet unpublished article by Bruce Epperson, "The American Bicycle Industry, 1868–1900."

9. *Boston Globe*, 4 Nov. 1877, reprinted in *American Bicycling Journal*, 22 Dec. 1877, p. 7.

10. *New York Times*, 18 April and 11 May 1876.

11. *New York Times*, 30 Nov. 1876.

12. *Boston Herald* quoted in *American Bicycling Journal*, 5 Jan. 1878, p. 9. Booth was "born in England, and first took to velocipede riding in Paris by giving exhibitions of trick riding at the Cirque Napoleon, where from skilful tricks and fancy riding, he was called the great velocipedian Ducrow, after which he returned to England, to Agricultural Hall, London, which is one of the largest halls in the world... While there he beat all the celebrated riders, French and English... He has given exhibitions of fancy and trick riding at all the principal theatres in England and some of the first in America. He arrived in New York in 1870, and travelled throughout the country and Canada giving exhibitions. At last he settled in Boston, and has been a constable in this city four years."

13. Charles Pratt, "Our First Bicycle Club," *The Wheelman*, March 1883, p. 401.

14. *American Bicycling Journal*, 22 Dec. 1877.

15. These "Rules and Regulations" were printed in full in *American Bicycling Journal*, 2 Feb. 1878.

16. Pratt, op. cit., p. 402. Another account, in *Boston Globe*, 27 Jan 1878 (quoted *in American Bicycling Journal*, 16 Feb.1878) underlined this upper-middle-class orientation: "Four gentlemen—a journalist, an architect, a lawyer and a merchant—were the first to introduce the bicycle here."

17. Pratt, op. cit., pp. 404–405.

18. See "Bicycle Clubs," in *American Bicycling Journal*, 2 Feb.1878, "A federation of individuals for the purpose of extracting from some particular sport or mode of exercise a greater amount of benefit or enjoyment than could be otherwise obtained, is a practical example of the old adage that 'Union is Strength.'"

19. Pratt, op. cit., p. 402.

20. Pratt, op cit., p. 403.

21. Pratt, op. cit., p. 403.

22. *American Bicycling Journal*, 30 March 1878.

23. Pratt, op. cit., p. 404.

24. "Rules and Regulations of the Boston Bicycle Club," *American Bicycling Journal*, 2 Feb. 1878.

25. The Suffolk Bicycle Club, the Montreal Bicycle Club and the San Francisco Bicycle Club were founded in 1878. Amhurst, Brockton, Essex, Fitchburg, Hartford, Harvard, Lynn, Massachusetts, New Haven, Princeton, Providence, Salem, Waltham and Worcester, clubs were formed in 1879. Outside New England, in 1879–80 clubs

were founded in Baltimore, Brooklyn, Buffalo, Chicago, Detroit, Germantown, New York, Philadelphia, Providence, Rochester, Trenton, Utica and Washington D.C.

26. Hawley, op. cit.

27. *American Bicycling Journal*, 9 Aug. and 18 Oct. 1879.

28. "American Bicycle Clubs, March 1880," in Charles Pratt, *The American Bicycler* (1880, 2nd ed.), pp. 245–7.

29. *Bicycling World*, 10 Dec. 1880, p. 67.

30. C.W. Nairn and Henry Sturmey, *The Cyclist and Wheel World Annual for 1882*. These approximate numbers are confirmed by A.D. Chandler and J.C. Sharp, *A Bicycle Tour in England and Wales*, who in an Appendix list 360 clubs in England and 130 in the U.S. They also give the "number of bicycle and tricycle riders in England" as 250,000 and in the U.S. as "8,000, and rapidly increasing."

31. "Bicycle Clubs," *Bicycling World*, 1 Jan. 1883, p. 6. The establishment of so many clubs in such a short time shows that there was exceptional initial burst of energy in the bicycling movement in the United States. It was particularly strong in urban and suburban areas, where there was an emphasis on organized recreational group riding and competition. For city dwellers, bicycling offered a rediscovery of the outdoors, and easy access to previously inaccessible places.

32. *American Bicycling Journal*, 19 Jan, 1878, p. 10, quoting the *Boston Globe*.

33. *American Bicycling Journal*, 25 Jan. 1879, p. 4.

34. *Bicycling World*, 13 Dec. 1879.

35. *Boston Herald*, newspaper clipping datelined 29 Oct. 1879, in Pratt scrapbook, Smithsonian Institution.

36. "Bicycling at the Colleges," Editorial in *Bicycling World*, 26 Nov. 1880.

37. Op. cit., 25 Jan. 1879, p. 4.

38. Op. cit., 25 Jan. 1879, p. 7.

39. *American Bicycling Journal*, 2 Feb. 1878, p. 3.

40. Op. cit., 9 Aug. 1879. These races led to an inquiry, conducted by Charles Pratt in Boston, into the amateur status of winner William Pitman, who was subsequently declared to be a professional and disqualified. The similar disqualification of another racer, W. M. Wright, by the New York Athletic Club led to a protest by Wright that "he did not transgress any rule of bicycling athletics in force," (*American Bicycling Journal*, 9 Aug. 1879), which was true since the N.Y.A.C. had no formal jurisdiction over bicycle racing. The N.Y.A.C. sustained the disqualification, but Wright went on to be reinstated as an amateur by the National Association of Amateur Athletes.

41. Advertising flyer in Charles Pratt scrapbook, Smithsonian Institution, Washington, D.C.

42. *American Bicycling Journal*, 1 Nov. 1879.

43. Pratt, op. cit., p. 411.

44. Hawley, op. cit.

45. *New York Times*, 18 May 1879.

46. *New York Times*, 19 May 1879.

47. *San Francisco Morning Chronicle*, 16 May 1869.

49. *Bicycling World*, 1 May 1880.

50. *American Bicycling Journal*, 9 August 1879.

51. *San Francisco Examiner*, 24 Feb. 1879.

52. *Bicycling World*, 1 May 1880.

53. *Bicycling World*, 10 Dec., 1880.

54. Biographical details from Karl Kron, *Ten Thousand Miles on a Bicycle*, pp. 546–8; *Bicycling Times*, 9 Oct. 1879 and *St. Stephen's Review*, 30 April 1887.

55. *Bicycling Times*, 31 Oct. 1878.

56. *Bicycling Times*, 20 Nov. 1879.

57. *Icycles–Wheel World Christmas Annual for 1880*. This advertisement shows the remarkable range of Etherington's publishing interests, which included the following titles:

   a) *Wheel World*, edited by Etherington and Lacy Hillier, "A Bicycling and Tricycling Illustrated Monthly Magazine of Sport." Etherington started *Wheel World* in 1880, ran it for eighteen months, then sold it to Iliffe and continued as editor of both that publication and *The Cyclist*;

   b) *The Cyclist*, edited by Henry Sturmey and C.W. Nairn in 1880 and later by Etherington himself;

   c) Henry Sturmey's *The Indispensable Handbook* and *Complete Guide to Bicycling*;

   d) *Hotel Charges Directory*, "no traveller should be without this work";

   e) *The Bicycle Annual for 1879* and *1880*;

   f) Charles Pratt's *The American Bicycler* was also advertised.

58. Information from Etherington scrapbook in Lorne Shields collection, Toronto. Etherington's cycling interests subsequently diversified into the promotion of other events related to marketing and selling leisure-time activities, among them an annual "Sportsman's Exhibition and Exhibition of Sporting and other Dogs," and "Arcadia, A Veritable Fairyland," at the Royal Agricultural Hall in Islington and Olympia.

59. *Bicycling Times*, 28 Nov. 1878.

60. *Bicycling Times*, 11 Sept. 1879 and *American Bicycling Journal*, 18 Oct. 1879. Details of these three Six Day promotions were as follows. Nov. 1878 event: competitors included Cann, Edlin, Lees, Terront, Higham, Stanton, Keen, Markham; 1st—Cann, 1,060 ½ miles, 2nd—Edlin, 1,025 miles. April-May 1879 event: competitors included Waller, Terront, Lees, Stanton, Higham; 1st—Waller, 1,172 miles, 2nd—Terront, 1,128 miles, 3rd—Lees, 1,102 miles; 4th—Stanton, 1,100 miles. Sept. 1879 event: competitors were Waller, Terront, Higham, Cann; 1st—Waller, 1,404 miles, 2nd—Terront, 1,390 miles.

61. *The Referee*, Sept. 1879, exact date unknown, advertisement reproduced in *The Years of the High Bicycle* (compilation of catalogues), Pinkerton, 1980.

62. "An Interview with John Keen," (conducted in Boston, 16 Nov. 1879), originally published in *Bicycling World* and reprinted in *Bicycling Times*, 1 Jan. 1880.

63. Address of President Gerard Cobb to the Bicycle Union, *The Country*, 21 Dec. 1878. Cobb disapproved of "this new form of contest, for which there has recently been a kind of mania elsewhere." Referring to his efforts to achieve a reform of amateur versus professional restrictions, Cobb regretted that "whilst we have been endeavouring to make our new pastime the occasion of a change calculated to influence beneficially other forms of athletics as well, our own domain should at the same time have been invaded by this utterly aimless, and in the opinion of many, most mischievous type of contest."

64. *Bicycling Times*, 25 Sept. 1879.

65. *American Bicycling Journal*, 25 Jan. 1879.

66. *Bicycling News*, 22 Nov. 1878.

67. See Chapter 7, "Six-Days Go-As-You-Please," in

John Cumming, *Runners and Walkers: A Nineteenth Century Sports Chronicle*. British pedestrian champions had visited America as early as the 1840s; England versus America sold tickets. English runner John Barlow attracted a crowd of 25,000 people to Hoboken, New Jersey to watch him compete for a $1,000 purse. At a return match in November the same year, the *Spirit of the Times* reported an even larger crowd, estimated at 40,000 (quoted in Ted Vincent, *The Rise and Fall of American Sport*, University of Nebraska, 1981, p. 34). Perhaps the most famous Six Day contest had been that between Edward Weston and Daniel O'Leary, both of whom had accomplished great walking feats on the road. In 1876, at the Agricultural Hall in Providence, Rhode Island, O'Leary defeated Weston, setting a world record of 519 miles. In 1876, Manchester's *Athletic News* carried an article entitled "Long Distance Walking," which confirmed the fashionable popularity of such events: "At the present time, when the public mind is much exercised with regard to the feats of endurance exhibited by American and English pedestrians, a few details of long distance walking may prove interesting to our readers." The same paper carried reports of the earliest Six Day bicycle races in the English Midlands (*Athletic News*, Manchester, 30 Sept., 21 Oct. and 2 Dec. 1876). By the 1880s, the Six Day pedestrian record was 568 miles, and by 1890, 619 miles. In the United States, a pioneer pedestrian marathon was staged at Madison Square Garden in 1878. The American Institute 500 mile endurance race had been presented in May 1879. In October 1879, just before Etherington's party arrived in the States, the *New York Times* reported that another Six Day foot-race "for the O'Leary belt" had just begun at Madison Square Garden (*New York Times*, 6 Oct. 1879). Etherington, riding the sporting wave of the times, eyed the Garden unsuccessfully for his 1879 American cycling Six Day debut.

68. *New York Times*, 6 Oct. 1879.

69. *Bicycling Times*, 9 Oct. 1879; this article was also printed as an "Extract" to be used for advertizing purposes.

70. Frenchman Charles Terront, who would become one of the most famous cyclists of the 1880s and 1890s, was only twenty-two but, according to *Bicycling Times*, had already won 500 medals. He had placed second in two of the Six Day races, and won a 26-hour race. William Cann, from Sheffield, was twenty-six, and a graduate of the intense north of England professional scene. He had won Etherington's first Six Day in November 1878, and beaten the Mexican horseman, Leon, riding 19 separate horses, with a total of 960 miles: "Cann is a bit of a wit, and is cram-full of Shakespeare, portions of which he rolls forth at opportune moments, much to the amusement of his friends." London bicycle manufacturer John Keen, who had an unrivaled record in the English 1 mile championships—winner in 1873, 1876, 1878 and 1879, runner-up in 1870, 1872 and 1874–was thirty years old, one of the veterans of English cycling, having first raced on the velocipede in 1869. "His reputation as being THE man has enabled him to secure an immense number of patrons for his make of bicycle, known as the Eclipse, and richly he deserves it. We anticipate that when our American cousins see Keen moving along with his easy, graceful and mechanical-like action, they will open their eyes a bit." (*Bicycling Times*, op. cit). *Bicycling World* interviewed Keen in Boston and found him "a gentlemanly, practical man, who knows the art and the business of bicycling in all their phases, and is ready in imparting his knowledge to others." David Stanton, at 31 the veteran of the four, born in South Wales, was the first rider to have ridden 1,000 miles in the Six Day race of March 1878 and had made a previous, 1876, visit to America (*Bicycling World*, 13 Dec. 1879).

71. *American Bicycling Journal*, 18 Oct. 1879.

72. *Bicycling Times*, 27 Nov. 1879.

73. *American Bicycling Journal*, 1 Nov. 1879.

74. Ibid.

75. Hawley, op. cit.

76. On the first, Etherington and Cann returned home because of "the vile state of the roads. In drawing a comparison with the English roads, a ploughed field and a billiard table would not be wide of the mark." On the second, however, "the riding of the visitors was much admired, that of Cann being particularly fleet and graceful. Terront's riding was plucky and rapid and very skilful, as was shown by his riding a very light racing machine steadily over the roughest country roads." (*Bicycling Times*, 13 Nov. and 27 Nov. 1879).

77. "The Massachusetts Bicycle Club," *The Wheelman*, June 1883, p. 166.

78. *Boston Globe*, 3 Nov. 1879,

79. All quotes from *Boston Globe*, 6–12 Nov. 1879.

80. *Bicycling World*, 15 Nov. 1879.

81. *Boston Globe*, 14 Nov. 1879.

82. *Chicago Tribune*, 20 Nov.-7 Dec, 1879.

83. In San Francisco, a row of six tents was erected, in which a new track, 15 feet wide and six laps to the mile, was built and six riders were recruited. "The bicycle as a racing vehicle has not been greatly used in this country, though much in vogue in England," reported the *San Francisco Chronicle*: "The interest in bicycle-racing in this country centers chiefly in Boston, though the love of locomotion on two wheels is widespread. The Suffolk Bicycle Club of Boston numbers 78 members and contains the best long and short-distance riders in this country. It was organized in the spring of last year, and has developed a very strong interest in the sport. From this nucleus, twenty-seven bicycle clubs have sprung up... Whether the San Francisco representatives of the eminently healthful and gentlemanly sport will gain as prominent a name for the State as the pedestrians and race-horses the contest which opens tonight at the Pavilion will tell." (*San Francisco Chronicle*, 29 Nov. 1879). The racing, for a first prize of $500, was heavily advertised in the local press. "It is a peculiar fact in connection with this diversion that the longer one gazes at the swiftly-gliding wheels and riders the more fascinated he becomes," commented the *San Francisco Chronicle*: "horse-racing and pedestrianism pale into insignificance in comparison with this novel mode of rapid transit." Dunbar, one of the riders, was "an acrobat by profession, and is one of the acrobatic team of Dunbar and Fox." Another, Bennett, was "a plumber by occupation, and has had but a brief experience with the bicycle, but has already attained an astonishing degree of proficiency." Royston, "a tall and slender youth, a native of England, was at one time a member of the famous London Bicycle Club, but has had no practice for four years." (*San Francisco Chronicle*, 30 Nov. 1879). Eggers, the winner, covered 543 miles;

Merrill, 2nd, 512 miles. Eggers, who "contested the race for his own amusement solely," gave his $500 prize to "the German and other hospitals" in San Francisco. Eggers rode "in the stiff English style–breast protruding, arms akimbo and at a most amazingly sharp angle... But he knows how to ride the bicycle." (*San Francisco Chronicle*, 3 Dec. 1879).

84. *San Francisco Chronicle*, 3 Dec. 1879.

85. *San Francisco Chronicle*, 12 Dec. 1879.

86. Baudry de Saunier, *Les Mémoires de Terront*.

87. Stanton's 50 mile (Aug. 1879, 2h 54m 34 3/5s) and 100 mile (Oct. 1876, 6h 45m) records were advertised as proof of the superiority of the "Humber." Stanton's advertising flyer was included as evidence among the legal documents described in footnote 90.

88. In an interview in *Bicycling World* (15 May 1880), Pope stated that he was first attracted to the bicycle when he was visited by "an English gentleman" in the summer of 1877, and he claimed to have had a bicycle made by July or August 1877. His first models were made by the Weed Sewing Machine Company at a factory in Hartford, Connecticut, and by the date of this interview he was able to claim that the Weed Company had "more tools, dies and machinery used for the exclusive manufacture of bicycles than any other maker in the world; our facilities at the present time are equal to turning out twice as many bicycles as that of any other manufacturer." In addition, he claimed to have 80 agencies "in almost every State," and that "three-quarters of the bicycles now sold in the United States are of our manufacture." An article in *Bicycling World* ("A Great American Manufacture," 1 April 1881) gives details and pictures of an already substantial industrial enterprise.

89. Charles Pratt scrapbook, Smithsonian Institution, Washington D.C.

90. Advertising flyer and "Motion papers for Restraining Order and Preliminary Injunction," filed 5 Feb.1880, motion granted 13 March 1880, both from National Archives, Washington D.C., copy supplied to me by David Herlihy. An interview with Colonel Albert A. Pope, conducted by the Editor Charles Pratt, was published in *Bicycling World*, 15 May 1880.

91. Henry Sturmey, in *The Indispensable Bicyclist's Handbook*, for 1887, pp. 346, "The Trade in America," had the following to say about Pope: "The oldest firm in the American trade is the Pope Manufacturing Company, who commenced business some ten years since, and for a long time retained a monopoly by the purchase of every American patent touching on velocipede construction which could by any course of argument be construed to cover any vital portion of the modern machine. From time to time opponents sprang up, and although for a long time, by the expenditure of thousands of dollars, they were either crushed, bought off, or beaten out of the field, the company have at last found it advisable, either on the score of expediency or as a paying transaction, to grant licenses in certain quarters, and put up with the competition produced. The greatest rival of the Pope Company was for a long time the Overman Wheel Company... This firm is one of the most go-ahead in the States, and after a long and expensive litigation with the original firm, has arranged an armistice on mutual terms by which both firms use each other's patents."

92. "A Great American Manufacture," *Bicycling World*, 1 April 1881, pp. 326–31. It is not surprising that the article, written by *Bicycling World* editor Charles Pratt, was uncritical of Pope's rapacious business methods, since Pratt also worked as one of Pope's attorneys!

93. Capt. Fred. Whittaker, *Handbook of Summer Athletic Sports* (New York, Beadle and Adams, 1880), p. 46.

94. Charles Pratt, *The American Bicycler: A Manual for the Observer, the Learner, and the Expert* (2nd Edition, 1880), p. 228.

95. *Journal of Sport History* 13, 1986.

96. *St. Stephen's Review*, 30 April 1887.

97. Prior to the founding of the L.A.W., there was in fact an American Division of the Cyclists Touring Club, and one of the founding fathers of the L.A.W., Frank W. Weston, continued as Chief Consul of the C.T.C. in the United States. See letter written by Weston, "The C.T.C. and the L.A.W.," in *L.A.W. Bulletin*, 24 Dec. 1886.

98. *Bicycling World*, 20 March 1880.

99. Charles Pratt, *The American Bicycler*, op. cit., pp. 245–247.

100. The history of the founding and early days of the L.A.W. is well documented and is told in a number of places. One reliable account is in Karl Kron, *Ten Thousand Miles on a Bicycle*, Chap. XXXVI, "The League of American Wheelmen," pp. 615–633. *Bicycling World* (successor to the *American Bicycling Journal*) contained ongoing accounts of L.A.W. activity and racing, and for a short time was the official publication of the League, which later contracted with *Amateur Athlete* before publishing its own house journal, *League of American Wheelmen Bulletin*, in July 1885. A useful summary of League activity can be found in an editorial, "The League in 1886," published in *L.A.W. Bulletin*, 31 Dec. 1886. The *Springfield Wheelmen's Gazette* is another important source. A wide-ranging chronological account of the L.A.W. from 1880 to 1896 was written by Abbot Bassett: published as "League of American Wheelmen: A Concise History of the Great Bicycle Organization," in the *Louisville Courier-Journal*, 9 Aug. 1896.

101. Quoted in Karl Kron, op. cit., p. 616. 102 *Bicycling World*, 12 Oct. 1883.

103 Pratt, *The American Bicycler*, op. cit., p. 155–6. An account of a ride from Fitchburg to Boston in April 1878 contained the following comments on the roads: "We had a half-mile walk through gravel and loose stones ... there was not a distance of two successive miles that we could ride without a dismount," and "I dismounted by a side fall owing to an attempt to ride through sand several inches deep." Road maintenance was done by the local authorities and was not kind to bicycles: "For the past few weeks the country people have been doing what they call "making" roads; that is, hauling sand and dirt on the road and leaving carriages to roll it down, and it was an utter impossibility for anyone to ride through the stuff. Part of the way we rode on the turf in preference to the road, and for miles we rode in the wheel tracks about seven or eight inches wide." *American Bicycling Journal*, 27 April 1878.

104. *L.A.W. Handbook*, quoted in Karl Kron, op. cit., p. 622.

105. Charles E. Pratt, op. cit., p. 203–205. If any one book could be said to constitute an authority on early bicycling in the United States, it is *The American Bicycler*, published with the support of the Pope Manufacturing

Company. 2,000 copies of the 1879 edition were sold, making a second edition necessary in April 1880. On the expansion of the American industry, Pratt wrote, p. 205: "The Pope Manufacturing Company, which had during the year 1878 made a large plant and struck out with an energy and enterprise which was far-sighted, has continued to increase its facilities, and may still be called the only manufacturer proper in the United States. During the year 1878 they devoted their attention to one style of machine ... which has been sold throughout this country and even in foreign parts. They have special agencies in all the principal cities and many of the smaller ones, throughout the States. It ought to be noted, to the credit of the American enterprise, that although they have had in Europe ten years of development and accumulation against our two or so, the works of the Pope Manufacturing Company are already said to be larger and richer in facilities than those of any other bicycling establishment in the world. During the past year, with only one pattern of their machine in the market, this company has furnished three-quarters of all the bicycles sold in the United States."

Pratt (1845-1898) was recognized upon his death at the relatively young age of 53 as "a well-known lawyer and literary man... Mr. Pratt's talents were largely bent towards mechanical matters, admirably fitting him for his specialty, that of a patent lawyer." (Obituary, *Boston Sunday Globe*, 21 Aug., 1898). Another obituary can be found in *The Wheel*, 25 Aug., 1898. The Pratt scrapbook in the Smithsonian Institution contains many interesting letters related to Pratt's central involvement in early cycling, as well as photographs of him. An auction of Pratt's "large and valuable library" was held in Boston on 4th-7th April 1899 (copy of Catalogue title-page in author's collection; whereabouts of original unknown).

106. "The Political Power of the L.A.W.," *Outing* Vol. 2, No. 2, May 1883.

107. Detailed accounts of several of the largest and most prestigious clubs of this early period can be found as follows: "The Massachusetts Bicycle Club," *The Wheelman*, June 1883, pp. 161-172; "The Springfield Bicycle Club," *Outing*, Aug. 1883, pp. 337-344; "The Capital and the Capital Club," *The Wheelman*, Nov. 1883, pp. 82-96.

108. The most extensive account of the Good Roads Movement is by Philip P. Mason, "The League of American Wheelmen and the Good Roads Movement, 1880-1905" (Ph. D. thesis, University of Michigan, 1957), which also has an excellent bibliography. See also W.H. Wheeler, "The Repair and Maintenance of Roads," *L.A.W. Bulletin*, 26 Nov. 1886, pp. 534-537. A good recent account can be found in Glen Norcliffe, *The Ride to Modernity, The Bicycle in Canada, 1869-1900*, Chap. 5, "Bad Roads, Good Roads," pp. 149-177.

109. Precise wording of the New York Athletic Club definition was as follows: "An amateur athlete is one who does not enter in an open competition, or for a stake, public money, or admission-money, or entrance-fee, or compete with or against a professional for any prize; or has never taught, pursued, or assisted in the pursuit of exercises as a means of livelihood." (quoted Pratt, op. cit., p. 162)

110. *L.A.W. Bulletin*, 21 May 1886. The duties of the Racing Board were spelled out in detail in League regulations for 1886 published in this issue:

"(a) to the Racing Board are referred all matters pertaining to racing and the championships. They shall make all arrangements for the annual championships which are held under League auspices, and shall assign such other championships as are now or may be established, to be run under the auspices of such clubs or associations as they may consider most desirable, and under such conditions as they may deem expedient.

(b). It shall be their duty to make inquiry regarding any wheelman whose amateur status is questioned, and all protests or charges shall be entered with the Chairman of that Board, who will provide for an investigation by a member or members of that Board. Suspicious circumstances, which are in the judgement of any member of the Board sufficient to make the status of any wheelman a matter of reasonable doubt, shall be the basis of an investigation in the absence of formal protests or charges...

(c). It shall be within the province of the Racing Board to receive the request of any wheelman for reinstatement as an amateur...

(d). It shall also be within the province of the Racing Board to suspend from the race track ... any wheelman guilty of unfair dealings or ungentlemanly conduct on the track, or any wheelman who competes in a race not governed by the rules of the L.A.W....

(e). The Racing board shall have the power to make such rules for its government and the government of race meetings as may be deemed expedient..."

111. Karl Kron, op. cit., p. 629, and *L.A.W. Bulletin* for May-June 1886.

112. *L.A.W. Bulletin*, 4 June 1886. An extended discussion of the problems of the Racing Board with the "maker's amateur" problem, and the 1886 ruling declaring that many of the leading amateurs were "professionals" is contained in the report presented by Abbot Bassett to the General Meeting of the L.A.W. in Boston, 29 May 1886 and reported verbatim in *L.A.W. Bulletin*, 11 June 1886, where a "Legal opinion regarding the action of the Racing Board against the suspected parties" was also printed.

113. *L.A.W. Bulletin*, 19 March 1886.

114. Bates in *Bicycling World*, 9 July 1886, quoted in Karl Kron, op. cit., p. 629.

115. Advertisement in *L.A.W. Bulletin*, 6 August 1886.

116. "The Springfield Bicycle Club," *The Wheelman*, Vol. 2, No. 5, Aug. 1883.

117. "One Man's Work for Cycling," *Outing*, Vol. 13, No. 1, Oct. 1888.

118. "Speech of the Right Hon. R. Lowe, M.P.," *American Bicycling Journal*, 11 May 1878. There seems to have been the belief among some that Americans in general were backward in their approach to physical exercise compared to the British. An article in the *Boston Advertiser* commented: "With the hindrances which our climate and modes of life present to a rounded physical development, it is no wonder that the attainment of it is less common than it should be. Unlike the Englishman, who has in the atmosphere and traditional usages of his country a continual inducement to life in the open air, the American has to create under difficulties the needed disposition for such experience... The truth is, there is much to be done in order to educate American men and women up to that condition of physical health and vigor in which athletic exercises are undertaken with pleasure,

rather than a sense of duty." The truth was that the British predisposition towards organized athletic activity was located more in its educational and social structures, rather than in "climate and modes of life." *Boston Advertiser*, date unknown, quoted in *American Bicycling Journal*, 11 May, 1878.

119. E.P. Prial, "Cycling in the United States," *Harper's Weekly*, 30 Aug. 1890. See also the following core articles on Pope's participation in the early American bicycle industry: "Col. Pope's Response to the Toast, 'The Wheel,' at the League of Ohio Wheelmen Banquet," *The Wheelman*, Vol. 1, No. 1, Oct. 1882, pp. 69–72.; "Interview with Colonel Albert A. Pope," *Bicycling World*, 15 May 1880, p. 222–23 and "A Great American Manufacture," *Bicycling World*, 1 April 1881, pp. 326–331.

Chapter Four

1. "Resume for 1880," in Lacy Hillier and Harry Etherington, *Icycles, The Christmas Annual of the Wheel World*, p. 11.

2. *The Bazaar, Exchange and Mart*, 17 April 1878. Griffin's figures refer to total production over the years to date of just these 3 important firms. He also reported here that 300 machines per week were made by the three Coventry firms quoted, a total of 500 per week total Coventry production. Wolverhampton (12 firms) made 100 per week; Birmingham (10 firms) also 100 a week; London (nearly 30 firms) added another 150 a week; the rest of the country (45 firms) added another 150 a week—making a total of 1,000 machines per week. If the average value of a bicycle was assumed to be £10, then bicycles worth £10,000 were produced each week. Griffin thus calculated that 25,000 bicycles were being made in a year, worth £250,000. The 1877 total he estimated at 20,000 bicycles, 1876—15,000, 1875—10,000, prior to 1875—10,000, giving a total of about 80,000 bicycles manufactured up to 1878.

3. "Introductory Notes," H.H. Griffin, *Bicycles of the Year 1877*.

4. Quoted at the A.G.M. of the Southampton Bicycle Club, *Bicycling News*, 12 Oct. 1877.

5. Viscount Bury, *19th Century Magazine*, Jan. 1885.

6. "A Great American Manufacture," *Bicycling World*, 1 April 1881.

7. C.W. Nairn and Henry Sturmey, *The Cyclist and Wheel World Annual*, 1882.

8. Bury and Hillier, Badminton *Cycling*, 1889 ed., pp. 3 and 307.

9. It is difficult to assess the number of cyclists who took part in formal competition as opposed to those who participated in club and recreational activities. One might reasonably estimate that the proportion of enthusiasts who raced in formal competition on a regular or occasional basis (as distinct from participating in club runs) would not have exceeded 10% of the total number of cyclists (see Chapter 9 for further discussion of this issue).

10. Editorial "A Cosmopolitan Club," in *Bicycling News and Sport and Play*, 8 April 1896.

11. A.J. Wilson, *The Pleasures, Objects and Advantages of Cycling* (1887), p. 65.

12. The French sport did not undergo a similar polarization of amateur and professional competitors in the 1880s. Competition was organized according to experience level, and prizes consisted either of cups and medals, equipment or cash. The participation of the industry was not regarded as intrusive and the categorization of the two classes, and their separation in competition, was not considered a priority.

13. "Britain" was not a simple geographical category. Scottish and Irish cyclists resented control from London and argued for a measure of regional autonomy in the management of their affairs. There was an Irish Cyclists' Union and a Scottish Cyclists' Union. Even working-class Birmingham rebelled against the centralized control of the National Cyclists' Union. Through the 1880s, the Amateur Athletic Association continued to claim its right to promote bicycle racing as part of its athletic meetings, and there were occasional outbreaks of squabbling between the N.C.U. and the A.A.A.

14. This organization still exists.

15. See S.H. Moxham, *Fifty Years of Road Riding (1885-1935): A History of the North Road Cycling Club* (Diemer and Reynolds, Bedford, 1935).

16. "The Trade and Racing," W.J. Grew, *The Cycle Industry* (Pitman, London, 1921), p. 67.

17. Discussion of the state of American roads can be found in Philip Mason, "The League of American Wheelmen and the Good Roads Movement, 1880–1905," Ph. D. thesis, University of Michigan, 1957. Mason writes, "At the beginning of the 19th century the roads in the United States were so bad that it was cheaper to send goods by ship 3,000 miles to Europe than to transport the same commodities overland for more than 30 miles. One road authority declared in 1854 that "the common roads of the United States are inferior to those of any other civilized country."

18. Thomas Stevens, *Around the World on a Bicycle* (Scribner's, New York, 1889).

19. See, for example, the report—"The Notable Runs and Excursions of 1883," *Outing and The Wheelman*, Feb. 1884. The writer conducted a survey of "over three hundred clubs in the United States" in compiling this article. Non-competitive, organized century runs tended to level the distinction between racing and recreation—they were athletically challenging, but did not record finishing times. Many accounts of races and rides over American roads were published in *Bicycling World* in the 1880s.

20. Quoted in Philip Mason (see note 17 above), Chapter 3, "Origins of the Good-Roads Campaign of the League of American Wheelmen, 1880–1888." See also Lewis Bates, "Effect of the Bicycle on Our Highway Laws," *The Wheelman*, Oct. 1882, pp. 40–44 and Lewis Bates, "Good Common Roads and How to Make Them," *Outing*, Dec. 1884, pp. 194–200.

21. Quoted in *L.A.W. Bulletin*, Feb. 1887. This wider political involvement of the League played an essential role in the growth of the sport.

22. Stevens, op. cit., p. 104–5.

23. "A Frenchman on French cycling," *Wheeling*, 28 Sept. 1887.

24. "Racing at Bordeaux," p. 799 and "Racing Under the Electric Light at Bordeaux," *The Cyclist*, 10 June 1885, p. 800. This French visitor's "only three" tracks in France may not be an accurate estimate, since the citation in note 23 mentions a fourth track at Agen, near Bordeaux.

25. *The Cyclist*, 1 July 1885, p. 895.

26. The electric lighting is also reported in H.O. Duncan, *The World on Wheels*, p. 319.

27. Author's translation: *La Vélocipédie Pour Tous, par Un Vétéran*, Paris, 1892 (reprinted by Éditions du Layet, Cavalière, 1987), p. 245.

28. *The Cyclist*, 26 Aug. 1885, p. 1110. *The Cyclist* (9 Sept. 1885, p. 1185) reported that the Berlin track (organized by resident English entrepreneur, T.H.S. Walker) was "a real beauty, and would very decidedly open the eyes of some of the English riders who fancy the Germans know little or nothing of racing. The path is over 19 feet wide and about 400 yards round, with excellently planned corner-ends, well banked, and two long straights." It was surfaced with "broken bricks, clay and ashes, which apparently binds well, and makes an excellent surface, standing the enormous amount of work thrown upon it well, as there are some 55 share-holders in the company owning the path, and they all have the right to go and bang round by the hour."

29. Alfred Howard, *The Bicycle for 1877*, p. 10.

30. See G. Lacy Hillier, "The Classic Tracks of London. Their history, peculiarities, legends, and frequenters, with brief notes of feats accomplished and records made thereon," a series of articles in *The Wheel World*, March, April, May and September, 1886.

31. A.J. Wilson, *The Pleasures, Objects and Advantages of Cycling*, op. cit., p. 63.

32. Duncan, op. cit., pp. 316–320.

33. Wilson, op. cit., p. 63. An index of British tracks in Lacy Hillier's Badminton *Cycling* (1889 edition) lists tracks at the following locations, several of which were indoors: Agricultural Hall, London; Alexander Palace, London; Aylestone Road Grounds, Leicester; Belgrave Road Grounds, Leicester; Bridlington Quay; Cambridge; Sophia Gardens, Cardiff; Coventry; Crystal Palace; Hampden Park, Glasgow; Jarrow; Kennington Oval, London; Lillie Bridge, London; Lincoln; Long Eaton; Lower Aston Grounds, Birmingham; North Durham, Newcastle; Oxford; Paignton; Stamford Bridge, London; Surbiton; Taunton Athletic Grounds; Wallsend; Weston-super-Mare; Molineux Grounds, Wolverhampton. An account of the building of a significant track in Nijmegen, Holland in 1885 is found in Gertjan Moed, "The First Cycle Track in the Nederlands," *Cycle History 10, Proceedings, 10th International Cycling History Conference*.

34. See *Wheeling*, 25 July, 8 and 29 Aug., 5, 12, 19 and 26 Sept., 3, 10 and 17 Oct., 19 and 26 Dec. 1894. The debate was also conducted in *The Sportsman* and *Sporting Life*, and the issue was further discussed in H.O. Duncan, *Vingt Ans de Cyclisme Pratique,* Introduction, p. iii.

35. "Track Measurement," *Bicycling World*, 2 March 1883, p. 199.

36. "The Broken Records at Hartford and Springfield," *Outing and The Wheelman*, November 1884, p. 128.

37. "The Great International Races in America," *Wheeling*, 12 Sept. 1885.

38. A.J. Wilson, op. cit, p. 64.

39. *The Cycle* (Boston, Mass.), 28 May 1886.

40. *The Cycle*, 20 August 1886. Later discussion of track building can be found in M. P. Paret, "How to build a cycle track," *The Wheel and Cycling Trade Review*, 30 March 1894. In the United States in the 1890s, prominent tracks were built at the following locations: Woodside Park, Philadelphia; Willow Grove, Philadelphia; Tioga Park, Philadelphia; Asbury Park, New Jersey; Waverley Park, Newark, New Jersey; Vailsburg, Newark, New Jersey; Charles River Park, Cambridge, Mass.; Manhattan Beach, New York; Crescent Park, Providence, Rhode Island; Hampden Park, Springfield, Mass.; Coliseum, Worcester, Mass., and The Oval, Rochester, New York. Temporary tracks were also frequently built for indoor, winter events.

41. When should the stop-watch be started and stopped? Should it be started by visual or aural response to the starter's gun? How accurate were various makes of stop-watches? Could fifths of a second be relied upon? How many timer-keepers should be used, and would the average of three results be the means of deciding the result? All this discussion was much more crucial for short-distance events, where time-gaps were much smaller.

42. *La Vélocipédie Pour Tous, par Un Vétéran*, Paris, 1892, op. cit., pp. 239–40.

43. Alfred Howard, *The Bicycle for 1878: A Record of Bicycling During the Past Year*, "The Year's Bicycling," pp. 7–23.

44. Charles Spencer, *Bicycles and Tricycles*, p. 125

45. *The Cyclist and Bicycling and Tricycling Trades Review*, 25 May 1881. *The Cyclist* was an influential weekly journal edited in London by C.W. Nairn and in Coventry by Henry Sturmey.

46. Alfred Howard, *The Bicycle for 1877: A Record of Bicycling for the Past Year*, "The Year's Bicycling," pp. 7–10.

47. A systematic analysis of annual racing events is certainly feasible from the extensive press documentation available. This analysis of just one issue of *The Cyclist* in 1881 might well be contradicted by the patterns in a publication directed at a north of England spectatorship. There was also professional racing in the winter months in the north.

48. National Cyclists' Union race programme from 26 July 1884 (author's collection).

49. N.C.U. program for 1-mile bicycle and 5-mile tricycle national championships; Aston Lower Grounds, Birmingham, 13 June 1885, author's collection.

50. Nahum Salamon, *Bicycling: Its Rise and Development*, p. 77 prints the following: "Rules to be observed by professional riders. (These are the oft quoted Wolverhampton Rules).

1. Riders must pass each other on the outside, and be a clear length of the bicycle in front before taking the inside; and the inside man must allow room for his competitor to pass.

2. One attendant only shall be allowed in the dressing room, or on the course, with each rider, and he must not touch the machine at starting.

3. If the judge is convinced that two riders arrange for the winner to divide any prize, they shall be disqualified, and the prize given for a race at the next meeting.

4. If a rider fails to appear in time, his partner shall run with another. No walk over will be allowed.

5. In order that the course may be in as good condition as possible for competitors, no practising will be allowed on the day of the race. The number of each rider will be shown on the telegraph-board at starting, and the number of the winner of each heat."

Considering the range of competitive situations

that were likely to be encountered in professional contests (especially concerning the organization of money and questions of sporting behavior during races), these "Rules" quoted by Salamon appear somewhat sparse and inadequate. This suggests that specific contests may have had their own sets of rules.

51. "British cycling in 1884," *Springfield Wheelmen's Gazette*, Dec. 1884.

52. Letter from J. R. Hogg, of North Shields Bicycle Club, in *Springfield Wheelmen's Gazette*, March 1886.

53. It is difficult to estimate accurately the number of professionals competing in Britain in the 1870s and 1880s. Alfred Howard's *The Bicycle for 1877* listed dozens of riders who competed in professional races at Molineux Grounds, Wolverhampton, but many of those were probably ordinary working-class athletes ineligible to race as amateurs. The number of professionals capable of earning a full-time living in the sport was probably rather small. A list of leading British high-wheel professionals from the 1870s and 1880s must certainly include: Tom Battensby (Newcastle), William Cann (Sheffield), F. Cooper, H.O. Duncan (mostly living in France), Harry Etherington (London), H. Higham (Nottingham), Richard Howell (Manchester, later moved to U.S.A.), Robert James (Birmingham), John Keen (London), F. Lees (Sheffield), James Moore (usually living in Paris), R. Patrick (Wolverhampton), Walter Phillips (Wolverhampton), John Prince (London, later emigrated to the U.S.), S. Rawson (Derby), E. Shelton (Wolverhampton), David Stanton, George Waller (Newcastle) and Fred Wood (Leicester).

54. "Death of Mr. G.W. Waller," *Newcastle Daily Chronicle*, 7 Nov. 1900.

55. *Bicycling Times*, 11 Sept. 1879.

56. Howard, *The Bicycle for 1877*, op. cit., listed Waller as competing at Molyneux Grounds, Wolverhampton in April, August and September 1876.

57. *Newcastle Daily Chronicle*, op. cit.

58. Many of the details of Waller's life have been taken from Helen Sinclair, *Cycle-Clips, A History of Cycling in the North-East*.

59. H.O. Duncan, *The World on Wheels*, Paris, 1927, pp. 315–22 and 329–38. Duncan's career is chronologically documented in two places: *World on Wheels*, pp. 316–320 and in *Le Sport Vélocipédique*, 6 Feb., 13 Feb. and 27 Feb. 1885.

60. Duncan, op. cit., p. 315; see also Andrew Ritchie, "The Cycling World of Paris," *The Boneshaker*, No. 143, Spring 1997.

61. Duncan, op. cit., p. 316.

62. Duncan's early career is documented at length in four biographical articles by L. Saint-Savin and G. de Moncontour in *Le Sport Vélocipédique*: 6 Feb. 1885, pp. 77–79; 13 Feb. 1885, pp. 91–93; 20 Feb. 1885, pp. 100–101; and 27 Feb. 1885, pp. 114–115.

63. Duncan, op. cit., p. 335.

64. Duncan, op. cit., p. 336.

65. Several histories of French cycling were written in the 1890s, the most significant of which are L. Baudry de Saunier, *Histoire Générale de la Vélocipédie*; Bonneville, *Le Vélo, Fils de France* (Etac, Nice, 1938); H.O. Duncan, *Vingts Ans de Cyclisme Pratique* (Juven, Paris, 1897).

66. See Nick Clayton, "The Cycling Career of James Moore," *The Boneshaker* No. 125, Spring 1991.

67. *Le Vélocipède Illustré*, 11 April 1874.

68. *Bicycle Journal*, 8 Feb. 1878.

69. In 1887, a French visitor was asked, "There are very few French manufacturers, and most of the machines are of English make, are they not?" He replied, "Yes, the only good French makers are Clement and Co, the others getting their machines manufactured in England, and the safety is chiefly ridden." "A Frenchman on French Cycling," *Wheeling*, 28 Sept. 1887.

70. Duncan, op. cit., p. 336.

71. An account of French cycling club formation and its social and cultural background is: Poyer, Alex, *Les Premiers Temps des Véloce-Clubs: apparition et diffusion du cyclisme associatif français entre 1867 et 1914* (Paris: L'Harmattan, 2003).

72. *La Vélocipédie Pour Tous, par Un Vétéran*, Paris, 1892, op. cit., p. 225.

73. Statistics from *Véloce-Sport*, 1 June 1893.

74. L. Baudry de Saunier, *Histoire Générale de la Vélocipédie*, pp. 301–309.

75. *La Vélocipédie Pour Tous, par Un Vétéran*, Paris, 1892, op. cit., p. 225.

76. Duncan, op. cit., p. 320. Walker was influential in the export of English cycling to Germany in the 1880s. See Rüdiger Rabenstein, "T.H.S. Walker—English Cycling Pioneer in Germany," *Proceedings of the 5th International Cycle History Conference*. Walker's career is further documented in Christiane Eisenberg, *"English Sports" und Deutsche Bürger, Eine Gesellschaftsgeschichte, 1800–1939*, p. 225 and Rüdiger Rabenstein, *Radsport und Gesellschaft*, p. 225–228.

77. "A Few Words on the French N.C.U.," *Wheeling*, 2 Nov. 1892.

78. Charles Spencer, *Bicycles and Tricycles* (Cycling Classics reprint, pp. 72–73).

79. Alfred Howard, *The Bicycle for 1877*, op. cit., pp. 7–10.

80. Howard, *The Bicycle for 1878*, op. cit., p. 22; "The Hampton Court Meet," *Bicycling News*, 16 May 1879.

81. Hillier and Etherington, *Icycles*, op. cit., "Resume for 1880," p. 15

82. "Hampton Court Meet, 1880," *The Cyclist*, 26 May 1880.

83. Charles Spencer, op. cit., pp. 73–74.

84. Advertisement, *The Cyclist*, 11 June 1884, p. 593.

85. "With the League of American Wheelmen at Washington," *Outing*, Sept. 1884, p. 425.

86. The L. A. W. Meets were held as follows between 1880 and 1892:

1. Newport, Rhode Island, May 31, 1880; 2. Boston, Mass., May 30–31, 1881; 3. Chicago, Ill., May 30–31, 1882; 4. New York, N. Y., May 27–28, 1883; 5. Washington, D. C., May 19–20, 1884; 6. Buffalo, N. Y., May 26–27, 1885; 7. Boston, Mass., May 27–29, 1886; 8. St. Louis, Missouri, May 20–21, 1887; 9. Baltimore, Maryland, June 18–20, 1888; 10. Hagerstown, Maryland, July 2–4, 1889; 11. Niagara Falls, N. Y., Aug. 25–27, 1890; 12. Detroit, Mich., July 16–18, 1891; 13. Washington, D. C., July 18–20, 1892

87. *The Wheel*, 13 April 1883, p. 6.

88. *Springfield Wheelmen's Gazette*, May 1884, p. 9. *The Springfield Wheelmen's Gazette*, first published in April 1883 as a club magazine, quickly achieved national prominence, with an 1885 circulation of more than 15,000, telling evidence of the quickly expanding American bi-

cycle racing scene. An advertisement in the July 1884 issue stated that the *Gazette* "will be national in its character, furnish the news in a compact and well-classified form, a firm upholder of the League of American Wheelmen, and an able exponent of the ideas and wishes of gentlemanly amateurs." It also aimed "to spread the feeling of good fellowship now existing among wheelmen."

89. "Wheel News, The Springfield Meet," *Outing*, Oct. 1883, p. 69.

90. *Springfield Wheelmen's Gazette*, May 1884.

91. *Springfield Wheelmen's Gazette*, May 1884.

92. *Bicycling World*, 28 Sept. 1883.

93. Advertisement, *The Cyclist*, 11 June 1884, p. 594.

94. *Springfield Wheelmen's Gazette*, July 1884.

95. These British cyclists all fell into the category of "maker's amateurs" since their travel was paid for by the makers of the machines they rode. The L.A.W. did not object, but a strict interpretation of the N.C.U. amateur rules would have branded them as "professionals." The N.C.U. was still in occasional heated discussion with the Amateur Athletic Association about who had the right to define and legislate amateurism in cycling.

96. "The Broken Records at Hartford and Springfield," *Outing and The Wheelman–An Illustrated Monthly Magazine of Recreation*, Nov. 1884, pp. 128–131. Sanders Sellers' father was "a prosperous manufacturer of Preston, England." Sellers' records in Springfield in 1884 were reported to have "electrified and astonished the wheel world," but at the end of the year, "having beaten the best men on the path."

97. *Springfield Wheelmen's Gazette*, Oct. 1884.

98. *Outing and The Wheelman*, Nov. 1884, p. 145.

99. *Springfield Wheelmen's Gazette*, July 1884.

100. Editorial in *Springfield Wheelmen's Gazette*, Nov. 1884.

101. *Springfield Wheelmen's Gazette*, March 1885.

102. *Springfield Wheelmen's Gazette*, April 1885.

103. The complete team consisted of amateurs Percy Furnival, R.H. English, M.V.J. Webber, W.A. Illston, R. Cripps, R. Chambers, A.P. Engleheart, F.W. Allard and professionals Richard Howell, Fred Wood and Robert James (see *The Cyclist*, 26 Aug. 1885, p. 1131).

104. *Springfield Wheelmen's Gazette*, Nov. 1885.

105. *Springfield Wheelmen's Gazette*, Nov. 1885.

106. "The Springfield Tournament," *The Cyclist*, 30 Sept. 1885, p. 1255.

107. Quoted in *Springfield Wheelmen's Gazette*, Nov. 1885. A London correspondent to *Bicycling World* (10 Sept. 1886, p. 464) wrote: "It seems to many men on this side that the American papers have an exaggerated idea of the importance of Mr. Lacy Hillier's utterances. You may rest assured that his following is a very small one, and diminishing daily. International snobbery, as manifested by the pen of a small stockjobber, in an unpopular cycling paper, is as offensive to English as to American eyes … the man who prostitutes his paper to air his malice against America is a very poor journalist, a very ordinary Stock Exchange operator and merely a figure head to the paper."

108. Accounts of this ride across America were serialized in *Outing* from April to July 1885, and were continued as "Around the World on a Bicycle," from Oct. 1885 to June 1888. Stevens arrived back in California in Jan. 1887. The full account of the trip was published as *Around the World on a Bicycle* in 1889.

109. Op. cit., Nov. 1885.

110. *Mirror of American Sports* was the official publication of the Illinois division of the League of American Wheelmen; quoted in *Springfield Wheelmen's Gazette*, Nov. 1885.

111. *Springfield Wheelmen's Gazette*, Dec. 1885.

112. Howard P. Merrill, "One Man's Work for Cycling," *Outing*, Oct. 1888, pp. 32–39.

113. *The Cycle* (Boston), 9 April 1886, p. 22.

114. "Misguided Wheelmen. The Pure (?) Amateurs—Where Are They?," *Springfield Wheelmen's Gazette*, April 1887. Since Ducker was the editor of the paper, this was probably written by Ducker himself.

115. "Cycling in England in 1888. A Retrospect of the Past Season," *The Wheel and Cycling Trade Review*, 9 Nov. 1888, pp. 240–41.

116. Merrill, op. cit., *Outing*, Oct. 1888, and "Our Monthly Record," *Outing*, Oct. 1888, pp. 88–89.

117. "Senator Morgan on the Buffalo Cycling Tournament," *The Cyclist*, 3 Oct. 1888, pp. 1377–78.

118. *The Cyclist*, 5 Sept. 1888, pp. 1249–50

119. *Providence Journal*, quoted in *Springfield Wheelmen's Gazette*, August 1884.

120. *Springfield Wheelmen's Gazette*, August 1884.

121. Gherardo Bonini rightly points out that the British-American alliance which conceived the idea and wished to preside over the institution of "world" championships was seen as despotic by another European alliance consisting of Austria-Hungary, Germany, France and Italy, which promoted various "European championships" to contest supremacy within their own bloc. See Gherardo Bonini, "National Identity and Ethnicity in European Cycling before 1914," *Annual of the European Committee for the History of Sport*, 2001.

122. "The Crown of Wild Olive," *Outing and The Wheelman*, Jan. 1884.

123. Advertisements, *Wheeling*, 23 Sept. 1885; *The Cycle*, 20 Aug. 1886, p. 346 and *L.A.W. Bulletin*, 6 Aug. 1886, p. 137.

124. See Maarten Van Bottenburg, *Global Games* (Chicago, University of Illinois Press, 2001).

125. *Wheeling*, 12 Sept. 1885, p. 325 and *Wheeling*, 9 June 1886, p. 136.

126. All references from *The Cyclist*, 1888.

127. The first tricycle made and marketed was Haynes and Jefferis' "Coventry" Tricycle, advertised in *Bicycling Journal*, 23 March 1877. But earlier, sophisticated experimentation had taken place, particularly machines made in Paris by English maker William Jackson, who had competed on one in the 1869 Paris–Rouen race (see Nick Clayton, "William Jackson, A Forgotten Pioneer of the Modern Tricycle," *Proceedings of the 9th Cycling History Conference*, 1999). Willard Sawyer's quadricycle velocipedes were extremely fine and light, built with speed and athletic performance in mind; see Andrew Ritchie, *King of the Road*, pp. 38–45. Looking more broadly at the evolution of cycles, it appears that three- and four-wheeled cycles were a central preoccupation of human-powered vehicle makers from early in the 19th century. The development of these cycles spanned the emergence of the two-wheeled velocipede, the high-wheel bicycle and the "safety" bicycle, and in effect led directly to motorized

tricycles and the first automobiles. This suggests that the tricycle activity of the 1880s was not a technological byway, as is frequently suggested, but a main road. The chain technology developed for tricycles led to the successful "geared-up ordinaries," and in the later 1880s to the emergence of the "safety" bicycle.

128. "Resume for 1880," in Lacy Hillier and Harry Etherington, *Icycles, The Christmas Annual of the Wheel World*, 1880, p. 16.

129. Henry Sturmey, *Tricyclists' Indispensable Annual and Handbook (a Guide to the Pastime, Record of the Sport, and Complete Cyclopedia on the Subject)*, 4th Edition, 1884.

130. See *The Ironmonger* (exact date unknown) quoted in *The Cyclist*, 10 Feb. 1886, p. 395: "At the first blush a trade which turns out only two classes of machines, one with two wheels and the other with three, might seem incapable of much variety, yet there is in reality hardly any other industry which presents as varied a series of products and so much good workmanship of a fine description. The different makers vie with each other so keenly that the patterns in use are counted by the hundred, and every season brings its crop of novelties and more or less marked improvements. The bicycle is still a favourite with young and active men, and its construction is always being altered and improved... It is in respect of the tricycle, however, that the modern cycling geniuses find their great field, that machine having a much wider constituency than its two-wheeled rival. Of tricycles there seems to be literally no end, and the ingenuity displayed in accomplishing new combinations and variations is almost astonishing... For all these numerous varieties there appears to be a demand, and, no matter how excellent the novelties of one season may have been, there is an apparently insatiable call for the super-excellent products of the new year... The modern cycle is a splendid specimen of modern workmanship, and probably embodies more skill–certainly more patented inventions–than any other single mechanical production of the time being. The industry is one of which we may well be proud. It virtually originated with ourselves, has been developed by us, and, so far as can be seen, is likely to remain in our own hands in every branch of the business requiring even moderately good work."

131. *Bicycling World*, 19 Nov. 1880. Cyclists in the United States were less enamored of the tricycle than were those in Britain, where it was extremely popular.

132. *Bicycling News*, 31 May 1878.

133. Quoted in *The Boneshaker*, No. 8, Summer 1957. There is extended discussion of the tricycle in Andrew Ritchie, *King of the Road*, Chap. 5, "Tricycling and 'Sociable' Cycling," *The Tricyclist*, a periodical devoted to exclusively to tricycling matters, was published from 1882 to 1885.

134. See Anon., "The True History of the Tricycle Union," *Wheel World*, June, 1883 and A.J. Wilson, "A complete and impartial history of the Tricycle Union," *Wheel World*, Jan. 1885, pp. 315–318. Racing was one of the most important issues in the organization of the independent Tricycle Association because in 1882 the N.C.U. had refused to promote a 50 mile tricycle road race, which it considered illegal.

135. "The Tricycle for American Women," *Outing and The Wheelman*, March 1885, pp. 423–426.

136. "Tricycling for Ladies," G. Lacy Hillier, Badminton *Cycling*, 2nd Edition, 1889, pp. 266–70. See also Miss F.J. Erskine's *Tricycling for Ladies*, first published in 1885.

137. H.W. Bartleet, *Bartleet's Bicycle Book*, p. 133.

138. Roy Green, *100 Years of Cycling Roads Records*. The Land's End to John o'Groats marathon, from southwest to north-east extremity of Great Britain, continued to be the ultimate test of endurance in bicycle and tricycle racing in the late 1800s.

139. G. Lacy Hillier, "Editorial," *The Tricyclist*, Vol. 1, No. 1, 30 June 1882.

140. H.W. Bartleet, op. cit., p. 133.

141. H.H. Griffin, *Bicycles and Tricycles of the Year 1888*.

142. The events and trends within cycling just described were part of a larger process of institutionalization and globalization of modern sport in Britain, France and America. Eric Hobsbaum refers to this process as "the mass-production of tradition," which he sees as occurring on both a social and a political level. He comments on the speed with which "in Europe sport in the modern form was a conscious import of social values and life-styles from Britain, largely by those influenced by the educational system of the British upper class." (see Eric Hobsbaum, "Mass-Producing Traditions: Europe, 1870–1914," in Eric Dunning and Terence Ranger, *The Invention of Tradition*).

CHAPTER FIVE

1. For a discussion of the reasons for Coventry's dominance, see Glenn Norcliffe, "The Rise of the Coventry Bicycle Industry and the Geographical Construction of Technology," *Proceedings of the 15th International Cycle History Conference* (Cycle Publishing, San Francisco, 2005).

2. Since the essential design changes examined in this chapter took place first in Great Britain, most of the discussion here relates to Britain except where otherwise noted. In general, there seems to have been an outward flow of new technological ideas from Britain to France, Germany and the United States, although American production techniques may well have been more advanced than their British counterparts. In spite of the attention Bijker has given it (see Introduction, endnote 7), this exhaustively documented period has received little attention from historians of technology. Recently, Paul Rosen (*Framing Technology*, 2002) has concentrated on two periods of cycle history in the 20th century to examine aspects of the economy, design and production of bicycles and their impact on technological development.

3. "Advertising Road Rides," *Wheeling*, 16 Sept. 1885, an editorial by editor Harry Etherington.

4. The "Xtraordinary" had the dimensions of an ordinary bicycle but threw the weight of the rider further behind the front axle, thereby increasing stability and decreasing the possibility of "headers." The American-made "Eagle" and "Star" safeties attempted to solve the same problem by reversing the wheels of the ordinary, and putting the small wheel in front. The new style of front-wheel-driven smaller-front-wheel safety bicycles were for a short time referred to as "dwarf safeties" because they

were much lower to the ground than the high-wheel bicycle. For further general discussion of the rise of the safety bicycle, see Andrew Ritchie, *King of the Road*, Chapter 6, "The Search for Safety."

5. The strength of this design was a reasonable wheel-size with the rider's weight and pedaling pressure located behind the center-point of the front wheel, giving road performers much greater safety at higher speeds. ("Land's End to John O'Groats on a Facile," *Wheeling*, 4 June 1884, p. 70). The history of "End-to-End" record rides is covered in Alan J. Ray, *Cycling: Land's End to John o'Groats* and Roy Green, *100 Years of Cycling Road Records*.

6. *Wheeling*, 4 June 1884 and 30 July 1884; an advertisement publicizing the "Facile" appeared in *The Cyclist*, 4 June 1884.

7. R.J. Mecredy and Gerald Stoney, *The Art and Pastime of Cycling*, Second Edition, 1890, p. 22. The reason for the choice of the word "Kangaroo" for this bicycle is not known.

8. "Progress and Invention," *Wheel World*, March 1886, pp. 133–135. The same article refers to an 1879 attempt at constructing a rear-driven safety bicycle, the Rudge "Bicyclette," which "lacked the perfection which is possible, in 1886, as the results of tricycle-making experience." The chronology of chain technology is a crucial aspect of the emergence of the safety bicycle. Advertisements from 1886 confirm the significance of contemporary chain developments: Frank Simons, a company in Birmingham, advertised "Morgan's Patent Roller Chain, for Tricycles and Safety Bicycles. Over 100 firms are now using it. Champion racers use no other;" W. Bown, also in Birmingham, advertised "Bown's New Patent Lower Chain Wheel Bearings–The Requirement of the Times for all Safety Bicycles" (see *Wheeling*, 14 April and 29 Sept. 1886). See also Nick Clayton, "Hans Renold and the Birth of the Bicycle Chain," *Proceedings of the 3rd Bicycle History Conference* (Neckarsulm,1992).

9. "The Kangaroo 100 Miles Road Ride," *Wheeling*, 1 October 1884, p. 276.

10. *Cyclists' Touring Club Monthly Gazette*, April 1885.

11. *Wheeling*, 4 June 1884.

12. "The 'Coventry Rotary' Race–Adams Beats the 24 Hours Record," *Wheeling*, 30 Sept. 1885, pp. 369–70.

13. "The Kangaroo 100 Miles Road Ride," *Wheeling*, 1 October 1884, p. 276, and "The North Road Club's All-Day Race," *Wheeling*, 7 Sept. 1887, pp. 347–48.

14. Mecredy and Stoney, op. cit., pp. 22–23.

15. *C.T.C. Monthly Gazette*, Feb. 1885.

16. *C.T.C. Monthly Gazette,* April 1885. The "Rover" illustrated in this advertisement was the short-lived first design, with a steering rod connecting the handlebars to the front wheel, a feature that was quickly substituted with direct steering in a second design revealed before the end of 1885.

17. Details of the introduction of the "Rover safety" are discussed in John Pinkerton and Derek Roberts, *A History of Rover Cycles*. The Starley letter is quoted on p. 36, but the source for it is not given.

18. W.K. Starley, "The Evolution of the Cycle," *Journal of the Society of Arts*, 20 May 1898, pp. 601–16.

19. "The 'Rover Safety' Race–Wonderful Record," *Wheeling*, 30 September 1885, p. 371. It is worth noting the original significance of the brand-name "Rover," based on the verb to rove or to move around freely far from home, a suggestion of independence and mobility.

20. H.O. Duncan, *World on Wheels*, p. 307.

21. "Stanley Show Supplement," *Wheeling*, 2 Feb. 1887, p. 265.

22. The use of the word "Bicyclette" was acquired from a previous machine of the same name made by H.J. Lawson. The French-sounding
brand-name was in fact English in origin, and appears to have been used in England in the period 1880–1886 in a generic sense to refer to the idea of a small-wheeled, rear-driven bicycle. As rival brands of safety bicycle entered the French marketplace, the appropriately French-sounding word transferred into everyday usage and became "bicyclette" with a small "b".

23. This ride is reported in H.O. Duncan, *The World on Wheels* (p. 307); *Véloce-Sport*, 15 April 1886 (p. 147); "Across France on a Rudge Bicyclette," *Wheeling*, 24 March 1886; "Continental Cycling Clippings," *The Cyclist*, 24 March 1886; "Across France on a Safety," *The Cyclist*, 31 March 1886; *Bicycling News*, 9 April 1886; "Johnny Crapaud A-wheel–A Chat with H.O. Duncan," *Bicycling News*, 23 April 1886.

24. This important meeting for the French bicycle industry is discussed in André Vant, *L'Industrie du Cycle dans la Région Stéphanoise* (Musée des Arts et Métiers, St. Etienne, 1993).

25. The creation of a professional cyclists' "Union" or "Syndicat" was mentioned in *Véloce-Sport*, 22 July 1886.

26. H.O. Duncan, op. cit., p. 307. Further research is needed in French sources to establish a detailed chronology of the introduction of the safety in France, but the main outlines as given in Duncan and the other French sources cited here appear to be reliable. Possibly there are rival French claims for French precedence in safety designs.

27. *C.T.C. Monthly Gazette*, Nov. 1885.

28. Advertisements quoted from *Wheeling*, 26 August 1885 and 7 October 1885; the illustration of the "Rover" safety racing was in *Wheeling*, 5 May 1886.

29. "British Correspondence," *Springfield Wheelmen's Gazette*, Nov. 1885; "The Maker's-Amateur Question," *Wheeling*, 4 March 1885, p. 279.

30. *Wheeling*, 28 October 1885; see also "The 'Kangaroo' Race," *The Cyclist*, 28 Oct. 1885, pp. 59–61.

31. "Progress and Invention," *Wheel World*, Nov. 1886.

32. *The Cyclist*, Special Show Supplement, 26 Jan. 1887.

33. Henry Sturmey, *Indispensable Guide to the Safety Bicycle*, 1885, "Introductory Notes" and description of "Rover," pp. 70–71. Sturmey's choice of the four words, "safety, speed, ease and elegance" can be seen as an expression of the dominant considerations in bicycle design. But acceptance of the safety was by no means universal at the time. This can be seen in a comment from a columnist in *Wheeling*, 15 June 1887: "Why is it, I wonder, that men will persist in racing on Safety machines… Safety machines are not adapted for path racing… The time is not far distant when the real racing men will make an energetic protest against these duffers on dwarfs, and the N.C.U. will have to legislate and prevent them riding except in Safety races. They will be no loss, for, as I have said before, no really good man rides one." The writer's opinions resulted in "a perfect avalanche of correspondence." *Wheeling*, 22 June 1887.

34. Henry Sturmey, *Indispensable Bicyclist's Handbook, A Complete Cyclopedia upon the Subject of the Bicycle and Safety Bicycle and Their Construction*, 1887, "Introductory Notes" and description of "Rover" on pp. 326–28. At least 35 different makes of "Rover"-type safeties are illustrated here.

35. "Analysis of Cycles at the Stanley Show, 1887," *Wheeling*, 9 Feb. 1887, p. 291.

36. "British Cycling in 1884," *Springfield Wheelmen's Gazette*, Dec. 1884 and "British Correspondence," Nov. 1885

37. Underwood advertisement, *L.A.W. Bulletin*, 12 March 1886; Spalding advertisement, *L.A.W. Bulletin*, 21 May 1886; Starley and Sutton advertisement, *L.A.W. Bulletin*, 9 July 1886.

38. *Outing*, Oct. 1888, p. 88.

39. All quotations from A.J. Wilson ('Faed'), "Record-breaking on the North Road," *Wheel World*, Oct. 1886, pp. 442–46 and Nov. 1886, pp. 503–09.

40. A.J. Wilson, "How Cycling Road Records Are Made in England," *Outing*, July 1889, pp. 300–05 and Sept. 1889, pp. 435–39.

41. Rule 1 of Records Committee of the National Cyclists Union stated in 1886 that–"The N.C.U. will adjudicate upon path and road records claimed by amateurs within the meaning of the definition and rules, but it shall be in the discretion of the Records Committee to decline to accept any claim where they consider that the interests of the sport would not be promoted thereby," quoted in A.J. Wilson, op. cit., p. 442 and p. 444.

42. S. H. Moxham, *Fifty Years of Road Riding (1885-1935)–A History of the North Road Cycling Club*, p. 11.

43. A.J. Wilson, *Wheel World*, Oct. 1886, p. 442 and p. 443.

44. A.J. Wilson, op. cit.

45. "Long-distance riding in the Liverpool district during 1886," *Wheeling*, 10 Nov. 1886.

46. "How the Wheel World Wags," *Wheel World*, Nov. 1886., pp. 522–23. Mills' 1886 rides, all accomplished on solid-tired machines, are listed here in chronological order (see table below)

47. "The North Road Club's All-Day race," *Wheeling*, 7 Sept. 1887, p. 347 and advertisement, 21 Sept. 1887.

48. "National Cyclists' Union–Full Report of Council Meeting," *Wheeling*, 15 Dec. 1886.

49. *Wheeling*, 28 Sept. 1887, p. 393.

50. "Road Racing. A Climax Reached," Editorial in *Wheeling*, 5 Oct. 1887.

51. Roy Green, *100 Years of Cycling Road Records*. The 14 clubs represented at the inaugural meeting of the R.R.A., were: North Road C.C., Anfield B.C., Bath Road Club, Anerley B.C., Polytechnic C.C., Catford C.C., North London C.C., Stanley B.C., Stoke Newington C.C., City of London C.C., Biggleswade and District C.C., Kingsdale C.C., Carleton C.C. and Pioneer C.C.

52. The abundance of documents relating to cycling clubs throughout Britain provides an opportunity to look at issues of class in cycling in the period 1880 to about 1900. How much did the cost of a bicycle affect the ability of lower income riders to participate in cycling? To what extent did working-class people embrace cycling because of the lack of other opportunities for sport? Did they get lured into cycling as a sport because they first used a bicycle for utilitarian purposes? Was the appeal in fact broader across the middle- and working-classes than might be supposed? Once again, Lowerson's assertion that cycling was "more distinctly pan-class as a participatory recreation than any other late Victorian boom sport" should be kept in mind. He sees cycling from the 1880s as "spreading downwards" socially, although he acknowledges the fashionable upper-classes' brief flirtation with cycling in the mid–1890s, when it spread briefly upwards. He also correctly identifies one of the principal problems in analyzing cycling as "a tension between the recreational and athletic values." See John Lowerson, *Sport and the English middle classes, 1870-1914*, pp. 116–21, and David Rubinstein, "Cycling in the 1890s," *Victorian Studies* (Indiana University), Autumn 1977, Vol. 21, No. 1.

53. As late as 1892–93, the Persil Flexible Wheel Tire Co. Syndicate Ltd was attempting to provide an alternative to the pneumatic tire with an elaborate sprung metal wheel, which "the Company hopes to fit to cabs, omnibuses, perambulators, and all sorts of carriages." This attempt to provide a sprung solution to the problem of vibration, which now looks so improbable as to be almost a joke, underlines the fact that in the early 1890s the absolute historical dominance of the pneumatic tire was not as yet assured. (see "The Persil Flexible Wheel," *The Boneshaker*, Spring 2001; "Roues suspendues 'Persil,'" *Véloce-Sport*, 17 Aug. 1893). Another such sprung wheel was made by Eastham and Haworth, Leyland (see *Wheeling*, 4 Jan. 1893.)

54. The best technical, chronological and legal account of the development of the pneumatic tire in Britain is Sir

Date	Route/Record	Time/Distance
1886		
July 5–10 (ordinary bicycle)	Land's End to John o'Groats	5 days 1h 45m
Aug. 4	24 hour record	268 miles (ordinary bicycle)
Aug. 15–20	Land's End to John o'Groats	5 days 10h (tricycle)
Sept. 4	1st North Road C.C.	24 hour 227 miles (ordinary bicycle)
Sept. 22	50 mile record	2h 46m 3s (tandem tricycle, with A.J. Wilson)
Oct 2	50 mile record	2h 47m 36s ("Ivel" safety bicycle)
Oct 5/6	24 hour record	295 miles ("Ivel" safety bicycle)
1887		
Sept. 2/3	2nd North Road C.C.	24 hour, 268 miles ("Ivel" tricycle)
Sept. 24	100 mile record	7h 46m 33s ("Ivel" tricycle)

[Table showing long-distance record road rides of G.P. Mills in 1886 and 1887.]

Arthur du Cros, *Wheels of Fortune–A Salute to Pioneers* (Chapman and Hall, London, 1938). Early American pneumatic developments are discussed in *The Cyclist* (May, 1890, p. 54), which said: "There is no little curiosity amongst those interested in cycling to see a wheel on this side of the ocean fitted with the Pneumatic Tire that has caused so much discussion in England. It is the invention of Mr. J.B. Dunlop... There is no doubt but what this invention is even yet in its experimental stage, although a number of racing men and others are using wheels with pneumatic tires in England. If it proves anything like a substantial success it will no doubt make its appearance in this country during the present season, and if its great advantages as a speed-maker are true, a progressive rider may catch the other napping by entering the races with a pneumatic tired wheel."

55. R.J. Mecredy and Gerald Stoney, *The Art and Pastime of Cycling*, 2nd Edition, 1890, pp. 229–31, "The Pneumatic Tyre." The Special Stanley Show Number of *The Irish Cyclist and Athlete* (30 Jan. 1891) contained an advertisement of two full pages for The Pneumatic Tyre and Booth's Cycle Agency, in Dublin listing all the advantages of the pneumatic tire, which included, "Comfort, Conservation of power, Speed, Less weight to carry, Frames will last longer, Invincible on grass, Requires little attention, Absence of nervous exhaustion, Anti-vibration contrivances unnecessary, Absence of noise, Absence of side-slipping."

56. Mecredy and Stoney, op. cit., Third Edition, 1893.

57. W.J. Grew, *The Cycle Industry*, p. 53.

58. Facts discussed in this general account of the beginnings of the pneumatic tire are taken from: *The History of the Pneumatic Tyre* by J.B. Dunlop (published after his death by his daughter Mrs Jean McClintock, Dublin, 1924); Sir Arthur du Cros, *Wheels of Fortune–A Salute to Pioneers* (Chapman and Hall, London, 1938); Francis J.J. Glynn, *The History of the Clincher Tyre and Rim* (North British Rubber Co., Edinburgh, c.1900); H.W. Bartleet, "The First Race on Pneumatic Tyres–How the Air Tyre Jumped into Fame," *Bartleet's Bicycle Book* (London, 1931), pp. 121–29, reprinted from *Cycling*, 28 Oct. 1920). See also: H.D. Higman, "The Founding of the Dunlop Tyre Company," *Proceedings of the 5th International Cycle History Conference*, September 1994, pp. 91–94.

59. Knowledge of a previous patent taken out by R.W. Thomson, from 1845, was denied by Dunlop: "Oh yes, I heard of Thomson's old patent several months ago," he told *The Wheelman and Irish Athletic and Cycling News* (21 Oct. 1890), "but was quite unaware of it at the time I patented my own invention. Thomson's patent, however, differs very materially from my own, and as far as I can understand, was a complete failure."

60. It is important to emphasize that Dunlop's initial work on the pneumatic principle was subsequently dependent upon the development of the detachable tire principle (Welch, 1890; Bartlett, 1890 and others), the design of a rim which would allow detachability (Westwood, 1892–3), the development of an effective valve (Woods, 1891), and the design of a strong, pliable cord case for the rubber tire, all of which were necessary for the universal adoption of the "clincher" tire.

61. An excellent account of the impact of Harvey du Cros, an enthusiastic athlete and cyclist, upon his six sons, who were all very close in age, is given in Chapter Seven,

"We Were Seven," of Du Cros, *Wheels of Fortune*, op. cit., pp. 70–78.

62. *Bartleet's Bicycle Book*, op. cit., p. 126.

63. Record times for these distances were as follows: ¼ mile–36 3/5s; ½ mile–1m 11s; 1 mile–2m 26 4/5s; 5 miles–13m 16 2/5s; 10 miles–27m 28 4/5s.

64. This sudden increased demand for rubber also had a huge impact on the international rubber market. In *King Leopold's Ghost–A Story of Greed, Terror, and Heroism in Colonial Africa* (Houghton Mifflin, New York, 1998, p. 159), Adam Hochschild writes of the appalling horrors committed by Belgian traders in the Congo in their greed for rubber during the rubber boom, a perspective on the 1890s middle-class bicycle boom in Western Europe which has not previously been explored: "The industrial world rapidly developed an appetite not just for rubber tires, but for hoses, tubing, gaskets, and the like, and for rubber insulation for the telegraph, telephone, and electrical wiring now rapidly encompassing the globe. Suddenly factories could not get enough of the magical commodity and its price rose throughout the 1890s. Nowhere did the boom have a more drastic impact on people's lives than in the equatorial rain forest..." Hochschild thus suggests that the sport and recreational pleasures indulged in by the middle-classes of the developed nations were bought at the expense of colonial exploitation and suffering.

65. H. Hewitt Griffin, "The Tiring Tyre Problem," *Cycling*, 31 Jan. and 7 Feb. 1891.

66. "Safety or Ordinary–Why is the safety so popular?" *Cycling*, 23 May 1891, p. 288.

67. Evidence of the impact of this technological revolution in bicycle design and in the sport of cycling can be seen in the amateur competition track records recognized by the N.C.U. during these crucial years, in which the precise moment of the proven superiority of the speed of the pneumatic-tired safety bicycle can be pinpointed in the 1890 figures. The ordinary bicycle figures remained the same while the safety record times are all lowered in 1890, 1892 and 1893. See Tables 5.1 and 5.2 at the end of chapter 5.

During 1893, new world records were set on the pneumatic safety bicycle at every distance on the track from ¼ mile to 24 hours. Commenting on the 1893 English records and the 1893 world record figures, James Blair, an N.C.U. official, wrote: "The record season, just closed, has been a remarkable one. Thanks to the improved surface at Herne Hill and tandem safety pacing, we are able to show up much better than last season, when only one World's path record stood to England's credit. The Americans still lead in the shorter distances. We must admit that in sprinting the Yankees can show us the way, but in long distance riding they do not appear to have any riders of promise. All World's safety records have been lowered. Turning to English path records we find all safety times and distances have been beaten at Herne Hill. The Ordinary Bicycle Records remain unchanged. All Tricycle Records, with one exception, have gone by the board. All the old Tandem Safety figures have been obliterated." ("The Records of '91,"*Cycling*, 24 Jan. 1891, p. 11.)

Long-distance records on the road during this period were similarly much improved. By 1893, Frank Shorland had ridden 195 miles in 12 hours and 370 miles in 24 hours, and in a grueling 1894 Land's End to John O'Groats ride, G.P. Mills reduced his 1886 ordinary bicycle record of 5days 1hour 45mins to 3days 5hours 49mins on a pneumatic safety.

68. H.H. Griffin, "Show Statistics for 1895 and 1896,"*Cycle Census of 19th Annual Stanley Show*. "Cushions" were various kinds of experimental suspension tires with an air-filled chamber, though not fully pneumatic. They were soon abandoned.

69. Henry Sturmey, "Introduction" to G.D. Leechman, *Safety Cycling*.

CHAPTER SIX

1. There were significant cycling movements in Belgium, Holland, Germany and Italy, as well, which should not be discounted in a consideration of the wider European scene.

2. Early race meetings between England and France were described in G. de Moncontour, "Les coureurs français en Angleterre" and "Les coureurs anglais en France," *Le Sport Vélocipédique*, 27 March 1885 and 10 April 1885.

3. *Véloce-Sport*, 16 and 23 March 1893.

4. "Les coureurs français en Angleterre," *Le Sport Vélocipédique*, 27 March 1885, pp. 159–160.

5. See S.H. Moxham, *Fifty Years of Road Riding (1885–1935), A History of the North Road Cycling Club* (Bedford: Diemer and Reynolds, 1935).

6. Among the sources which document the French sport, the following have been especially helpful: L. Baudry de Saunier, *L'Histoire de la Locomotion Terrestre* (Paris, 1935); H.O. Duncan, *Vingt Ans de Cyclisme Pratique–Étude complète du Cyclisme de 1876 à ce jour* (F. Juven, Paris, 1897); G. de Moncontour, *Les Champions Français* (Paris, 1892). The periodicals *Le Sport Vélocipédique* (Official publication of the Union Vélocipédique de France), *Le Véloce-Sport, La Bicyclette* and *La Revue des Sports* are also important primary sources.

7. There has been very little research done into American road racing in the 1890s and the early 20th century, although it was well documented in the daily press and cycling periodicals. It appears to have declined significantly after about 1900, but on the other hand, a small number of massed- start races and long-distance record-breaking individual rides continued after that. An Elgin-Chicago "Classic," for example was held between 1926 and 1953. There are also many accounts in the period 1900–1920 of trans-continental rides by young men.

8. The Irvington–Millburn 25-mile Handicap road race was held continuously between 1889 and 1908 (*Otto Eisele's Cycling Almanac*, 1953).

9. Jean Durry, for example, in his *La Véridique Histoire des Géants de la Route* (1973), gives the title "Le Grand Départ" to the chapter which begins with an account of this race (p. 26). Bordeaux-Paris began in 1891 and continued unbroken (except for the two World Wars) until it was finally abandoned in 1987. For many years after 1945 it was run as a two-part race, the riders being paced for the final 200 kilometres into Paris by small motor-cycles called "Dernys."

10. *Cycling*, 30 May 1891. It should be pointed out that such use of superlatives was characteristic of partisan journalistic reporting. The affiliations of the riders were: G.P. Mills (Anfield Bicycle Club and North Road Cycling Club); M.A. Holbein (Catford Cycling Club and North Road Cycling Club); S.F. Edge (Surrey Bicycle Club and London County Cycling and Athletic Club) and J.E.L. Bates (Surrey Bicycle Club and London County Cycling and Athletic Club)

11. *Bicycling News*, 13 February 1892. It is assumed here that editorials in *Bicycling News* were in general written by Lacy Hillier himself.

12. Victor Breyer, "How G.P. Mills won the first Bordeaux–Paris," *Cycling*, 19 March 1947.

13. According to an account in *The Wheel and Cycling Trade Review* (U.S.), 12 June 1891, Mills' ride was far from easy due to several equipment problems: "The machine he started on, the Humber, was a new one. He had not gone very far when he was knocked off his machine; the framework was twisted... Mills practically rode five different wheels. The first change he made was on to an R and P, which he rode for 30 miles, then he mounted a Humber, but as the tires were not blown out, and the machine did not suit him at all, he exchanged for a Stroud's racer; on this machine he could have gone through, but for the fact that the tire punctured when he had ridden 300 kilometres. He then mounted a Humber roadster, and rode to the end of the journey. He argues that the changes he made were rather disadvantageous than otherwise, because all the machines were of a different height and length of crank." The article further stated that: "perhaps no race of such long duration has been ridden with fewer and shorter stoppages... He ate but little solid food, except for the first seventy or eighty miles, though he ate as much fruit as he could get on the journey."

14. H.O. Duncan, *World on Wheels* (Paris, 1927), p. 351.

15. *Cycling*, 30 May, 1891.

16. "Depuis quelques années, une nouvelle classe d'hommes a surgi, qui semble avoir devoir prendre une place importante au soleil du sport. Ces hommes dont les premiers spécimens sont venues d'Amérique s'intitulent un peu pompeusement managers, ce qui veut dire directeurs, administrateurs." [For some years now, a new kind of person has sprung into existence, who has had a important role in the limelight of the sport. The first of these specimens came from America and called themselves a little bit pompously "managers," or in other words directors or administrators.] H.O. Duncan, *Vingt Ans de Cyclisme*, p. 154. Others who occupied a similar role were Harry Etherington (GB), Choppy Warburton (GB), Tom Eck (US) and W.J. Morgan (US) who were all Duncan's contemporaries. The modern *directeur sportif* is the manager of a professional cycling team, and takes charge of technical aspects of training and equipment. Duncan's role was an even wider one, in that he was responsible for all aspects of the riders' participation in competition and was active in promoting bicycle racing as a publicity tool for the bicycle industry.

17. Duncan, *World on Wheels*, p. 357.

18. See L. Baudry de Saunier, *Les Mémoires de Terront* (with Charles Terront, Paris, 1893); reprinted with an Introduction by Jacques Seray (Prosport, Paris, 1980). The *Mémoires de Terront* was a publishing sensation. Baudry de Saunier wrote the book in six days, it was immediately rushed into print, and on the strength of Terront's fame and popularity as winner of Paris–Brest–Paris, it sold 3,000 copies while the March 1893 1,000 km race between

Terront and Corre was taking place in Paris. See also Andrew Ritchie, "The Cycling World of Paris in 1893," *The Boneshaker* No. 143, Spring 1997 and Andrew Ritchie, "Charles Terront and Paris–Brest–Paris in 1891," *The Boneshaker* No. 150, Summer 1999. Duncan's accounts of Paris–Brest–Paris can be found in *World on Wheels*, pp. 354–357 and in *Vingt Ans de Cyclisme Pratique* (F. Juven, Paris, 1897), pp. 132–3.

19. This detail offers a revealing insight into the difference between British and French attitudes towards competition at the time. In British ideological amateurism, only the athlete was openly recognized as being tested; the importance of the machine was recognized but downplayed. In France, with the acceptance of industry sponsorship, a particular machine was considered to be an important component of the overall athletic contest; both man and machine were to be tested and therefore should start and finish the race together. This attitude persisted well into the 20th century in France and was applied in the early Tours de France.

20. "Paris to Brest and back–An extraordinary race," *Cycling*, 12 Sept.1891; "Terront's experiences–How he won the Paris–Brest race," *Cycling*, 26 Sept.1891. Significantly, as a statement about the contemporary relationship between bicycle and automobile technology, the Paris–Brest–Paris route was covered by a gasoline-powered, two cylinder quadricycle, made by Peugeot, which did a total of 2047 km in 139 hours. This was probably the first time that a motor vehicle had been involved in a bicycle race (see Baudry de Saunier, *Histoire de la Locomotion Terrestre*, Paris, 1935, p. 178; also reported in *La Nature*, 20 Oct. 1891).

21. "Long-distance Competitions," *Cycling*, 19 September 1891. In fact, such objections to the severely strenuous endurance events which characterized bicycle racing in the 1890s, and the extreme physiological stresses they were thought to impose, are frequently encountered in the popular press and the medical literature of the period. See Chapter 2, "The Medical Debate" in Christopher Thompson, "The Third Republic on Wheels" (Ph. D. thesis, 1997), and John Hoberman, *Mortal Engines* (1992).

22. Baudry de Saunier, "Match Terront-Corre," in *Véloce-Sport*, 2 March 1893.

23. H.O. Duncan and Pierre Lafitte, *En Suivant Terront de St. Petersbourg à Paris* (Flammarion, Paris, 1894); "Match Cody-Meyer," *La Bicyclette*, 27 Oct. 1893.

24. *Bicycling News*, 21 May 1892.

25. "Bordeaux–Paris–Victoire de Cottereau et Stéphane, roue dans roue," *Véloce-Sport*, 1 June 1893.

26. "The Bordeaux–Paris Road Race," *Bearings*, 3 June 1897, p. 1898. As Philippe Gaboriau points out in "The Tour de France and Cycling's Belle Epoque" (in Hugh Dauncey and Geoff Hare, eds., *The Tour de France 1903–2003: A Century of Sporting Structures, Meanings and Values*, Frank Cass, 2003), long-distance automobile races were also popular at exactly this time.

27. *La Bicyclette*, 12 June 1892.

28. The organization and running of Paris–Brussels is documented in *La Bicyclette*, 21 July, 28 July, 18 Aug. and 25 Aug. 1893. The willingness of Leopold the Second, King of Belgium, to be associated with this heavily promoted race was especially significant in light of the monarch's role in the brutal exploitation of the rubber resources in the Belgian Congo. The demand for rubber in a variety of industries—particularly to supply the increased need for tubes and tyres in the bicycle industry—led to the genocidal plundering of the native population of the Congo, as documented in Adam Hochschild, *King Leopold's Ghost* (Houghton, Mifflin, New York, 1998).

29. *La Bicyclette*, 25 Aug. 1893.

30. *Wheeling*, 8 Aug. 1894.

31. See *Journal de Roubaix*, 21 April 1896, documented in Pascal Sergent, *A Century of Paris–Roubaix* (Bromley Books, 1996).

32. Table 6 A, which shows the principal place-to-place road races inaugurated between 1891 and 1896, with approximate distances, sponsorship (where known) and winners, can be found at the end of Chapter 6.

33. This fact could also, of course, create the conditions for a "fix," an arrangement for the local rider to win.

34. Table 6 B, which shows the first 12 years of the Bordeaux-Paris road race, with winners, times, average speeds, and whether paced or not, including automobile pace between 1897 and 1899, can be found at the end of Chapter 6.:

35. Baudry de Saunier, *Le Cyclisme théorique et pratique*.

36. See L. Baudry de Saunier, *L'Art de la Bicyclette* (Paris, 1896). Baudry de Saunier (1865–1938) earned the title of "the historian of French cycling" as a young man with a series of major works. Associated in the 1890s with the leading French cycling newspaper, *Véloce-Sport*, his 1892 work, *Le Cyclisme Théorique et Pratique*, was described there as "the greatest literary monument and most interesting defence ever written in honour of cycling." His 1893 *Mémoires de Terront* was an overnight best-seller. In a significant literary and sporting career, he also wrote in a similar style about the beginnings of the automobile, and later was editor of *La Revue du Touring Club de France*. Baudry de Saunier's other cycling publications include the following titles: *Histoire générale de la Vélocipédie* (Paris, 1891); *Le Cyclisme théorique et pratique* (Paris, 1892); *Recettes utiles et procédés vélocipédiques* (Paris, 1893); *Les Mémoires de Terront*, with C. Terront (Paris, 1893, reprinted with an Introduction by Jacques Seray, Prosport, Paris, 1980); *L'Art de bien monter la Bicyclette* (Paris, 1894); *L'Art de la Bicyclette* (Paris, 1896); *Ma petite bicyclette, son anatomie* (Paris, 1925); *Ma petite bicyclette, sa pratique* (Paris, 1925); *L'Histoire de la Locomotion Terrestre* (Paris, 1935).

37. "The Pleasures of Road Racing," *Cycling*, 22 July 1893, p. 8.

38. G. Lacy Hillier, "Cycle Racing," *The Encyclopaedia of Sport* (London, 1911).

39. "To Overcome Public Prejudice," *Cycling*, 3 Sept. 1892, p. 104.

40. "Road racing," *Bicycling News*, 21 May 1887.

41. Quoted in Roy Green, *100 Years of Cycling Road Records* (Road Records Association, 1988).

42. "The Union and Road Records," Editorial, *The Cyclist*, 14 March 1888, p. 521.

43 "Road Records Association," *The Cyclist*, 9 May 1888, pp. 740–1.

44. "Road Racing," *The Cyclist*, 1 Aug. 1888, pp. 1081–2. Lacy Hillier voiced a similar opinion in an 1892 *Bicycling News* editorial: "The fate of road racing appears to be decided," he wrote, "Each day news reaches us that some club or other has decided to abandon its pro-

gramme of road events, and in future to hold its speed competitions on the path. It is a matter for congratulation that the clubs themselves are taking the initiative instead of waiting until the scandal has been made the subject of legislative action, either in the Council Chamber of the National Cyclists' Union or in the Houses of Parliament." It was better for the sport, argued Lacy Hillier, for it to police itself than for others to have to do it; road racing was "a scandal," it was "necessary for the welfare of the pastime of cycling that it should cease" ("The Beginning of the End," *Bicycling News*, 4 June 1892).

45. "Road-racing," *Bicycling News*, 9 March 1889.

46. "Concerning Road-racing–A Serious Note of Warning," *Bicycling News*, 16 March 1889.

47. "Road-racing–A Reply," *Bicycling News*, 16 March 1889.

48. "More About Road Racing," *Bicycling News*, 23 March 1889.

49. "English Amateurs in France," *Bicycling News*, 13 February 1892.

50. *Irish Cycling News*, date unknown, quoted in *American Wheelman*, Oct. 1887.

51. "Causerie du Jour–George Lacy Hillier," *La Bicyclette*, 16 Oct. 1892 (author's translation).

52. "Sport," *Bicycling News*, 28 May 1892.

53. Another of Hillier's statements of faith in the amateur cause can be found in an earlier *Bicycling News* editorial (9 Oct. 1885): "On the great question of the day—Amateurism—we once and for all record our complete and irreconcilable dissent from the doctrines preached by the disciples of "Get money honestly, if possible, but get money;" we refuse to accept what is called the inevitable, because we cannot believe that the present state of amateurism is the inevitable, and all our efforts shall be directed to the reform of the abuse amateurism suffers from. If straight- forward cutting criticism can kill, we hope to be in at the death."

54. "The Amateur Question in France," *Bicycling News*, 23 April 1892. This article was written by "our Paris correspondent," perhaps H.O. Duncan.

55. "Road-Racing," *Wheeling*, 26 Sept. 1894, p. 605.

56. *Cycling*, 15 September 1894.

57. *Cycling*, 27 October 1894.

58. *The Times*, 15 June 1895.

59. *The Times*, 27 October and 1 November 1897.

60. *The Times*, 8 November 1897.

61. *The Times*, 26 November 1897.

62. The Road Racing Council was established in 1922. In 1937, this body became the Road Time Trials Council, the controlling body of a peculiarly British approach to road racing which for many years defined road racing mainly as time trialling and kept an essentially working-class, club and community-based, sport out of sight and mind by racing on Britain's roads as early as possible on Sunday mornings, when everybody else was still in bed, as it still does today.

63. A thorough study of sponsorship and advertising in sport in the 1890s would no doubt show that bicycle racing during this period played a significant and innovative role in defining the potential of sport to sell products to consumers. Cuca Cocoa's participation in long-distance bicycle racing is also interesting in that it was an early commercial expression and acknowledgment of the need for stimulants in extreme athletic effort.

64. "Famous Racing Trophies—The CUCA Cup," *The Hub*, 31 Oct. 1896, p. 501. The use of the term "scientifically cultivated" here indicates that specific techniques were developed to gain maximum speed both from the pacing-machine and from the method the cyclist used to follow it. Pacing in general terms had been understood in the high-wheel period, but these long races allowed further intense experimentation.

65. "How a Twenty-Four Hours Contest is Managed," *The Hub*, 26 Dec. 1896, p. 315.

66. "The Great All Day Path-Race," *Cycling*, 30 July 1892.

67. The CUCA races were sponsored by Messrs. Root and Co. Ltd, proprietors of the Cuca Cocoa and Chocolate Company. "The CUCA Cup Race. Marvellous performance by Shorland," *Wheeling*, 1 August 1894; "The Cuca 24. Shorland breaks World's Records and makes the Cuca Cup his own," *Cycling*, 4 Aug. 1894; "An Historic Race," editorial in *Wheeling*, 1 August 1894. The winners of the events were as follows: 1892, Shorland, 413m 1615 yds; 1893, Shorland, 426¼ miles; 1894, Shorland, 460m 1296 yds; 1895, George Hunt, 450m 1459 yds; 1896, F.R. Goodwin, 476m 1702 yds.

68. "Long-Distance Competitions," *Cycling*, 19 Sept. 1891.

69. *Véloce-Sport*, 3 August 1893.

70. "International Courtesy," *Véloce-Sport*, 17 August 1893.

71. "Timing and Timers. Comparative articles on timing at home and abroad. England and America," *Cycling*, 15 Sept. 1894.

72. *The Times*, 30 March 1896.

73. *Bicycling World*, 11 Sept 1896. Hillier was born in Chichester in 1856, started riding the bicycle in 1874, joined the Stanley Bicycle Club in 1878 and was involved in the foundation of both the Bicycle Union and the Bicycle Touring Club the same year. In 1880, he first became involved in cycling journalism as founder and editor, with Harry Etherington, of *Wheel World* (see "George L. Hillier," *Bicycling and Athletic Journal*, 25 March 1880). In 1881, he won the English high-wheel championships at all distances. Later, he was the editor of *The Cyclist*. Upon his death in 1941, an obituary commented: "One of the greatest figures in cycling history was removed by the death last month of George Lacy Hillier, cycling journalist, author, sports promoter, and active participant in the pastime almost to the end of his days… A fierce controversialist in his younger days, he mellowed into a kindly and dignified old gentleman." (*C.T.C. Gazette*, March 1941).

74. "Words from the 'Prophet'" *Wheeling*, 3 Oct. 1894.

75. "Rational," "Is Amateurism Possible?" *Wheeling*, 10 October 1894; G.L. Hillier, letter to the Editor, "Is Amateurism Possible? Yes!," *Wheeling*, 17 October 1894.

76. "Editorial Notes," *Wheeling*, 15 Aug. 1894.

77. American roads were notoriously unpredictable, and the size of the country and greatly differing weather made it difficult for cyclists to chart and anticipate conditions. Good roads could in fact be found in surprising places. George Nellis, for example, who crossed the continent on a high-wheel bicycle in 1887, found smooth, hard roads on the prairies near North Platte, Nebraska on which he was able to ride 44 miles in 5 1/2 hours. He called it "the finest stretch for that distance in the entire United States." See Kevin J. Hayes, *An American Cycling*

Odyssey, 1887 (University of Nebraska Press, Lincoln and London, 2002), p. 109.

78. See Hayes, *An American Cycling Odyssey, 1887* and Thomas Stevens, *Around the World on a Bicycle* (Scribner, New York, 1887).

79. A telling juxtaposition of two club photographs in Glen Norcliffe, *The Ride to Modernity* (Figs. 6.2 and 6.3) illustrates how the exclusively masculine club world of the mid-1880s had broadened by the mid-1890s to include women and younger members. The hard-line road riding clubs (such as the English North Road Cycling Club) remained very much a male preserve, however, throughout the 1890s.

80. *Bicycling World*, 5 June 1885, p. 103.
81. *Bicycling World*, 7 Aug. 1885.
82. *Boston Globe*, 1 Aug. 1885.
83. *L.A.W. Bulletin*, 16 April and 22 Oct. 1886.
84. *Springfield Wheelmen's Gazette*, April 1887, p. 5.
85. *The American Wheelman*, May and June 1887; *Bicycling World*, 24 June, 1887.
86. "Is Road Racing Wrong?," *The American Wheelman*, Sept. 1887. It should not be forgotten, of course, that the paper expressing this opinion was clearly pro-cycling.
87. *The Wheelmen's Gazette* (Indianapolis), April 1892, p. 92.
88. *The Wheel*, 1 June 1894. Even allowing for the element of exaggeration in such an account, it is clear that the crowds must have been unusually large, since the novel event would have attracted unusual attention. *The Referee* (1 June 1894) reported that this race had been run seven years previously, "promoted by R.D. Garden, manager of the Chicago branch of the Pope company, to boom cycling, which was, of course, then in swaddling clothes." The entries and actual starters were as follows: 1887 race–41 entrants, 35 starters; 1888–86 entries, 71 starters; 1889–123 entries, 67 starters; 1890–186 entries, 77 starters; 1891–223 entries, starters unknown; 1892–387 entries, starters unknown; 1893—351 entries, 271 starters; 1894–421 entries, 329 starters. The Associated Cycling Clubs of Chicago promoted the event in 1894. The race was run as a handicap.
89. *The Wheel and Cycling Trade Review*, 1 June 1894 and *Buffalo Daily Courier*, 31 May 1894.
90. *Worcester Telegram*, ? May 1896 (exact date unknown).
91. *Worcester Telegram*, 14 June 1896. No in-depth study of this aspect of American sport history at the turn of the century has as yet been attempted. Road racing was extensively documented in the cycling press and in the urban newspapers of the period, where races often received several pages of coverage. In the absence of the automobile, cycling was a major presence in the urban landscape.
92. *New York Times*, 15 July 1894.
93. *The American Cyclist*, June 1892.
94. *The Referee*, 1 June 1894.
95. *Indianapolis Sentinel*, 8 Sept. 1895.
96. *The Wheel*, 1 June 1894.
97. *San Francisco Chronicle*, 17 August 1894.
98. *Bicycling World*, 11 Sept 1896.
99. *New York Evening Journal*, 7 Nov. 1898.
100. A much stronger, universal resistance—leading in fact to severe restrictions because of the danger to other road-users—was encountered by motor-racing pioneers. Fatal accidents occurred in many of the long-distance automobile races, Paris–Amsterdam, Paris–Berlin and Paris–Vienna, but the most notorious fatalities occurred in the Paris–Madrid race of 1903, which was ordered to be stopped by the French government at Bordeaux after a terrible first day of carnage. See Chapter 10, "Paris–Madrid," in Charles Jarrott, *Ten Years of Motors and Motor Racing* (London, Grant Richards, 1906) and Chapter 3, Philippe Gaboriau, "The Tour de France and Cycling's Belle Epoque," in Dauncey and Hare, *The Tour de France, 1903–2003*.
101. *La Bicyclette*, 28 Aug. 1892.
102. L. Baudry de Saunier, *Le Cyclisme Théorique et Pratique* (Librairie Illustrée, Paris, 1892), p. 11 and p. 16.
103. *La Bicyclette*, 2 June 1893, p. 1169. The cultural, moral and spiritual aspects of sport were emphasized in the "Courses d'Artistes" and the "Café-Concerts" organized in Parisian cycling circles in the mid-1890s. *La Bicyclette* and *Le Vélo* sponsored a "Course d'Artistes, Peintres, Sculpteurs et Architectes ... reserved exclusively for those who can prove convincingly that they are painters, sculptors or architects," a road race held on a 40 km course which included Versailles (*La Bicyclette*, 30 June, 7 and 14 July 1893). Later the "Café-Concerts" staged a mixture of serious bicycle racing, women's racing, costume competitions and other festivities, a Bohemian celebration of alternative life-styles. Sport was integrated into other cultural activities, rather than separated from them.
104. See Philippe Gaboriau, *Le Tour de France et Le Vélo—Histoire sociale d'une épopée contemporaine*, L'Harmattan, Paris, 1995 and Paul Boury, *La France du Tour—Un espace sportif à géographie variable*, L'Harmattan, Paris, 1997. In fact, roads in France, Belgium and Italy are routinely closed for the big professional races, and even for minor races, indicating a general acceptance by the authorities of the sport.

CHAPTER SEVEN

1. Much has been published on the process by which sport has evolved or advanced to its present-day structure and organization. See, for example, Dunning, E. and Sheard, K., *Barbarians, Gentlemen and Players: A Sociological Study of the Development of Rugby Football* (New York, New York University Press, 1979); Guttmann, A., *From Ritual to Record—The Nature of Modern Sports* (New York, Columbia University Press, 1978); Hargreaves, John, *Sport, Power and Culture—A Social and Historical Analysis of Popular Sports in Britain* (Cambridge, Polity Press, 1986). Dunning and Sheard publish a chart showing the structural properties of folk games and modern sports, and emphasize that the structural properties of sport are cultural constructions, socially shaped. Central to the discussion is the distinction between "pre-industrial" and "modern" sport, and it can easily be seen that cycling, which began in 1868–69, falls in every respect into the category of a "modern" sport.

2. The dual use of the word "record" as both a verb (to record) and a noun (a record) should be noted here. The original meaning implied by the word was that "a record" was kept of a particular performance, or that a particular performance "was recorded," and thus was "on

record." From this comes the contemporary use of the word as a noun as in "a world record," as meaning the best time performance ever achieved for a particular distance.

3. See "Championships and Records," in F.T. Bidlake, *Cycling* (Routledge, London, 1896), p. 117.

4. The phrasing of this clause in the stated objectives of the N.C.U. in the earlier days did not include the professional class.

5. F.T. Bidlake, op. cit., p. 111. Bidlake was not a fan of the N.C.U. and its many committees. In 1898, when the N.C.U. was finally successful in prohibiting its licenced riders from taking part in road-racing, Bidlake was "stumping the country haranguing sympathetic audiences of road-racing club members." Bidlake, a life-long member of the North Road C.C., suggested that road-racing clubs should secede from the N.C.U. The N.C.U. responded: "The results of Bidlake's new association ... will be the promotion of road-racing in defiance of the law of the land, in opposition to public opinion and the cycling and general press, and with more danger to pedestrians, to drivers of carriages and other vehicles, and to 99% of cyclists themselves, who neither-road race nor have any sympathy with this discredited branch of the sport." (*N.C.U. Review and Official Record*, Jan. 1898, Vol. 4, No. 38). It may still be argued that Britain's failure to become a world cycling power on a par with France, Italy or Belgium in the later 1890s can be traced to the obsessive concern of the National Cyclists' Union bureaucrats to uphold amateur "respectability" during this formative period and to fail to promote and encourage "open" road racing.

6. For information on James Moore, see Nick Clayton, "The cycling career of James Moore," *The Boneshaker* No. 125, Spring 1991.

7. *Morning Advertiser*, 11 and 16 Sept. 1869.

8. The earliest Six Day races I have been able to document took place in 1876. *The Athletic News*, a Manchester paper (30 September 1876) reported two six day rides by individual cyclists, Thuillet of France at the Molineux Grounds, Wolverhampton, and Frank White at the Arboretum, Walsall. These were pure audience-grabbing endurance events, the Thuillet ride attracting 10,000 spectators: Thuillet was paced by John Keen on the final day. On 21 October 1876 the same paper reported the logical conclusion to the earlier reports, a six-day race between Thuillet and White, again at Walsall.

9. H.O. Duncan, *World on Wheels*, Paris, 1927; N. Salamon, *Bicycling: Its Rise and Development*, London, 1874; *Le Vélocipède Illustré*, 11 April 1874; A. Howard, *The Bicycle for 1874*, London, 1874.

10. *New York Times*, 18 April and 11 May 1876; Michael Wells, "America and the Ordinary: In the beginning, 1876," *The Wheelmen*, Nov. 1992.

11. "International Competition," *Bicycling World*, 20 Jan. 1882, p. 123.

12. "The Policy of the N.C.U." and "Report of the Committee for Promoting Professional Racing," *N.C.U. Review and Official Record*, April 1887, Vol. 4, No. 1.

13. *N.C.U. Review and Official Record*, March 1894, Vol. 2, No. 23.

14. "Resume for 1880," *Wheel World Christmas Annual*, London, 1880.

15. *Cycling*, 9 July 1892.

16. Sellers was called "a rider who had landed in New York but three days before, and whose name had never been heard outside the Midland counties of England." Sellers was only 21 years old, "the son of a prosperous manufacturer of Preston." The British, said *Outing* (Nov. 1884) "came to ride, not to disgust people with swaggering remarks, as some of the Britons did last year."

17. See "The Broken Records at Hartford and Springfield," pp. 128–131, and "Monthly Record," pp. 145–6, *Outing and The Wheelman*, Nov. 1884.

18. "International Championships," *The Cyclist*, 24 Feb. 1886, pp. 431–32.

19. *The Cycle* (Boston), 9 April 1886.

20. These included tricyclist E. Kiderlein (Holland, 1887, 1-mile), August Lehr (Germany, 1889, 1-mile), P. Scheltema-Beduin (Holland, 1891, 1-mile safety), A.A. Zimmerman (U.S.A., 1892, 1-mile, 5-miles and 50-miles), C. Ingeman-Petersen (Denmark, 1894, 1-mile) and M. Diakoff (Russia, 1896, 5-miles and 25-miles).

21. The German Deutsche Radfahrer Bund, founded in 1884, also included Austria, German-speaking Bohemia and German-speaking Switzerland. This table shows governing bodies established by 1890. The dates of other national governing bodies are provisionally listed as: Argentina—Union Velocipedistica Argentina, 1902 (one of two national bodies struggling for representation at 1902 U.C.I. Congress); South Africa—South African Cycling Federation (date of founding unknown); Spain—Federacion Espanola do Ciclismo, 1893 (?). The pioneering technological and organizational role of Britain in disseminating interest in the sport is well-documented in the cases of the United States (see Chapter 3), of Australia (see "Under the Southern Cross," *Outing*, Feb. 1884, Vol. 3 No. 5) and of Germany (see Heiner Gillmeister, "English Editors of German Sporting Journals at the Turn of the Century," *The Sports Historian*, May 1993, pp. 38–65). According to Theo Stevens, "The Elitist Character of Early Dutch Cycling" (*Proceedings of the 12th International Cycling History Conference*, Van der Plas Publications, San Francisco, 2002), this pattern of English participation in the diffusion of cycling into northern Europe and the formation of athletic clubs devoted to cycling was also repeated in Holland. In 1883, C.H. Bingham, the captain of the Ooievaar Club (Stork Club) of The Hague, was instrumental in the founding of Het Nederlandsche Velocipedisten Bond and became its first president, while another Englishman, D. Webster, captain of the Haarlemsche Velocipede Club, became vice-president. Both were members of the C.T.C. The French appear to have been more influential in the spread of cycling into Italy and Spain.

22. Thus, in 1885, a "Nordic championship" took place in Copenhagen and in 1892 and 1893 a Sokol association in Zagreb held a "Championship of the Kingdom of Croatia, Slavonia and Dalmatia." In 1886 the Deutsche Radfahrer Bund held the first, higher-profile "European championship" in Berlin, when the Viennese newspaper, *Allgemeine Sport Zeitung*, expressed support for the concept of a united, multi-ethnic, multi-liguistic "Mitteleuropa." And beginning in 1894 a "European championship," or a "Grand Prix of Europe" was a prominent part of the professional European track-racing season, contested as an alternative and rival to official world championships. Quoted in Gherardo Bonini, "National

Identity and Ethnicity in International Cycling before 1914," *Annual* of European Committee for the History of Sport, 2001. The 1886 Berlin "Championship of Europe" was the brain-child of T.H.S. Walker, the English editor of *Der Radfahrer*, the journal of the Deutsche Radfahrer Bund, and was held on the occasion of the annual meeting of the D.R.B. The fact that the winner of the 10,000m high-wheeler event, Edward Hale, was not one of the best British cyclists was underlined in *Sporting Life*. See Rüdiger Rabenstein, "T.H.S. Walker—English Cycling Pioneer in Germany," (*Proceedings*, International Cycle History Conference, 1994).

23. "1887," *The Cyclist*, 28 Dec. 1887 and "Professional Racing Prospects," *The Cyclist*, 11 April 1888 (editorials probably by Henry Sturmey).

24. Mentioned in issues of *The Cyclist* and *Bicycling World* in 1888.

25. American Rowe had recently turned professional, and was thus a new challenge to Howell, the well-established English professional champion. *The Cyclist*, 11 April 1888, wrote of this contest that Howell and Rowe had been, "for the last two years at least, the acknowledged and practically undefeated champions of the Eastern and Western hemispheres."

26. "Cowboys v. Bicyclists at the Agricultural Hall, Islington," *The Cyclist*, 16 Nov. 1887, "Cowboys v. Cyclists at Birmingham," *The Cyclist*, 4 Jan. 1888 and "Cyclists v. Cowboys," *The Cyclist*, 28 March 1888. At the Birmingham race. The "Cyclists" rode 804 miles, while the "Cowboys" rode 795 miles.

27. "Battensby Challenges the Yankees," *The Cyclist*, 18 April 1888.

28. According to *The Cyclist*, ("R. Howell v. W. Wood for £100," 4 April 1888), Wood's performances had "evidently tickled the perceptive faculties of Mr. Robert Mould, of the Marquis of Lorne Hotel, North Shields," who "seems to have taken Wood in hand, and has proved a most consistent and generous supporter to him. Mr. Mould's great ambition seemed to be in meeting the world's recognized champion, and he lost no time in issuing a challenge which was promptly accepted by Howell." W. Wood should not be confused with Leicester professional Fred Wood, who in April 1888 returned home from an extended racing trip to the United States, Australia and New Zealand which had begun in Aug. 1886 (see "Interview with Fred Wood," *The Cyclist*, 25 April 1888).

29. "International Race at Leicester. Howell v. Rowe," *The Cyclist*, 18 April 1888.

30. "International Race at Jarrow-on-Tyne," *The Cyclist*, 25 April 1888.

31. René Jacobs and Hector Mahau, *Le Prestige de la Route* (Éditions Eeclonaar, Belgium, 2002).

32. See Minutes of a Meeting of General Committee, National Cyclists' Union, 12 Aug. 1892 (Modern Records Centre, Warwick University): "Inter-National Championships—Mr. Sturmey proposed and Mr. Church seconded: That a Committee be appointed to consider the question of Inter-National Championships (Carried). Messrs. Sturmey, Hillier and Turner were appointed as the first members of the Committee."

33. The Scottish organization, although invited, could not send an official representative, though J.R.Nisbet, editor of *The Scottish Cyclist*, attended. There was continued dissension about the position of the Irish, Scottish and Welsh Cyclists' Unions within the umbrella of the N.C.U. The full list of delegates was as follows: Henry Sturmey and W.M. Appleton (National Cyclists' Union); A.E. Kemplen (Union des Sociétés Françaises de Sports Athlétiques); Heinrich Kleyer (German Cyclists' Union); Franz Netcher (Dutch Cyclists' Union); G. Bonetti (Italian Cyclists' Union); W.F. McCourt (Irish Cyclists' Association); A. Choisy (Belgian Cyclists' Union); Dr. P.E. Doolittle (Canadian Cyclists' Assocation); H.E. Raymond (League of American Wheelmen). Also present were Messrs. Marais, Rousseau and Paul Hardy representing the Union Vélocipédique de France. See "Formation of an International Cyclists' Association," *The Scottish Cyclist*, 30 Nov. 1892.

34. Sturmey's committee reported back to the N.C.U. (see *N.C.U. Review and Official Record*, Dec. 1892): "Your Committee have to report that, in accordance with instructions, they communicated with the various ruling bodies of Cycling on the Continents of Europe and America, laying before them, briefly, the suggested basis on which it was proposed to work, and asking that if the idea met with their approval they should appoint committees to deal with the details of a draft scheme which would be submitted ... for the consideration of the various Unions... This was provided and copies sent to each... A meeting was accordingly held on Wednesday, Nov. 23rd, at the Agricultural Hall, at which officially appointed delegates were present."

35. Source unknown.

36. Editorial, "International Championships," *The Scottish Cyclist*, 30 Nov. 1892; see also the report in the same issue, "Formation of an International Cyclists' Association."

37. *Cycling*, 3 Dec. 1892.

38. A letter from Henry Sturmey, Secretary of the International Cyclists' Association mentions a 1-mile professional race at the 1894 Championships, which was probably not a full Championship event. Sturmey also mentions "a conference on international amateurism and an International Exhibition in Antwerp" (see *Wheeling*, 25 July 1894).

39. "Paris versus Chicago," *La Bicyclette*, 1 Jan. 1893, pp. 590–592.

40. "Course Internationale d'Amateurs, Paris–Brussels," *La Bicyclette*, 25 Aug. 1893, pp. 1594–1601.

41. The championships were reported in the *New York Times*, 23, 30 July, 1, 7, 8, 9, 10, 11, 12, 13 Aug. 1893; also in *Bearings*, 4, 11 and 18 Aug. 1893 (with excellent photographs).

42. "Arrangements for the Big International Meet," *New York Times*, 30 July 1893.

43. See "The Year 1897 in Cycling," *Spalding's Official Bicycle Guide for 1898*.

44. See Andrew Ritchie, *Major Taylor*, pp. 125–128.

45. See "Report of the General Committee—Report of the International Championships and the First International Congress at Antwerp and Brussels," *N.C.U. Review and Official Record*, March 1895, Vol. 3, No. 27: "The Board of the I.C.A. were desired by the Congress to draft rules for, and establish Cycling World's Championships for professionals ... professional championships will be included in the I.C.A. programme at Cologne this season." An account by Henry Sturmey of the confusion

and appeals following the 1 mile professional race at the 1895 Cologne championships can be found in the *N.C.U. Review and Official Record*, Dec. 1895, Vol. 3, No. 30.

46. *N.C.U. Review and Official Record*, March 1897, Vol. 3, No. 35.

47. *The Wheel* quoted in "International Championships," Editorial in *Wheeling*, 12 Sept. 1894.

48. See discussion in *Bicycling News*, 15, 22 and 29 April 1896.

49. Quoted in Gherardo Bonini, "National Identity and Ethnicity in International Cycling before 1914," *Annual* of European Committee for the History of Sport, 2001.

50. The creation of the U.C.I. was effected at the Aug. 1900 Congress of the I.C.A. in Paris. Reported in *Allgemeine Sport Zeitung*, 12 Aug. 1900, quoted in Gherardo Bonini, op. cit. There was a brief period of overlap between the two bodies, during which the I.C.A. lingered on as an N.C.U.-controlled organization. A dispute over voting rights at first prevented resolution of British membership in the new U.C.I., since the N.C.U. wanted a vote for each of the constituent national members of the United Kingdom—England, Scotland, Ireland and Wales—which was finally agreed upon in 1903.

51. Bonini points out that the professionals were less concerned with the "official" World Championships since their competition in the open marketplace of sport was already determining their pecking order. The professionals. Attitude towards the nationalism fostered by official World Championships was also ambivalent—they raced wherever they were most popular and could obtain the highest fee. In effect, track owners and promoters (of whom the most powerful were in Paris, Antwerp, Copenhagen, Berlin and New York) were a challenge to the authority of the national federations.

52. A fuller account of Zimmerman's life and career has been expanded from this shorter account and published as Andrew Ritchie, *Flying Yankee: The International Cycling Career of Arthur Augustus Zimmerman* (John Pinkerton Memorial Publishing Fund, 2009).

53. *Wheelmen's Gazette*, Nov. 1893; *The Wheel*, 4 Jan. 1895; Gregory Houston Bowden, *The Story of the Raleigh Bicycle* (W.H. Allen, London, 1975).

54. Introduction by Frank Bowden in A. A. Zimmerman, *Points for Cyclists with Training* (F.W.S. Clarke, London, 1893).

55. Bowden, op. cit.

56. Bowden, *Points for Cyclists*, op. cit.

57. *British Sport*, quoted in *American Cyclist*, April 1892.

58. "L.A.W. re. Zimmerman," Minutes of General Committee of N.C.U., 29 April 1892, Mss. 328/B, Modern Records Centre, University of Warwick, Coventry.

59. Bowden, in Zimmerman, op. cit.

60. *Irish Cyclist*, quoted in *American Cyclist*, Aug. 1892.

61. "Zimmerman's Latest," *American Cyclist*, Sept. 1892.

62. *Wheeling*, quoted in *American Cyclist*, Aug. 1892.

63. *American Cyclist*, Sept. 1892, op. cit.

64. Bowden, in Zimmerman, op. cit.; *New York Times*, 30 June 1893.

65. Zimmerman Treated Unfairly," *New York Times*, 25 June 1893.

66. A revealing insight into attitudes within the National Cyclists' Union following Zimmerman's victories in the 1892 championships is given in the report of a Committee meeting of 17 Dec. 1892 (reported in *N.C.U. Review and Official Record*, March 1893). E.B. Turner proposed the motion, which was seconded by Hillier, that: "In the opinion of this Council the time has now arrived when it is advisable that no person connected with the trade of making, selling, or letting on hire cycles or their essential parts, should be eligible to act as a representative … on the Council or on the Appeals or General Committees of the Union." The proposal was voted down, 31 for, 39 against. E.B. Turner addressed the meeting: his proposal was "a first step towards the purification of the sport," which "was being dragged in the mire by those men who were suborned by the makers. The Union was being held up to derision by foreign countries… It was a prostitution of a most noble sport… They must keep the sport free from any trade influence whatever. The moment that pounds, shillings and pence came in at the door, amateur sport flew out at the window."

67. Interview with Zimmerman, *New York Times*, 12 July 1893. The interview gives further revelations of the hypocrisy and double-dealing within the power structures of English "shamateurism," and is particularly interesting on the role of Lacy Hillier and Zimmerman's reactions to him. See Andrew Ritchie, *Flying Yankee*, pp. 63–65.

68. *Véloce-Sport* (Paris), 15 June 1893.

69. Quoted in "American Comments on the Zimmerman Incident," Editorial in *Cycling*, 8 July 1893.

70. *New York Times*, 14, 25 and 26 June; 12 and 29 July 1893; *Wheelmen's Gazette* (Indianapolis), July 1893.

71. This poster is published in various places, most accessibly in Jack Rennert, *100 Years of Bicycle Posters* (Harper and Row, New York, 1973). The art for the poster was drawn by George Moore, the doyen of cycling commercial artists, and the copy in Rennert advertises the Paris agency of the Raleigh company.

72. *Indianapolis Sentinel*, 25 August 1893. Another interesting description of Zimmerman was published in *Véloce-Sport*, 15 June 1893: "In riding, Zimmerman is very interesting to study, especially since he has a style and a position completely different from our best riders. When he is going slowly, he is balanced on his machine with a side-to-side movement of his shoulders, although his hips are completely still. But when the pace picks up, all his body movement stops as it is an obstacle to speed. Our best riders tend to bend their arms, to arch their backs, to move their head and shoulders, but Zimmerman simply pedals faster, without any visible sign of effort. Rather than lowering his head, like the others, he stretches it forwards, looking straight in front of him, his nose in the air, rather like a hare or a thoroughbred horse. He doesn't bend his arms, but holds them close to his body, while his legs rotate with absolute regularity like the pistons of a locomotive. His ankles are extraordinarily supple, and you have the impression that his feet press the pedals with a smooth and continuous motion, such a difficult perfection to achieve. When he begins his sprint, it is not sudden, and you can't tell when it begins, and you have the impression that it is just his normal style, and not exceptionally fast. He is certainly the best rider at the moment, perhaps the best ever. Everyone who has seen him agrees that it is a new experience, that he deserves to be called the king of the track."

73. Editorial, *The Wheel and Cycling Trade Review*, 6 April 1894.
74. "Zimmie," *The Wheel and Cycling Trade Review*, 6 April 1894.
75. Bowden, in *Zimmerman*, op. cit.
76. *The Wheel and Cycling Trade Review*, 6 April 1894.
77. *Bearings*, 27 April 1894; *Outing*, May 1894.
78. *The Wheel*, 13 April 1894.
79. *Cycling Life*, 19 April 1894.
80. Information quoted from J.-M. Erwin and A.A. Zimmerman, *Conseils d'Entrainement par Zimmerman et Relation de son Voyage en Europe* (Librarie du Vélo, Paris, 1894); also published in English as J.M. Erwin and A.A. Zimmerman, *Zimmerman Abroad and Points on Training* (Chicago, Blakeley Printing Co., 1895).
81. *The Wheel*, 31 Aug. 1894.
82. Quoted from Erwin and Zimmerman, op. cit. (author's translation).
83. Interview published in *Chicago Evening Post*, date unknown, quoted in *The Wheel*, 18 Jan. 1895.
84. *The Wheel*, 7 Sept. 1894.
85. *Cycling*, 18 Aug. 1894.
86. *The Wheel*, 7 Sept. 1894.
87. Interview published in *Chicago Evening Post*, date unknown, quoted in *The Wheel*, 18 Jan. 1895; *New York Times*, 13 Nov. 1894.
88. *New York Times*, 18 Feb 1896.
89. *Bearings*, 27 May 1897.
90. See "The Cycle Racing of 1893," *Wheelmen's Gazette*, Nov. 1893 and "A Resume of the Racing Season," *Wheelmen's Gazette*, Nov. 1894.
91. "The Men of the Year," *The Wheel*, 4 Jan. 1895.
92. *Rules, Regulations and Instructions of the N.C.U.*, 1895 edition.
93. Quoted from Bidlake, op. cit., pp. 111–113.
94. F.T. Bidlake, op. cit., pp. 113–114.
95. G. Lacy Hillier, "The Chances of the New Professionalism," *Cycling*, 23 Dec. 1893.
96. Cartoon from *Cycling*, 27 April 1895.
97. Dr. E. B. Turner, "The New Professionalism," *Cycling*, 30 Dec. 1893. It is not clear exactly what the nature of the objections to professionalism voiced by a critic such as Turner actually were. Was professional bicycle racing really as dishonest, as prone to deceptions, vices and disappointments as amateur proponents suggested, or was it in these suspicions that the class-based antipathies and prejudices were most tellingly expressed?
98. "Mass Meeting of Racers," *Cycling*, 30 June 1894 and "The Racing Men's Revolt," *Cycling*, 14 July 1894.
99. Editorial, *Cycling*, 23 June 1894.
100. *La Revue Athlétique*, 25 Dec. 1890, quoted in Mandell, op. cit., p. 32.
101. J. Astley Cooper, "An Anglo-Saxon Olympiad," *Nineteenth Century*, Sept. 1892, quoted in Mandell op. cit., p. 32.
102. Richard Mandell, *The First Modern Olympics* (University of California Press, 1976), p. 82; see also Chap. 7, "Mass-Producing Traditions," in Eric Hobsbawm and Terence Ranger, *The Invention of Tradition* (Cambridge U.P., 1983). See also Douglas Brown, "Modern Sport, Modernism and the Cultural Manifesto: De Coubertin's *Revue Olympique*," *International Journal of the History of Sport*, June 2001.
103. Mandell, ibid., p. 83.
104. *Bulletin du Comité International des Jeux Olympiques*, Oct. 1894 [author's translation].
105. The sports represented at the 1896 Olympic Games were those that were popular among the expanding European upper and middle-class, though team sports were not as yet included. The sports included track and field (100m, 400m, 800m, 1500m, marathon, 110m hurdles), jumping and throwing (high jump, long jump, pole vault, triple jump, shot put, discus), wrestling, swimming, weight-lifting, fencing, gymnastics, rowing, cycling, shooting and tennis. Of the original 15 members of the International Olympic Committee, 12 were European, and the other three were from the United States, Argentina and New Zealand. See David Wallechinsky, *The Complete Book of the Summer Olympics* (Little, Brown and Co., 1984).
106. Mandell, op. cit., p. 144.
107. *Bulletin du Comité International des Jeux Olympiques*, April 1895, p. 4.
108. A search for the earliest dates of the founding of world governing bodies of other major sports has provided the following information: the Fédération Internationale Gymnastique was formed in 1881, but no world championships were held until 1903. The International Skating Union was formed in 1892 and began holding world championships in 1893. The Fédération Internationale des Sociétés d'Aviron (rowing) was also formed in 1892, though only European championships were held from 1893. F.I.F.A., the world soccer body, was formed in 1904.
109. See Andrew Ritchie, *Major Taylor*, pp. 176–183.
110. Gherardo Bonini, "National Identity," op. cit.
111. Figures for N.C.U. from *N.C.U. Review and Official Record*, March 1897 and for C.T.C. from *C.T.C. Monthly Gazette*, Jan. 1897. A figure for total membership of national cycling organizations for the whole of Great Britain would also have to include membership of the Scottish Cyclists' Union and the Irish Cyclists' Union. There was, of course, a considerable overlap in membership of the N.C.U. and the C.T.C. since some cyclists joined both organizations.

Chapter Eight

[A note on distances, speeds and salary amounts discussed in Chapter 8. Distances and average speeds are expressed in both miles and kilometers, and no attempt has been made to convert them because of conversion anomalies. If necessary, miles may be converted into kilometers and kilometers into miles using the formulas: 1 mile = 1.6 km and 1 km = 0.63 miles.]

1. An extended discussion of concepts of "modernism" and how they relate to modern sport, and in particular the modern Olympic movement, can be found in Douglas Brown, "Modern Sport, Modernism and the Cultural Manifesto: De Coubertin's Revue Olympique," *International Journal of the History of Sport*, June 2001, pp. 78–109.
2. *Sport-Album der Rad-Welt* (1904), p. 124; J.- M. Erwin and A.A. Zimmerman, *Conseils d'Entraînement et Relation de son voyage en Europe* (Paris: Librairie du Vélo, 1894) ; *Berliner Illustrirte Zeitung* 13, p. 199 and 16, p. 241.

3. Tracks were built in the 1890s in every country where cycling was popular: especially in Britain, France, Belgium, Germany, Italy and the United States. In England, Herne Hill Track was described as "the nursery of the majority of our leading riders of the present day." It was conveniently located in south London, and "possesses rare facilities for the successful attacking of records." It was "fringed by a belt of trees on one side, and beneath the shelter of a tall railway viaduct on another, and it is seldom indeed that a breeze is blowing in sufficient force to seriously interfere with the comfort of riders." Most important, the track was resurfaced in 1893 with "the then newly invented and now well-known "battens," strips of wood laid upon a substratum of concrete and cement, and banked at each end sufficiently to allow of its successful negotiation at even the highest rate of speed." The cost of the new facility was from £5–6,000. ("The cost of a famous racing track," *The Hub*, 22 Aug. 1896). This wooden track was severely criticized as cement became increasingly popular and was generally recognized as being faster. New tracks were also built in London at Wood Green and Catford, and that at Putney improved. The Wood Green track cost a total of £18,000, including £3,000 for the cement track itself and £3,600 for the grandstand ("Famous racing tracks," *The Hub*, 29 Aug. 1896, p. 147). In Paris and Berlin new tracks were generally constructed of cement. By 1903, *Sport-Album der Rad-Welt* listed 19 leading continental tracks outside Germany, including Amsterdam, Antwerp, Brussels, Copenhagen, Florence, Rome, Turin, Zurich and three in Paris. The same publication for 1904 lists 54 tracks in Germany!

4. "The National Circuit of 1897," *The Referee*, 10 Dec. 1896.

5. See Chapter 7, pp. 127–141, "Let him ride to death—The Crazy Fringe," in Robert A. Smith, *A Social History of the Bicycle* (New York: American Heritage Press, 1972).

6. *Illustrirte Zeitung* 2366, 1888.

7. Op. cit., 1893, 2598, p. 408; 2607, p. 660 and 2608, p. 688; J.R. de Bruycker, *Das Abenteuer der grossen Distanzritte* (Kiel: Moby Dick Verlag, 1985).

8. The oldest of these "classics" are Bordeaux–Paris (1891), Paris–Roubaix (1896), Paris–Tours (1896) and Paris–Brussels (1896).

9. *Deutscher Radfahrer-Bund*, 1891, p. 510.

10. The record was set on 27 July 1882 at Crystal Palace, London; 20 miles in 59m 31 4/5s, or 20 miles 300 yds in the hour. See G. Lacy Hillier, "A succinct and critical history of the One Hour's Cycle Path Record from the earliest authenticated record to the present day," *The Cyclist Annual and Year Book for 1892*.

11. *Deutscher Radfahrer-Bund*, 1891, p. 312. Journalist Victor Breyer recollected later that "this race was an eye-opener for the masses... That human beings had been capable of riding nearly 400 miles on their frail machines, almost without a dismount, filled everybody with admiration. It came as a tremendous revelation." ("How G. P. Mills won the first Bordeaux–Paris," *Cycling*, 19 March 1947). The North Road Cycling Club had promoted 12 hour and 24 hour time trials since its foundation in 1885, having been formed specifically to take advantage of the fine condition of the Great North Road, and its suitability for bicycle racing. The first North Road C. C. 24-hour race was held in 1886, and was won on an ordinary bicycle by G. P. Mills (227 miles), the same rider who won the Bordeaux–Paris race in 1891.

12. See Andrew Ritchie, "Charles Terront and Paris–Brest–Paris in 1891," *The Boneshaker* 150, Summer 1999 and Andrew Ritchie, "The French Classics and British opposition to road racing in the 1890s," *The Boneshaker* 151, Winter 1999.

13. Philippe Tissié, *Guide du Vélocipédiste pour l'Entraînement, la Course et le Tourisme* (Paris: Octave Doin Editeur, 1893); H.O. Duncan, *The World on Wheels* (Paris: Self-published, c.1926); Versnick, op. cit.; L. Baudry de Saunier, *Les mémoires de Terront* (1893; modern edition Paris: Prosport, 1980).

14. *Sport-Album der Rad-Welt* (1903); Fredy Budzinski, *Taschen-Radwelt—Ein radsportliches Lexikon* (Berlin, 1908/9).

15. Höfer, op. cit., p. 43.

16. Höfer, op. cit., pp. 50 and 58.

17. Höfer, op. cit., p. 53; Detlev Sierck, *Das Tourenfahren*, in Paul von Salvisberg, *Der Radfahrsport in Bild und Wort* (Munich: Academischer Verlag, 1897).

18. *Illustrirte Zeitung* 2810 (1893), p. 45; *Deutscher Radfahrer-Bund* (1893), p. 424.

19. *Vossische Zeitung* (30 June 1893).

20. *Illustrirte Zeitung* 2610 (1893), p. 46.

21. *Morning Advertiser*, 26 Oct. 1875. Laumaillé and Richard, from the club named Vélo-Sport of Paris, encountered terrible weather conditions, but still beat the record time of Count von Zubowitz and his mare Caradoc, which "inspired the members of the Paris club with the ambition of rivalling it," by nearly 3 days. They rode bicycles made by the Coventry Machinists Company. "All along the route the light machines were the admiration and the envy of the people who had hitherto known of no other bicycles than the wooden-wheeled "boneshakers" which are now abandoned in this country." See also *Bicycling: Its Rise and Development, A Text Book for Riders*, London: 1876, pp. 34–40.

22. H. O. Duncan and Pierre Lafitte, *En Suivant Terront de St. Petersburg à Paris à Bicyclette* (Paris: 1894).

23. "Terront's Record Ride Across Europe," *The Cyclist*, 18 Oct. 1893.

24. See Robert Louis Jefferson, *To Constantinople on a Bicycle* (1894), *Roughing It in Siberia* (1895), *Awheel to Moscow and Back* (London: Sampson, Low, Martin, 1895), *Across Siberia on a Bicycle* (London: Cycle Press, 1896) and *A New Ride to Khiva* (London: Methuen, 1899). See also Thomas Allen and William Sachleben, *Across Asia on a Bicycle* (New York: Century Co., 1894).

25. Jacques Seray, *1904–Ce Tour de France qui faillit être le dernier* (Abbeville, 1994).

26. *L'Auto*, date unknown, quoted in Seray, op. cit., p. 118. The early Tour de France is explored in Hugh Dauncey and Geoff Hare, "The Tour de France: A Pre-Modern Contest in a Post-Modern Context" (pp. 1–29), and Philippe Gaboriau, "The Tour de France and Cycling's Belle Epoque" (pp. 57–78), both in Dauncey and Hare, *The Tour de France 1903–2003: A Century of Sporting Structures, Meanings and Values* (London: Cass, 2003). Gaboriau rightly makes the connection between the beginning of the Tour de France and the series of well publicized road races involving both bicycles and cars between 1891 (date of the first Bordeaux–Paris bicycle

race) and 1903. Both bicycle and automobile industries were deeply and competitively involved in these events. Following a series of appalling fatalities and serious injuries on the road between Paris and Bordeaux during the French leg of the Paris–Madrid car race in May 1903, car racing was banned on the roads of France. The publicity potential of such events had been amply demonstrated, however, before the Paris–Madrid tragedies. Says Gaboriau: "a whole series of road races can be considered as a single category of competitions linking sports, newspapers and industries to the values of endurance, record-breaking and mechanical modernity." But with the Paris–Madrid fatalities, "this fantastic race towards progress ended in drama and chaos," writes Gaboriau. The first Tour de France, therefore, although it down-played speed and sensation, emphasized the human and heroic values of tenacity and endurance.

27. *Deutsche Turn-Zeitung*, Leipzig, 1904, p. 647; W. Gronen and W. Lemke, *Geschichte des Radsports und des Fahrrades* (Eupen: Edition Doepgen Verlag, 1978), p. 239 (referred to throughout as Gronen/Lemke).

28. G. Lacy Hillier, in *The Cyclist Annual and Yearbook for 1892* (see Note 12), wrote that Cortis' unsuccessful attempt on 2 Sept. 1880 to break the 20 mph time for the hour was "the earliest recorded instance of pacemakers being used in an attempt to make good time." Hillier himself was one of the four pacers. An analysis of psychological aspects of pacing was conducted in 1898 by Norman Triplett, of Indiana University, and published as "The Dynamogenic Factors in Pacemaking and Competition," *American Journal of Psychology*, Vol. IX, July 1898. A more recent analysis of tactical aspects of pacing in bicycle racing is found in Edward Albert, "The Sociology of Bicycle Racing—Group Sport with a Difference," *Cycling Science*, Sept.–Dec. 1991.

29. *The Hub*, 10 Oct. 1896, p. 363. The article continues: "To get good results out of a multi-cycle, the men riding it must, as it is termed, "nick" perfectly together, that is to say, they must work with that mechanical unison of movement that alone brings out the highest speed. For this reason it is that the "professionals" are most to be relied upon. They are men specially picked on account of an ability to ride best in particular company, just in the same way as a university eight [in rowing] is selected."

30. "The Year 1897 in Cycling," *Spaldings Official Bicycle Guide for 1898*. Spaldings goes on to comment on Jimmy Michael: "He is the most marvellous athlete the world has ever seen, for with his diminutive size he combines a power and an ability that is gigantic, and during the last season has duplicated in this country his record in England, France and Germany. He has been the bright particular star of the match racing season. He has met defeat only once during the entire season, and he met all who were brave enough to face him in a race."

31. "Revolution in Cycle Racing," newspaper unknown, from early 1898, author's collection; *New York Times*, 2 Jan. 1898.

32. "Record-breaking as a science," *The Hub*, 7 Nov. 1896, p. 3.

33. "Motor Pacing Possibilities," *Cycling*, 13 Feb. 1897.

34. Gronen/Lemke, 1978, have many interesting photographs of pacing-machines from the period. The link between bicycle racing and the emerging automobile and aviation industries was both in the technology of large, powerful gasoline-powered engines and the skilled personnel with expertise in working with them. Many bicycle racers, after their cycling careers, went into the automobile and aviation industries.

35. "Dies Making Records," *Bicycling World*, 8 June 1903. This article also explained that following the accident, American paced riders were compelled to use heavier American-made tires in races: "Most of the accidents to pace followers have been due to tires bursting. The racing men during the last two years have nearly all been using French made tires. These they discovered when they went to race abroad. They are very finely made tires, resilient and speedy, but their fast quality is largely due to their being made exceedingly thin and with a web that is silky in its fineness. The heat generated by the speed at which the men go now is enough to make such tires explode." Belgian star Verbist was another cyclist killed during a race, and British star Jimmy Michael died of a brain hemorrhage on an Atlantic crossing following a serious accident. Gronen/Lemke, *Geschichte des Radsports*, estimate that between 1899 and 1928, 33 riders and 14 pacemakers were killed on European and American tracks. *Sport-Album der Rad-Welt* listed the deaths of "stayers" almost routinely between 1903 and 1905, the toll including Alfred Gornemann, Paul Albert, Harry Elkes and Edouard Taylor in 1903, Karl Kaser and Paul Dangla in 1904 and Charles Brecy, George Leander, Jimmy Michael, Hubert Sevenich and Willy Schmitter in 1905. American riders Johnnie Nelson and Archie McEachern also died. American Bobby Walthour managed to escape with his life from a seemingly endless series of spectacular crashes

36. Hogenkamp, op. cit., 1916, p. 387; *Sport- Album der Rad-Welt* No. 8 (1910) printed an article on the accident, "Die Rennbahn- katastrophe und ihre Folgen," which Rabenstein excerpts on his p. 295. At a meeting on 17 August 1909 between ministers and representatives of bicycle racing organizations, a complete ban on the sport was lifted on the condition that windshields were not used and that a roller had to be installed at a distance of 40 cm from the back wheel of the pacing-machine, to slow the cyclist. See Gronen/ Lemke, p. 223.

37. "The Track Tragedy at Berlin," *Bicycling World and Motorcycle Review*, 7 Aug. 1909, p. 745. See also, Renate Franz, "The "Black Sunday" of Berlin, or Death at the Cycle Track," *Cycle History 19, Proceedings of the 19th International Cycling History Conference*, 2010.

38. S. H. Moxham, *Fifty Years of Road Riding, the North Road Cycling Club, 1885–1935* (Bedford: Diemer and Reynolds, 1935).

39. Cuca Cocoa races were as follows: 1892, Shorland, 414 miles; 1893, Shorland, 426 1/4 miles; 1894, Shorland, 460 miles 1296 yards; 1895, George Hunt, 450 miles 1459 yards; 1896, F. R. Goodwin, 476 miles 1702 yards.

40. Hogenkamp, 1916, p. 180; photo in Gronen/Lemke, 1978, p. 216.

41. *L'Auto*, 16 Sept. 1909; see also Gronen/Lemke, p. 228. Guignard's world record, set on 15 Sept. 1909, was the reason for the publication of the retrospective record list.

42. *Berliner Illustrierte Zeitung* 38 (1898), p. 5.

43. For an account of the American Six-Day sport, see Peter Nye, *The Six-Day Bicycle Races: America's Jazz-Age Sport* (Van der Plas Publications, San Francisco, 2006).

44. *Athletic News* (Manchester), 30 Sept. 1876 and 21

Oct. 1876. At the first event, Thuillet "was accompanied by his friend Keen, the long-distance champion, and the enthusiasm of the spectators rose to a great pitch as the race drew near the end, for the champions were running at the astonishing pace of 16 miles an hour."

45. See *American Bicycling Journal*, 18 Oct. 1879. The young Charles Terront was one of the leading contenders in these contests. See Andrew Ritchie, "The Beginnings of Trans-Atlantic Bicycle Racing: Harry Etherington and the Anglo-French Team in America, 1879–80," *International Journal of the History of Sport*, Dec. 1998; see also *Cycle-Clips, A History of Cycling in the North-East* (Tyne and Wear County Museums, 1985).

46. *Deutsche Illustrirte Zeitung* 28 (1884–85), Vol. 2, p. 47.

47. Kaufmann, op. cit., p. 67; Andrew Ritchie, *Major Taylor* (Bicycle Books, San Francisco, 1989).

48. Editorial, *New York Times*, 12 Dec. 1896.

49. Kaufmann, op. cit., p. 76; Gronen/Lemke, p. 163; Budzinski, *Taschen-Radwelt—Ein radsportliches Lexikon* (Berlin: Verlag der Rad-Welt, 1908–09).

50. *New York Times*, 6–13 Dec. 1897.

51. Kaufmann, op. cit., p. 69.

52. Kaufmann, op. cit., p. 71 and 76.

53. *Bühne und Sport* 29, 1907, p. 15.

54. Kaufmann, op. cit, pp. 72 and 76; Hogenkamp, op. cit., pp. 462 and 472; *Sport-Album der Rad-Welt*, 1912, 1913 and 1914.

55. See Andrew Ritchie, "The Origins of Bicycle Racing in England: Technology, Entertainment, Sponsorship and Advertising in the Early History of the Sport," *Journal of Sport History*, Vol. 26, No. 3, Fall 1999.

56. Fredy Budzinski, "Radsport und Turnen," in Edmund Neuendorf, *Die deutschen Leibesübungen* (Berlin-Essen: W. Andermann Verlag, 1928), p. 665.

57. *Amtliche Liste der Deutschen Berufsfahrer* (1899); *Spaldings Official Bicycle Guide for 1898, p. 5.*; *The Cycle Age and Trade Review*, 16 Feb. 1899, p. 488. *Spaldings* for 1899 said, "There are perhaps 25,000 amateur and professional racing men in the United States."

58. C. Rintelen, "Sport und Industrie," in *Amtliche Fest-Schrift zum 12. Bundestage des DRB*, 1895, pp. 49.

59. For example, in the Vienna–Berlin long-distance race in 1893; see *Deutscher Radfahrer-Bund*, 1893, p. 351.

60. Thaddäus Robl, *Der Radrennsport* (Leipzig: Verlag Grethlein, 1905), p. 18.

61. *Deutsche Turn-Zeitung*, 1894, p. 204.

62. "Looking Backward–A Review of '93 Racing," *Bearings*, 22 Dec. 1893.

63. "What a Champion Cyclist Earns," *Cycling*, 31 Dec. 1898. The article gives the following details: Michael received £300 from the company whose machine he rode and the same amount from his tyre suppliers. He also received between £10–300 for each record he broke, depending on the importance of the event. In a record attempt, however, the expense of paying pace-makers had to be borne by the record-breaker. In France, the prizes were "exceedingly tempting"; a first prize in the Grand Prix de Paris was £250, while in Australia a major race could pay as much as £300. French racer Huret, once a baker, "now rides about in his brougham, and has a villa that many a proud merchant might well covet. Morin, Jacquelin, and Bourillon, three more Parisian idols, are in the same enviable position." Huret had an annual income of 4,000 francs, and was known to have won about £1,000 in one 24-hour race. Dutch racer Cordang, however, made even more when he broke the 24-hour record in London in 1897, earning £1,600 for that one event.

64. *Bearings*, 25 Feb. 1897, p. 390.

65. *Worcester Spy*, 22 Nov. 1898 and unidentified Philadelphia newspaper in author's collection. See also, Andrew Ritchie, *Major Taylor*, pp. 108–10.

66. Ritchie, *Major Taylor*, p. 143.

67. H. Naundorf, "Radfahren," in C. Diem, H. Sippel, F. Breithaupt, *Stadion, Das Buch von Sport und Turnen—Gymnastik und Spiel*, (Berlin: Neufeld and Henius Verlag, 1928), p. 272.

68. *Sport-Album der Rad-Welt*, 1903, 1904, 1905 and 1907.

69. *Bühne und Sport* 5 (1907), p. 8.

70. Eduard Bertz, *Die Philosophie des Fahrrads* (Dresden: Verlag Reissner, 1900), p. 86.

71. Adolph Schulze, "Radfahren," in H. Richard, *Sport und Körperpflege* (Verlag J.J. Arnd, Leipzig, 1908), p. 580.

72. "Popular professionals and their salaries," *The Hub*, 7 Nov. 1896.

73. *Spaldings Official Bicycle Guide for 1898.*

74. *Bühne und Sport*, 1907.

75. *Scientific American* 361 (1899), p. 292.

76. Joseph Jiel-Laval, "Une course à bicyclette. Paris–Brest et retour" (Bordeaux, 1892): in Philippe Tissié, op. cit. (Note 15), p. 227.

77. Karl Planck, *Fusslümmelei. Über Stauchballspiel und englische Krankheit* (Stuttgart: 1898), p. 15.

78. Paul von Salvisberg, *Der Radfahrsport in Bild und Wort* (Munich: Academischer Verlag, 1897; reprinted by Olms Presse, Hildesheim and New York, 1980), p. 260.

79. *Monatsschrift für das Turnwesen*, 1898, p. 247.

80. *Sport-Album der Rad-Welt*, 1909, p. 6.

81. Bertz, op. cit., p. 84.

82. H. Boruttau, "Radfahren und Automobilsport," in Siegfried Weissbein, *Hygiene des Sports* (Leipzig: Verlag Grethlein, c. 1911), p. 184.

83. Jim McGurn, *On Your Bicycle* (London: John Murray, 1987), p. 122.

84. Adolphe Schulze, "Radfahren," in Richard Nordhausen, *Sport und Körperpflege* (Leipzig: J.J. Arnd, 1908), p. 574.

85. The event was reported in the *Buffalo Express*, 26 Aug. 1869 and the *New York Times*, 27 Aug. 1869 and imaginatively illustrated in *L'Illustration*, 25 August 1869. In fact, as a series of contemporary stereograph photographs makes clear, the exploit was less dangerous than was apparent from the written accounts because the "velocipede" consisted of two heavy wheels between which Professor Jenkins was positioned so that much of his weight and a heavy balance-bar were below the tight-rope. The machine was not a normal velocipede (see *The Boneshaker* No. 158, Spring 2002, p. 46).

86. *Berliner Illustrierte Zeitung*, 1900, p. 695.

87. *Sport-Album der Rad-Welt*, 1906, p. 34.

88. *Bearings*, 13 April 1896; *The Hub*, 3 Oct. 1896.

89. Among them; the *New York Times*, 1 July 1899, the *Chicago Daily Tribune*, 1 July 1899, the *Louisville Courier-Journal*, 1 July 1899, the *San Francisco Examiner*, 1 July 1899. Bertz, op. cit., p. 90; photos in Gronen/Lemke, pp. 132 and 174. See also Andrew Ritchie, *Major Taylor*, op. cit., pp. 118–120.

90. "Murphy's Bicycle Ride a Hint to the Railroads," p. 34 and "A Mile in Less than a Minute on a Bicycle," p. 41, *Scientific American*, 15 July 1899.

91. See Rüdiger Rabenstein, "Sensational Bicycle Acts Around 1900," *Proceedings of the 9th International Cycle History Conference* (San Francisco: Van der Plas Publications, 1999), pp. 62–68.

92. Barry Hecla, "Racing as a Business. The Evolution of the Racing Team, Its Causes and Effects," *The Referee*, 26 Oct. 1894.

93. *Cycle Age and Trade Review*, 16 Aug. 1900.

94. "Money Spent by Circuit Chasers," *Bearings*, 2 Sept. 1897.

95. "Cycle Racing Reforms," *New York Times*, 6 Feb. 1898.

96. An article in the *New York Times*, 23 Sept., 1892 ("Tempting the Wheelmen—Baseball Magnates after the Amateur Cyclists") explained that "a syndicate of baseball magnates was forming to manage bicycle racing on a professional basis. The future of this scheme depends largely upon engaging all the prominent amateur riders, thus inducing them to compete for cash prizes." The plan was evidently to bolster the slow winter baseball season by building cycling tracks within existing baseball fields. H.E. Raymond, Chairman of the Racing Board of the League of American Wheelmen told the *Times*: "It has been known for some time that such a plan was afoot, and it is intended by the baseball people as a shift to use their grounds. Baseball has been steadily on the decrease as a paying investment, and the rapid growth of cycle racing has directed the speculation in sports to our quarter. I am aware that cement tracks are talked of for all baseball fields, and of course that means that they must be made to pay by securing the services of all the fast riding men on the path at the present time in the amateur ranks." There is no evidence that such a scheme was actually carried out, but the existence of the plan underlines the speculative nature of sport promotion at the time.

97. See Ritchie, *Major Taylor*, pp. 101–108, pp. 115–116, pp. 128–129 and pp. 140–143. A summary of the conflict between the opposing sides can be found in "Outlaw Racing Movement Elucidated," *The Wheel and Cycling Trade Review*, 1 June 1899, pp. 20–26 and in "Racing Situation Summed Up—Strength of Opposing Sides," *The Cycle Age and Trade Review*, 30 March 1899, pp. 680–81. The issue was partially resolved at the League of American Wheelmen convention in Philadelphia in February 1900. "The speed and facility with which that vital matter was disposed of savored of the manner in which a hot potato is popularly supposed to be dropped. Anyone who heard the hearty cheer which followed the announcement of the vote (it was practically unanimous) would have imagined that the assemblage had at last rid itself of an incubus that was fast sapping its vitality."; "L.A.W. National Assembly—Delegates Vote to Abandon Race Control Without Discussion," *Cycle Age*, 22 Feb. 1900.

98. *Cycle Age and Trade Review*, 1 March 1900.

99. For a definition of "modern" and "modernity," Glen Norcliffe's *The Ride to Modernity* is useful and apposite. On pp. 248–249, "modernity" is described as follows: "Although the bicycle era was only a brief episode in the complex drama of modernity, it provides a number of insights into the workings of the broader cultural movement... During its turbulent (and still incomplete history) modernity has passed through many phases as new technologies and fashions were discovered, modified, diffused, and then discarded, one after another, each in turn being replaced by new ideas that revived the project, and relaunched it in a new direction." Norcliffe then highlights four aspects of modernity: "First, modernity is antagonistic to the status quo. Second, and paradoxically, although local traditions form a part of the established practices that are inimical to modernity, modernity itself becomes locally embedded... Third, a part of this geographical embeddedness has resulted from the ability of modernity to seduce the 'crowd,' in slightly different ways in different places, mainly because it is able to create spectacles that have a local resonance. Finally, the practical manifestation of modernity has been most firmly based in industry; the abstract rhetoric of rationality and reason has found its most decisive incarnation in factories, in the industrial workforce, and in the production of a succession of consumer goods of varying utility. The essential subtext to the discussion is that modernity has become massively important because it grew from its metaphysical origins into a popular and diversified movement that progressively infiltrated every practical aspect of western civilization."

Chapter Nine

1. *Cyclist Year Book* for 1895.

2. *N.C.U. Review and Official Record*, March 1897.

3. While recognizing this general dynamic–that competition had a strong affect on design–it is important to recognize that certain kinds of technological change certainly occurred with no need to be tested within competition. The introduction in the late 1880s of female-specific open frame design, for example (the woman's bicycle), was an innovation related to practical usage and was unrelated to speed. Similarly, the introduction of the luxury touring bicycle of the mid–1890s was directed specifically at the affluent recreational rider. But by the mid–1890s, bicycle design had solidified around the diamond-frame, which had by that time become the bicycle for all kinds of riding. Many smaller details of style were directed at a particular kind of consumer.

4. A valuable summary discussion on differences between American and French cycling patterns and on class and fashion elements in the development of recreational and utility cycling in those two countries is found in Thomas Burr, "French Expansion, American Collapse, 1890-1910," *Proceedings of the 16th International Cycling History Conference* (2006). This is expanded in Burr's doctoral dissertation, "Markets as Producers and Consumers: The French and U.S. national Bicycle Markets, 1875–1910" (unpublished Ph. D. in Sociology, U.C. Davis, 2005).

5. *Cassell's Complete Book of Sports and Pastimes* (London: Cassell, 1888).

6. *Sporting Goods Dealer*, May 1900, quoted in Burr, op. cit.

7. *Bicycling World*, 21 Nov. 1903, quoted in Burr, op. cit.

8. *The Hub*, 8 May 1897 and 14 Aug. 1897.

9. "The Bicycle in 1900," *Leslie's*, 24 Feb. 1900.

10. According to A.E. Harrison, in his economic analysis of the British industry, "there were 2 manufacturers of completed cycles in Coventry in 1874, 14 in 1882, 22 in 1890 and 35 in 1892. Birmingham had 6 makers in

1875, 43 in 1880, 54 in 1886 and 114 in 1891. Nottingham had 8 in 1878, 13 in 1886 and 33 in 1892." The number of "makers of complete cycles" for 1896–97 is given as "Birmingham–309, Coventry–75, London–390 and Nottingham–59." On the American industry, Harrison gives the following figures: in 1889, there were 27 "cycle-making firms," with an output of $2,568,326; by 1895, there were 500 factories, by 1897, 700; the 1899 Census showed 312 "bicycle-making establishments," with a production worth nearly $32 million. See A. E. Harrison, "The Competitiveness of the British Cycle Industry, 1890–1914," *Economic History Review*, 1969 (Economic History Society, London). It is not clear whether these figures also include component manufacturers.

11. Quoted in Karl Kron, *Ten Thousand Miles on a Bicycle*, p. 648, reporting *Wheeling*, 6 Oct. 1886.

12. *N.C.U. Review and Official Record*, April 1887, Vol.4, No. 1.

13. *N.C.U. Review and Official Record*, April 1887, Vol.4, No. 1.

14. *N.C.U. Review and Official Record*, Jan. 1887, Vol.3, No. 1.

15. They were: *La Revue des Sports, La Revue du Sport Vélocipédique, Le Véloce-Sport, Le Cycle, Le Monde Cycliste, La France Cycliste, Les Sports Athlétiques, L'Industrie Vélocipédique, Le Cycliste, Le Bulletin Officiel de l'Union Vélocipédique de France, Le Cycliste Belge, Le Cyclisme, La Bicyclette* and *L'Écho des Sports de Paris.*

16. Exceptions include: "Lawyer Won the Bet—2,836 Wheels Passed between Fourth and Walnut from 5.30 to 8.30 o'clock," *Louisville Courier-Journal*, 11 July 1897 (published in *The Boneshaker*, Summer 2001) and accounts of a census taken in Manchester, reported in the *Manchester Guardian*, 11 May 1896 and 17 May 1897 (published in *The Boneshaker*, Summer 2000). Burr (see Footnote 5) also mentions reports of widespread utility use in Minneapolis, and in Indianapolis there were "large bicycle storage rooms in the downtown district."

17. See Mason, P.P. "The League of American Wheelmen and the Good Roads Movement, 1880–1905" (University of Michigan: Ph. D. thesis, 1957).

18. *Harper's Weekly*, 17 August 1895.

19. The role of women riders in the history of the bicycle, and the question of the bicycle's contribution to the social emancipation of women in the 1880s, 1890s and the turn of the century period has been touched on occasionally here, although it has not been a central concern. The literature of the subject has now become quite large, as the significant but problematic role of the bicycle in the history of women's sport and recreation is better understood. An almost universal attention to the controversial question of women's participation in cycling can be found in the British and American general and cycling press in the later 1890s. The following are some of the publications on the topic: P. Marks, *Bicycles, Bangs and Bloomers: The New Woman in the Popular Press* (Kentucky: University of Kentucky, 1990); P. Vertinsky, *The Eternally Wounded Woman: Women, Doctors and Exercise in the Late Nineteenth Century* (Urbana and Chicago: Illinois University Press, 1994); Claire Simpson, "Respectable Identities: New Zealand Nineteenth-Century 'New Women' on Bicycles," *International Journal of the History of Sport*, June 2001 (excellent bibliography). Rational Dress Societies were created and the press contained extensive discussion of the propriety of the novel "divided" skirts and fashionable bloomers worn by women riders, see, for example, Mrs F.W. Harburton, *Reasons for Reform in Dress* (London: Hutchings and Crowsley, 1885) and *Rational Dress Society Gazette* (1880s); "A Minister Writes of Bicycle Skirts" and "The Women Bicycle Riders of Louisville–How and Where They Ride and What They Wear," *Louisville Courier-Journal*, 17 Oct. 1897. The mid–1890s saw the rise of periodical publications specifically directed at the woman cyclist, the most significant of which are listed in Note 14 of the Conclusions. That cycling was not the only sport where women were asserting themselves is confirmed by an article such as: "Women who Shoot, Drive and Ride–Equal to the Most Expert of Their Friends," *Louisville Courier-Journal*, 7 Feb. 1897, which said, "American woman are rapidly taking to out of door sports."

20. *Harper's Weekly*, 12 Jan. 1895.

21. Sturmey continued: "Of the Metropolitan clubs, the London takes first numerical rank, numbering over 250. The Temple, Stanley, Birmingham, and St. Helen's clubs have each above 100 members, whilst the Touring Club numbers some 500, most of whom belong to other clubs as well. In age the Pickwick takes the lead, having been founded in 1870. Of Provincial clubs, the Dungarvan claims seniority, having commenced its existence also during 1870, but a few months later. Three or four date back to '71 and '72; but by far the greater number are quite of recent origin, nearly half having been formed during '76, between 60 and 70 in '77, and about as many in '78; facts which speak for themselves of the gigantic strides with which this invigorating pastime is gaining ground in popular favour." Henry Sturmey, *Indispensable Bicyclist's Handbook*, 1879 edition.

22. Henry Sturmey (ed.), *The Cyclist Annual and Year Book for 1893* (London: Iliffe, 1893). Further examination of the information contained in these publications can be found in the author's Ph.D. thesis (Strathclyde University, Glasgow, 2009). I have had access only to the 1893, 1894, 1895 and 1899 editions of this publication. In his "Introduction" to the 1893 edition, Sturmey writes that it is the thirteenth year he has presented his *Annual and Year Book*.

23. By way of comparison, A.J. Wilson, *The Pleasures, Objects and Advantages of Cycling* (1887) quotes 1876 club figures as 60 total, with 11 in London, 39 in provinces, 9 in Ireland and 1 in Scotland.

24. A detailed examination of this mass of clubs, geographically well distributed all over the country, nearly all of which included the words "Cycling Club," "Bicycle Club," "Road Club" or "Wheelers" in their titles, but whose social activities nevertheless extended well beyond cycling, might be the opportunity for a significant study of the role of sport in British working- and middle-class life at the end of the 19th century, and give rich insights into patterns of leisure and recreation. A similar study of urban cycling clubs in the United States would also shed interesting light on patterns of urban and suburban recreation and mobility. Chicago, for example, appears to have been an especially active cycling city, but also significant were Boston, New York, Buffalo, Cleveland, Indianapolis and Milwaukee.

25. In London, these racing clubs included: Anerley B.C. (150 members), Bath Road Club (120), Catford C.C. (450), Dover Road C.C. (180), Holborn C.C. (290), Lon-

don County C. and A.C. (300), North Road C.C. (178), Polytechnic C.C. (250). See, for example, S.H. Moxham, *Fifty Years of Road Riding (1885-1935)—A History of the North Road Cycling Club* (Bedford: Diemer and Reynolds, 1935) and E.J. Southcott, *The First Fifty Years of the Catford Cycling Club* (London: Foulis and Co., 1939).

26. See Denis Pye, *Fellowship is Life; The National Clarion Cycling Club, 1895-1995*, (Clarion Publishing, Bolton, Lancashire, 1995). The nature of the extra-cycling interests of cycling clubs tended to widen, of course, during the 20-year period under examination, being particularly broad and varied during the cycling boom of the mid-1890s.

27. Titles include *The Lady Cyclist* (1896-97) and *Wheelwoman and Society Cycling News* (1896-1899) in Britain and *The Wheelwoman* in the United States.

28. This total has to be treated with caution, however, because it probably excluded a significant number of riders who competed in time trials on the road, and who did not need an N.C.U. affiliation because the N.C.U. did not sanction road racing. It should also be noted that the figures quoted here were for a period of maximum activity within the cycling movement in general, a boom lasting from about 1896 to about 1900.

29. Sturmey, *Cyclist Year Book* for 1895, pp. 17-28.

30. Advertising supplement in *Wheeling*, 20 July 1892. This claim is contradicted by the N.C.U. figures given previously. However, C.T.C. membership may have been counted as individual subscriptions, whereas the vast majority of N.C.U. members had joined automatically through the affiliation to the N.C.U. of a local club.

31. A.W. Rumney, *A Cyclist's Notebook* (Johnston, Edinburgh, 1900), p. 122.

32. *C.T.C. Gazette*, March 1897, p. 99, noted that total membership for the end of 1896 was 34,655 members, an increase of 18,312 members over the 1895 total, "a truly phenomenal increase." This number was still less than the membership in the N.C.U. for the same year, contradicting the C.T.C. claim that it was "the largest athletic or quasi-athletic institution in the world."

33. Karl Kron, *Ten Thousand Miles on a Bicycle* (New York: self-published, 1887).

34. Mason, op. cit., p. 48.

35. See Alex Poyer, *Les Premiers Temps des Véloce-Clubs: apparition et diffusion du cyclisme associatif français entre 1867 et 1914* (Paris: L'Harmattan, 2003). Poyer shows that of this total number of clubs, only some became affiliated with the national governing body of racing, the Union Vélocipédique de France: clubs affiliated with the U.V.F. in 1888—27, in 1895—186, in 1901—203, in 1903—474, in 1914—521.

36. Once again Burr (op. cit., Note 5) is useful and provocative on the dynamics in France.

37. A. Lloyd Owen, "Club life of today," *Cycling*. 7 Dec., 1901.

38. See, for example, H.G. Wells, *The Wheels of Chance*, first published 1896.

39. A valuable contribution to the discussion of bicycle production and use statistics is Bruce Epperson, "How Many Bikes?," *Cycle History 11, Proceedings of the 11th Cycling History Conference* (San Francisco: Van der Plas, 2000).

40. Since the L.A.W. was also the governing body, through its Racing Committee, of bicycle racing in the United States, it was similar in its function to the English N.C.U. and different from the C.T.C., which had no racing functions whatsoever.

Epilogue

1. According to Maurice Martin, editor of *Le Véloce-Sport*, writing in 1890, there were approximately 25-30,000 cyclists in France, among whom were only about 500 "coureurs" (racing cyclists). The rules governing racing were tightly controlled by the U.V.F., which forbade multiple-gearing in racing until well into the 20th century, while the T.-C. de F. promoted competitive trials of new technology. See Maurice Martin, *Voyage de Bordeaux à Paris par trois vélocipédistes* (Bordeaux: Véloce-Sport, 1890); "Le cyclisme français à la fin du XIXème siècle," in Raymond Henry, *Du Vélocipède au Dérailleur Moderne* (Saint-Etienne, Association des Amis du Musée d'Art et d'Industrie de Saint-Etienne, 1998), pp. 22-23; Henri Bosc, "Il y a cent ans: Les précurseurs du cyclotourisme et les premiers récit de voyages—Maurice Martin," in *Proceedings of the Second International Conference on Cycle History* (Saint-Etienne, 1995), pp. 120-127.

2. Maurice Martin, *Grande Enquête Sportive du journal Le Vélo* (Paris: Brocherioux, 1898), quoted in Bosc, see Note 1.

3. Maurice Martin, in *Voyage de Bordeaux à Paris* (see Note 1) complained of rowdy scenes at hotels frequented by racers on the nights of important races in France and how he and other tourists had been refused accommodation at certain hotels on the road because racers had recently stayed there and created havoc.

4. H. Graves, G. Lacy Hillier and Susan, Countess of Malmesbury, *Cycling* (Lawrence and Bullen, London, 1898), quoted in *C.T.C. Gazette*, June 1898.

5. Christopher Thompson's, "The Third Republic on Wheels: A Social, Cultural and Political History of Bicycling in France from the Nineteenth Century to World War II" (Ph.D. thesis, New York University, 1997), has been helpful in this respect, but Thompson does not explore very far the bicycle racing and industrial sources of the 1870s and 1880s.

6. Neil Tranter, *Sport, economy and society in Britain, 1750-1914*, "The revolution in sport," p. 13.

7. G.L. Hillier, Badminton *Cycling*, 1896 edition, Appendix, p. 339.

8. It is fascinating to observe that even today, more than a century after the events discussed in this text, bicycle technology advances with unrestrained curiosity and inventiveness. Every component of the bicycle is subjected to microscopic examination, new materials are put to use and both fashion and technological change play their part in determining what contemporary bicycles look like. As always, competition (including, today, mountain biking) plays a crucial part in designing and testing the industry's products.

9. In general, early motor-cycles and cars were at first viewed as a technological extension of the bicycle. Like the bicycle, they were technologically "modern" and gave a similar mobility. Unlike the bicycle, they were at first very expensive and highly unreliable. This continuity of perception is especially apparent in the press and in the persons of editors and journalists who made the transition from cycling to motoring. For a brief period in

1901, the weekly *Cycling* changed its name to *Cycling and Moting* (not "Motoring"—AR), before reverting to *Cycling*. The history of the Temple Press, publishers of *Cycling*, and its role in the emergence of the car and of the popular specialized press is well told in Arthur C. Armstrong, *Bouverie Street to Bowling Green Lane* (Hodder and Stoughton, London, 1946).

People who moved from the bicycle industry to the car industry included, for example, in England, S.F. Edge, Montague Holbein, Allard; in France, Henri Fournier, Peugeot, Adolphe Clément; in the United States, Albert Champion (French/American racer who founded spark-plug company). There were many others. A study of the transferral of personnel, technology, economic organization and manufacturing expertise from the bicycle industry to the young motor-cycle and automobile industries in Britain, France, Germany and the United States is still very much needed. From a manufacturing point of view, the industries appear to have meshed organizationally and geographically. Machine tools used to produce bicycles were in general appropriate for early motor-cycle and car production. The manufacture of larger engines was something new in scale and technique. Gearing systems had been considerably developed during the tricycle boom of the 1880s. Electrical components were a new departure, but built on lighting systems developed for the bicycle in the 1890s, Joseph Lucas being important.

As with the early days of the bicycle, racing played a crucial role in the development of the automobile. Charles Jarrott, *Ten Years of Motors and Motor Racing* (Grant Richards, London, 1906), is particularly informative on the period 1896–1906, and is especially interesting in its accounts of racing on French roads, many of which were the same roads used for bicycle races in the later 1890s, Bordeaux–Paris, for example. Because the 1903 Paris–Madrid car race caused an unacceptable number of fatal accidents on its first day, the race was banned by the French government.

From Jarrott's final chapter, "The Future," the following passage is a vibrant expression of modern (or perhaps "futurist") ideas: "If I were asked to state what new element has most greatly influenced the habits, sympathies and characteristic of the people of the world during the past fifty years, I would unhesitatingly reply that it is the science of mechanism, the development of the ingenuity of the human mind and brain in combating the laws of nature and in conquering the stupendous forces which sway and affect the lives of all inhabitants of the globe. The labour of the beast, the manual work of the slave, and the expenditure of human labour, are being swept away. The age of the machine is upon us. The soulless and subservient mechanism is the great power of today and of the future, and in the years to come we shall forget the why and wherefore, we shall forget the conditions under which our forefathers lived, and we shall fail to understand the measure and immensity of the influence on our everyday life of the science of mechanism... Of all the great and far-reaching discoveries in the science of mechanism, that of the self-propelled road vehicle is the greatest. It is safe to say this, because we have as yet merely touched the fringe of this mighty discovery."

10. Hillier, op. cit., 1889 edition, p. 1.
11. Hillier, op. cit., 1896 edition, p. 110 and Preface, pp. ix and x.
12. Hillier, op. cit, 1896 edition, Appendix, p. 339.
13. H.H. Griffin, "Cycling under Three Heads. II—The Sport," *Baily's Magazine*, May and June 1892. Griffin was a journalist and reviewer of bicycle industry products whose experience of the trade went back to its very beginnings. In the early 1870s, he contributed a column, "Bicycling Notes," to *Bazaar, Exchange and Mart* at a time when a specialized cycling press did not yet exist. In the later 1870s and 1880s, he produced an important annual, *Bicycles and Tricycles of the Year*. His *Cycles and Cycling* was published in four editions, 1890, 1893, 1897 and 1903.
14. H.H. Griffin, "Cycling Twenty Years Ago," *The Cycle Magazine*, April 1896.
15. *The Times*, 2 Sept. 1897.
16. J.A. Mangan, ed., *A Sport-Loving Society: Victorian and Edwardian Middle-Class England at Play* (Abingdon: Routledge, 2006), p. 2, quoting Tranter, *Sport, Economy and Society in Britain, 1750–1914*, p. 16.
17. "Cycle Racing Today," *New York Tribune Bicycle Day Supplement*, 22 Feb. 1898.
18. *Cycle Age and Trade Review*, 16 Feb. 1899. It should be noted, of course, that these ambitious figures were given during a "boom" which was about to collapse.
19. Tranter, op. cit., Introduction, p. 1
20. Griffin, ibid.
21. Griffin quoted four 1 mile records between 1876 and 1891 as examples of faster times. They were:

2m 16s–F.J. Osmond, Herne Hill, London, 13 July 1891
2m 35 2/5s—W.A. Rowe, Springfield, USA, 23 Oct. 1885
2m 47 4/5s—I. Keith-Falconer, University Ground, Cambridge, 21 May 1879
3m 10s—I. Keith-Falconer, Lillie Bridge, London, 6 April 1876

In fact, the 1 mile record was to continue to fall through the 1890s as the fashion for pacing gained momentum. The debate here about what constitutes athletic excellence when it is expressed through radical improvements in technology continues to this day, most recently about what constitutes an acceptable 1 hour record. The Union Cycliste Internationale has recently, in effect, declared invalid the last 25 years of 1 hour records set on super-streamlined, "unacceptable" bicycles, and turned the clock back to a record established by Eddy Merckx in 1972 on a "conventional" bicycle. Before the UCI ruling, Chris Boardman's hour record, set in 1996 using the "superman" position, stood at 56.375 km. Merckx's 1972 record of 49.431 kms was broken by a mere 10 metres by Chris Boardman in October 2000, when he established a new "standard" bicycle 1 hour record of 49.441 km.
22. See Max Weber, *From Max Weber: Essays in Sociology* (Oxford: Oxford University Press, 1973).
23. H.H. Griffin, "Cycling Twenty Years Ago," *The Cycle Magazine*, April 1896.
24. H.H. Griffin, *Cycles and Cycling*, London, George Bell and Sons, 4th Edition, 1903.
25. In fact, it had been accepted from about 1890 on that two categories of cycling records had to be recognized, unpaced and paced, and the question was also addressed in road racing, whether the individual competitor was allowed to be helped by non-competing pacers.
26. R.J. Mecredy and A.J. Wilson, *The Art and Pastime of Cycling* (Iliffe and Son, London); 3rd Edition, 1893; Chapter 1, "Pleasures and Advantages of Cycling."

Bibliography

A. Archives (original documents consulted)

Minute Book of the Bicycle Union, 1878–81 (Modern Records Centre, University of Warwick Library, Mss. 328/B/Temp).

Minute Books of the National Cyclists' Union, 1882 onwards (Modern Records Centre, University of Warwick Library, Mss. 328/B/Temp).

Papers relating to Cambridge University Bicycle Club, including Minute Books, scrap-books, advertising material, correspondence and accounts for the building of the Club track (Cambridge University Library, Add. 7628).

Indianapolis Historical Museum, Indianapolis, Indiana—Major Taylor scrapbooks and family memorabilia.

Charles Pratt scrapbook and Abbott Bassett scrapbook, Smithsonian Institution, Washington D.C.

Advertising flyer and "Motion papers for Restraining Order and Preliminary Injunction," filed 5 Feb.1880, motion granted 13 March 1880, both from National Archives, Washington D.C.

B. Printed Publications

Abrahams, H.M., and Kerr, J.B., *Oxford v. Cambridge, A Record of Inter-University Contests from 1827–1930* (London, 1931).

Armstrong, Arthur C., *Bouverie Street to Bowling Green Lane* (London: Hodder and Stoughton, 1946).

"A Working Mechanic," *The Modern Velocipede: Its History and Construction* (London: George Maddick, 1869).

Bailey, Peter, *Leisure and Class in Victorian England (Rational Recreation and the contest for control, 1830–1885)* (London, 1978).

Bartleet, H.W., *Bartleet's Bicycle Book* (London: Ed. Burrow and Co., 1931).

Bassett, Abbott, "League of American Wheelmen—Items from Its History," in Porter, Luther H., *Wheels and Wheeling—An Indispensable Handbook for Cyclists* (Boston: Wheelman Company, 1892), pp. 10–26.

_____, "Outdoor Season—Revival of Cycling," *Harper's Weekly* (U.S.A.), 11 June 1904, p. 906.

Baudry de Saunier, *L'Art de Bien Monter la Bicyclette* (Paris: 1894).

_____, *Le Cyclisme Théorique et Pratique* (Paris: Flammarion, 1892).

_____, *L'Histoire de la Locomotion Terrestre* (Paris: 1935)

_____, L., *Histoire Générale de la Vélocipédie* (Paris: Paul Ollendorf, 1891).

_____, *Les Mémoires de Terront* (Paris, 1893; reprinted Paris: Prosport, 1980).

_____, *Recettes Utiles et Procédés Vélocipédiques* (Paris: 1893).

Baxter, Sylvester, "Economic and Social Influences of the Bicycle," Arena (U.S.A.), Oct. 1892, p. 583.

Berryman, Jack, and Park, Roberta, *Sport and Exercise Science—Essays in the History of Sports Medicine* (Urbana and Chicago: University of Illinois Press, 1992).

Berto, Frank, *The Birth of Dirt—Origins of Mountain Biking* (San Francisco: Cycling Resources, 1999).

Bertz, Eduard, *Die Philosphie des Fahrrads* (Dresden: Verlag Reissner, 1900).

Bettmann, S. "Cycle Finance (An Episode in Coventry's History)," *Readers' Bulletin—Coventry Public Libraries*, May–June 1923, Vol 1, No. 4.

Bijker, Wiebe J., "King of the Road: The Social Construction of the Safety Bicycle," in *Of Bicycles, Bakelites and Bulbs—Toward a Theory of Sociotechnical Change* (Cambridge: MIT Press, 1997).

Bishop, Joseph B, "Social and Economic Influences of the Bicycle," *The Forum* (U.S.A.), Aug. 1896, p. 684.

Bonneville, L., *Le Vélo, Fils de France* (Nice: Etac, 1938).

Boury, P., *La France du Tour: Le Tour de France—un espace sportif à géométrie variable* (Paris: L'Harmattan, 1997).

Bowden, Gregory Houston, *The Story of the Raleigh Cycle* (London: W.H. Allen, 1975).

Budzinski, Fredy, *Taschen-Radwelt—Ein radsportliches Lexikon* (Berlin: Verlag der Rad-Welt, 1908–09).

Burr, Thomas, "Markets as Producers and Consumers: the French and U.S. National Bicycle Markets, 1875–1910" (Ph. D. thesis, Davis, California, 2005).

Calvet, Jacques, *Le Mythe des Géants de la Route* (Grenoble: Presses Universitaires de Grenoble, 1981).

Carlsson, Chris (ed.), *Critical Mass: Bicycling's Defiant Celebration* (Edinburgh and Oakland, California: AK Press, 2002).

Carr, E. H., *What Is History?* (New York: Knopf, 1961).

Chandler, A. D., *Scale and Scope: The Dynamics of Industrial Capitalism* (Cambridge, Mass., MIT Press, 1990).

Chandler, A.D. and Sharp, J.C., *A Bicycle Tour in England and Wales* (Boston: A. Williams and Co., 1881).

Chany, Pierre, *La Fabuleuse Histoire du Cyclisme des Origines à 1955* (Paris: Nathan, 1988).

———, *La Fabuleuse Histoire du Tour de France* (Paris: Nathan, 1991).

Cortis, H.L., *Principles of Training, for Amateur Athletes* (Coventry: Iliffe, 1882).

Crawford, T. C., "Ernest Terah Hooley and His Guinea-Pigs," *Cosmopolitan Magazine* (U.S.A.), Nov. 1898, pp. 97–104.

Cumming, John, *Runners and Walkers—A Nineteenth Century Sports Chronicle* (Chicago: Regnery Gateway,1981).

Dauncey, Hugh, and Hare, Geoff, (eds.), *The Tour de France 1903–2003: A Century of Sporting Structures, Meanings and Values* (London: Frank Cass, 2003).

Dawson, Samuel., *Incidents in the Course of a Long Cycling Career* (Lancaster: Beeley Bros, 1906).

De Koven, Mrs. Reginald, "Bicycling for Women," *Cosmopolitan Magazine* (U.S.A.) 19, (1892–96), p. 394.

Demaus, A.B., and Tarring, J.C., *The Humber Story, 1868–1932* (Gloucester: Alan Sutton, 1989).

Déon, Bernard and Seray, Jacques, *Les Revues Cyclistes, des origines à nos jours* (Saint-Étienne: Association des Amis du Museé d'Art et d'Industrie de Saint-Étienne, 1996).

Desgrange, Henri, *La Tête et les Jambes* (Paris: L. Pochy, 1898).

———, *Alphonse Marcaux* (Paris: L. Pochy, 1899).

Dickinson, R.I., "Bicycling for Women. Some Hygenic Aspects of Wheeling," *The Outlook* (U.S.A.), 28 March 1896, p. 553.

———, "Bicycling for Women: The Puzzling Question of Costume," *The Outlook*, 25 April 1896.

Ducros, Sir Arthur, *Wheels of Fortune: A Salute to Pioneers* (London: Chapman and Hall, 1938).

Duncan, H.O., *Vingt Ans de Cyclisme Pratique* (Paris: F. Juven, 1897).

———, *The World on Wheels* (Paris: privately printed, 1927).

Duncan, H.O., and Lafitte, Pierre, *En Suivant Terront de Saint-Pétersbourg à Paris à Bicyclette* (Paris: Flammarion, 1894).

———, and Mousset, E., *L'Entraînement Théorique et Pratique* (Paris: 1894).

———, and Superbie, L., *L'Entraînement à l'usage des Vélocipédistes, Coureurs et Touristes* (Paris: Librairie du Véloce-Sport, 1892)

Dunham, Norman, "The Bicycle Era in American History" (Harvard University: Ph. D. thesis, 1956).

Dunning, E. and Sheard, K., *Barbarians, Gentlemen and Players: A Sociological Analysis of Popular Sports in Britain* (New York: New York University Press, 1979).

Durry, Jean, *La Véridique Histoire des Géants de la Route* (Lausanne: Edita, 1973).

Eisenberg, Christiane, *"English Sports" und Deutsche Bürger, Eine Gesellschaftsgeschichte, 1800–1939* (Paderborn: Ferdinand Schöningh, 1999).

Elias, Norbert and Dunning, Eric, *Quest for Excitement: Sport and Leisure in the Civilizing Process* (Oxford and New York: Blackwell, 1986).

Erskine, Miss F.J., *Lady Cycling* (London: Walter Scott, 1897).

———, *Tricycling for Ladies* (London: Iliffe, 1885).

Etherington, H., "Bicycling," *Sporting Mirror*, Feb. 1881.

"Etiquette of the Road," *Harper's Weekly*, 3 Oct. 1896, p. 973.

Evans, Richard J., *In Defence of History* (New York and London: Norton, 1997).

"An Experienced Velocipedist," *The Velocipede, its history, and practical hints how to use it* (London: J. Bruton, 1869).

Firth-Bottomley, J., *The Velocipede, its past, present and its future* (London: Simpkin, Marshall, 1869).

Fitzpatrick, Jim, *The Bicycle and the Bush: Man and Machine in Rural Australia* (Melbourne: Oxford University Press, 1981).

Gaboriau, Philippe, *Le Tour de France et Le Vélo: Histoire sociale d'une épopée contemporaine* (Paris: L'Harmattan, 1995).

Garrigues, Harry J., "Woman and the Bicycle," *The Forum*, 20, 1896, p. 973.

Giffard, Pierre, *La Fin du Cheval* (Paris: Colin, 1899).

———, *La Reine Bicyclette. Histoire du vélocipède depuis les temps les plus reculés jusqu'à nos jours* (Paris: Firmin-Didot, 1891).

Gillmeister, Heiner, "English Editors of German Sporting Journals at the Turn of the Century," *The Sports Historian*, No, 13, May 1993, pp. 38–56.

Glynn, Francis J.J., *The History of the Clincher Tyre and Rim* (Edinburgh: North British Rubber Co., c.1900).

Goddard, J.T., *The Velocipede: Its History, Varieties and Practice* (New York: Hurd and Houghton, 1869).

Green, Roy, *100 Years of Cycling Roads Records* (Road Records Association, 1988).

Grew, W.J., *The Cycle Industry* (London: Isaac Pitman and Sons, 1921).

Griffin, H.H., *Cycles and Cycling* (London: George Bell, 1903 and subsequent editions).

———, "Cycling Twenty Years Ago," *The Cycle Magazine*, April 1896.

———, "Cycling under Three Heads. 2. The Sport," *Baily's Magazine*, June 1892.

Gronen, Wolfgang and Lemke, Walter, *Geschichte des Radsports—von den Anfängen bis 1939* (Eupen: Edition Doepgen, 1978).

Guttman, Allen, *From Ritual to Record: The Nature of Modern Sports* (New York: Columbia University Press, 1978).

———, *Sports Spectators* (New York: Columbia U.P., 1986).

———, *Games and Empires* (New York: Columbia U.P., 1994).

Hardy, Stephen, "Entrepreneurs, Organizations, and

the Sport Marketplace: Subjects in Search of Historians," *Journal of Sport History*, Vol. 13, No. 1, Spring 1986.

Harris, Michael, and Lee, Alan, "Sporting News, 1860–1914," in, *The Press in English Society from the 17th to 19th Century* (Associated University Presses, 1986).

Harrison, A.E., "The Competitiveness of the British Cycle Industry, 1890–1914," *Economic History Review*, Vol. XXII, 1969, pp. 287–303.

_____, "F. Hopper and Co., the problems of capital supply in the cycle manufacturing industry, 1891–1914," *Business History*, XXIV, 1982.

_____, "Growth, Entrepreneurship and Capital Formation in the United Kingdom's Cycle and Related Industries, 1870–1914" (York University, Ph. D. thesis, 1977).

_____, "The Origins and Growth of the UK Cycle Industry to 1900," *The Journal of Transport History*, Vol. 6, March 1985, pp. 41–70.

Henry, Raymond, *Du Vélocipède au Dérailleur Moderne* (Saint-Etienne: Association des Amis du Musée d'Art et d'Industrie de Saint-Etienne, 1998).

Herlihy, David. V., *Bicycle—The History* (Yale University Press: New Haven and London, 2004).

Hillier, George Lacy, "A Brief and Critical Account of the One Mile Amateur Bicycle Path Record," *Cyclist Christmas Number*, 1891.

_____, "Cycle Racing," in *The Encyclopaedia of Sport*, 1911.

_____, "Cycles Past and Present," *Transactions of the Royal Scottish Society of Arts* 13, 1892, pp. 243–257.

_____, "A General Survey of Long-Distance Cycle Riding," *Cyclist Annual and Year Book for 1893*.

_____, and Bramson, W.G.H., *Amateur Cycling: with Hints on Training* (London: Dean and Sons, 1893).

_____, and Viscount Bury, *Cycling* (Badminton Series) (London: Longman, Green and Co., 1887 and subsequent editions).

_____, and Etherington, Harry, *Icycles, The Christmas Annual of the Wheel World* (London: Etherington, 1880).

Hoberman, John, *Mortal Engines: The Science of Performance and the Dehumanization of Sport* (New York, Singapore and Sydney; The Free Press, 1992).

Hobsbawm, Eric, "Mass-Producing Traditions: Europe, 1870–1914," in Eric Hobsbaum and Terence Ranger, *The Invention of Tradition* (Cambridge: Cambridge University Press, 1983).

_____, *On History* (London: Weidenfeld and Nicholson, 1997).

Hooley, E.T., *Confessions* (1924).

Holt, Richard, "The Bicycle, the Bourgeoisie and the Discovery of Rural France, 1880–1914," *British Journal of Sports History*, 2 (1985), 127 ff.

_____, *Sport and Society in Modern France* (London: Macmillan, 1981).

_____, "Women, Men and Sport in France, c. 1870–1914: An Introductory Survey," *Journal of Sport History*, Vol. 18, No. 1, Spring 1991.

Hounshell, David, *From the American System to Mass Production, 1800–1932: The Development of Manufacturing Technology in the United States* (Baltimore: Johns Hopkins University Press, 1984).

Howard, Alfred, *The Bicycle for 1874: A Record of Bicycling for the Year* (London: Henry Causton, 1874).

_____, *The Bicycle for 1876: A Record of Bicycling for the Past Year* (London: Bicycle Journal, 1877).

_____, *The Bicycle for 1877: A Record of Bicycling for the Past Year* (London: Bicycle Journal, 1878).

Howard, Charles, *The Handy Route Book of England and Wales* (London: Letts, 1885).

_____, *The Roads of England and Wales; An Itinary for Cyclist, Tourists and Travellers* (London: Mason and Payne, 1889).

Hubert, Philip G., "The Wheel of Today," *Scribner's Magazine* (U.S.A.), 17, 1895, p. 702.

Jacobs, René, and Mahau, Hector, Le Prestige de la Route (Éditions Eeclonaar: Belgium, 2002).

Jeanes, Walter, "Des origines de vocabulaire cycliste français" (Sorbonne, Paris: Ph. D. thesis, 1950).

Hudson, Derek, *Munby, Man of Two Worlds* (London: Sphere Books, 1974).

Humphrey, Mrs., "Women on Wheels," *The Idler* (U.S.A.) 8, (1892–96), p. 73.

Jarrott, Charles, *Ten Years of Motors and Motoring* (London: Grant Richards, 1906).

Kobayashi, Keizo, *Histoire du Vélocipède de Drais à Michaux, 1817–1870* (Tokyo: Bicycle Culture Center, 1993).

_____, *Pour une Bibliographie du Cyclisme: répertoire des livres en langue française édités entre 1818 et 1983* (Paris: Fédération Française de Cyclotourisme and Fédération Française de Cyclisme, 1984).

Kron, Karl (Lyman Hotchkiss Bagg), *Ten Thousand Miles on a Bicycle* (New York: self-published, 1887).

Ladies' World, "Outing and Bicycle Number," New York, July 1896.

Leechman, G.D., *Safety Cycling* (London: Iliffe, 1895).

Leonard, Irving, *When Bikehood Was In Flower—Sketches of Early Cycling* (South Tamworth, New Hampshire: Bearcamp Press, 1969).

Lessing, Hans-Erhard, *Karl Friedrich Drais von Sauerbronn, 1785–1851* (Exhibition catalogue: Karlsruhe and Mannheim, 1985).

_____, *Erste deutsche illustrirte Vélocipède Brochüre vom Hippolyt de Wesez*: reprint of *Andeutungen über das Vélocipède*, first published 1869 (Hannover: Schäfer, 1995).

Lightwood, J.T., *The Romance of the Cyclists' Touring Club* (London: C.T.C. 1928).

Lloyd-Jones, Roger, and Lewis, M.J., *Raleigh and the British Bicycle Industry: An Economic and Business History, 1870–1960* (Aldershot: Ashgate, 2000).

Low, F.P., "The Cost of Cycles," *Badminton Magazine*, X, 1900, p. 516.

Lowerson, John, *Sport and the English Middle Classes, 1870–1914* (Manchester: Manchester University Press, 1993).

MacAloon, John J., *This Great Symbol: Pierre Coubertin and the Origins of the Modern Olympic Games* (Chicago and London: University of Chicago Press, 1981).

Mandell, Richard, *The First Modern Olympics* (Berkeley: University of California press, 1976).

____, *Sport: A Cultural History* (New York: Columbia University Press, 1984).

Mangan, J.A., *Athleticism in the Victorian and Edwardian Public School* (Cambridge: Cambridge University Press, 1981; new ed., London: Frank Cass, 2000).

____, *The Games Ethic and Imperialism—Aspects of the Diffusion of an Ideal* (London: Penguin, 1986, new ed., London: Frank Cass, 1998).

____, "Oars and the Man: Pleasure and Purpose in Victorian and Edwardian Cambridge," *British Journal of Sports History*, Dec. 1984, pp. 245–271.

____, "Social Darwinism, Sport and English Upper Class Education," *Stadion* VII, Autumn 1982, pp. 93–116.

____, *A Sport-Loving Society: Victorian and Edwardian middle-class England at Play* (Abingdon: Routledge, 2006).

____, and Park, Roberta (eds.), *From "Fair Sex" to Feminism: Sport and the Socialization of Women in the Industrial and Post-Industrial Eras* (London: Frank Cass, 1987).

Martin, Maurice, *Grande Enquête Sportive du Journal Le Vélo* (Paris: Brocherioux, 1898).

____, *Voyage de Bordeaux à Paris par trois vélocipédistes* (Bordeaux: Véloce-Sport, 1890).

Mason, P.P. "The League of American Wheelmen and the Good Roads Movement, 1880–1905" (University of Michigan: Ph. D. thesis, 1957).

Mason, Tony, "Sporting News, 1860–1914," from Michael Harris and Alan Lee, *The Press in English Society from 17th to 19th Century* (Associated University Presses, 1986).

McClintock, Jean, *The History of the Pneumatic Tyre* (Dublin: 1924).

McCrone, Kathleen E., *Playing the Game: Sport and the Physical Emancipation of English Women, 1870–1914* (Lexington: Kentucky University Press, 1988).

McGurn, Jim, *On Your Bicycle: The Illustrated Story of Cycling* (York: Open Road Publishers, 2nd edition 1999).

Mecredy, R.J., and Stoney, Gerald (revised and enlarged by R.J. Mecredy and A.J. Wilson), *The Art and Pastime of Cycling* (Dublin: Mecredy and Kyle, 2nd Edition, 1890).

Miah, Andy and Eassom, Simon (eds.), *Sport Technology: History, Philosophy and Policy*. Research in Philosophy and Technology, Vol. 21. (Oxford: Elsevier, 2002).

Millward, Andrew, "The Cycle Trade in Birmingham, 1890–1920," *Proceedings of the 3rd International Cycle History Conference* (Neckarsulm, Germany, 1992).

____, "Factors contributing to the sustained success of the UK cycle industry, 1870–1939" (Birmingham University, Ph.D. thesis, 1999).

____, "The Genesis of the British Cycle Industry, 1867–1872," *Proceedings of the 1st International Cycle History Conference* (Glasgow: Museum of Transport, 1990).

Moncontour, G. de, *Les Champions Français* (Paris, 1892).

Moxham, S.H., *Fifty Years of Road Riding (1885–1935)—A History of the North Road Cycling Club* (Bedford: Diemer and Reynolds, 1935).

Munslow, Alun, *Deconstructing History* (London: Routledge, 1997).

Nairn, C.W., "Bicycling," *The Pictorial World*, May 1881.

____, and Fox, C.J., *The Bicycle Annual* (London: Etherington, 1878, 1879 and 1880).

____, and Sturmey, H., *The Cyclist and Wheel World Annual* (Coventry: Iliffe, 1882). Contains a "Bibliography of Cycling" compiled by H. Blackwell (pp. 195–208), which may well be the earliest bibliography of the subject.

New York Tribune "Bicycle Day Supplement," New York, 22 Feb. 1898.

Norcliffe, Glen, *The Ride to Modernity—The Bicycle in Canada, 1869-1900* (Toronto: University of Toronto Press, 2001).

Nye, Peter, *Hearts of Lions—The History of American Bicycle Racing* (New York and London: Norton, 1988).

Pallant, Annie, *A Sporting Century, 1863-1963* (Callington, Cornwall: self-published, 1997).

Palmer, Arthur Judson, *Riding High: The Story of the Bicycle* (New York: Dutton, 1956).

Park, Roberta, "British Sports and Pastimes in San Francisco, 1848-1900," *British Journal of Sports History*, Dec. 1984.

Pennell, J., "Cycles and Cycling," *Fortnightly Review*, LXIII, 1898, p. 67.

Petiton, C., *Histoire du Véloce-Club Rouennais: Son origine, son but, ses présidents, ses courses, ses travaux* (Cagniard, Rouen, 1896).

Pfister, Gertrud, "Sport, Technology and Society: From Snow-shoes to Racing Skis," *Sport in Society*, Vol. 4, No. 1, Spring 2001, pp. 73–98.

Phillips, R.E., *Things a Cyclist Ought to Know—A resume of the leading events in the cycling world during the year 1883, and a compendium of useful information for bi- and tri-cyclists.* (London: Houlston, 1882 and subsequent editions).

Pinch, Trevor J., and Bijker, Wiebe E., "The Social Construction of Facts and Artifacts: Or How the Sociology of Science and the Sociology of Technology Might Benefit Each Other"; Chapter 1 of *The Social Construction of Technological Systems–New Directions in the Sociology and History of Technology* (Cambridge, Mass. and London: MIT Press, 1996).

Pinkerton, John, and Roberts, Derek, *A History of Rover Cycles* (Birmingham: privately printed, 1998).

Porter, Luther H., *Wheels and Wheeling—An Indispensable Handbook for Cyclists* (Boston: Wheelman Company, 1892).

Poyer, Alex, *Les Premiers Temps des Véloce-Clubs: apparition et diffusion du cyclisme associatif français entre 1867 et 1914* (Paris: L'Harmattan, 2003).

Pratt, Charles E., *The American Bicycler: A Manual for the Observer, the Learner, and the Expert* (Boston: private publication, 1879).

Pye, Denis, *Fellowship Is Life: The National Clarion Cycling club, 1895–1995* (Bolton, Lancashire: Clarion Publishing, 1995).

Rabenstein, Rüdiger, *Radsport und Gesellschaft—Ihre sozialgeschichtlichen Zusammenhänge in der Zeit von 1867 bis 1914* (Hildesheim, Munich and Zurich: Weidmann, 1991).

Rabinbach, Anson, *The Human Motor: Energy, Fatigue and the Origins of Modernity* (Berkeley: University of California Press, 1990).

Ray, Alan, J., *Cycling: Land's End to John o'Groats* (London: Pelham Books, 1971).

Ritchie, Andrew, "Amateur World Champion, 1893: The International Cycling Career of American Arthur Augustus Zimmerman, 1888–1896," in ed. Boria Majumdar and Fan Hong, *Modern Sport: The Global Obsession, Essays in Honour of J.A. Mangan* (series: Sport in the Global Society, London: Routledge, 2007).

_____, *Flying Yankee—The International Cycling Career of Arthur Augustus Zimmerman* (John Pinkerton Memorial Publishing Fund, 2009)

_____, *King of the Road* (London: Wildwood House, 1975).

_____, "The League of American Wheelmen, Major Taylor and the 'Color Question' in the United States in the 1890s," in ed. J.A. Mangan and Andrew Ritchie, *Ethnicity, Sport, Identity—Struggles for Status* (series: Sport in the Global Society, London, Frank Cass, 2004).

_____, *Major Taylor—The Extraordinary Career of a Champion Bicycle Racer* (San Francisco: Bicycle Books, 1988; reprinted Baltimore: Johns Hopkins University Press, 1996; 2nd edition, revised, *Major Taylor, The Fastest Bicycle Rider in the World*, San Francisco, Cycle Publishing, 2009).

_____, "Marshall "Major" Taylor—The Fastest Bicycle Rider in the World," in ed. Wiggins, David, *Out of the Shadows—A Biographical History of African American Athletes* (Fayetteville: University of Arkansas Press, 2006).

_____, "The Origins of Bicycle Racing—Technology, Entertainment, Sponsorship and Publicity (John Pinkerton Memorial Publishing Fund, 2007).

_____, *The Origins of the Bicycle—Kirkpatrick Macmillan, Gavin Dalzell, Alexandre Lefebvre—Documentation, memory, craft tradition and modern technology* (John Pinkerton Memorial Publishing Fund, 2009)

_____, with Rabenstein, Rüdiger, "Mostly Middle-Class Cycling Heroes: The Fin de Siecle Commerical Obsession with Speed, Distance and Records," in Ed. J. A. Mangan, *Reformers, Sport, Modernizers—Middle-Class Revolutionaries* (European Sports History Review, Vol. 4, 2002).

Roberts, Derek, *Cycling History—Myths and Queries* (London: Pinkerton, 1991).

Robl, Thaddäus, *Der Radrennsport* (Leipzig: Verlag Grethlein, 1905).

Roosevelt, Dr. J. West, "A Doctor's View of Bicycling," *Scribner's Magazine*, June 1895.

Rosen, Paul, *Framing Production—Technology, Culture, and Change in the British Bicycle Industry* (Cambridge and London: MIT Press, 2002).

Rubinstein, David, "Cycling in the 1890s," *Victorian Studies* (Indiana University), Autumn 1977, Vol. 21, No. 1, pp. 47–71.

Rumney, A.W., *Cycle Touring* (London: George Bell, 1898).

_____, *A Cyclist's Notebook* (Edinburgh: Johnston, 1900).

Russell, Stewart, "The Social Construction of Artefacts: A Response to Pinch and Bijker," and Pinch and Bijker respond with "Science, Relativism and the New Sociology of Technology: Reply to Russell," both in *Social Studies of Science* (London, Beverley Hills and New Delhi: Sage, Vol. 16, 1986).

Salamon, Nahum, *Bicycling: Its Rise and Development* (London: Tinsley Bros., 1st ed. 1874; 2nd ed. 1876). Reprint by Newton Abbot, Devon: David and Charles, 1970).

Salvisberg, Paul von, *Der Radfahrsport in Bild und Wort* (Munich: Academischer Verlag, 1897).

Schwinn, F.W., *Fifty Years of Schwinn-Built Bicycles, 1895–1945* (Chicago: Arnold, Schwinn and Company, 1945).

Seray, Jacques, *Deux Roues: La Véritable Histoire du Vélo* (Rodez: Éditions Rouergue, 1988).

Sharp, Archibald, *Bicycles and Tricycles: An Elementary Treatise on their Design and Construction* (London: Longman, 1896; reprint Cambridge, Mass. and London: MIT Press, 1977).

Sinclair, Helen, *Cycle-Clips, A History of Cycling in the North-East* (Newcastle: Tyne and Wear County Council Museums, 1985).

Sinker, Rev. Robert, *Memorials of the Hon. Ion Keith-Falconer* (Cambridge: Deighton and Bell, 1888).

Smith, Robert A., *A Social History of the Bicycle—Its Early Life and Times in America* (New York: American Heritage Press, 1972).

"The Social Effect of Cycling," *The Spectator*, May 30 1896, p. 769.

Southcott, E.J., *The First Fifty Years of the Catford Cycling Club* (London: Foulis and Co., 1939).

Spencer, Charles, *The Bicycle: Its Use and Action* (London: Warne, 1870).

_____, *The Bicycle Road Book* (London: Griffith and Farren, various editions from 1880 on).

_____, *Bicycles and Tricycles: Past and Present* (London: Griffith and Farran, 1883), reprinted by Oakland, California: Cycling Classics, 1996. Contains a "List of publications in connection with cycling" (pp. 132–52 in reprint).

_____, *The Modern Bicycle* (London: Frederick Warne, 1870).

_____, *The Modern Gymnast* (Lomdon: Frederick Warne, 1866).

Sport—a Guide to Historical Sources in the UK (London: Sports Council Information Series No.9, 1983).

Stables, W. Gordon, *Health upon Wheels; or, Cycling as a Means of Preserving and Restoring the Vital Powers* (London: Iliffe, 1887)

Stevens, Thomas, *Around the World on a Bicycle* (New York: Scribner's, 1889).

Street, Roger, *The Pedestrian Hobby-Horse at the Dawn of Cycling* (Christchurch, Dorset: Artesius Publications, 1998).

Sturmey, Henry, *The Indispensable Bicyclist's Handbook* (Coventry: Iliffe, various dates from 1878).

____, *Indispensable Bicyclist's Handbook: A Complete Cyclopedia upon the Subject of the Bicycle and Safety Bicycle and Their Construction*, (London: Iliffe and Son, 1887).

____, *Indispensable Guide to the Safety Bicycle* (Coventry: Iliffe, 1885).

____, *Tricyclists' Indispensable Annual and Handbook—A Guide to the Pastime, Record of the Sport, and Complete Cyclopedia on the Subject*, (Coventry: Iliffe, 1881 and subsequent editions).

____, *The Tricyclists' Indispensable Handbook and Guide* (London: Etherington, 1881).

Taylor, Marshall Walter, *The Fastest Bicycle Rider in the World—An Autobiography of Marshall "Major" Taylor* (Worcester, Mass.: Wormley Publishing, 1928).

Thompson, Christopher S., "Controlling the Working-Class Sports Hero in Order to Control the Masses? The Social Philosophy of Henri Desgrange," *Stadion* XXVII, 2001.

____, "The Third Republic on Wheels: A Social, Cultural and Political History of Bicycling in France from the Nineteenth Century to World War II" (New York University: Ph. D. thesis, 1997).

Tobin, G.A., "The Bicycle Boom of the 1890s: the Development of Private Transportation and the Birth of the Modern Tourist," *Journal of Popular Culture*, Vol. 7, No. 4 (1974), p. 838.

Townsend, James B., "The Social Side of Bicycling," *Scribner's Magazine*, June 1895.

Tranter, Neil, *Sport, Economy and Society in Britain, 1750–1914* (Cambridge: Cambridge U.P., 1998).

"Un Vétéran," *La Vélocipédie pour Tous* (May and Motteroz, 1892), reprinted by Cavalière: Éditions du Layet, 1987.

Van Bottenburg, Maarten, *Global Games* (Chicago: University of Illinois Press, 2001).

Vant, Andre, *L'Industrie du Cycle dans le Région Stéphanoise* (St. Etienne: Musée des Arts et Métiers, 1993).

Vaughan, Graham, and Guerin, Bernard, "A Neglected Innovator in Sports Psychology: Norman Triplett and the Early History of Competitive Performance," *International Journal of the History of Sport*, Vol. 14, No. 2 (Aug. 1997), pp. 82–99.

"Velox," *Velocipedes, Bicycles and Tricycles: How to make and how to use them, with a sketch of their history, invention and progress* (London: Routledge, 1869).

Vertinsky, Patricia, *The Eternally Wounded Woman: Women, Doctors and Exercise in the Late Nineteenth Century* (Urbana and Chicago: University of Illinois Press, 1994).

Vigarello, G., "Le Tour de France," in P. Nora (ed), *Les Lieux de Mémoire*, Vol. II, *Les Traditions* (Paris: Gallimard, 1992). Translated as *Realms of Memory: Rethinking the French Past* (New York: Columbia University Press, 1997), vol. 2, p. 271.

Viollette, Marcel, et al., *Le Cyclisme* (Paris: Pierre Lafitte, 1912; facsimile by Editions Slatkine, Geneva, 1980).

Wallechinsky, David, *The Complete Book of the Summer Olympics* (Boston and New York: Little, Brown and Co., 1984).

Ward, Mrs M.E., *Bicycling for Ladies* (New York: Brentano's, 1896).

Weaver, John, and Weaver, Joan, "'We've had no punctures whatsoever': Dunlop, Commerce and Cycling in fin de siecle Australia," *International Journal of the History of Sport*, Vol. 16, No. 3 (Sept. 1999), pp. 94–112.

Weber, Max, *From Max Weber: Essays in Sociology* (Oxford: Oxford University Press, 1973).

Wells, H.G., *The Wheels of Chance*, first published 1896 (many different editions).

Whitt, F.R. and Wilson, David Gordon, *Bicycling Science—Ergonomics and Mechanics* (Cambridge, Mass. and London: MIT Press, 1974).

Whittaker, Capt. Fred., *Handbook of Summer Athletic Sports* (New York: Beadle and Adams, 1880).

Whorton, James C., "'Athlete's Heart': The Medical Debate over Athleticism," *Journal of Sport History*, Vol. 9, No. 1, Spring 1982, pp. 30–52.

Wigglesworth, Neil, *The Evolution of English Sport* (London: Frank Cass, 1996).

Willard, Frances E., *A Wheel Within a Wheel: How I Learned to Ride the Bicycle, with Some Reflections by the Way* (Chicago: Women's Temperance Publishing Association, 1895).

Williams, Edward, *A Bibliography of Cycling Books* (Birmingham: National Cycling Archive Publication, 1993).

Williamson, John A., *The Rights and Liabilities of Cyclists* (London: Iliffe, 1885).

Wilson, A.J., *The Pleasures, Objects and Advantages of Cycling* (London: Iliffe, 1887).

Zimmerman, A.A. *Zimmerman on Training, with Points for Cyclists* (Leicester: F.W.S. Clarke, 1893).

____, and Erwin, J.-M., *Conseils d'Entrainement et relation de son voyage en Europe* (Paris: Librarie du Vélo, 1894).

C. Newspapers and Journals

This bibliography does not attempt to list completely all the publishing details of journals which included cycling as both sport and recreation either as their primary focus or one of their primary foci in the period covered by this book. Those listed here are, therefore, the most prominent and those most used in this research. The exact dates of publication runs, title changes, publishers, etc, are often difficult to establish. Dates given here reflect those issues actually seen by the author, rather than the historical run of the periodical as published.

Journals Consulted

British:

Badminton Magazine of Sports and Games, 1895–1900 (London: Longman's, Green and Co.).
The Bazaar, Exchange and Mart., published throughout 1870s–1890s.
Bicycle Gazette (Coventry: Feb.–Aug. 1879).
Bicycle Journal (London: 1876–1878).
Bicycle Touring Club Monthly Gazette and Official Record (1882 et seq.).
Bicycling—A Monthly Provincial Magazine and Country Club Gazette (Newcastle: Aug. 1878).
Bicycling News (1876–1900).
Bicycling Times and Touring Gazette (eds. C.J. Fox and A.J. Wilson), (London: 1875–1887).
The Bicyclist (London, Nov. 1875–1876).
Cycle Magazine (1895–1897).
Cycling (Newcastle: 1878–1880). *Cycling/Cycling Weekly* (London, 1891–present). *Cycling World Illustrated* (1896).
Cyclist and Bicycling and Tricycling Trades' Review (eds. H. Sturmey and C.W. Nairn), (London and Coventry: Iliffe, 1879–1902).
Cyclist Annual and Yearbook, ed. Henry Sturmey (1882–1900).
Cyclists' Touring Club Monthly Gazette (London: 1880–1898).
The Engineer.
English Mechanic and Mirror of Science (London, 1865–1870).
The Hub (London: 1896–1899)
Irish Cyclist (1885–1931).
The Ironmonger (used for early period, 1869–1870).
Ixion: A Journal of Velocipeding, Athletics and Aerostatics (Jan.–May 1875).
Lady Cyclist (1895).
Mechanic's Magazine.
National Cyclists' Union Review and Official Record (1886–?).
Northern Wheeler (Bolton: 1892–1899).
Rational Dress Society's Gazette (London: 1890s).
Scottish Cyclist (Glasgow: 1888–1918).
Tricycling Journal (London: Cordingley, 1881–1886).
The Tricyclist, (Ed: G. Lacy Hillier), (Coventry: 1882–1885).
Wheel and Cycle Trade Review (1898–1899).
Wheel World (Eds: H. Sturmey and C.W. Nairn), (Coventry: Iliffe, 1880–1886).
Wheeling (1884–1901).
The Wheelman and Irish Athletic and Cycling News (1890–1892).
The Wheelwoman and Society Cycling News (1896–1899).

American:

American Bicycling Journal (Boston: 1877–79).
American Cyclist (Hartford, Conn., 1891–1892).
Bearings (Chicago: 1890–1897).
Bicycling World (Boston: 1879–1897): "A Great American Manufacture" (Pope Manufacturing Co.), 1 April 1881.
The Cycle (Boston, Mass.: 1886–1887).
Cycle Age and Trade Review (Chicago: 1897–1901).
The Cyclist (Boston: 1889–1891)
Good Roads (various dates in the 1890s, sometime included with the League of American Wheelmen Bulletin).
Harper's Weekly (New York: late 1860s–1890s).
League of American Wheelmen Bulletin (Various location and titles: 1886–1894); "The Founding of the L.A.W." August, 1887, p. 83.
Outing: "The Notable runs and Excursions of 1883," Feb. 1884, pp. 366–373; With the League of American Wheelmen at Washington," Sept. 1884, pp. 425–431; "The Broken Records at Hartford and Springfield," Nov. 1884, pp. 128–131; Charles Pratt, "The L.A.W. and Legal Rights," Jan. 1886, pp. 454–56; Howard Merrill, "One Man's Work for Cycling" (concerning Henry Ducker), Oct. 1888, pp. 32–39; 'Faed,' "How Cycling Road Records Are Made in England," July 1889, pp. 300–305; Charles Clay, "Fair Riders on Modern Wheels," Jan. 1891, pp. 305–307; P.N. Jaconsen, "The Detroit Wheelmen," July 1891, pp. 335–341; Charles Pratt, "A Sketch of American Bicycling and its Founder," July 1891, pp. 342–349; A.H. Godfrey, "Cycling Clubs and Their Spheres of Action," July 1897, pp. 341–351 and Aug. 1897, pp. 488–494.
The Pacific Cyclist (San Francisco: 1894–95)
The Referee (Chicago: 1893–1896).
Scientific American. Spirit of the Times.
Springfield Wheelmen's Gazette (Springfield, Mass., 1884–1886)
The Wheel and Cycling Trade Review (Chicago: 1888–1900).
The Wheelman (Boston: 1882–1883): Charles Pratt, "A Wheel Around the Hub," Oct. 1882, pp. 3–21; "The Uses of the Bicycle," Dec. 1882. Charles Pratt, "Our First Bicycle Club," March 1883, pp. 401–412; President Bates, "The Political Power of the L.A.W.," May 1883, pp. 98–100; Albert S. Parsons, "The Massachusetts Bicycle Club," June 1883; G. Johnstone Stoney, "On the Energy Expended in Propelling a Bicycle," July 1883, pp. 269–278; A.L. Fennessy, "The Springfield Bicycle Club," Aug. 1883, pp. 337–344; Charles Pratt, "Pierre Lallement and His Bicycle," Oct. 1883, pp. 4–13; "The Capital and the Capital Club," Nov. 1883, pp. 82–96.
Wheelmen's Gazette (Indianapolis: 1892–1896).

French:

La Bicyclette (Paris: 1892–1895).
Bulletin du Comité International des Jeux Olympiques.
Le Bulletin Officiel de l'Union Vélocipédique (1890–1903).

Le Cycle (1891–1895).
Le Cycliste (1888–1914).
Le Cycliste Belge (1889–1892).
La France Cycliste (1890–1894).
L'Industrie Vélocipédique (1882–?).
Le Journal des Vélocipédistes (Paris: 1893–1895).
Le Monde Cycliste (1888–1893).
Paris-Vélo (Paris: 1893–1897).
La Revue des Sports (Paris: 1876–1895).
La Revue Vélocipédique (Paris: 1882–1886).
Le Sport Vélocipédique (Paris: 1880–1886).
Le Vélo (Paris: 1892–1904).
Le Véloce-Sport (Bordeaux: 1885–1895).
Le Vélocipède Illustré (Paris: April 1869–1872).
La Vie au Grand Air (Paris: 1898–1922)

German:

Sport-Album der Rad-Welt—Ein radsportliches Jahrbuch (Berlin: 1902–1905).
Das Velociped (ed. T.H.S. Walker), (Berlin: 1881).

Newspapers Consulted

British:

Athletic News (Manchester).
Bell's Life, London (1822–1886).
Birmingham Daily Post.
Coventry Herald and Free Press.
Coventry Standard.
Daily News.
Daily Telegraph.
The Field.
Liverpool Mercury.
Liverpool Weekly Courier.
Manchester Guardian.
Morning Advertiser.
Newcastle Daily Chronicle
North London News.
Ripon Gazette.
Sporting Life.
Sydenham Times.
The Times.
Wolverhampton Chronicle.

American:

Boston Globe.
Boston Herald.
Buffalo Daily Courier.
Chicago Tribune.
Daily Alta California.
Indianapolis Sentinel.
Louisville Courier-Journal.
Louisville Times.
New York Times.
New York Evening Journal.
New York Tribune Bicycle Day Supplement.
San Francisco Chronicle.
San Francisco Examiner.

German:

Berliner Illustrirte Zeitung.
Deutsche Turn-Zeitung
Illustrirte Zeitung.

D. SPECIALIST CYCLING PUBLICATIONS

The Boneshaker
(journal of the Veteran Cycle Club).

Clayton, Nick, "The Cycling Career of James Moore" (No. 125, Spring 1991).
_____, "The First Bicycle" (No. 113, Spring 1987).
_____, "The Hon. Ion Keith-Falconer and the Cambridge University Bicycle Club" (No. 140, Spring 1996).
Parker, E.B., "The Honourable Ion Keith-Falconer" (No. 65, Winter 1971).
Ritchie, Andrew, "Professional World Championships," No. 142, Winter 1996).

Proceedings of International Cycle History Conferences (Cycle Publishing / Van der Plas Publications, San Francisco):

1990, 1st Conference:

Millward, Andrew, "The Genesis of the British Cycle Industry, 1867–1872," pp. 59–79.
Oddy, Nicholas, "Kirkpatrick McMillan, The inventor of the pedal cycle or the invention of cycle history," pp. 24–32.

1991, 2nd Conference:

Bosc, Henri, "Il y a cent ans: Les précurseurs du cyclotourisme et les premiers récits de voyages—Maurice Martin," pp. 120–127.

1993, 4th Conference:

Bowerman, Les, "John Keen–The Life of a Cycling Pioneer," pp. 89–98.

1994, 5th Conference:

Higman, H.D., "The Founding of the Dunlop Tyre Company," pp. 91–94.
Rabenstein, Rüdiger, "T.H.S. Walker—English Cycling Pioneer in Germany," pp. 155–160.
"Colonel Pope and the Founding of the U.S. Cycle Industry," pp. 95–98

1996, 7th Conference:

Clayton, Nick, "Who Invented the Penny-Farthing?," pp. 31–42.
Ritchie, Andrew, "The Origins of Bicycle Racing in England, 1868–1870," pp. 43–56.

1997, 8th Conference:

Berto, Frank, "Who invented the mountain bike?," pp. 25–48.

1999, 10th Conference:

Clayton, Nick, "Of Bicycles, Bijker, and Bunkum," pp. 11–24.

The Wheelmen

Cameron, Frank, "The Pacific Coast Velocipede," No. 31, Nov. 1987.

Friedlander, Suzan D., "Popularization of the Bicycle in the United States in the Late 1890s: Its Effect on Women's Dress and Social Codes," No. 45, Nov. 1994.

Graber, Jacques, "The Lefebvre Bicycle," No. 58, May 2001.

Herlihy, David, "The Pickering export controversy: its resolution and some pertinent lessons," No. 47, November 1995.

Ritchie, Andrew, "The velocipede of Alexandre Lefebvre and problems of historical interpretation," No. 59, Nov. 2001.

Wells, Michael, "Ordinary Women: High Wheeling Ladies in Nineteenth Century America," No. 43, Nov. 1993, pp. 2–14.

Index

Agricultural Hall, Islington, London 102; exhibitions of machines staged at 35; "Grand Bicycle Races" held in 1869 34; races held at in 1869 38–39
Amateur Athletic Association 125
Amateur Athletic Club 70, 331n1; applies "mechanic, artisan or labourer" clause 50; foundation of 8; holds earliest amateur championships 45–46
Amateur Athletic Union 88
amateur bicycle championships: earliest amateur championships 45; first official amateur championship 46–47, 50; first official championships 72–73; jurisdiction of Amateur Athletic Club 70–71; *see also* championships; competition, international
amateur versus professional races: 76, 76
amateurism: definition agreed by I.C.A. 210–11; ideals of 210–11
Anglo-Americans: founding of American cycling 88
Arend, Willy 263, 283

Banker, George 216
Bartleet, H.W. 186
Bassett, Abbot: 116, 151, 218
Battensby, Tom 138
bicycle industry: economic boom 121–22; estimates of total value of trade and numbers of bicycles 298; production figures for 360n10; statistics concerning production and patents 294
bicycle racing: against horses 312; categories of races held in England in 1874 59–61; concentration of early racing in manufacturing centers 34–35; earlier in San Francisco than in London 24–26; earliest races in France 21–22; early competition in America 327–28n26; earning power of professional cyclists 282–84; numbers of professional cyclists 280; training methods 288–89; *see also* competition, international; velocipede racing; velocipedes
bicycle technology: light and strong 124–25; racing as primary testing ground for technology 205
Bicycle Touring Club: claims to be the largest athletic organization in world 82; founded 5, 50, 70, 81–82, 122
"bicycle tournament" 38
Bicycle Union 133–34, 295; founded 5, 45–46, 50, 69–76; rejects definition of "mechanic, artisan and labourer" clause 74–75; sponsors amateur championships 50; *see also* National Cyclists' Union
bicycle: "bicycle" accepted 63; first uses of term 15
Bowden, Frank 246

California: roads 100; velocipedes in 7, 24
Cambridge University: acceptance of amateur sport at 50; cycling at 62–65
Cambridge University Bicycle Club: first cycling tracks in England 62; formed 1874 65; membership figures for 62
Cann, William 102, 138
century rides 126
chains: first used for safety bicycle 166; need for chains in tricycle technology 156–57; use in tricycles and "Kangaroo" make safety bicycle possible 166–68
championships: importance of in evolution of high-wheel bicycle 46–47; races between Cooper, Moore, Keen and Stanton 52; *see also* world championships
championships, American: first official championships 98; 20-mile amateur championship 147
championships, French: inadequate facilities for in Bordeaux 127–28
championships, professional: Aston Cross Grounds, 1871 45; between known champions 60; first official ones held in England 231–2; unofficial between England and France 142–3
championships, world *see* world championships
Charles Spencer's gymnasium, London 27–30

club houses 120
clubs, American: Boston Bicycle Club 89–90, 93, 94–97; Brown University Athletic Association 96; Century Road Club of America 195; Cincinnati Velocipede Club 24; Columbia University Club 96; Connecticut Bicycle Club 131; Essex Bicycle Club 98; Harvard 96; Lynn Cycle Club 132; Massachusetts Bicycle Club 106; New Haven Bicycle Club 148; New York Athletic Club 98; Oakland Bicycle Club 100–101; Princeton Bicycle Club 96; Providence Bicycle Club 96–97, 105–6; San Francisco Bicycle Club 100, 100–01; Springfield Bicycle Club 131, 143–155; Suffolk Bicycle Club 100
clubs, British: Anfield Bicycle Club 164, 178; Belfast Cruisers Cycling Club 184; Cambridge University Bicycle Club 332n26; Dark Blue Bicycle Club, Oxford University 60, 63; formation of early velocipede clubs in London 57–58; Liverpool Velocipede Club 332n14; London County Cycling and Athletic Club 213, 214; North Road Cycling Club 177, 180; numbers of clubs in England 48–49; Pickwick Bicycle Club 58; Sturmey records numbers of 298–303; Wolverhampton Velocipede Club 35, 57
clubs, French: details of 305; earliest formation of 21, 326n14–15; early clubs and racing 21, 141–3; number of clubs affiliated with U.V.F. 141; Union Velocipedique de France 141; Union Velocipedique Parisienne 141; Velo-Sport de Paris 141; Veloce Club Bordelais 159–60, 193
Cobb, Gerard 66, 71–72, 75, 102, 333n62, 335n94; as President of Bicycle Union 62, 75
competition, international: American and British professionals in England 237–8; American riders cross to Europe 231; between England and France compli-

373

cated by definitions of amateurism and professionalism 232–3; between England and the United States 143–55; British riders cross Atlantic 231; "champions" 231; N.C.U. championships 236
Cooper, Fred 17, 52, 57
Cortis, H.L. 334n70; attempts to ride 20 miles in an hour 129–30
Cotterell, Stanley 82
cycling in France: numbers of cyclists 362n1
cycling press: emergence of 50; expansion of 163, 296
Cyclists' Touring Club 122–23; claims to be largest athletic institution in world 303; membership statistics for 302–03

De Civry, Baron Frederic 140, 193–4, 240
De Coubertin, Pierre 203, 257–60
definitions, of amateurism and professionalism: as proposed by Bicycle Union 72–73
De Saunier, Baudry: *Memoires de Terront* 349n18; publications 350n36; writes best-selling *Memoires* of Charles Terront 200; writing on bicycle technology 205
Desgrange, Henri 270
Ducker, Henry E. 150–51; pushes world status for American cycling events 151–55
Du Cros family: early pneumatic racing 184–87
Duncan, Herbert O.: agent for Humber and Rudge companies in Paris 138; on difference between British and French racing 138–40; manager for Terront ride from St. Petersburg to Paris 269–70; preference for France 139; on qualities needed to win important races in France 198–99; Rover safety as "wonderful commercial proposition" 170; sets record on Rudge "Bicyclette" between Montpellier and Paris 170–72; writes *World on Wheels* 138
Dunlop, John Boyd: invention of pneumatic tire 183–88; *see also* pneumatic tires
Dunlop Company: 187

earning power of professional cyclists 359n63; increases in 1890s 263–4
Edge, S.F. 196
electric lighting: 129
Elkes, Harry 276
Etherington, Harry 101–13; impact of visit to U.S. 112; leads British "invasion" to U.S. 149; promoted Six Day race at Agricultural Hall 138–39; publications 337n57; on road races as tests of bicycles and tricycles 164

Fournier, Henri 193

Garin, Maurice 204
Gaskell, H.W. 147
geared-up ordinary racing 165–68
geared-up ordinaries 123; the Facile and the Kangaroo 165–68; Xtraordinary, Facile and Kangaroo development 165
Giffard, Pierre 199
Good Roads Movement 126, 296, 340n108; League of American Wheelmen 115–16
governing bodies of cycling: dates of formation of in various countries 353n21
Great North Road 125; used for record-breaking rides 176–77
Griffin, Harry Hewitt 39, 48; bicycle production figures 341n2; extent of the press 51; industry statistics 121–22; safety bicycles as four-fifths of the market 161; "vast revolution" has swept the bicycle industry 190

Hamelle, Paul: criticizes British amateurism 210
Hendee, George 117, 145
high-wheel bicycle: 38–39, 68; on cutting edge of sport 50, 124–25
Hillier, George Lacy 214–7, 351n73; controversy concerning timing at 1893 Cuca Cocoa Challenge 213–4; debate on merits of wood and cement for track construction 131; distinction between C.T.C. and N.C.U. 71; invites Zimmerman to become member of London County Cycling and Athletic Club 245–6; on Keith-Falconer's ride from Bournemouth to Hitchen 64–65; opposes road racing 205–7; proponent of amateurism in sport 209–16
Holbein, M.A. 196
Howard, Alfred 49, 50, 59, 74, 83–84, 332n23; difference between amateur and professional categories 61
Howell, Richard 147, 233, 237
Humber, Thomas 28, 36
Hume, W. 184
Huret, Constant 204, 277

improvements, technological 36–8, 124
International Cyclists' Association 203; accepts amateur definition 211; first world championships 238–45; foundation of 5; list of delegates at 354n33; *see also* world championships
International Velocipede and Loco-machine Exhibition 57

Jarrott, Charles 362n9
Jiel-Laval 196, 267
Johnson, J.T. 45
Johnson, L.H. 98

Kangaroo *see* geared-up ordinaries
Keen, John 45, 50, 52, 60, 105–7, 138, 141–2, 334n69–70, 334n75–78; as champion rider and manufacturer 36–37; as technological innovator and small manufacturer 77–78; championship record 77–78; contests amateur-professional races 66; financial "testimonial" to 37; "probably the best-known bicyclist in the world" 79; significance of life and career of 77–79; technical improvements realized by 56
Keith-Falconer, Ion 62–68, 333n38–39; breaks record for ride from Land's End to John o'Groats 66; contests amateur-professional races 76
Kron, Karl 25, 304

League of American Wheelmen 122; annual Meets and races 113–16, 144–46, 343n86; foundation of 92, 113–16, 339n100; Good Roads Movement 126, 296; *Handbook* 115; inaugural meeting 114; membership statistics 304–5; political power 115–16; Racing Board 117–18, 340n110
legislative restrictions 69–70
Lesna, Lucien 204
licensing schemes 254–57
Liverpool: early velocipeding in 32–34
Liverpool Velocipede Club: "Bicycle Tournament and Assault at Arms" 33
long-distance races 200
long-distance rides, in Britain 331n4; Land's End to John o'Groats (Keith-Falconer) 66; Land's End to John o'Groats (Mills) 333; Liverpool to London 39; London to Brighton 39; London to John o'Groats 30, 40; *see also* "place-to-place" record rides
long-distance rides, in Europe 334n24; Paris to Vienna 333; St. Petersburg to Paris 270
Lowe, Robert, M.P. 84; speaks about progress of cycling i118

Macmillan, Kirkpatrick 19, 323n11
"maker's amateurs" 116, 125, 152,

Index

197–98, 281–2; G.P. Mills becomes a prominent example of 178
managers: names and details of 349n16
manufacturers: Arthur Markham 56; Coventry Machinists' Company 51, 56, 117, 121; Cunningham, Heath and Co 92; Eugene Meyer 47; Gormully and Jeffrey 112, 117; Hillman, Herbert and Cooper 166–68; Humber Company 197–200; John Keen 36–37, 57; Meyer tension-wheel bicycle with toe-pedals 47; Palmer, Knox and Co. 24–25; Pope Manufacturing Company 90, 105, 107, 110, 112, 122; Starley and Sutton 169–73; Thomas Humber, Nottingham 28, 56, 57; W.H.J. Grout, London 57
Markham, Arthur 42
Mayall, John: 28–9; and beginnings of bicycle in England 328n31; ride to Brighton 39
McGregor, O.E. 42, 52–54; see also Wolverhampton
"mechanic, artisan and labourer clause" 47
Mecredy, Alexander 182–3
Mecredy, Richard 183; impact and advantages of pneumatic tire 182–3; "Kangaroo" and development of chain technology 166; "Rover safety" and popularity of the "Kangaroo" 169; wins four N.C.U. championships 186
Medinger, Paul 128, 142, 194
"Meets" 58, 143–47
Miller, Charlie 278
Mills, George P. 178–9, 196–98
Moore, James 17, 22, 23, 34, 45–7, 52, 60; wins unofficial "world championships" in France and England 141
Morgan, W.J. ("Senator") 153, 237
Mott, Albert 280; see also League of American Wheelmen
mountain bikes: development of 324n13
Munger, L.D. (Birdie) 218

National Circuit, U.S. 264
National Cycling Association 221; wrests control of professional sport from L.A.W. 290
National Cyclists' Union 122, 125, 295; anti-road racing attitude 310–11; big clubs threaten to secede on question of road racing 212; championships 134–5; disapproval of racing on public roads 207–8; disapproval of road racing 179–80; holds professional championships in 1894 231–2; imposes suspensions of riders 256; legislation abolishing road racing 212; membership statistics 302–4; ordinary and safety championships 189; votes to prohibit British amateurs from racing in France 210; see also Bicycle Union
national governing bodies of cycling 235
non-competitive cyclists: difficulty of knowing numbers of 291–2
numbers of cyclists: estimated in U.K. 121–2

Old Welsh Harp Inn, Hendon, north London: 42
Olympic Games 257–60, 323n2; English "Anglo-Saxon Olympiad" or "Pan-Britannic Gathering" 257; first Games 257–60; origin of awarding cups related to old Olympic Games 147
"open" sport: organization of 335n85
opposition to road racing 211
ordinaries, geared-up 163–5
Oxford University 8, 50, 62–65

pace-making 213, 358n28
paced racing: accident at Botanical Gardens, Berlin 276; element of danger and drama 276; fatalities during 358n35; growth and evolution of 272–77; Guignard ride of more than 100 kms in an hour 277; introduction of electric, steam-powered and gasoline-powered pacing machines 272–77; in high-wheel era discussed 76
pacing machines 275
pedestrianism 16, 99, 104, 324n11; and Six Day racing 337–8n67
periodicals and newspapers, American: *American Bicycling Journal* 89–90, 92–93, 98, 100, 105–6, 118; *Bicycling World* 96, 100, 107, 112, 113–14, 131, 159, 218, 276; *League of American Wheelmen Bulletin* 176; *Outing* 154; *Spaldings Official Bicycle Guide for 1898* 273, 284; *Springfield Wheelmen's Gazette* 143–55, 343–44n88; *The Wheel and Cycling Trade Review* 120; *The Wheel-man* 154; *Wheelmen's Gazette*, Indianapolis 253
periodicals and newspapers, British: earliest English cycling journals 331n2; *Sport-Album der Rad-Welt* 286; *The Times* 23, 39, 85–86
periodicals and newspapers, French: *La Bicyclette* 203; *Veloce-Sport* 193; *Le Velocipede Illustre* 21, 22, 48, 141
place-to-place record rides: Land's End to John o'Groats (Adams) 165–6; Land's End to John o'Groats (Marriott and Mills) 160; Montpellier to (Duncan) 171–2; see also long-distance rides, in Britain
pneumatic tires: experimental bicycles built 184; first Irish rider to compete on pneumatics in England in 1889 186; first used in competition 184–7; invention 181–8; key factor in bicycle racing and recreational cycling boom 181–2; see also Dunlop
Pneumatic Tyre and Booth's Cycle Agency, Dublin 182
Pope, Col. Albert: commercial tactics in American marketplace 112; interview with 339n88
Pratt, Charles E. 89, 92–4, 97–8, 113–15, 339–40n105; on aims of Boston Bicycle Club 94
Prince, John S. 233

Queen's College, Belfast: 184
Queen's Ground, Sheffield 60

racers, American: Banker, George 216; Elkes, Harry 276; Hendee, George 117, 145; Miller, Charlie 278; Munger, L.D. (Birdie) 218; Prince, John S. 233; Rollins, Wentworth 112; Rowe, William A. 117, 150, 152; Taylor, Major 243–4, 263, 282–3; Walthour, Bobby 276; Wheeler, George 216; Zimmerman, Arthur 216, 239–45
racers, British: Battensby, Tom 138; Cann, William 102, 138; Cooper, Fred 17, 52, 57; Cortis, H.L. 334n70; Edge, S.F. 196; Gaskell, H.W. 147; Holbein, M.A. 196; Howell, Richard 147, 233, 237; Hume, W. 184; Mills, G.P. 178, 196–98; Sellers, Sanders 147, 233; Shorland, Frank 213; Smith, George 167; Whiting, H.P. 334n64; Wood, Fred 45
racers, French: De Civry, Baron Frederic 140, 193–4, 240; Fournier, Henri 193; Garin, Maurice 204; Huret, Constant 204, 277; Jiel-Laval 196, 267; Lesna, Lucien 204; Medinger, Paul 128, 142, 194; Moore, James 141; Terront, Charles 102, 105, 109, 128, 138, 142, 193, 225, 267–8
races: Irvington-Millburn, New Jersey 216; Martin Road Race, Buffalo, New York 220; Pullman Race, Chicago 220–1; Telegram Trophy Race 220; Vienna-Berlin 268; see also races, French
races, French: Bordeaux-Paris 195–206, 267, 357n11; Paris-Brest-Paris 198–201, 267–68; Paris-Brussels 203; Paris-Clermont Ferrand 202; Paris-

Roubaix 203; Paris-Rouen 22, 326n18
racing, French: beginnings of 325n4; disrupted by Franco-Prussian War of 1870-1, 141; earliest occurrences of 325-6n14; early development 141-42; nature and organization of 232-33
racing, professional: in England 59, 137; numbers of professionals in Britain 343n53; outside N.C.U. control 136
Rational Dress Society 335n89
record-breaking: as prominent in bicycle racing 285
road conditions 125-7; in America 126, 216-18, 341n17, 351n77, 339n103; crowds on British roads versus French 206; in France 127; well-maintained roads used to break records 125
road racing, in America: Chicago, Pullman, Martin and Irvington-Millburn races 194-5; Clarksville Road Race 218; crowds of spectators at start and finish of 218-19; first 100-mile road race held in 1883 114; general summary of 216-18; on high-wheel bicycle 216-18; surge of interest in Chicago 220-22
road racing, in Britain: attitude toward 207-9; between Oxford and Cambridge 63; early racing in Liverpool 40-41; foundations of modern road racing 193-227; "Great Bicycle Race" between Chester and Liverpool 1869 32-33; N.C.U. and discouragement on public roads 125-6; the problem of "scorching" and public image 194; road riders threatened by racing on public roads 179
road racing, in France: foundation of modern 194-205; presented as epic sporting battle of heroic contestants 180; road races inaugurated during 1891-96 225; 12 years of Bordeaux-Paris 224
Road Records Association 125, 207, 223-4; formation 180
Roads Improvement Association: in Britain 126; within N.C.U. 296
Rollins, Wentworth 112
"Rover safety" bicycles: capabilities and potential 171-2; development of 169-76; first introduced at Stanley Show 169; George Smith breaks 100-mile record 171-73; introduced in America 176; *see also* safety bicycles
Rowe, William A. 117, 150, 152
Rowley Turner 28

safety bicycles: 123-4, 161, 181; *see also* Rover safety bicycles

Salamon, Nahum 49, 51, 72, 331n3; *Bicycling: Its Rise and Development* 51
San Francisco, Mechanic's Pavilion: early arrival of velocipedes 24-5; racing at 100, 108
"scorchers" 80
Sellers, Sanders (Preston) 147, 233
Shorland, Frank 213
Simpson lever chain 202
Sinker, Rev. Robert 67
"Six Day" bicycle races 89, 102-3, 337n60, 338n70; in Boston 106-7; earliest examples of 329n62, 353n8; growth and evolution of 277-80; at Madison Square Garden 277-80; in San Francisco 338n83; Waller rides 1,404 miles 104
Smith, George 167
Snoxell and Spencer, London 29, 38
spectators: at Agricultural Hall 39; at club runs of Boston Bicycle Club in 1878 94; at first bicycle race on Pacific coast 100; at Oxford-Cambridge road race 64; at race meetings in Wolverhampton 52-4; at races in London and the Midlands 50; at racing in Bordeaux 128; at Springfield Tournament 117
Spencer, Charles 27-30, 38, 58, 54; rides from London to Brighton 29-30, 40-41; rides from London to John o'Groats 51-52
Springfield Tournaments 117, 143-55, 233-36; advertised as "world championships" in 1886 143-49; organized by Springfield Bicycle Club 143-55
Stanley Show, London: 1887 exhibits 175; on success of "Rover safety" 170
Stanton, David 17-18, 45, 50, 52, 77, 97, 105
"Star" bicycle 176
Starley, James 169-70
Stevens, Thomas 126, 217, 269; completes journey across America on a bicycle 150
Sturmey, Henry 135; on annual international championships 153; *Indispensable Handbook and Cyclist Annual and Year Book* 298-302; and International Cyclists' Association 297; on international meetings 234; *Tricyclists' Indispensable Manual and Handbook* 157, 163

Taylor, Major 243-4, 261, 263, 282-3
Terront, Charles 102, 105, 109, 128, 138, 142, 193, 225, 267-8
Tour de France 270-2; foundation of and car racing 357n26; riders who participated in first 204-5

track construction: banked 132; in Berlin and Leipzig 129; *Bicycling World* discussion about 131; and consistent results 132; in England, France, Germany 130; material 131; in Wolverhampton 129
tracks: American 131-2, 342n40; Belgrave Road Grounds, Leicester 134; in Britain 342n33; Bordeaux 128; construction of in Britain and Europe 357n3; Crystal Palace 130; faster speeds 263-4; French, lack of 127; Hampden Park, Springfield 145-49; in Hartford and Springfield 130; Lillie Bridge 130; Paris 129; Stamford Bridge 130; Surbiton 130; Surbiton Recreation Grounds Bicycle Track 129; Velodrome Buffalo, Paris 226
trains, rides behind: Charles "Mile-a-Minute" Murphy 287; E.E. Anderson 287
Tricycle Association: 159-60
tricycle racing: 160
tricycles: 155-62; design of 163; development of 160; evolution of 344n127, 345n130; recreation and utility 156; role in transportation technology 155-6
Troy, Willis B. 251
Turner, Rowley brings French velocipede to London 28; ride to Brighton 39

Union Cycliste Internationale: formation of 355n50; succeeded International Cyclists' Association 244-5
Union Velocipedique de France 296; foundation of 5; no distinction between amateur and professional 193; rules 171-2; stays outside I.C.A. 240
utility cycling 12, 55, 86-7, 165

Velocipede "Derbys" 32
velocipedes: 5, in America 26-7, 91, 327n24, 327n25; development of 20-21; diffusion from U.S. to England 26-7; early 3 and 4-wheeled 19-20; exhibition 43; racing 30, 31, 48; use of the term 325n2

Walker, T.H.S. 129, 143;
Waller, George 45, 102, 138; builds Bicycle Ground in Byker, Newcastle 138; Six Day race 138
Walthour, Bobby 276
Warburton, "Choppy" 216
Welsh Harp Hotel 330n73
Weston, Frank L. 89, 94
Wheeler, George 216
Whiting, H.P. 48, 74-5, 334n64
Wilson, A.J. 124; on long-distance road riding as distinctively En-

glish sport 176–7; on number of tracks in England 130; on of road racing 208; on Springfield Tournament 131

Wolverhampton, Molineux Grounds 35, 52–4, 60

"Wolverhampton Rules" 137, 342n50

women and cycling 298, 326n17, 335n89; early racing 18–19, 22; Lady Cyclists' Association 301–2; membership in C.T.C. 82–3; overview of literature on 361n19; and the "Rational Dress" movement 159–60; and the "sociable" tricycle 160; in San Francisco in 1879 109; tricycles 157; velocipede races 327n24

Wood, Fred 45

world championships 242–3, 330n86; amateur championships, Antwerp 242; amateur championships, Chicago 241–2; difficulties of defining and organizing, distance and location 238–9; events from 1893 to 1900 243; first official 8; first professional 241; logistical problems of organizing 244; need for world governing body of cycling 238–9; possibility of Springfield Tournaments recognized 234–5; unofficial 5, 233; *see also* International Cyclists' Association

Zimmerman, Arthur Augustus 118, 176, 216, 239–45, 245–54, 263, 348; after retirement 253–4; clubs 245–6; in England 252–3; in Europe 251; on Hillier 248–9; in Indianapolis 250–1; praises French tracks 253; riding style 355n72; treatment at hands of N.C.U. 249–50; turns professional 251–2; victories 252–3; wins world championships 250

www.ingramcontent.com/pod-product-compliance
Lightning Source LLC
Chambersburg PA
CBHW081534300426
44116CB00015B/2629